T0137838

IFIP Advances in Information and Communication Technology   **634**

Editor-in-Chief

Kai Rannenberg, Goethe University Frankfurt, Germany

IFIP – The International Federation for Information Processing

IFIP was founded in 1960 under the auspices of UNESCO, following the first World Computer Congress held in Paris the previous year. A federation for societies working in information processing, IFIP's aim is two-fold: to support information processing in the countries of its members and to encourage technology transfer to developing nations. As its mission statement clearly states:

IFIP is the global non-profit federation of societies of ICT professionals that aims at achieving a worldwide professional and socially responsible development and application of information and communication technologies.

IFIP is a non-profit-making organization, run almost solely by 2500 volunteers. It operates through a number of technical committees and working groups, which organize events and publications. IFIP's events range from large international open conferences to working conferences and local seminars.

The flagship event is the IFIP World Computer Congress, at which both invited and contributed papers are presented. Contributed papers are rigorously refereed and the rejection rate is high.

As with the Congress, participation in the open conferences is open to all and papers may be invited or submitted. Again, submitted papers are stringently refereed.

The working conferences are structured differently. They are usually run by a working group and attendance is generally smaller and occasionally by invitation only. Their purpose is to create an atmosphere conducive to innovation and development. Refereeing is also rigorous and papers are subjected to extensive group discussion.

Publications arising from IFIP events vary. The papers presented at the IFIP World Computer Congress and at open conferences are published as conference proceedings, while the results of the working conferences are often published as collections of selected and edited papers.

IFIP distinguishes three types of institutional membership: Country Representative Members, Members at Large, and Associate Members. The type of organization that can apply for membership is a wide variety and includes national or international societies of individual computer scientists/ICT professionals, associations or federations of such societies, government institutions/government related organizations, national or international research institutes or consortia, universities, academies of sciences, companies, national or international associations or federations of companies.

More information about this series at http://www.springer.com/series/6102

Alexandre Dolgui · Alain Bernard ·
David Lemoine · Gregor von Cieminski ·
David Romero (Eds.)

Advances in Production Management Systems

Artificial Intelligence for Sustainable and Resilient Production Systems

IFIP WG 5.7 International Conference, APMS 2021
Nantes, France, September 5–9, 2021
Proceedings, Part V

Springer

Editors
Alexandre Dolgui (iD)
IMT Atlantique
Nantes, France

Alain Bernard (iD)
Centrale Nantes
Nantes, France

David Lemoine (iD)
IMT Atlantique
Nantes, France

Gregor von Cieminski (iD)
ZF Friedrichshafen AG
Friedrichshafen, Germany

David Romero (iD)
Tecnológico de Monterrey
Mexico City, Mexico

ISSN 1868-4238   ISSN 1868-422X (electronic)
IFIP Advances in Information and Communication Technology
ISBN 978-3-030-85916-9   ISBN 978-3-030-85914-5 (eBook)
https://doi.org/10.1007/978-3-030-85914-5

This Springer imprint is published by the registered company Springer Nature Switzerland AG
The registered company address is: Gewerbestrasse 11, 6330 Cham, Switzerland

Preface

The scientific and industrial relevance of the development of sustainable and resilient production systems lies in ensuring future-proof manufacturing and service systems, including their supply chains and logistics networks. "Sustainability" and "Resilience" are essential requirements for competitive manufacturing and service provisioning now and in the future. Industry 4.0 technologies, such as artificial intelligence; decision aid models; additive and hybrid manufacturing; augmented, virtual, and mixed reality; industrial, collaborative, mobile, and software robots; advanced simulations and digital twins; and smart sensors and intelligent industrial networks, are key enablers for building new digital and smart capabilities in emerging cyber-physical production systems in support of more efficient and effective operations planning and control. These allow manufacturers and service providers to explore more sustainable and resilient business and operating models. By making innovative use of the aforementioned technologies and their enabled capabilities, they can pursue the triple bottom line of economic, environmental, and social sustainability. Furthermore, industrial companies will be able to withstand and quickly recover from disruptions that pose threats to their operational continuity. This is in the face of disrupted, complex, turbulent, and uncertain business environments, like the one triggered by the COVID-19 pandemic, or environmental pressures calling for decoupling economic growth from resource use and emissions.

The International Conference on Advances in Production Management Systems 2021 (APMS 2021) in Nantes, France, brought together leading international experts on manufacturing, service, supply, and logistics systems from academia, industry, and government to discuss pressing issues and research opportunities mostly in smart manufacturing and cyber-physical production systems; service systems design, engineering, and management; digital lean operations management; and resilient supply chain management in the Industry 4.0 era, with particular focus on artificial intelligence-enabled solutions.

Under the influence of the COVID-19 pandemic, the event was organised as online conference sessions. A large international panel of experts (497 from 50 countries) reviewed all the submissions (with an average of 3.2 reviews per paper) and selected the best 377 papers (70% of the submitted contributions) to be included in these international conference proceedings. The topics of interest at APMS 2021 included artificial intelligence techniques, decision aid, and new and renewed paradigms for sustainable and resilient production systems at four-wall factory and value chain levels, comprising their associated models, frameworks, methods, tools, and technologies for smart and sustainable manufacturing and service systems, as well as resilient digital supply chains. As usual for the APMS conference, the Program Committee was particularly attentive to the cutting-edge problems in production management and the quality of the papers, especially with regard to the applicability of the contributions to industry and services.

The APMS 2021 conference proceedings are organized into five volumes covering a large spectre of research concerning the global topic of the conference: "Artificial Intelligence for Sustainable and Resilient Production Systems".

The conference was supported by the International Federation of Information Processing (IFIP), which is celebrating its 60th Anniversary, and was co-organized by the IFIP Working Group 5.7 on Advances in Production Management Systems, IMT Atlantique (Campus Nantes) as well as the Centrale Nantes, University of Nantes, Rennes Business School, and Audecia Business School. It was also supported by three leading journals in the discipline: Production Planning & Control (PPC), the International Journal of Production Research (IJPR), and the International Journal of Product Lifecycle Management (IJPLM).

Special attention has been given to the International Journal of Production Research on the occasion of its 60th Anniversary. Since its foundation in 1961, IJPR has become one of the flagship journals of our profession. It was the first international journal to bring together papers on all aspects of production research: product/process engineering, production system design and management, operations management, and logistics. Many exceptional scientific results have been published in the journal.

We would like to thank all contributing authors for their high-quality work and for their willingness to share their research findings with the APMS community. We are also grateful to the members of the IFIP Working Group 5.7, the Program Committee, and the Scientific Committee, along with the Special Sessions organizers for their support in the organization of the conference program. Concerning the number of papers, special thanks must be given to the local colleagues who managed the reviewing process as well as the preparation of the conference program and proceedings, particularly Hicham Haddou Benderbal and Maria-Isabel Estrepo-Ruiz from IMT Atlantique.

September 2021

Alexandre Dolgui
Alain Bernard
David Lemoine
Gregor von Cieminski
David Romero

Organization

Conference Chair

Alexandre Dolgui   IMT Atlantique, Nantes, France

Conference Co-chair

Gregor von Cieminski   ZF Friedrichshafen, Germany

Conference Honorary Co-chairs

Dimitris Kiritsis   EPFL, Switzerland
Kathryn E. Stecke   University of Texas at Dallas, USA

Program Chair

Alain Bernard   Centrale Nantes, France

Program Co-chair

David Romero   Tecnológico de Monterrey, Mexico

Program Committee

Alain Bernard   Centrale Nantes, France
Gregor von Cieminski   ZF Friedrichshafen, Germany
Alexandre Dolgui   IMT Atlantique, Nantes, France
Dimitris Kiritsis   EPFL, Switzerland
David Romero   Tecnológico de Monterrey, Mexico
Kathryn E. Stecke   University of Texas at Dallas, USA

International Advisory Committee

Farhad Ameri   Texas State University, USA
Ugljesa Marjanovic   University of Novi Sad, Serbia
Ilkyeong Moon   Seoul National University, South Korea
Bojan Lalic   University of Novi Sad, Serbia
Hermann Lödding   Hamburg University of Technology, Germany

Organizing Committee Chair

David Lemoine   IMT Atlantique, Nantes, France

Organizing Committee Co-chair

Hichem Haddou Benderbal   IMT Atlantique, Nantes, France

Doctoral Workshop Chairs

Abdelkrim-Ramzi   IMT Atlantique, Nantes, France
  Yelles-Chaouche
Seyyed-Ehsan   IMT Atlantique, Nantes, France
  Hashemi-Petroodi

Award Committee Chairs

Nadjib Brahimi   Rennes School of Business, France
Ramzi Hammami   Rennes School of Business, France

Organizing Committee

Romain Billot   IMT Atlantique, Brest, France
Nadjib Brahimi   Rennes School of Business, France
Olivier Cardin   University of Nantes, France
Catherine Da Cunha   Centrale Nantes, France
Alexandre Dolgui   IMT Atlantique, Nantes, France
Giannakis Mihalis   Audencia, Nantes, France
Evgeny Gurevsky   University of Nantes, France
Hichem Haddou Benderbal   IMT Atlantique, Nantes, France
Ramzi Hammami   Rennes School of Business, France
Oncu Hazir   Rennes School of Business, France
Seyyed-Ehsan   IMT Atlantique, Nantes, France
  Hashemi-Petroodi

David Lemoine   IMT Atlantique, Nantes, France
Nasser Mebarki   University of Nantes, France
Patrick Meyer   IMT Atlantique, Brest, France
Merhdad Mohammadi   IMT Atlantique, Brest, France
Dominique Morel   IMT Atlantique, Nantes, France
Maroua Nouiri   University of Nantes, France
Maria-Isabel Restrepo-Ruiz IMT Atlantique, Nantes, France
Naly Rakoto   IMT Atlantique, Nantes, France
Ilhem Slama   IMT Atlantique, Nantes, France
Simon Thevenin   IMT Atlantique, Nantes, France
Abdelkrim-Ramzi   IMT Atlantique, Nantes, France
  Yelles-Chaouche

Scientific Committee

Erry Yulian Triblas Adesta	International Islamic University Malaysia, Malaysia
El-Houssaine Aghezzaf	Ghent University, Belgium
Erlend Alfnes	Norwegian University of Science and Technology, Norway
Hamid Allaoui	Université d'Artois, France
Thecle Alix	IUT Bordeaux Montesquieu, France
Farhad Ameri	Texas State University, USA
Bjørn Andersen	Norwegian University of Science and Technology, Norway
Eiji Arai	Osaka University, Japan
Jannicke Baalsrud Hauge	KTH Royal Institute of Technology, Sweden/BIBA, Germany
Zied Babai	Kedge Business School, France
Natalia Bakhtadze	Russian Academy of Sciences, Russia
Pierre Baptiste	Polytechnique de Montréal, Canada
Olga Battaïa	Kedge Business School, France
Farouk Belkadi	Centrale Nantes, France
Lyes Benyoucef	Aix-Marseille University, France
Bopaya Bidanda	University of Pittsburgh, USA
Frédérique Biennier	INSA Lyon, France
Jean-Charles Billaut	Université de Tours, France
Umit S. Bititci	Heriot-Watt University, UK
Magali Bosch-Mauchand	Université de Technologie de Compiègne, France
Xavier Boucher	Mines St Etienne, France
Abdelaziz Bouras	Qatar University, Qatar
Jim Browne	University College Dublin, Ireland
Luis Camarinha-Matos	Universidade Nova de Lisboa, Portugal
Olivier Cardin	University of Nantes, France
Sergio Cavalieri	University of Bergamo, Italy
Stephen Childe	Plymouth University, UK
Hyunbo Cho	Pohang University of Science and Technology, South Korea
Chengbin Chu	ESIEE Paris, France
Feng Chu	Paris-Saclay University, France
Byung Do Chung	Yonsei University, South Korea
Gregor von Cieminski	ZF Friedrichshafen, Germany
Catherine Da Cunha	Centrale Nantes, France
Yves Dallery	CentraleSupélec, France
Xavier Delorme	Mines St Etienne, France
Frédéric Demoly	Université de Technologie de Belfort-Montbéliard, France
Mélanie Despeisse	Chalmers University of Technology, Sweden
Alexandre Dolgui	IMT Atlantique, Nantes, France
Slavko Dolinšek	University of Ljubljana, Slovenia

Sang Do Noh	Sungkyunkwan University, South Korea
Heidi Carin Dreyer	Norwegian University of Science and Technology, Norway
Eero Eloranta	Aalto University, Finland
Soumaya El Kadiri	Texelia AG, Switzerland
Christos Emmanouilidis	University of Groningen, The Netherlands
Anton Eremeev	Siberian Branch of Russian Academy of Sciences, Russia
Åsa Fasth-Berglund	Chalmers University of Technology, Sweden
Rosanna Fornasiero	Consiglio Nazionale delle Ricerche, Italy
Xuehao Feng	Zhejiang University, China
Yannick Frein	INP Grenoble, France
Jan Frick	University of Stavanger, Norway
Klaas Gadeyne	Flanders Make, Belgium
Paolo Gaiardelli	University of Bergamo, Italy
Adriana Giret Boggino	Universidad Politécnica de Valencia, Spain
Samuel Gomes	Belfort-Montbéliard University of Technology, France
Bernard Grabot	INP-Toulouse, ENIT, France
Gerhard Gudergan	RWTH Aachen University, Germany
Thomas R. Gulledge Jr.	George Mason University, USA
Nikolai Guschinsky	National Academy of Sciences, Belarus
Slim Hammadi	Centrale Lille, France
Ahmedou Haouba	University of Nouakchott Al-Asriya, Mauritania
Soumaya Henchoz	Logitech AG, Switzerland
Hironori Hibino	Tokyo University of Science, Japan
Hans-Henrik Hvolby	Aalborg University, Denmark
Jan Holmström	Aalto University, Finland
Dmitry Ivanov	Berlin School of Economics and Law, Germany
Harinder Jagdev	National University of Ireland at Galway, Ireland
Jayanth Jayaram	University of South Carolina, USA
Zhibin Jiang	Shanghai Jiao Tong University, China
John Johansen	Aalborg University, Denmark
Hong-Bae Jun	Hongik University, South Korea
Toshiya Kaihara	Kobe University, Japan
Duck Young Kim	Pohang University of Science and Technology, South Korea
Dimitris Kiritsis	EPFL, Switzerland
Tomasz Koch	Wroclaw University of Science and Technology, Poland
Pisut Koomsap	Asian Institute of Technology, Thailand
Vladimir Kotov	Belarusian State University, Belarus
Mikhail Kovalyov	National Academy of Sciences, Belarus
Gül Kremer	Iowa State University, USA
Boonserm Kulvatunyou	National Institute of Standards and Technology, USA
Senthilkumaran Kumaraguru	Indian Institute of Information Technology Design and Manufacturing, India

Thomas R. Kurfess	Georgia Institute of Technology, USA
Andrew Kusiak	University of Iowa, USA
Bojan Lalić	University of Novi Sad, Serbia
Samir Lamouri	ENSAM Paris, France
Lenka Landryova	Technical University of Ostrava, Czech Republic
Alexander Lazarev	Russian Academy of Sciences, Moscow, Russia
Jan-Peter Lechner	First Global Liaison, Germany
Gyu M. Lee	Pusan National University, South Korea
Kangbok Lee	Pohang University of Science and Technology, South Korea
Genrikh Levin	National Academy of Sciences, Belarus
Jingshan Li	University of Wisconsin-Madison, USA
Ming K. Lim	Chongqing University, China
Hermann Lödding	Hamburg University of Technology, Germany
Pierre Lopez	LAAS-CNRS, France
Marco Macchi	Politecnico di Milano, Italy
Ugljesa Marjanovic	University of Novi Sad, Serbia
Muthu Mathirajan	Indian Institute of Science, India
Gökan May	University of North Florida, USA
Khaled Medini	Mines St Etienne, France
Jörn Mehnen	University of Strathclyde, UK
Vidosav D. Majstorovich	University of Belgrade, Serbia
Semyon M. Meerkov	University of Michigan, USA
Joao Gilberto Mendes dos Reis	UNIP Paulista University, Brazil
Hajime Mizuyama	Aoyama Gakuin University, Japan
Ilkyeong Moon	Seoul National University, South Korea
Eiji Morinaga	Osaka Prefecture University, Japan
Dimitris Mourtzis	University of Patras, Greece
Irenilza de Alencar Naas	UNIP Paulista University, Brazil
Masaru Nakano	Keio University, Japan
Torbjörn Netland	ETH Zürich, Switzerland
Gilles Neubert	EMLYON Business School, Saint-Etienne, France
Izabela Nielsen	Aalborg University, Denmark
Tomomi Nonaka	Ritsumeikan University, Japan
Jinwoo Park	Seoul National University, South Korea
François Pérès	INP-Toulouse, ENIT, France
Fredrik Persson	Linköping Institute of Technology, Sweden
Giuditta Pezzotta	University of Bergamo, Italy
Selwyn Piramuthu	University of Florida, USA
Alberto Portioli Staudacher	Politecnico di Milano, Italy
Daryl Powell	Norwegian University of Science and Technology, Norway
Vittaldas V. Prabhu	Pennsylvania State University, USA
Jean-Marie Proth	Inria, France
Ricardo José Rabelo	Federal University of Santa Catarina, Brazil

Rahul Rai	University at Buffalo, USA
Mario Rapaccini	Florence University, Italy
Nidhal Rezg	University of Lorraine, France
Ralph Riedel	Westsächsische Hochschule Zwickau, Germany
Irene Roda	Politecnico di Milano, Italy
Asbjörn Rolstadås	Norwegian University of Science and Technology, Norway
David Romero	Tecnológico de Monterrey, Mexico
Christoph Roser	Karlsruhe University of Applied Sciences, Germany
André Rossi	Université Paris-Dauphine, France
Martin Rudberg	Linköping University, Sweden
Thomas E. Ruppli	University of Basel, Switzerland
Krzysztof Santarek	Warsaw University of Technology, Poland
Subhash Sarin	VirginiaTech, USA
Suresh P. Sethi	The University of Texas at Dallas, USA
Fabio Sgarbossa	Norwegian University of Science and Technology, Norway
John P. Shewchuk	Virginia Polytechnic Institute and State University, USA
Dan L. Shunk	Arizona State University, USA
Ali Siadat	Arts et Métiers ParisTech, France
Riitta Smeds	Aalto University, Finland
Boris Sokolov	Russian Academy of Sciences, Russia
Vijay Srinivasan	National Institute of Standards and Technology, USA
Johan Stahre	Chalmers University of Technology, Sweden
Kathryn E. Stecke	The University of Texas at Dallas, USA
Kenn Steger-Jensen	Aalborg University, Denmark
Volker Stich	RWTH Aachen University, Germany
Richard Lee Storch	University of Washington, USA
Jan Ola Strandhagen	Norwegian University of Science and Technology, Norway
Stanislaw Strzelczak	Warsaw University of Technology, Poland
Nick Szirbik	University of Groningen, The Netherlands
Marco Taisch	Politecnico di Milano, Italy
Lixin Tang	Northeastern University, China
Kari Tanskanen	Aalto University School of Science, Finland
Ilias Tatsiopoulos	National Technical University of Athens, Greece
Sergio Terzi	Politecnico di Milano, Italy
Klaus-Dieter Thoben	Universität Bremen, Germany
Manoj Tiwari	Indian Institute of Technology, India
Matthias Thüre	Jinan University, China
Jacques H. Trienekens	Wageningen University, The Netherlands
Mario Tucci	Universitá degli Studi di Firenze, Italy
Shigeki Umeda	Musashi University, Japan
Bruno Vallespir	University of Bordeaux, France
François Vernadat	University of Lorraine, France

Agostino Villa   Politecnico di Torino, Italy
Lihui Wang   KTH Royal Institute of Technology, Sweden
Sabine Waschull   University of Groningen, The Netherlands
Hans-Hermann Wiendahl   University of Stuttgart, Germany
Frank Werner   University of Magdeburg, Germany
Shaun West   Lucerne University of Applied Sciences and Arts,
                                     Switzerland
Joakim Wikner   Jönköping University, Sweden
Hans Wortmann   University of Groningen, The Netherlands
Desheng Dash Wu   University of Chinese Academy of Sciences, China
Thorsten Wuest   West Virginia University, USA
Farouk Yalaoui   University of Technology of Troyes, France
Noureddine Zerhouni   Université Bourgogne Franche-Comte, France

List of Reviewers

Abbou Rosa

Abdeljaouad Mohamed Amine

Absi Nabil

Acerbi Federica

Aghelinejad Mohsen

Aghezzaf El-Houssaine

Agrawal Rajeev

Agrawal Tarun Kumar

Alexopoulos Kosmas

Alix Thecle

Alkhudary Rami

Altekin F. Tevhide

Alves Anabela

Ameri Farhad

Andersen Ann-Louise

Andersen Bjorn

Anderson Marc

Anderson Matthew

Anholon Rosley

Antosz Katarzyna

Apostolou Dimitris

Arica Emrah

Arlinghaus Julia Christine

Aubry Alexis

Baalsrud Hauge Jannicke

Badulescu Yvonne Gabrielle

Bakhtadze Natalia

Barbosa Christiane Lima

Barni Andrea

Batocchio Antonio

Battaïa Olga

Battini Daria

Behrens Larissa

Ben-Ammar Oussama

Benatia Mohamed Amin

Bentaha M.-Lounes

Benyoucef Lyes

Beraldi Santos Alexandre

Bergmann Ulf

Bernus Peter

Berrah Lamia-Amel

Bertnum Aili Biriita

Bertoni Marco

Bettayeb Belgacem

Bevilacqua Maurizio

Biennier Frédérique

Bititci Umit Sezer

Bocanet Vlad

Bosch-Mauchand Magali

Boucher Xavier

Bourguignon Saulo Cabral

Bousdekis Alexandros

Brahimi Nadjib

Bresler Maggie

Brunoe Thomas Ditlev

Brusset Xavier

Burow Kay

Calado Robisom Damasceno

Calarge Felipe
Camarinha-Matos Luis Manuel
Cameron David
Cannas Violetta Giada
Cao Yifan
Castro Eduardo Lorenzo
Cattaruzza Diego
Cerqueus Audrey
Chang Tai-Woo
Chaves Sandra Maria do Amaral
Chavez Zuhara
Chen Jinwei
Cheng Yongxi
Chiacchio Ferdinando
Chiari da Silva Ethel Cristina
Childe Steve
Cho Hyunbo
Choi SangSu
Chou Shuo-Yan
Christensen Flemming Max Møller
Chung Byung Do
Ciarapica Filippo Emanuele
Cimini Chiara
Clivillé Vincent
Cohen Yuval
Converso Giuseppe
Cosenza Harvey
Costa Helder Gomes
Da Cunha Catherine
Daaboul Joanna
Dahane Mohammed
Dakic Dusanka
Das Dyutimoy Nirupam
Das Jyotirmoy Nirupam
Das Sayan
Davari Morteza
De Arruda Ignacio Paulo Sergio de
De Campos Renato
De Oliveira Costa Neto Pedro Luiz
Delorme Xavier
Deroussi Laurent
Despeisse Mélanie
Di Nardo Mario
Di Pasquale Valentina
Dillinger Fabian
Djedidi Oussama

Dolgui Alexandre
Dolinsek Slavko
Dou Runliang
Drei Samuel Martins
Dreyer Heidi
Dreyfus Paul-Arthur
Dubey Rameshwar
Dümmel Johannes
Eloranta Eero
Emmanouilidis Christos
Ermolova Maria
Eslami Yasamin
Fast-Berglund Åsa
Faveto Alberto
Federico Adrodegari
Feng Xuehao
Finco Serena
Flores-García Erik
Fontaine Pirmin
Fosso Wamba Samuel
Franciosi Chiara
Frank Jana
Franke Susanne
Freitag Mike
Frick Jan
Fruggiero Fabio
Fu Wenhan
Fujii Nobutada
Gahan Padmabati
Gaiardelli Paolo
Gallo Mosè
Ganesan Viswanath Kumar
Gaponov Igor
Gayialis Sotiris P.
Gebennini Elisa
Ghadge Abhijeet
Ghrairi Zied
Gianessi Paolo
Giret Boggino Adriana
Gloeckner Robert
Gogineni Sonika
Gola Arkadiusz
Goodarzian Fariba
Gosling Jon
Gouyon David
Grabot Bernard

Grangeon Nathalie
Grassi Andrea
Grenzfurtner Wolfgang
Guerpinar Tan
Guillaume Romain
Guimarães Neto Abelino Reis
Guizzi Guido
Gupta Sumit
Gurevsky Evgeny
Habibi Muhammad Khoirul Khakim
Haddou Benderbal Hichem
Halse Lise Lillebrygfjeld
Hammami Ramzi
Hani Yasmina
Hashemi-Petroodi S. Ehsan
Havzi Sara
Hazir Oncu
Hedayatinia Pooya
Hemmati Ahmad
Henchoz El Kadiri Soumaya
Heuss Lisa
Hibino Hironori
Himmiche Sara
Hnaien Faicel
Hofer Gernot
Holst Lennard Phillip
Hovelaque Vincent
Hrnjica Bahrudin
Huber Walter
Husniah Hennie
Hvolby Hans-Henrik
Hwang Gyusun
Irohara Takashi
Islam Md Hasibul
Iung Benoit
Ivanov Dmitry
Jacomino Mireille
Jagdev Harinder
Jahn Niklas
Jain Geetika
Jain Vipul
Jasiulewicz-Kaczmarek Małgorzata
Jebali Aida
Jelisic Elena
Jeong Yongkuk
Johansen John

Jones Al
Jun Chi-Hyuck
Jun Hong-Bae
Jun Sungbum
Juned Mohd
Jünge Gabriele
Kaasinen Eija
Kaihara Toshiya
Kalaboukas Kostas
Kang Yong-Shin
Karampatzakis Dimitris
Kayikci Yasanur
Kedad-Sidhoum Safia
Keepers Makenzie
Keivanpour Samira
Keshari Anupam
Kim Byung-In
Kim Duck Young
Kim Hwa-Joong
Kim Hyun-Jung
Kinra Aseem
Kiritsis Dimitris
Kitjacharoenchai Patchara
Kjeldgaard Stefan
Kjersem Kristina
Klimchik Alexandr
Klymenko Olena
Kollberg Thomassen Maria
Kolyubin Sergey
Koomsap Pisut
Kramer Kathrin
Kulvatunyou Boonserm (Serm)
Kumar Ramesh
Kurata Takeshi
Kvadsheim Nina Pereira
Lahaye Sébastien
Lalic Danijela
Lamouri Samir
Lamy Damien
Landryova Lenka
Lechner Jan-Peter
Lee Dong-Ho
Lee Eunji
Lee Kangbok
Lee Kyungsik
Lee Minchul

Lee Seokcheon
Lee Seokgi
Lee Young Hoon
Lehuédé Fabien
Leiber Daria
Lemoine David
Li Haijiao
Li Yuanfu
Lim Dae-Eun
Lim Ming
Lima Adalberto da
Lima Nilsa
Lin Chen-ju
Linares Jean-marc
Linnartz Maria
Listl Franz Georg
Liu Ming
Liu Xin
Liu Zhongzheng
Lödding Hermann
Lodgaard Eirin
Loger Benoit
Lorenz Rafael
Lu Jinzhi
Lu Xingwei
Lu Xuefei
Lucas Flavien
Lüftenegger Egon
Luo Dan
Ma Junhai
Macchi Marco
Machado Brunno Abner
Maier Janine Tatjana
Maihami Reza
Makboul Salma
Makris Sotiris
Malaguti Roney Camargo
Mandal Jasashwi
Mandel Alexander
Manier Hervé
Manier Marie-Ange
Marangé Pascale
Marchesano Maria Grazia
Marek Svenja
Marjanovic Ugljesa
Marmolejo Jose Antonio

Marques Melissa
Marrazzini Leonardo
Masone Adriano
Massonnet Guillaume
Matsuda Michiko
Maxwell Duncan William
Mazzuto Giovanni
Medić Nenad
Medini Khaled
Mehnen Jorn
Mendes dos Reis João Gilberto
Mentzas Gregoris
Metaxa Ifigeneia
Min Li Li
Minner Stefan
Mishra Ashutosh
Mitra Rony
Mizuyama Hajime
Mogale Dnyaneshwar
Mohammadi Mehrdad
Mollo Neto Mario
Montini Elias
Montoya-Torres Jairo R.
Moon Ilkyeong
Moraes Thais De Castro
Morinaga Eiji
Moser Benedikt
Moshref-Javadi Mohammad
Mourtzis Dimitris
Mundt Christopher
Muši Denis
Nääs Irenilza De Alencar
Naim Mohamed
Nakade Koichi
Nakano Masaru
Napoleone Alessia
Nayak Ashutosh
Neroni Mattia
Netland Torbjørn
Neubert Gilles
Nguyen Du Huu
Nguyen Duc-Canh
Nguyen Thi Hien
Nielsen Izabela
Nielsen Kjeld
Nishi Tatsushi

Nogueira Sara
Noh Sang Do
Nonaka Tomomi
Noran Ovidiu
Norre Sylvie
Ortmeier Frank
Ouazene Yassine
Ouzrout Yacine
Özcan Uğur
Paes Graciele Oroski
Pagnoncelli Bernardo
Panigrahi Sibarama
Panigrahi Swayam Sampurna
Papakostas Nikolaos
Papcun Peter
Pashkevich Anatol
Pattnaik Monalisha
Pels Henk Jan
Pérès François
Persson Fredrik
Pezzotta Giuditta
Phan Dinh Anh
Piétrac Laurent
Pinto Sergio Crespo Coelho da
Pirola Fabiana
Pissardini Paulo Eduardo
Polenghi Adalberto
Popolo Valentina
Portioli Staudacher Alberto
Powell Daryl
Prabhu Vittaldas
Psarommatis Foivos
Rabelo Ricardo
Rakic Slavko
Rapaccini Mario
Reis Milena Estanislau Diniz Dos
Resanovic Daniel
Rey David
Riedel Ralph
Rikalović Aleksandar
Rinaldi Marta
Roda Irene
Rodriguez Aguilar Roman
Romagnoli Giovanni
Romeo Bandinelli
Romero David

Roser Christoph
Rossit Daniel Alejandro
Rudberg Martin
Sabitov Rustem
Sachs Anna-Lena
Sahoo Rosalin
Sala Roberto
Santarek Kszysztof
Satolo Eduardo Guilherme
Satyro Walter
Savin Sergei
Schneider Daniel
Semolić Brane
Shafiq Muhammad
Sharma Rohit
Shin Jong-Ho
Shukla Mayank
Shunk Dan
Siadat Ali
Silva Cristovao
Singgih Ivan Kristianto
Singh Sube
Slama Ilhem
Smaglichenko Alexander
Smeds Riitta Johanna
Soares Paula Metzker
Softic Selver
Sokolov Boris V.
Soleilhac Gauthier
Song Byung Duk
Song Xiaoxiao
Souier Mehdi
Sørensen Daniel Grud Hellerup
Spagnol Gabriela
Srinivasan Vijay
Stavrou Vasileios P.
Steger-Jensen Kenn
Stich Volker
Stipp Marluci Andrade Conceição
Stoll Oliver
Strandhagen Jan Ola
Suh Eun Suk
Suleykin Alexander
Suzanne Elodie
Szirbik Nick B.
Taghvaeipour Afshin

Taisch Marco
Tanimizu Yoshitaka
Tanizaki Takashi
Tasić Nemanja
Tebaldi Letizia
Telles Renato
Thevenin Simon
Thoben Klaus-Dieter
Thurer Matthias
Tiedemann Fredrik
Tisi Massimo
Torres Luis Fernando
Tortorella Guilherme Luz
Troyanovsky Vladimir
Turcin Ioan
Turki Sadok
Ulrich Marco
Unip Solimar
Valdiviezo Viera Luis Enrique
Vallespir Bruno
Vasic Stana
Vaz Paulo
Vespoli Silvestro
Vicente da Silva Ivonaldo
Villeneuve Eric
Viviani Jean-Laurent
Vještica Marko
Vo Thi Le Hoa
Voisin Alexandre
von Cieminski Gregor
Von Stietencron Moritz
Wagner Sarah
Wang Congke
Wang Hongfeng
Wang Yin

Wang Yingli
Wang Yuling
Wang Zhaojie
Wang Zhixin
Wellsandt Stefan
West Shaun
Wiendahl Hans-Hermann
Wiesner Stefan Alexander
Wikner Joakim
Wiktorsson Magnus
Wimmer Manuel
Woo Young-Bin
Wortmann Andreas
Wortmann Johan Casper
Wuest Thorsten
Xu Tiantong
Yadegari Ehsan
Yalaoui Alice
Yang Danqin
Yang Guoqing
Yang Jie
Yang Zhaorui
Yelles Chaouche Abdelkrim Ramzi
Zaeh Michael Friedrich
Zaikin Oleg
Zambetti Michela
Zeba Gordana
Zhang Guoqing
Zhang Ruiyou
Zheng Feifeng
Zheng Xiaochen
Zoitl Alois
Zolotová Iveta
Zouggar Anne

Contents – Part V

Improvement of Design and Operation of Manufacturing Systems

Crossdock and Transportation Issues

Maintenance Improvement and Lifecycle Management

Additive Manufacturing and Mass Customization

Frameworks and Conceptual Modelling for Systems and Services Efficiency

Optimization of Production and Transportation Systems

Optimization of Supply Chain Agility and Reconfigurability

AI-Based Approaches for Quality and Performance Improvement of Production Systems

Risk and Performance Management of Supply Chains

Data-Driven Platforms and Applications in Production and Logistics: Digital Twins and AI for Sustainability

Assembly Line Worker Assignment and Balancing Problem with Positional Constraints

Hyungjoon Yang⑩, Je-Hun Lee⑩, and Hyun-Jung Kim$^{(\boxtimes)}$⑩

Korea Advanced Institute of Science and Technology (KAIST),
Daejeon 34141, Republic of Korea
hyunjungkim@kaist.ac.kr

Abstract. One of the most important operational issues in the assembly line is to assign tasks and workers to stations while balancing the workload of the workers. We consider the assembly line worker assignment and balancing problem (ALWABP) where the process time of a task depends on worker skill levels. We also consider new positional constraints in the ALWABP to secure the working area of the workers. Two mathematical programming models are proposed to assign workers and tasks when new products are introduced and when a worker is absent or leaves a position temporary, respectively. A heuristic algorithm for the first model is proposed due to its extremely high complexity. The experimental results show the efficiency of the proposed methods. Finally, we explain how the proposed models can be used with a real-time dashboard of a digital twin.

Keywords: Assembly line · Line balancing · Worker skill level · Positional constraints · Digital twin

1 Introduction

An assembly line balancing problem (ALBP) which distributes tasks to workstations was introduced in 1955 [1]. The problem is known to be NP-hard due to its high complexity [2]. The early studies have focused on the ALBP to balance task times on each station while neglecting the heterogeneity of the workers. Later, many studies have considered practical environments, such as mixed-model assembly lines [3], multi-manned stations [4], and various shapes of assembly lines [5]. An assembly line worker assignment and balancing problem (ALWABP) further considers the different task time of each worker to the ALBP and assigns workers and tasks to stations [6]. Many studies have developed exact methods [7–9] and heuristic algorithms [10–12] for the ALWABP. ALWABP also has been.

We address the ALWABP with new positional constraints which are required from one of the automotive parts manufacturing companies in Korea. Since multiple workers perform tasks in a workstation simultaneously, it is important to secure the working area of the workers. In addition, it is preferred not to assign tasks located far from each other to a worker [13]. These positional constraints are newly considered as well as task

A. Dolgui et al. (Eds.): APMS 2021, IFIP AICT 634, pp. 3–11, 2021.
https://doi.org/10.1007/978-3-030-85914-5_1

precedence constraints. We propose two mathematical models, for the assignment, which can be used when new products are introduced and when a worker is absent or leaves a position temporary, respectively. Absenteeism is one of the significant factors that break the balance of assembly lines. Some workers are absent for the whole day while some others may leave the position for a while during work hours. It happens unexpectedly and is hard to predict in advance. Therefore, it is important to quickly and effectively respond to such a situation [14], and the second model we propose addresses this problem. We finally explain how the proposed models can be used in practice with a digital twin.

2   Problem Definition

The problem we consider has been motivated from one of the automotive parts manufacturing companies in Korea. The company assembles a wiring harness which consists of wires, terminals, and connectors and runs throughout the entire vehicle. The wiring harness is assembled on a panel which moves on a conveyor belt. We assume the assembly line produces a single type of wiring harness. Figure 1 shows assembly tasks on a panel and the precedence graph of the tasks, and Fig. 2 shows the assembly line we consider.

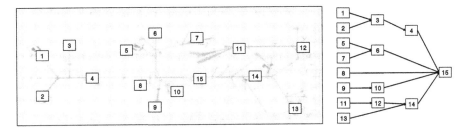

Fig. 1. An example of tasks and their precedence graph

Fig. 2. Photo of an assembly line

We consider two positional constraints required from the company. The first one is a task positional constraint which restricts the assignment of tasks located far from each other to a worker. The other one is a worker positional constraint where the working areas of adjacent workers are not overlapped. The objective is to minimize the cycle time.

3 Solution Approach

3.1 Mathematical Programming Model for Regular Assignment

Table 1 below shows the indices, parameters and decision variables we use for the mathematical model.

Table 1. Notations of a mathematical model for regular assignment

Indices & sets	
$h, i (\in I)$	Indices of tasks (Set of tasks)
$j (\in J)$	Index of stations (Set of stations)
$k (\in K)$	Index of workers (Set of workers)
P	Set of task pairs with precedence
P_t	Set of task pairs that are too far to be assigned to the same worker
P_w	Set of task pairs that are too close to be assigned to the adjacent worker
Parameters	
t_{ik}	Process time of task i when performed by worker k
M	Total number of tasks (used as a sufficiently big number)
Decision variables	
x_{ijk}	1 if task i is performed by worker k at station j, otherwise 0
y_{jk}	1 if worker k is assigned to station j, otherwise 0
C	Cycle time of the line

$$\min C \qquad (1)$$

Subject to:

$$\sum_{j \in J} \sum_{k \in K} x_{ijk} = 1, \qquad \forall i \in I \qquad (2)$$

$$\sum_{j \in J} y_{jk} = 1, \qquad \forall k \in K \qquad (3)$$

$$\sum_{k \in K} y_{jk} = 1, \qquad \forall j \in J \qquad (4)$$

$$\sum_{j\in J}\sum_{k\in K}jx_{hjk} \leq \sum_{j\in J}\sum_{k\in K}jx_{ijk}, \qquad \forall(h,i)\in P \tag{5}$$

$$\sum_{i\in I}\sum_{j\in J}t_{ik}x_{ijk} \leq C, \qquad \forall k\in K \tag{6}$$

$$\sum_{i\in I}x_{ijk} \leq My_{jk}, \qquad \forall j\in J, k\in K \tag{7}$$

$$\sum_{j\in J}\left(x_{hjk}+x_{ijk}\right) \leq 1, \qquad \forall k\in K, (h,i)\in P_t \tag{8}$$

$$\sum_{k\in K}\left(x_{h(j-1)k}+x_{ijk}\right) \leq 1, \qquad \forall j\in J\backslash\{1\}, (h,i)\in P_w \tag{9}$$

This formulation derives the optimal assignment of tasks and workers to reduce the cycle time. Objective function (1) and Constraints (2)–(7) are the basic formulation of the ALWABP. Constraint (2) indicates that each task is assigned to exactly one station. Constraints (3) and (4) mean that each worker should be assigned to one station and each station should have only one worker, respectively. Constraint (5) is used for the precedence relation of the tasks. Constraint (6) computes the cycle time which takes the maximum value among the completion times of all workers, and Constraint (7) makes sure that tasks are assigned to a worker and a station when the worker is assigned to the station. Constraints (8) and (9) are the task positional constraint and worker positional constraint, respectively. After obtaining a solution, the workstations are then assigned to panels evenly.

3.2   Mathematical Programming Model for Task Reassignment

We now propose another mathematical model that adjusts the initial assignment obtained in Sect. 3.1. When a worker is absent at the beginning of the day or leaves a position during work hours, the tasks assigned to the worker should be reassigned. The following notations and formulation are used for this case. We note that x_{ijk} and y_{jk} used in this section are obtained from the model in Sect. 3.1 (Table 2).

Table 2. Notations of a mathematical model for task reassignment

Set	
I_U	Set of unassigned tasks (tasks that should be reassigned)
Parameter	
k_a	Absent worker
Decision variable	
a_{ik}	1 if reassign task i to worker k, otherwise 0

$$\min C \tag{10}$$

Subject to:

$$\sum_{k\in K\setminus\{k_a\}} a_{ik} = 1, \qquad \forall i \in I_U \tag{11}$$

$$\sum_{j\in J}\sum_{k\in K} j a_{hk} y_{jk} \leq \sum_{j\in J}\sum_{k\in K} j x_{ijk}, \qquad \forall (h,i) \in P, h \in I_U, i \notin I_U \tag{12}$$

$$\sum_{j\in J}\sum_{k\in K} j x_{hjk} \leq \sum_{j\in J}\sum_{k\in K} j a_{ik} y_{jk}, \qquad \forall (h,i) \in P, h \notin I_U, i \in I_U \tag{13}$$

$$\sum_{j\in J}\sum_{k\in K} j a_{hk} y_{jk} \leq \sum_{j\in J}\sum_{k\in K} j a_{ik} y_{jk}, \qquad \forall (h,i) \in P, h, i \in I_U \tag{14}$$

$$a_{ik} + \sum_{j\in J} x_{hjk} \leq 1, \qquad \forall (h,i) \in P_t, k \in K, i \in I_U \tag{15}$$

$$\sum_{k\in K}\left(a_{hk} y_{(j-1)k} + a_{ik} y_{jk}\right) \leq 1, \qquad \forall (h,i) \in P_w, j \in J\setminus\{1\}, h, i \in I_U \tag{16}$$

$$\sum_{i\in I}\sum_{j\in J} t_{ik}\left(a_{ik} y_{jk} + x_{ijk}\right) \leq C, \qquad \forall k \in K\setminus\{k_a\} \tag{17}$$

Constraint (11) reassigns the tasks of the absent worker. Constraints (12), (13) and (14) are used for the precedence relation of tasks after the reassignment. Constraints (15) and (16), respectively, are for the task positional constraint and worker positional constraint after the reassignment. Constraint (17) calculates the cycle time.

3.3 Heuristic Algorithm for Regular Assignment

Since it takes a long time to obtain an optimal solution of the model in Sect. 3.1, a heuristic algorithm is proposed. We note that an optimal solution of the model in Sect. 3.2 is easily obtained within a short period of time. The proposed algorithm consists of the initial solution generation step and improvement step with local search.

First, the tasks with no predecessor are randomly selected and assigned to the first station. The number of tasks assigned to each station is either $|I|/|k|$ or $|I|/|k|$. Similarly, the remaining tasks are also randomly assigned to the stations by considering the precedence constraints and positional constraints. After that, workers who can finish the tasks in a station at the earliest time are assigned. Then an initial solution is obtained.

A local search process is applied to the initial solution with task shift, task swap, and worker swap operators to reduce the cycle time. If there is any improvement after applying the three operators, the current best solution is updated. Otherwise, a new neighbor solution is obtained from the current solution by randomly changing the task assignment regardless of the solution quality. Then the local search process is again applied to the neighbor solution. This procedure is repeated until a give number of iterations or the given maximum computation time.

4   Computational Results

The two optimization models in Sects. 3.1 and 3.2 were programmed and solved by using OR-Tools, an open source software for optimization. The maximum number of iterations of the heuristic algorithm is set to 10,000, and the time limit is 10 min. Experiments are performed by comparing the proposed heuristic algorithm to an optimal solution for initial assignment and by comparing the reassignment result of the proposed mathematical model to the current practice. Table 3 shows the comparison result of the model solved with OR-Tools and the proposed heuristic algorithm for regular assignment. Table 4 shows the effectiveness of the model for task reassignment by comparing the result with the current practice. The average cycle time (CT) and computation time with 30 instances are presented in the tables.

In Table 3, the model for regular assignment found optimal solutions with up to 10 tasks with OR-Tools. When the number of tasks is more than 20, it is not able to provide optimal solutions within one hour. The best cycle time found so far is written in the CT column in the table. We can observe that the proposed heuristic algorithm provides optimal solutions with 10 tasks and 5 workers. In addition, it gives a better solution than OR-Tools with more than 40 tasks and 10 workers when there is a time limit of one hour. The computation time of the heuristic algorithm is less than 2 min. This is enough for practical use because the heuristic algorithm is required to run in the early morning of the day when a new product is assembled, which does not occur frequently.

In Table 4, the current practice indicates the results from the simple rule used in the company. The operations manager reassigns tasks based on his/her experience in the company. We can see that the proposed model can reduce the cycle time at most 17.5% with 100 tasks and 20 workers. The computation time of the optimization model with OR-Tools is within 10 s even for the large-sized instances.

Table 3. Computation results for OR-Tools and heuristic algorithm

Number of tasks	Number of workers	Optimization model		Heuristic algorithm	
		CT(s)	Computation time(s)	CT(s)	Computation time(s)
7	3	378*	<1	378*	<1
10	5	341*	35	341*	<1
20	7	524	>3,600	524	8
40	10	714	>3,600	**703** **(−1.5%)**	28
100	20	910	>3,600	**874** **(−3.9%)**	110

*: optimal solution

Table 4. Comparison of the proposed model and current practice for task reassignment

Number of tasks	Number of workers	Current practice CT(s)	Optimization model CT(s)
10	5	555	543 (−2.1%)
20	7	739	679 (−8.1%)
40	10	951	833 (−12.4%)
100	20	1,249	1,031 (−17.5%)

5 Applications to Practice

With the advancement of IoT, it is possible to identify the real-time position of workers and to detect whether a worker is away from the assembly line and returns to the line. In the company we consider, the workers wear a bracelet with a sensor, and the real-time position of each worker is collected by a beacon system.

Our proposed method is implemented in the digital twin which collects real-time data and monitors the current operations state. Figure 3 shows a scenario of our method applied with a digital twin. All the information about the current position of workers and their task assignment are described in the dashboard of a digital twin. Step 1 in Fig. 3 shows the optimal worker-task assignment when all workers are present in the assembly line. When a worker leaves his/her position for a certain period, absenteeism is automatically recognized (Step 2 in Fig. 3) and the proposed model in Sect. 3.2 is run with the real-time information of the task assignment, remaining workers, and tasks requiring the reassignment. Then an optimal solution to minimize the cycle time is obtained with a commercial solver and displayed in the dashboard with the modified

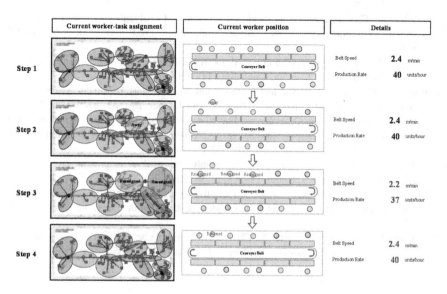

Fig. 3. Use of proposed methods in practice

conveyor belt speed and production rate (Step 3 in Fig. 3). The conveyor belt then decreases its speed according to the solution obtained. When the worker returns to the assembly line, the initial assignment is again applied (Step 4 in Fig. 3).

6 Conclusion

We have addressed the ALWABP with new positional constraints to minimize the cycle time. Two mathematical programming model and one heuristic algorithm have been proposed, and the experimental results have shown their effectiveness. We have also provided a scenario of using the proposed model with a digital twin by detecting the real-time position of workers. We further need to compare the digital twin result with the actual result, to develop exact algorithms for the regular assignment, to consider the work efficiency of an individual operator, and to develop AI models for solving the problem.

References

1. Salveson, M.E.: The assembly line balancing problem. J. Ind. Eng. **6**(3), 18–25 (1955)
2. Gutjahr, A.L., Nemhauser, G.L.: An algorithm for the line balancing problem. Manage. Sci. **11**(2), 308–315 (1964)
3. Thomopoulos, N.T.: Line balancing-sequencing for mixed-model assembly. Manage. Sci. **14**(2), B59–B75 (1967)
4. Fattahi, P., Roshani, A., Roshani, A.: A mathematical model and ant colony algorithm for multi-manned assembly line balancing problem. Int. J. Adv. Manuf. Technol. **53**(1–4), 363–378 (2011)
5. Miltenburg, G.J., Wijngaard, J.: The U-line Line Balancing Problem. Manage. Sci. **40**(10), 1378–1388 (1994)
6. Miralles, C., García-Sabater, J. P., Andrés, C., Cardos, M.: Advantages of assembly lines in sheltered work centres for disabled. A case study. Int. J. Prod. Econ. **110**(1–2), 187–197 (2007)
7. Vilà, M., Pereira, J.: A branch-and-bound algorithm for assembly line worker assignment and balancing problems. Comput. Oper. Res. **44**, 105–114 (2014)
8. Borba, L., Ritt, M.: A heuristic and a branch-and-bound algorithm for the Assembly Line Worker Assignment and Balancing Problem. Comput. Oper. Res. **45**, 87–96 (2014)
9. Li, Z., Kucukkoc, I., Tang, Q.: Enhanced branch-bound-remember and iterative beam search algorithms for type II assembly line balancing problem. Comput. Oper. Res. **131**, 105235 (2021). https://doi.org/10.1016/j.cor.2021.105235
10. Blum, C., Miralles, C.: On solving the assembly line worker assignment and balancing problem via beam search. Comput. Oper. Res. **38**, 328–339 (2011)
11. Mutlu, Ö., Polat, O., Supciller, A.A.: An iterative genetic algorithm for the assembly line worker assignment and balancing problem of type-II. Comput. Oper. Res. **40**, 418–426 (2013)
12. Moreira, M.C.O., Ritt, M., Costa, A., Chaves, A.A.: Simple heuristics for the assembly line worker assignment and balancing problem. J. Heuristics **18**(3), 505–524 (2012)

13. Gansterer, M., Hartl, R.F.: One- and two-sided assembly line balancing problems with real-world constraints. Int. J. Prod. Res. **56**(8), 3025–3042 (2018)
14. Ritt, M., Costa, A.M., Miralles, C.: The assembly line worker assignment and balancing problem with stochastic worker availability. Int. J. Prod. Res. **54**(3), 907–922 (2016)

Design and Implementation of Digital Twin-Based Application for Global Manufacturing Enterprises

Jonghwan Choi[1] , Jinho Yang[1] , Joohee Lym[1] ,
Sang Do Noh[1(✉)] , Yong-Shin Kang[2], Yu La Joe[3],
Sang Hyun Lee[3], Jeong Tae Kang[3], Jungmin Song[4], Dae Yub Lee[4],
and Hyung Sun Kim[4]

[1] Sungkyunkwan University, Suwon 16419, Republic of Korea
sdnoh@skku.edu
[2] Advanced Institutes of Convergence Technology,
Suwon 16229, Republic of Korea
[3] Yura, Seongnam 13494, Republic of Korea
[4] Dexta Inc., Suwon 16419, Republic of Korea

Abstract. Nowadays, global competition in the manufacturing sector is increasingly fierce. Thus, global manufacturing companies must have a manufacturing system that ensures the production of reasonably priced, high-quality products, while meeting the needs of various customers. To address this issue, smart manufacturing should be implemented by adopting various information and communication technologies and convergence with existing manufacturing industries. One of the key technologies required for the implementation of smart manufacturing is a cyber-physical system (CPS). One of the major factors for the successful construction of a CPS is digital twin (DT). In this paper, we propose a standards-based information model for building a DT application, which is a key technology of a CPS-based integrated platform, by overcoming the heterogeneous device environment of global manufacturers and using data collected from various manufacturing sites. Furthermore, we propose a concept of modeling and simulation-based DT application. The DT application proposed in this study facilitates monitoring, diagnosis, and prediction at manufacturing sites using real-time data collected from various environments by ensuring interoperability. Moreover, its validity is verified by applying the technology to a global manufacturing company of automotive parts.

Keywords: Cyber-physical system (CPS) · CPS-based platform · Digital twin · Information model · Smart manufacturing

1 Introduction

Nowadays, global competition in the manufacturing sector is increasingly fierce, and companies need to implement smart manufacturing systems that support effective and accurate decision-making through the adoption of various information and communication technologies (ICT) and convergence with existing manufacturing industries to

© IFIP International Federation for Information Processing 2021
Published by Springer Nature Switzerland AG 2021
A. Dolgui et al. (Eds.): APMS 2021, IFIP AICT 634, pp. 12–19, 2021.
https://doi.org/10.1007/978-3-030-85914-5_2

produce reasonably priced high-quality products, while meeting the needs of various customers [1, 2]. To address this issue, many advanced manufacturing countries are leading the advancement of manufacturing at the national level, starting with Germany's Industrie 4.0 [1–3]. The major technologies that drive the Fourth Industrial Revolution include the Internet of Things (IoT) and cyber-physical systems (CPSs) implemented in the manufacturing environment [1]. In the future, manufacturing companies will build global networks to integrate and manage various manufacturing resources, such as their products, machines, and production facilities [1].

A CPS is based on a concept of managing systems where physical resources and the cyberspace are interlinked through a communication network [1, 4]. In such an environment, each physical device is represented as a virtual representation defined as a digital twin (DT), which comprises various types of models and data [4]. A DT is appraised as a next wave of simulation and optimization technology for products and production systems [5, 6]. By applying a DT to the production system, the field information and functions are synchronized, facilitating the analysis, evaluation, optimization, and prediction of the current situation [7]. The implementation of a CPS allows global manufacturing companies producing products in multiple countries to increase the efficiency of the whole production process by recognizing, adapting, and flexibly responding to situations based on the data collected in real time from the field beyond the conventional static manufacturing systems [8, 9]. However, various problems, such as heterogeneous device environments, need to be overcome to integrate and utilize the information of the distributed environment using CPS and DT technologies. Global manufacturing companies must overcome heterogeneous environments that have not been standardized in various geographically distributed manufacturing sites.

Accordingly, to solve this problem, studies have been conducted on CPS-based integrated platforms reflecting international standards [10]. In this paper, we propose an information model for building a DT by overcoming the heterogeneous environment of global manufacturing companies and using data collected from various manufacturing sites. This information model is designed based on Open platform communication unified architecture (OPC UA) proposed by the OPC Foundation to overcome the heterogeneous environment of distributed manufacturing systems. Furthermore, we propose a concept of modeling and simulation-based DT. Then, the technology is applied to a global manufacturer of automotive parts to verify its effectiveness.

2 Research Background

Since the introduction of the concept of DT in a study by Grieves in 2003, it has been continuously evolving to date [11]. A DT is a virtual representation of a physical asset and synchronizes the physical asset's information and functions, and it can be used to perform simulations accurately and quickly [7]. Because a DT enables the integration of simulation-based approaches with the technology that analyzes big data collected in massive quantities, it is considered a key technology for the adoption of CPS [12].

A DT facilitates the construction of a model that quickly reflects field information by incorporating ICT, which will allow dynamic diagnosis and prediction, unlike conventional simulation models [13]. To evolve from conventional discrete event simulation to DT, technologies, such as synchronization with networking devices and pattern identification, should be developed [6]. Moreover, the technology for linking data collected from manufacturing sites in real time is an important technology for building a DT [14, 15]. In a virtual space, a DT is built as a simulation model with components for a physical shop floor and requires the establishment of a mapping information model for the shop floor elements based on the Unified Modeling Language or another information modeling method [16]. These information and simulation models are integrated, providing a basic environment where the operational information of the shop floor is synchronized [16]. However, it is not necessary to model all physical assets depending on the cost and time constraints, and only the physical assets required for the purpose of DT should be modeled [17].

To build the aforementioned DT technology, a CPS-based platform that provides various services by integrating the information in the distributed environment should be built, and the interoperability for exchanging information on the platform is crucial [10, 15]. Grieves who first proposed DT also mentioned the data interface between the DT and physical assets as the third component of the DT system. If the data interface is not available, then the interaction between the DT and physical assets will be impossible, and consequently, the intelligentization of DT will not be achieved [11, 17]. A DT should comprise a variety of information collected from heterogeneous systems, and it can be used to support decision-making by monitoring and predicting the manufacturing sites. Accordingly, this study introduces a DT technology that can be used on an integrated platform, which secures interoperability and provides various services by integrating data collected from distributed manufacturing sites.

3 DT-Based Application

3.1 Concept of the DT-Based Application

The DT-based application proposed in this study integrates and virtualizes the real-time information collected in a distributed manufacturing environment; evaluates key performance indicators (KPIs), such as productivity; and predicts various situations and results based on simulations and big data. The application mainly comprises (1) a DT library composed of base models predefined for a fast construction of a virtual model; metadata showing the definitions of the data and the relationships between data; and production logics, such as dispatching rule and scheduling; (2) a manufacturing database that keeps a variety of production management information; (3) a simulation engine for performing diagnosis and prediction based on the information; (4) component modules of the DT; and (5) a DT interface for exchanging data with the system's external environment and the legacy system. Figure 1 shows the components and concept diagram of the aforementioned DT-based application.

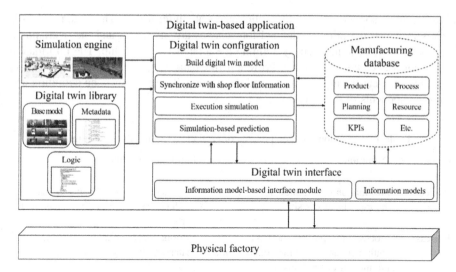

Fig. 1. Components and concept of the DT-based application system

There are four main stages in the construction process of a DT. In the first stage, a DT model suitable for the purpose is created using the DT library, manufacturing database's information, and simulation engine. In the second stage, synchronization is performed, which combines the created DT model and the information model collected from the field in real time. This stage facilitates dynamic modeling by reflecting abnormal situations, such as various equipment problems occurring in the field. In the third stage, a simulation stage exists, in which the DT model reflecting the on-site situation in real time is simulated, thereby facilitating the prediction of simulation-based results in the last stage to support the decision-making of decision-makers through the calculation of KPIs appropriate for the purpose.

3.2 Information Model for the DT Application

A key factor for the successful application of a DT is the description of physical and synchronized assets, which is entailed in a standardized information modeling.

OPC UA is a communication standard that provides information modeling and real-time data exchange for manufacturing systems [18]. OPC UA provides a relatively simple and flexible information modeling method to deal with a wide range of industrial equipment and production systems [18–20]. Liu, Chao, et al. proposed a CPMT (Cyber-Physical Machine Tools) Platform based on OPC UA that enables standardized, interoperable and efficient data communication among machine tools and various types of software applications [20]. In this paper, we propose an OPC UA-based information model to overcome the heterogeneous environment of a distributed manufacturing system and secure versatility. It contains various elements composing the production site, relationship between the elements, and planning information for manufacturing processes and production, etc. It consists of five classes, i.e., Product, Process, Plan, Resource, and Instance. Excluding the Instance class, the remaining four classes contain some dynamic information and static information. The Instance class is a class in which the other predefined four classes are instanced, and the overlapping information can be minimized by defining the reference relationship. The information model consists of the node name, browse name, data type, access level, parent node, modeling rule, cardinality, manifest, and description. Table 1 shows the definition and major components of each class.

Table 1. Definition and components of each class in the information model

Class name	Definition	Major components
Product	Information on products produced at the manufacturing site	Information on the bill of materials, products, semi-finished products, and parts
Process	Process information, such as equipment and input materials, for the production of products	Information, such as process, input materials, and logistics
Plan	Information on part and product procurement and production plans	Information, such as material procurement plan, targeted production volume, job schedules, and non-operation plan
Resource	Information on manufacturing resources for the production of products	Information on equipment, buffer, moving equipment, and workers, etc.
Instance	A class that creates and synchronizes the above four classes in a DT model	Layout, physical locations of manufacturing resources, and on-site information collected in real time

4 Implementation

We apply the proposed DT application and information model to an actual industrial site to verify their validity. This study was conducted as a part of the international joint research of South Korea and Sweden to develop a key technology of a CPS-based integrated platform to integrate and use information collected from a distributed manufacturing environment of a global manufacturer, as described above. Figure 2 shows a screen of the platform's user interface for visualizing and monitoring the data collected based on the information model from the distributed manufacturing sites. The center of the screen shows the status of the manufacturing site through the Google Map application programming interface. On the right side, various events occurring at the distributed manufacturing sites can be checked, and at the bottom of the screen, the user-defined comprehensive KPIs can be checked.

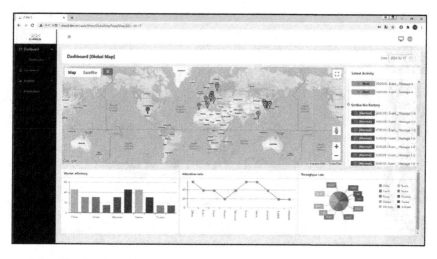

Fig. 2. User interface screen of the CPS-based integrated platform

The proposed model and application are applied in a factory of a South Korean global automotive part manufacturer, which produces automotive junction boxes. After producing printed circuit boards, which are semi-finished products, finished products are produced by the workers in this plant using automated processing and assembly equipment. Most equipment is automated, and the data collected from the equipment and the information on the products under production are stored on the production management server. Afterward, the server sends the data suitable for the proposed information model to the interface module of the DT application. Hence, real-time monitoring is facilitated by visualizing the data collected from the site. When a process failure or abnormal situation occurs, a simulation model that reflects the situation is created to perform the diagnosis and prediction. Figure 3 shows a screen of a DT model based on the real-time data collected from the plant site. The right side of the figure shows a screen where the information collected from the on-site equipment and products is recorded as event logs.

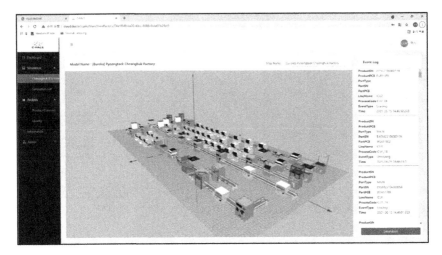

Fig. 3. Real-time monitoring screen of the subject plant

5 Conclusions

In this paper, we propose a DT-based application, a key technology of CPS-based integrated platform, for the smart manufacturing for global manufacturing companies. We designed and implemented DT-based application technologies and proposed an OPC UA-based standardized information model to secure interoperability in a heterogeneous device environment. Finally, we applied the proposed technologies to the production plant of a South Korean global automotive part manufacturer to validate this study. In the future, we will expand the application scope of the information model and DT technologies proposed in this study from the current scope of production lines, extending from the product level to the supply chain level. Furthermore, the big data analytics technology will be integrated with the monitoring and simulation-based prediction technologies to improve the DT model's intelligence.

Acknowledgement. This research was supported by the Ministry of Trade, Industry and Energy (MOTIE) and the Korea Institute for Advancement of Technology (KIAT) in South Korean through the International Cooperative R&D program [P0009839, the Cyber Physical Assembly and Logistics Systems in Global Supply Chains (C-PALS)]. In addition, it was supported by the Ministry of SMEs and Startups through the WC300 Project [S2482274, Development of Multi-vehicle Flexible Manufacturing Platform Technology for Future Smart Automotive Body Production].

References

1. Kagermann, H., Wahlster, W., Helbig, J.: Securing the future of German manufacturing industry: Recommendations for implementing the strategic initiative INDUSTRIE 4.0. Final report of the Industrie 4.0 (2013)

2. Kang, H.S., et al.: Smart manufacturing: past research, present findings, and future directions. Int. J. Precision Eng. Manuf.-Green Technol. **3**(1), 111–128 (2016). https://doi.org/10.1007/s40684-016-0015-5

3. Wiktorsson, M., Noh, S.D., Bellgran, M., Hanson, L.: Smart factories: South Korean and Swedish examples on manufacturing settings. Procedia Manuf. **25**, 471–478 (2018)

4. Schroeder, G.N., Steinmetz, C., Pereira, C.E., Espindola, D.B.: Digital twin data modeling with automationml and a communication methodology for data exchange. IFAC-PapersOnLine **49**(30), 12–17 (2016)

5. Park, K.T., Lee, J., Kim, H.-J., Noh, S.D.: Digital twin-based cyber physical production system architectural framework for personalized production. Int. J. Adv. Manuf. Technol. **106**(5–6), 1787–1810 (2019). https://doi.org/10.1007/s00170-019-04653-7

6. Flores-García, E., Kim, G.-Y., Yang, J., Wiktorsson, M., Do Noh, S.: Analyzing the characteristics of digital twin and discrete event simulation in cyber physical systems. In: Lalic, B., Majstorovic, V., Marjanovic, U., von Cieminski, G., Romero, D. (eds.) APMS 2020. IAICT, vol. 592, pp. 238–244. Springer, Cham (2020). https://doi.org/10.1007/978-3-030-57997-5_28

7. Tao, F., Zhang, M., Nee, A.Y.C.: Digital Twin Driven Smart Manufacturing. Academic Press (2019)

8. Miclea, L., Sanislav, T.: About dependability in cyber-physical systems. In: 2011 9th East-West Design & Test Symposium (EWDTS), pp. 17–21. IEEE (2011)

9. Ribeiro, L., Björkman, M.: Transitioning from standard automation solutions to cyber-physical production systems: an assessment of critical conceptual and technical challenges. IEEE Syst. J. **12**(4), 3816–3827 (2017)

10. Yang, J., et al.: Integrated platform and digital twin application for global automotive part suppliers. In: Lalic, B., Majstorovic, V., Marjanovic, U., von Cieminski, G., Romero, D. (eds.) APMS 2020. IAICT, vol. 592, pp. 230–237. Springer, Cham (2020). https://doi.org/10.1007/978-3-030-57997-5_27

11. Grieves, M.: Digital twin: manufacturing excellence through virtual factory replication, White paper, pp. 1–7 (2014)

12. Monostori, L., et al.: Cyber-physical systems in manufacturing. CIRP Ann. **65**(2), 621–641 (2016)

13. Liu, Q., Zhang, H., Leng, J., Chen, X.: Digital twin-driven rapid individualised designing of automated flow-shop manufacturing system. Int. J. Prod. Res. **57**(12), 3903–3919 (2019)

14. International Standard, 008–01–2012: Standard for Core Manufacturing Simulation Data–XML Representation, Simulation Interoperability Standards Organization (2012)

15. Yun, S., Park, J.-H., Kim, W.-T.: Data-centric middleware based digital twin platform for dependable cyber-physical systems. In: 2017 Ninth International Conference on Ubiquitous and Future Networks (ICUFN), pp. 922–926. IEEE (2017)

16. Zheng, Y., Yang, S., Cheng, H.: An application framework of digital twin and its case study. J. Ambient. Intell. Humaniz. Comput. **10**(3), 1141–1153 (2018). https://doi.org/10.1007/s12652-018-0911-3

17. Kim, Y.-W., Lee., H., Yoo, S., Han, S.: Characterization of Digital Twin, Technical report, Electronics and Telecommunications Research Institute, Daejeon, South Korea (2021)

18. IEC 62541–1: OPC Unified Architecture Specification Part1: Overview and Concepts, ver.1.04, OPC Foundation (2017)

19. IEC 62541–5: OPC Unified Architecture Specification Part5: Information Model, ver. 1.04, OPC Foundation (2017)

20. Liu, C., Vengayil, H., Lu, Y., Xu, X.: A cyber-physical machine tools platform using OPC UA and MTConnect. J. Manuf. Syst. **51**, 61–74 (2019)

Exploring Economic, Environmental, and Social Sustainability Impact of Digital Twin-Based Services for Smart Production Logistics

Goo-Young Kim[1] ![ORCID], Erik Flores-García[2] ![ORCID], Magnus Wiktorsson[2] ![ORCID], and Sang Do Noh[1(✉)] ![ORCID]

[1] Sungkyunkwan University, Suwon 16419, South Korea
`sdnoh@skku.edu`
[2] KTH Royal Institute of Technology, 15136 Södertälje, Sweden

Abstract. Digital Twins are increasingly perceived as critical enablers for improving operational performance and sustainability of Smart Production Logistics. Addressing the lack of empirical research on this topic, this study explores the economic, environmental, and social sustainability impact of Digital Twin-based services for Smart Production Logistics. The study presents findings from a Smart Production Logistics demonstrator in an academic environment and underscores the contributions and limitations of current understanding about Digital Twin-based services in relation to their impact on economic, environmental, and social sustainability. The study presents valuable implications for managers responsible for material handling.

Keywords: Digital twin-based services · Sustainability · Smart Production Logistics

1 Introduction

Digital technologies are considered an enabler for achieving superior operational performance and contributing to impact in economic, environmental, and social sustainability [1]. In particular, the literature suggests that Digital Twins (DTs) may contribute to achieving this dual-purpose [2]. DTs refer to a set of linked operations, data artifacts, and simulation models representing and predicting behaviors, and involve a bi-directional relation between a physical production system and its virtual counterpart [3]. For example, recent findings contend that DTs may enhance sustainable development, and predict and material handling in Smart Production Logistics (SPL) [4, 5]. Current research about DTs focuses on developing DT-based services. Yet, current understanding about DT-based services focuses on the performance of SPL, and efforts about the economic, environmental, and social impact of DT-based services remain insufficient. Consequently, the purpose of this paper is to explore the impact of economic, environmental, and social sustainability of DT-based services for SPL in material handling. Empirical data is drawn from an SPL demonstrator.

© IFIP International Federation for Information Processing 2021
Published by Springer Nature Switzerland AG 2021
A. Dolgui et al. (Eds.): APMS 2021, IFIP AICT 634, pp. 20–27, 2021.
https://doi.org/10.1007/978-3-030-85914-5_3

The results of this study suggest that the current understanding of DT-based services in SPL may contribute to achieving all impacts in economic, environmental, and social sustainability, but is insufficient.

2 Related Works

Recent research shows that DTs are a way to implement smart manufacturing, and DT-based services improve current circumstances and hurdles. Grieves proposed the concept of DTs in 2003 including three parts, physical space, virtual counterpart, and data connection between two spaces [6]. The physical and virtual models and data in DTs describe the characteristics of the physical object and its digital replica. These are used in diagnosis, analysis, prediction, and optimization of the manufacturing system to support decision-making. DT-based services refer to the components of DT providing intuitive understanding of target objects through multiple data, resources, and distributed computing [7]. In other words, DT-based services offer value-adding services to non-professional users with limited technical expertise. Accordingly, DT-based services assist non-professional users to manage cost, capacity, and real-time status issues [8]. For example, DT-based services include predicting, diagnosing, or reducing the cost and downtime of transport operations in SPL to help staff in charge of operational, tactical, and strategic decisions [9, 10]. To implement DT, the literature provides not only guidelines regarding how to use the Internet of Things (IoT) devices such as networks and sensors [11], but also identifies that the production logistics simulation model needs networking devices and synchronization to develop into DT [12]. Additionally, the recent research discusses the use of DT to support the decision-making process in the field of production and logistics through testbeds containing the IoT infrastructure and simulation software [13]. In relation to sustainability, the literature posits that DTs enhance sustainable development by reducing energy consumption and predict material handling by optimizing transportation equipment in SPL [5].

Sustainability is divided into three interrelated aspects: Economic, Environmental, and Social. Figure 1 based on [15] shows the impact of Industry 4.0 on three sustainability areas. Importantly, impact on one aspect of sustainability affects another. For example, increasing resource efficiency has the effect of reducing the amount of energy used by resources on the environmental aspect, and brings other effects of increasing productivity through the efficient use of resources on the economic aspect.

The literature offers several examples evidencing how DTs and DT services enhance sustainability. For example, prior studies propose applying DTs in data flow systems and develop a sustainability indicator for improving the performance of the sustainable design of products [16]. Additionally, the literature highlights the use of DT services for improving efficiency and productivity of existing processes, and reducing energy consumption and associated costs in small and medium sized companies [17]. Finally, recent efforts propose a DT-driven sustainable manufacturing framework analyzing the impact of DTs in economic, environmental, and social sustainability for equipment systems, and services [18].

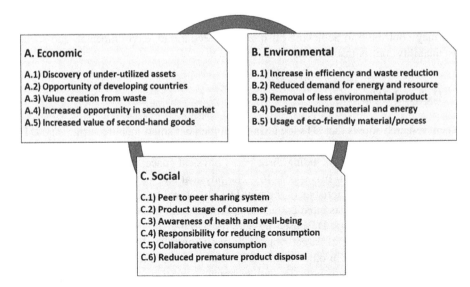

A. Economic

A.1) Discovery of under-utilized assets
A.2) Opportunity of developing countries
A.3) Value creation from waste
A.4) Increased opportunity in secondary market
A.5) Increased value of second-hand goods

B. Environmental

B.1) Increase in efficiency and waste reduction
B.2) Reduced demand for energy and resource
B.3) Removal of less environmental product
B.4) Design reducing material and energy
B.5) Usage of eco-friendly material/process

C. Social

C.1) Peer to peer sharing system
C.2) Product usage of consumer
C.3) Awareness of health and well-being
C.4) Responsibility for reducing consumption
C.5) Collaborative consumption
C.6) Reduced premature product disposal

Fig. 1. Economic, environmental, and social sustainability

3   Digital Twin-Based Services and Sustainability

This section describes a DT for material handling in production logistics and its services addressing economic, environmental, and social sustainability. The DT includes five dimensions according to [19, 20] involving a physical world, digital world, data storage, networking, and DT-based services. The proposed DT-based services comprehend monitoring, prescription and prediction of material handling tasks. Finally, we describe the relation of the proposed DT-based services to sustainability.

The DT comprehends a physical world, digital world, data storage, networking, and DT-based services for material handling. The physical world includes three warehouses, up to three forklifts, and three production processes composed of six stations. Ultra-Wideband (UWB) radio tags and Radio Frequency Identification (RFID) sense points collect data in real-time from the forklifts. The virtual world provides a digital representation of the physical world. The virtual world encapsulates, processes, and synchronizes information including resource (forklift name, distance travelled, location, speed, time stamp), and order (product, order, confinement and delivery location, pickup and delivery time). Databases in a server store real-time data and information processed in the virtual world. Additionally, the DT utilizes a Node-Red application for transferring data from the factory floor, and communicating across DT-based services.

This study proposes DT-based services including monitoring, prescription and prediction for material handling. These services target distinct functions in logistics organizations. Monitoring services involve a web-based application displaying the real-time movement and plotting of spaghetti diagrams and heat maps of forklifts. Additionally, the monitoring service presents the utilization, distance travelled, and collisions incurred by forklifts. The monitoring services benefit managers responsible for supervising and assigning resources in material handling. Prescriptive service applies a task scheduling optimization algorithm that arranges material handling tasks according to position of a forklift, its distance to a station, and the time for picking and delivering material. The algorithm minimizes the delivery time, makespan, and distance travelled by a forklift when delivering material handling tasks. The prescriptive services support forklift drivers responsible for picking and delivering material in the factory. Finally, the predictive service utilize historical information including number of forklifts and material handling tasks as an input to a discrete event simulation model. The model tests scenarios including changes to number of tasks, forklifts and their availability providing a prognosis delivery, makespan, and distance for material handling. Figure 2 present the monitoring, prescriptive, and predictive DT-based services for material handling.

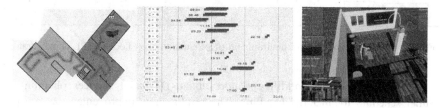

Fig. 2. Monitoring, prescriptive, and predictive DT-based services for material handling

DT meets the requirement of personalized manufacturing and has the environmental sustainability benefits of not only increasing resource efficiency but also reducing the waste of energy, and the social sustainability benefits of focusing on user use. DT services make it easier for members of the shop-floor and factory to share information, discover underutilized resources, and remove products or processes damaging the environmental aspect. The use of real-time location information enables operators to grasp in advance the collision that may occur during logistics movement and material handling at the production site and creates a safe environment for operators and manufacturing resources.

4   Case Study

This section presents a case from an automotive company in Sweden. Forklifts operators perform material handling tasks manually including delivery of part from warehouse to production stage and transfer of part from previous to next production stage. However, forklifts operators are in trouble when locating the point of confinement and delivery of parts and determining the sequence of scheduled tasks. Moreover, managers struggle with understanding the reasons for deviations of scheduled tasks, and improving delivery, makespan, and distance of material handling. The case applies the proposed SPL demonstrator (Fig. 3) including the DT-based services for material handling.

The forklift executes a schedule including 25 material handling tasks specifying the order number, pick and delivery time, and pick and delivery locations. We planned two scenarios before (As-Is) and after (To-Be) using the DT-based services. In the before scenario, operators execute the schedule ad hoc. Forklift operators arrange and deliver chronologically material handling tasks according to the earliest consumption time.

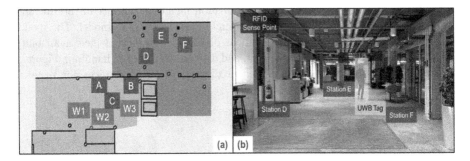

Fig. 3. (a) Layout and (b) IoT environment of production shop floor in SPL demonstrator

In the after scenario, forklift operators utilize DT-based services obtaining an optimal schedule for material handling. The results show improvement on key performance indicators involving on time deliveries, distance, and makespan when applying the DT-based services. The late deliveries decrease from two late deliveries to zero late deliveries. The total distance travelled by forklifts also decreases from 850 m to 670 m. Finally, the makespan decreases from 23:48 min to 23:42 min. Table 1 presents the results of the DT-based services demonstrator.

Table 1. Results of DT-based services system demonstrator

Scenario	Late deliveries (# of tasks)	Distance (meters)	Makespan (minutes)
As-Is	2	850	23:48
To-Be	0	670	23:42

5 Discussions

The findings of this study suggest that current understanding about DT-based services in SPL may contribute to, but is insufficient for, achieving all impacts of sustainability. The results indicate that current understanding about DT-based services may contribute to, one out of five type of impact on economic sustainability, two out of five types of impact in environmental sustainability, and two out of five types of impact in social sustainability. Table 2 presents the sustainability impact and empirical results of this study. A description each DT-based services contributing to impact in economic, environmental, and social sustainability follows.

Table 2. Sustainability impact and empirical results

Sustainability impact	Empirical result
A.1) Discovery of under-utilized assets	Increase of the number of forklifts required
B.1) Increase in efficiency and waste reduction	Reduction of the number of delayed deliveries
B.2) Reduced demand for energy and resource	Reduction of the travelled distances of forklifts
C.3) Awareness of health and well-being	The traffic and collisions history of forklifts
C.4) Responsibility for reducing consumption	Information of resource utilization for tasks
A. Economic; B. Environmental; C. Social	

The results of this study suggest that DT-based services in SPL may contribute to achieving impact on economic sustainability. In this study, monitoring and prescriptive DT-based services apply real-time location and task scheduling optimization showing the position of individual forklifts with respect to time and their execution of material handling tasks. Furthermore, the results suggest that managers applying real-time location and task scheduling optimization may recapture the value of forklift utilization. For example, DT-based services may be essential for logistics planners responsible for allocating forklifts to specific areas of a factory or sharing forklifts across different processes in material handling.

Additionally, the results of this study suggest that prescriptive DT-based services for SPL contribute to impact on environmental sustainability. In particular, this study argues that scheduling optimization is crucial for reducing the distance travelled by forklifts in material handling, and thereby contribute to increasing resource efficiency and waste reduction. However, the findings of this study suggest that energy spent in material handling may be decreased in relation to the distance travelled by forklifts. This finding may be essential for manufacturing organizations concerned with reaching environmental sustainability goals. DT-based services revealing travelled distance may be essential for identifying and reducing unnecessary delivery routes, minimizing forklifts, and motivating the choice of material handling equipment with improved energy efficiency. Consequently, this study posits that current understanding about DT-based services in SPL may reduce demand for energy.

Furthermore, this study argues that existing understanding about monitoring and predictive DT-based services in SPL may lead to impact in social sustainability. Empirical results suggest that DT-based services may contribute to increased awareness toward health and well-being in two ways. Firstly, DT-based services including path traces register traffic and heat maps reveal the frequency of travel of forklifts. Path traces and heat maps indicate areas of high risk for staff in logistics and operations who may be ex-posed to forklift collisions. Secondly, DT-based services register the location and number of collisions of forklifts during material handling. Collisions are registered in real-time and historic data in a layout of the factory. Consequently, managers may implement corrective actions preventing future incidents threatening the wealth and well-being of staff. Furthermore, DT-based services may facilitate increased accountability towards reduced production and consumption. DT-based services show the number and distance travelled by forklifts in real-time for completing a delivery schedule. This information is critical for analyzing the utilization of resources and revealing waste (e.g. excess distance or forklifts) in material handling. Based on this information, manufacturing companies may increase awareness and implement policies increasing accountability towards the reduction of resources for material handling.

While having the advantage of meeting some of the three aspects of sustainability, we confirmed challenges. A.4) Increased opportunity in secondary market and A.5) Increased value of second-hand goods of Fig. 1 are insufficient to be supported by the DT service presented in this study. These are connected to the product life cycle. In other words, simulation services related to product usage scenarios, not for services for material handling, are necessary to check the life cycle of the product to disposal. B.5) Usage of eco-friendly material/process requires the development of new material for product and process design. This is because the product design is decided and the manufacturing process changes depending on the material. C.5) Collaborative consumption and C.6) Reduced premature product disposal are accomplished by the product design services. Therefore, DT should design products with the requirements of consumers offered from online and produce and execute a production process. Virtual experiment services to determine the durability of the designed product is necessary to reduce premature product disposal.

6 Conclusions

This study developed a demonstrator of SPL in an academic environment based on current understanding about DT-based services. Empirical results indicated that current understanding about DT-based services in SPL may contribute to, but is insufficient for, achieving all impacts in economic, environmental, and social sustainability described in literature. This study presents important contributions to practice including a description of benefits of DT-based services in SPL for operators, and logistics and factory managers, and their implications to economic, environmental, and social sustainability. Future research could focus on verifying results by drawing data from different industrial segments, and different aspects of SPL for example automated guided vehicles, forklift fleets, and different levels of the automation. Furthermore, the findings of this study underscore the need for extending current understanding about and proposing DT-based services leading to impact in economic, environmental, and social sustainability.

Acknowledgement. This research was supported by the Ministry of Trade, Industry and Energy (MOTIE) and the Korea Institute for Advancement of Technology (KIAT) in South Korean, and Eureka SMART and Vinnova in Sweden through the International Cooperative R&D program [P0009839, the Cyber Physical Assembly and Logistics Systems in Global Supply Chains (C-PALS)]. In addition, it was supported by the Ministry of SMEs and Startups through the WC300 Project [S2482274, Development of Multi-vehicle Flexible Manufacturing Platform Technology for Future Smart Automotive Body Production].

References

1. Abubakr, M., Abbas, A.T., Tomaz, I., Soliman, M.S., Luqman, M., Hegab, H.: Sustainable and smart manufacturing: an integrated approach. Sustainability. **12**(6), 2280 (2020)
2. Beier, G., Ullrich, A., Niehoff, S., Reißig, M., Habich, M.: Industry 4.0: how it is defined from a sociotechnical perspective and how much sustainability it includes–A literature review. Journal of cleaner production, p. 120856 (2020)
3. Cimino, C., Negri, E., Fumagalli, L.: Review of digital twin applications in manufacturing. Comput. Ind. **113**, 103130 (2019)
4. Cao, J., Wang, J., Lu, J.: A referenced cyber physical system for compressor manufacturing. MATEC Web of Conferences **306**, 02005 (2020)
5. Wang, W., Zhang, Y., Zhong, R.Y.: A proactive material handling method for CPS enabled shop-floor. Robot. Comput. Integr. Manuf. **61**, 101849 (2020)
6. Grieves, M.: Digital twin: manufacturing excellence through virtual factory replication. White Paper **1**, 1–7 (2014)
7. Longo, F., Nicoletti, L., Padovano, A.: Ubiquitous knowledge empowers the smart factory: the impacts of a service-oriented digital twin on enterprises' performance. Annu. Rev. Control. **47**, 221–236 (2019)
8. Qi, Q., Tao, F., Zuo, Y., Zhao, D.: Digital twin service towards smart manufacturing. Procedia Cirp **72**, 237–242 (2018)
9. Zheng, P., et al.: Smart manufacturing systems for Industry 4.0: Conceptual framework, scenarios, and future perspectives. Front. Mech. Eng. **13**(2), 137–150 (2018)
10. Lu, Y., Liu, C., Kevin, I., Wang, K., Huang, H., Xu, X.: Digital twin-driven smart manufacturing: Connotation, reference model, applications and research issues. Robot. Comput.-Integrat. Manuf. **61**, 101837 (2020)
11. Uhlemann, T.H.J., Lehmann, C., Steinhilper, R.: The digital twin: realizing the cyber-physical production system for industry 4.0. Procedia Cirp **61**, 335–340 (2017)
12. Flores-García, E., Kim, G.Y., Yang, J., Wiktorsson, M., Noh, S.D.: Analyzing the characteristics of digital twin and discrete event simulation in cyber physical systems. In: IFIP International Conference on Advances in Production Management Systems, pp.238–244. Springer, Cham (2020). Dio: https://doi.org/10.1007/978-3-030-57997-5_28
13. Baalsrud Hauge, J., Zafarzadeh, M., Jeong, Y., Li, Y., Khilji, W.A., Wiktorsson, M.: Employing digital twins within production logistics. In: IEEE International Conference on Engineering, pp.1–8 (2020)
14. Kusiak, A.: Smart manufacturing. Int. J. Prod. Res. **56**(1–2), 508–517 (2018)
15. Strandhagen, J.W., Alfnes, E., Strandhagen, J.O., Vallandingham, L.R.: The fit of Industry 4.0 applications in manufacturing logistics: a multiple case study. Adv. Manuf. **5**(4), 344–358 (2017). https://doi.org/10.1007/s40436-017-0200-y
16. He, B., Cao, X., Hua, Y.: Data fusion-based sustainable digital twin system of intelligent detection robotics. J. Clean. Prod. **280**, 24181 (2021)
17. Park, K.T., Im, S.J., Kang, Y.S., Noh, S.D., Kang, Y.T., Yang, S.G.: Service-oriented platform for smart operation of dyeing and finishing industry. Int. J. Comput. Integr. Manuf. **32**(3), 307–326 (2019)
18. He, B., Bai, K.J.: Digital twin-based sustainable intelligent manufacturing: a review. Adv. Manuf. **9**(1), 1–21 (2021)
19. Tao, F., Zhang, M., Liu, Y., Nee, A.Y.C.: Digital twin driven prognostics and health management for complex equipment. CIRP Ann. **67**(1), 169–172 (2018)
20. Tao, F., Zhang, H., Liu, A., Nee, A.Y.: Digital twin in industry: state-of-the-art. IEEE Trans. Industr. Inf. **15**(4), 2405–2415 (2018)

Applying Machine Learning for Adaptive Scheduling and Execution of Material Handling in Smart Production Logistics

Erik Flores-García[(⊠)] ⓘ, Yongkuk Jeong ⓘ,
and Magnus Wiktorsson ⓘ

Department of Sustainable Production Development,
KTH Royal Institute of Technology, 15136 Södertälje, Sweden
efs01@kth.se

Abstract. Combining Smart Production Logistics (SPL) and Machine Learning (ML) for adaptive scheduling and execution of material handling may be critical for enhancing manufacturing competitiveness. SPL and ML may help identify, adapt, and respond to scheduling changes originating from disturbances in and enhance the operational performance of material handling. However, the literature combining SPL and ML for material handling is scarce. Accordingly, the purpose of this study is to propose a framework applying ML for the dynamic scheduling and execution of material handling tasks in SPL. The study proposes an architecture including Cyber Physical System (CPS) and Internet of Things (IoT) applying ML for the dynamic scheduling and execution of material handling. Then, we describe the ML inputs, interactions, and work flow for realizing the proposed architecture. Finally, the study presents digital services in a simulation environment exemplifying the dynamic scheduling and execution of material handling in SPL. The study concludes with essential implications to the manufacturing industry.

Keywords: Smart production logistics · Adaptive scheduling · Machine learning

1 Introduction

Combining Smart Production Logistics (SPL) and Machine Learning (ML) offers advantages essential for addressing unexpected events that arise during material handling and enhancing the competitiveness of manufacturing companies [1]. On the one hand, SPL involves applying digital technologies including Cyber Physical Systems (CPS) and Internet of Things (IoT) for making machines and material handling equipment smart [2]. Accordingly, SPL facilitates the perception, active response, and autonomous decision-making for the movement of materials and information within the boundaries of a factory [3]. Particularly, SPL is essential for identifying, adapting, and reducing costly mistakes originating from disturbances or machine breakdowns affecting material handling. On the other hand, ML is a subset of artificial intelligence focusing on autonomous computer knowledge gain [4]. ML includes algorithms

© IFIP International Federation for Information Processing 2021
Published by Springer Nature Switzerland AG 2021
A. Dolgui et al. (Eds.): APMS 2021, IFIP AICT 634, pp. 28–36, 2021.
https://doi.org/10.1007/978-3-030-85914-5_4

identifying and extracting valuable patters in data, and allows computers to solve problems without explicit programming [5]. One area of increasing interest in SPL is applying ML for adapting the scheduling and execution of material handling as a response to unexpected events including malfunctioning machines, changing priorities, illness of staff, delays, defects, or shortage of materials [6].

ML provides distinct benefits essential for addressing unexpected disturbances and adapting scheduling and execution of material handling tasks. For example, ML provides fast acceptable solutions that conform to the operation of a dynamic environment [7]. The timeliness of response in ML is advantageous over current alternatives such as simulation approaches requiring intensive computational effort and lacking adaption to changes in the factory floor. Additionally, ML reduces the effort to acquire knowledge, identify a strategy, and adapt to changes of environments automatically [8]. Finally, ML can classify and predict responses based on knowledge learned from training examples [9].

Recent research efforts advance the use of ML in SPL, yet address scheduling and material handling separately [10, 11, 13]. These studies are critical for addressing unexpected events arising in material handling, yet the manufacturing industry may obtain only partial benefits when applying scheduling and execution of material handling independently. Instead, manufacturing companies require adaptive scheduling capable of identifying disturbances, adjusting changes instantly, and executing material handling.

Addressing this need, the purpose of this study is to propose a framework applying ML for adaptive scheduling and execution of material handling in SPL. The main contribution of this work includes a CPS architecture containing a physical, virtual, and an adaptive control layer. We apply ML in the adaptive control layer for knowledge learning, and adaptive adjustment including scheduling and execution of material handling. Additionally, the study includes the description of the phases in ML for a achieving a closed loop adaptive scheduling based and execution of material handling. Finally, the study presents the visualization of a SPL system including the proposed framework in a laboratory environment. The remainder of this paper includes the following sections. Section 2 reviews related works about SPL in material handling and ML. Section 3 describes the proposed framework applying ML for adaptive scheduling and execution of material handling. Section 4 presents the visualization of a SPL system. Section 5 draws the conclusions of this study and suggests future research.

2   Related Works

This section presents current understanding about SPL essential for addressing unexpected events in material handling. The section describes the importance of IoT devices and CPS for adaptive scheduling and execution of material handling. Then, the section outlines key elements of existing architectures of CPS in SPL. The section finalizes identifying essential aspects for applying ML to existing IoT and CPS architectures.

CPS are critical for developing the vision of SPL including the acquisition, handling, and use of real-time data facilitating autonomous decisions in the shop floor. CPS and IoT involve multi-layered architectures that facilitate acquiring, handling, and using real-time and historic information essential for adapting scheduling and executing material handling as events occur. In relation to scheduling, Rossit et al. [14] propose a decision-making schema for smart scheduling intended to yield flexible and efficient production schedules on the fly. Feng et al. [15] suggest a dynamic scheduling system based on CPS improving the energy efficiency of the job-shop. Jha et al. [16] present a CPS for manufacturing processing in IIoT environments, in which physical actor resources take part in the scheduling process. In relation to material handling, Zhang et al. [2] investigate the mechanism of intelligent modeling and active response of manufacturing resources in the infrastructure layer; and present a self-organizing configuration for SPL. Zhang et al. [17] design a CPS control model for material handling.

The literature on CPS and IoT underscores key elements of existing architectures that may be essential for adaptive scheduling and execution of material handling. For example, Guo et al. [6] propose a three layered approach of a SPL system including a physical, virtual, and control layers addressing self-adaptive collaborative control. The virtual layer involves IoT technologies, sensors and automatic identification sensors for acquiring and transmitting real-time information about physical devices in the literature terms a physical layer. The virtual layer comprehends synchronizing real-time information and dynamic behavior of physical devices, the encapsulation of information, and digital services for the use of information by staff. Finally, a control layer detects external and internal exceptions using real-time status information and a knowledge base. The control layer identifies and proposes strategies for addressing known exceptions. Additionally, the control layer analyzes new exceptions, extracts knowledge, and updates the database.

Recent advances suggest applying ML for adapting scheduling to unexpected events in combination with IoT and CPS [10]. Applying ML requires developing a knowledge base for simultaneously acquiring different information from the manufacturing system in real-time and selecting an appropriate strategy for responding to unexpected events [18]. There are four essential aspects for developing and using a knowledge base for the adaptive scheduling and execution of material handling. Firstly, acquiring information including system structure and capacity (static data) and manufacturing process, material handling and behavior (dynamic data). Secondly, processing information including the identification and classification of status of the manufacturing system and real-time and historical disturbances. Thirdly, knowledge learning involving the selection of a best response for each disturbance and evaluation of each response in relation to scheduling and execution of material handling. Fourthly, applying an adjusted scheduling strategy and the execution of material handling tasks.

3 Applying ML for Adaptive Scheduling and Execution of Material Handling in SPL

This section proposes a framework applying ML for the adaptive scheduling and execution of material handling in SPL. The framework presents a direct response to the need of the manufacturing industry for addressing unexpected events arising in material handling. Accordingly, the framework includes a CPS architecture together with an adaptive control layer involving ML. Figure 1 presents the proposed SPL framework applying ML for adaptive scheduling and execution of material handling.

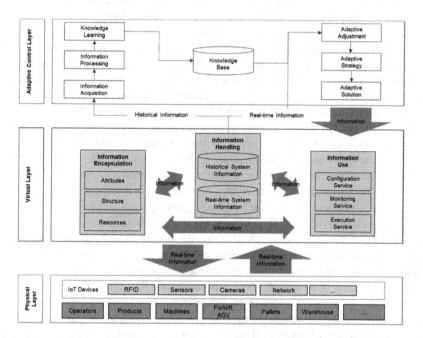

Fig. 1. Proposed SPL framework applying ML for adaptive scheduling and execution of material handling.

The CPS architecture for adaptive scheduling and execution of material handling includes a physical, virtual, and adaptive control layers. The physical layer comprehends the real-world manufacturing system. This layer contains machines, operators, products, forklifts, AGVs, pallets, and warehouses in the shop floor. Additionally, the physical layer comprises IoT devices such as RFIDs and sensors, cameras, and networking devices connected to forklifts and AGVs. The activities in the physical layer are two-fold. Firstly, the physical layer executes scheduled tasks in material handling. Secondly, IoT devices collect, transmit, and receive real-time information from the shop floor indispensable for applying ML for adaptive scheduling and execution of material handling.

The virtual layer contains elements and activities for synchronizing material handling in the shop floor with its virtual counterpart. The virtual layer contains three sets of activities focusing on information encapsulation, handling, and use. Information encapsulation refers to the segmentation of information from each device of the manufacturing system including its attributes, structure, and resources. Information encapsulation includes real-time and historical information involving resources, unexpected events, schedule of tasks, and performance in material handling. For example, resource data refers to type, time, position, distance travelled, and speed of an AGV. Information about unexpected events includes time, obstacle, and AGV downtime, and scheduling information comprehends order number, location and time for picking and delivering orders. Information about performance of material handling includes throughput, on time delivery, makespan, and distance travelled by forklifts or AGVs. Information handling comprehends the processing and analysis of historical and real-time information. Importantly, information handling targets the calculation and interrelation of information about resources, unexpected events, schedules and performance in material handling. Consider the case of the parameter for on time delivery requiring the integration of information about AGV location, schedule, and time. Finally, information use concerns the configuration, monitoring, and execution of scheduled tasks in material handling. Digital services provide an interface between staff and the virtual manufacturing system and facilitate automatic decisions. Accordingly, digital services facilitate the execution of the schedule for material handling, and determine how and when material handling resources carry out tasks in the shop floor.

ML is the core element of the adaptive control layer. Accordingly, real-time acquisition of information and a knowledge base detect and determine the impact of unexpected events. Figure 2 exemplifies addressing unexpected events with the proposed SPL framework applying ML. The knowledge base contains responses to unexpected events that occurred in the past. Additionally, the processing of real-time information detects new unexpected events and renews the knowledge base. The knowledge base presents an online decision adjusting the scheduling strategy based on the goals of the adaptive scheduling that maintain the performance of SPL. Then, the adaptive control layer transfers an adaptive solution including optimal schedule to the virtual layer. Finally, material handling resources execute the optimal schedule in the physical layer. The proposed framework applies ML in four phases for achieving a closed loop adaptive scheduling based and execution of material handling based on prior findings [10].

The four phases for applying ML in the adaptive control layer include acquiring information, identifying disturbances, adapting a scheduling strategy, and generating a schedule. Information acquisition requires two steps. Firstly, transferring information from the physical layer of a CPS to the adaptive control layer. Secondly, examining and selecting information critical for adaptive scheduling and execution of material handling is essential.

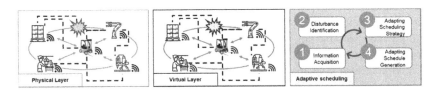

Fig. 2. Addressing unexpected events with the proposed SPL framework applying ML.

The identification of disturbances in the adaptive control layer involves three aspects. Firstly, determining the type of disturbance; secondly, recognizing the effects of a disturbance; and thirdly, establishing a response. Establishing a response involves analyzing dynamically and defining the limits of operational performance. Accordingly, adjustments to a schedule respond to maintaining or improving a level of operational performance.

The adapting scheduling strategy is an output of the knowledge base. Therefore, the scheduling strategy requires gathering knowledge learned from the manufacturing process including historical and real-time information. Additionally, the knowledge base provides real-time information consisting of updates to the scheduling strategy with the purpose of achieving a desired level of operational performance. Finally, the adaptive control layer presents an adaptive schedule of its execution in material handling. The adaptive schedule depends on the effects of disturbances on the operational performance of the manufacturing system. Additionally, the adaptive schedule presents information including material handling tasks, location and time for pickup and delivery, and the resource assigned to the execution of a task to the virtual layer.

4   Prototype Applications in SPL Test-Bed Environment

This section describes a prototype application for testing the proposed framework of this study. This prototype application includes a SPL test-bed environment, and a variety of robots and IoT devices. An internal network connects all robots and devices, and facilitate the transmission of material handling data including resource type, location, distance, speed, and status in real time.

A database stores real-time data used for the learning of the ML models and visualizing the execution of material handling by the AGV in the virtual world. Figure 3 shows the execution of material handling by the AGV in the SPL test-bed environment. Figure 3 (a) presents how the AGV finds the route in the as-is situation. In this case, the AGV receives the mission to deliver material from the planning system and performs the given mission according to the order. The AGV utilizes a radar sensor and pathfinding algorithm for identifying nearby obstacles, and determining the path during the execution of material handling. However, as shown in Fig. 3 (a) the AGV cannot react in real-time to events that occur during the execution of material handling. Upon encountering and unexpected event, the AGV will stop the execution of material handling, and recalculate the optimal path to its destination.

However, adaptive and predictive responses are possible by applying the framework proposed in this study. First, Fig. 3 (b) shows an adaptive response method when an unexpected event occurs while the AGV is moving. In this instance, the AGV can execute ML-based routing by combining real-time and historical data in the ML model. The ML model provides two advantages originating from its knowledge base and training including faster response than optimal path finding algorithms and alternatives to unexpected situations. Therefore, the AGV reacts to occurrences in real-time and does not require stopping and recalculating during the execution of material handling.

Next, Fig. 3 (c) shows the predictive response to a wide planning horizon in material handling. Traditionally, the AGV executes multiple missions sequentially. However, ML-based scheduling calculates in advance the total material handling time of all missions including different scheduling scenarios. Therefore, the proposed framework may contribute to real-time routing and a wide planning horizon in material handling.

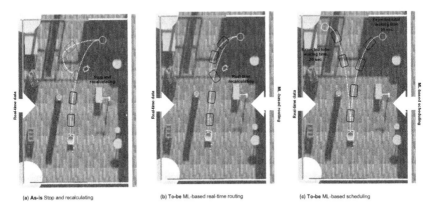

(a) **As-is** Stop and recalculating   (b) **To-be** ML-based real-time routing   (c) **To-be** ML-based scheduling

Fig. 3. Example of AGV with logistics tasks in SPL test-bed environment

ML-based real-time routing can be implemented through the framework we propose in this paper. Currently, AGV scans its surroundings and identifies obstacles before staring the delivery task, and the shortest is calculated based on this. If there is any obstacle in the path that was not recognized from the beginning, the operation is temporarily stopped, and the optimal path is recalculated as shown in Fig. 4 (a). This problem can be improved through online adaptive route planning by the framework prosed in this paper. The reinforcement learning (RL) algorithm can be used to respond to the dynamic situation of the SFL environment. Unlike any other ML models such as supervised and unsupervised learning models, the RL algorithm does not requires labeled or unlabeled data. But it trains the model by rewards when the agent performs an action appropriate for its purpose. The trained model can make the right decision by itself, not only in a given environment but also in a completely new environment. Figure 4 (b) represents this situation, and the continuous revised path can be calculated by periodically calling the trained RL model. Since the RL model has al-ready been trained, it can immediately calculate the revised path even for dynamic obstacles.

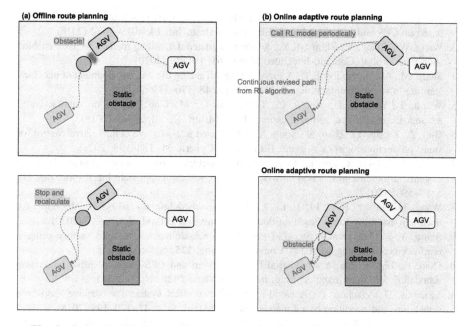

Fig. 4. Comparison between offline route planning and online adaptive route planning

5   Conclusions

The purpose of this study was to propose a framework applying ML for the adaptive scheduling and execution of material handling in SPL. The main contribution of this work included a CPS architecture containing a physical, virtual, and an adaptive control layer. We applied ML in the adaptive control layer for knowledge learning, and adaptive adjustment including scheduling and execution of material handling. The study presented the visualization of a SPL system including the proposed framework in a laboratory environment. Future research will focus on verifying the proposed framework in an industrial case. Additionally, future studies will involve additional tasks in including packaging, transportation, or warehousing.

Acknowledgments. The authors would like to acknowledge the support of the Swedish Innovation Agency (VINNOVA). This study is part of the Cyber Physical Assembly and Logistics Systems in Global Supply Chains (C-PALS) project. The SMART EUREKA CLUSTER on Advanced Manufacturing program funded this project.

References

1. Woschank, M., Rauch, E., Zsifkovits, H.: A review of further directions for artificial intelligence, machine learning, and deep learning in smart logistics. Sustainability **12**, 3760 (2020)

2. Zhang, Y., Guo, Z., Lv, J., Liu, Y.: A framework for smart production-logistics systems based on CPS and industrial IoT. IEEE Trans. Industr. Inf. **14**, 4019–4032 (2018)
3. Wang, W., Zhang, Y., Zhong, R.Y.: A proactive material handling method for CPS enabled shop-floor. Robot. Comput.-Integrated Manuf. **61**, 101849 (2020)
4. Sharp, M., Ak, R., Hedberg, T.: A survey of the advancing use and development of ma-chine learning in smart manufacturing. J. Manuf. Syst. **48**, 170–179 (2018)
5. Wuest, T., Weimer, D., Irgens, C., Thoben, K.-D.: Machine learning in manufacturing: advantages, challenges, and applications. Prod. Manuf. Res. **4**, 23–45 (2016)
6. Guo, Z., Zhang, Y., Zhao, X., Song, X.: CPS-Based self-adaptive collaborative control for smart production-logistics systems. IEEE Trans. Cybern. **51**, 188–198 (2021)
7. Shiue, Y.-R., Guh, R., Lee, K.: Development of machine learning-based real time scheduling systems: using ensemble based on wrapper feature selection approach. Int. J. Prod. Res. **50**, 5887–5905 (2012)
8. Wang, H., Sarker, B.R., Li, J., Li, J.: Adaptive scheduling for assembly job shop with uncertain assembly times based on dual Q-learning. Int. J. Prod. Res., 1–17 (2020)
9. Shiue, Y.-R., Lee, K.-C., Su, C.-T.: Real-time scheduling for a smart factory using a reinforcement learning approach. Comput. Ind. Eng. **125**, 604–614 (2018)
10. Qiao, F., Liu, J., Ma, Y.: Industrial big-data-driven and CPS-based adaptive production scheduling for smart manufacturing. Int. J. Prod. Res. **2020**, 1–21 (2020)
11. Mourtzis, D., Vlachou, E.: A cloud-based cyber-physical system for adaptive shop-floor scheduling and condition-based maintenance. J. Manuf. Syst. **47**, 179–198 (2018)
12. Umar, U.A., Ariffin, M.K.A., Ismail, N., Tang, S.H.: Hybrid multi objective genetic algorithms for integrated dynamic scheduling and routing of jobs and automated-guided vehicle (AGV) in flexible manufacturing systems (FMS) environment. Int. J. Adv. Manuf. Technol. **81**, 2123–2141 (2015)
13. Hu, H., Jia, X., He, Q., Fu, S., Liu, K.: Deep reinforcement learning based AGVs real-time scheduling with mixed rule for flexible shop floor in industry 4.0. Comput. Ind. Eng. **149**, 106749 (2020)
14. Rossit, D.A., Tohmé, F., Frutos, M.: Industry 4.0: smart scheduling. Int. J. Prod. Res. **57**, 3802–3813 (2019)
15. Feng, Y., Wang, Q., Gao, Y., Cheng, J., Tan, J.: Energy-efficient job-shop dynamic scheduling system based on the cyber-physical energy-monitoring system. IEEE Access **6**, 52238–52247 (2018)
16. Jha, S.B., Babiceanu, R.F., Seker, R.: Formal modeling of cyber-physical resource scheduling in IIoT cloud environments. J. Intell. Manuf. **31**(5), 1149–1164 (2019). https://doi.org/10.1007/s10845-019-01503-x
17. Zhang, Y., Zhu, Z., Lv, J.: CPS-based smart control model for shopfloor material handling. IEEE Trans. Industr. Inf. **14**, 1764–1775 (2018)
18. Qu, T., Lei, S.P., Wang, Z.Z., Nie, D.X., Chen, X., Huang, G.Q.: IoT-based real-time production logistics synchronization system under smart cloud manufacturing. Int. J. Adv. Manuf. Technol. **84**(1–4), 147–164 (2015). https://doi.org/10.1007/s00170-015-7220-1
19. Priore, P., Gómez, A., Pino, R., Rosillo, R.: Dynamic scheduling of manufacturing systems using machine learning: an updated review. Artif. Intell. Eng. Des. Anal. Manuf. **28**, 83–97 (2014)

When Softbots Meet Digital Twins: Towards Supporting the Cognitive Operator 4.0

Ricardo J. Rabelo[1]([⊠]), David Romero[2], Saulo P. Zambiasi[3],
and Luciano C. Magalhães[1]

[1] UFSC - Federal University of Santa Catarina, Florianópolis, Brazil
ricardo.rabelo@ufsc.br
[2] Tecnológico de Monterrey, Monterrey, Mexico
[3] UNISUL - University of Southern Santa Catarina, Florianopolis, Brazil

Abstract. Digital Twins (DT) represent one of the most powerful technologies related to Industry 4.0 implementation. Combined with the advances in Computer Science and Production Management, DTs have become an emerging trend in many applications. Despite the DT potentials, Industry 4.0 is pushing companies to adopt digital solutions that provide higher human satisfaction to increase operational excellence. One approach to handle this involves how workers should interact with systems and smart machines. Softbots is a prominent direction to underpin this goal. This paper presents ongoing results of a research that exploits how softbots can be combined with DTs to create a more "symbiotic" human-machine/computer interaction within a smarter decision-making environment.

Keywords: Industry 4.0 · Softbots · Digital Twin · Cognitive Operator 4.0

1 Introduction

Industry 4.0 paradigm involves the use and combination of several so-called "enabling technologies", being the *Digital Twin (DT)* one of them [1]. A *DT* can be defined as an intelligent and evolving digital model, following the lifecycle of its physical twin to monitor, control, simulate, and optimize its processes, at the same time that continuously predicts its future statuses for further decision-making upon that [2].

One of the most adopted strategies pursued in the *Industry 4.0 digital transformation path* is the development of "data-driven environments", where decision-makers are provided with access to integrated and more accurate information related to the diverse organisational areas, including the shop floor. Their ultimate goal is to support more agile, comprehensive, and confident decision-making, nowadays usually supported by management and real-time production dashboards [3].

Despite the potentials brought up by such data-driven environments (as smart shop floors), many decision-makers are not prepared at all to correctly understand the plethora of technical terminologies related to production management, to make wider analyses and correlations between different performance indicators, to go through data to glean insights for decision-making, among other limitations [4, 5]. Besides that, data-driven environments can bring more complexity to decision-makers if not

© IFIP International Federation for Information Processing 2021
Published by Springer Nature Switzerland AG 2021
A. Dolgui et al. (Eds.): APMS 2021, IFIP AICT 634, pp. 37–47, 2021.
https://doi.org/10.1007/978-3-030-85914-5_5

properly designed to avoid "information overload" [6]. The practice has been showing that decision-makers have been increasingly exposed to massive amounts of information about their companies' processes, systems (including different DTs), and equipment, where lots of checking (sometimes repetitive), analyses, supervision, reporting actions as well as critical decision-making need to be more and more often and rapidly performed. All this leaves managers' capabilities to a cognition and stress limit, jeopardizing the quality of their decision-making [5, 6].

In a *Smart Shop floor context,* although a DT can, for instance, show production data via *digital dashboards* and monitor in real-time the execution of the *Cyber-Physical Systems (CPSs)* it represents, there are some relevant issues to consider once the DT is implemented [7–11]:

- The data to be shown in a digital dashboard is typically predefined (and hence limited), including the way data will interact with its users.
- The set of data to be shown in a digital dashboard is designed for a generic user.
- The use of a predefined and generic set of data prevents different users from having access to information outside the DT data model's border in the case of ad-hoc questions or of the need for very particular situations. This means making users going through other information systems' GUIs (e.g., ERP or MEs) to pick the required information and to 'mentally' reason about it outside of the DT's environment. This can also be as difficult due to home office, as many corporate information systems are still only available as local and non-web-based systems.
- The human limitation to follow (with the eyes) many 'things' simultaneously in a DT visualization or CPS execution.
- The many 'hidden information' in a DT visualization because of poor GUI design.
- The current limitations of data and business analytics solutions, which are not yet able to provide much intelligence and effective decision-support, leaving to decision-makers the more sensible and business-context analyses out of the plenty of information and available dashboards.
- Most of the development tools in the market for DTs (especially those provided by big IT/OT players) are not so easy to interoperate with (besides being costly, and therefore, not affordable for most SMEs).

Regarding the strong impact Industry 4.0 has on the workforce, several authors have highlighted the importance of systems to evolve in a way to support the newer types of interactions between humans, machines, and systems towards boosting human satisfaction and operational excellence [e.g., 11, 12]. In this context, the emerging concept of *Operator 4.0* ascends to significance. Coined by [13], its vision refers to supporting a socially and cognitive sustainable manufacturing workforce environment in the factories of the future, where smart operators should work collaboratively and aided by machines via advanced human-machine/computer interaction (HMI/HCI) technologies.

The *Operator 4.0 concept* can be implemented using different technologies. When looking at the type 'Smarter Operator 4.0', software robots (or just *softbots*) are one of the most promising approaches [13, 14]. A *softbot* can be generally defined as a computer program that interacts with and acts on behalf of a user or another program [15]. This is in line with the Cognitive DT concept, described as a "digital reflection of the user, intended to make decisions and carry out tasks on the user's behalf" [16]. [17] have also pointed out the importance of improving the level of DT's autonomy and interactivity in smart manufacturing systems to quickly respond to unexpected events without central re-planning. [18] have called this next-generation of software robots as *Softbots 4.0* – due to their capabilities of assisting operators in the management and automation of business processes, computer systems, and production assets in an industrial networked environment.

The goal of this paper is to present the results of a research that tackles those DT issues. It addresses them by introducing softbots to intermediate the interactions between the DT and production managers in Industry 4.0 production scenarios. This does not mean replacing the native DT's user interfaces, but rather adding a complementary and more "symbiotic" way of HMI/HCI towards supporting and leveraging the "Cognitive Operator 4.0" [13, 20]. This concept refers to empowering workers with more capabilities, autonomy, resources, and interactivity to better perform their activities within smart manufacturing systems [13].

This paper is organised as follows: Sect. 1 highlights the problem to be tackled and the desired improvements; Sect. 2 summarizes the research methodology adopted in this work; Sect. 3 provides basic foundations and related works to softbots and DTs; Sect. 4 details the experimental setup and preliminary results; and Sect. 5 presents the preliminary conclusions of this research and its next short-term steps.

2   Research Methodology

Adopting the *Action-Research methodology,* the prototype was developed as a proof-of-concept with the primary goal of evaluating to which extent the addition of a softbot could cope with the DT issues mentioned in the previous section.

Three previous authors' works have been used as a basis for the prototype. In [14], a group of collaborative *softbots* was developed to interact with a shop floor composed of six workstations of a FESTO MPS system existing in a university lab. In [5], a set of new dialogues, production scenarios and analytics have been implemented, related to the integration of a *softbot* to a Manufacturing Execution System (MES) system from the market. In [10], a DT prototype was built up on top of the same FESTO MPS system, allowing users to remotely follow the production in real-time as well as to act on the system in some situations.

The prototype developed for this work took advantage of some codes and GUIs from those two previous *softbots* and has extended and adapted them to the new interaction scenario involving the developed DT.

3   Basic Foundations and Related Works

3.1   Basic Foundations

Most of the R&D works found out in the literature are not DTs, but "digital shadows" instead. There are three types of virtualizations of a system [21]:

- *Digital Model* – it is a digital representation of a physical object; there is no interaction between the physical and the virtual models.
- *Digital Shadow* – it is characterized by the unidirectional connection between physical and digital models; only the physical model updates the digital model.
- *Digital Twin* – it is also characterized by the bidirectional connection between physical and digital models; the physical and the digital models continuously interact and update each other.

A DT can *mirror* one or more entities of a physical environment, such as operators, machines, materials, and shop floor layouts. In its execution cycle, a DT needs to collect information from its CPSs and send information and commands back to them; CPSs need to send data to its DT, and users need to follow and visualize the CPSs operation via its DT as well as to interact with the DT itself. This involves functionalities for data management, analysis, and computing [22].

A comprehensive DT in a manufacturing domain should support the following general functionalities [21]: (i) real-time monitoring and updating of the DT with information about parts, products, operations, machines, and all the related shop floor entities; (ii) analysis and energy consumption forecast; (iii) intelligent optimization based on the analysis of users' operation and product and/or production process data; (iv) analysis upon users' operation to evaluate their behaviours; (v) virtual product maintenance, including testing, evaluations, and new maintenance plans set-ups; and (vi) failure analysis and forecasting for equipment and/or product maintenance.

A *softbot* can be defined as a *"virtual system deployed in a given computing environment that automates and helps humans in the execution of tasks by combining capabilities of conversation-like interaction, system intelligence, autonomy, proactivity, and process automation"* [23]. It interfaces with smart machines and robots, computers, databases, and other information systems, aiding the operator in the execution of different tasks in "human-like" interactions within Industry 4.0 production and management scenarios [5]. Depending on the softbot's purpose, intelligence, autonomy, architecture, and modelling approaches, a "softbot" can functionally be seen as equivalent to other concepts, such as an *agent, personal assistant, chatbot, bot, holon, or avatar* [18].

Softbots does not aim at replacing the native human-machine/computer interfaces between workers and machine tools, or the ones with enterprise information systems, such as ERP or MES. Instead, they represent a higher-level and new type of frictionless human interaction, also skipping fixed and predefined menus commonly accessed via keyboard and mouse. That interaction can be provided by different means, like web browsers, mobile devices, augmented reality, natural language, haptics, etc. [24].

3.2　Related Works

After a search in scientific databases, it could be observed that the use of softbots (or equivalent concepts) at the shop floor level in the context of Industry 4.0 got some attention since about five years ago [25]. Their use integrated into DTs is more recent. Actually, not many works were found out combining softbots (or equivalent terms) and

DTs. Among them, the large majority only mention it as a trend, both in scientific papers [e.g., 16, 26-30] and in whitepapers, like in[1,2].

To the best of our knowledge, only two works have considered that combination in a more concrete way. In [31], a reference architecture for DTs, called *JARVIS*, is proposed. Although a module to support the interaction with a "chatbot" has been designed, it seems that no implementation has been made yet. In [32], the *Alexa* chatbot (from *Amazon*) is used to interact with a product's digital counterpart (which represents a DT) via voice using a reference vocabulary as a basis. The authors [32] mention an implementation, but no examples are shown in their paper.

4   Experimental Setup and Preliminary Results

4.1   The FESTO MPS System

The manufacturing infrastructure used as the basis for the development of both DT and softbot is a FESTO MPS system. It is composed of six machines (or stations) that work in sequence. Each station is equipped with a *PLC Siemens S7-1200 full DC* and a set of sensors and actuators. They use the *Profinet network and OPC protocol*. Stations' tags statuses and production data are accessed via the *TIA Portal,* from Siemens.

4.2   General System's Architecture

Figure 1 illustrates the general architecture of the developed prototype.

At the local level environment, a *softbot* has been deployed to help local operators to interact with the MPS system more comfortably and informally. Operators can request many different types of data from the planned and ongoing production. Besides that, the softbot was programmed to proactively carry on some actions, for example, checking some predefined situations and going into alarm in some cases [14].

Still, at this level, the operator can be provided with past information (e.g., what has been produced, via accessing the ERP database), current information (e.g., what is being produced), and future information (basically in terms of what is planned to be produced). In these two last cases, the TIA Portal acts as the main source of information.

In terms of the DT, one of its parts is placed at the local level. A *wrapper* was implemented to grab information from the MPS's stations in real-time and store them in the DT database *(MongoDB)*. There is a total of 135 variables (tags) that indicate several aspects of the stations during their operation. The communication between the wrapper and the TIA Portal is done via OPC-DA protocol. All this layer runs with Windows 7 OS.

---

[1] Virtual Assistants and Digital Twins Advance Personalised Medicine. https://healthcare-in-europe.com/en/news/virtual-assistants-digital-twins-advance-personalised-medicine.html.

[2] Affective Computing. https://cmte.ieee.org/futuredirections/2020/11/27/megatrends-for-this-decade-x/.

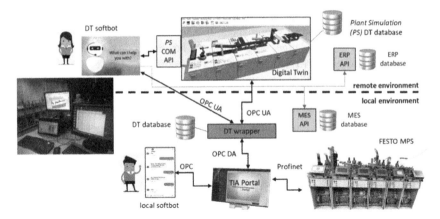

Fig. 1. General systems' architecture

At the remote level environment, a DT has been developed (in *Python*) on top of the MPS [10]. The MPS environment has been drawn up using the *Plant Simulation (PS) software,* from Siemens. The real-time visualization of the MPS operation is done via a permanent access to the DT's database using the OPC-UA protocol. It can be accessed via its Python/COM API, in the same way as its internal database. On the left side of Fig. 1, it can be shown the DT environment with a partial view of the MPS in the background. The monitor/PC on the right side has the DT wrapper/OPC server. The DT appears on the left side, with two screens (the one at the bottom is just a screen extension of the DT visualization environment).

Another *softbot* has been developed, acting as a kind of client application of the DT: the "DT softbot". It can access both other information that is not handled within the DT environment (e.g., the ERP) and the ones dealt with by the DT itself via its API. All this layer runs with Windows 10 OS. The DT and the softbot run on different servers, although in the same local network.

At this level, the operator: can be provided with past information (e.g., what has been produced, via accessing the Plant Simulation and/or the DT databases); can *visualize* current information (e.g., what is being produced, the machines in operation, bottlenecks formation, etc.); can have access to related information from other systems; can monitor and take care of the MPS execution; and can make some (current and future) analytics (e.g., prediction) based on some data and performance indicators.

Considering the objective of this paper and of the associated *proof-of-concept prototype,* the whole architecture and issues related to e.g., the integration approach and security, were simplified. Yet, only the most important MPS stations' entities were graphically represented in the DT software. However, the environment works for a real case, including facing all issues related to integrating different systems, interoperating with different technologies and protocols, and supporting real-time communication.

4.3   The ARISA NEST Platform for Softbots

Both "softbots" have been created using the *ARISA NEST*[3]. It is a PaaS-based-academic tool that allows the derivation and specialization of "instances of" both single and groups of *service-oriented softbots* [14]. They can be accessed via Web or mobile phone. ARISA is free and it is deployed in another cloud/server. It supports the communication between it and the derived softbots in various ways using open protocols/standards.

ARISA NEST supports three types of behaviour modes in its communication with end-users: (i) *Reactive* – when the softbot acts in direct response to users requests via chatting (e.g., to ask about more detailed information from a given machine); (ii) *Planned* – when the softbot acts in response to predefined scheduled tasks (of different types and complexities), bringing their results to users after their execution (e.g., to generate daily performance reports); and (iii) *Pro-active* – when the softbot performs predefined tasks autonomously on behalf of users or of some system it represents, bringing their results to users if needed (e.g., to continuously checking communication problems between data collectors and the DT wrapper - and to promptly take measures to solve them - or sending warnings and alarms).

4.4   The Use Cases

Several scenarios have been devised to preliminary assess this research. For this paper, due to space restrictions, scenarios were mixed, figures were condensed, and only two stations have been considered to leave the figures clearer. These scenarios show the combination of the reactive, planned, and pro-active behaviours, with the capabilities of doing some analytics, actuation on the real system (as a truly DT), and the gathering of information from different systems other than from the DT itself.

Use Case 1: Reactive + Request Decomposition + Access to other Systems + Analytics In this case, the user checks the DT's analytics module (developed in this prototype) and observes that the *Distribution station's OEE (Overall Equipment Effectiveness)* is strangely too unstable. He then realizes that some production orders will be delayed if this continues as the DT is predicting, but he does not know either which orders might be affected by that (this information is actually handled by the MES system) nor the respective customers' names (this information is handled by the ERP system) so that he could warn both customers and the company's CRM area in advance.

As the DT does not have all the required information, this request is got by the softbot, which "reacts" to attend it. The message is interpreted by the softbot (based on predefined keywords set up when the softbot is derived), it is decomposed into "sub-tasks" (one for each correct subsystem - the MES and ERP in this case - that should be accessed via calling their APIs to get the information), and each subtask is executed (within/by the softbot). This Use Case is shown in Fig. 2.

---

[3] ARISA NEST platform for softbots derivation – https://arisa.com.br/ [in Portuguese].

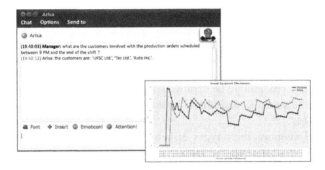

Fig. 2. Use Case 1: Reactive + Request Decomposition + Access to other Systems + Analytics

Use Case 2: Planned + Automatic Actions

In this case, there is no user request. The softbot simply executes the tasks that have been previously configured by the user, on behalf of him. In this scenario, the softbot should automatically generate the utilization level of the *Distribution and Testing stations* at the end of each working shift for his general analysis. As the *ARISA NEST* does not support internally graphical elements in its GUI, it does it calling the Plant Simulation's API to see the utilization level. This Use Case is shown in Fig. 3.

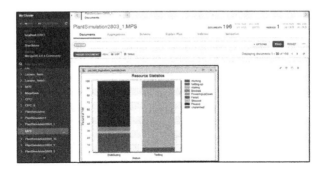

Fig. 3. Use Case 2: Planned + Automatic Actions

Use Case 3: Pro-Active + Actuation on the Real System

In this case, there is not a user request either. However, the pro-active mode relates to the possible autonomy level a softbot can have. For example, a softbot could always warn the user (e.g., sending him a message or getting into alarm) and order a given machine (the Distribution station, for example) to be turned off when its OEE gets lower than 20%. This value of 20% would be a result of a more sophisticated algorithm that calculated that after processing a long OEE historical series also considering the stored company's good practices knowledge base.

In the developed prototype this was just assumed, and a simple algorithm has been implemented to really act on the *physical Distribution station,* to be turned off in that OEE situation. Figure 4 zooms the moment when this situation occurs as well as it shows the change in the respective station's tag, from 'false' (i.e., it was turned on) to 'true' (i.e., it is now turned off).

The possibility to turn a given station off by the user is also allowed via pressing the red button of each station directly on the DT's graphical interface (see Fig. 1). Another example of this Case is to support the Use Case 1. Instead of doing the user to follow the OEE performance of the Distribution station "manually" over time, the softbot proactively and permanently checks that and warns the user when that situation happens. This Use Case is shown in Fig. 4.

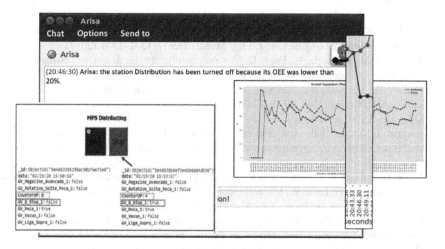

Fig. 4. Use Case 3: Pro-Active + Actuation on the real system

5   Conclusions

This paper has presented an approach for the use of *softbots* to improve the way users interact with DTs and on how they manage the production management in general with manufacturing DTs. An initial prototype has been developed, integrated into a near-real shop floor, which is composed of six machines that act as cyber-physical systems.

A set of scenarios was designed to evaluate the devised approach against the issues highlighted in the introduction. The scenarios were implemented and tested in a controlled environment. The evaluation was qualitative, given the nature of the issues.

Current results could confirm the potential of the approach, where the integration of a *softbot* with a DT environment helped to overcome the targeted issues.

Some open points have arisen from this research. One of the most critical issues refers to the autonomy level a softbot can have, especially when an actuation on the real system is needed. As this is a very sensitive situation, a kind of systems governance model should exist to determine the frontiers of operation and actuation among the most directed involved systems, namely the MES, the DT, and the softbot.

There are many possible further directions to be exploited from now on. Besides enriching the DT's graphical visualization with more MPS' elements, the main next short-term steps refer to enhancing the interaction between the *softbot* and the DT in terms of better aiding users in business analyses and decision-support based on the data the DT and other systems (including wearables) can jointly provide.

Acknowledgements. This work has been partially supported by CAPES Brazilian Agency for Higher Education, project PrInt "Automation 4.0".

References

1. Mittal, S., Khan, M.A., Romero, D., Wuest, T.: Smart manufacturing: characteristics, technologies and enabling factors. J. Eng. Manuf. **233**(5), 1342–1361 (2017)
2. Barricelli, B.R., Casiraghi, E., Fogli, D.: A survey on digital twin: definitions, characteristics, applications, and design implications. IEEE Access **7**, 167653–167671 (2019)
3. Romero, D., Vernadat, F.: Enterprise information systems state of the art: past, present and future trends. Comput. Ind. **79**, 3–13 (2016)
4. ASG: The ASG Technologies 2020 Survey Report – Barriers to Success with Information-Powered Business: Bad Data Burdens the Modern Enterprise. https://content.asg.com/MarketingCollateral/DataIntelligence/whitepaper-asg-data-intelligence-barriers-to-success.pdf
5. Abner, B., Rabelo, R.J., Zambiasi, S.P., Romero, D.: Production management as-a-service: a softbot approach. In: Lalic, B., Majstorovic, V., Marjanovic, U., von Cieminski, G., Romero, D. (eds.) Advances in Production Management Systems. Towards Smart and Digital Manufacturing, APMS 2020. IFIP Advances in Information and Communication Technology, vol. 592. Springer, Cham. https://doi.org/10.1007/978-3-030-57997-5_3
6. McDermott, A.: Information Overload Is Crushing You. Here are 11 Secrets That Will Help. https://www.workzone.com/blog/information-overload/
7. Jones, D., Snider, C., Nassehi, A., Yon, J., Hicks, B.: Characterising the digital twin: a systematic literature review. CIRP J. Manuf. Sci. Technol. **29**(1), 36–52 (2020)
8. Rabelo, R.J., Zambiasi, S.P., Romero, D.: Collaborative softbots: enhancing operational excellence in systems of cyber-physical systems. In: Camarinha-Matos, L.M., Afsarmanesh, H., Antonelli, D. (eds.) PRO-VE 2019. IAICT, vol. 568, pp. 55–68. Springer, Cham (2019). https://doi.org/10.1007/978-3-030-28464-0_6
9. Lua, Y., Liub, C., Xu, X.: Digital twin-driven smart manufacturing: connotation, reference model, applications and research issues. Robot. Comput. Integr. Manuf. **61**, 101837–101852 (2020)
10. Rabelo, R.J., Magalhaes, L.C., Cabral, F.G.: A proposal of a reference architecture for digital twins in industry 4.0 (in Portuguese). In: Proceedings of the XXIII Brazilian Congress of Automation (2020)
11. Rooein, D., Bianchini, D., Leotta, F., Mecella, M., Paolini, P., Pernici, B.: Chatting about processes in digital factories: a model-based approach. In: Nurcan, S., Reinhartz-Berger, I., Soffer, P., Zdravkovic, J. (eds.) BPMDS/EMMSAD-2020. LNBIP, vol. 387, pp. 70–84. Springer, Cham (2020). https://doi.org/10.1007/978-3-030-49418-6_5

12. Frazzon, E.M., Agostino, I.S., Broda, E., Freitag, M.: Manufacturing networks in the era of digital production and operations: a socio-cyber-physical perspective. Annu. Rev. Control. **49**, 288–294 (2020)

13. Romero, D., Stahre, J., Wuest, T., et al.: Towards an operator 4.0 typology: a human-centric perspective on the fourth industrial revolution technologies. In: International Conference on Computers & Industrial Engineering (CIE46), Tianjin, China, pp. 1–11 (2016)

14. Rabelo, R.J., Romero, D., Zambiasi, S.P.: Softbots supporting the operator 4.0 at smart factory environments. In: Moon, I., Lee, G.M., Park, J., Kiritsis, D., von Cieminski, G. (eds.) APMS 2018. IAICT, vol. 536, pp. 456–464. Springer, Cham (2018). https://doi.org/10.1007/978-3-319-99707-0_57

15. Schwartz, T., et al.: Hybrid teams: flexible collaboration between humans, robots and virtual agents. In: Klusch, M., Unland, R., Shehory, O., Pokahr, A., Ahrndt, S. (eds.) MATES 2016. LNCS (LNAI), vol. 9872, pp. 131–146. Springer, Cham (2016). https://doi.org/10.1007/978-3-319-45889-2_10

16. Somers, S., Oltramari, A., Lebiere, C.: Cognitive twin: a cognitive approach to personalized assistants. In: AAAI Spring Symposium: Combining Machine Learning with Knowledge Engineering (2020)

17. Rosen, R., Wichert, G., Lo, G., Bettenhausen, K.: About the importance of autonomy and digital twins for the future of manufacturing. IFAC-PapersOnLine **48**(3), 567–572 (2015)

18. Rabelo, R., Zambiasi, S.P., Romero, D., Abner, B.: Softbots 4.0: excelling smart production management. Int. J. Comput. Integr. Manuf. (to appear)

19. Brain. Chatbot Report 2019: Global Trends and Analysis. https://chatbotsmagazine.com/chatbot-report-2019-global-trends-and-analysis-a487afec05b/

20. Thorvald, P., Fast-Berglund, Å., Romero, D.: The cognitive operator 4.0. In: Proceedings of the 18th International Conference on Manufacturing Research. IOS Press (2021)

21. Kritzinger, W., Karner, M., Traar, G.: Digital twin in manufacturing: a categorical literature review and classification. IFAC PapersOnLine **15**(11), 1016–1022 (2018)

22. Zhong, R.Y., Xu, X., Klotz, E.: Intelligent Manufacturing in the Context of Industry 4.0: A Review. Engineering, 3(5):616–630 (2017)

23. Kim, J.H.: Ubiquitous robot. In: Reusch B. (eds.) Computational Intelligence, Theory and Applications. Advances in Soft Computing, vol. 33, pp. 451–459 (2005)

24. Papcun, P., Kajáti, E., Koziorek, J.: Human machine interface in concept of Industry 4.0. In: World Symposium on Digital Intelligence for Systems and Machines, pp. 289–296 (2018)

25. Preuveneers, D., Ilie-Zudor, E.: The intelligent industry of the future: a survey on emerging trends, research challenges and opportunities in Industry 4.0. J. Ambient Intell. Smart Environ. **9**(3), 287–298 (2017). https://doi.org/10.3233/AIS-170432

26. Rasheed, A., San, O., Kvamsdal, T.: Digital twin – values, challenges and enablers from a modeling perspective. IEEE Access **8**, 21980–22012 (2020)

27. Yarnold, J., Henman P., McEwan, C.: Artificial intelligence. https://policy-futures.centre.uq.edu.au/files/6128/PolicyFutures_Unpacking_Artificial_Intelligence.pdf

28. Guo, J.: Digital twins are shaping future virtual worlds. SOCA **15**(2), 93–95 (2021)

29. Boschert, S., et al.: Symbiotic Autonomous Systems. IEEE Digital Reality (2019)

30. Bolton, R., McColl-Kennedy, J., et al.: Customer experience challenges: bringing together digital, physical and social realms. J. Serv. Manag. **29**(5), 776–808 (2018)

31. Parri, J., Patara, F., Sampietro, S.: A framework for model-driven engineering of resilient software-controlled systems. Computing **103**, 589–612 (2021)

32. Wellsandta, S., Foosheriana, M., Thoben, K-D.: Interacting with a digital twin using Amazon Alexa. In: 5th International Conference on System-Integrated Intelligence, pp. 4–8 (2020)

New Approaches for Routing Problem Solving

The Implementation of Eulerian Coverings of a Graph for Solving Routing Problems

Tatiana A. Makarovskikh$^{(\boxtimes)}$ (iD)

South Ural State University, 76, Lenin Avenue, Chelyabinsk 454080, Russia
Makarovskikh.T.A@susu.ru

Abstract. In terms of graph theory, the urban transport network can be adequately represented as a graph. All crossroads in the city are considered to be the vertices of the graph, and streets are the edges. Using this model, one can set and effectively solve many routing problems: (1) constructing the routes between given starting and ending points, satisfying the rules of the road (allowed turns at crossroads and a given sequence of driving through the streets), (2) finding the way, passing through all the streets of the city in accordance with the rules of the road and a given sequence of turns at crossroads (an algorithm for constructing an permissible Eulerian chain), (3) constructing a minimal cardinality set of routes running through all the streets of the city (Eulerian cover of any graph with permissible chains). The paper provides a formalization of these problems and effective algorithms for solving them.

Keywords: Graphs · Trajectory planning · Polynomial algorithm · Transportation control

1 Introduction

Various problems of management and automation design often lead to solving the routing problem. So, for example, one of the most actively explored areas is a mathematical model based on choosing the optimal route between different objects. These objects can be considered to be the vertices of a directed graph, and the optimal routes in this case will represent the shortest paths in the graph, which is a mathematical model of the considered problem. [1] considers is the problem of modelling the closed queuing networks, for example, the placement of bicycle parking lots in the city, where parking lots are defined as the vertices of a directed graph, and possible paths between them be weighted arcs. When planning and managing the choice of a delivery route, it is possible to solve a problem based on representing a set of typical system states as graph vertices, the

The work was supported by the Ministry of Science and Higher Education of the Russian Federation (government order FENU-2020-0022).

routes of this graph correspond to the control decisions of the fuzzy situational network.

Let's consider the solution of the routing problem solved by [2]. It requires the distribution of transport and passenger flows and takes into account the specifics of driving in cities. To solve it, a correct description of the behaviour of the passenger (or the car) when choosing a route is required. Many factors influence his behaviour. For example, a special graph may be used to model the system of all possible paths within the city. Such a graph can be called communication graph. It is a superposition of the following subgraphs: subway routes, railway, pedestrian paths, highways, etc. Such a system of all possible displacements is not static, therefore it can be noted that all edges of the communication graph routes are characterized by the moments of creation and marking for deletion.

Routing problems complicated by various constraints are of the greatest theoretical interest. There are various methods for solving such problems and various constraints, for example, considered by [3], and [4].

In terms of graph theory, the transport network can be represented as a graph $G = (V, E)$, where the set of vertices V is the set of crossroads (cities, airports, warehouses, etc.), and the set of edges E is a set of connections between objects from V (roads, highways, flights, etc.). Thus, if there is an edge $e = \{v_1, v_2\}$, then there is a direct message between the objects corresponding to v_1 and v_2. The solution of the routing problem in the transport network assumes (1) construction of routes between the given starting and ending points, satisfying the traffic rules (allowed turns at crossroads and a given sequence of travel along the streets), (2) finding a path passing through all the city streets in accordance with the traffic rules and a given sequence of turns at crossroads (an algorithm for constructing an permissible Euler chain), (3) constructing a minimal cardinality set of routes passing through all the streets of the city (Euler's cover of an arbitrary graph by permissible chains). As mentioned above, the most interesting are routing problems with constraints, since the constraints introduced allow us to describe a fairly narrow class of applied problems. Since the graph corresponding to the transport network has a sufficiently large dimension, the most urgent are algorithms that make it possible to obtain a solution (or a feasible solution) in the shortest possible time. The preferred algorithms are the ones that solve the problem in polynomial time (if they exist for the declared class of problems).

Constraints on constructing of routes in graphs can be classified as local (when a condition is set at a fixed vertex or edge) and global (a constraint is set for the graph as a whole). Problems with **local constraints** include the problem of constructing a route that satisfies a fixed system of allowed transitions. In terms of the transport routing problem, the problem statement can be interpreted as follows. All crossroads of the city roads are considered as the vertices of the graph, and streets are considered as edges. It is necessary to get a route between the starting and ending points that meets the rules of the road (allowed turns at crossroads) or the specified sequence of driving along the streets.

To solve these problems we define the following graphs: (1) the graph corresponding to the map of the area, in which each vertex $v \in V$ corresponds to a crossroad, (2) transition graphs $T_G(v)$ defined at each vertex $v \in V$. The vertices of the transition graphs are edges incident to $v \in V$, i.e. $V(T_G(v)) = E_G(v)$, and the edges define the allowed transitions (the transitions correspond to the given traffic rules at a particular crossroad).

2 Constructing the Permissible Path Between Two Vertices

The constraints on routes in the graph G can be formulated in terms of the graph of allowed transitions. These definitions are given by [4]. Let us formulate them for completeness.

Definition 1. *Let G be a graph.* **Transitions graph** *$T_G(v)$ for vertex $v \in V(G)$ be a graph, the vertices of which are the edges incidentto vertex v, i.e. $V(T_G(v)) = E_G(v)$, and set of edges be the allowed transitions.* **The system of allowed transitions** *(or the* **transitions system** *for short) T_G be the set $\{T_G(v) \mid v \in V(G)\}$, where $T_G(v)$ be the transitions graph for v. Path $P = v_0 e_1 v_1 \ldots e_k v_k$ in G be T_G-compatible, if $\{e_i, e_{i+1}\} \in E(T_G(v_i))$ for each i $(1 \le i \le k-1)$.*

The following theorem proved by [5] holds for a problem of constructing the T_G-compatible chain, i.e. simple chain $C = v_0 e_1 v_1 \ldots e_k v_k$ in graph G, for which $\{e_i, e_{i+1}\} \in E(T_G(v_i))$ for each i $(1 \le i \le k-1)$.

Theorem 1. *If all transition graphs belong to class M of complete multipartite graphs, or class P of matchings, then the problem of constructing the T_G-compatible chain may be solved by time $O(|E(G)|)$. Otherwise, this problem is $\mathcal{NP}$-complete.*

If transitions system for vertex $v \in V(G)$ is a matching then the problem can be reduced to a problem for graph

$$G' : V(G') = V(G)\backslash\{v\},$$
$$E(G') = (E(G)\backslash E_G(v)) \cup \{\{v_i, v_j\} : \{\{v_i, v\}; \{v, v_j\}\} \in E(T_G(v))\}.$$

If $T_G(v)$ fro any vertex $v \in V(G)$ is a complete multipartite graph then to get a permissible chain we may use algorithm T_G-COMPATIBLE PATH [4].

Note that in the general, the direct application of this algorithm does not allow to solve the problem of finding a T_G-compatible route containing the maximum number of edges. Note that T_G-**COMPATIBLE PATH** algorithm cannot be used to construct routes that cover all edges of graph G.

Indeed, a maximum cardinality matching in the graph G' cannot contain a pair of edges forming a forbidden transition, since they are incident to one common vertex of graph G'. At the same time, in the general, there may be a T_G-compatible route containing such a pair of edges. Note that [5] does not consider the issue of recognizing the multipartition of graphs $T_G(v)$, as well as the problem of constructing an permissible route or a set of routes covering all edges of the original graph. This recognition is rather trivial, and it is advisable to use the concept of a partition system introduced by [6] and [7].

3   Algorithm for Constructing the Permissible Eulerian Chain

As noted, algorithm by [5] generally does not allow constructing compatible chains of maximum length. Compatible Eulerian chains are of particular interest. A necessary and sufficient condition for the existence of P_G-compatible chains is given by [7]. The complexity of checking the existence of P_G-compatible Euler chain is not greater than $O(|E(G)|)$.

To define P_G-compatible chain in terms of forbidden transitions the term of partition system is used.

Definition 2. *Let* $G = (V, E)$ *be a graph. Let* $P_G(v)$ *be some partition of set* $E_G(v)$. **The partition system** *of* G *be a system of sets* $P_G :=$ $\{P_G(v) \mid v \in V(G)\}$. *Let* $p \in P_G(v)$, $\{e, f\} \in p$. *Chain not containing the transitions* $e \to v \to f$ *and* $f \to v \to e$ *be called* P_G-**compatible**, *and transitions* $e \to v \to f$ *and* $f \to v \to e$ *be* **forbidden**.

Note that the graph of allowed transitions $T_G(v)$ uniquely determines the graph of forbidden transitions $\overline{T_G}(v)$ and vice versa. Obviously, $T_G(v) \cup \overline{T_G}(v) = K_{|V(G)|}$, i.e. the forbidden transition graph is the complement of the allowed transition graph to a complete graph. Thus, using the definition of 1, one can pose a problem with any graph of allowed (forbidden) transitions.

On the contrary, the graph of allowed transitions, defined using the partition system P_G, cannot be arbitrary, but belongs to the class M of complete multipartite graphs: the elements of the partition $P_G(v)$ determine the parts of the graph $T_G(v) \in M$, and the set of its edges

$$E(T_G(v)) = \{e, f \in E_G(v) : (\forall p \in P_G(v)) \{e, f\} \not\subset p\}.$$

In this case, the graph of forbidden transitions $\overline{T_G}(v)$ will be a set of $|P_G(v)|$ cliques, this fact can be used to recognize the belonging of $T(v)$ to M.

Thus, a partitioning system into subsets can be given on $E(v)$ (the set of edges incident to the vertex v). If the edges e_1 and e_2 belong to the same subset, then the edge e_2 cannot follow the edge e_1. The graph $G(V, E)$ will be defined as an adjacency list, the elements of which are structures. Each element of this structure consists of two fields: (1) numbers of the vertex v_i, adjacent to the current vertex; (2) the number c_i of the split element. Note that each edge e of the graph belongs to two adjacency lists: for vertices v_i and v_j, which are the ends of this edge. But for each vertex the edge e will belong to different partition systems.

To construct the compatible Eulerian chain we may use P_G-COMPATIBLE EULER CHAIN algorithm [4] that solves the problem of obtaining $P(G)$-compatible Euler chain by time $O\left(|E(G)| \cdot |V(G)|\right)$. This algorithm can be easily implemented using standard computational tools.

4   Eulerian Cover of a Graph by Permissible Chains

Let us consider the problem of constructing an Euler covering of a graph with compatible chains. We assume that the transition system T_G contains only matchings and complete multipartite graphs [4].

Definition 3. *Let the Euler cover be the minimal cardinality set of edge-disjoint paths, covering the set of edges of a given graph.*

In this case, the graph is completed to be Euler. One way to reduce a graph to Euler is given by [4]. The considered algorithm 1 for constructing a covering by feasible chains consists in introducing a fictive vertex v^* and connecting it with all odd vertices with fictitious edges. [4] proved that in this case it is possible to solve the problem in linear time. As a result, $l + 1$ chain covering the original graph will be constructed. Here $l = \deg(v^*)$.

Algorithm 1. COVERING BY T_G-COMPATIBLE CHAINS

Require: : $G = (V, E)$, transitions graphs $T_G(v)$ $\forall v \in V(G)$.
Ensure: : a set of chains T^i, $i = 1, 2, \ldots, k$, covering graph G, $m = 2k$ is the number of odd vertices.
1: $U = \{v \in V(G) \ : \ T_G(v) \text{is matching }\};$ ▷ **Step 1**
2: $V(G') = V(G)\backslash U,$ ▷ Reduce G to G'
3:
$$E(G') = \left(E(G)\backslash \bigcup_{v \in U} E_G(v)\right) \bigcup \left\{\bigcup_{v \in U} \{\{v_i v_j\} : \ \{v_i v, \ v v_j\} \in T_G(v)\}\right\};$$
4: $T_{G'}(v) = \textbf{Reduce}(T_G(v), U)$ ▷ Replace all entries of $u \in U$: $vu, wu \in E_{T_G}(u)$ by w
5: $G^* = \text{AddSupplementary}(G', v^*);$ ▷ **Step 2.**
6:      ▷ Introduce a supplementary vertex v^* adjacent to all odd vertices of G'
7: $T_{G^*} = \textbf{Modify}(T_{G'}(v));$ ▷ Introduce vertex vv^* adjacent to all vertices in the graph $T_{G^*}(v)$ for all $v \in V'(G) \ : \ \deg(v) \equiv 1 \pmod 2$ into the transition graph $T_{G^*}(v)$.
8: **for all** $v \in V(G)$: $\exists p \in P(v)$: $|p| > \deg(v)/2$ **do**   ▷ **Step 3.**
9:      **for all** $i = 1, 2, ..., 2|p| - \deg(v)$ **do**
10:          **AddEdge**($G^*, (vv^*)_i$);   ▷ introduce $2|p| - \deg(v)$ supplementary edges
11:          **Modify**($T_{G^*}((vv^*)_i)$);   ▷ Modify the transitions graph
12:      **end for**
13: **end for**
14: $T_{G^*} = P_G$-COMPATIBLE EULER CHAIN(G^*)▷ **Step 4.** Obtain compatible cycle
15: **for all** $v \in V(G)$ **do**   ▷ **Step 5**
16:      $T'(G') = \textbf{Delete}((vv^*))$ ▷ Delete supplementary edges from T^* and obtain T'
17: **end for**
18: **for all** $u \in U$ **do**   ▷ **Step 6**
19:      $T = \textbf{Modify}(T');$ ▷ Modify paths by adding the vertices deleted at Step 1.
20: **end for**

Theorem 2. *Algorithm 1* ***COVERING BY*** T_G***-COMPATIBLE CHAINS***
correctly solves the problem of constructing the Euler cover of graph G by
T_G*-compatible chains. Its computing complexity is not greater than* $O(|E(G)| \cdot |V(G)|)$.

In terms of the transport routing problem, this problem can be interpreted in
two ways: (1) the constructed cover is a set of permissible routes in the city, and
the vertex v^* is a depot; (2) the constructed cover is a solution of well-known
applied problems when certain constraints are put on the sequence of passed
streets/corridors.

5   Example

Let's consider the simple but visual example of constructing the cover by T_G-
compatible chains for graph in Fig. 1. The real life examples (maps of the cities
where vertices are cross-roads, and edges are streets) have $10^4 - 10^9$ vertices
and edges, and they are the subject of interest for another research concerning minimization of calculation time. So, the graph in Fig. 1 has odd vertices
$V_{odd} = \{v_1, v_7, v_8, v_9, v_{10}, v_{11}\}$. Hence, Euler cover contains three chains. Let us
introduce the supplementary vertex v^* and construct the edges incident to it,
the second ends of these edges be vertices

$$v \in V_{odd}: \ E_{odd} =$$
$$= \{\{v^*, v_1\}, \{v^*, v_7\}, \{v^*, v_8\}, \{v^*, v_9\}, \{v^*, v_{10}\}, \{v^*, v_{11}\}\}.$$

Thus, we obtain graph $G^* = G(V \cup V_{odd}, E \cup E_{odd})$. According to transitions
system T_G we complete transitions system T_{G^*} according to Step 2 of Algorithm
1. Splitting of graph G^* vertices according to T_{G^*} is given in Fig. 2. Hence, we

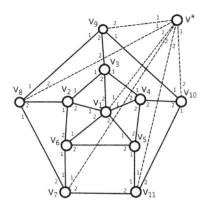

Fig. 1. Graph G with 6 odd vertices, partitions for each vertex, supplementary vertex
v^*, and supplementary edges adjacent to it

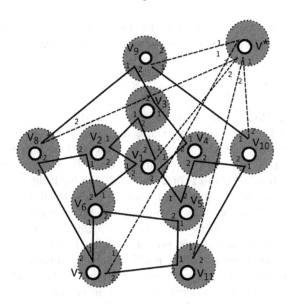

Fig. 2. Graph G^* all vertices of which are split according to the given transitions system. The gray circles round the split vertices

obtain T_G-compatible Euler cycle for G^* by algorithm P_G-COMPATIBLE EULER CHAIN.

$$(G^*) = \{v_8 v_9 v_3 v_4 v_1 v_5 v_4 v_{10} v_{11} v^* v_{10} v_9 v^* v_7$$
$$v_{11} v_5 v_6 v_7 v_8 v_2 v_6 v_1 v_2 v_3 v_1 v^* v_8\} \, .$$

When we delete edges $e \in E_{odd}$ from $C(G^*)$ we get the cover of initial graph G by compatible chains

$$C_1 = \{v_8 v_9 v_3 v_4 v_1 v_5 v_4 v_{10} v_{11}\}, \quad C_2 = \{v_{10} v_9\},$$
$$C_3 = \{v_7 v_{11} v_5 v_6 v_7 v_8 v_2 v_6 v_1 v_2 v_3 v_1\}.$$

Nevertheless, additional edges in the graph can also be introduced in accordance with additional constraints, for example, when solving a traffic problem, these edges may represent a planar extension and/or duplicate the existing edges. In this case, the number of constructed chains depends on the number of additional edges. So, if the graph from the considered example (Fig. 1) is a homeomorphic image of some area map, then the following auxiliary routes will be obtained between the chains C_i, $i = 1, 2, 3$: $C_{1,2} = v_{11} v_{10}$, $C_{2,3} = v_9 v_8 v_7$ (or $C_{2,3} = v_9 v_{10} v_{11} v_7$). In general, algorithm T_G-COMPATIBLE PATH to construct permissible chains between pairs of odd vertices.

In terms of the transport routing problem, this problem can be interpreted in two ways:

– the constructed cover is a set of permissible routes in the city, and the vertex v^* is a depot;

– the constructed cover is a solution of well-known applied problems when certain constraints are put on the sequence of passed streets/corridors.

6   Conclusion

The known algorithms make it possible to construct a simple chain between two different vertices that satisfies local constraints. The paper shows the possibility of recognizing a transition system, which allows solving the problem of constructing a compatible path in linear time. It is proved that using the developed algorithm P_G-COMPATIBLE EULER CHAIN for Euler graph G it is possible to obtain a P_G-compatible Euler cycle or to establish its absence in time $O(|V(G)| \cdot |E(G)|)$. Covering the graph G with compatible chains is also possible in time $O(|V(G)| \cdot |E(G)|)$ using algorithm COVERING T_G -COMPATIBLE CHAINS. The considered algorithms can be used, for example, to solve routing problems in transport, when the dimension of the problem is large enough and it is necessary to use algorithms that solve the problem in the shortest time. The directions for further research is the development of C++-library that implements the construction of routes with the local constraints discussed here.

References

1. Giuseppe, C., Portigliotti, C.F., Rizzo A.: A Network Model for an Urban Bike Sharing System. IFAC-PapersOnLine, vol. 50, issue 1, pp. 15633–15638 (2017)
2. Panyukov, A.V., Pivovarova, Yu.V., Chaloob, Kh.: Mathematical model for solving operational problem of regional cargo transportation. J. Comput. Eng. Math. **6**, 68–73 (2019)
3. Chentsov, A.G., Chentsov, P.A.: Routing under constraints: problem of visit to megalopolises. Autom. Remote Control **77**(11), 1957–1974 (2016)
4. Panyukova, T., Alferov, I.: The software for constructing trails with local restrictions in graphs. Open J. Discrete Math. **3**(2), 86–92 (2013)
5. Szeider, S.: Finding Paths in Graphs Avoiding Forbidden Transitions. Discrete Applied Mathematics, no. 126, pp. 261–273 (2003)
6. Fleischner, H.: Eulerian Graphs and Related Topics. Part 1, vol 1. Ann. Discrete Mathematics, no. 45 (1990)
7. Kotzig, A.: Moves without forbidden transitions in a graph. Mat.-Fiz. Casopis **18**(1), 76–80 (1968)

An Exact Method for a Green Vehicle Routing Problem with Traffic Congestion

Hongyuan Luo$^{(\boxtimes)}$, Mahjoub Dridi, and Olivier Grunder

Nanomedicine Lab, Univ. Bourgogne Franche-Comté, UTBM, 90010 Belfort, France
{hongyuan.luo,mahjoub.dridi,olivier.grunder}@utbm.fr

Abstract. This paper addresses a time-dependent green vehicle routing problem (TDGVRP) with the consideration of traffic congestion. In this work, the objective is to optimize the vehicle routing plan, with the goal of reducing carbon emissions, which has linear relationship with fuel consumption of vehicles. To deal with traffic congestion, travel time are considered to be time-dependent. We propose a branch-and-price (BAP) algorithm to precisely solve this problem. A tailored labeling algorithm is designed for solving the pricing sub-problem. Computational experiments demonstrate the effectiveness of the proposed BAP algorithm.

Keywords: Vehicle routing problem · Time-dependent · Carbon emissions · Branch-and-price

1 Introduction

The vehicle routing problem (VRP) is a practical and concerned issue in a wide range of application systems, including logistics, transportation, distribution, home health care, and supply chains [1]. Recently, the growing awareness of environmental concerns such as global warming and urban air pollution has led to increased efforts to protect the environment [2]. Many companies consider environmental-friendly operations throughout their supply chains. The motivation of being more environmental conscious is not only about legal constraints, but it also reduces costs and attracts customers who prefer green operations [3]. Therefore, some researchers have studied the green VRP (GVRP).

Nowadays, traffic congestion has become another common problem. Based on this limitation, [4] proposed the time-dependent VRP (TDVRP) in which the travel time changes with the departure time. In this paper, we focus on the time-dependent green vehicle routing problem (TDGVRP) with the time-varying vehicle speed and time windows. The cost of fuel consumption is one of the most significant part of the operation costs in logistics transportation. In the sense of the TDGVRP, we strive to minimize carbon emissions, which

The first author would thank the China Scholarship Council for the financial support gratefully (contract No. 201801810122).

© IFIP International Federation for Information Processing 2021
Published by Springer Nature Switzerland AG 2021
A. Dolgui et al. (Eds.): APMS 2021, IFIP AICT 634, pp. 59–67, 2021.
https://doi.org/10.1007/978-3-030-85914-5_7

has linear relationship with fuel consumption, as the objective to optimize the vehicle routing with the time-varying vehicle speed. An exact branch-and-price (BAP) algorithm is developed to solve the TDGVRP.

The rest of this paper is organized as follows. Section 2 introduces the problem and formulation. Section 3 develops an exact BAP approach to solve the problem. The computational experiments are described in Sect. 4. Section 5 concludes the paper.

2   Problem Description and Formulation

2.1   Problem Description

The studied TDGVRP addresses a key aspect regarding the impact of traffic congestion in terms of the feasibility, fuel consumption and carbon emissions of a route. Let $G = (N, A)$ be a directed graph with a set of vertices $N = \{0, 1, \ldots, n, n + 1\}$, in which $N_c = \{1, \ldots, n\}$ represent customers, and 0 and $n + 1$ represent the origin and the destination depot, respectively. The distance between vertex i and vertex j is denoted by d_{ij}. Each vertex $i \in N$ has a demand q_i, a service time s_i, and an associated hard time window $[a_i, b_i]$. Each vehicle has to wait until the earliest time a_i if it arrives at vertex i before time a_i, meanwhile the vehicle is prohibited to arrive after time b_i. For vertices $i \in \{0, n + 1\}$, it is assumed that $q_i = s_i = a_i = 0$ and $b_i = T$. Thus there is a fixed planning horizon $[0, T]$ in which vehicles are allowed to move along the route. A set of unlimited fleet of homogeneous vehicles with a limited capacity Q are employed to service the customers.

The impact of traffic congestion is captured by considering that the time required to travel from vertex i to vertex j, when departing from vertex i at time t, is given by a travel time function that is continuous, piecewise linear, and satisfies the FIFO property (i.e., a later departure always leads to a later arrival and thus overtaking will not happen). The traffic congestion at peak hours influences vehicle speed directly, thus affecting the travel time and fuel consumption of the vehicles. Under this setting, the cost minimizing the TDGVRP consists in finding a set of feasible routes minimizing the total carbon emissions, which has linear relationship with fuel consumption of vehicles.

2.2   Modeling Time-Dependent Travel Time and Carbon Emissions

The time dependence of the studied TDGVRP is based on the interaction between vehicle speed profiles determined by the traffic condition and travel time function [2]. According to the survey and literature, there are two peak traffic jam periods in a day, respectively are from 7 am to 9 am and from 5 pm to 7 pm. Figure 1(a) draws an average vehicle speed profile of departure time from 7 am to 7 pm. Figure 1(b) draws the corresponding travel time function for an arc of the distance 50 km. By using those stepwise speed functions, the FIFO property holds for each arc in the graph G. In this paper, let $\tau_{ij}\left(t_i^k\right)$ represent

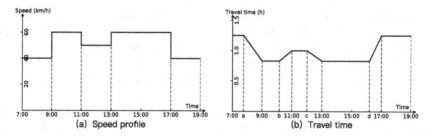

Fig. 1. Piecewise linear travel time function derived from stepwise speed function for an arc of length 50 km.

the travel time from vertex i to vertex j when vehicle k departs from vertex i at time t_i^k and so $\tau_{ij}(t)$ is a travel time function about the departure time t.

For each arc $(i,j) \in A$, there are several time periods of the corresponding travel time function $\tau_{ij}(t_i^k)$. In this paper, we define T_{ij} as the set of time periods. For example, if Fig. 1(b) is travel time function of an arc (i,j), then there will be 9 time periods in travel time function. We denote m as the index of the time periods, that is $T_{ij}^m \in T_{ij}$ for $m = 0, 1, \ldots, |T_{ij}| - 1$, which T_{ij}^m is defined by two continuous time breakpoints w_m, w_{m+1}, namely $T_{ij}^m = [w_m, w_{m+1}]$. Due to the travel time function $\tau_{ij}(t_i^k)$ is linear in each time period $T_{ij}^m \in T_{ij}$, it is easy to get the linear function expression by calculating the slope θ_m and intercept η_m, namely $\tau_{ij}(t_i^k) = \theta_m \times t_i^k + \eta_m$.

For a path $p = (v_0, v_1, \ldots, v_k)$ which $v_0 = 0$ is the original depot and v_i for $0 \le i \le k$ is the vertex at position i in the path p, the earliest time when the departure time at vertex v_0 is t and the service at v_i is completed is represented by the ready time function $\delta_{v_i}^p(t)$. The ready time function is nondecreasing in the domain t, and can be calculated for each vertex in the path p as follows:

$$\delta_{v_i}^p(t) = \begin{cases} t & \text{if } i = 0, \\ \max\{a_{v_i} + s_{v_i}, \delta_{v_{i-1}}^p(t) + \tau_{v_{i-1}v_i}\left(\delta_{v_{i-1}}^p(t)\right) + s_{v_i}\} & \text{otherwise.} \end{cases} \tag{1}$$

The ready time function is also piecewise linear, and similarly we can use the breakpoints, and the boundary values of the time window at vertex v_i to represent the ready time function.

The research addressed in this paper aims to minimize the carbon emissions by optimizing vehicle speeds and routes. Carbon emissions is used to provide an estimate of the exhaust generated by vehicles. To measure carbon emissions, the speed-emission coefficients should be applied first to estimate the fuel consumption. "Road Vehicle Emission Factors 2009" has reported a database of vehicle speed-emission factors for fuel consumption [5]. The general format of the vehicle fuel consumption function is presented as:

$$FC(v) = k\left(a + bv + cv^2 + dv^3 + ev^4 + fv^5 + gv^6\right)/v \tag{2}$$

where v is the speed in km/h, $FC(v)$ is the fuel consumption in $l/100\,\text{km}$, and k, a, b, c, d, e, f, g are different coefficients for estimating the fuel consumption. In this paper, we adopt the coefficients in [6], and the corresponding coefficients for each $l/100\,\mathrm{km}$ fuel consumption are $0.037, 12690, 16.56, 86.87, -3.55, 0.06146, -0.0004773$, and 0.000001385, respectively. The conversion factor of carbon emissions from fuel consumption is $3.1787\,\mathrm{kg}$ carbon per liter fuel consumed. Therefore, the formula of carbon emissions is $CE\left(v\right) = 3.1787 \times FC\left(v\right)$.

As for an arc $(i,j) \in A$, we define $f_{ij}\left(t_i^k\right)$ as the carbon emissions function when vehicle k departs from vertex i at time t_i^k. We denote v_m as the speed of time period $T_{ij}^m \in T_{ij}$ in travel time function. So there are same speeds in consecutive time periods, such as in Fig. 1(b), $v_0 = v_1 = 40$ km/h. Based on travel time function formula $\tau_{ij}\left(t_i^k\right) = \theta_m \times t_i^k + \eta_m$, if the slope θ_m of the time period to which the departure time t_i^k belongs is 0, namely $\theta_m = 0$, then there will be only one speed v_m used in the journey between vertex i and vertex j. Therefore $f_{ij}\left(t_i^k\right) = CE\left(v_m\right) \times d_{ij}/100$. And if the slope θ_m of the time period to which the departure time t_i^k belongs is not 0, namely $\theta_m \neq 0$, then there will be two speeds v_m, v_{m+1} used in the journey between vertex i and vertex j. Therefore

$$
\begin{aligned}
f_{ij}\left(t_i^k\right) = {} & CE\left(v_m\right) \times v_m \times \left(w_{m+1} - t_i^k\right)/100 \\
& + CE\left(v_{m+1}\right) \times v_{m+1} \times \left[t_i^k + \tau_{ij}\left(t_i^k\right) - w_{m+1}\right]/100.
\end{aligned} \tag{3}
$$

We analyze the formula 3 and find that the formula 3 is a linear function of t_i^k. Thus the carbon emissions function $f_{ij}\left(t_i^k\right)$ is also piecewise linear.

For a path $p = (v_0, v_1, \ldots, v_k)$ which $v_0 = 0$ is the original depot and v_i for $0 \leq i \leq k$ is the vertex at position i in the path p, the earliest time when the departure time at vertex v_0 is t, we define $F_{v_i}^p\left(t\right)$ as the total carbon emissions function up to vertex v_i in path p when the service at v_i is completed with the ready time $\delta_{v_i}^p\left(t\right)$. As mentioned before, the ready time function $\delta_{v_i}^p\left(t\right)$ is also piecewise linear. Thus in path p, we can use the composite function to denote $f_{v_{i-1},v_i}\left(t_{v_{i-1}}^p\right)$ for $i = 1, 2, \ldots, k$, namely $f_{v_{i-1},v_i}\left(t_{v_{i-1}}^p\right) = f_{v_{i-1},v_i}\left(\delta_{v_{i-1}}^p\left(t\right)\right)$. Therefore, the total carbon emissions function is denoted as:

$$
F_{v_i}^p\left(t\right) = \begin{cases} 0 & \text{if } i = 0, \\ F_{v_{i-1}}^p\left(t\right) + f_{v_{i-1},v_i}\left(\delta_{v_{i-1}}^p\left(t\right)\right) & \text{otherwise.} \end{cases} \tag{4}
$$

where the addition operation between functions only counts the domain intersection. If the intersection is an empty set, then the function has no domain.

3   Branch-and-Price Algorithm

3.1   Set-Partitioning Formulation

We define Ω as the set of feasible paths. Let y_p be a binary variable deciding whether path p is included in the optimal solution or not, and let σ_{ip} be a binary variable that denotes the customer i is visited by the path p or not.

We formulate the studied problem as a set partitioning formulation, which is presented as follows:

$$Z = \min \sum_{p \in \Omega} c_p y_p \tag{5a}$$

$$\text{s.t.} \sum_{p \in \Omega} \sigma_{ip} y_p = 1, \ \forall i \in N_c \tag{5b}$$

$$y_p \in \{0,1\}, \ \forall p \in \Omega \tag{5c}$$

where the objective function Z (5a) minimizes the carbon emissions of the chosen paths, constraint (5b) guarantees that each customer $i \in N_c$ is visited only once, and constraint (5c) ensures that the decision variables are binary.

We define the LP relaxation of the set-partitioning model as the master problem (MP). In the LP relation problem, the '=' in formula (5b) can be replaced by the '≥', and the formula (5c) is replaced by $y_p \geq 0, \ \forall p \in \Omega$. We use column generation [7] to solve the MP with a small subset $\Omega' \subseteq \Omega$ of feasible paths. The MP with the subset Ω' is denoted as the restricted MP (RMP).

After the initialization step, new columns are added iteratively until the algorithm converges to the optimal (fractional) solution. At each iteration, the LP relaxation of the RMP is computed to obtain the dual variables π_i associated with constraints (5b) for $i \in N_c$. If a feasible route p with negative reduced cost $c_p - \sum_{i \in N_c} \pi_i \sigma_{ip}$ exists, then it is added to the RMP and the procedure is repeated. Otherwise, the current fractional solution is optimal.

3.2 Branching and Node Selection Strategy

After column generation, a branching strategy on arcs is adopted in this paper. Let H_{ij} be the set of all columns that contain arc $(i,j) \in A, i, j \in N_c$. The sum of the flows on arc (i,j) is equal to $\sum_{p \in H_{ij}} y_p$. If there exists at least an arc (i,j) with fractional $\sum_{p \in H_{ij}} y_p$, then we branch on the value $\sum_{p \in H_{ij}} y_p$ which is the closest to the midpoint 0.5. Two new child nodes are generated accordingly by forcing arc (i,j) in one node and forbidding arc (i,j) in the other node. In the former case, all columns containing arcs (i,j') and (i',j) with $i' \neq i$ and $j' \neq j$ are deleted. In the latter case, columns using arc (i,j) have to be removed.

3.3 The Pricing Problem

The pricing sub-problem constructs a feasible route with a minimum reduced cost, using the dual values obtained from the LP solution of the RMP. If the constructed route has negative reduced cost, its corresponding column is added to the RMP. Otherwise, the LP procedure will be terminated with an optimal solution to the continuous relaxation of the MP. To sum up, at each iteration of the column generation algorithm, the pricing problem aims to find routes (columns) $r \in \Omega$ with negative reduced cost $\bar{c}_r$, if any exists. The pricing problem searches for the routes with a negative reduced cost, and its objective function is defined as $\min_{p \in \Omega'} \bar{c}_p = c_p - \sum_{i \in N_c} \pi_i \sigma_{ip}$, where $\bar{c}_p$ is the reduced cost of path p, and π_i is the dual variable associated with the formulation (5b). To solve the pricing problem, a forward labeling algorithm is developed.

The Labeling Algorithm. The labeling algorithm generates implicitly an enumeration tree where each node is named as a label L and denotes a partial path starting from the original depot. Aiming to overcome the huge exponential growth, domination rules are used to reduce the number of labels. Then we present the forward labeling algorithm for the TDGVRP. In labeling algorithm, we start generating labels from the start depot o to its successors. For each label L, the notations are presented in Table 1.

Table 1. The notations of a label.

Notation	Interpretation
$p(L)$	The partial path of label L, and $p(L) = (o, \dots, v)$
$v(L)$	The last vertex visited on the partial path $p(L)$
$S(L)$	The set of unreachable customers after visiting $v(L)$, and $S(L) \supseteq p(L)$
$L^{-1}(L)$	The parent label from which L originates by extending it with $v(L)$
$q(L)$	The total demand after servicing vertex $v(L)$ in path $p(L)$
$\delta_L(t)$	The piecewise linear function that represents the ready time at $v(L)$ if vehicle departed at the origin depot at t and reached $v(L)$ through partial path $p(L)$
$F_L(t)$	The piecewise linear function that represents total carbon emissions at $v(L)$ if the vehicle departed at the origin depot at t and reached $v(L)$ through path $p(L)$, namely $c_L(t)$
$\pi(L)$	The cumulative value of dual variable associated with the formulation (5b) in path $p(L)$

The labeling algorithm begins with the label $v(L) = 0$ that denotes the initial path $p(L) = (0)$, the algorithm iteratively processes each label L until no unprocessed labels remain. A label L' can only be extended to label L along an arc $(v(L'), j)$ when the extension is feasible with the constraints of time windows and capacity, namely $\delta_{L'}(t) + \tau_{v(L'),j} \leq b_j \; \forall \; j \in N \setminus S$, and $q(L') + q_j \leq Q \; \forall \; j \in N \setminus S$. If the extension along the arc $(v(L'), j)$ is feasible with the above conditions, then a new label L is created. The information of new label L is updated by using the following formulas: $p(L) = p(L') \cup \{j\}$, $v(L) = j$, $S(L) = p(L) \cup \{k \in N \lor \min\{\delta_{L'}(t) + \tau_{v(L'),k}\} > b_k \lor q(L') + q_k > Q\}$, $L^{-1}(L) = L'$, $q(L) = q(L') + q_j$, $\delta_L(t) = \max\{a_j + s_j, \delta_{L'}(t) + \tau_{v(L'),j} + s_j\}$, $F_L(t) = F_{L'}(t) + f_{v(L'),j}(\delta_{L'}(t))$, and $\pi(L) = \pi(L') + \pi_j$.

For a partial path $p(L)$, if the path $p(L)$ is feasible, then it will always be feasible with a departure time 0 from the origin depot o. In other words, if the path $p(L)$ is feasible, $dom(\delta_L)$ is always a time interval $[0, t_0]$ for $t_0 \geq 0$ with $dom(\delta_L)$ is the domain of δ_L.

After an extension to vertex j, if the last vertex in the new path $p(L)$ is $n+1$, that is $v(L) = n+1$, then the minimal cost c_L and the reduced cost $\bar{c}_L$ of the complete path associated with the label L are calculated by $c_L = \min_{t \in dom(F_L)}\{F_L(t)\}$, and $\bar{c}_L = \min_{t \in dom(F_L)}\{F_L(t)\} - \pi(L)$, where $dom(F_L)$ is the domain of the total carbon emissions function $F_L(t)$. Define $dom(\delta_L)$ and $img(\delta_L)$ be the domain and image of the ready time function $\delta_L(t)$, and let $dom(F_L)$ and $img(F_L)$ be the domain and image of the total carbon emissions function $F_L(t)$, respectively. Based on the definitions of $dom(\delta_L)$ and $dom(F_L)$, we can get that the domain of ready time function $\delta_L(t)$ is equal to the domain of total carbon emissions function $F_L(t)$, namely $dom(\delta_L) = dom(F_L)$.

In general, the labeling algorithm is similar to enumeration method and dynamic programming, and all possible extensions are handled and stored for each label. With the iteration of the labeling algorithm, the number of labels will exponentially increase. In order to overcome the exponential growth, dominance rules are used to reduce the number of labels enumerated. [8] define that three requisites must be met if Label L_2 is dominated by label L_1. These requirements are (1) $v(L_1) = v(L_2)$; (2) all of the feasible extensions $E(L_2)$ of the label L_2 to vertex $n+1$ must be the subset of label $E(L_1)$, namely $E(L_2) \subseteq E(L_1)$; (3) $\bar{c}_{L_1 \oplus L} \leq \bar{c}_{L_2 \oplus L}, \forall L \in E(L_2)$. Therefore, in the developed forward labeling algorithm, dominance rule is proposed as follows.

Proposition 1. *(Dominance rule) Label L_2 is globally dominated by label L_1 if (1) $v(L_1) = v(L_2)$, (2) $S(L_1) \subseteq S(L_2)$, (3) $dom(F_{L_2}) \subseteq dom(F_{L_1})$, (4) $\delta_{L_1}(t) \leq \delta_{L_2}(t), \forall\ t \in dom(\delta_{L_2})$, (5) $F_{L_1}(\arg\{\delta_{L_1} = \delta_{L_2}(t)\}) - \pi(L_1) \leq F_{L_2}(t) - \pi(L_2), \forall t \in dom(F_{L_2})$, and (6) $q(L_1) \leq q(L_2)$.*

4 Numerical Experiments

In this section, we conduct the experiments to test the performance of the BAP algorithm. The algorithms are coded in C++. The RMPs are solved by CPLEX 12.10.0. Computational experiments are conducted on a PC with an Inter(R) Core(TM) i7-7700 CPU @3.60 GHz ×8 and a 16 GB RAM, under a Linux system. Computation times are reported in seconds on this machine.

There are no similar problems in the existing researches, so we generate the test instances based on the classical Solomon VRPTW benchmark instances [9]. In this paper, we test the instances with 25 customers. In the basis of Solomon VRPTW instances, the rules of generating the test instances are as follows: (1) we set the start depot and the end depot as the same point; (2) the planning horizon was set as 12 h, therefore, the time window $[a_i, b_i]$ of vertex i in the Solomon instances was modified as $[a_i \times (12/b_0), b_i \times (12/b_0)]$; (3) the distance d_{ij} was not changed, but we set the unit as km; (4) the service time was set to 0.5h for all customers; (5) the other parameters were not changed.

Table 2. The results of BAP algorithm on instances with 25 customers.

Instance	Root LB	Root time	Best LB	UB	Time	Final gap (%)	Nodes
C101	285.96	0.08	294.82	294.82	0.26	0	5
C102	250.66	0.62	260.94	260.94	1.94	0	9
C103	237.51	7201.7	238.94	238.94	7208.36	0	1
C104	208.88	7201.76	208.88	208.88	7201.76	0	1
C105	260.43	0.04	260.43	260.43	0.04	0	1
C106	284.87	7201.49	294.85	294.85	7210.04	0	1
C107	215.99	0.09	244.62	244.62	1.73	0	17
C108	200.88	0.2	200.88	200.88	0.2	0	1
C109	199.98	0.79	199.98	199.98	0.79	0	1

The BAP algorithm is terminated with a time limit of 7200 s. Table 2 reports our computational results for solving TDGVRP using the proposed BAP algorithm. Column 1 reports the name of instances. Column 2 reports the lower bound (LB) at the root node. Column 3 reports the root time. Column 4 reports the best LB (BLB) after branching. Column 5 reports the upper bound (UB) corresponding to the best integer solution. Column 6 reports the total Cpu time. Column 7 reports the optimality gap $(Gap = (UB - BLB)/BLB * 100\%)$. Column 8 reports the number of explored branch-and-bound tree nodes (Nodes). From Table 2, we can know that the proposed BAP algorithm can solve 6 out of 9 instances effectively, which proves the effectiveness and efficiency of the proposed BAP algorithm.

5   Conclusion and Future Research

We studied a TDGVRP with the consideration of traffic congestion. In order to solve the TDGVRP, we propose an exact BAP algorithm, where the master problem and the pricing sub-problem are solved by a CG algorithm and a labeling algorithm, respectively. The CG algorithm embedded within branch-and-bound framework is used to obtain feasible integer solution. Computational results prove the effectiveness and efficiency of the proposed BAP algorithm. At last, the work is worthy of further study. We can verify the BAP algorithm on larger scale instances, and we can also design an acceleration strategy to improve the algorithm.

References

1. Liu, R., Tao, Y., Xie, X.: An adaptive large neighborhood search heuristic for the vehicle routing problem with time windows and synchronized visits. Comput. Oper. Res. **101**, 250–262 (2019)

2. Zhu, L., Hu, D.: Study on the vehicle routing problem considering congestion and emission factors. Int. J. Prod. Res. **57**(19), 6115–6129 (2019)
3. Çimen, M., Soysal, M.: Time-dependent green vehicle routing problem with stochastic vehicle speeds: an approximate dynamic programming algorithm. Transp. Res. Part D Transp. Environ. **54**, 82–98 (2017)
4. Malandraki, C., Daskin, M.S.: Time dependent vehicle routing problems: formulations, properties and heuristic algorithms. Transp. Sci. **26**(3), 185–200 (1992)
5. Figliozzi, M.A.: The impacts of congestion on time-definitive urban freight distribution networks co2 emission levels: results from a case study in portland, oregon. Transp. Res. Part C Emerg. Technol. **19**(5), 766–778 (2011)
6. Qian, J., Eglese, R.: Finding least fuel emission paths in a network with time-varying speeds. Networks **63**(1), 96–106 (2014)
7. Desaulniers, G., Desrosiers, J., Solomon, M.M.: Column Generation, vol. 5. Springer, Boston (2005). https://doi.org/10.1007/b135457
8. Dabia, S., Ropke, S., Van Woensel, T., De Kok, T.: Branch and price for the time-dependent vehicle routing problem with time windows. Transp. Sci. **47**(3), 380–396 (2013)
9. Solomon, M.M.: Algorithms for the vehicle routing and scheduling problems with time window constraints. Oper. Res. **35**(2), 254–265 (1987)

Investigating Alternative Routes for Employee Shuttle Services Arising in a Textile Company: A Comparative Study

İbrahim Miraç Eligüzel$^{(\boxtimes)}$ ⓘ, Nur Sena Yağbasan ⓘ, and Eren Özceylan ⓘ

Industrial Engineering Department, Gaziantep University, 27100 Gaziantep, Turkey

Abstract. For the big companies, picking up a number of employees from various places (residential areas or common places) within a neighborhood and brought to the factory should be a challenging task. Potential improvements for this constantly repeated service planning may result in cost and total traveled distance reduction. To search and provide the aforementioned potential savings, three different scenarios with three different bus capacities are generated for a textile company in this paper. In the first scenario that is also the current application of the company, an integer programming model for the capacitated vehicle routing problem (CVRP) is applied. In this scenario, shuttle buses with a certain capacity are routed by picking up the employees from their homes. In the second scenario, the employees are clustered (cluster size is equal to the vehicle capacity) using P-median model to minimize the total walking distance of employees to the meeting point, then the shuttle buses are routed by visiting the clustered zones (meeting points). In the last scenario, the employees are clustered using K-means model and then, shuttle buses transport workers to factory from the center points of each cluster. Three scenarios with different bus capacities (20, 30 and 50 people) are applied to a textile company (the depot) that includes 1,361 employees. The models are run using Gurobi 9.1.1 with Python 3.8 and the results are discussed. According to the results, second and third scenarios reduce the total traveled distance by 46.90% and 44.10% (averagely) compared to the first scenario, respectively.

Keywords: Employee shuttle services · Vehicle routing problem · P-median · K-means · Clustering

1 Introduction

Service planning of workers between factory and their homes are required to be managed efficiently and effectively in order to reduce costs. Therefore, our motivation in this study can be considered under service routing due to its crucial part in the operation of businesses.

As a solution approach, CVRP is taken into consideration. CVRP is one of the main problems in logistics management aims to generate routes to visit all nodes and turn back to the initial node with pre-decided capacities. CVRP also can be applied on

© IFIP International Federation for Information Processing 2021
Published by Springer Nature Switzerland AG 2021
A. Dolgui et al. (Eds.): APMS 2021, IFIP AICT 634, pp. 68–76, 2021.
https://doi.org/10.1007/978-3-030-85914-5_8

shuttle routing to gather people for carrying them to point of arrival. For instance, school bus routing is solved by CVRP and 28.6% travel cost saving is managed [1]. In that aspect, another study focuses on picking students from the eight points with eight buses on campus via solving with genetic algorithm [2]. Results indicate that shorter distance for two routes is achieved and savings in the distance becomes greater with respect to the total distances. In addition, CVRP is utilized on problem required for associated costs with touristic distribution networks of low demand by solved with genetic algorithm [3]. There are also studies which concern real-life applications; for instance, pharmaceutical and herbalist product delivery [4], waste collection [5], and office furniture delivery [6]. All in all, CVRP can be used for reducing the transportation cost to deliver people to the destination.

Facilities with a large number of workers should use analytic tools to reduce worker picking costs. Therefore, CVRP integration with different approaches can be utilized as another solution method for the facilities which have a large amount of work to provide cost reduced and effective carrying model. From this point of view, workers can be clustered with respect to their home addresses, and routes for vehicles can be decided to gather workers from the center point of each cluster. In literature, there are several studies that consider the clustering before applying routing by aiming more effective solution. One of the studies proposed a method that consists of two mainframes as clustering and optimization and results demonstrate that node clustering before applying CVRP effectively reduces the problem space which leads to quick convergence to the optimum solution [7]. In this aspect, clustered VRP is conducted, in which two exact algorithms, a branch and cut as well as a branch and cut and price is applied, and computational performance is significantly improved [8]. Another in-stance of study in the aforementioned perspective presents the algorithm integrates the Bat algorithm with a modified K-means clustering, which is based on clustering first route second to convert the original VRP into traveling salesman problems with reduced complexity [9]. In addition to the aforementioned studies with clustering and CVRP, there are several studies in literature such as using K-means with the cheapest link algorithm for routing the Indian cooperative dairy distribution network [10], K-means with grey wolf algorithm [11], and recursive K-means with Dijkstra algorithm [12].

For the applied methods, some assumptions are made. One of them is the there is no traffic density during the service operation. Secondly, whole considered vehicles and workers expected to travel at the same speed. Therefore, elapsed times are assumed to be proportional to distances.

In this study, service problem is handled under three scenarios and compared with each other for picking workers from their home addresses. Also, for each scenario, three different capacity variants are considered, which are decided as 20, 30, and 50 people.

Three solution scenarios in this study are explained as follows. In the first scenario, CVRP is solved by linear programming without clustering for collecting workers from their home addresses. In the second scenario, the P-median method is applied to cluster the addresses and gather central addresses for each cluster. Distance between connected nodes and their centers are obtained to calculate walking distance. Then, distances between centers and facilities are summed to have total distances for transportation. Therefore, total walking distance minimization is accomplished and transportation cost is reduced. Lastly, K-means is applied to cluster home addresses to minimize walking distance and obtain the center point for each cluster. After that, the distance between each center and factory is calculated and summed, and then the walking distance (objective value of K-means) is added to the total distance between centers and factory. Mentioned three scenarios are illustrated in Fig. 1. For each aforementioned method, three different capacities are concerned. The paper is organized as follows: Sect. 2 formally defines the applied methodologies. Input data and the solution of the three scenarios are discussed in Sect. 3. Finally, the last section presents our conclusions.

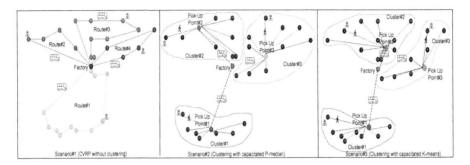

Fig. 1. Representation of the considered three scenarios

2   Methodologies

As mentioned in the previous section, three different scenarios are considered in this study. To generate the scenarios, three different models namely CVRP, P-median, and K-means are used and described below.

2.1   Capacitated Vehicle Routing Problem

CVRP refers to a class of problems in which a series of routes for a fleet of vehicles located at one depot must be calculated for a number of geographically scattered customers, and the vehicles must have the maximum loading capacity. CVRP's goal is to reduce overall cost (i.e., a weighted function of the number of routes and their travel distance) while serving a group of customers with known needs. CVRP is a one of the well-known combinatorial problems that belongs to the NP-Hard problem set [13]. Let $G = (V, E)$ be a directed graph with vertices $V = \{0, 1, \ldots n\}$ and edges $H = \{(i, j) : i, j \in V, i \neq j\}$. The depot is represented by vertex 0, and each remaining vertex i represents a customer with a positive demand d_i. There is a fleet of p vehicles with the same capacity Q. The non-negative cost/distance c_{ij} is associated with each arc $(i, j) \in H$. The minimum number of vehicles needed to serve all customers is $\sum_{i=1}^{n} d_i / pQ$.

x_{ij} takes value 1 if edge belongs to the optimal solution, and value 0 otherwise, $\forall i, j \in V : i \neq j$. u_i is an additional continuous variable representing the load of the vehicle after visiting customer i [14]. The mathematical formulation which is used in this study is described below [15].

Objective function

$$Min \sum_{i=0}^{n} \sum_{j=0}^{n} x_{ij} c_{ij} \tag{1}$$

Subject to

$$\sum_{i \in V} x_{ij} = 1 \quad \forall j \in V \tag{2}$$

$$\sum_{j \in V} x_{ij} = 1 \quad \forall i \in V \tag{3}$$

$$\sum_{i \in V} x_{i0} = p \tag{4}$$

$$\sum_{j \in V} x_{0j} = p \tag{5}$$

$$u_i - u_j + Q x_{ij} \leq Q - d_i \quad \forall i,j \in V, i \neq j \tag{6}$$

$$d_i \leq u_i \leq Q \quad \forall i \in V \tag{7}$$

$$x_{ij} \in \{0,1\} \quad \forall i,j \in V \tag{8}$$

The CVRP consists of finding a collection of simple circuits (corresponding to vehicle routes) with minimum cost, defined as the sum of the costs of the arcs belonging to the circuits (Eq. 1). Constraints (2) and (3) (indegree and outdegree of nodes) impose that exactly one edge enters and leaves each vertex associated with a customer, respectively. Analogously, Constraints (4) and (5) ensure the degree requirements for the vertex of depot. Constraints (6) and (7) impose the capacity requirements of CVRP while eliminating the sub-tours [4]. Finally, Constraint (8) is the integrality conditions.

2.2 Capacitated P-median Approach

The P-median model is applied to minimize the employees' total walking distance to the meeting point by clustering the employees. Due to a limited capacity of clusters, capacitated P-median on a discrete space is considered in this study. The capacitated P-median problem seeks to define the number of P candidate facility (clusters) to be opened, and which customers (employees) will be assigned to each facility (cluster). In the model, every cluster has a limited employee capacity and each employee has one demand. The problem should consider that each cluster can serve only a limited number of demands so that the sum of distances between each demand point (employee home) and the facility (cluster center) assigned to that demand point is minimized. In the model, i and $j = 1, 2, ..., n$ is the set of employees and also of possible medians where P clusters will be located, d_i is the demand of employee i, Q_j is the capacity of the median (cluster) j, $d_{ij} > 0$ $(i \neq j)$ is the distance between employee i and cluster median j. x_{ij} is a binary decision variable that takes 1 if an employee i is assigned to a cluster j, otherwise it is 0. y_j is also a binary decision variable that takes 1 if an employee is selected as a cluster median j, otherwise it is 0. The problem formulation is given as follows [16]:

Objective function

$$Min \sum_i^n \sum_j^n x_{ij} d_{ij} d_i \tag{9}$$

Subject to

$$\sum_j x_{ij} = 1, \forall_i, \tag{10}$$

$$\sum_j y_j = p, \tag{11}$$

$$x_{ij} d_i \leq Q_j y_j, \ \forall_{i,j}, \tag{12}$$

$$x_{ij}, y_j \in \{0, 1\}. \tag{13}$$

The objective function (Eq. 9) aims to minimize total walking distance of all employees. Constraint (10) imposes that each employee is assigned to one and only one cluster median, Constraint (11) guarantees that P cluster medians are selected, Constraint (12) forces that a total median capacity to be respected and Constraint (13) prepares the binary integer conditions.

2.3   Capacitated K-means Approach

Capacitated K-means is also applied to cluster the employees. The capacitated K-means approach seeks to define K amount candidate cluster centers to be decided and which employees will be assigned to each cluster center while employees attended to nearest the cluster center. The capacitated K-means problem formulation is given as follows [17]:

Objective function

$$Minimize \sum_{i=1}^n \sum_{h=1}^k T_{i,h} * \left(\frac{1}{2} (x_i - \mu_{h,t})^2 \right) \tag{14}$$

Subject to

$$\sum_{i=1}^n T_{i,h} \geq \tau_h, h = 1, 2, \ldots, k \tag{15}$$

$$\sum_{h=1}^k T_{i,h} = 1, i = 1, 2, \ldots, n \tag{16}$$

$$T_{i,h} \geq 1, i = 1, 2, \ldots, n h = 1, 2, \ldots, k \tag{17}$$

where, Given a database X of n points, minimum cluster membership values $\tau_h \geq 0$, $h = 1, \ldots, k$ and cluster centers $\mu_{1,t}, \mu_{2,t}, \ldots, \mu_{k,t}$ at iteration t. $T_{i,h}$ is binary variable that demonstrates attendance of data point x_i is to nearest center μ_h or not [17]. Objective function (14) aims to attend nodes to its nearest cluster center. Constraint (15) ensures the attendance of minimum number of nodes to one cluster. Constraint (16) ensures that one node is allowed to attend just one cluster center and constraint (17) forces all nodes to attend cluster.

3   Case Study and Results

The service plan of Kartal carpet, which operates in Gaziantep province, is taken into consideration. Utilized case comprehends the 1,362 nodes (including the factory) with its GPS coordinates and GPS coordinates converted into longitude and latitude values in order to gather nodes' positions in X-Y axis. After gathering X-Y axis, the distance matrix is generated by utilizing Euclidian distance. For instance, "a1" has longitude and latitude "37.1383, 37.3716" values. Distance between "a1" and "a2" (37.0898, 37.3676) is calculated by Euclidian distance and it is equal to 4.86 km. Normally, there are three shifts for workers per day. However, the picking of workers for only one shift is focused on in this paper. The geographical locations of 1,362 nodes in terms of X-Y values from the GPS coordinates are shown in Fig. 2.

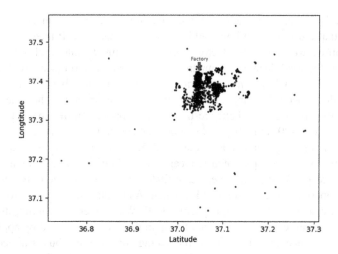

Fig. 2. Illustration X-Y coordinates of home addresses in Gaziantep providence

The aforementioned three methods, which are P-median, K-means and CVRP, are applied by using Python 3.8- Gurobi 9.1.1 with the time limit set to three hours with a computer that has Intel Core i7 9750H CPU with 8 GB RAM features. Capacities of vehicles are selected as 20 (e.g. VW Crafter), 30 (e.g. Isuzu Turkuaz) and 50 (e.g. Mercedes - Benz Tourismo). The number of routes and clusters is decided by the total number of workers divided by capacities and decimals are rounded up which are 69 (20 capacity), 46 (30 capacity) and 28 (50 capacity). For instance, if a bus with 30 people capacity is chosen, and then scenario#1 has to visit 1,361 workers with 46 routes/buses. Scenario#2 and #3 divide 1,361 workers into 46 (1,361/30) clusters then the buses have to pick 30 workers from each cluster then back to the factory.

Table 1. Results of the three methods (in meters)

Capacity	Scenario	Total walking distance	Average distance per worker	Total bus distance	Average distance per bus	Total distance
20	#1	0.00	0.00	118,900.00	1,723.19	118,900.00
	#2	5,305.70	3.89	56,900.00	824.63	62,205.70
	#3	4,984.00	3.66	58,700.00	850.70	63,684.00
30	#1	0.00	0.00	82,700.00	1,797.83	82,700.00
	#2	5,762.70	4.23	38,600.00	839.10	44,362.70
	#3	3,639.50	2.67	38,555.10	838.20	42,194.60
50	#1	0.00	0.00	55,700.00	1,989.29	55,700.00
	#2	4,131.00	3.03	25,540.00	912.10	29,671.00
	#3	9,546.30	7.01	24,258.40	866.40	33,804.70

In Table 1, the feasible results of three scenarios are given. From Table 1, it can be easily said that clustering the home addresses with capacitated P-median (scenario#2) and transporting workers to the factory from the obtained centers (clusters) outstandingly reduces the total distances compared to CVRP application (scenario#1). When it comes to capacitated K-means (scenario#3), it demonstrates better performance for capacity with 30 people compared to the other two scenarios. On the other hand, the capacitated P-median gives a better result than the application of capacitated K-means for the capacity of 20 and 50 people. From the general view, there is a significant difference between capacitated P-median and K-means approaches. Capacitated P-median outperforms the capacitated K-means by 1.48 km and 4.13 km with capacities 20 and 50, respectively. However, capacitated K-means shorten the distance by 2.17 km compared to the capacitated P-median. As result, the minimum total distance is obtained by scenario2# with a capacity of 50. When average walking distance per worker is taken into consideration, the minimum distance is gathered by application of scenario3# with capacity 30. Lastly, if the average distance per bus is aimed, the best result is obtained by applying scenario2# with the capacity of 20. Therefore, decision-makers are able to select the best alternative with respect to their objectives.

4   Conclusion

In the proposed study, three methods are utilized in order to minimize the total distances to carry workers to the factory. Three different scenarios are considered and generated. In the first scenario, without clustering, 1,361 workers are picked with a CVRP model. In the following two scenarios, 1,361 workers are clustered using capacitated K-means and P-median approaches, and then the buses are directed to the cluster centers. All three scenarios are run with three different vehicle capacities as 20, 30 and 50. Because of the problem size, a time limit is considered and feasible solutions are obtained. Results demonstrate that the total distance (vehicle distance + walking distance) decreases with the increments in capacity. However, capacitated P-median and K-means show different performances with respect to given capacity and CVRP has the longest total distance for all three scenarios. The minimum total distance is obtained when the workers are clustered with P-median and 50 people capacitated bus is used. On the other hand, clustering with the K-means approach with 30 people capacitated bus yields the minimum total walking distance. As an extension of this paper, the authors will focus on the simultaneous application of VRP and clustering approaches rather than the hierarchal approach. In addition, the problem will be handled as a bi-level programming where the upper and lower levels are represented by the company and workers, respectively. Finally, traffic congestion that affects the traveling time will be considered to reflect the real-life dynamics.

References

1. Bektaş, T., Elmastaş, S.: Solving school bus routing problems through integer programming. J. Oper. Res. Soc. **58**(12), 1599–1604 (2007)
2. Mohammed, M.A., et al.: Solving vehicle routing problem by using improved genetic algorithm for optimal solution. J. Comput. Sci. **21**, 255–262 (2017)
3. Medina, J.R., Yepes, V.: Optimization of touristic distribution netwoorks using genetic algorithms. SORT Stat. Oper. Res. Trans. **27**(1), 0095–0112 (2003)
4. Fischetti, M., Toth, P., Vigo, D.: A branch-and-bound algorithm for the capacitated vehicle routing problem on directed graphs. Oper. Res. **42**(5), 846–859 (1994)
5. Franca, L.S., Ribeiro, G.M., de Lorena Diniz Chaves, G.: The planning of selective collection in a real-life vehicle routing problem: a case in Rio de Janeiro. Sustain. Cities Soc. **47**, 101488 (2019)
6. Kır, S., Yazgan, H.R., Tüncel, E.: A novel heuristic algorithm for capacitated vehicle routing problem. J. Ind. Eng. Int. **13**(3), 323–330 (2017)
7. Abdillah, U., Suyanto, S.: Clustering nodes and discretizing movement to increase the effectiveness of HEFA for a CVRP. Int. J. Adv. Comput. Sci. Appl. (IJACSA) **11**(4), 774–779 (2020)
8. Battarra, M., Erdoğan, G., Vigo, D.: Exact algorithms for the clustered vehicle routing problem. Oper. Res. **62**(1), 58–71 (2014)
9. Kassem, S., et al.: A hybrid bat algorithm to solve the capacitated vehicle routing problem. In: 2019 Novel Intelligent and Leading Emerging Sciences Conference (NILES), vol. 1. IEEE (2019)
10. Rautela, A., Sharma, S.K., Bhardwaj, P.: Distribution planning using capacitated clustering and vehicle routing problem. J. Adv. Manag. Res. **16**, 781–795 (2019)
11. Korayem, L., Khorsid, M., Kassem, S.S.: Using grey wolf algorithm to solve the capacitated vehicle routing problem. IOP Conf. Ser. Mater. Sci. Eng. **83**(1), 012014 (2015)
12. Moussa, H.: Using recursive K-means and Dijkstra algorithm to solve CVRP. arXiv preprint arXiv:2102.00567 (2021)
13. Lin, S.-W., et al.: Applying hybrid meta-heuristics for capacitated vehicle routing problem. Expert Syst. Appl. **36**(2), 1505–1512 (2009)

14. Borcinova, Z.: Two models of the capacitated vehicle routing problem. Croatian Oper. Res. Rev. **8**, 463–469 (2017)
15. Toth, P., Vigo, D.: Models, relaxations and exact approaches for the capacitated vehicle routing problem. Discrete Appl. Math. **123**, 487–512 (2002)
16. Shamsipoor, H., Sandidzadeh, M.A., Yaghini, M.: Solving capacitated P-median problem by a new structure of neural network. Int. J. Ind. Eng. **19**(8), 305–319 (2012)
17. Demiriz, A., Bennett, K.P., Bradley, P.S.: Using assignment constraints to avoid empty clusters in k-means clustering. In: Constrained Clustering: Advances in Algorithms, Theory, and Applications, vol. 201 (2008)

Two Variants of Bi-objective Vehicle Routing Problem in Home (Health)-Care Fields

Salma Hadj Taieb[1(✉)], Taicir Moalla Loukil[1],
Abderrahman El Mhamedi[2], and Yasmina Hani[2]

[1] Faculty of Economics and Management of Sfax, University of Sfax,
3018 Sfax, Tunisia
taicir.loukil@fsegs.usf.tn
[2] University of Paris 8 Vincennes-Saint-Denis, Saint-Denis, France
{a.elmhamedi,y.hani}@iut.univ-paris8.fr

Abstract. In this research paper, we consider two bi-objectives models, the Vehicle Routing Problem Preferences with Time windows, temporal dependencies, multiple structures and multiple specialties "VRPPTW-TD-2MS" and the Vehicle Routing Problem Balance with Time windows, temporal dependencies, multiple structures and multiple specialties "VRPBTW-TD-2MS", in Home (Health)-Care "HHC" service field. In this context, The HHC services is mostly assigned to certain persons such as people who have a chronic disease or who have difficulty leaving their houses by offering them medical, social, and/or medico-social services like nursing, dressing, bathing, toileting, feeding, shopping, hygiene assistance, etc. These several services are provided by different public and private home care structures. These structures work together in coordination to provide high HHC quality for patients. Therefore, patients are not in a single structure anymore, but rather at home and need to be served by caregivers. As a result, the problem is no longer limited to the care organization, but also to the construction of optimal tours for the caregivers, the delivery of medicines, and the equipment needed for care. According to our knowledge, our work is different from those made in the literature. Our problem consists to determine the caregivers' tours while optimizing bi-objective function, which aims to minimize the total traveling time and the total negative preference or the maximal difference workload of caregivers under set of constraints such as time window, synchronization, precedence and disjunction constraints with multiple structures and multiple caregivers' skills. A benchmark of instances is considered from literature. Cplex (Optimization Software package) is used to solve our problems to obtain efficient solutions.

Keywords: VRPPTW-TD-2MS · VRPBTW-TD-2MS · Bi-objective · Home (Health)-Care

1 Introduction

Some challenges related to care recipient, care provider, artifacts (equipment/ technology and supplies) and health care environment (especially affective challenges, cognitive challenges, physical challenges, degraded quality, the home

© IFIP International Federation for Information Processing 2021
Published by Springer Nature Switzerland AG 2021
A. Dolgui et al. (Eds.): APMS 2021, IFIP AICT 634, pp. 77–86, 2021.
https://doi.org/10.1007/978-3-030-85914-5_9

environment, work environment, etc.) [1] raise from the strategic, tactic and operational perspectives by the incorporation of home care in logistics and transports activities. In this context, we are interested to shed light on HHC services, which is a growing sector in the society. It becomes increasingly legitimate [2, 3] due to the evolution of an aging population [4] and the crisis context like Covid-19 [5] This sector is still witnessing numerous evolutions according to demographic, political, and economic factors. In many countries, scientific researchers place great importance on the people's satisfactions, needs and the improvement of the living conditions [6–8].

For several years, the scientific study has been dealing with the care organization in hospitals ([9, 10] etc.). The follow-up of some patients' health does not require their presence in the hospital. There is no need to the continuous presence of the nurse or specific materials to take care of them. In this case, the follow-up can be carried out with patients at their home. This service aims to avoid the unnecessary hospitalizations, to reduce convalescence periods and hospital infections. Some patients needs other services such as cleaning, cooking and shopping etc. These types of services are provided by different home care structures belonging to the social, medical and/or medico-social fields. Therefore, optimizing those resources (materials and human levels) is among companies' top priorities and considerable efforts. The objective of our research is to propose a model to assign patients (visits) to nurses (caregivers) and determine the routing of each caregiver. So, we are interested in designing decision support tools to provide solutions for decision-makers and to arrange vehicle routing to serve geographically distributed patients under various constraints (synchronization, precedence, disjunction, multiple structure and multiple skills) in order to minimize the total transportation time and the total negative caregiver's preference or balance their workload.

This paper begins with the problem description and a literature review of Vehicle Routing Problem's "VRP" variants based on different approaches. Modelization of the problem and experimental results will be presented in the next section.

2   Problem Description and Literature Review

2.1   Problem Description

The growing old population and the increasing demand of care take overtaken the capacity of health institutions, which generates a developing trend in home care. In the Operational Research community, many authors have adressed by this issue, which interests aspects are related to VRP [11, 12]. The VRP is considered an excellent application for different programs not only HHC but also offering different social services [13–16]. It aims to define a set of ways to manage the group of patients. The goals may vary and depend on each context and institution. Among the most common, we can find, minimizing the cost measure (about travelling time/distance) and maximizing the preference of stakeholders (patient/caregivers) to ensure their satisfaction level. In this context, a group of caregivers should visit a set of geographically dispersed customers (patients) respecting time windows and time-dependent constraints such as synchronization that requires more than one vehicle to serve a patient at the same time, precedence that requires a fixed order between home care workers and disjunction that means the precedence of the precedence. These couples of visits are carried out on the same patient and with two home care workers having different specialties. These home care workers can be from the same structure or from different structures. Thus, their accessibility, their skills and their structures must also be taken into account. About the service of each caregiver, each one leaves his structure and return to his starting point taking into consideration a limited number of hours per day.

2.2   Literature Review

In this section, we present a survey work related to HHC. We take a look at research work that addresses the routing problem as Vehicle Routing Problem (VRP) in the HHC context. We can find a very large number of VRP variants, which present many similarities, but differ in structures. Each problem variant is designed using parameters describing the assumptions, the constraints, and the objectives.

[17] considered the routing and/or scheduling nurses problem which minimizes the cost objective function, the total of extra time, and the part-time work that is scheduled taking into consideration time windows, breaks, multi-skills, and multi-structure constraints. They proposed two heuristic methods to solve the problem.

[18] optimized Home Health Care services respecting patients' preference, caregivers' preference and their qualifications. They solved the problem with Tabu Search and simulated annealing meta-heuristics.

[19] modelled the Home Care Crew Scheduling problem as a problem of a partitioning set with temporal dependencies and time windows constraints. The latter is solved with column generation in a Branch-and-Price framework.

[20] surveyed the vehicle tour problem with time windows and synchronization constraint. A home care environment, one depot, and a unique period are crucial elements to formulate and solve the problem. They considered three objective functions: reducing travel time, minimizing negative preference patients, or minimizing caregivers workload difference. To solve this problem, they developed a heuristic approach.

[21] developed a MILPwhich aims to minimize the total travel time of nurses under constraints of time windows, staff lunch breaks, patient-staff regularity, and synchronization visits between home workers. Two solvers were presented by authors to solve one instance of the model, which are: LINGO from LINDO SYSTEMS and OPL-CLPEX from ILOG Studio.

[22] respected the same considerations of [20] but they solve their problem using the LINGO of LINDO SYSTEMS solvers.

[23] tried to solve Health Care routing problem under; time windows, caregivers' skills, breaks and patients' dislikes constraints using a Variable Neighborhood Search algorithm. Their goal is either maximizing the satisfaction level of patients/home workers or minimizing the traveling times of the caregivers.

[11] used Branch-and-Price method to solve the generalization of the Vehicle Routing Problem with Time Windows (VRPTW). Time windows, synchronization, preferences and precedence constraints are modelled as services provided to patients. Their objectives is to minimizing uncovered visits, maximizing caretaker-visit preferences and minimizing the total travelling costs.

[24] established daily home care planning with visits synchronization respecting the patients' time windows.

[25] have proposed a decision support tool based on a simulated annealing method. Their method was tested on the instances of [20] with the latest criterion.

[26] presented a case study for HHC. They developed a linear program taking into account Time Windows and caregivers' skills constraints while the main objective is to find an optimal route for visits scheduled every day.

[27] treated a chance-constrained home-caregiver scheduling and routing problem with stochastic travel and service times. The problem is modelled as a bi-objective function, which minimizes the expected total operational cost of selected routes and a penalty cost for unserved customers, subject to the following constraint: Time windows and a chance constraint. As a solution method, they combined the branch and price algorithm and the discrete approximation method.

[28] introduce the HHC routing and scheduling problem (HHCRSP) for two separate services set of HHC and Home Delivery Vehicles that are affected by the different staff because of operational constraints. Consequently, the proposed MILP solved by the heuristic method suggests minimizing the total travel cost and route affectation cost for nurse and vehicle routes. The synchronization between different services considered.

[29] formulated a MIP model as new variant of "VRPTW" named "VRPTW-TD-2MS" the vehicle routing problem with time windows, time dependencies, multi-structures, and multi specialities problem. They proposed Variable Neighborhood Search; General Variable Neighborhood Search; and General Variable Neighborhood Search with Ejection Chains-based for solving their model.

[30] treated the Stochastic Districting−Staff Dimensioning−Assignment−Routing Problem, the objective is to minimize the hiring, violation of the neighbourhood constraint, and estimated travel costs. The constraints considered in this work are; skill levels of the caregivers, time window. A novel met-heuristic algorithm offered to solve the model of this problem.

[4, 31–34]; etc. have proposed relatively a complete review of the literature on Home Health Care routing and scheduling issues.

3 Modelization and Experimental Results

3.1 Modelization

We extend the mathematical modeling Vehicle Routing Problem with Time Window, Temporal dependencies, multiple structures and multiple specialties "VRPTW-TD-2MS" of [29] to deal with two bi-objective optimization models (the first model is "VRPPTW-TD-2MS", and the second model is "VRPBTW-TD-2MS"). The purpose of our first model is to design the least-cost routes for units caregivers (vehicles), taking into consideration the maximal preference of patients. The purpose of our second model is to design the least-cost routes for caregivers, taking into consideration the minimization of the maximal difference workload of home care workers.

Notations

$G = \bigcup_{s=1..S} (S^s, E^s)$	Undirected graph
$S^s = V^s \cup C^s$	The node set
$C^s = \{0, n_s + 1\}$	The initial and final structure s
$V^s = \{1, .., n_s\}$	The visit points of structure s
E^s	The edge-set for structure s
P	The set of speciality
T^s_{ij}	The travel duration
D^s_i	The time duration
$Pref^s_{jk}$	The preference measure
$[a^{sk}_i, b^{sk}_i]$	Time window preference where a^{sk}_i and b^{sk}_i respectively the earliest start time and the latest start time of visit i
P^{synch}	The set of couple of visits that are synchronized
P^{pred}	The set of couple of visits subject to precedence constraints
P^{disj}	The set of couple of visits subject to disjunction
w	The balancing variable
$W^s_{ijk} = D^s_i$	The measure is in service duration
$W^s_{ijk} = T^s_{ij}$	The measure is in traveling time
$\alpha 1, \alpha 2$	Weights of the objectives

Parameters

z^s_{pk}: A binary parameter that is equal to 1 if home care worker k from structure s has a specialty p, 0 otherwise. y^s_{ip}: A binary parameter that is equal to 1 if visit i is to be carried out by a home care worker from structure s with specialty p, 0 otherwise.

Decision Variables

x^s_{ijk}: A binary decision variable that is equal to 1 if the vehicle k from structure s goes from visits i to j, 0 otherwise. t^s_{ik}: A real decision variable indicates the starting time of visit i if this latter is visited by vehicle k from structure s, 0 otherwise.

A detailed solution example for our problems is shown in the figure below:

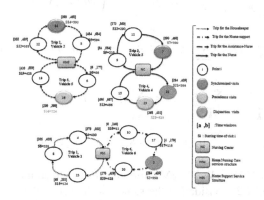

Fig. 1. Example for VRPPTW-TD-2MS or VRPBTW-TD-2MS problems.

A detailed solution example see in the (Fig. 1), for a simple instance with NC structure, HSS structure and HNC structure, hold in total 19 points (Patients or visits). Point 7 from NC structure and point 14 from HNC structure are two synchronized visits that have the same starting time of services. Point 16 from HNC structure and point 23 from NC structure are two precedence visits that visit 16 have to precede visit 23. Point 21 from NC structure and point 2 from HSS structure are two disjunction visits that have the same time windows but cannot be performed at the same time. Six caregivers with four skills carry out these visits.

The mathematical modeling of the VRPPTW-TD-2MS formulated as follows (Model 1):

$$\text{Minimize } \alpha 1 \sum_{s \in S} \sum_{k \in K^s} \sum_{(i,j) \in E^s} T^s_{ij} x^s_{ijk} + \alpha 2 \sum_{s \in S} \sum_{k \in K^s} \sum_{(i,j) \in E^s} Pref^s_{jk} x^s_{ijk} \tag{1}$$

Subject to

$$y^s_{ip} = 1 : \sum_{k \in K^s} \sum_{j \in V^{s+}} y^s_{jp} x^s_{ijk} z^s_{pk} = 1 \quad \forall s \in S, p \in P^s, i \in V^s \tag{2}$$

$$z^s_{pk} = 1 : \sum_{i \in V^s} x^s_{0ik} y^s_{ip} = \sum_{i \in V^s} x^s_{i(n_s+1)k} y^s_{ip} = 1 \quad \forall s \in S, k \in K^s, p \in P^s \tag{3}$$

$$y^s_{ip} z^s_{pk} = 1 : \sum_{j \in V^{s+}} x^s_{ijk} y^s_{jp} = \sum_{j \in V^{s-}} x^s_{jik} y^s_{jp} \quad \forall s \in S, i \in V^s, k \in K^s, p \in P^s \tag{4}$$

$$t^s_{ik} + (D^s_i + T_{ij}) x^s_{ijk} \le t^s_{jk} + \left(1 - x^s_{ijk}\right) b^{sk}_i \quad \forall s \in S; k \in K^s; (i,j) \in E^s \tag{5}$$

$$a^{sk}_i \sum_{j \in V^s} x^s_{ijk} \le t^s_{ik} \le b^{sk}_i \sum_{j \in V^s} x^s_{ijk} \quad \forall s \in S; i \in V^s; k \in K^s \tag{6}$$

$$a^{sk}_i \le t^s_{ik} \le b^{sk}_i \quad \forall s \in S, i \in \{0, n_s + 1\}, k \in K^s \tag{7}$$

$$\sum_{k \in K^s} t^s_{ik} = \sum_{k \in K^{s'}} t^{s'}_{jk} \quad \forall (i,j) \in P^{synch}\left(\text{with } i \in V^s, j \in V^{s'}\right) \tag{8}$$

$$\sum_{k \in K^s} t^s_{ik} + D^s_i \le \sum_{k \in K^{s'}} t^{s'}_{jk} \quad \forall (i,j) \in P^{pred}\left(\text{with } i \in V^s, j \in V^{s'}\right) \tag{9}$$

$$\sum_{k \in K^s} t^s_{ik} + D^s_i \le \sum_{k \in K^{s'}} t^{s'}_{jk} \text{ or } \sum_{k \in K^s} t^s_{jk} + D^s_j \le \sum_{k \in K^{s'}} t^{s'}_{ik} \quad \forall (i,j) \in P^{disj}\left(i \in V^s, j \in V^{s'}\right) \tag{10}$$

$$x^s_{ijk} \in \{0, 1\} \quad \forall s \in S; k \in K^s; (i,j) \in E^s \tag{11}$$

The second model VRPBTW-TD-2MS formulated as Mixed-integer linear programming (MILP) (**Model 2**) considering the same constraints of the (**Model 1**).

$$Minimize \; \alpha 1 \sum_{s \in S} \sum_{k \in K^s} \sum_{(i,j) \in E^s} T_{ij}^s x_{ijk}^s + \alpha 2 w \qquad (1')$$

$$\sum_{(i,j) \in E^s} W_{ijk1}^s x_{ijk1}^s - \sum_{(i,j) \in E^s} W_{ijk2}^s x_{ijk2}^s \leq w \quad \forall s \in S, k_1 \in K^s, k_2 \in K^s \backslash k_1 \qquad (12)$$

The bi-objective function (1) of Model 1 is about, to minimize the total traveling time of set of vehicles and the total negative preference of patient for caregivers, the bi-objective function (1') of Model 2 is to minimize the total distance traveled by a set of vehicles and the maximal difference workload of caregivers. Constraint (2) ensures that each visit point is served by one caregiver with the corresponding specialty and the given structure. Constraint (3) states that each vehicle begins from the depot, and returns to it at the same structure. Constraint (4) ensures the equality of the inflow and outflow arcs at every point. Constraint (5) is about the time continuity constraint of routes. According to constraint (6) and (7), each vehicle of given structure must respect visits time windows and caregivers' time windows respectively. Constraints (8), (9), and (10) are about synchronization's visits, precedence's visits, and disjunction's visits, respectively, of different structures. Constraint (11) concerns the nature of the variable definition. Constraint (12) is about the balancing constraint.

The impact of our two models will be twofold: **Model 1** for the patients for their satisfaction levels and **Model 2** for the caregivers in their workload balancing while taking into account the cost criterion as a main objective.

3.2   Experimental Results

In order to test our formulated models (**Model 1** and **Model 2**), we consider the benchmark of [29] for "VRPTW-TD-2MS" and the benchmark of [20] for Vehicle Routing Problem with Time Window and Synchronization constraint "VRPTWSyn" to generate new instances, based on the same rules provided by the latter, for VRPPTW-TD-2MS and VRPBTW-TD-2MS problems. The below generated instances are clustered according to visits and vehicles number (in our data instance, we use 60 visits and 12 vehicles).

We use Cplex 12.5 coupled with C++ language to solve **Model 1** and **Model 2**.

Table 1. Solutions and computational times for the VRPPTW-TD-2MS generated instances.

Data	Weight Obj 1	Weight Obj 2	MIP	
			SOL	CPU
1-60-2 (Small time window)	0.9	0.1	−87.06	24.30
	0.5	0.5	−716.25	33.19
	0.1	0.9	−1352.00	24.45
1-60-3 (Meduim time window)	0.9	0.1	−96.30	3600
	0.5	0.5	−787.45	878.87
	0.1	0.9	−1485.84	1129.49
1-60-4 (Large time window)	0.9	0.1	−106.01	3598.80
	0.5	0.5	−865.12	50.02
	0.1	0.9	−1631.17	45.23

Obj1: Minimize traveling time, Obj2: Minimize Preference of customers.

Table 2. Solutions and computational times for the VRPBTW-TD-2MS generated instances.

Data	Weight Obj 1	Weight Obj 3	MIP	
			SOL	CPU
1-60-2 (Small time window)	0.9	0.1	15.77	3600
	0.5	0.5	29.09	3597.91
	0.1	0.9	40.95	3600
1-60-3 (Meduim time window)	0.9	0.1	15.82	3600
	0.5	0.5	30.35	3600
	0.1	0.9	41.78	3600
1-60-4 (Large time window)	0.9	0.1	15.46	3600
	0.5	0.5	30.17	3596.95
	0.1	0.9	43.68	3594.64

Obj1: Minimize traveling time, Obj3: Minimize workload of caregivers.

Note that the addition of the second objective function makes the problem more complex than the traditional one. All combinations of time windows and weights objective functions, i.e. 9 test problems, are presented in these tables. The problem size is defined through the number of constraints and the number of variables, varying according to time windows classes. The objective function values from these runs are shown in the "SOL" column and the processing time values are presented in the "CPU" column. To obtain solutions as good as possible within the time limit, we solve instances with 60 min as a time limit. CPLEX solves Model 1 and Model 2 but when we solve some of the larger data, we find that Cplex has problems of finding solutions in a reasonable time.

4   Conclusion

Our occupation aimed to model "VRPPTW-TD-2MS" and "VRPBTW-TD-2MS" problems and solve them with Cplex. Two MILP have been formulated as bi-objective models to determine the caregivers' tours while optimizing the objective functions minimizing the total traveling distance and the total negative preference or the maximal difference workload of home care workers. The output of our programs provides care services to a geographically dispersed population while assigning visits to each caregiver and defining the tour of each vehicle. The set of efficient solutions (for each combination of objectives weights) have been obtained with Cplex within one hour. Note that our problems include the VRP, which is known to be NP-Hard. When we solve *Model 2*, we obtain a result with a larger CPU time. Therefore, *Model 2* is more complex than *Model 1*. For that reason, we will propose a metaheuristic method to solve these models and larger instances in shorter CPU time as future work.

References

1. Beer, J.M., McBride, S.E., Mitzner, T.L., Rogers, W.A.: Understanding challenges in the front lines of home health care: a human-systems approach. Appl. Ergon. **45**, 1687–1699 (2014). https://doi.org/10.1016/j.apergo.2014.05.019
2. Gershon, R.R., et al.: Home health care challenges and avian influenza. Home Health Care Manag. Pract. **20**, 58–69 (2007)
3. En-nahli, L., Allaoui, H., Nouaouri, I.: A multi-objective modelling to human resource assignment and routing problem for home health care services. IFAC-PapersOnLine **48**, 698–703 (2015)
4. Di Mascolo, M., Espinouse, M.-L., Hajri, Z.E.: Planning in home health care structures: a literature review. IFAC-PapersOnLine **50**, 4654–4659 (2017). https://doi.org/10.1016/j.ifacol.2017.08.689
5. Atashi, A., Nejatian, A.: Challenges of home health care during COVID-19 outbreak in Iran. Int. J. Commun. Based Nurs. Midwifery **8**, 360 (2020)
6. Algamdi, S.J.: Older patients' satisfaction with home health care services in Al-Baha Region, Saudi Arabia. Ph.D. thesis, University of Salford (2016)
7. Aydin, R., et al.: An evaluation of home health care needs and Quality of Life among the elderly in a semi-rural area of Western Turkey. Eur. Geriatr. Med. **7**, 8–12 (2016)
8. Zhang, L., et al.: Home health care daily planning considering the satisfaction of all the stakeholders. In: 2019 International Conference on Industrial Engineering and Systems Management (IESM), pp. 1–6 (2019)
9. Adan, I., Vissers, J.M.H.: Patient mix optimisation in hospital admission planning: a case study. Int. J. Oper. Prod. Manag. **22**, 445–461 (2002)
10. You, L., et al.: Hospital nursing, care quality, and patient satisfaction: cross-sectional surveys of nurses and patients in hospitals in China and Europe. Int. J. Nurs. Stud. **50**, 154–161 (2013)
11. Rasmussen, M.S., Justesen, T., Dohn, A., Larsen, J.: The home care crew scheduling problem: preference-based visit clustering and temporal dependencies. Eur. J. Oper. Res. **219**, 598–610 (2012). https://doi.org/10.1016/j.ejor.2011.10.048
12. Decerle, J., Grunder, O., El Hassani, A.H., Barakat, O.: A memetic algorithm for a home health care routing and scheduling problem. Oper. Res. Health Care **16**, 59–71 (2018)
13. Toth, P., Vigo, D.: The vehicle routing problem. SIAM (2002)
14. Chen, S., Jiang, T.: Design of logistic zones for the vehicle routing problem (VRP): application to water distribution. 전자무역연구 **8**, 89–103 (2010)
15. Zamorano, E., Stolletz, R.: Branch-and-price approaches for the multiperiod technician routing and scheduling problem. Eur. J. Oper. Res. **257**, 55–68 (2017)

16. Mathlouthi, I., Gendreau, M., Potvin, J.-Y.: Mixed integer linear programming for a multi-attribute technician routing and scheduling problem. INFOR Inf. Syst. Oper. Res. **56**, 33–49 (2018)
17. Cheng, E., Rich, J.: A Home Health Care Routing and Scheduling Problem (1998)
18. Bertels, S., Fahle, T.: A hybrid setup for a hybrid scenario: combining heuristics for the home health care problem. Comput. Oper. Res. **33**, 2866–2890 (2006)
19. Dohn, A., Rasmussen, M.S., Justesen, T., Larsen, J.: The home care crew scheduling problem. ICAOR 1–8 (2008)
20. Bredström, D., Rönnqvist, M.: Combined vehicle routing and scheduling with temporal precedence and synchronization constraints. Eur. J. Oper. Res. **191**, 19–31 (2008). https://doi.org/10.1016/j.ejor.2007.07.033
21. Bachouch, R.B., Fakhfakh, M., Guinet, A., Hajri-Gabouj, S.: Planification des tournées des infirmiers dans une structure de soins à domicile (2009)
22. Rabeh, R., Saïd, K., Eric, M.: Collaborative model for planning and scheduling caregivers' activities in homecare. IFAC Proc. Vol. **44**, 2877–2882 (2011). https://doi.org/10.3182/20110828-6-IT-1002.01043
23. Trautsamwieser, A., Hirsch, P.: Optimization of daily scheduling for home health care services. JAOR **3**, 124–136 (2011)
24. Afifi, S., Dang, D.-C., Moukrim, A.: A simulated annealing algorithm for the vehicle routing problem with time windows and synchronization constraints. In: Nicosia, G., Pardalos, P. (eds.) LION 2013. LNCS, vol. 7997, pp. 259–265. Springer, Heidelberg (2013). https://doi.org/10.1007/978-3-642-44973-4_27
25. Afifi, S., Dang, D.-C., Moukrim, A.: Heuristic solutions for the vehicle routing problem with time windows and synchronized visits. Optim. Lett. **10**(3), 511–525 (2015). https://doi.org/10.1007/s11590-015-0878-3
26. Yuan, Z., Fügenschuh, A.: Home health care scheduling: a case study. Helmut-Schmidt-Univ., Professur für Angewandte Mathematik Hamburg (2015)
27. Liu, R., Yuan, B., Jiang, Z.: A branch-and-price algorithm for the home-caregiver scheduling and routing problem with stochastic travel and service times. Flex. Serv. Manuf. J. **31**(4), 989–1011 (2018). https://doi.org/10.1007/s10696-018-9328-8
28. Nasir, J.A., Kuo, Y.-H.: A decision support framework for home health care transportation with simultaneous multi-vehicle routing and staff scheduling synchronization. Decis. Support Syst. **138**, 113361 (2020)
29. Frifita, S., Masmoudi, M.: VNS methods for home care routing and scheduling problem with temporal dependencies, and multiple structures and specialties. Int. Trans. Oper. Res. **27**, 291–313 (2020)
30. Nikzad, E., Bashiri, M., Abbasi, B.: A matheuristic algorithm for stochastic home health care planning. Eur. J. Oper. Res. **288**, 753–774 (2021)
31. Castillo-Salazar, J.A., Landa-Silva, D., Qu, R.: Workforce scheduling and routing problems: literature survey and computational study. Ann. Oper. Res. **239**(1), 39–67 (2014). https://doi.org/10.1007/s10479-014-1687-2
32. Fikar, C., Hirsch, P.: Home health care routing and scheduling: a review. Comput. Oper. Res. **77**, 86–95 (2017)
33. Cissé, M., Yalçındağ, S., Kergosien, Y., Şahin, E., Lenté, C., Matta, A.: OR problems related to home health care: a review of relevant routing and scheduling problems. Oper. Res. Health Care **13**, 1–22 (2017)
34. Grieco, L., Utley, M., Crowe, S.: Operational research applied to decisions in home health care: a systematic literature review. J. Oper. Res. Soc. 1–32 (2020)

Inventory Routing Problem with Transshipment and Substitution for Blood Products Using the Case of the Belgian Blood Distribution

Christine Di Martinelly[1]([⊠]) , Nadine Meskens[2] ,
Fouad Riane[3,4,5] , and Imane Hssini[6]

[1] IESEG School of Management, Univ. Lille, CNRS, UMR 9221 - LEM - Lille
Economie Management, 59000 Lille, France
c.dimartinelly@ieseg.fr
[2] Université Catholique de Louvain, Louvain School of Management, LOURIM,
Chaussée de Binche 151, 7000 Mons, Belgique
nadine.meskens@uclouvain.be
[3] SCI Ecole Centrale de Casablanca, Casablanca, Morocco
[4] LMMII Laboratory, LGI CentraleSupélec Paris Saclay University,
Gif-sur-Yvette, France
[5] FST Settat, Hassan Premier University, Settat, Morocco
[6] LSI, Ecole Nationale des Sciences Appliquées d'Oujda, Oujda, Morocco

Abstract. In this paper, we deal with a blood supply chain management problem. We focus in particular on blood distribution routes design and optimization. Blood is a scarce and perishable product, made of multiple components, each with specific compatibility rules. We would like to investigate the impact of compatible products substitution and transshipment between hospitals on blood demand satisfaction. We use the case of the blood supply chain in Belgium as an application. We model the case as an Inventory Routing Problem with transshipment and substitution for perishable products in a capacity constrained environment. We implement the model and conduct experimentations to evaluate the contribution of both transshipment and substitution with regards to shortages and distribution and inventory costs reduction. In a capacity constrained environment, at equivalent cost, mismatching/substitution is preferred to transshipment to satisfy the demand and avoid backorders.

Keywords: Inventory routing · Blood supply chain · Sensitivity analysis

1 Introduction

In this paper, we are interested in the Inventory Routing Problem (IRP) with transshipment and substitution for blood products in a capacity constrained environment. The IRP problem arises in several industries and services when decisions on inventory management, vehicle routing and delivery-scheduling decisions are integrated; it is encountered typically in the case of vendor managed inventory in which the supplier/

© IFIP International Federation for Information Processing 2021
Published by Springer Nature Switzerland AG 2021
A. Dolgui et al. (Eds.): APMS 2021, IFIP AICT 634, pp. 87–96, 2021.
https://doi.org/10.1007/978-3-030-85914-5_10

vendor is given the responsibility of managing the customer's inventory [1]. As seen in the literature review of [2], the IRP has received considerable attention from researchers over the years and multiple variants, taken into account multiple attributes of the problem, have been studied. Among those attributes, we focus on transshipment and substitution.

Transshipment occurs when products can be shipped between customers; this feature is interesting in a deterministic context when no lost sales occur as it is a way to reduce distribution and inventory costs [3]. Substitution may offer the opportunity to sell a substitute product in case a product is out-of-stock; it enables a company to satisfy the demand and reduce excess inventory; however, in a capacity constrained environment, products are competing for the space available and the advantages linked to substitution are dependent on the parameters of the model [4].

Both transshipment and substitution have a positive effect on the amount of inventory kept and are ways to avoid shortages, yet the trade-offs when both are taken into account are not clear. We aim to perform a sensitivity analysis to understand those and determine lines for future research.

To perform this analysis, we use the case of the Belgium blood supply chain, which is typically the case of an IRP for multiple perishable products with transshipment and substitution in a capacity constrained environment. Blood is a particular commodity, which is perishable and scarce, with an irregular supply, and whose shortage may be life-threatening. Blood, or whole blood, is made of 4 components (red blood cells, platelets, plasma and cryo), which are separated mechanically or by apheresis [5]. Those different components have each specific shelf-live and usage. Additionally, they are tested for blood groups and have their own rules for compatibility. The study of the blood supply chain focuses on various stages of the process from donors to patients, as it can be seen in the literature reviews made by [5, 6] and [7]. In this paper, we focus on the distribution and inventory management problem between the blood bank and the hospitals, on which the authors presented a state of art in [8]. Relevant papers to our research are summarized in Table 1, following the problem characterization proposed by [2]. The setting under study is close to the research of [9], in which the authors consider only one vehicle and of [10], in which the authors do not take into account inventory holding cost nor substitution.

As additional characteristics, we consider multiple vehicles and if the demand cannot be satisfied, it is backordered. The problem is modeled as a mixed integer program; as the IRP in its basic version is NP-hard [2], a decomposition-based heuristic is developed and tested on multiple instances. The model is additionally used to lead extensive experimentations on key parameters of the model; this last part is presented in the present paper.

2   Problem Description and Assumptions

In this section, we analyze an IRP with transshipment and substitution for the red blood cell products over a finite discrete time horizon, using multiple vehicles with limited capacity. We consider two echelons of the supply chain as products are delivered between the blood bank and the different hospitals. At each time period, the routing problem seeks to identify which hospitals to visit; multiple vehicles are required due to distances between hospitals and time limit on each tour. The inventory at each hospital is managed under a Maximum Level (ML) policy meaning that the blood bank determines how much to deliver as long as the holding capacity is respected.

Table 1. Relevant papers to the IRP for blood products.

Authors	Product number		Demand		Time horizon		Routing		Inventory decision			Fleet composition		Fleet size			Objectif				Solution method				Problem characteristics	
	Single	Multiple	Stochastic	Deterministic	Finite	Infinite	Direct	Multiple	Non negative	Lost sales	Back order	Homogeneous	Heterogeneous	Single	Multiple	unconstrained	Cost	Profit	Env. impact	other	Exact method	Heuristic	Meta-heuristic	Simulation	Transfer	Substitution
[11]	*		*		*			*	*			*			*		*					*			*	
[12]	*		*		*			*			*				*		*	*	*		*		*			
[13]	*		*		*			*		*	-	-			*					*	*				*	
[14]	*			*	*			*	*	*	*	*			*		*				*	*				
[15]	*		*		*			*		-	-	*		*			*				*					*
[16]	*			*	*			*	*			*			*		*				*					
[17]	*		*		*			*		-	-	*	*								*	*				
[18]		*	*		*			*			*	*		*			*							*		
[9]		*		*	*			*	*	-	*	*			*						*	*			*	*
[10]		*		*	*			*	*		-	*			*						*	*			*	

The demand for blood cell products is considered deterministic, and is expressed in number of blood bags. As the supply of blood cell products at the blood bank may vary over the time period, there may be periods in which the blood supply is not sufficient to cover the demand. In this case, hospitals have the possibility to substitute the blood cell products (the term of mismatching can be encountered in place of substitution and describes the use of a compatible blood product when the patient's blood type is unavailable at the time of the request), use transshipment to get the product from another hospital or backorder the demand (meaning the surgical intervention requiring the blood is postponed). At each period, a percentage of the products hold on inventory becomes obsolete.

Notation	
Set	
$\mathcal{H}$	Set of hospitals only
$\mathcal{H}^+$	Set of hospitals and blood bank
$\mathcal{V}$	Set of vehicles
$\mathcal{S}$	Set of visited hospitals during a period
$\mathcal{T}$	Set of time periods over the planning horizon
$\mathcal{P}$	Set of blood products
Parameters	
D_{irt}	Demand of product r during period t at hospital i
C_i	Storage capacity at hospital i
Z_{rt}	Quantity of product r available at the depot during each period t
θ_{ri}	Outdating rate of product r stored at each location i
cap	Vehicle capacity
φ_{ij}	Transportation time between 2 locations $i, j \in H^+$
τ_t	Maximum working time during period t
$dist_{ij}$	Distance (in km) between 2 locations $i, j \in H^+$
I_{ri0}	Initial inventory of product r at hospital i
CST_{ri}	Inventory holding cost of product r at location i
$CTRAV$	Transportation cost, in €/KM
CT_{ri}	Transshipment penalty cost of product r from location i
CR_{ri}	Backorder cost of product r at location i
CS_{ru}	Substitution cost between products r and u
MC_{ur}	Compatibility matrix; equal to 1 if product u is compatible with product r; 0 otherwise
e_r	Blood type distribution per product r in the Belgian population
Variables	
Q_{rit}	Quantity of product r delivered to location i during period t
q_{rijt}	Quantity of product r transported between location i and j at period t
I_{rit}	Inventory of product r at hospital i at period t
x_{ijt}	Binary variable equal to 1 if during period t the location j is directly visited after location i
S_{rit}	Quantity of product r in backorder at location i during period t
T_{rit}	Quantity of product r transshipped from location i during period t
SU_{urit}	Quantity of product u, substitute of product r, from inventory of location i at period t (to satisfy demand D_{irt})

2.1 Mathematical Modelling

$$Min \sum_{\substack{i \in \mathcal{H} \\ }} \sum_{\substack{j \in \mathcal{H} \\ i \neq j}} \sum_{t \in \mathcal{T}} CTRAV * dist_{ij} * x_{ijt} + \sum_{j \in \mathcal{H}} \sum_{r \in \mathcal{P}} \sum_{t \in \mathcal{T}} CST_{rj} * I_{rjt} \quad (1)$$

$$+ \sum_{j \in \mathcal{H}} \sum_{r \in \mathcal{P}} \sum_{t \in \mathcal{T}} CR_{rj} * S_{rjt}$$

$$+ \sum_{j \in \mathcal{H}} \sum_{t \in \mathcal{T}} \sum_{r \in \mathcal{P}} \sum_{u \in \mathcal{P}} CS_{ru} * SU_{rujt} + \sum_{j \in \mathcal{H}} \sum_{t \in \mathcal{T}} \sum_{r \in \mathcal{P}} CT_{rj} * T_{rjt}$$

Subject to :

$$\sum_{i \in \mathcal{H}} x_{ijt} \leq 1 \quad \forall j \in \mathcal{H}, t \in \mathcal{T} \tag{2}$$

$$\sum_{\substack{i \in \mathcal{H} \\ i \neq j}} x_{ijt} - \sum_{\substack{m \in \mathcal{H} \\ m \neq j}} x_{jmt} = 0 \quad \forall j \in \mathcal{H}, t \in \mathcal{T} \tag{3}$$

$$\sum_{i \in \mathcal{S}} \sum_{\substack{j \in \mathcal{S} \\ j \neq i}} x_{ijt} \leq |\mathcal{S}| - 1 \quad \forall S \subset \mathcal{H}, \mathcal{S} \neq \phi, t \in \mathcal{T} \tag{4}$$

$$\sum_{i \in \mathcal{H}} \sum_{\substack{j \in \mathcal{H} \\ j \neq i}} x_{ijt} * \varphi_{ij} \leq \tau_t \quad \forall t \in \mathcal{T} \tag{5}$$

$$\sum_{j \in \mathcal{H}} x_{0jt} \leq |\mathcal{V}| \quad \forall t \in \mathcal{T} \tag{6}$$

$$\sum_{\substack{i \in \mathcal{H} \\ i \neq j}} q_{rijt} - \sum_{\substack{m \in \mathcal{H} \\ m \neq j}} q_{rjmt} = Q_{rjt} - T_{rjt} \quad \forall j \in \mathcal{H}, r \in \mathcal{P}, t \in \mathcal{T} \tag{7}$$

$$\sum_{r \in \mathcal{P}} q_{ri0t} = 0 \quad \forall i \in \mathcal{H}, t \in \mathcal{T} \tag{8}$$

$$\sum_{r \in \mathcal{P}} q_{rijt} \leq Cap * x_{ijt} \quad \forall i \in \mathcal{H}^+, j \in \mathcal{H}, i \neq j, t \in \mathcal{T} \tag{9}$$

$$T_{rit} \leq (1 - \theta_{ri}) * I_{rit-1} \quad \forall i \in \mathcal{H}, r \in \mathcal{P}, t \in \mathcal{T} \tag{10}$$

$$I_{rit} = (1 - \theta_{ri}) * I_{rit-1} + Q_{rit} - S_{rit-1} - T_{rit} \quad \forall i \in \mathcal{H}, r \in \mathcal{P}, t \in \mathcal{T}$$
$$- \sum_{u \in \mathcal{P}} MC_{ru} * SU_{ruit} + S_{rit} \tag{11}$$

$$D_{rit} = \sum_{u \in \mathcal{P}} MC_{ur} * SU_{urit} + S_{rit} \quad \forall i \in \mathcal{H}^+, r \in \mathcal{P}, t \in \mathcal{T} \tag{12}$$

$$I_{r0t} = (1 - \theta_{r0}) * I_{r0t-1} - \sum_{i \in \mathcal{H}} q_{r0it} + Z_{rt} \quad \forall r \in \mathcal{P}, t \in \mathcal{T} \tag{13}$$

$$\sum_{r \in P} (1 - \theta_{ri}) * I_{rit-1} + \sum_{r \in P} Q_{rit} - \sum_{r \in P} T_{rit} \leq C_i \quad \forall i \in \mathcal{H}^+, t \in \mathcal{T} \qquad (14)$$

$$\sum_{r \in P} I_{rit} \leq C_i \quad \forall i \in \mathcal{H}, t \in \mathcal{T} \qquad (15)$$

$$x_{ijt} \epsilon \{0, 1\} \quad \forall i, j \in \mathcal{H}^+, i \neq j, t \in \mathcal{T} \qquad (16)$$

$$Q_{rit}, I_{rit}, q_{rijt}, SU_{urit}, T_{rit} \geq 0 \quad \forall i, j \in \mathcal{H}^+, i \neq j, r, u \in \mathcal{P}, t \in \mathcal{T} \qquad (17)$$

The objective function (1) minimizes the total cost (costs of transportation, inventory holding, backorder, substitution, and transshipment penalty). Constraints (2) assure that each hospital is visited at most once during each period. Constraints (3) guarantee that the vehicle moves to the next hospital after serving the current one. Constraints (4) delete subtours. Constraints (5) ensure that the time to complete each tour does not exceed working hours. Also, during each period, the number of tours cannot be superior to the number of vehicles (as a vehicle completes maximum a tour during each period) (6). Constraints (7) determine the quantities delivered at each hospital and quantities transshipped. Constraints (8) make sure the vehicle is empty when returning to the depot. Constraints (9) are vehicle capacity constraints. Constraints (10) determine the maximum quantities of products that can be transshipped. Constraints (11) and (12) are inventory balancing constraints at the hospitals. Constraints (13) are inventory balancing constraints at the depot. Constraints (14) are capacity constraints for each hospital. Constraints (14) are capacity constraints for each time period. Constraints (16) and (17) define the domain of the variables.

3   Computational Results

The mathematical model has been coded with CPLEX and implemented on a computer with Windows XP, 2,9 GHz Intel Core i5 and 8 Go RAM. The models are run with an optimality gap of 2%.

3.1   Data Set

The data set has been constructed following a similar approach to [9], mixing both real data and generated data. We consider hospitals located in the South part of Belgium. The number of hospitals considered for the computational experiment varies between 5 and 15. The distances between hospitals, $dist_{ij}$ are estimated via a GIS software. There are 4 vehicles with the same capacity. The planning horizon is 7 days, considering 8 products, each one representing a blood type. Table 2 presents the percentages per product in the Belgian population.

Table 2. Blood type distribution per product r in the Belgian population, e_r

Product	O^+	O^-	A^+	A^-	B^+	B^-	AB^+	AB^-
%	36%	6%	37%	7%	9%	1%	3%	1%

- The demand D_{irt} is randomly generated in an interval $[a * e_r * L_i, b * e_r * L_i]$ where L_i is the number of beds in the hospital i and e_r is the blood type distribution per product r in the Belgian.
- The quantity of products r, available at time t, at the blood bank, Z_{rt}, is uniformly generated in the interval $\left[c * e_r * \sum_i L_i, d * e_r * \sum_i L_i \right]$.

Different demand scenarios over the time horizon are considered and analyzed by varying the values of a, b and c, d. In this paper, we focus on a scenario where the demand is high compared to the blood supply, thus requiring the use of transshipment and mismatching to satisfy the demand of blood products. The values are set to $a = 20$, $b = 30$ and $c = 30$, $d = 35$.

- The initial inventory at each hospital, I_{ri0}, is randomly generated in the interval $[0,..,50]$.
- The maximum working time during period t, τ_t, is fixed at 10 h/day.
- The capacity of each vehicle, cap, is fixed at a total of 5000 products.
- The outdating rate, θ_{ri}, is 1%.
- The holding cost, CST_{ri}, is fixed at 1 €/product, the transportation cost, $CTRAV$, at 0.5 €/KM, and the transshipment penalty cost, CT_{ri}, at 1.5 €/product.
- The backorder cost, CR_{ri}, is set at 5 €/product and the substitution cost, CS_{ru}, at 2 €/product.

3.2 Sensitivity Analysis

A sensitivity analysis is conducted on some key parameters of the objective function with the aim of testing their influence on the elements under study: mismatching cost, transshipment penalty and backorder cost.

The holding cost is an important element of an inventory management model. One would expect that if the holding cost increases, hospitals will use mismatching and transshipment to keep inventory as low as possible.

The holding cost has an impact on mismatching; when the holding cost increases, hospitals use more mismatching to satisfy the demand (chart on the left in Fig. 1) and avoid shortages. Obviously, if the holding cost is superior to the mismatching cost, there is more mismatching.

The quantities transshipped are in comparison very limited. Transshipment is used to satisfy the demand and avoid shortage in complement of mismatching when transshipment penalty is inferior to holding cost.

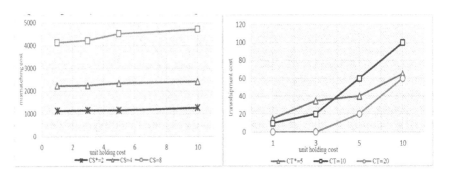

Fig. 1. Impact of holding cost on transshipment and mismatching (CT: unit transshipment penalty and CS: unit mismatching cost)

The impact of transportation cost on mismatching is very limited (chart on the left in Fig. 2). When transportation cost increases, the number of units mismatched slightly increases. When transshipment penalty is high (20€), there is no transshipment, whatever the transportation cost. Transshipment penalty is adding up to the cost of transportation and thus hospitals will try to minimize distribution costs as much as possible to satisfy the demand. Similar results where put forward by [3].

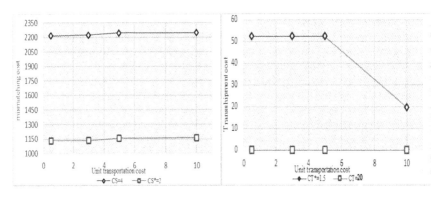

Fig. 2. Impact of unit transportation cost on transshipment and mismatching (CT: unit transshipment penalty and CS: unit mismatching cost)

Interestingly, the transshipment penalty has little impact on the quantities backordered. There is however a clear link between an increase in mismatching cost and the number of items that are backordered (chart on the right in Fig. 3). Interestingly, the 2 lines representing the total backorder costs are nearly superimposed meaning that there is nearly a direct relation between mismatching and backorder. If the mismatching cost doubles, the number of backorders doubled; this relation remains stable when the backorder cost increases.

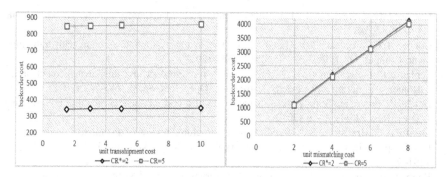

Fig. 3. Impact of transshipment and mismatching on backorder cost (CR: backorder cost)

In the computational experiments led, at an equivalent cost per unit, mismatching/ substitution is preferred to transshipment to satisfy the demand and avoid backorders. This will increase the demand for products with the highest mismatching rate (blood product type O⁻ can be a substitute for any product demand). This also raises the question of how to properly estimate substitution and transshipment unit cost in order to avoid bias in the derived inventory and routing policy. As blood products are vital, it pleads in favor of a multi-objective approach allowing the decision maker to give priority to the components of the objective function.

4 Conclusion and Perspectives

In this paper, we studied the IPR with transshipment and substitution for multiple products in a capacity constrained environment. Due to the complexity of the problem, a decomposition-based heuristic was developed; this heuristic solved the problem in 3 phases, based on the complexity induced by the characteristics of the problem: the routing problem, the classical IRP and then the transshipment and substitution. The focus of this paper is on the sensitivity analysis led on the key components of the objective function of the IRP. This study put forward that mismatching is preferred to transshipment to satisfy the demand and avoid backorder. Mismatching and backorder quantities are also directly linked.

Our future work is on a multi-objective approach to solve the problem under study and give different priorities to the components of the objective function.

Also, currently the outdating of the products is considered through an outdating rate applied to the products on inventory at the hospitals. The age of the products will be included.

References

1. Disney, S.M., Towill, D.R.: The effect of vendor managed inventory (VMI) dynamics on the Bullwhip Effect in supply chains. Int. J. Prod. Econ. **85**(2), 199–215 (2003)

2. Coelho, L.C., Cordeau, J.-F., Laporte, G.: Thirty years of inventory routing. Transp. Sci. **48** (1), 1–19 (2014)

3. Coelho, L.C., Cordeau, J.-F., Laporte, G.: The inventory-routing problem with transshipment. Comput. Oper. Res. **39**(11), 2537–2548 (2012)

4. Schlapp, J., Fleischmann, M.: Technical note—multiproduct inventory management under customer substitution and capacity restrictions. Oper. Res. **66**(3), 740–747 (2018)

5. Beliën, J., Forcé, H.: Supply chain management of blood products: a literature review. Eur. J. Oper. Res. **217**(1), 1–16 (2012)

6. Osorio, A.F., Brailsford, S.C., Smith, H.K.: A structured review of quantitative models in the blood supply chain: a taxonomic framework for decision-making. Int. J. Prod. Res. **53**(24), 7191–7212 (2015)

7. Pirabán, A., Guerrero, W.J., Labadie, N.: Survey on blood supply chain management: models and methods. Comput. Oper. Res. **112**, 104756 (2019)

8. Hssini, I., Meskens, N., Riane, F.: Optimisation du stockage des produits sanguins labiles: revue et analyse de la littérature. Génie industriel et productique **2**(Numéro 1), 22 (2019). https://doi.org/10.21494/ISTE.OP.2019.0421

9. Jafarkhan, F., Yaghoubi, S.: An efficient solution method for the flexible and robust inventory-routing of red blood cells. Comput. Ind. Eng. **117**, 191–206 (2018)

10. Zahiri, B., et al.: A multi-stage stochastic programming approach for blood supply chain planning. Comput. Ind. Eng. **122**, 1–14 (2018)

11. Bashiri, M., Ghasemi, E.: A selective covering-inventory- routing problem to the location of bloodmobile to supply stochastic demand of blood. Int. J. Ind. Eng. Prod. Res. **29**(2), 147–158 (2018)

12. Eskandari-Khanghahi, M., et al.: Designing and optimizing a sustainable supply chain network for a blood platelet bank under uncertainty. Eng. Appl. Artif. Intell. **71**, 236–250 (2018)

13. Hemmelmayr, V., et al.: Vendor managed inventory for environments with stochastic product usage. Eur. J. Oper. Res. **202**(3), 686–695 (2010)

14. Hemmelmayr, V., et al.: Delivery strategies for blood products supplies. OR Spectrum **31**(4), 707–725 (2009)

15. Hendalianpour, A.: Mathematical modeling for integrating production-routing-inventory perishable goods: a case study of blood products in Iranian Hospitals. In: Freitag, M., Kotzab, H., Pannek, J. (eds.) LDIC 2018. LNL, pp. 125–136. Springer, Cham (2018). https://doi.org/10.1007/978-3-319-74225-0_16

16. Kazemi, S.M., et al.: Blood inventory-routing problem under uncertainty. J. Intell. Fuzzy Syst. **32**(1), 467–481 (2017)

17. Kochan, C.G., Kulkarni, S.S., Nowicki, D.R.: Efficient inventorying and distribution of blood product during disasters. In: Zobel, C.W., Altay, N., Haselkorn, M.P. (eds.) Advances in Managing Humanitarian Operations. ISORMS, pp. 185–204. Springer, Cham (2016). https://doi.org/10.1007/978-3-319-24418-1_9

18. Federgruen, A., Prastacos, G., Zipkin, P.H.: An allocation and distribution model for perishable products. Oper. Res. **34**(1), 75–82 (1986)

Improvement of Design and Operation
of Manufacturing Systems

Improving Manufacturing System Design by Instantiation of the Integrated Product, Process and Manufacturing System Development Reference Framework

José Ramírez$^{(\boxtimes)}$ and Arturo Molina

Tecnologico de Monterrey, 14380 Mexico City, Mexico
a00995924@itesm.mx, armolina@tec.mx

Abstract. With Industry 4.0 and the changing dynamics of markets, assisting in designing, modifying, or improving manufacturing systems at different scales becomes necessary, both in large manufacturers and SMEs. Enterprise modelling architectures support the specific description of various layers to assist in the product lifecycle development by reusing general models that can be tailored to particular scenarios through instantiation processes. This work improves the development of manufacturing systems through partial and particular instantiated models based on the Integrated Product, Process and Manufacturing System Development reference framework. Furthermore, this model benefits from the characterization of different industrial sectors to collect tools and activities to avoid developing manufacturing systems anew. In this way, the proposed solution is to create partial models to assist in the design of different manufacturing scenarios: (i) product transfer, (ii) technology transfer and (ii) manufacturing system design. Case studies are instantiated to prove the effectiveness of this framework, in which the particular project activities are developed, and finally, the results assessed by qualitative and quantitative parameters to allow performance measurement.

Keywords: Industry 4.0 · Enterprise engineering · Manufacturing system modelling · Reference model · Instantiation

1 Introduction

Manufacturing capabilities have always depended on available technology [1]. The evolution of electronics and computational systems allowed greater control and precision in transformation processes, as well as faster and more continuous production of products demanded by society [2]. Specific and coordinated activities are required to optimise resources as market behaviour pushes preferences towards differentiated and personalised products to meet particular consumer needs [3]. Industry must be able to react to changes quickly and cost-effectively to survive in this new manufacturing environment, thus, creating new challenges for the construction and management of manufacturing systems (MS) [4]. MS require strategic and multidisciplinary planning that design methodologies must assist. It is essential to emphasise the structured

A. Dolgui et al. (Eds.): APMS 2021, IFIP AICT 634, pp. 99–107, 2021.
https://doi.org/10.1007/978-3-030-85914-5_11

creation of these systems as that is where most companies fail in a given time, either due to poor planning or incorrect management of available resources, as considerable investments are required for the creation of a manufacturing plant. It becomes imperative to improve MS development by gathering tools and structuring design activities to be used across different industrial sectors to streamline the processes of creation, construction and evaluation of these complex organisations. Acquiring the necessary strategic skills represent a challenge that many manufacturing companies are facing for speeding up the production system design and optimisation and some appropriate tools and models must be provided that are easily adapted to the needs and unique characteristics of some enterprises. Section 2 is a brief summary of the IPPMD, its roots on enterprise engineering and how it is used to develop the product lifecycle. Section 3 centres on the instantiation for different manufacturing system designs, the workflow of the methodology from decision diagrams to instantiation mappings. Furthermore, Sect. 4 synthesizes three case studies that elaborate on the development of the proposal to three different design scenarios. Lastly, in Sect. 5, the conclusions and future work of this article are reported.

2   IPPMD to Design Integrated Manufacturing Systems

Enterprise Architecture frameworks have been created to allow the structured creation of enterprises to deploy systematic engineering practices. The ISO-19439 standard provides a unified concept for enterprise engineering activities that enable the interoperability of various modelling architectures [5]. However, these heavyweight frameworks create a problem increasing the complexity of its adoption among diverse industry sectors. Then, fully customization for a given scenario, utilizing instantiation, allows to inherit the main characteristics and structures of a core model to be adapted to specific characteristics in different levels: (i) general, (ii) partial and (iii) particular. General models gather an extensive set of knowledge that is useful to design any enterprise from different viewpoints. Then, partial models gather common characteristics for a given context with a reusable set of characteristics to develop solutions in certain engineering activities. The Integrated Product, Process and Manufacturing System Development (IPPMD), is a lightweight framework that arises from Enterprise Engineering standards and allows straightforward creation of particular instances to assist in the development of the product lifecycle in different sized enterprises operating in a diversity of productive sectors [6–8]. IPPMD has been successfully implemented in several environments, and there is extensive literature that delves into the use of the methodology [9–12]. The IPPMD consists of three entities that constitute the product lifecycle: (i) product design, (ii) process selection and (iii) manufacturing system development [13]. The third entity supports the design and development of MS with different characteristics, diverse progress stages and operating under specific business scopes to optimise resources, detect opportunity areas and gain competitive advantage. To this extent, instantiation advantage is gained by the integration of different tools guided by decision workflows to include a specific set of engineering activities focused on improving: (i) strategic planning, (ii) resource management, and (iii) outcome validation.

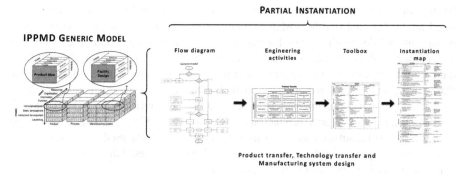

Fig. 1. Methodology to generate partial instances of the IPPMD general model for manufacturing system design.

3 Manufacturing System Development Instantiation

IPPMD instantiation for manufacturing system development is divided into three categories or subentities that guide the path of development of an MS according to the following characteristics: (i) product transfer when an MS already exists, and a new product is meant to be produced using existing processes in the facilities; (ii) technology transfer when an MS already exists, and a new product is to be manufactured, but new processes must be installed at the plant; and (iii) MS design, when there is the need to create a plant from scratch to allocate the production of a new product.

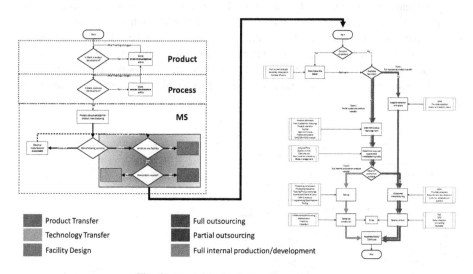

Fig. 2. Partial instantiation flow diagrams

In this way, the methodology elaborates in the development of partial instantiations for each one of the three subentities of the MS development following the structure:

(i) flow diagrams, (ii) engineering activities, (iii) toolbox and (iv) instantiation maps (see Fig. 1). The first step for instantiation consists of detecting current manufacturing conditions and developing plans for the company. Once product and process entities are completed, documentation is transferred to MS development, where detailed conditions for every case should determine the best route of action aided by decision flow diagrams. Then, each subentity is classified into the following scenarios or types, representing how production will be organised: (i) full outsourcing, (ii) partial outsourcing and (iii) full internal production/development (see Fig. 2). These variations go according to the manufacturing company's strategy to create the product, the conditions under which it operates and its core values to understand in detail the series of activities that will be carried out during the instantiation.

The second step consists of structuring engineering activities in four stages that will depend heavily on the previous route selection (see Fig. 3a). Each stage is organized in a progressive basis cycle of (i) analysis where data is gathered, (ii) synthesis where vital information is filtered and (iii) evaluation to assess if tollgates are appropriately met. If the results are satisfactory, the project can move to the next stage until completion. Nevertheless, constant iteration and concurrency among stages are needed to include feedback from the system to improve previously designated objectives. This characteristic allows the model to go back and forth between the different points of the instantiated engineering activities.

The toolbox specification is the third essential step of the methodology, allowing each engineering activity to be performed. It is a collection of design, administrative and computer tools that together speed up the progress of activities. The suggested toolbox is a tiny subset of all possible and available existing solutions in the manufacturing industry. Figure 3b, for instance, displays a set of tools applicable to each engineering activity. The toolset availability and definition will depend on the application area and the expertise of the company, and that can be added to the related activity, as some enterprises have their preferred or custom toolset. Although activities are bound to a toolset for structuring reasons, they are not restricted to each paired activity; then, they can be used whether they are available and could prove results in other stages.

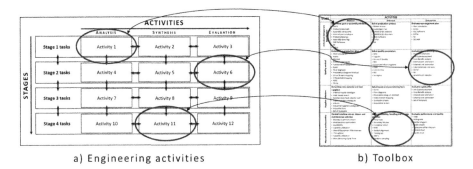

a) Engineering activities   b) Toolbox

Fig. 3. Partial instantiation engineering activities and toolbox

In order to consolidate engineering activities and toolboxes, maps allow instances of development for any scenario to generate the MS design variant in the final step. The instantiation map lists the series of activities explored in much greater detail and links the tools and tollgates expected by each phase of work. Tollgates are the documentation that allows access to the subsequent activities as they combine the series of data and details that will serve as a starting point to the following stages. The different scenarios ought to have the necessary activities to continue the MS development, but tollgates will indicate whether the activity has been successfully completed or if it is required to elaborate on the stage or the activity. When needed, multiple iterations of stages are necessary to refine the workflow. All in all, the partial instantiation derived following the methodology can be used in a specific design that will generate a particular instantiation ad hoc to the development process.

4   Case Studies

In order to test the development potential and advantage of using MS design using IPPMD, partial models were further instantiated to carry out three case studies to assess planning, resource management, and validation of the methodology. Each case study addressed one of the manufacturing criteria with a defined expected outcome (see Fig. 4).

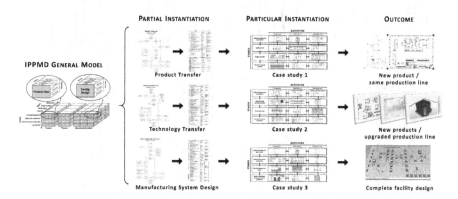

Fig. 4. IPPMD particular instantiations applied in three case studies

4.1   Product Transfer

An enterprise specialized in removing processes has a query to produce a thousand pieces per month of a new component that requires precise custom cutting and some counterbored holes. A product transfer case is detected with flow diagrams where just revamping existing processes is necessary to achieve new production goals. As all the manufacturing activities are being carried out within the facility, it was a whole internal production route. Following the partial instantiated model (see Fig. 5), it was possible to successfully deploy the production of the new piece by adapting current milling machines to produce the needed amount of production per month.

PROJECT DESIGN VISION ASSESSMENT (columns: Results, Effects, Impacts, Benefits)

STAGE	ACTIVITIES	TOOLS	TOLLGATES	RESULTS	EFFECTS	IMPACTS	BENEFITS
1 — Individual Component Specification	**Analysis: Determine part or assembly attributes** • Decompose design, Get datasheets of the components, Determine material, Determine shape and geometry, Determine dimensions **Synthesis: Select production process** • Search the internal catalogue for similar products, Group components or subprocess (from raw to finish), parts matching current machine tools, Map required process and **Evaluation: Evaluate rearrangement plan** • Determine if machine capabilities suit required characteristics of volume, tolerances and finish, Determine if processing times match available machinery	• Product Datasheet • Product drawings • PRIMA Matrix • Custompart.net • Plant simulation	• Documentation about part and assembly key characteristics and candidate processes • Documentation about machine tool selection along tools, jigs and fixtures needed • Report of technological capacity and projected physical rearrangement to manufacture the new part or assembly	• Part and assembly key characteristics and candidate processes • More flexibility in the production line tool selection and • Increased knowledge and experience	**Business process** • Strategic planning **Machinery and equipment** **Human capital**	**Performance indicators** • Less raw material and parts expenses • increased running machine hours • Less total machine set-ups • Higher % of processing hours	**Strategy** • New product sales • Reduced time for developing new products • Economic feasibility • Order fulfilment • Better process costs • Productivity increase • Quality assurance **Economic** • Higher productivity • Higher sales • Higher value-added for invested capital • New investment feasibility
2 — Quality control	**Analysis: Evaluate manufacturing costs** • Evaluate processing costs, Calculate energy consumption, Calculate labour costs **Synthesis: Select quality parameters** • Define internal quality indicators according to volume, scrap and production schedules **Evaluation: Determine a production plan** • Determine a production programme including volume and machine availability	• Part Cost Estimator • Internal cost estimation • Internal quality policies • Value Stream Mapping	• Report of cost analysis • Documentation on performance indicators and expected quality • Report with volume, processing times, routes and manufacturing supplies needed.	• Performance and quality indicators hand by hand with production data cost analysis reports	**Organisation structure** • Better procedures and practices • Top-notch manufacturing techniques	**Performance indicators** • On-time supplies • Less WIP inventory • Better manufacturing lead time	
3 — Supplier selection	**Analysis: Determine raw material and tool suppliers** • Search for suppliers in the internal database, Search for internal and external suppliers, Candidate suppliers for internal production route, Candidate a contingency supply route **Synthesis: Select query and provisioning basis** • Request quotations, Determine a provision programming, Determine delivery conditions **Evaluation: Evaluate supply offer** • Evaluate prices • Evaluate candidates according to previous experience and ratings	• Internal supply catalogue • Public supplier catalogues • Alibaba • Quotation sheets • Acquisition orders • Internal cost estimation • External cost estimation • Bill of Materials	• Report with supply candidates for internal and external production • Quotation reports and detailed information about suppliers provisioning scheme • Rating documentation and supply contracts	• Reports and supply candidates for internal and external production • Quotation, ratings and contracts	**Human capital** • Communication • Decision making • Best practices	**Performance indicators** • On-time deliveries • increase gross profit margin • Reduced manufacturing services	
4 — Manufacturing and assembly	**Analysis: Control machine set-up, labour and maintenance activities** • Set up machine programming, Set up processing sequences, Set up flow lines, Set up buffers and handling equipment, Implement labour shifts, Gather production data **Synthesis: Control assembly, handling and storage activities** • Complete assembly of components and subcomponents, Handle finished parts, Store finished parts, Gather production data **Evaluation: Evaluate performance and quality** • Evaluate production data • Compare performance to expected values	• Discrete Event Simulation • Discrete Event Simulation • Discrete Event Simulation	• Production process documentation • Assemblies and storage documentation • Report on actual vs expected performance and quality	• Process, assemblies and storage documentation • Actual vs expected performance assessment	**Business process** • Order fulfilment	**Performance indicators** • On-time deliveries • Fewer downtimes • Reduced scrap and rejection rate	

Fig. 5. Product transfer particular instantiation map

Engineering activities such as evaluate a rearrangement plan, determine a production schedule, quality and costs analysis, along with a correct supplier selection, among others, were used concurrently and iteratively in order to fulfil the production objectives. Furthermore, it allowed to reuse current equipment and apply the already mastered processing capabilities. Some tools used included: datasheets specs, PRIMA matrix, Value Stream Mapping (VSM), Cost estimators, suppliers catalogues and Discrete Event Simulation (DES). The latter was used to model production parameters to assess feasibility for the project as only 10% of the facility's capacity was available. Different scenarios forecasting allowed to reduce bottlenecks to accommodate new production requirements within the capacity of the plant. Project design vision assessment indicated increased strategic planning, more flexibility in the production line, increased knowledge and expertise, and better order fulfilment. It also impacted performance indicators such as increased running machine-hours, better manufacturing lead time, increased gross profit margin and reduced scrap and rejection rate. At the same time, positive strategic benefits went from and increased productivity to new product sales, to say a few.

4.2   Technology Transfer

An SME specialising in removing processes was asked to produce a thousand pieces per month of three unique components. One required turning (available in the facility), the other required milling (also available), but the third one was based on plastic extrusion, a process not available so far. Flow diagram assessment detected a technology transfer case. The company decided that it was a unique opportunity to invest in some industrial 3D printing machines as some of their clients were requesting this service. However, production scenario valuation revealed that to achieve the objectives to produce the three new components partial outsourcing route was necessary. Engineering activities included determining part attributes, process selection, determining raw material, machine and tools suppliers, equipment routing and flowlines design, production scheduling and labour evaluation, saying a few. Particular instantiation allowed reusing current equipment while adding a new production line. Some tools used during the development included: OPITZ, CAD/CAM, PRIMA Matrix, cost estimators, bill of materials, process time charts, VSM, and DES. In this case, simulation modelling was used to assess the impact of installing the new production line, the integration of the outsourced parts in the assembly line, process availability times and whether it was justifiable to hire new personnel; thus, forecasting scenarios was necessary to optimise resources in the plant and assist decision making. After project vision assessment, some remarkable effects on the business processes, human and technological capital, and organisation structure were new process development, adapting top-notch manufacturing techniques, adapting to new production lines, and personnel experience gathering. There was also a high impact and improvement in performance indicators such as on-time supplies, better communication and decision making, optimised processes and increased flexibility in the production line. Last but not least, higher sales and higher value-added for invested capital were some of the reported economic benefits, while new product sales and reduced time for developing new products boosted the strategic advantage.

4.3   Manufacturing Facility Design

This case is about a Mexican manufacturing project focusing on the creation of versatile small-scale CNC machines. So far, the business strategy had been to outsource all manufacturing while engineering centres on the design and assembly of components. However, they had become interested in mounting a small facility for prototyping and testing small batches of their recently designed extrusion module. It included a whole set of processes beneficial for the scope of the project. After following flow diagrams, it became evident that the construction of the entire manufacturing facility could not be affordable due to the expenses of buying equipment. This fact led to a hybrid case where a facility was mounted, and likewise, outsourcing manufacturing was needed due to strategic reasons. Engineering activities focused on two branches. The first three stages allowed to structure the project, mainly relying upon information gathering and projections, then little investment was necessary. The fourth stage is all about plant construction and production ramp-up. As higher investments are necessary, then previous stages had to be thoroughly validated to measure the impact of project tollgates per stage. The toolbox was extensive and included most of the tools used in the other cases. In this regard, DES was a milestone and succeeded in developing the digital model of all the stages while forecasting different scenarios to suit the production target. Computations allowed to determine the best equipment arrangement, labour optimization and machinery expected performance to fulfil the production. The instantiation outcome was the complete facility design (physical and virtual) to master the required processing capabilities of the project and the integration of outsourcing production in the assembly lines. Some remarkable business, human and technological effects using design vision were: projection of capabilities of the production line, better selection of equipment, strategic planning and optimised digital models. At the same time, positive performance indicators included less material and part expenses, less total machine set-ups, on-time supplies, reduced WIP inventory and reduced scrap and rejection rate. At the end of the day, new product sales and new investment feasibility were some strategic benefits, while better process costs, quality assurance and higher value-added for invested capital were some of the economic advantages.

5   Conclusions

IPPMD lightweight framework can be shaped to create partial instantiations that can be used to create particular case studies in different industrial environments. Entities and subentities allow for better classification of manufacturing systems according to the different characteristics, diverse development stages and specific business scopes to set the roadmap and improve strategic planning and resource management. Tollgates deliver qualitative and quantitative parameters to allow performance measurement during the design for outcome validation. Some of the most critical metrics are obtained from DES in the toolbox. It allowed for graphical and numerical interpretation of the complex dynamics and interactions when designing an MS. This powerful tool can forecast different scenarios and design model optimization. Programming the parameters obtained during process design and administrative data using different mathematical approaches expands understanding and sets real-life expectations. Thus, decision making is improved, and better results can be obtained with available resources.

Since necessities from large enterprises are very different to those from SMEs, it would be essential to future-proof the methodology by improving particular instantiations to accommodate a wider variety of manufacturing systems requirements. This strategy will include revising current engineering activities, a more extensive catalogue of the toolboxes and improved tollgates assessment. Furthermore, the inclusion of sensing, smart and sustainable indexes could directly align with current Industry 4.0 modelling trends to cope with increasingly rigid government regulations to include sustainable features spanning the entire product lifecycle.

References

1. Allen, R.C.: The British Industrial Revolution in Global Perspective. Cambridge University Press, New York (2009).
2. Schwab, K.: The fourth industrial revolution. Currency (2017)
3. Sousa, R., da Silveira, G.J.C.: The relationship between servitization and product customization strategies. Int. J. Oper. Prod. Manag. (2019)
4. Chryssolouris, G.: Manufacturing Systems: Theory and Practice. Springer, New York (2013). https://doi.org/10.1007/978-1-4757-2213-4
5. Li, Q., Chan, I., Tang, Q., Wei, H., Yudi, P.: Rethinking of framework and constructs of enterprise architecture and enterprise modelling standardized by ISO 15704, 19439 and 19440. In: Debruyne, C., Panetto, H., Weichhart, G., Bollen, P., Ciuciu, I., Vidal, M.-E., Meersman, R. (eds.) OTM 2017. LNCS, vol. 10697, pp. 46–55. Springer, Cham (2018). https://doi.org/10.1007/978-3-319-73805-5_5
6. Molina, A., Carrasco, R.: The use of GERAM to support SMEs development in Mexico. In: Bernus, P., Nemes, L., Schmidt, G. (eds.) Handbook on Enterprise Architecture. Springer, Heidelberg (2003). https://doi.org/10.1007/978-3-540-24744-9_22
7. Bernus, P., Noran, O., Molina, A.: Enterprise architecture: twenty years of the GERAM framework. Annu. Rev. Control (2015). https://doi.org/10.1016/j.arcontrol.2015.03.008
8. Kamio, Y.: globeman21: enterprise integration for global manufacturing for the 21st century. IFAC Proc. Vol. (1998). https://doi.org/10.1016/s1474-6670(17)40608-2
9. Mauricio-Moreno, H., Miranda, J., Chavarria, D., Ramirez-Cadena, M., Molina, A.: Design S3-RF (Sustainable x Smart x Sensing - Reference Framework) for the future manufacturing enterprise. IFAC-PapersOnLine $28(3)$, 58–63 (2015). https://doi.org/10.1016/j.ifacol.2015.06.058
10. Miranda, J., Pérez-Rodríguez, R., Borja, V., Wright, P.K., Molina, A.: Integrated product, process and manufacturing system development reference model to develop cyber-physical production systems-the sensing, smart and sustainable microfactory case Study. IFAC-PapersOnLine (2017). https://doi.org/10.1016/j.ifacol.2017.08.2006
11. Cortes, D., et al.: Integrated Product, Process and Manufacturing System Development (2018). https://doi.org/10.1109/ICE.2018.8436275
12. Cortés, D., Ramírez, J., Chavarría-Barrientos, D., Miranda, J., Molina, A.: Integrated product, process and manufacturing system development reference model: research summer as case study (2018). https://doi.org/10.18687/LACCEI2018.1.1.278
13. Molina, A., Ponce, P., Miranda, J., Cortés, D.: Enabling Systems for Intelligent Manufacturing in Industry 4.0. Springer, Cham (2021). https://doi.org/10.1007/978-3-030-65547-1

A Formal Skill Model Facilitating the Design and Operation of Flexible Assembly Workstations

Lauren Van De Ginste[1,2](✉) [iD], Alexander De Cock[3], Axl Van Alboom[1,2],
Yogang Singh[1,2], El-Houssaine Aghezzaf[1,2], and Johannes Cottyn[1,2]

[1] Department of Industrial Systems Engineering and Product Design, Ghent
University, Technologiepark 46, 9052 Gent-Zwijnaarde, Belgium
Lauren.VanDeGinste@UGent.be
[2] Industrial Systems Engineering (ISyE), Flanders Make vzw, 8500 Kortrijk, Belgium
[3] CodesignS, Flanders Make vzw, 3920 Lommel, Belgium
https://www.UGent.be, https://www.FlandersMake.be

Abstract. In the Industry 4.0 area, there is an increasing demand for
highly customized products in small batch sizes. Final assembly operations are frequently targeted to embed flexibility and compensate for the
growing manufacturing uncertainties. Therefore, an adequately designed
and operated flexible assembly workstation is crucial. Converting the
flexibility needs into design and operational decisions requires versatile formal models delivering generic descriptions of needs and capacities. Skills form the central connector between products, processes and
resources. Here, a skill-centered model for describing resource activities,
the related production needs and flexibility impacts is introduced. The
model fits both plug and produce and design optimization settings and
goes beyond current skill-based modelling by offering a framework which,
by design, does not limit the applications and easily adapts to the desired
level of detail. One key strength is its ability to combine abstract and
executable skills. Next to the product-action skills, also assistive skills
related to operator support, parts storing, ergonomics etc. can be easily
modelled. The use of the model is illustrated by an example based on an
industrial use case from Flemish industry.

Keywords: Assembly workstation flexibility · Skill-based
engineering · Resource modelling

1 Introduction

In today's highly competitive environments, manufacturing deals with a lot of
challenges. One of them is increasing flexibility while keeping cost low and quality high. Final assembly operations are frequently targeted to embed flexibility
and compensate for the increased manufacturing uncertainties and customization [15]. The individual resources and configurations in an assembly workstation

© IFIP International Federation for Information Processing 2021
Published by Springer Nature Switzerland AG 2021
A. Dolgui et al. (Eds.): APMS 2021, IFIP AICT 634, pp. 108–116, 2021.
https://doi.org/10.1007/978-3-030-85914-5_12

setting directly impact the overall plant-level flexibility through base flexibility dimensions relating to the key components of a manufacturing company (personnel, equipment and material) [17]. Also, not only directly value-adding resources have a high impact, but also resources related to operator support, part storing, ergonomics etc. have an not to be neglected effect.

In [9] it is recognised that a common formal capability-based resource model is needed to allow rapid system design and reconfiguration decisions in heterogeneous multi-vendor production environments. This model should allow a well thought-out design, objective resource selection and further reasoning during operations and reconfigurations [5]. A lot of research in manufacturing is focused on the development of models to describe products with information as design, geometry and required processes. A standardized and universal applicable model for resources producing or assembling these products is frequently neglected and application- or vendor-specific [18]. In [7] the potential and importance of formal ontologies to capture and share assembly knowledge is illustrated. They support collaboration across the assembly design and process planning domains. Because skills are identified as a connector between products, processes and resources, the here-introduced model could form a building-block between product requirements, assembly sequences, resources, operations and their impact on flexibility in an assembly knowledge store [1].

The paper is organised as follows. Section 2 describes the current state-of-art in skill-based assembly resource modelling. Section 3 introduces the formal skill model and illustrates it's use and key strengths with some clarifying examples. Finally, conclusions and further research directions are found in Sect. 4.

2   State-of-Art

Several research projects have recently looked into skill- or capability-based modelling in the manufacturing and assembly domain. Before further elaborating on the current state-of-the-art (Sect. 2.2), the different viewpoints on the meaning and use of the term 'skill' versus 'capability' are highlighted (Sect. 2.1).

2.1   Capabilities Versus Skills

It is recognised in literature that, for manufacturing and assembly, resources can be best described by their skills or capabilities which mimic their capacities and ability to complete tasks [11]. Resources in manufacturing are seen quite broad and can be any physical entity, representing hardware and software, that is involved by the execution of a process [5]. This includes equipment, operators, parts, sub-assemblies etc.

The term 'capability' was first used in literature together with the term 'competence' to describe high-level human qualifications in manufacturing. However today it is also frequently used in more general formal models for the manufacturing domain [11]. A capability is in this context defined by [6] as "the inherent ability of the manufacturing system to perform change in the properties of a material in order to produce tangible products". According to [8] this definition falls short on not including assembly operations and those capabilities which don't change the properties of the product but are required during production. Capabilities however remain closely related to adding value to products [6].

The term 'skill' is sometimes used interchangeably with 'capability' but is mostly more focused on executable machine functionalities working bottom up [8,11]. In [14] skills are identified in the robot programming context as "re-occuring actions that are needed to execute standard operation procedures". In [10] the term skill is specifically used for the superiority features of an operator defining it's worker performance in performing tasks. More broadly, skills are seen as a connector between products, processes and resources enriched with additional information [1,14]. A skill is also very broadly defined as "the potential of a manufacturing resource to achieve an effect within a domain [12]". A lot of overlap is found between both terms. Small connotation differences can be identified but no real consensus can be found in literature. Skills seem to be more frequently used on the lower execution level than capabilities, while capabilities rather start from value-adding activities.

The focus of the here-introduced model is broad and in fact spans both terms. Nevertheless, one term should be chosen. Because a more bottom-up approach is envisioned allowing higher levels of detail for execution activities (but at the same time also more abstract design activities), the term 'skill' will be used.

2.2 Skill-Based Modelling

When looking into the development of skill-based models, Kocher et al. [11] states that it is important to keep the model as general and open as possible to enable reuse and future extensions. Next to models solely focusing onto the skill- or competence-level of operators, two main categories of skill-based modelling approaches can be identified [10,11].

The first category are formal models such as ontologies to create skill structures that can be used as a shared vocabulary or for optimization and reasoning purposes. Most contributions start from the process or task that is translated into a required skill [3,4,9,14]. Järvenpää et al. [9] developed a model to support 'capability matchmaking' between product requirements and resource skills. Later on it is extended with 'executable capabilities' for task programming but without a direct link between both [16]. Hashemi-Petroodi et al. developed a three-step methodology to automatically reconfigure reconfigurable manufacturing systems (RMS) [4]. Feasible assembly plans are set-up using a skill-based comparison of the product requirements and RMS. The skill comparison is based on a semantic matching process. The assigned resources are only afterwards checked through a quantitative parameter analysis. Hoang et al. [5] proposed as one of the first a more product-oriented approach to limit modelling and communication effort during reasoning. In their model the skills of resources are represented as ranges of product property values. However, the efforts needed to deduce the important properties and keeping them updated is a disadvantage compared to the process-oriented approach. In [11] a formal model of machine skills that directly includes both a description of high-level and executable skills is presented. Their model is an alignment ontology, built upon different sub-ontologies based on industry standards. Because of the inter-linking between various sub-ontologies, modelling is complex and does not adapt quickly to the desired level of detail. In [13] equipment is uniformly identified via high level skills which can be matched with the product-specific manufacturing requirements embedded in the product's bill of processes. From these high-level descriptions, executable skills are derived and made available as services.

The second category focuses on the execution level including plug and pro-duce environments where skills are used to encapsulate machine functionalities for task-level programming [11]. In [1] a similar concept as in [13] is implemented, but more focused on task-oriented programming. Here, skill descriptions are used for the vendor-independent modelling of resources, processes and products. Their taxonomy is mainly built on 5 top-level skills which can be subdivided into more specific skills. Danny et al. [3] actively developed an openly accessible plug-and-produce system using AutomationML and OPC UA. The concept of skill recipes and skill requirements is used to execute the resource skills to fulfil the assem-bly requirements. Rovida et al. [14] focus on an even more narrow scope and specifically targets task level robot programming by providing robots with a set of movement primitives on the controller level and skills operating as standard operating procedures. The skills are implemented by the primitives which are mostly inferred through autonomous reasoning by the robot.

All aforementioned approaches differ in their level of granularity, implemen-tations, applications and modelling languages which makes it difficult to merge and reuse them. The only common ground between all above models is the uncoupling between products and resources via skills. However, none of them is application independent and easily adapts to the desired level of detail.

3   Formal Skill-Model

The proposed skill-centered model describes and links resource capacities to the related production needs via skills showing their impact on the 'world'. The model is meant to be versatile and can be used during both the design and exe-cution phase to suggest reconfigurations or other optimisations. It is perfectly suited for skill-based programming and scheduling of machine functionalities, but also for the matchmaking between tasks and resources including constraints. Fur-thermore it can link to operational data and serve as a base to analyse operations and asses the performance and robustness. It is meant as a core model which connects with different other models (resource model, skill condition model and task model) and allows for application specific extensions.

3.1   Conceptual Model

Figure 1 shows the conceptual skill-model. It is displayed using the Unified Mod-eling Language (UML) notation to deliver an abstract view on the high-level meta-model. This way, it easily shows the links between different aspects and

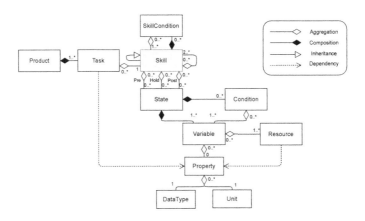

Fig. 1. Conceptual skill-model, represented in UML

aids for easy problem understanding, analysis and documentation [2]. Different software implementations are possible. Because of the high-level of interlinking, ontology based graph databases seem the best suited for large examples and data storage (Sect. 3.2).

Skills are the central element describing the applicable transitions between states. The model recognizes the four dimensional nature of the skill concept. Skills can be atomic or composed, process-independent or process-specific, product-independent or product-specific and even resource-independent or resource-specific [12]. First, it is easy to understand that skills can be decomposed into subskills until they cannot be decomposed any further. When this atomic point is reached, depends on the required level of granularity and is thus application specific. An example is the skill 'transport' that is composed of a 'pick' and 'place' skill. However, composition is also closely related to refinement, if different compositions are possible, a refinement is required. Refinements add detail to the skills based in the other 3 dimensions. The process dimension embeds more detail of the related process in the states. An example is when the skill 'connect' is specified into 'welding' or the even more specific 'arc-welding' skill. The same applies to the product and resource dimension, they both add more detail to the skill when becoming more product- or resource-dependent.

The concept of states is used to model the impact of an action on the world model. There can be different pre-, post- and hold-states with each it's variables and related conditions. Only the parameters actively used in the post state can be changed by the skill and define the end state. Other parameters can be tracked but will not change permanently because of the skill. In other words, skill states contain the subset of resource parameters with additional conditions important for describing the temporary and definite impact of the skill in the world model.

Specifically in this model, states are modelled by variables and conditions. The variables should always be linked to properties of resources in the world model. If a resource is not yet specified, the root object 'resource' is used. Variable conditions impose constraints on the variable, e.g. end state - position equal to end position. In contrast to variable conditions, skill conditions stay on the level of skills and lay links and constraints between skills. Skill conditions form a separate model and act as a blackbox within the skill model. Behaviour trees and other constraints related to assistive skills are modellable via skill conditions. By not limiting the number of refinements, the user can go as detailed as necessary. By leaving the interpretation of 'skills' open, different viewpoints can be embedded. The next section further clarifies the model with an example.

3.2   Example Application

The concepts of the model are illustrated based on an industrial use case from Flemish Industry. The assembly of a compressor serves as an example, more specifically the insertion of a rotor into the main housing is worked out. Figure 2 gives a detailed description of the skill 'insert', worked out towards operators and filled-in specifically for the compressor assembly.

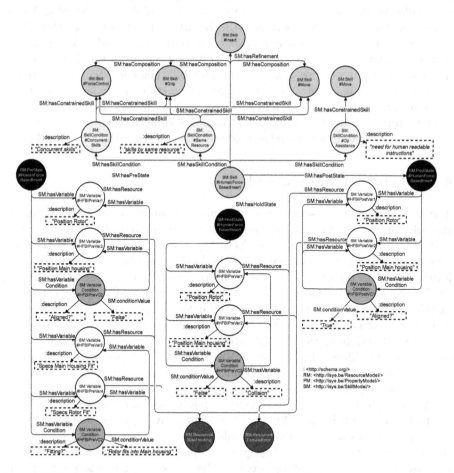

Fig. 2. Skill model example: executable operator insert applied on compressor assembly

During the pre-state the position of both objects that have to be inserted is important together with the shape. Do the objects fit? Are they insertable? The variables directly link to the parts that are manipulated during the insertion. After the skill has taken place, the positions should again be checked and the objects should be aligned. It can be seen that the shape of the objects is important to check if the insertion is possible, but the skill does obviously not change the shape. Therefore 'shape' is not embedded in the post-state. The hold state is used to prevent collisions between the parts during insertion. The model is that detailed that sensors and operator input could be linked to the model to follow up execution. At the same time, in depth information related to assistive skills is available. Because the insert is specified for operators a skill condition is added which imposes the need for a resource which instructs the operator e.g. pick-to-lights, smart glasses etc. Skill conditions can be used to add that kind of assistive skills, but skill conditions can also ask for resources which can store the parts, for tables etc. The skill conditions also impose that the sub-skills should be handled by the same executing resource and be available concurrently. A less refined model of the skill insert can also be added to all resources that have the capacity to insert. This way a process-, resource- and product-independent model will allow easy comparisons between different resources. Can I use a robot, or is an operator more appropriate? The states will then only highlight the more general variables and related conditions. No information on e.g. specific parts or assistive skills will be added. Note that the example is somewhat simplified to keep it printable. Additional states and variables could be added. Nevertheless, this example shows in a comprehensible way the key-strengths of the model.

4   Conclusion and Outlook

The design of flexible assembly workstations and optimisation of the execution thereof requires multidimensional and versatile formal models. Skills form the central factor in describing all manufacturing resources and easily link them to production requirements and product flows. In this contribution, a skill-centered formal model is presented which stands out by combining different concepts coming from both the design and execution point of view. The model combines high-level and executable skills and opens the door for assistive skills required to embed, not directly value-adding, peripheral equipment. The model should be further validated, however the applications seem broad and the model seems to easily adapt to different levels of granularity and detail. It is also not obligatory to fill in all details, which is an advantage in contrast to existing models to manage the complexity.

A major drawback of formal models remains however that they always in the first place result in an additional effort. They have to be created next to the real implementations. The strength should come from a broader knowledge store combining all info and facilitating optimisations and new designs in the future. Because of the decoupling of resources, products and processes via a central skill model, data should be more easily and consistently changeable and extendable.

This way experience and knowledge can be consolidated and will not be lost. Firstly, the model will be further validated via additional use cases from industry and adjusted where necessary.

In future work, the task, resource and skill condition model will also be further elaborated. Extra arrangements will be proposed for the definition and meaning of skills, this is key for a neat and well-ordered assembly knowledge store but is nowadays application specific. Nevertheless the formal model will remain the core which opens up compatibility with future plug-ins and to create a shared vocabulary links to standard terminology found in literature and recognized standards will be added.

References

1. Backhaus, J., Reinhart, G.: Digital description of products, processes and resources for task-oriented programming of assembly systems. J. Intell. Manuf. **28**(8), 1787–1800 (2015). https://doi.org/10.1007/s10845-015-1063-3
2. Ciccozzi, F., Malavolta, I., Selic, B.: Execution of UML models: a systematic review of research and practice. Softw. Syst. Model. **18**(3), 2313–2360 (2018). https://doi.org/10.1007/s10270-018-0675-4
3. Danny, P., Ferreira, P., Lohse, N., Guedes, M.: An AutomationML model for plug-and-produce assembly systems. In: Proceedings - 2017 IEEE 15th International Conference on Industrial Informatics, INDIN 2017, pp. 849–854 (2017). https://doi.org/10.1109/INDIN.2017.8104883
4. Hashemi-Petroodi, S.E., Gonnermann, C., Paul, M., Thevenin, S., Dolgui, A., Reinhart, G.: Decision support system for joint product design and reconfiguration of production systems. In: Ameri, F., Stecke, K.E., von Cieminski, G., Kiritsis, D. (eds.) APMS 2019. IAICT, vol. 566, pp. 231–238. Springer, Cham (2019). https://doi.org/10.1007/978-3-030-30000-5_30
5. Hoang, X.L., Hildebrandt, C., Fay, A.: Product-oriented description of manufacturing resource skills. In: IFAC-PapersOnLine, vol. 51, pp. 90–95. Elsevier B.V. (2018). https://doi.org/10.1016/j.ifacol.2018.08.240
6. Holmström, P.: Modelling manufacturing systems capability. Ph.D. thesis, Kungliga Tekniska Högskolan (2006)
7. Imran, M., Young, B.: The application of common logic based formal ontologies to assembly knowledge sharing. J. Intell. Manuf. **26**(1), 139–158 (2013). https://doi.org/10.1007/s10845-013-0768-4
8. Järvenpää, E.: Capability-based adaptation of production systems in a changing environment (2012)
9. Järvenpää, E., Siltala, N., Hylli, O., Lanz, M.: The development of an ontology for describing the capabilities of manufacturing resources. J. Intell. Manuf. **30**(2), 959–978 (2018). https://doi.org/10.1007/s10845-018-1427-6
10. Katiraee, N., Calzavara, M., Finco, S., Battini, D., Battaïa, O.: Consideration of workers' differences in production systems modelling and design: state of the art and directions for future research. Int. J. Prod. Res. **59**(11), 3237–3268 (2021). https://doi.org/10.1080/00207543.2021.1884766
11. Kocher, A., Hildebrandt, C., Vieira da Silva, L.M., Fay, A.: A formal capability and skill model for use in plug and produce scenarios. In: 2020 25th IEEE International Conference on Emerging Technologies and Factory Automation (ETFA), pp. 1663–1670 (2020). https://doi.org/10.1109/etfa46521.2020.9211874

12. Malakuti, S., et al.: Challenges in skill-based engineering of industrial automation systems. In: IEEE International Conference on Emerging Technologies and Factory Automation, ETFA, pp. 67–74 (2018). https://doi.org/10.1109/ETFA.2018.8502635
13. Pfrommer, J., Stogl, D., Aleksandrov, K., Escaida Navarro, S., Hein, B., Beyerer, J.: Plug & produce by modelling skills and service-oriented orchestration of reconfigurable manufacturing systems. At-Automatisierungstechnik **63**(10), 790–800 (2015). https://doi.org/10.1515/auto-2014-1157
14. Rovida, F., Krüger, V.: Design and development of a software architecture for autonomous mobile manipulators in industrial environments. In: Proceedings of the IEEE International Conference on Industrial Technology, pp. 3288–3295, June 2015. https://doi.org/10.1109/ICIT.2015.7125585
15. Salunkhe, O., Fast-Berglund, A.: Increasing operational flexibility using Industry 4.0 enabling technologies in final assembly. In: 2020 IEEE International Conference on Engineering, Technology and Innovation (ICE/ITMC), pp. 1–5 (2020). https://doi.org/10.1109/ICE/ITMC49519.2020.9198630
16. Siltala, N., Järvenpää, E., Lanz, M.: An executable capability concept in formal resource descriptions. IFAC-PapersOnLine. **51**, 102–107 (2018). https://doi.org/10.1016/j.ifacol.2018.08.242
17. Van De Ginste, L., et al.: Defining flexibility of assembly workstations through the underlying dimensions and impacting drivers. In: Procedia Manufacturing, vol. 39, pp. 974–982. Elsevier B.V. (2019). https://doi.org/10.1016/j.promfg.2020.01.391
18. Vichare, P., Nassehi, A., Kumar, S., Newman, S.T.: A unified manufacturing resource model for representing CNC machining systems. Robot. Comput. Integr. Manuf. **25**(6), 999–1007 (2009). https://doi.org/10.1016/j.rcim.2009.04.014

Multi-criteria Filtering Approach for Comparison and Analysis of Scheduling Alternative Scenarios: Case Study on an Open Pit Phosphate Mine

Najoua Alaoui[1,2](✉) 🔟, Ahlam Azzamouri[1] 🔟, Selwa ElFirdoussi[1] 🔟,
and Pierre Féniès[1,2]

[1] EMINES, Mohammed VI Polytechnique University,
43150 Ben Guerir, Morocco
{Najoua.Alaoui,Ahlam.Azzamouri,Selwa.Elfirdoussi,
Pierre.Fenies}@emines.um6p.ma
[2] Pantheon-Assas, Paris II University, 75006 Paris, France

Abstract. Open-pit phosphate mine is characterized by a stack of layers with different chemical characteristics (Source qualities SQ). The extraction process involves various elementary operations performed by a dedicated or polyvalent machines. The tactical mining scheduling consists to define the blocs to be extracted and assign the machines over the planning horizon. However, the interdependencies and complexity characterizing this problem make the decision-making process so difficult. This paper proposes a multi-criteria approach integrated in an Interactive Decision Support System (IDSS) based on an original sequential approach selecting the most performant mining scenarios. Indeed, a discrete event simulation-based model developed and encapsulated in this IDSS proposes various scenarios. With a developed multi-criteria filtering approach, each scenario is approved by a feasibility study to verify that a scenario can satisfy the demand for merchantable qualities (MQ). Then, the feasible scenarios are analyzed based on their robustness when facing disturbed demand vectors and compared by other effectiveness and efficiency criteria. To preserve only the two or three most performant scenarios.

Keywords: Mining scheduling · Interactive Decision Support System IDSS · Alternative scenarios · Multi-criteria decision making

1 Introduction

The planning of ore mining in an open-pit mine is widely studied in the literature since the 1960's based on optimization and/or simulation approaches. Researchers have focused on the long-term mining planning issue [1]. However, studies based on medium- and short-term scheduling are relatively limited [2]. The spatiotemporal interdependencies and the various characteristics of the mining sector make the decision-making process more difficult.

© IFIP International Federation for Information Processing 2021
Published by Springer Nature Switzerland AG 2021
A. Dolgui et al. (Eds.): APMS 2021, IFIP AICT 634, pp. 117–126, 2021.
https://doi.org/10.1007/978-3-030-85914-5_13

Our field of study is based on an open-pit phosphate mine from the OCP group, whose supply chain is made up of several entities allowing the transition from ore to a finished or semi-finished product. The sedimentary nature of the mine means that the extraction of a layer can only be carried out if the upper level is already removed. From a transverse view, the mine is divided into panels, each of which is divided into blocs, the blocs on the same line represent the trench [3, 4]. The extracted SQ are transported to the down-stream mechanical processing units to subsequently enter a mixing or blending process [5] to constitute the MQ. A discrete event simulation-based (DES) model was developed considering the different constraints (geology, qualities, machines, etc.) of the mine to reproduce the extraction process and propose the extraction planning (scenario) [2]. The integration of the priority indexes of the extracted SQ as control parameters in the simulation, led to the possibility of generating various scenarios in a rapid and coherent way, based on a variation of parameters.

This paper aims to answer the following research question: How can we evaluate a set of generated scenarios, considering a multi criteria filtering approach, to select 2 or 3 most performant scheduling programs for the planning team to choose from and apply in the field? To answers this question, we have started by exposing the research works proposed in the scenario concept and the multi-criteria analysis approaches in Sect. 2. Then, Sect. 3 will propose the multi-criteria filtering approach developed. Thereafter, Sect. 4 will be dedicated to the case study illustrating the experimental results based on real field data before concluding in Sect. 5.

2 Literature Review

The scenario analysis has been widely applied in several sectors and disciplines [6, 7]. Defining a scenario has been a challenge [8]. Bell affirmed in [9] that "scenario" gives methodological unity to futures studies. Today a diverse group of decision-makers, consultants, and researchers develop and use scenarios in a variety of ways [7, 10]. The scenario-based research methodology is considered among the most used in various fields and is used for many purposes as highlighted by [11]. Notten et al. proposed [12] an updated typology and explain how the typology was tested for its robustness in a comparative analysis of recent scenario projects. Borjeson et al. [13] regroup and reconcile several typologies, to distinguish three main categories based on the main questions asked by a decision-maker: i) what will happen? (Predictive), ii) what can happen? (Exploratory), iii) how to achieve a specific objective? (Normative).

Information about the past and the present lead to different alternative possibilities about the future. Thus, a need for evaluation and comparison to perceive to what extent each alternative is plausible, desirable and beneficial for the decision-maker is necessary [9] p. 317.The complexity of analyzing and comparing multidimensional alternatives scenarios leads to considering explicitly several criteria and objectives to be optimized simultaneously in the analysis of preferences. Thus, defining a Multi-criteria decision problem consisting on the comparison of solutions and the determination of one or more optimal solution (s). Several approaches are used to guide the decision-making process in this case, by offering an analysis allowing to deepen the reflection on the studied scenarios and identify a consensus on the choice of one or more best scenarios. In this literature review, we studied three main approaches: the statistical response surface methodology (RSM), the aggregated and Pareto methods as main categories of multi objective optimization (MOO).

The RSM aims to evaluate the impact of decision variables as inputs on the response obtained as output, in order to determine the set of optimal decision parameters allowing to lead to the best scenario in relation to an objective function [14] and providing an exact answer to an approximate problem [15]. Some authors [16–18], having used or compared the RSM method with other methods, explain that this technique also represents multiple limitations to consider. Concerning the MOO approaches, there is a general consensus that it can be broadly broken down into two basic categories: Aggregation methods and Pareto methods [19]. The formulation of the aggregate objective function requires the assignation of preferences or weights to criteria converging towards the choice of a single scenario. Guo et al. ensure in [20] that in the world of industrial production and when making decisions, it is common for several production objectives to be considered and achieved simultaneously. Some authors use the weighted sum method to transform multi-objective problems into single-objective problems like [21, 22]. However, it is difficult for some problems to determine the weight of the different lenses. It is also impossible to have a single solution that can simultaneously optimize all goals when multiple goals conflict. To deal with this problem, some researchers have used the concept of Pareto optimality to provide more feasible solutions (optimal solutions in the Pareto sense) to the production decision maker such as authors in [23–25] affirmed that the advantage of the Pareto method lies in the possibility of separately taking into account several conflicting criteria in the evaluation and the selection of the best scenarios, thus allowing a richer critical analysis of the potential scenarios.

Based on this literature review, we conclude that this paper deals with a specific problem that have not been yet studied in the context of multi-criteria decision making related to the short and midterm scheduling of ore extraction problem taking into account different criteria. Indeed, The RSM is not applied in our case given the weak link between inputs parameters, their interdependence, and the response. The aggregation method is also not adequate because of the absence of a synthetic indicator that can express the multidimensional complexity of a mining scheduling scenario. Thus, considering the conflicting efficiency and effectiveness criteria, the Pareto method seems to be the best to keep this complexity while determining a reduced subset of the best scenarios located on the Pareto front. Furthermore, it is necessary to note that considering the complexity of this problem, we will define other levels to our multi criteria approach before using the Pareto method at the end. All in all, this IDSS is an enriching contribution to the few decision support systems dealing with the mining industry, using a DES model as a resolution module and following an original problem tailored sequential approach instead of the classical traditional. This sequential approach will guarantee the consideration of all the technical mining constraints by encapsulating the SED model. On the other hand, it will ensure that significant criteria for the decision makers will be taken into consideration. Thus, we will guarantee an alignment with complex mining objectives and make our approach feasible in the practical case of the mine.

3 Multi-criteria Approach: Proposition and Integration

In order to generate a set of technically feasible scenarios for ore extraction scheduling, we feed the DES model with real mine data. Then simulate a set of scenarios each based on distinct control parameters (priority indexes), on an annual scheduling horizon as presented in [26, 27]. The possibility of rapidly and coherently constructing extraction scenarios based on the variation of priority indexes of each SQ, made it possible to respect deposit, process and machines constraints but also explore several alternative scenarios. Thus, we were confronted with a decisional challenge to support the decision makers in their choice of the 2 or 3 most performant scenarios from a hundred alternatives. This decision making process goes beyond the technical coherence of the generated scenarios, by considering other criteria to evaluate different aspects of the alternatives scenarios. The first criteria as suggested in [27] focuses on the satisfaction of the client's demand on several scheduling horizons. We calculate the demand satisfaction rate (SR$_s$) per scenario such as:

$$SR_s = \frac{\sum_h F_{s,h}}{N} \tag{1}$$

s: Index of scenario.

h: Index of scheduling horizon.

N: Number of the scheduling horizon tested.

$F_{s,h}$: Binary variable which is equal to 1 if the scenario s tested on horizon h is feasible, and null otherwise.

Nevertheless, this criterion, alone, is not sufficient for decision makers to make a final choice. Because, even if a scenario is coherent and assures a satisfaction of the client's demand, it is acceptable as a viable solution, but is not necessarily the most efficient of the alternative scenarios. Thus, we integrate more significant criteria in our proposed multi-criteria approach, aiming to support the decision maker to choose the best scenario while taking into account the complex multidimensional nature of the latter.

Figure 1 depicts the proposed multi-level filtering approach serving the purpose of evaluating and comparing alternative scenarios. Level 1 consists on data wrangling, structuring and synthesizing important needed information from simulation output. Level 2 aims to study the feasibility of the scenario as explained in [27]. Level 3 deals with the study of scenario's robustness which is the important aspect to consider while deciding for the scheduling program to apply. In fact, the robustness of a scenario reflects its ability to deal with a stochastic MQ demand. In the mine, this fluctuation of the demand can disturb the execution of the scheduling program, leading to necessary perpetual adjustments. The integration of this aspect in the decision-making process will allow us to assess the robustness of the acceptable scenarios regarding a fluctuated demand character. Therefore, to avoid weaker scenarios that may satisfy the initially formulated demand but would fail meet it, if a fluctuation occurs.

In order to formulate level 3, we had to understand how the demand fluctuates then verify if a significant data history is available to quantify the disturbances in volume and nature. The MQ demand fluctuates in two fundamental forms: temporal and quantitative. Four sub-types follows: *i)* temporal disturbance based on an anticipation of one or more MQ demand, *ii)* temporal disturbance based on delaying of one or more MQ demand *iii)* quantitative disturbance based on an increase of the required volume of one or more MQ over a specific period, *iv)* quantitative disturbance based on a reduction of the required volume of one or more MQ over a specific period. According the experience of miners, time anticipation *(i)* and quantity augmentation *(ii)* are the two most critical types of disruption. In this case, they may not be able to satisfy the demand if the SQ to produce it are not extracted yet or available in volume and nature. Note that the availability of SQ in a period is linked to the succession of elementary operations of the extraction process, to the assignments and availability of the extraction machines as well as to the time necessary to access and extract the desired SQ.

Another challenge we encountered during the formulation of this level, is the lack of a significant data history that can be exploited in the quantitative formulation of disturbances. To get around it, we decided to set up a Generator of Disturbed Demand vectors called GDD. The role of this component is to generate different types of disturbances to help us perceive the behavior of acceptable scenarios when facing disturbed demand vectors. In fact, based on the initial demand vector, the generator chooses each time: *i)* two MQs and two periods to be modified if it is a temporal disturbance or, *ii)* two MQs and one period in the case of a quantitative disturbance. In the first case, an addition or subtraction of the volume from one period to the next is introduced but the total volume required remains intact. However, in the second case we introduce two parameters α and β specific to the selected MQ's. These parameters serve to specify the percentage of increase or reduction of the initially requested volume applied to generate the disrupted demand vectors. We made it possible that these parameters can be specified by default between a minimum and maximum values or else defined by decision-makers if a more precise information is communicated ahead. The GDD allows us to create several sets of disrupted demand vectors, where each vector comprise the 4 types of disturbance, which we specify as test bundles. We try to test alternative scenarios on different test bundles, in order to evaluate and assess their robustness while dealing with disturbances that are different in nature.

So, the purpose of this robustness study is to test the capacity of feasible scenarios to respond to disturbed demand vectors, with the same SQ supplies proposed to satisfy the initial demand. It is based on the same formulation as the feasibility study (a linear programing blending formulation), but the demand is not fixed this time. Moreover, to analyze the results of the robustness study, it was necessary to synthesize a Robustness Rate (RR_s) per scenario, such as:

$$RR_s = \frac{\sum_k \sum_v F_{s,v,k}.w_v}{N} \tag{2}$$

s: Index of scenario.
v: Index of perturbed demand vector.
k: Index of test bundle.
N: Number of tested bundles

$F_{s,v,k}$: Binary variable which is equal to 1 if the scenario s tested on perturbed demand vector v from test bundle k is possible, and null otherwise.

w_v: attributed weight for the perturbed demand vector v.

The scenarios are then ranked according to their RR_s, to select only the ones with a RR_s above 80% (a rate considered as an acceptable threshold according to the industrials).

At level 4, alongside the robustness study component, other criteria are synthesized from each scenario, to explore the multidimensional complexity of scheduling program through a Pareto method. This criteria are related to the displacement time and occupation of the extraction machines.

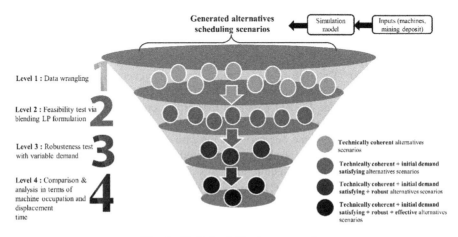

Fig. 1. Multi-level filtering approach

4   Experimental Analysis

We have tested the relevance of the IDSS designed on real data in collaboration with the mine's planning and method team [27] of OCP group. We were able to generate and validate an acceptable scheduling program ensuring technical consistency and allowing the satisfaction of the annual demand for 2020 over all planning horizons. Subsequently, our vision turned towards the search for a scheduling program based on the approach proposed.

Therefore, we started by generating a set of 20 scheduling scenarios relating to the same 2020 demand data, by varying the control parameters. In order to have 20 different scenarios the control parameters related to the SQ were given each time a different value from 1 to 10, at the start of the simulation as. Then, we carried out the feasibility study presented in [27] for each scenario. The obtained results in Table 1 show that six out of twenty scenarios are efficient in the short term, but failed to meet the initial demand in the medium term. The black dots meaning the scenario is feasible on the scheduling horizon, the white dots insinuating the infeasibility. These six scenarios are considered irrelevant ones and are therefore eliminated for the remainder of the study. Thereafter, we illustrate the creation of the disturbed demands via the GDD, through which behavior of the scenarios is studied.

Table 1. The satisfaction rate (SR$_s$) for the feasibility study per scenario i per month m

m/s	S1	S2	S3	S4	S5	S6	S7	S8	S9	S10	S12	S13	S14	S15	S16	S17	S18	S19	S20	S21
M1	•	•	•	•	•	•	•	•	•	•	•	•	•	•	•	•	•	•	•	•
M2	•	•	•	•	•	•	•	•	•	•	•	•	•	•	•	•	•	•	•	•
M3	•	•	•	•	•	•	•	•	•	•	•	•	•	•	•	•	•	•	•	•
M6	•	•	•	•	•	•	•	•	•	•	○	•	•	○	•	•	•	•	•	•
M9	•	•	•	•	•	•	•	•	•	•	○	○	•	○	•	•	•	•	•	•
M12	•	•	•	•	•	•	•	•	•	•	○	○	○	○	○	•	•	•	•	○
SRs (%)	100.0	100.0	100.0	100	100.0	100.0	100.0	100.0	100.0	100.0	50.0	66.7	83.3	50.0	83.3	100.0	100.0	100.0	100.0	83.3

Table 2 shows the creation of two different vectors of disturbed demand. The first vector representing one-month time anticipation of the requested volume of MQ 2 and 3. The second vector reflecting a quantity increase of the initial demand by 15% and 10% respectively regarding MQ 1 and 4 on the 9th month.

Table 2. Example of demand disruptions

Cumulated demand	MQ 1	MQ 2	MQ 3	MQ 4	MQ 5
M1	190932	132682	13441	25641	1282
M2	381865	265364	26882	51282	2564
M3	572797	398046	40323	76923	3846
M6	1145596	796092	80645	153846	7693
M9	1718394	1194137	120968	230769	11539
M12	2291191	1592183	161290	307692	15385
Time anticipation	Anticipation of the requested volume of the 3rd month on the 2nd month				
M1	190932	132682	13441	25641	1282
M2	381865	398046	40323	51282	2564
M3	572797	398046	40323	76923	3846
M6	1145596	796092	80645	153846	7693
M9	1718394	1194137	120968	230769	11539
M12	2291191	1592183	161290	307692	15385
Quantity addition	Quantity addition of the initial demand by 15% & 10% respectively for MQ 1 and MQ 4				
M1	190932	132682	13441	25641	1282
M2	381865	265364	26882	51282	2564
M3	572797	398046	40323	76923	3846
M6	1145596	796092	80645	153846	7693
M9	1976153	1194137	120968	253846	11539
M12	2291191	1592183	161290	307692	15385

For this study we create 3 test bundles (Table 3), each one containing 16 vectors of disturbed demands of all four types, to maintain a heterogeneous nature of the disruptions in each test bundle. The weights attributed to each disruption nature is defined by the decision makers, taking in consideration the criticality factor. In fact, as we explained earlier time anticipation and quantity augmentation are considered most critical, since it requires more SQ in a specific period. We thus attribute a more important weight to the more critical disturbances.

Table 3. The weight and disruption type for the generated disturbed vectors (V)

V / S	S1	S2	S3	S4	S5	S6	S7	S8	S9	S10	S17	S18	S19	S20	Weight	Disruption type
V1	1	1	1	1	1	1	1	1	1	1	1	1	1	1	0.075	Time_Anticipation
V2	1	1	1	1	1	1	1	1	1	1	1	1	1	1	0.075	Time_Anticipation
V3	0	0	0	1	0	0	0	0	0	0	0	0	0	0	0.075	Time_Anticipation
V4	0	0	0	1	0	0	0	0	0	0	0	0	0	0	0.075	Time_Anticipation
V5	1	1	1	1	1	1	1	1	1	1	1	1	1	1	0.05	Time_Retardation
V6	1	1	1	1	1	1	1	1	1	1	1	1	1	1	0.05	Time_Retardation
V7	1	1	1	1	1	1	1	1	1	1	1	1	1	1	0.05	Time_Retardation
V8	1	1	1	1	1	1	1	1	1	1	1	1	1	1	0.05	Time_Retardation
V9	0	1	1	1	0	1	0	0	0	0	0	0	0	0	0.085	Quan_Augmentation
...	...	...	...	...	...	...	...	...	...	...	...	...	...	...		...
V46	1	1	1	1	1	1	1	1	1	1	1	1	1	1	0.04	Quan_Reduction
V47	1	1	1	1	1	1	1	1	1	1	1	1	1	1	0.04	Quan_Reduction
V48	1	1	1	1	1	1	1	1	1	1	1	1	1	1	0.04	Quan_Reduction

The robustness test is carried out for each scenario 48 times (the number of test vectors). As shown in Table 4, from the remaining 14 scenarios only 5 have a RR_s above 80% that is considered acceptable for the decision makers.

Table 4. The results of robustness rate per scenario

Test (%) / S	S4	S3	S6	S8	S17	S9	S10	S18	S1	S2	S5	S7	S20	S19
Test bundle 1	100.00	100.00	100.00	92.50	92.50	92.50	80.50	92.50	92.50	100.00	92.50	92.50	72.00	60.00
Test bundle 2	100.00	85.00	85.00	76.50	76.50	63.50	76.50	76.50	76.50	70.00	76.50	56.50	76.50	50.50
Test bundle 3	92.50	77.50	77.50	77.50	77.50	80.50	77.50	63.50	60.50	55.50	55.50	63.50	63.50	50.50
RRs (%)	97.50	87.50	87.50	82.17	82.17	78.83	78 .17	77.50	76.50	75.17	74.83	70.83	70.67	53.67

In this case study, we explain how the first 3 levels of the proposed multi-level filtering approach permits us to guide the decision makers through the choice of 2 or 3 performant scenarios. We started by generating 20 technically coherent scenarios via a DES model. We proceeded to eliminate those not satisfying the initial demand on all planning horizons (1, 2, 3, 6, 9, 12 months). Then, we integrated the stochastic aspect of the demand and evaluated the robustness of the remaining scenarios, to end up with only 5 acceptable scenarios out of 20 as shown in Table 5. This approach helps the decision makers consider different aspects of a performant scenario, all while reducing the number of scenarios to be discussed.

Table 5. Synthesis of the results of each step per scenario

Scenario	S1	S2	S3	S4	S5	S6	S7	S8	S9	S10	S12	S13	S14	S15	S16	S17	S18	S19	S20	S21
Respect of technical mining constraints																				
Satisfaction of the initial demand																				
Acceptable robustness facing demand fluctuations																				

5 Conclusion

The open-pit mine extraction process is characterized by a spatiotemporal constraints and a conflictual criteria who make the tactical scheduling complex. A DES model was developed to generate a feasible extraction program (scenario) considering technical constraints. The integration of priority indexes of SQ as control parameters made it possible to generate several technically coherent scenarios by means of variations of the latter. Consequently, an evaluation and comparison of the generated set of alternatives scenarios was necessary. Thus, this paper, presents a multi-criteria filtering approach integrated on an IDSS aiming to propose the two or three most performant extraction planning. The approach proposed was tested and experimented based on a real data from the phosphate mine. The results obtained show the significance of the approach making it possible to evaluate and compare the 20 generated scenarios. In addition to the respect of technical constraints assured by the simulation model, many scenarios failed to ensure the satisfaction of the client's demand in the short as in the midterm (1, 2, 3, 6, 9, 12 months) and thus they were be eliminated. Other scenarios, even if feasible, showed weakness while facing fluctuations of the demand. We continue working on the fourth level to integrate criteria giving decision makers insight on occupational, displacement time of the extraction machines and SQ stock residue. Exploring the complexity of a scenario and understanding the challenges of the mining decision makers, will help us guide the choice of the most performant 2 or 3 scenarios. The development of a visualization component based on advanced data analytic tools is on progress to facilitate the visualization and comparison of the different indicators.

References

1. Chicoisne, R., Espinoza, D., Goycoolea, M., Moreno, E., Rubio, E.: A new algorithm for the open-pit mine scheduling problem. Oper. Res. **60**, 517–1028 (2009)
2. Azzamouri, A. : Construction de méthodes et d'outils de planification pour l'industrie minière du phosphate en contexte de Lean Management. Thèse de doctorat, Université Paris Nanterre (France) (2018)
3. Azzamouri, A., Fénies, P., Fontane, F., Giard, V.: Scheduling of open-pit phosphate mine. Int. J. Prod. Res. **56**(23), 7122–7141 (2018)
4. Azzamouri, A., Bamoumen, M., Hilali, H., Hovelaque, V., Giard, V.: Flexibility of dynamic blending with alternative routings combined with security stocks: a new approach in a mining supply chain. Int. J. Prod. Res. (2020). https://doi.org/10.1080/00207543.2020.1814443
5. Azzamouri, A., Giard, V.: Dynamic blending as a source of flexibility and efficiency in managing phosphate supply chain. In: ILS Conference, Lyon, France (2018)
6. Kleiner, A.: The Age of Heretics. Doubleday, New York (1996)
7. Ringland, G.: Scenario Planning. John Wiley & Sons, Chichester (1998)
8. Spaniol, M.J., Rowland, N.J.: Defining scenario. Futures Foresight Sci. **1**(1), e3 (2019)
9. Bell, W.: Foundations of Future Studies: History, Purposes, and Knowledge, p. 317 (2009)
10. European Environment Agency and ICIS. Cloudy crystal balls: an assessment of recent Europea and global scenario studies and models (2000)
11. Ramirez, R., Malobi, M., Simona, V., Arnoldo, M.K.: Scenarios as a scholarly methodology to produce "interesting research". Plann. Future Stud. **71**, 70–87 (2015)

12. Notten, P.W.F., Rotmans, J., van Asselt, M.B.A., Rothman, D.S.: An updated scenario typology. Futures **35**, 423–443 (2003)
13. Borjesona, L., Hojera, M., Dreborg, K.H., Ekvallc, T., Finnvedena, G.: Scenario Types and Techniques: Towards a User's Guide. Futures **38**(7), 723–739 (2006)
14. Mongometry, D.C: Design and Analysis of Experiments, 8th edn., chapter 11 (2012)
15. Khuri, A.I.: A general overview of response surface methodology. Biometrics Biostatistics Int. J. **5**(3), 87–93 (2017)
16. Downing, D.J., Gardner, R.H Hoffman F.O.: An examination of response-surface methodologies for uncertainty analysis in assessment models. Technometrics **27**(2), 151–163 (1985)
17. Kiran, M.D., Shrikant, A., Parag, S.S., Lele, S.S., Rekha, S.S.: Comparison of artificial neural network (ANN) and response surface methodology (RSM) in fermentation media optimization. Biochem. Eng. J. **41**, 266–273 (2008)
18. Cassettari, L., Roberto, M., Roberto, R., Fabio, R.: Effectiveness and limits of response surface methodology in application to discrete and stochastic simulation of manufacturing plants. Appl. Math. Sci. **7**, 4137–4172 (2013)
19. Weck, O.L.D: Multiobjective optimization: history and promise. In: Proceedings of 3rd China-Japan-Korea Joint Symposium on Optimization of Structural and Mechanical Systems, Kanazawa, Japan (2004)
20. Guo, Z.X., Wong, W.K., Li, Z., Ren, P.: Modeling and Pareto optimization of multiobjective order scheduling problems in production planning. Comput. Ind. Eng. **64**, 972–986 (2013)
21. Guo, Z.X., Wong, W.K., Leung, S.Y.S., Fan, J.T., Chan, S.F.: Genetic optimization of order scheduling with multiple uncertainties. Expert Syst. Appl. **35**(4), 1788–1801 (2008)
22. Ishibuchi, H., Murata, T.: A multi-objective genetic local search algorithm and its application to flowshop scheduling. IEEE Trans. Syst. Man Cybern. Part C Appl. Rev. **28**(3), 392–403 (1998)
23. Chitra, P., Rajaram, R., Venkatesh, P.: Application and comparison of hybrid evolutionary multiobjective optimization algorithms for solving task scheduling problem on heterogeneous systems. Appl. Soft Comput. **11**(2), 2725 (2011)
24. Jozefwska, J., Zimniak, A.: Optimization tool for short-term production planning and scheduling. Int. J. Prod. Econ. **112**, 109–120 (2008)
25. Yan, H., NaiQi, W., MengChu, Z. and ZhiWu, L.: Pareto-optimization for scheduling of crude oil operations in refinery via genetic algorithm. IEEE Trans. Syst. **47**(3), 517–530 (2017)
26. Alaoui, N., Azzamouri, A., Elfirdoussi, S., Fenies, P., Giard, V.: Interactive scheduling decision support system for ore extraction at a phosphate mine. In: The 8th International Conference on Industrial Engineering and Systems Management (IESM), Shangai, China (2019)
27. Alaoui, N., Azzamouri, A., Elfirdoussi, S., Fenies, P.: Conception d'un SIAD pour la planification minière : mise en œuvre dans le contexte minier de l'extraction du phosphate. In: 13ème Conférence Francophone de Modélisation, Optimisation et Simulation- MOSIM 2020 – 12 au 14 novembre (2020)

Evaluation of Complex Manufacturing Systems in the Context of Aggregated Operating Curves

Ulf Bergmann[1]([⊠]), Matthias Heinicke[2], Gerd Wagenhaus[1], and Sascha Schmidt[1]

[1] Otto-Von-Guericke University, 39106 Magdeburg, Germany
ulf.bergmann@ovgu.de
[2] Targus Management Consulting AG, Dechenstraße 7,
40878 Ratingen, Germany

Abstract. For the right configuration of production systems it is crucial to know the optimum operating point by way of a functional correlation between work in process and output rate or throughput time respectively.

As a matter of fact, executives and managers are quite familiar with this correlation which, however, rarely leads to its formal-mathematical application. Among others, this is due to the specific prerequisites arising from the application of general laws from queuing theory and operating curve theory.

Therefore, this paper will discuss our approach for a practical determination and description of suitable reference value systems using aggregated operating curves. The main focus will be directed towards the system's behaviour of complex production systems in versatile batch production, as it is frequently encountered in mechanical and plant engineering.

Keywords: Aggregated operating curve · Simulation · Production system control · Modeling procedure

1 Introduction

In order to adequately evaluate the performance of operating systems it is necessary to have significant parameters. Especially useful in this context are models and parameters of both the queuing theory and the curve theory. In the course of evaluating and configurating production structures, an increasing need for aggregated system description is noticeable, which goes beyond familiar bottleneck analyses focusing on one operating system.

Based on the general principles of operating curve theory, this paper will present a practical approach for the aggregated determination and application of a funnel model's parameters. Finally, the verification of the approach will be shown by reviewing a complex production system.

A. Dolgui et al. (Eds.): APMS 2021, IFIP AICT 634, pp. 127–135, 2021.
https://doi.org/10.1007/978-3-030-85914-5_14

2 Theoretical Aspects

The evaluation of the system's behaviour is usually based on input-output modeling (I/O). With these kind of model significant parameters like work in process (WIP), output rate and throughput time can be ultimately derived from the formal I/O presentation of production systems. The interdependencies between these three parameters are known as Little's Law and, in its modified version, as Funnel Model (see Fig. 1).

2.1 Little's Law

The methodological groundwork of Little's Law is the queuing theory. A so-called queue is defined by a number of units (jobs) waiting for their processing at a single workstation. The arrival rate indicates how many units (jobs) are arriving the system on average in a certain period of time. The service rate indicates how many units (jobs) can be served by the system on average in a certain period of time. The realised service rate, then, yields the system's output in terms of quantity (number of jobs) [1].

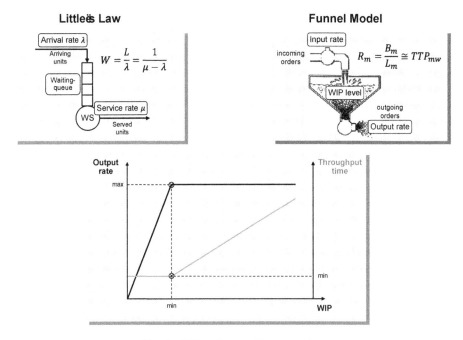

Little's Law

$$W = \frac{L}{\lambda} = \frac{1}{\mu - \lambda}$$

Funnel Model

$$R_m = \frac{B_m}{L_m} \cong TTP_{mw}$$

Fig. 1. Little's law vs. Funnel model.

Depending on the amount of already waiting units (jobs), Little's Law shows how long on average a newly arrived unit (job) will have to stay within the operating system until being processed (waiting time W). As long as the three parameters are measured in consistent units, Little's Law can be universally applied, with these findings coming chiefly from the observation of production lines and single workstations. If the WIP is then taken as an independent variable (WIP = the number of units L in the system), the interdependencies of Little's Law can be presented as an operating curve (sometimes called production-flow graph) [1].

There will be an ideal operating curve if no system variability is apparent. Once a minimally required WIP has been established, maximum system output rate will be provided accordingly. Underneath this critical WIP level, the system output rate will drop proportionally to the average amount of jobs [1, 2]. According to Little's Law, the curve of the throughput time is contrary (see Fig. 1).

2.2   Funnel Model

Extending Little's Law, [2] define what is called the Funnel Model, thereby referring to flow processes in chemical engineering. Here, production units (in general individual workstations) are regarded as funnels out of which the processed orders will flow out (cf. Fig. 1 right). Depending on the maximum capacity available, the funnel opening, therefore, illustrates the performance of the observed production unit (incoming orders). The queuing orders together with the newly arriving orders within the funnel comprise the WIP of orders yet to be processed (outgoing orders).

Provided that there is no new order entering the system, the funnel model states how long it will take on average to completely finish processing the WIP with consistent mean performance [2]. This will result in so-called operating points which describe respective operating modes of a production system for specific reference periods (e.g. one week). When, in addition to that, output rate and throughput time are shown as a function of the WIP level, the system behaviour might be modelled accordingly ([2] refers to them as production or operating curves, cf. Fig. 1).

Such operating curves describing a system-specific behaviour that occurs individually for the production type depending on the formation conditions. It might even vary according to the determination coefficient of influencing factors. Therefore, a quantitative statement concerning the WIP makes only sense when having just a few influencing parameters, and will be used for the simulative design of production systems as well. It is crucial for such designs that the variance of the input parameters is deterministic in a way that these parameters are stipulated as design restrictions for the future management model. For existing systems that are subject to a certain change of input parameters it is highly useful to know – or determine for that matter – the progression of its operating curve.

2.3   Short Synopsis

A crucial characteristic of the Funnel Model is its time evaluation of WIP and output rate. Provided that the evaluation intervals are of sufficient length, the change of the WIP will, therefore, only be influenced by the output rate of the evaluated system when using the Funnel Model. The completion behavior of orders (resp. the sequencing rule) as well as the variance of its work contents actually have no direct impact for the Funnel Model.

The situation is different for Little's Law. As regards the modelling and calculation as a queuing formula, WIP and output rate are given as count variables. Especially when faced with a multitude of different jobs with many different work contents respectively, the measuring by means of count variables proves to be unsuitable [3]. On top of that, when it comes to applying queuing models, form and parameters of distribution for arrival and service times as well as their necessary stochastic independence have to be described in correlation with each other [2]. This is crucially disadvantageous when modelling complex production processes since both the arrival and service times can rarely be described in an exact manner with classical distribution functions.

However, it is precisely the adjustment of the completion rate to the WIP which is the core task of production planning and control, in other words the essential control to influence the system performance, be it as a form of capacity adjustment or by means of load balancing. And this is exactly what queuing models will not enable with their modelling assumptions [2].

Consequently, with regard to practical questions concerning the configuration of production systems, queuing models do not comply with the requirements needed, which is why we will use the factual connections of the Funnel Model in the course of this paper.

3   Approach for the Aggregation of Operating Curves

3.1   Prerequisites

Our focus is set on the aggregated evaluation of complex production systems, especially versatile batch production scenarios in mechanical and plant engineering. Due to the production programmes and technological sequences typical for these scenarios, such systems are characterised by a complex organisational structure that has to deal with shifting bottleneck situations. Therefore, we will show in which way the relevant production parameters can be determined as an aggregation of specific individual parameters in order to describe the operating systems involved in the manufacturing process.

The aggregated evaluation of a production system with the help of the Funnel Model requires, above all, a determination of measuring points for evaluating the jobs that enter and leave the system. Basically, this determination can be performed starting with the smallest operating system which cannot be reasonably broken down any further, and then continued for each higher aggregation level. Provided that the WIP can be determined with acceptable precision, it is irrelevant at this point how the individual workstations are linked with each other.

These measuring points (defined as input and output) are used as referential points for the aggregated evaluation of the work content per job in planned hours and will literally cover the scope of the evaluation, accordingly. Based on this, the present system state will then be determined by using the Funnel Model, and will be termed operating point. Here, ideal operating curves represent the suitable "reference coordinate system" for a present system state [4, 5].

Such state values are only helpful as a benchmark or reference values for decisions in production controlling if the statistical correlations of relevant system parameters are taken into account [6]. Consequently, a so-called black-box-approach is not feasible. It is rather necessary to aggregate the specific individual parameters from the workstations involved in the system processing according to their material flow-based interconnectedness. Using an intensity index, the material flow structure will be simplified to become a direct line of weighted predecessor-successor-relationships, when the aggregated parameters can ultimately be determined via the identified bottleneck [5, 7].

The description of the inner system structure is necessary and detailed, requiring a lot of effort and background knowledge. Since a long-term stable bottleneck is also required, such a white-box-approach is not feasible, either. The same goes for shifting bottlenecks, as is the case in our evaluation scenario. Therefore, this is our modified approach: We call it grey-box-approach for the aggregated evaluation of reference values for WIP (a), output rate (b) and throughput time (c).

3.2   Grey-Box-Approach

(a) The ideal minimum WIP is the minimally required WIP necessary for the full utilisation of all operational means within the evaluated system. When performing an aggregated I/O evaluation of a production system by means of the Funnel Model, the amount of available work (work load) within a production system can be regarded as its temporally evaluated total WIP level. Because of this system-wide perspective, it is irrelevant to determine which working step has been made for individual products according to their specific technological sequence on the production system's individual workstations. In fact, the cumulative process time of the individual jobs rather indicates their respective work load that they load the production system with, both in total and, consequently, each workstation according to their technological sequence. Therefore, the calculation of the so-called medium work content (WC_m) at first occurs as weighted mean by weighting the work content of each workstation i against the related quantity of given jobs m_p:

$$WC_{m,i} = \frac{\sum m_p \cdot WC_{p,i}}{\sum m_p} \tag{1}$$

It is necessary to include this aggregated work content because the minimum WIP is considered here for the entire production system and not for a single workstation. As a next step, the respective variation coefficients (WC_v) can be derived for each workstation:

$$WC_{v,i} = \frac{\sigma\left(WC_{p,i}\right)}{\overline{WC_{p,i}}} \tag{2}$$

Then, by taking the system's composition (type i and number n of workstations) into account, the resource-based values can be accumulated to provide the minimum critical WIP_{min}:

$$WIP_{min} = \sum_i \left(n_i \cdot WC_{m,i} \cdot \left(1 + WC_{v,i}\right)^2 \right) \tag{3}$$

Subsequently, this theoretically derived value will work as a system-wide parameter of the WIP, for which the production system will reach its maximum possible output rate; always in accordance with the planned production programme and performance losses inherent to the production system due to its complex interrelationship between various jobs.

(b) Viewed from the perspective of the planning manager, the scheduled production programme results in a medium workload that determines the maximum required output rate $OR_{req, prod}$ of the system in a certain period of time T:

$$OR_{req,prod} = \frac{\sum_p \sum_i WC_{p,i}}{T} \tag{4}$$

Since in the long run the average release rate is always less than the average capacity of the production programme [1, 2], the planning manager can determine the maximum achievable output rate $OR_{max, prod}$. Hence, for a fixed variety of jobs the following applies:

$$OR_{req,prod} \leq OR_{max,prod} \leq OR_{max,theo} \tag{5}$$

In this context, $OR_{max, theo}$ represents the theoretical optimum of the maximum possible output rate of a production system, resulting from the installed capacity. Basically, in practical circumstances, this maximum possible output rate $OR_{max, theo}$ is impossible to achieve, even without taking into account unforeseeable breakdowns.

(c) The fundamental basis, of course, for determining a reference value for the throughput time is again the production programme featuring the type and number of products m_p to be manufactured. Aggregated to a weighted mean, the lowest possible throughput time TTP_{min} can be determined according to their technological sequence, and will arise from the total of product-specific work content at each workstation i plus required transport times:

$$TTP_{min} = \frac{m_p \cdot TTP_{min,p}}{\sum m_p} \text{ with } TTP_{min,p} = \sum WC_{p,i} \tag{6}$$

Therefore, this minimum value – which is mostly a theoretical value, especially in complex production systems – serves as an ideal reference value for the throughput time in the course of events.

4   Practical Verification and Findings

We verified the feasibility of the grey-box-approach by using a lab-sized production system. This multi-agent controlled system is composed of various Fischertechnik components simulating machining processes on work pieces. The use case was based on real-world production scenarios for which we gained the following aggregated reference values (see Table 1), using the given Eqs. 1, 2, 3, 4, 5 and 6 of the grey-box-approach (note: the simulating processes were running with a reduced time scale in seconds).

Table 1. Data and aggregated reference values of the analysed production scenarios.

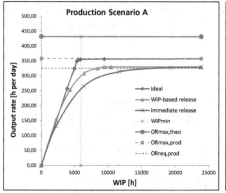
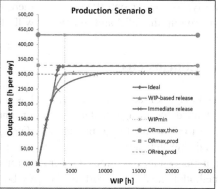

	Production Scenario A						T_{av} = 250 d/a with 16 h/d		Production Scenario B						
A-10	A-20	A-30	A-40	A-50	A-60	Product	B-100	B-200	B-300	B-400	B-500	B-600	B-700	B-800
600	600	600	450	360	360	Order size	225	600	375	600	600	600	600	450
60	60	60	80	100	100	No. of orders	160	60	96	60	60	60	60	80

Production sequence and time per order [h]	Process (No. of machines)	Production sequence and time per order [h]

| dc = 1.29 | WIP_min = 6365 h | WIP_min = 3973 h | dc = 0.92 |
| dl = 0.85 | OR_req,prod = 326 h/d | OR_req,prod = 300 h/d | dl = 1 |

The reference values have been verified using simulation data. In order to do so, the system behaviour was first determined as a "perfect world simulation". After that, the empirical system behaviour was simulated in a "real world scenario", which took place, firstly, as a result of an immediate job release ("uncontrolled system") and, secondly, by means of a WIP-based job release ("controlled system"). Figure 2 illustrates the results as output rate operating curve.

Fig. 2. Aggregated operating curves of the simulated production scenarios.

Here it becomes clear again how important a detailed evaluation of the output rate as crucial parameter is (cf. Eq. 5). Based on a fixed mix of type and number of product variants (different jobs to be done), $OR_{max,\ prod}$ is determined as the maximum achievable output rate of the evaluated production system, resulting from the bottleneck in the production system. Correlating with the product variants to be produced, shifting bottlenecks often complicate this determination (cf. Ch. 3.1).

Apart from bottleneck-based analyses, we are using in our grey-box approach the maximum required output rate $OR_{req,\ prod}$ as a reference value; that is the output rate required for completing the given production programme. Regardless of other impact factors, $OR_{req,\ prod}$ serves as the saturation limit. According to economical considerations, it is by definition unprofitable to exceed $OR_{req,\ prod}$ significantly, except for additional work beyond the regular production programme.

A crucial parameter in this respect is the critical WIP determined by means of aggregation. Our investigations have shown that the interdependency between the output rate and WIP are specific to the system, which will individually appear according to the formation conditions of the production structure. It might even vary in accordance with the determination coefficient of those formation conditions. In order to assess the system behaviour imminent in both production scenarios, we can use two significant indicators: the degree of complexity dc and the degree of linearity dl (for further calculation details see [8]). Then the following can be stated.

- If dc is high and dl is low (Production Scenario A): trending towards a complex system structure = critical WIP works as lower threshold; i.e. a required output max will only be achieved by a multiple of the critical WIP (maximum 100%)
- If dc is low and dl is high (Production Scenario B): trending towards a simple system structure = critical WIP acts as upper threshold; i.e. a required output max will materialize within a narrow tolerance zone around the critical WIP level ($\pm$ 10%)

On top of that, our investigation illustrates very well the sensitivity of the critical WIP as a control variable. As for the controlled system, even minor modifications in the critical WIP will lead to considerable changes in the system's performance. Contrarily, for the uncontrolled system, there is no immediate cancellation of jobs, which will run-up the WIP and, therefore, will affect the throughput time in a negative way.

5   Conclusions

As a matter of fact, our investigation has confirmed the basic principles of curve theory, extended by an aggregated evaluation and management of necessary parameters. It goes to show that the combination of $OR_{req,\ prod}$ as a saturation limit and critical WIP is a suitable indicator for setting a feasible operating point. This is much in line with experience-based routines of operation for the present application and also validates the methodological framework of the grey-box-approach introduced here.

Compared to the immediate job release, the advantages of the WIP-based job release are clearly visible. The latter benefits from the design parameters of the approach presented here.

Especially when viewed against the background of the WIP-oriented approach that is frequently used in industrial practice as production control, the introduced critical WIP proves its controlling effect as reference value. Furthermore, by using the present data base of a real production programme, it is relatively easy to determine the highest necessary output rate (saturation limit). The correlation of WIP and output rate limit quickly results in an operating point that seems ideally suited to get closer to the theoretical optimum in a WIP-controlled production system.

References

1. Hopp, W.J., Spearman, M.L.: Factory Physics: Foundations of Manufacturing Management, 3rd edn. Irwin McGraw-Hill, New York (2008)
2. Nyhuis, P., Wiendahl, H.P.: Fundamentals of Production Logistics: Theory Tools and Applications. Springer, Berlin (2014)
3. Pound, E.S., Bell, J.H., Spearman, M.L.: Factory Physics for Managers: How Leaders Improve Performance in a Post-Lean Six Sigma World. McGraw-Hill Education, New York (2014)
4. Bergmann, U., Heinicke, M.: Resilience of productions systems by adapting temporal or spatial organization. Procedia CIRP **57**, 183–188 (2016)
5. Nyhuis, P.: Beiträge zu einer Theorie der Logistik. Springer, Berlin (2008)
6. Kemmner, A.: Ein heimlicher Leitfaden für ständig kritisierte Fertigungssteuerer. Abels & Kemmner Homepage. https://www.ak-online.de/de/2008/06/ps2008-14/. Accessed 9 Apr 2021
7. Weigert, G.: Operating curves of manufacturing systems: a theoretical discourse. In: Azevedo, A. (ed.) Advances in Sustainable and Competitive Manufacturing Systems. LNME, pp. 887–897. Springer, Heidelberg (2013). https://doi.org/10.1007/978-3-319-00557-7_73
8. Bergmann, U., Heinicke, M.: Approach for the evaluation of production structures. In: Lödding, H., Riedel, R., Thoben, K.-D., von Cieminski, G., Kiritsis, D. (eds.) APMS 2017. IAICT, vol. 514, pp. 176–183. Springer, Cham (2017). https://doi.org/10.1007/978-3-319-66926-7_21

Conceptual Maps of Reliability Analysis Applied in Reconfigurable Manufacturing System

Tian Zhang[(⊠)], Lazhar Homri, Jean-yves Dantan, and Ali Siadat

LCFC Laboratory, Arts Et Metiers Institute of Technology, Metz, France
{tian.zhang, lazhar.homri, jean-yves.dantan,
ali.siadat}@ensam.eu

Abstract. Reliability has always been an important factor for any manufacturing companies. An appropriate level of reliability in a manufacturing system could mean less maintenance cost, higher efficiency and steadier production state. Because each machine in a manufacturing system has its individual level of reliability, reliability on the system level would depend largely on how the machines are configured. In traditional efforts on reconfigurable manufacturing system (RMS) reliability assessments, mean time between failure (MTBF) is usually adopted as reference index of reliability. Also, in existing research efforts of applying reliability analysis in manufacturing system, reliability is merely a single and over-simplified index in the framework. But there exist various forms of reliability inside a RMS, and the complexity of this concept would keep increasing with the development of new technology in manufacturing industry. To analyze reliability in RMS in a more comprehensive way, we built conceptual maps as first step for research agenda – from the perspective of general layer, reliability analysis and RMS.

Keywords: Reconfigurable manufacturing system · Reliability analysis · Conceptual map · Mean time between failure

1 Introduction

Most of the existing research efforts on the reliability of manufacturing systems are analysis on system topology, and the reliability attributes of the components are relatively less considered. Analytical method and computer simulation method are the two main directions when analyzing reliability of a manufacturing system. Among various analytical methods, Fault tree analysis (FTA) and Failure mode and effect analysis (FMEA) are quite usually applied for systems with relatively smaller scale in earlier research [2]. With the development of modern industrial technology, more methods are gradually being proposed and applied into analyzing the reliability of the systems, such as Petri net and Markov chain [10, 13]. In the system reliability assessment of large complexity, simulation method such as Monte Carlo combined with various algorithms plays an important role [9].

© IFIP International Federation for Information Processing 2021
Published by Springer Nature Switzerland AG 2021
A. Dolgui et al. (Eds.): APMS 2021, IFIP AICT 634, pp. 136–145, 2021.
https://doi.org/10.1007/978-3-030-85914-5_15

It is important to adapt reliability analysis to the specific case of Reconfigurable Manufacturing Systems (RMS). RMS fits the current market trend, which is varying quite fast and cost limit. Although cost is a constraint, quality is a big issue at the same time. Taking china as an example, a national strategic plan "Made in China 2025" mentioned quality as a key focus [16]. Thus, to fit the fast-varying market with the cost and quality requirement, reliability analysis in RMS is important. Succinctly saying, when compared with regular manufacturing system, RMS would involve more module interactions/interfaces due to the nature of the system. In an RMS, reliability not only matters on the modules of tools, machines and system, but also between these modules. Thus, it is more reasonable to distinguish the reliability of an RMS from a regular manufacturing system.

RMS is a machining system which can be created by incorporating basic process modules including both hardware and software that can be rearranged or replaced quickly and reliably [6]. The basic features of an ideal RMS include modularity, integrability, customized flexibility, scalability, convertibility and diagnosability, in which diagnosability is the ability to automatically read the current state of a system for detecting and diagnosing the root-cause of output product defects, and subsequently correct operational defects quickly. Diagnosability has two application directions during manufacturing process. One is the diagnosability of machine failures, and another is the diagnosability of non-conforming products. The latter is quite necessary when one considers the frequent rearrangements happening in an RMS which causes higher uncertainties of product qualities than that happening in a traditional manu-facturing system. Regarding the hardware equipment, fast diagnosability could be realized by reconfigurable inspection machine (RIM). Then control methods, statistic methods and signal processing techniques could be led-in for further analysis on sources of reliability and quality problems. Therefore, diagnosability – among the main 6 features mentioned above – has the strongest linkage with reliability analysis in RMS.

In traditional efforts on RMS reliability assessments, mean time between failure (MTBF) is usually adopted as the reliability performance reference index. Besides MTBF, several similar index such as failure rate (reciprocal of MTBF), mean down time and availability were also adopted in extensive research [7]. But there were doubts whether this is suitable for industrial applications. Calculation of MTBF requires that failure mode being based on exponential distribution, which does not always fit the real case, especially not for a RMS case.

For an RMS, the characteristic of reconfiguration could be realized in many forms. As shown in Fig. 1, reconfigurations could be on layout, machine tools or planning, either simultaneously or separately according to specific assumptions. Hence, reliability could be interpreted in many ways with different form of reconfigurations not limited to the only index – MTBF.

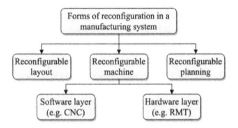

Fig. 1. Reconfiguration in various forms

Based on the considerations and discussions above, we proposed to interpret the idea of reliability in a more reasonable and comprehensive way. The problem formalization is as follows:

To address the increasing complexity of manufacturing systems, we try to include various forms of reliability inside a reconfigurable manufacturing system, its machines and products during the whole period of time: from the beginning of manufacturing to product's end of life. In this paper, our main contribution is constructing conceptual maps as an informational basis for an issue we proposed.

To clarify the proposed research issue, we made an example with automobile for illustration as shown in Fig. 2. The whole life of the automobile, from manufacturing to usage were included in our research time span. When the automobile order arrives, the production requirements would occur automatically, thus we make selection of the configurations, which could be presented as the period called "usage of RMS". During this step, performance index of a system such as scalability is also renewed. Then the manufacturing process starts, during which the state of the system is diagnosed, along with the reliability such as MTBF for a maintainable automobile manufacturing system. After the automobile has been verified by the quality control and put into usage, environmental factors such as road quality, maintenance of the engine and usage weather etc. could all influence the final reliability of the automobile.

In the following part of this paper, chapter 2 includes the discussion of existing related works and highlighted two firmly related papers to our research issue; chapter 3 presents the conceptual maps we built for the research issue; and chapter 4 includes conclusion and future research perspectives.

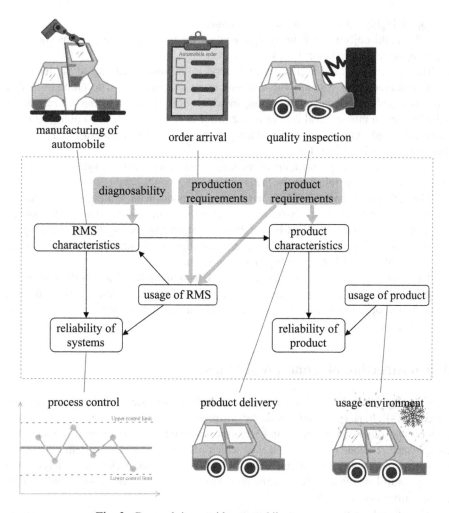

Fig. 2. Research issue with automobile as an example

2 Relevant Research

After formalizing our problem, we did a literature searching in Web of Science. The searching condition was set very strictly, and we applied snowballing method for more related papers. We ended up with 25 papers as the review paper database, in which there were 2 papers highly related to the issue we proposed. This number proves the scarcity of reliability analysis in RMS, in which reliability is taken as a main criterion. Yet as we have mentioned in chapter 1, reliability plays a rather important role in current manufacturing systems, especially in systems with reconfigurable characteristics. Therefore, it is quite important to build conceptual maps for this issue as a start.

Papers highly related to the proposed issue:

– 《A multi-objective reliability optimization for reconfigurable systems considering components degradation》 [14].

The authors proposed an integrated method to improve reliability of the reconfigurable manufacturing system, with cost-efficiency as constraint. The problem in this paper is a multi-objective optimization, in which objectives are to maximize system reliability and minimize total cost or performance lost. In this article, reconfiguration is realized through rearranging and replacing components, which accords to the reconfigurable layout branch in Fig. 1.

– 《Research and optimization of reconfigurable manufacturing system configuration based on system reliability》 [12].

The authors presented a hybrid parallel-series model with waiting system characteristics, in which reliability is set as the criterion. Also, other system performances including productivity, and cost by combining system engineering theory are adopted for evaluation. Same as the former paper, reconfiguration form also accords to the reconfigurable layout branch in Fig. 1 in this research.

These two papers share the same form of reconfiguration, and both worked on algorithms to solve the performance optimization. But the difference is in the 1st research, the optimization is multi-objective but in the 2nd research, reliability is the only objective in optimization.

3   Construction of Conceptual Maps

A conceptual map is a graphical tool that depicts suggested relationships between concepts [4]. It is commonly used by instructional designers, engineers, technical writers, and others to organize and structure knowledge. It could help organize the complicated relations between concepts, which fits our need since the definition of the reliability and quality in our research is of multiple layers. Reliability analysis and quality control enable a manufacturing company to precisely control the manufacturing process from two key aspects.

The advantage of CM is its stimulation of idea generations, which could aid in brainstorming of potential research topics. But as the same time, it can only be seen as a first step in a scientific research and there could be individual differences when it comes to the definition of one same word. This often happens when the researchers are from different countries, or even sometimes different labs.

By constructing conceptual maps, we intended to aid researchers by increasing clarity of reliability analysis and RMS concepts and thus, the probability of successful implementation. At the same time, it will help clarifying for our own research topic in the later works. CM is preferred to be built with reference to a few particular questions that researchers would like to answer as a start. The focus question we ask is consistent to the research issue we proposed: How do we conduct reliability analysis on RMS in a more reasonable and comprehensive way?

The elements in CM are concepts, propositions, cross-links and hierarchical frameworks [8]. Concept is defined as a perceived regularity in events or objects, or records of events or objects, designated by a label. Cross-links helps connect two concepts from various segments of the CM, it is often where the creative leaps would occur. Propositions are statements about some object or event in the universe, either naturally occurring or constructed. Propositions contain two or more concepts connected using linking words or phrases to form a meaningful statement.

In the following parts, we are going to present the CM of the 2 concepts "reliability analysis" and "reconfigurable manufacturing system" separately and then combine the two concepts for a more general CM. The former two CMs are buit the 2 main questions: why and how? "Why" leads to the concepts that's related to the reason why this main concept is built and "how" leads to the concepts those are more related to the methods and approaches.

As shown in Fig. 3, reliability analysis could be broadly interpreted as analysis on the ability for a system to perform its intended function [11]. As discussed in the former contents, the importance of reliability in a system is nonnegligible, especially with the increasing of size and complexity of systems. With functionality of manufacturing operations becoming more essential, there is also a growing need for reliability analysis. Definition of reliability could be adapted into many forms based on the essence of the systems. Reliability could be presented by many indexes, the common definition of reliability function is R(t), and also there could be MTTF, maintainability– which could also be presented by mean time to repair (MTTR), mean time between failure (MTBF), failure rate and availability. The techniques in RA that's quite often applied are reliability block diagrams, network diagrams, fault tree analysis (FTA) and Monte Carlo simulation. FTA has the advantage of describing the fault propagation in a system, but it might not come into effect in a system with high-complexity and maintenance characteristic. Monte Carlo simulation could be applied to evaluate MTBF when the possible distribution function is already given.

It is noteworthy that the concepts in Fig. 3 could keep unchanged or change according to the system type (regular/reconfigurable manufacturing system). To identify those concepts which might be significantly impacted by system type, we highlighted them in Fig. 3 by deep color. (When one concept is highlighted, all the concepts located on its branches could be affected by system type logically.) When a system is reconfigurable rather than dedicated, there would certainly involve more possible **failures** due to its higher system complexity. Yet when compared to overly complicated flexible manufacturing system, it could contain less failures – either in law of the failure, causes of failure or consequences of failure. Thus, the **reliability** for regular and reconfigurable manufacturing system would vary identically. And as shown in Fig. 3, the **hardware system**, **software system** and **machines** for processing could all be special for a reconfigurable manufacturing system when compared with regular ones.

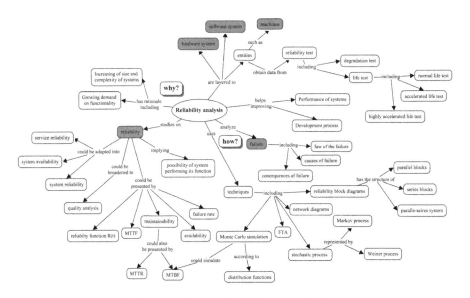

Fig. 3. Conceptual map of reliability analysis in a system

We constructed the CM of RMS as shown in Fig. 4. The parts where RMS is different from a regular manufacturing system have been highlighted by darker color in the figure. RMS was introduced as a response to volatile global markets that instigated large uncertainty in product demand [5]. RMS has the reconfigurable characteristics, and they are commonly concluded to 6 features for enabling rapid responsiveness [1]. The feature customized flexibility enables the system to manufacture part families. One of the main reason RMS is different from dedicated manufacturing system (DMS) or flexible manufacturing system (FMS) is its focus on producing part families. Integrability could be realized either on the system level or machine level. At the machine level, reconfigurable machine tools (RMT) could be applied; at the system level, machines are seen as modules that could be integrated through transport systems. Diagnosability is the feature closely related to reliability, it could be detection on either product quality or system reliability. In the phase of problem formalization, both these two elements are taken into consideration in the model. Typically, RMS contains computer numerically controlled (CNC) machines and in-line inspection stations. RMS could be the study object in many applications: configuration selection, planning and scheduling, product family formation, layout configuration analysis and configuration design. In configuration design, it could be applied to level of systems, machines or other modules such as transportation/controlling equipment etc. [3], which concords with the feature of integrability.

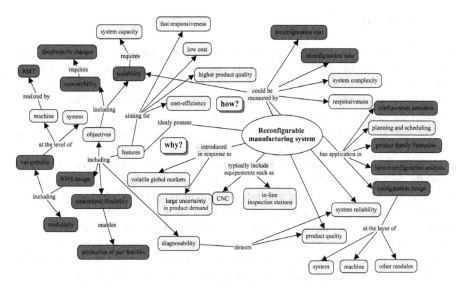

Fig. 4. Conceptual map of reconfigurable manufacturing system

As show in the Fig. 5, combination of the conceptual maps includes general concepts for our research issue – applying reliability analysis in reconfigurable manufacturing system, in which we show the factors that attributes to the comprehensive research characteristics. Attributions to comprehensiveness of our research have two parts: the variety of reliability indexes and the variety of the studied layers. And the scope of time, which has not been added into the map, is also an attribution to comprehensiveness.

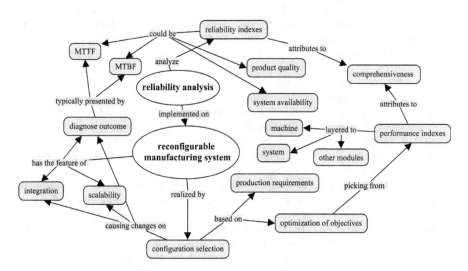

Fig. 5. Top layer of the conceptual maps

4 Conclusion

The conceptual maps we have developed are based on the study literatures of RMS and reliability. The validation of the conceptual map could be realized in 2 ways in future work. One way is to validate by comparing conceptual maps generated by others. The other way is to observe the behavior in a relevant situational context. This could be summarized as application validity approach [15].

The aim of this study was to clarify the conceptual ambiguity when applying reliability analysis in reconfigurable manufacturing systems. In support of this aim, we provided a visual representation of this topic in the form of conceptual maps in chapter 3. While the map provides a necessary first step towards clarification, the results could be continuously improved based on up-to-date findings in those fields.

The construction of the conceptual maps is a basis for our research agenda. In future work, we could keep developing the methodology and models for the research issue we proposed. As mentioned in chapter 3, each cross-link in the conceptual maps could imply a potential research topic. Besides the issue we proposed, how the usage period together with manufacturing period impact on the reliability of products could also be an interesting direction for researching.

References

1. Andersen, A.-L., Nielsen, K., Brunoe, T.D., Larsen, J.K., Ketelsen, C.: Understanding changeability enablers and their impact on performance in manufacturing companies. In: Moon, I., Lee, G.M., Park, J., Kiritsis, D., von Cieminski, G. (eds.) APMS 2018. IAICT, vol. 535, pp. 297–304. Springer, Cham (2018). https://doi.org/10.1007/978-3-319-99704-9_36
2. Baig, A.A., Ruzli, R., Buang, A.B.: Reliability analysis using fault tree analysis: a review. Int. J. Chem. Eng. Appl. 4(3), 169 (2013)
3. Capawa Fotsoh, E., Mebarki, N., Castagna, P., Berruet, P., Gamboa, F.: Towards a reference model for configuration of reconfigurable manufacturing system (RMS). In: Lalic, B., Majstorovic, V., Marjanovic, U., von Cieminski, G., Romero, D. (eds.) APMS 2020. IAICT, vol. 591, pp. 391–398. Springer, Cham (2020). https://doi.org/10.1007/978-3-030-57993-7_44
4. Hager, P.J., Scheiber, H.J., Corbin, N.C.: Designing & Delivering: Scientifific, Technical, and Managerial Presentations. John Wiley & Sons (1997)
5. Koren, Y.: The emergence of reconfigurable manufacturing systems (RMSs). In: Benyoucef, L. (ed.) Reconfigurable Manufacturing Systems: From Design to Implementation. SSAM, pp. 1–9. Springer, Cham (2020). https://doi.org/10.1007/978-3-030-28782-5_1
6. Koren, Y., Gu, X., Guo, W.: Reconfifigurable manufacturing systems: principles, design, and future trends. Front. Mech. Eng. 13(2), 121–136 (2018)
7. Kumar, U.D., Knezevic, J., Crocker, J.: Maintenance free operating period – an alternative measure to MTBF and failure rate for specifying reliability. Reliab. Eng. Syst. Saf. 64(1), 127–131 (1999)
8. Novak, J.D., Cañas, A.J.: The theory underlying concept maps and how to construct them. Florida Institute for Human and Machine Cognition (2008)
9. Pan, Q., Dias, D.: An effificient reliability method combining adaptive support vector machine and monte carlo simulation. Struct. Saf. 67, 85–95 (2017)

10. Wu, X.Y., Wu, X.Y.: Extended object-oriented petri net model for mission reliability simulation of repairable PMS with common cause failures. Reliab. Eng. Syst. Saf. **136**, 109–119 (2015)
11. Xie, M., Dai, Y.S., Poh, K.L.: Computing System Reliability: Models and Analysis. Springer (2004)
12. Xiong, H., Chen, M., Lin, Y., Lv, C., Li, A., Xu, L.: Research and optimization of reconfigurable manufacturing system configuration based on system reliability. Kybernetes (2010)
13. Ye, Y., Grossmann, I.E., Pinto, J.M., Ramaswamy, S.: Modeling for reliability optimization of system design and maintenance based on Markov chain theory. Comput. Chem. Eng. **124**, 381–404 (2019)
14. Zhao, J., Si, S., Cai, Z.: A multi-objective reliability optimization for reconfigurable systems considering components degradation. Reliab. Eng. Syst. Saf. **183**, 104–115 (2019)
15. Albert, D., Steiner, C.M.: Empirical validation of concept maps: preliminary methodological considerations. In: Fifth IEEE International Conference on Advanced Learning Technologies (ICALT 2005), pp. 952–953 (2005)
16. Li, L.: China's manufacturing locus in 2025: With a comparison of "Made-in-China 2025" and "Industry 4.0". Technol. Forecast. Soc. Chang. **135**, 66–74 (2018)

Crossdock and Transportation Issues

Berth Allocate Problem with Multi-entry Considering Marine Fish Freshness

Jing Zhu[1]($\boxtimes$), Wang Yan[2], and Xuehao Feng[3]

[1] School of Management, Zhejiang University,
Hangzhou, People's Republic of China
11820014@zju.edu.cn
[2] ZPMC, Shanghai, People's Republic of China
wangyan_wy@zpmc.com
[3] Ocean College, Zhejiang University,
Hangzhou, People's Republic of China
fengxuehao@zju.edu.cn

Abstract. In this paper, we analyze the berth allocation problem for vessels calling at fishing ports by considering the current higher consumer demand for seafood freshness in the vast inland areas of China. At first, according to the previous investigation on the site of Zhoushan Fishing Port, we propose a mathematical model to maximize the overall profit with a multiple-entry policy of the vessels. The optimal berth allocation and re-entry of vessels can be obtained. We integrate the vessel's owner, the manager of the port, and the fish market vendor together, regarding the tripartite overall profit as the objective function. Based on this, taking into account the relationship between seafood unloading time and overall income, a mathematical model of mixed-integer linear programming (MILP) is constructed to accurately describe the berth allocation decision framework under which fishing vessels are allowed multiple arrivals.

Keywords: Fish port · Berth allocation · Mathematical programming · Multiple-entry policy

1 Introduction

Berth allocation problem (BAP, also known as the berth scheduling problem) is a well-known NP-complete problem. In this problem, fishing vessels arrive over time and the terminal operator needs to assign them to berths to be served (loading and unloading cargos) as soon as possible. Discrete berth allocation refers to the scenario that the shoreline of the port is artificially divided into multiple different sections [1, 2]. On the contrary, a continuous berth means the shoreline of the port is not divided into different subsections [3, 4].

Some scholars are dealing with uncertainty. A lot of works of literature considered uncertain arrival time [5]). And some preview research focused on the uncertain operation time [6–9], while others aimed at the integrated uncertain factors [10–12].

In this work, we studied a BAP with a multi-entry policy (BAMEP) to maximize the total profit with consideration of the time value of seafood. Although there exists a

A. Dolgui et al. (Eds.): APMS 2021, IFIP AICT 634, pp. 149–157, 2021.
https://doi.org/10.1007/978-3-030-85914-5_16

large body of literature in the field of the BAP. Few studies considering Loss of seafood value and multi-entry policy for the berth allocation in fishing ports.

2 Problem Description

The assignment of berth for calling vessels at the port is berth planning. Port has several types of resources, including berth, equipment, and staff. The BAMEP aims at assigning arriving vessels to berth and make full and proper use of the resources mentioned above to get the optimal profit. In each cycle (e.g. one day), vessels arrive at one port at different time points. Each vessel is loaded with at least one type of seafood. We assume the sharing of information under which the port knows the exact amounts of seafood of different types on each vessel. The number of berths in the port is limited, each of which can serve only one vessel at the same time. The unloading process of one vessel can be interrupted by another vessel when the former one finishes the unloading process of one type of seafood. It can wait at a specific area (e.g. anchorage) until one berth becomes available where it can continue to unload the seafood. Some types of seafood can only be unloaded at the specific berth and the efficiency of unloading goods varies according to berths.

As for the fishing port, the fishing goods to transport need to be fresh. Thus, we have to consider freshness when constructing profit formulation. We assume that the prices of the seafood are respectively non-increasing with the time when the seafood is unloaded from the corresponding vessel. Because sailing inbound and out more than one time is permitted, the cost of each time sailing inbound should be taken into account. In terms of further profit, we want to satisfy as many owners of fishing vessels as possible. Thus, we cannot let one vessel waiting for too long. To simplify this problem, making the makespan as early as possible is a proper way. As a consequence, the BAMEP aims to minimize the overall penalty cost resulting from the waiting time and decreasing of the prices.

3 Mathematic Model

3.1 The Assumptions

When we are dealing with problems, we have to make some assumptions as the reality is so changeable and unpredictable.

The fishing vessels are allowed to arrive at the port any time but their arriving time is deterministic. And the prices of seafood are non-increasing with the time when they are unloaded at the port, respectively.

We care about neither the length of the berth nor the length of the vessel. For the reason that we are aiming at dealing with the problem in the fishing port, the fishing boats are almost of equal size. Accordingly, we regard all the sizes as the same length and make our problem easier and clearer. Moreover, no crossing constraints and safety space between berths must be obeyed.

A berth may not have the capacity to serve all categories of fishing goods. Consequently, the capacity of the berth can constrain the berth allocating.

The vessels are permitted to sail into the berth more than once until all the goods have been unloaded. In this paper, we let it possible for the vessels to sail into the berth more than once. The operation of one vessel can be interrupted only when all seafood of one type on that vessel is unloaded.

In this model, we regard a certain berth each time been arranged like a box. Under that consequence, if a certain berth has been arranged for n times, then we have n boxes here. With this assumption, we transfer the original problem to the problem to arrange the vessel to the berth's box, not merely the berth itself.

For a certain box of a berth, there is an independent start service time and ending service time. Relatively, for every kind of seafood in any vessel, there is an independent start service time and ending service time, too.

3.2   The Mathematical Formulation for the Model

As we have assumed, the work we have to do is to arrange each box of berth properly. The approach MILP is proposed, so a basic formulation deciding the arrangement to get the optimal objective is presented here. But before that, the following notation should be introduced first. And the variables and parameters notation is shown in Table A1 in the Table 1.

Table A1. Notations in the formulation

Parameters	
w_{ij}	The amount of jth goods in the ith vessel
c_{mj}	1, for the mth berth can serve the jth goods; 0, otherwise
v_i	The number of times that the vessel i can sail in the berth and out
R^A	The penalty parameter of the price reduced to the freshness decreasing
R^T	The transforming parameter to convert the ending time to the value
R^I	The cost parameter the vessel sailing inbound one time
T_i	The arrival time of the ith vessel
p_j	The price of the jth goods when totally fresh
E_m	The efficiency of unloading goods in the mth berth
M	A large enough number
s_{ij}	1 for there is jth goods in the ith vessel; 0, otherwise
m_1	The proportion parameter of the profit in the objection formulation
m_2	The proportion parameter of the maximize of the ending time in the objection formulation
N_{berth}	The total number of all the berths in the port
N_{goods}	The total number of the kinds of all the fishing goods
N_{vessel}	The total number of all the vessels to be arranged
N_{order}	The maximum number of the times which the berth can be arranged
Variables	
t_{mk}^s	The start time, the time when the mth berth starts to be used in the kth time
t_{mk}^e	The ending time, the time when the mth berth has been used in the kth time
T_{ij}^s	The start time, the time when the jth kind of seafood of the ith vessel starts to be unloaded
T_{ij}^e	The ending time, the time when all of the jth goods of the ith vessel unloaded
x_{ijmk}	1 for the mth berth is used for ith vessel at the kth order to unload the jth goods; 0, otherwise
y_{ijl}	1 means that in terms of the ith vessel, the jth kind of seafood is unloaded right followed by the lth goods
z_{mk}	1 for the mth berth has been arranged for k times,0, otherwise
π_{ijmk}	1 for before the mth berth is used for ith vessel at the kth order to unload the jth goods, the vessel should sail into the berth; 0, otherwise
τ_i	The number of times that the vessel i truly sail in the berth and out

The object function can be formulated as below.

$$Minimize: m_1 \sum_i \sum_j R^A w_{ij} p_j T^e_{ij} + m_2 \left(R^T \times \max_{i,j}(T^e_{ij}) \right) + R^l \sum_i \tau_i \tag{1}$$

The set of constraints is given below.

$$\sum_m \sum_k x_{ijmk} = s_{ij}, \ \forall i, \ \forall j \tag{2}$$

$$z_{mk} = \sum_i \sum_j x_{ijmk}, \ \forall m, \forall k \tag{3}$$

$$z_{mk} \leq 1, \ \forall m, \forall k \tag{4}$$

$$z_{mk} \leq z_{mk-1}, \ \forall m, \ \forall k, k \neq 1 \tag{5}$$

$$\sum_i \sum_k x_{ijmk} \leq M \times c_{mj}, \ \forall m, \ \forall j \tag{6}$$

$$t^s_{mk} \geq t^e_{mk-1}, \ \forall m, \ \forall k, k \neq 1 \tag{7}$$

$$t^e_{mk} = t^s_{mk} + \sum_i \sum_j x_{ijmk} \times \frac{w_{ij}}{E_m}, \ \forall m, \ \forall k \tag{8}$$

$$t^s_{mk} \geq \sum_i \left(\sum_j x_{ijmk} \times T_i \right), \ \forall m, \ \forall k \tag{9}$$

$$T^s_{ij} \geq \left(x_{ijmk} - 1 \right) \times M + t^s_{mk}, \ \forall i, \forall j, \ \forall m, \ \forall k \tag{10}$$

$$T^s_{ij} \leq \left(1 - x_{ijmk} \right) \times M + t^s_{mk}, \ \forall i, \ \forall j, \ \forall m, \ \forall k \tag{11}$$

$$T^e_{ij} \geq \left(x_{ijmk} - 1 \right) \times M + t^e_{mk}, \ \forall i, \ \forall j, \ \forall m, \ \forall k \tag{12}$$

$$T^e_{ij} \leq \left(1 - x_{ijmk} \right) \times M + t^e_{mk}, \ \forall i, \ \forall j, \ \forall m, \ \forall k \tag{13}$$

$$T^s_{ij} \leq s_{ij} \times M, \ \forall i, \ \forall j \tag{14}$$

$$T^e_{ij} \leq s_{ij} \times M, \ \forall i, \ \forall j \tag{15}$$

$$\sum_{j=0}^{N_{goods}} \left(y_{ijl} \times s_{ij} s_{il} \right) = 1, \ \forall i, \ \forall l, l \neq j \tag{16}$$

$$\sum_{j=0}^{N_{goods}} y_{ijl} = 1, \ \forall i, \ \forall l, l \neq j \tag{17}$$

$$\sum_{l=1}^{N_{goods}+1} \left(y_{ijl} \times s_{ij}s_{il}\right) = 1, \ \forall i, \ \forall j, l \neq j \tag{18}$$

$$\sum_{l=1}^{N_{goods}+1} y_{ijl} = 1, \ \forall i, \ \forall j, l \neq j \tag{19}$$

$$T_{ij}^e \leq T_{il}^s + \left(1 - y_{ijl}\right) \times M, \ \forall i, \ \forall j, \ \forall l, l \neq j \tag{20}$$

$$T_{ij}^s \geq T_{il}^e + \left(y_{ilj} - 1\right) \times M, \ \forall i, \ \forall j, \ \forall l, l \neq j \tag{21}$$

$$\pi_{ijm1} = x_{ijm1}, \ \forall i, \ \forall j, \ \forall m \tag{22}$$

$$\pi_{ijmk} \leq x_{ijmk}, \ \forall i, \ \forall j, \ \forall m, \ \forall k, k > 1 \tag{23}$$

$$\pi_{ijmk} \leq \left(1 - x_{ijmk}\right) - \left(\sum_{l,l \neq j} x_{ilmk-1} - 1\right), \ \forall i, \ \forall j, \ \forall m, \forall k, k > 1 \tag{24}$$

$$\pi_{ijmk} \geq x_{ijmk} - \sum_{l,l \neq j} x_{ilmk-1}, \ \forall i, \ \forall j, \ \forall m, \ \forall k, k > 1 \tag{25}$$

$$\sum_j \sum_m \sum_k \pi_{ijmk} = \tau_i, \ \forall i \tag{26}$$

$$\tau_i \leq v_i, \ \forall i \tag{27}$$

$$T_{ij}^e \geq 0, \ \forall i, \ \forall j \tag{28}$$

$$T_{ij}^s \geq 0, \ \forall i, \ \forall j \tag{29}$$

$$t_{mk}^e \geq 0, \ \forall m, \ \forall k \tag{30}$$

$$t_{mk}^s \geq 0, \ \forall m, \ \forall k \tag{31}$$

$$y_{ijl} \in \{0, 1\}, \ \forall i, \ \forall j, \ \forall l, j \neq l \tag{32}$$

$$x_{ijmk} \in \{0, 1\}, \ \forall i, \ \forall j, \ \forall m, \ \forall k \tag{33}$$

$$z_{mk} \in \{0, 1\}, \ \forall m, \ \forall k \tag{34}$$

$$\pi_{ijmk} \in \{0, 1\}, \ \forall i, \ \forall j, \ \forall m, \ \forall k \tag{35}$$

Accordingly, we are aiming at making it a win-win situation for each aspect. We regard them all as a whole and care about the overall interest including the vessels arriving and unloading the goods, and the goods selling from the port to the market. However, sometimes we not only care about the profit we have but also the waiting time the vessels spend. In terms of the long-term profit, the manager of the port will never let one of the fishing vessels wait for too long. In the above, the objective function (1) minimizes the integration of the sum of the profit, the max of the ending time, and the times for all the vessels sailing inbound and out.

Constraint (2) is a usual constraint which only if the kind of seafood is on the vessel, we will assign it. Constraint (4) is a bind that one box of a berth cannot be arranged twice or even more. Constraint (5) lets the arrangement of the berth be ordered, which means you cannot arrange a box before the smaller numbered box has been arranged. Constraint (6) enforces the seafood can only be unloaded if the berth has the capacity.

Constraint (9) requires that the starting time of service should be larger equal than the arriving time of the vessel which is common sense. Constraints (10) to (13) define the variables T_{ij}^s and T_{ij}^e by using the relationship with t_{mk}^e and t_{mk}^s. Constraints (14) and (15) also uses big M constraints to require that the variables T_{ij}^s and T_{ij}^e should be zero if there's no seafood here. Constraints (16) to (21), the variable y_{ijl} is been introduced to let us get the unloading sequence of different seafood of the same vessels. We use the virtual start point seafood with the index 0, and the virtual ending point seafood with the index $N_{goods} + 1$.

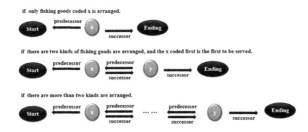

Fig. 1. The berth plan on the timeline

With the virtual start point and ending point, every point from 1 to N_{goods}, which means every kind of goods on a certain vessel, will have a predecessor and a successor. Some examples are shown in Fig. 1.

We also want to control the times that every vessel sails into the berth and out. To let the model closer to reality, the times that the vessel sails in and out can be limitless. Accordingly, a new binary variable π_{ijmk} is been introduced to show whether Seafood j on the Vessel i is unloaded at Berth m in the order of k or not.

Constraints (23) to (25) defines the variable π_{ijmk} when the index k larger than one. We can use some mathematical techniques to define π_{ijmk} with the comparison to x_{ijmk} and x_{ijmk}. We use a new variable τ_i to record the times that Vessel i sail into the berth in total, which is Constraint (25). Constraint (26) requires that the times that every vessel in and out to the berth should less equal than the parameter v_i.

4 Experimental Results and Analysis

In this section, we conducted comprehensive numerical experiments to illustrate the optimal solution and how it is influenced by parameters. The solution is obtained using ILOG CPLEX 12.9 optimizer coded with JAVA. The computational experiments were conducted on a computer with Core™ i5-630HQ CPU with 2.30 GHz processors and 8.00 GB RAM.

We assume that there are 10 fishing vessels to arrange with four categories of seafood, assumed to be lobster, salmon, octopus, and fish, and coded from 1 to 4 in order. At first, a sensitivity analysis on capacity is introduced below. Types of berth in different scenarios are shown in Table 1.

Table 1. The experiments about the berth.

No.	Scenario	Efficiency			Profit ($)	Time used
		Berth 1	Berth 2	Berth 3		(quarter-hour)
		General	Lobster	Octopus		
1	1A	1	9	9	53401.50	247.11
2		5	9	9	54417.42	76.80
3		6	9	9	54441.62	64
4		9	9	9	54519.59	64
5	2 (three berth are general)	1	9	9	54518.17	64
6		5	9	9	54527.27	64
7		9	9	9	54542.71	64
8	3	1	9	9	52750.67	276.44
9		5	9	9	54417.85	84.36
10		9	9	9	54513.97	64
11	4	1	9	9	52768.57	399.11
12		5	9	9	54323.39	97.51
13		9	9	9	54485.79	64
14	5	1	9	9	52693.67	520.89
15		5	9	9	54099.59	109.69
16		9	9	9	54441.62	64
17	1B	5	9	8	54452.56	78.7
18		5	9	9	54460.52	76.80
19		5	9	10	54465.59	75.18
20		5	9	11	54472.03	74.03

In terms of the five scenarios, we conduct three experiments each with the efficiency of Berth 1 changing. We set the efficiency of the Berth 1 in the three experiments respectively as low efficiency, medium efficiency, and high efficiency with the numbers 1, 5, and 9. Using the arrangement data, the objective profit and the total working time can be calculated. Conclusions can be easily found in the scatter plot.

As shown in and Table 1, we can find that when we improve the efficiency of the general berth from low efficiency to medium efficiency, the profit has relatively significant growth. There is still a growth between high efficiency and a medium one. As expected, general berths are more valuable to profits when berths have the same efficiency. However, as we have mentioned that too many general berths are easy to cause waste. Besides, a unique berth always has a relatively higher efficiency than the general berth. Thus, choose a proper unique berth is of high importance. Comparing Scenarios 3, 4, and 5, we can find that the right combination of unique berths can help maximize profits. In a real port assignment, the number of the berth is limitless and much lower than the number of fishing goods. Thus, by no means we can have each fishing goods a unique berth. Choosing the right combination of the unique berth can be a valuable problem for the management of the port company. Furthermore, Compare Scenario 1B with Scenario 1A, the results imply that the effect of improving the efficiency of general berths is better than that of improving the efficiency of private berths. Considering that the costs of them are different, so further work could be done when deciding the efficiency of which berth to improve.

What kind of berth should be constructed, the general one or the unique one can be a valuable question for the management of the port to dealing with. We also conducted the experiments by adding a berth.

Table. 2. The experiments about adding a berth.

No.	Scenario	Efficiency	The maximum order				Obj ($)	Time used (quarter-hour)
			Berth 1	Berth 2	Berth 3	Berth 4		
1	1	5	3	3	7	2	54489.23	84.08
2		6	1	6	4	4	54497.07	82.92
3		7	1	5	6	3	54500.37	80.62
4		8	2	6	2	5	54509.65	75.00
5		9	3	5	1	6	54522.79	72.78
6	2	9	3	5	4	3	54514.71	73.68
7	3	9	0	6	3	3	54508.79	73.42
8	4	9	4	7	1	3	54486.96	77.67
9	5	9	3	7	3	2	54485.79	77.56

As Table 2 implies, the following messages can be found. When a unique berth is added, the high the price of the kind of seafood aimed at, the more the profit is. The significant trend is shown in Column 6 to Colum 9 of Table 2. However, the gap is not simply related to price. Other factors such as the amount of each kind of fishing goods and the conditions of other berths may influence the profit as well. Besides, the rise of efficiency of berth helps the increase of profit. Adding the cost of construction of berth of different efficiency can make the problem clearer. And proper kinds of unique berth (Experiment 7 and Experiment 6) works better than general berth with not high enough efficiency (Experiment 1, Experiment 2, and Experiment 3). Thus, building multifunctional berths is not necessarily better than unique berths. We also found from

Table 2 that the maximum order in the results of some experiments varies in a relatively large gap. It means that some berths are overworking while some are idle. So it is not rational to make all the berth multifunctional.

5 Conclusion and Future Research

This paper introduces a berth allocation problem to solve the fishing port berth arrangement for fishing vessels. Some activities including inbound, outbound, transshipment and fishing goods selling in the market are taken into consideration. To maximize the total profit to get a win-win situation is our objective. Besides, the decision we make can get the industrial development and benefit fishermen and consumers as well.

Acknowledgements. This work was supported by the by National Natural Science Foundation of China (no. 71801191).

References

1. Imai, A., Nishimura, E., Papadimitrou, S.: The dynamic berth allocation problem for a container port. Transp. Res. Part B Methodol. **35**(4), 401–417 (2001)
2. Cordeau, J.F., Laporte, G., Legato, P., et al.: Models and tabu search heuristics for the berth-allocation problem. Transp. Sci. **39**(4), 526–538 (2005)
3. Park, K.T., Kim, K.H.: Berth scheduling for container terminals by using a sub-gradient optimization technique. J. Oper. Res. Soc. **53**(9), 1054–1062 (2002)
4. Lee, D.-H., Wang, H., Miao, L.: Quay crane scheduling with non-interference constraint in port container terminals. Transp. Res. Part E Logist. Transp. Rev. **44**(1), 124–135 (2008)
5. Umang, N., Bierlaire, M., Vacca, I.: Exact and heuristic methods to solve the berth allocation problem in bulk ports. Transp. Res. Part E Logist. Transp. Rev. **54**, 14–31 (2013)
6. Hendriks, M., Laumanns, M., Lefeber, E., Udding, J.T.: Robust cyclic berth planning of container vessels. OR Spectr. **32**(3), 501–517 (2010)
7. Golias, M.M.: A bi-objective berth allocation formulation to account for vessel handling time uncertainty. Marit. Econ. Logist. **13**(4), 419–441 (2011)
8. Karafa, J., Golias, M.M., Ivey, S., Saharidis, G.K., Leonardos, N.: The berth allocation problem with stochasti c vessel handling times. Int. J. Adv. Manuf. Technol. **65**, 1–12 (2013). https://doi.org/10.1007/s00170-012-4186-0
9. Ursavas, E., Zhu, S.X.: Optimal policies for the berth allocation problem under stochastic nature. Eur. J. Oper. Res. **225**, 380–387 (2016)
10. Han, X., Lu, Z., Xi, L.: A proactive approach for simultaneous berth and quay crane scheduling problem with stochastic arrival and handling time. Eur. J. Oper. Res. **207**, 1327–1340 (2010)
11. Zhen, L., Chang, D.: A bi-objective model for robust berth allocation scheduling. Comput. Ind. Eng. **63**, 262–273 (2012)
12. Xu, Y., Chen, Q., Quan, X.: Robust berth scheduling with uncertain vessel delay and handling time. Ann. Oper. Res. **192**(1), 123–140 (2012)

Cross-Dock Location: An Airbus Helicopters Case Study

David Arturo Pardo Melo[1,2(✉)] ⓘ, Vincent Bernier[2] ⓘ,
Yannick Frein[1] ⓘ, and Bernard Penz[1] ⓘ

[1] Univ. Grenoble Alpes, CNRS, Grenoble INP, G-SCOP,
38000 Grenoble, France
david-arturo.pardo-melo@grenoble-inp.fr
[2] Airbus Helicopters, 13700 Marignane, France

Abstract. In this paper, we evaluate the implementation of a cross-docking strategy at Airbus Helicopters (AH). To this end, firstly, we conduct a literature review on cross-dock location, and the facility location problem (FLP). Then, we describe briefly the AH current supply chain and based on literature review we develop a mixed integer linear programming (MILP) model adapted to this case. We apply this model to optimize the AH current supply chain. Results show that total costs could be potentially reduced by 21% by implementing a cross-docking strategy at AH. Finally we conduct a sensitivity analysis on input costs in order to evaluate the robustness of the solution obtained. It is found that results obtained are sensitive to variations on the input transportation costs.

Keywords: Airbus · Supply chain network design · Cross-dock location · Logistics · Transportation

1 Introduction

Cross-docking is a logistics strategy very often used by companies in order to optimize supply chain networks. It consists in implementing intermediary facilities in order to consolidate shipments coming from several suppliers that have the same destination with no storage. This strategy has proven to be successful in industries such as the automobile industry (*i.e.* Toyota case [9]). Currently at Airbus Helicopters (AH), inbound transportation is directly managed by suppliers in 80% of the cases that leads to direct transportation to AH's warehouses. For these suppliers there's no visibility over transportation costs and transportation operations. This results in a non-optimized inbound supply chain. In this article we evaluate the possibility to implement a cross-docking strategy at AH. The aeronautic industry is characterized by small production rates (More or less 30 helicopters per year for a product line) compared to the automobile industry. In the next section, we conduct a literature review on cross-dock location, particularly we are interested in models that allow determining the optimal location of cross-docking facilities within a supply chain, that determine the product flow through the supply chain network. Then we describe the AH current supply chain and we develop a MILP cross-dock location model for the AH case. Finally we use this model in order to evaluate the implementation of a cross-docking strategy at AH.

© IFIP International Federation for Information Processing 2021
Published by Springer Nature Switzerland AG 2021
A. Dolgui et al. (Eds.): APMS 2021, IFIP AICT 634, pp. 158–167, 2021.
https://doi.org/10.1007/978-3-030-85914-5_17

2   Literature Review

Belle et al. [1] define cross-docking as "the process of consolidating freight with the same destination (but coming from several origins), with minimal handling and with little or no storage between unloading and loading of the goods". In that way, the main difference between cross-docking facilities and the traditional warehousing – distribution centers, is the fact that in cross-docking facilities products are temporally stored for a small amount of time. In literature, some authors define 24 h as the storage time limit in cross-docking facilities [14]. However, in some companies, even if products are stored for a longer time, they still considering logistics platforms as cross-docks as long as "products move from supplier to storage to customer virtually untouched except for truck loading" [1]. Compared to point-to-point transportation the main advantages of cross-docking are: transportation costs reduction, consolidation of shipments and improved resource utilization. By locating cross-docks, several Less than Truck Load (LTL) shipments can be consolidated in a Full Truck Load (FTL) shipment. In this way, transportation cost is reduced due to LTL transportation distances reduction and truck capacity use rate is improved through the consolidation of LTL shipments in a FTL shipment. We can find some successful cases of cross-docking implementation as the Toyota Case [9] and the Walt Mart Case [12]. According to Belle et al. [1], mainly two factors can influence the suitability of a cross-docking strategy in a company: demand stability and unit stock out costs. Cross-docking is a good alternative when demand is stable and unit stock-out costs are low. If unit stock-out costs are important, cross-docking stills being a good solution if it is supported by appropriate planning tools and information systems.

In this study, we are particularly interested in determining the optimal location of cross-docking facilities within a supply chain network and the way the suppliers deliver their components. Facility location problem (FLP) is a well-established research area within operations research [5] which deals with this kind of problems. The simplest versions of the FLP are the p-median problem and the uncapacitated facility location problem (UFLP). The p-median problem consists in a set of customers and a set of potential facility locations distributed in a space. Each customer has its own demand, and distances or costs between each customer and each potential facility location are known. The objective is to locate N facilities at N locations of the set of potential locations in order to minimize total cost for satisfying the demand of customers. The UFLP is similar to the p-median problem. The only difference is that the number of facilities to be located is not predetermined. In the UFLP, a fixed opening cost is defined per potential facility and thus, the number of facilities located is an output of the model [10]. Moreover, the capacity of the facilities is not limited. The p-median and the UFLP problems are characterized by having deterministic parameters, a single product and a single period planning horizon.

There exists many variants of the facility location problem. The main of them are: the capacitated facility location problem [15] in which the capacity of the facilities is included in the problem, the multi-period facility location problem [6] used for problems where parameters evolve over time, the multi-product facility location problem [4] for problems were facility requirements vary in function of the type of product, the multi-level facility location problem in which location is decided at several layers of the supply chain [7], the stochastic facility location problem in which parameters behavior is modelled using probability functions and the robust facility location problem in which parameters are uncertain and there is no information about the probability function of the parameters [11]. In the AH case, parameters are deterministic, location needs to be determined only for cross-docking facilities and capacity constraints must be included. Additionally due to the strategic nature of the problem, the AH problem is a single period problem and demand can be aggregated in one single product.

Supply Chain Network Design (SCND) models can also integrate facility location decisions as well as other tactical decisions such as transportation mode selection, routing decisions, etc. However, in this study we are interested in models dealing only with location and allocation decisions.

3 Airbus Case Study

3.1 Current Supply Chain

AH has incorporated the modularity concept in its products. Hence, different modules are produced separately in the different Airbus sites: Albacete (Spain), Donauworth (Germany), Marignane (France) and Paris Le Bourget (PLB) (France). The rear fuselage is produced at Albacete, the Airframe is produced at Donauworth, the main rotor and the tail rotor are produced at Marignane and the blades are produced at PLB. Final product assembly takes place at Marignane or Donauworth. Each one of the Airbus sites has its own suppliers; they are located in three different continents: America, Africa and Europe. The scope of this study is limited to inbound flow: parts flow between suppliers and the different Airbus sites.

Recently Airbus launched a project in order to transfer all the stock to Albacete. Hence all the suppliers will deliver a warehouse at Albacete and after products will be forwarded to the final destination. We assume that this is the current scenario in our study. In other words, we evaluate the implementation of cross-docking facilities between suppliers and Albacete.

For this study, we select a panel of 152 suppliers located in Europe, America and Morocco, which are representative of product variety. Only a supplier that provides engines is excluded. This supplier delivers very expensive and bulky parts that are subject to a dedicated transportation mode managed separately. These suppliers were selected based on parts needed for the assembly of one helicopter. They represent 32% of the turnover of the company. For these suppliers we retrieved deliveries made in 2018 for Donauworth and Marignane from a database provided by the procurement department. Optimizations are conducted using this data which is representative of the AH current situation.

In the current supply chain, in 80% of the cases, suppliers manage transportation separately and AH does not have visibility over transportation operations and transportation costs (included in parts cost). Hence, the current inbound supply chain is non-optimized as a whole. Here, we evaluate the implementation of a cross-docking strategy. This would require the modification of the current AH transportation management system.

3.2   Delivery Methods and Transportation Modes

Mainly three delivery methods are used by suppliers depending on the shipment weight:

- Parcel and Courier Services (PCS): Door to door method of delivery. Freight companies suggest using this kind of solution for transport weights smaller than 70 kg [3].
- Less than Truck Load solutions (LTL): These solutions are used when transportation weight is not significant enough to use all the transportation mode capacity. Freight transportation companies suggest using this kind of solutions for transport weights bigger than 70 kg [3] and smaller than 11 loading meters (~ 11 tons, [8]).
- Full Truck Load solutions (FTL): All the transportation capacity is used. This is the best and cheapest solution for big transportation quantities. Transportation companies suggest using this delivery method for transportation weights bigger than 11 loading meters (~ 11 tons, [8]).

Additionally, suppliers use three transportation modes: road freight, sea freight and airfreight. For suppliers located in Europe parts are 100% delivered using road freight. Suppliers located in United States and Canada deliver 100% of their parts using airfreight. There is one supplier located in Mexico: Airbus Mexico. It delivers parts for Marignane using airfreight and parts for Donauworth using sea freight for 80% of the shipments and airfreight for the remaining 20%. Finally, suppliers located in Morocco deliver 100% of their parts using sea freight.

3.3   Current Supply Chain Total Cost

We estimate total transportation cost, storage cost and work in progress (WIP) cost for the current supply chain. Concerning transportation cost, as it was mentioned before, it is not known for 80% of the suppliers. For that reason, we estimate it using UPS tariffs [13] retrieved online for the PCS shipments and DHL tariffs [2] retrieved online for LTL shipments. FTL costs are estimated based on AH inter-sites transportation costs. Transportation costs from Albacete to the final destinations (Marignane and Donauworth) are included. Regarding the storage cost only capital cost is taken into account. At Airbus it is assumed in 2018 to be equal to 10% of parts cost (figure provided by the finance department). Finally, we estimate WIP cost for sea freight shipments due to important transportation delays using the Little's Law:

$$WIP\ cost = Throughput * Lead\ Time * 10\% * parts\ cost \tag{1}$$

The throughput represents the demand per day (kg/ per day) and the lead time represents the transportation delay in days. The last part of the formula (1) represents the storage cost (capital cost) which is 10% of parts cost. In this case parts cost is estimated in € per kg. Current total costs are presented in Table 1. Because of **Airbus privacy policies**, total costs in the study have been normalized.

Table 1. Current total costs

Transportation cost	92
Storage cost	5
WIP cost	3
Total cost	100

3.4 Cross-Dock Location Model for AH

In this study we are interested in evaluating at a strategic level, if it is cost-efficient or not to implement a cross-docking consolidation strategy in a supply chain taking into account total delivery volumes (small in the AH case). In that way, the objective of this model is to support strategic decision-making process concerning transport organization. For this reason, we decide to develop a single period deterministic cross-dock location model. The supply chain considered in this case is composed by a set of suppliers N, a set of potential cross-docking facilities M and a set of warehouses P. Suppliers must satisfy warehouses demand. They have the option of delivering directly all the warehouses or passing through a cross-docking facility in order to deliver all of them. A supplier cannot deliver parts using both flow alternatives. Products are transported using PCS, LTL or FTL solutions between suppliers and warehouses and using LTL or PCS solutions between the suppliers and the cross-docking facilities. FTL solutions or LTL sea freight solutions are used between the cross-docking facilities and the warehouses (consolidation). Volume delivered by each supplier i to a warehouse k (V_{ik}), total cost of delivering products from supplier i through the cross-docking facility j (C_{ij}) and total cost of delivering products from supplier i directly to all the warehouses (C_{i0}) are known. FTL delivery frequency between the cross-docking facilities and the warehouses is fixed (FTL_{jk}), hence, storage cost at the cross-docking facilities is calculated in function of it and FTL transportation cost between the cross-docking facilities and the warehouses is fixed (t_{jk}). The MILP is presented below:

Sets

$N = \{1 .. n\}$: The set of suppliers.

$F = \{0 .. m\}$: The set of delivery alternatives for each supplier. 0 represents delivering all the warehouses directly and j represents delivering all the products for all the warehouses through the cross-docking facility j.

$M = \{1 .. m\} \subseteq F$: The set of potential cross-docking facilities.

$P = \{1 .. p\}$: The set of Warehouses.

Parameters

C_{ij} $(i \in N \text{ and } j \in M)$: Total cost per year of delivering all the products from supplier i using cross-docking facility j. This cost includes transportation costs between the supplier i and the cross-docking facility j, handling costs and storage cost at the cross-docking facility j and at the warehouses in function of FTL_{jk}.

C_{i0} ($i \in N$): Total cost per year of delivering products directly to all the warehouses from supplier i. This cost includes transportation cost between the supplier i and all the warehouses and storage cost at all the warehouses.

V_{ik} ($i \in N$ and $k \in P$): Total volume (kg) delivered per year by supplier i to warehouse k.

K_{jk} ($j \in M$ and $k \in P$): Capacity of the transportation mode used between the cross-docking facility j and the warehouse k.

FTL_{jk} ($j \in M$ and $k \in P$): Fixed delivery frequency between the cross-docking facility j and the warehouse k (Times per year).

t_{jk} ($j \in M$ and $k \in P$): Total fixed transportation cost per year of delivering warehouse k from the cross-docking facility j with a fixed delivery frequency FTL_{jk}.

f_j ($j \in M$): Fixed opening cost of the cross-docking facility j.

Decision Variables

X_{i0} ($i \in N$): Takes a value of 1 if supplier i delivers all its products directly to all the warehouses, 0 otherwise.

X_{ij} ($i \in N$ and $j \in M$): Takes a value of 1 if supplier i delivers all its products through the cross-docking facility j to all the warehouses and 0 otherwise.

X'_{jk} ($j \in M$ and $k \in P$): Takes a value of 1 if the cross-docking facility j delivers the warehouse k, 0 otherwise.

Y_j ($j \in M$): Takes a value of 1 if the cross-docking facility j is used, 0 otherwise.

q_{jk} ($j \in M$ and $k \in P$): Volume delivered from the cross-docking facility j to the warehouse k.

Model

$$\textbf{\textit{Objective Function}} : Min \sum_{i=1}^{n}\sum_{j=0}^{m} C_{ij}X_{ij} + \sum_{j=1}^{m}\sum_{k=1}^{p} t_{jk}X'_{jk} + \sum_{j=1}^{m} f_jY_j \qquad (2)$$

Subject to

$$\sum_{j=0}^{m} X_{ij} = 1 \ \forall i \in N \qquad (3)$$

$$X_{ij} \leq Y_j \qquad \forall i \in N, \forall j \in M \qquad (4)$$

$$q_{jk} = \sum_{i=1}^{n} X_{ij}V_{ik} \qquad \forall j \in M, \forall k \in P \qquad (5)$$

$$q_{jk} \leq X'_{jk}FTL_{jk}K_{jk} \qquad \forall j \in M, \forall k \in P \qquad (6)$$

$$X_{ij} \in \{0,1\} \qquad \forall i \in N, \forall j \in F \qquad (7)$$

$$Y_j \in \{0, 1\} \qquad \forall j \in M \tag{8}$$

$$q_{jk} \in \mathbb{R}^+ \qquad \forall j \in M, \forall k \in P \tag{9}$$

$$X_{jk} \in \{0, 1\} \qquad \forall j \in M, \forall k \in P \tag{10}$$

The objective function (2) minimizes the sum between the total cost of delivering products from suppliers to warehouses or cross-docking facilities, the FTL transportation cost between the cross-docking facilities and the warehouses and the fixed opening costs. Constraint (3) ensures that for each supplier only one alternative is chosen between delivering products through a cross-docking facility and delivering them directly. Constraint (4) represents the fact that a supplier can deliver a cross-docking facility only if it is used. Constraint (5) ensures that products volume that goes from one cross-docking facility to one warehouse per year corresponds to the products volume delivered by suppliers using the cross-docking facility to this warehouse per year. Constraint (6) ensures that the quantity delivered from cross-docking facilities to warehouses respect the transportation mode capacity. Constraints (7–10) precise the validity domain of each decision variable.

4 Analysis of the Airbus Case Study

We run the model using Supply Chain Guru X (a supply chain design software which uses Xpress-Mosel as its mixed integer linear program solver) on the AH instance composed by 152 suppliers and one warehouse (Albacete) described in Sect. 3.1. Concerning cross-docking facilities, AH already counts with several distribution centers already installed in its supply chain. Based on these already existing AH distribution centers we define a set of 7 potential cross-docking facilities. In that way, there are not fixed opening costs in this case. Potential cross-docking facilities are located in: London (England), Paris (France), Toulouse (France), Saint-Etienne (France), Vitrolles (France), Zurich (Switzerland) and New York (United States). We assume that LTL sea freight is used between the cross-docking facility at New York and Albacete (taking into account volume delivered by North American suppliers) and FTL road freight is used between the rest of the cross-docking facilities and Albacete. Based on figures provided by the AH logistics department we assume that handling cost per pallet at the cross-docking facilities is equal to 16 €. We run the model for several values of FTL_{jk}: twice per month, once per week, twice per week and three times per week. Mean running time is 11 s. The minimum cost is obtained for FTL_{jk} equal to 96 times per year/ twice per week and the cross-docking facilities used are Toulouse and New York. This is called the cross-docking scenario. Results are presented in Table. 2.

Table 2. Cross-docking scenario total cost results

Transportation cost	57
Storage cost	9
WIP cost	6
Handling cost	7
Total cost	79

By using the cross-docking facilities at Toulouse and New York, with a LTL sea transportation mode between New York and Albacete, a FTL road transportation mode between Toulouse and Albacete, and a delivery frequency between the cross-docking facilities and Albacete equal to twice per week, total cost could be potentially reduced by 21%. Total cost reduction is driven by transportation cost reduction thanks to the consolidation of FTL shipments at the cross-docking facility at Toulouse and the consolidation of LTL sea freight shipments at New York (taking into account low sea freight transportation costs). 107 suppliers deliver the cross-docking facility at Toulouse and 12 suppliers deliver the cross-docking facility at New York (which explains WIP cost increase). In total 1696 tons per year are delivered to the cross-docking facilities. Supplementary storage cost in the cross-docking scenario is due to products storage at the cross-docking facilities. It is assumed that two times per week, the FTL truck used between Toulouse and Albacete, and the LTL sea transportation mode used between New York and Albacete are able to pick all the products available on stock. In other words it is assumed that workload at the cross-docking facilities is smoothed.

5   Sensitivity Analysis

In order to evaluate the robustness of the results obtained in the cross-docking scenario, we conduct a sensitivity analysis by varying input costs: transportation costs, storage cost and handling cost. We evaluate impact on total cost reduction achieved, the volume delivered to the cross-docking facilities and the cross-docking facilities used. Four levels of variation are evaluated for the input costs: −50%, −25%, +50% and +100%. Results are presented in Fig. 1 and Fig. 2. For all the variation levels on all the input costs, the same cross-docking facilities are used: Toulouse and New York. When transportation costs are reduced by 50% total cost reduction achieved in the cross-dock location scenario decreases from 21% to 8%, and when transportation costs increase by 100% total cost reduction achieved is increased from 21% to 32%. Volume delivered per year to the cross-docking facilities is reduced by 2.5% when transportation costs are reduced by 50% and it is increased by 0.9% when transportation costs are increased by 100%. Concerning storage cost, cost reduction achieved in the cross-dock location scenario is increased from 21% to 24% when it is reduced by 50% and it is reduced from 21% to 16% when it is increased by 100%. Volume delivered per year to the cross-docking facilities is increased by 0.8% when storage cost is reduced by 50% and it is reduced by 0.1% when storage cost is increased by 100%. Finally, total cost reduction achieved in the cross-dock location scenario is increased from 21%

to 25% when handling cost is reduced by 50% and it is reduced from 21% to 14% when handling cost is increased by 100%. Volume delivered per year to the cross-docking facilities does not change when handling cost is reduced by 50% and it is reduced by 0.2% when handling cost is increased by 100%.

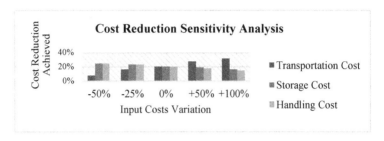

Fig. 1. Cost reduction sensitivity analysis

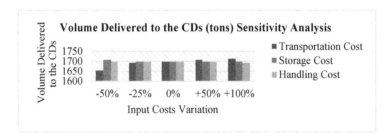

Fig. 2. Volume delivered sensitivity analysis

In conclusion, results obtained are sensitive to variations on transportation costs. Conversely, for big variations of the storage cost and the handling cost results do not change significantly.

6   Conclusions

In this article, we evaluate the implementation of a cross-docking strategy at AH, a helicopter manufacturer in the aeronautic industry, which is characterized by small production rates. To this end, based on literature, we developed a MILP cross-dock location model and we apply it to an AH instance composed by 152 suppliers, 7 potential cross-docking facilities and one warehouse (Albacete). We assume that LTL sea freight is used between the cross-docking facility at New York and Albacete and FTL road freight is used between the European cross-docking facilities and Albacete. As a result, by implementing two cross-docking facilities at Toulouse and New York, total cost could be potentially reduced by 21%. This demonstrates that a cross-docking strategy can be a cost-efficient solution in the helicopters industry despite the small production rates. Results obtained suppose that workload is smoothed at the cross-docking facilities. In order to evaluate the robustness of the results obtained, we conducted a sensitivity analysis by varying input costs. It was found that results obtained are sensitive to variations on transportation costs. Conversely, for big variations of the storage cost and the handling cost results do not change significantly. Finally, due to small delivery volume (1750 tons per year) included in this study only two cross-docking facilities are used. To go further in this analysis, it is recommendable to conduct a case study including 100% of the AH suppliers. This may increase cross-dock location cost reduction potential.

References

1. Belle, J.V., Valckenaers, P., Cattryse, D.: Cross-docking: state of the art. Omega **40**, 827–846 (2012)
2. DHL Freight Quote Tool. https://www.logistics.dhl/fr-en/home/our-divisions/freight/road-freight/road-freight-quote-tool.html. Accessed 9 Sept 2018
3. Freight Center, https://www.freightcenter.com, last accessed 2018/07/09
4. Klose, A., Drexl, A.: Facility location models for distribution system design. Eur. J. Oper. Res. **162**(1), 4–29 (2005)
5. Melo, M.T., Nickel, S., Saldanha-da-Gama, F.: Facility location and supply chain management – a review. Eur. J. Oper. Res. **196**, 401–412 (2009)
6. Nickel, S., Saldanha-da-Gama, F.: Multi-period facility location. In: Location Science, pp. 289–310. Springer (2015). https://doi.org/10.1007/978-3-319-13111-5_11
7. Ortiz-Astorquiza, C., Contreras, I., Laporte, G.: Multi-level facility location problems. Eur. J. Oper. Res. **267**, 791–805 (2017)
8. Projektgruppe Standardbelieferungsformen: Standardbelieferungsformen der Logisitik in der Automobilindustrie. In: Recommandation 5051 VDA - German Association of the Automotive (2008)
9. Rechtin, M.: Why Toyota cross-docks. https://www.autonews.com/article/20010806/ANA/108060766/why-toyota-cross-docks. Accessed 25 Feb 2020
10. Reese, J.: Methods for Solving the p-Median Problem: An Annotated Bibliography. Mathematics Faculty Research (2005)
11. Snyder, L.V.: Facility location under uncertainty: a review. IIE Trans. **38**(7), 547–564 (2006)
12. Stalk, G., Evans, P., Shulman, L.E.: Competing on capabilities: the new rules of corporate strategy. Harvard Bus. Rev. **70**(2), 57–69 (1992)
13. UPS Zones and Rates. https://www.ups.com/fr/fr/shipping/zones-and-rates.page. Accessed 9 Sept 2018
14. Vahdani, B., Zandieh, M.: Scheduling trucks in cross-docking systems: robust meta-heuristics. Comput. Ind. Eng. **58**(1), 12–24 (2010)
15. Wu, L.-Y., Zhang, X.: Capacitated facility location problem with general setup cost. Comput. Oper. Res. **33** 1226–1241 (2006)

A Hierarchical Network Approach for Long-Haul Parcel Transportation

Camille Gras[1,2(✉)] ⓘ, Van-Dat Cung[1] ⓘ, Nathalie Herr[2] ⓘ,
and Alantha Newman[1]

[1] Univ. Grenoble Alpes, CNRS, Grenoble INP, G-SCOP,
38000 Grenoble, France
{camille.gras,van-dat.cung,alantha.newman}@grenoble-inp.fr
[2] Probayes, 38330 Montbonnot, France
{camille.gras,nathalie.herr}@probayes.com

Abstract. In this work, we study the long-haul stage of parcel transportation, which involves the integration of the sorting operation allowing better consolidation of parcels in containers. The transportation is optimized over a complex two-level hybrid hub-and-spoke network and is conducted with a heterogeneous fleet; there are two types of vehicles which are balanced over the network on a daily basis with the management of empty trucks. We are not aware of a framework for long-haul parcel transportation in the literature that is sufficient to handle all aspects of the industrial problem we address. In terms of finding a solution, we propose a hierarchical algorithm with aggregate demands whose performance is related to the value of a truck filling rate threshold. Roughly speaking, the demands above this threshold can be routed directly while the ones below this threshold follow the hierarchical structure of the network. The routing of the two types of demands is optimized, first separately and then together in a multi-step process in which the subproblems are solved via Mixed Integer Linear Programs. Numerical experiments are carried out on datasets provided by a postal company (225 sites with 2500 demands). Various threshold values are tested to find out which one is the best, in terms of solution quality obtained and computational time.

Keywords: Operations research · Network design · Long-haul transportation · Parcel delivery · Hierarchical network

1 Introduction

E-commerce has experienced sustained growth over the last two decades. In 2019, an estimated 1.92 billion people purchased goods or services online[1]. This provides motivation for parcel delivery companies to constantly adapt and optimize

---

[1] Statista: E-commerce worldwide - Statistics & Facts Feb. 2021.

Grenoble INP—Institute of Engineering, Univ. Grenoble Alpes.

© IFIP International Federation for Information Processing 2021
Published by Springer Nature Switzerland AG 2021
A. Dolgui et al. (Eds.): APMS 2021, IFIP AICT 634, pp. 168–178, 2021.
https://doi.org/10.1007/978-3-030-85914-5_18

their transportation networks. The parcel delivery process is composed of four steps: collection, long-haul transportation, distribution and delivery [10]. The optimization of the long-haul transportation (defined as intercity transportation [4]) on a road network is addressed in this work. This means that neither how parcels reach an initial sorting center (the first-mile collection problem), nor how parcels are delivered from depots to final clients (the last-mile delivery and distribution problems) are considered. As long-haul parcel transportation addresses transportation of large volumes of parcels over long distances, a better use of vehicles and logistics operations such as sorting results in economies of scale.

In this paper, we define the Long-Haul Parcel Transportation Problem (LHPTP) in which the input is made of transportation demands expressed by the triple (origin, destination, number of parcels), and the road network composed of possible origin, destination and intermediate sites and links between them. The objective of the LHPTP is to minimize the costs for the postal company while delivering all of the demands. The predesigned road network has two sets of sites, sorting centers and delivery depots within a two-level (inner and outer level) hierarchical structure presented in Sect. 2.1. Over this hierarchical network, demands must be routed from sorting centers to delivery depots directly or through at most two other sorting centers. The transportation of parcels is made via two types of vehicles: trucks with one or two containers. As a daily transportation plan is designed, the vehicles have to be balanced over the course of a day for each site: empty vehicles need to be returned to appropriate locations.

1.1 Background and Previous Works

Hierarchical networks are composed of sites which are of different types of varying importance. The sites of a same type (inner-hubs, sorting centers, depots) form a **layer** [5]. Each pair of layers constitutes one **level** of the hierarchical network (and is sometimes referred to as an echelon). In the LHPTP, a two-level hierarchical network is given as input as there are three types of sites.

In our network, we have a **hub-and-spoke** configuration on each level. In a hub-and-spoke network, all links either begin or end at a hub, the other extremities of the links being the spokes [2]. A hub-and-spoke network in which there are possibilities to bypass the hubs with direct links is called **hybrid hub-and-spoke network**. Lin and Chen [8] define a hierarchical hub-and-spoke network in which each site is assigned to exactly one hub. It corresponds to our network without inner-hubs. Baumung and Gunduz [1] propose a heuristic for parcel transportation. They send fully filled trucks with parcels for the same destination (sorting center) until there are not enough parcels in the origin sites to fill a truck. The parcels which remain (called **residual volumes**) are consolidated into trucks. These residual volumes routing is optimized with an MILP. This method cannot be used to solve the LHPTP as it uses only one vehicle type, has one level of network (our inner level) and empty vehicle balancing is not considered.

Other work related to the LHPTP can be found in [6, 11–13] although none of these works exactly captures our problem formulation. Briefly, the LHPTP has more than one vehicle type and a two-level network in which the costs of parcel long-haul transportation are minimized on both levels simultaneously. A key feature of LHPTP is that there is no tour between sorting centers and delivery depots, while in previous work, this transportation stage often involves a tour [11]. We do not consider sorting capacity, as each sorting center has appropriately-sized sorting capacity. We simultaneously optimize the long-haul transportation and the balance of vehicles in the course of day on a two-level network which seems to be a unique aspect in the scope of parcel transportation.

1.2   Contributions

The LHPTP is really a family of problems based on various parameters (e.g., allowed logistic operations, limited fleet versus unlimited fleet, arc capacity, vehicle balancing constraints, vehicle types, etc.). None of the problems modeled in the literature is sufficient to model the specific problem that we want to solve nor to solve the variations that could arise based on the various parameters that we consider. For example, other works treat the long-haul stage of parcel delivery as a single level; there is very little treatment of two-level networks with logistics operations on parcels permitted between the levels. Moreover, in a two-level network, certain issues arise that do not apply to a simpler model; for example, balancing vehicles between intermediate sites (i.e., not origin/destination sites).

In this work, we take advantage of the hierarchical structure of our network to design good transportation plans by dividing the whole problem into tractable subproblems. We directly send large demands and consolidate residual demands. Indeed, it seems natural to maximize the truck filling rate and minimize the number of parcels sorted. Therefore, we do not impose a sorting (as in [6]) on all the demands, which incurs extra costs. Instead, we require a sorting for a subset of the demands while sending the other demands directly. We send directly (bypassing all sorting operations) trucks filled more than a **truck filling rate threshold**, rather than only the fully filled ones (like [1]). The LHPTP has two levels which can both be bypassed by direct paths, and a heuristic is used to optimize this decision for bypassing the two sortings. But this heuristic is not used within the inner level as the MILP reaches the optimum for the inner level optimization.

In Sect. 2, the LHPTP is introduced and an MILP formulation for it is presented. In Sect. 3, an algorithm which solves the LHPTP via the aggregation of demands and the MILP is presented. Finally, in Sect. 4, we show that the algorithm with aggregate demands can handle our large real data instances.

2   Problem Description

The LHPTP defined in this section is basically a Service Network Design problem [3] with Hub-and-Spoke structure. However, the LHPTP has distinct properties such as demands have both fixed origin and destination, and the sorting operation has a cost per parcel. Moreover, the problem we tackle is an industrial problem containing strong constraints. Thus, after the presentation of the application framework of our problem, we introduce an MILP for the LHPTP, which can be adapted to solve other long-haul parcel transportation problems.

2.1 Application Framework and Optimization Problem

In our application framework, we are presented with the problem of delivering parcels via trucks with one or two containers in a national postal network composed of sites with around 2500 demands per day being routed between these sites. There are two **sets of sites**: each site of our network is either a delivery depot or a sorting center but cannot be both. There are on average 17 sorting centers and 208 delivery depots. Among the sorting centers, some are also inner-hubs fixed by the transportation managers.

Parcels are physical objects which must be routed from a specified origin sorting center to a designated delivery depot. As each container can transport a significant amount of parcels, all parcels are assumed to be of equal (average) size. Parcels having the same origin and destination are grouped in a **demand**. Demands are represented by the triple (origin, destination, number of parcels). We assume that the demands are known for an average day. Our goal is to design a **transportation plan** to deliver all the demands at a minimum cost. The cost of a solution is composed of transportation costs and logistics operations' costs.

Indeed, only one logistics operation is considered – the **sorting** – which occurs in sorting centers. When parcels are sorted, all parcels in a container are grouped according to the next site served on their operational path. When a set of demands destined for different final sites are put in the same container it is called **consolidation**. The parcels are shipped in **bulk** in containers. A container cannot be partially unloaded, thus it carries parcels headed for one site, which is either an intermediate sorting center or a final delivery depot depending on the parcel's destination. This means that when there is consolidation between demands, there is always a sorting operation afterwards.

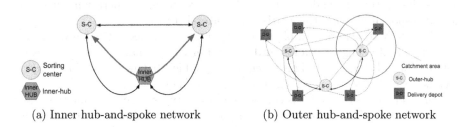

(a) Inner hub-and-spoke network   (b) Outer hub-and-spoke network

Fig. 1. The two levels of the hybrid hub-and-spoke network

The parcels are delivered on a road network composed of two hierarchically nested **hub-and-spoke networks** (see Fig. 1). The inner level of this network is made of sorting centers. A sorting center on a path between two sorting centers is called inner-hub. The outer level of the network is composed of sorting centers and delivery depots. Indeed, each delivery depot is assigned to a sorting center (an outer-hub), usually the closest (with respect to travel time). The area which contains the delivery depots affiliated to a sorting center, including this sorting center, is called a **catchment area**. The mapping of the catchment areas, created with the experience of transportation managers, is used in the current operational strategy in which the parcels are handled regionally. They are sent to the catchment area containing their delivery depot, sorted in their corresponding outer-hub and sent to their delivery depot.

The **inner network** connects the sorting centers (see Fig. 1a). It is a hybrid hub-and-spoke network as the sorting centers either send parcels directly to other sorting centers or they can use an inner-hub to sort and/or consolidate demands. The **outer network** arises when the final destinations of parcels, are the delivery depots (see Fig. 1b) are added. They are the spokes in a hybrid hub-and-spoke network in which the outer-hubs are the corresponding sorting centers. Indeed, parcels can either be sent directly from their origin sorting center or consolidated and then sorted before reaching their delivery depots.

There are two types of **vehicles**: trucks with one container and trucks with two containers (also called twin trailers). The number of vehicles or containers is not limited and can be adapted appropriately in the optimization process. Note that the performance standard is the same for all the vehicles and does not depend on the vehicle type. The vehicle type changes only the capacity and the cost.

An **operational path** is a set of consecutive physical links between sites. Each of the links on the operational path is associated with a schedule and each site is associated with an operation (sorting or delivery) performed on a parcel flow at a time slot. Moreover, each link is served with a vehicle type (i.e., a vehicle with one or two containers). Each parcel is either (i) sent on a direct path from a sorting center to a delivery depot, or (ii) it undergoes a single sorting at a sorting center (not mandatorily an inner-hub), or (iii) it undergoes two sortings, one at an inner-hub and one at the corresponding sorting center of the destination. Each demand can be split over multiple operational paths in the transportation plan: this is **disaggregate shipping** [7].

As a daily transportation plan is designed, there is a need to balance vehicles to ensure that enough **vehicles and containers** are available each day on each site to send all the parcels. This is achieved by vehicle balancing: sending **empty trucks** back from sites in which there were too many vehicles.

In summary, the LHPTP is composed of three types of constraints: the delivery constraints, the capacity constraints and the design-balance constraints. The delivery constraints (1b) state that all the parcels have to be delivered. The link capacity constraints (1c) associate the number of parcels and the number of vehicles on each link. There are such constraints for each vehicle type and each link in the network. Finally, the design-balance constraints (1d) balance both containers and trucks between sites on a daily basis.

2.2 MILP Formulation

The MILP formulation for the LHPTP is a path-based model; the number of possible operational paths for each demand is bounded. Indeed, each operational path is allowed to have at most two sorting operations after the initial sorting (done immediately upon collection), which limits each path's length and thus the number of possible paths. The notations in our model are: D is the set of demands, V the set of vehicle types, S the set of sites composed of $S_{s.c}$ the set of sorting centers and $S_{d.d}$ the set of delivery depots. L is the set of links between sites whose element $l_{i,j}$ is the link between site i and site j, P_d is the set of possible operational paths for the demand d in D, P_d^l is the set of possible operational paths using the link l in L for demand d in D.

The variables are of two types: (1) $x_p^d \in [0, 1]$, with $d \in D$ and $p \in P_d$, represent **parcel flows**. It is the percentage of a demand d using an operational path p; (2) $y_l^{veh} \in \mathbb{N}$, with $l \in L$ and $veh \in V$, represent **vehicle flows**. They are integers which represent the number of vehicles of type veh on each link l. The cost of the operational path p is denoted c_p. c_l^{veh} is the cost of the link l with vehicle veh, v_d the number of parcels of demand d, and C_{veh} the capacity of vehicle veh.

$$\min \sum_{d \in D} \sum_{p \in P_d} c_p x_p^d + \sum_{veh \in V} \sum_{l \in L} c_l^{veh} y_l^{veh} \tag{1a}$$

s.t.:

$$\forall d \in D, \sum_{p \in P_d} x_p^d = 1 \tag{1b}$$

$$\forall l \in L, \forall veh \in V, \sum_{d \in D} \sum_{p \in P_d^l} v_d x_p^d \leqslant y_l^{veh} \cdot C_{veh} \tag{1c}$$

$$\forall s \in S, \sum_{i \in S} y_{l_{i,s}}^{veh} = \sum_{j \in S} y_{l_{s,j}}^{veh} \tag{1d}$$

with: $x_p^d \in [0, 1]$ \hfill (1e)

$$y_l^{veh} \in \mathbb{N} \tag{1f}$$

LHPTP-MILP

Due to the usage of consolidation, a container can carry parcels with different origins and destinations; a demand might not be routed on its shortest path. Indeed, consolidation is a crucial strategy used to reduce costs, but its usage makes the problem computationally difficult (since it is not simply a shortest path problem). Different sorting centers and different time slots can be used for the sorting operations. Moreover as the possibility of disaggregate shipping is added, there is a combinatorial explosion on the number of possible operational paths, which prevent the MILP from giving an optimal solution on realistic sized datasets (with around 225 sites and 2500 demands) in reasonable time.

3   Hierarchical Algorithm with Aggregate Demands

The LHPTP can be formulated as an MILP which does work well on small instances. Therefore, the Hierarchical Algorithm with Aggregate Demands (henceforth HAAD) divides the problem into smaller subproblems, each of which can be solved optimally via an MILP or other means, and then adds these solutions together to obtain a final solution of good quality, although it can be suboptimal.

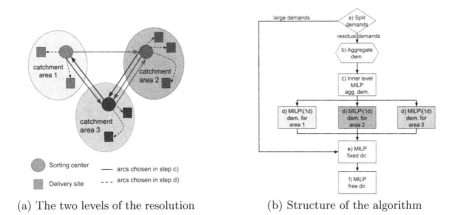

(a) The two levels of the resolution   (b) Structure of the algorithm

Fig. 2. Hierarchical Algorithm with Aggregate Demands (HAAD)

We first find an optimal transportation plan on the inner level (see Fig. 1), which involves choosing the inner-hubs. We allow all sorting centers to be candidate inner-hubs in order to test whether or not the inner-hubs proposed by the transportation managers are actually the best ones. Then the extension of this transportation plan is optimized on the outer level. Finally, in the last steps of the algorithm, these solutions are combined and refined to obtain a transportation plan for the whole network (see Fig. 2). Recall that the original demands of the LHPTP are from sorting centers to delivery depots. For the inner problem, we create aggregate demands which are demands from sorting centers to sorting centers (in order to separate the two levels). The last sorting is required to be done in the corresponding sorting center of the delivery depot of destination. An aggregate demand is the sum of demands from a sorting center to all the corresponding delivery depots of another (destination) sorting center.

Algorithm 1: Hierarchical Algorithm with Aggregate Demands (HAAD)

---

1 a) Split demands
2 **for** each demand d **do**
3 | **if** $v_d < \sigma \cdot C_{veh}$ **then** **Add** d to the set of residual demands
4 | **else** $k = \lceil v_d/C_{veh} \rceil$
5 | | **if** $k \cdot \sigma \cdot C_{veh} \leq v_d \leq k \cdot C_{veh}$ **then** **Add** d to the set of large demands
6 | | **else Split** d into a large demand of volume $(k-1)C_{veh}$ and a residual demand (twin demands)

7 b) Aggregate demands
8 **for** each residual demand d **do**
9 | **Aggregate** it with the demands with the same corresponding sorting center as destination

10 c) Solve the aggregate subproblem (inner level)
11 **Solve the MILP** which is made only of links between sorting centers
12 d) Extend for each catchment area (outer level)
13 **for** each one of the n catchment areas **do**
14 | **Solve the MILP without constraints (1d)** to route the demands towards their catchment area

15 e) Add the solutions for residual demands, large demands (on direct paths) and the balance of trucks
16 **Solve the MILP** with all the residual demands and with only the chosen operational paths to optimize the vehicle flow. The large demands are enforced to use a direct paths (for up to 1h).
17 f) Add the large demands
18 **Solve the MILP** with all the demands, the solution of the previous MILP fixed and the option for the large demands to follow a direct path or an already chosen operational path. (for up to 1h)

The algorithm chooses the links between sorting centers first (plain arcs in Fig. 2a), then it chooses the links from sorting centers to delivery depots in each zone around each sorting center (dotted arcs on Fig. 2a) and finally it assembles the solutions. But if all the demands are aggregated, we lose the possibility of using direct paths from a sorting center to a delivery depot, which have been proven to be useful [9,11]. Therefore the following approach is considered: if a demand is large enough to nearly fill a truck (above a threshold σ), then sending a truck with this demand directly from the origin to the destination is considered. Thus the HAAD first splits the demands into large demands, whose operational paths are actually determined in the last step (deferred demands), and residual demands whose operational paths are specified by the transportation plan constructed on the inner and outer levels of the network. These residual demands are either routed through an inner-hub and subject to an additional sorting, or they are routed directly from their initial sorting center to their final sorting center. This latter determination is made during the single call to the LHPTP-MILP on the set of aggregate residual demands.

This approach gives a solution for the complete instance in reasonable time but might be globally suboptimal because the choice between performing at least one sorting or sending the parcel on a direct path is handled in a heuristic way. Thus, for a parcel sent directly, it could be the case that some possible operational paths that could be chosen in a global optimal solution are not considered.

4   Numerical Experiments and Results Analysis

Simulations are run on a Linux server with 32 CPU and 150 Gbytes of RAM using CPLEX 12.8 solver. The data, provided by a postal company, contains six datasets which represent six different configurations of the network with logistics sites spread across mainland France. A dataset is made of: (1) a set of sites with their type, location and the travel times between each pair of sites; (2) a set of demands (origin, destination, number of parcels) between these sites; (3) costs: kilometric cost and the costs of all the logistics operations (sorting, entering sites, leaving sites etc.). The number of sites varies from 154 sites to 292 and the number of demands varies from 2312 to 3627. Note that the kilometric cost for a vehicle is thrice the cost to sort one parcel in a sorting center.

In the network on which the parcel transportation is optimized, there are from two to four inner-hubs fixed by the transportation managers. In this section, we ignore this constraint and assume that all the sorting centers can be inner-hubs in order to enhance the possibilities of consolidation and to confirm if the four inner-hubs chosen by the transportation managers are the right ones.

Table 1. Comparison of the thresholds (NEV = No Empty Vehicles)

σ (%)	Time (h)			Sol fix. dir e)			Built sol f)			Gap (%)			Fill. rate (NEV)			Global fill. rate		
	min	avg	max	min	avg	max	min	avg	max	min	avg	max	min	avg	max	min	avg	max
none		6			—		377	406	426	10.2	13.7	17.4	70.0	71.3	73.2	42.7	43.4	44.4
100	1.0	1.1	1.3	376	415	444	376	414	442	13.4	15.5	16.7	82.6	84.0	86.0	52.4	54.1	55.7
80	1.0	1.2	1.2	374	406	429	374	406	429	12.2	13.8	14.9	81.6	83.9	85.9	51.4	53.4	54.8
60	1.0	1.1	1.2	367	399	419	367	399	419	10.1	12.2	13.9	79.5	81.8	83.6	49.3	50.9	52.0
40	1.1	1.2	1.5	374	406	426	374	406	426	11.5	13.8	15.7	75.4	76.0	77.1	45.5	45.7	46.4
20	1.0	1.3	1.5	436	463	480	436	463	480	19.9	24.5	27.7	60.1	61.5	63.3	34.1	34.7	35.4

We first compare results obtained with several thresholds (σ in Algorithm 1) for splitting demand volumes into large and residual demands. In this algorithm, each MILP is solved with 1 h time limit and all sorting centers are considered as inner-hubs. The gap presented in Table 1 is with respect to the best lower bound computed by the solver (after a 6 h run).

The results in Table 1 show that compared to the LHPTP-MILP when run without any heuristic for 6 h (line with threshold none), the HAAD can provide better solution values in 5 to 6 times less computational time for the appropriate thresholds. The threshold which provides the best results is 60% ±10%. The solutions obtained in step e) and step f) are nearly the same and in these steps the optimal solution is reached most of the time (with respect to the variables fixed as inputs). If a large demand does not have any twin demand, it cannot use a non-direct path. For these demands, there is no difference between the solutions of steps e) and f). And the lower the threshold is, the less there are demands which are split into twin large and residual demands. Note that steps e) and f) are run for much less than one dedicated hour.

In the solutions presented in Table 1, nearly all the sorting centers are used as inner-hubs. It is because the demands are small compared to the vehicle capacity and because the sorting costs are not very high compared to the kilometric cost. Consolidation of demands is then interesting as it reduces the number of vehicles used, even if this leads to more sortings. This might not be the case with much higher sorting costs. To check this we compare results obtained with several sorting costs with a threshold of 60% for the activation of direct paths. The number of inner-hubs used decreases when the sorting cost increases. Moreover, the inner-hubs selected by the HAAD are not the one selected by transportation managers and this results in better solutions. Thus the HAAD can be an interesting decision support tool for the managers. With $\sigma = 60\%$, the vehicle filling rates with and without considering returns of empty vehicles are respectively 50,9% and 81,8%. Slightly higher vehicle filling rates (like 84%) can be obtained with higher filling rate thresholds but at the expense of sorting cost for more consolidation.

The simulations show that in parcel transportation, due to sorting costs and empty balancing of vehicles, greater truck filling does not obviously result in lower cost. Indeed, the cheaper solutions are not the ones in which the trucks have the highest filling rate. The best threshold to decide if a demand should use a direct path is when it fills 60% of a container, not 100%. This result seems counter-intuitive for someone on the ground with only a local point of view, as they do not have a global perspective, which leads to a different conclusion. But it allows to optimize the network globally and to minimize the total cost.

We also show that the advantages of consolidation in inner-hubs depends strongly on the sorting costs and kilometric costs. Thus the optimal threshold found empirically depends on the datasets and would need to be recomputed if the algorithm were to be applied on another dataset.

With the data we used, greater truck filling rates do not correspond to the cheapest solution. It means, in general, that in long-haul parcel transportation, it is not always better to send fully-filled trucks.

5   Conclusion

In this work, the Long-Haul Parcel Transportation Problem (LHPTP) is defined. It consists of optimizing the long-haul transportation of parcels on a two-level hybrid hub-and-spoke network with three types of sites. We present a new hierarchical algorithm which exploits the two-level structure of the network to solve this problem which contains strong industrial constraints. As the hybrid hub-and-spoke network offers the possibility to use direct paths, we offer this option for large demands (over a threshold). The residual demands (lower than the threshold) are gathered into aggregate demands which stay on the inner-level of the network. The HAAD divides the problem into subproblems solved through MILPs. It has been tested with success on real data instances at the scale of a country (around 225 sites and 2500 demands) which are too large to be solved efficiently with a single global MILP.

We have tested various thresholds of truck filling rate to divide the demands to find which one suits our datasets the best. This constitutes a tailored heuristic which permits us to have better quality solutions for the LHPTP that can be obtained more efficiently. One perspective for future work is to investigate the impact of using different thresholds on different network areas or/and for different demands. These thresholds can integrate other criteria than the truck filling rate such as distances and transportation costs.

Acknowledgments. This work is funded by ANRT, CIFRE n°2019/0351. We thank Nicolas Teypaz and Sylvain Ducomman (Probayes) for their comments.

References

1. Baumung, M.N., Gündüz, H.I.: Consolidation of residual volumes in a parcel service provider's long-haul transportation network. In: Corman, F., Voß, S., Negenborn, R.R. (eds.) ICCL 2015. LNCS, vol. 9335, pp. 437–450. Springer, Cham (2015). https://doi.org/10.1007/978-3-319-24264-4_30
2. Bryan, D.L., O'kelly, M.E.: Hub-and-spoke networks in air transportation: an analytical review. J. Reg. Sci. **39**(2), 275–295 (1999)
3. Crainic, T.G.: Service network design in freight transportation. Eur. J. Oper. Res. **122**(2), 272–288 (2000)
4. Crainic, T.G.: Long-Haul Freight Transportation. In: Hall, R.W. (eds) Handbook of Transportation Science. International Series in Operations Research Management Science, vol. 56. pp. 451–516. Springer, Boston (2003) https://doi.org/10.1007/0-306-48058-1_13
5. Cuda, R., Guastaroba, G., Speranza, M.G.: A survey on two-echelon routing problems. Comput. Oper. Res. **55**, 185–199 (2015)
6. Lee, J.H., Moon, I.: A hybrid hub-and-spoke postal logistics network with realistic restrictions: A case study of korea post. Expert Syst. Appl. **41**(11), 5509–5519 (2014)
7. Leung, J.M.Y., Magnanti, T.L., Singhal, V.: Routing in point-to-point delivery systems: formulations and solution heuristics. Transp. Sci. **24**(4), 245–260 (1990)
8. Lin, C.C., Chen, S.H.: The hierarchical network design problem for time-definite express common carriers. Transp. Res. Part B: Methodological **38**(3), 271–283 (2004)
9. O'Kelly, M.E.: A geographer's analysis of hub-and-spoke networks. J. Transp. Geogr. **6**(3), 171–186 (1998)
10. Sebastian, H.-J.: Optimization approaches in the strategic and tactical planning of networks for letter, parcel and freight mail. In: Dolk, D., Granat, J. (eds.) Modeling for Decision Support in Network-Based Services. LNBIP, vol. 42, pp. 36–61. Springer, Heidelberg (2012). https://doi.org/10.1007/978-3-642-27612-5_3
11. Zäpfel, G., Wasner, M.: Planning and optimization of hub-and-spoke transportation networks of cooperative third-party logistics providers. Int. J. Prod. Econ. **78**(2), 207–220 (2002)
12. Zhang, J., Wu, Y., Liu, P.: Routing problem for hybrid hub-and-spoke transportation network: a case study of a ltl carrier. In: 2007 IEEE International Conference on Automation and Logistics, pp. 170–175. IEEE (2007)
13. Zhang, W., Payan, A.P., Mavris, D.N.: Improving courier service network efficiency through consolidations. In: AIAA Scitech 2021 Forum. p. 1233 (2021)

Assessment of MaaS (Mobility as a Service) Apps in Metropolitian Area of São Paulo, Brazil

Gabriel Santos Rodrigues[1], João Gilberto Mendes dos Reis[1](✉), Regis Cortez Bueno[2], Wilson Yoshio Tanaka[2], Adriano Maniçoba da Silva[2], and Sivanilza Teixeira Machado[2]

[1] RESUP - Research Group in Supply Chain Management - Postgraduate Program in Production Engineering, Universidade Paulista, São Paulo, Brazil
joao.reis@docente.unip.br

[2] Instituto Federal de Educação, Ciência e Tecnologia de São Paulo - Câmpus Suzano, Suzano, Brazil

Abstract. The popularization of mobile internet and transport applications making passenger transport real-time information available to the general public. In the Metropolitan Area of São Paulo (MASP), the largest urban agglomeration in South America with 21 million inhabitants carrying out their activities every day, these systems have been changing the user's behaviour. The purpose of this study is to evaluate the perception and use of these applications called Mobility as a Service (MaaS) for the passenger in MASP. To do so, we conducted a survey with 138 respondents that live in MASP in May 2020 regarding the services: Google Maps, Moovit and Citymapper. They evaluated what the application they prefer to, how the applications functions are used by theirs and the public transportation frequence of use and after the anwers were used in a descripitive statistics analysis. The results indicated a predominance of youth users that plan their trips using public transportation and seek real-time information through by these applications.

Keywords: Passenger transport · Journey planning · Mobile technology

1 Introduction

The Metropolitan Area of São Paulo is the main Brazilian metropolitan region and the largest urban agglomeration in South America. It is composed of 39 municipalities geographically interconnected to the city of São Paulo, a global metropolis that concentrates 21 million inhabitants in an area of approximately and generates approximately 18% of the Brazilian GDP [1]. This region concentrate approximately 9.4 million jobs and 5.5 million enrolled students whom generates 42 million journeys daily [2].

© IFIP International Federation for Information Processing 2021
Published by Springer Nature Switzerland AG 2021
A. Dolgui et al. (Eds.): APMS 2021, IFIP AICT 634, pp. 179–187, 2021.
https://doi.org/10.1007/978-3-030-85914-5_19

MASP has its public transport network based on Subway service, Metropolitan Train and Bus. The subway network is 101 km long with six lines carrying four million passengers per day. The metropolitan train network has seven lines with 271 km of extension and 94 stations that serve 23 of the 39 municipalities of the MASP transporting over 3 million passengers per day. Finally, bus network is made up of 1,336 municipal lines and 587 intercity lines that are operated by approximately 18,000 vehicles [3–6].

With the popularization of smartphones and high-speed mobile internet several applications have emerged that allow users to make decisions based on information provided. These applications are named Mobility as a Service (MaaS) [7] and has been used by passenger in metropolitan areas.

MaaS can help users to move around making use of GPS (Global Positioning System) and information collected in real-time from operators and other passengers [8]. They can be informed of the waiting time for a certain passenger transport system or just regarding the itinerary; and those that provides services such as taxis and ridesharing.

In this article, we evaluated MaaS that works as an aid to decision-making for the transportation users. Real-time information reduces the inconvenience caused by waiting for a long time and makes them feel safer while waiting for transport [9]. Moreover, it shows in real-time the position of the transport vehicle reducing passenger wasting time [10, 11].

With these ideas in mind, the aim of this study is to analyze the perception of users of the public passenger transport system in the Metropolitan Region of São Paulo on the efficiency of three MaaS: Google Maps, Moovit and Citymapper. They were selected based on the availiability in many global and important areas such as London, Tokyo and New York. And how they can assist in the user's decision-making about their daily commuting planning.

To do so, we conducted an online survey with 138 people in 2020, divided into three parts: profile of users, the main modes of transport adopted and which are the most important functions. The data were analyzed using two statistical methods: descriptive statistics and factor analysis.

The article is divided as follows: Section is formed by this introduction, Sect. 2 the methodology approach, Sect. 3 our results, Sect. 4 our main conclusions.

2   Methodology

2.1   Survey

We conducted a survey to obtain empirical information beyond those found in scientific documents on urban mobility. The purpose was to evaluate the efficiency of the use of MaaS by users of passenger public transportation in MASP.

The survey was carried out in May 2020 with 138 users living in MASP. It was divided into three parts: (i) Socioeconomic characteristics such as gender, age, educational level and income; (ii) Transport systems use such as frequency, purpose and integration mode, transport mode, integration with other modes of transport, and travel time; and (iii) User's perception of mobile applications such as key applications used, the main objective of its use, frequency of use, and evaluation of the main services offered.

Among the MaaS offered we studied: TP = Travel planner (Routes, Timetable, Journey time, Fare); RS = Route sharing; OFFMAP = Off-line maps; JP = Journey planner: Origin and Destination; JF = Journey fare; MP = Mode preference; PC = Passenger capacity; RTI = Real time information; DF = Delay forecast; TI = Traffic information; AMI = Active mobility integration; ICA = Integration car app (ridesharing) and taxi; UCI = User Collaborative Integration.

The research sample was calculated based on Eq. 1 [12]. We considered the population in MASP, degree of homogeneity 50/50, sampling error of 10%, and confidence level of 95%.

$$n = \frac{NZ^2P(1-p)}{(N-1)e^2 + Z^2p(1-p)} \tag{1}$$

Where, n = sample size, N = population, Z = abscissa of the normal standard, p = estimated homogeneity, e = sample error.

2.2   Validation and Survey Application

Data collection was performed using an electronic form, using the Google Forms tool. First, a pre-test was carried out with seventeen (17) participants, to validate the structure. After this process, the link for participation was sent via social networks and email groups, WhatsApp, Instagram and Facebook. The volunteers, before answering the form, underwent reading about the research clarifications and guidelines, and later, signed the Informed Consent Form. The survey was only open to participants who agreed to voluntarily participate.

Data Analysis

The softwares Microsoft Excel 2016 ©and Statistics v.13.3 ©were used to tabulate and process the data, being organized as follows:

- **1st step:** Raw data were collected and participants who were not users of MaaS applications were excluded for descriptive analysis since the research interest was the group of users. Thus, 35 respondents were excluded from the sample, which totalled 103 participants.
- **2nd step:** We applied descriptive statistics to characterize the profile of users and analyze the perception regarding the efficiency of MaaS applications (Google, Moovit and Citymapper).
- **3rd step:** A processing of the normality test was carried out, observing the Kolmogorov-Smirnov test ($p > 0.05$) [13], due to the sample size. Afterwards, a non-parametric analysis was performed, using the Kruskal-Wallis [13] test to verify the occurrence of a significant difference among the perception of participants with frequencies of use of passenger public transport.

- **4th step:** A Cronbach [14], Kaiser-Meyer-Olkin (KMO) [15], Bartlett Sphericity [16] tests were performed before conduct a Factor Analysis.
- **5th step:** To perform the Factor Analysis parameterized by varimax rotation, and the extraction of factors by Principal Component, participants who did not carry out the evaluation of the applications of interest to the study were excluded, totalling 15 respondents and reducing the sample to 88 participants.

3 Results

3.1 Sample Characterization

In order to explore all participants of the research, the sample characterization examined all the 138 participants. In our survey 75% of participants express to do use of some type of MaaS application. This result indicate a dissemination of this application due to high degree of mobile phone users and internet access. In São Paulo state that include MASP, in 2019, more than 53% of 30.5 million internet users connect only through mobile phones [17].

In our survey, it is observed that 51% of MaaS users are male and 49% female. This result means the MaaS access are almost identical between gender. Moreover, around 60% are in the age group between 18 and 35 years old, with a majority of women between 18 and 25 years old, and men between 26 and 35 years old. The result is consistent with data from Brazilian Institute of Geography and Statistics who shows that 80% of people in these groups presents a high level of access a internet via mobile phones [18].

By large, 41% have a household income between 3 and 4 minimum Brazilian wages (Brazilian minimum wage is USD 188,18 in 13/03/21), Table 1.

Table 1. Sample distribution

Variable	n	Participation (%)	Variable	n	Participation (%)
Gender			Education		
Female	50	48.5	Fundamental	3	2.9
Male	53	51.5	High School	31	30.0
Age group			Undergraduate	50	48.5
<17	2	1.9	Graduate	19	18.5
18 a 25	32	31.1	Income household		
26 a 35	30	29.1	<2	26	25.3
36 a 45	24	23.3	3 a 4	42	40.8
>46	15	14.5	5 a 7	17	16.5
			8 a 9	5	4.8
			>10	13	12.6

Among the respondents 51 % are from city of São Paulo, and the others are distributed among the cities of Metropolitan Area, such as: Aruja, Diadema, Ferraz de Vasconcelos, Guarulhos, Itaquaquecetuba, Maua, Mogi das Cruzes, Osasco, Poa, São Bernardo do Campo, São Caetano do Sul and Suzano. As an expected result, we found out 52% of users use the system with the main purpose of commuting to work, followed by study, leisure and services. These results are in accordance with what was observed by Giuliano et al. [19] in which the displacement has as its main purpose work.

3.2 Descriptive Statistics

Our results indicate a preference for bus service (43%) over others such as subway (22%), train (19%), ridesharing (15%) and taxi (1%). The result prove bus service as more comprehensive system with easy access in MASP, on the other hand cause great impact in congestions [20]. More than 60% of the participants have a high frequency of public transport use service - considering people that uses it every day, six days a week and on working days. There was no significant difference ($p > 0.05$) by the Chi-square between the variables analyzed, Table 2.

Table 2. Frequency of use by transport mode

Transport mode						
Frequency	Subway	Bus	Taxi	Ridesharing	Train	Total
Everyday	21.43	64.29			14.29	13.59
Six days a week	28.57	57.14		7.14	7.14	13.59
Weekdays	31.43	48.57			20.00	33.98
Between one and three days/semana	23.08	30.77		7.69	38.46	12.62
Weekends		57.14		42.86		6.80
Rarely	10.00	10.00	5.00	50.00	25.00	19.42

In addition, we observed that ridesharing service as Uber and 99 (Brazilian local company service) have been gaining ground among users, mainly regarding of those that rarely travelled by public passenger transport and those that travel exclusively on the weekends.

When participants were query about the ways of displacement between residence to the departure point (first mile), we found that 64% travel on foot, 15.5% by bus, 12.5% by private vehicle (motorcycle) and/or car), 7% ridesharing, and 1% per local area minibuses. And when compared to the frequency of use of the public transport system, a significant difference was noted (Chi-squared = 9.93; p = 0.0416). Similar results were obtained when comparing the data for the last mile (Chi-squared = 11.09; p = 0.0255).

Regarding the last mile we identified that 66% of perform on foot, 17.5% by bus, 8.5% by private vehicle (motorcycle and/or car), 7% ridesharing and 1% per local area minibuses. The increase in the use of ridesharing is a reality that straight affect public passenger transport operators that will need to reinvent their services. Our results confirm a trend in all suburbs of the country regarding ridesharing [21].

3.3   MaaS Adoption

In this study, we query respondents based on three MaaS apps, Google Maps, Moovit and Citymapper. In Fig. 1 we have the use by level.

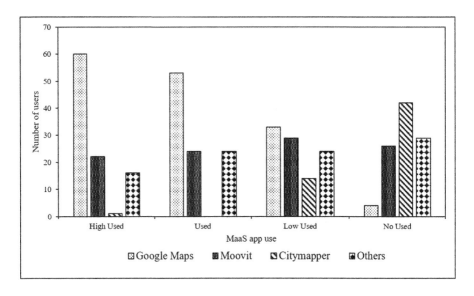

Fig. 1. Proportion of distribution of MaaS app use

The easiness of access and the multiplatform availability means Google Maps the MaaS app more utilized by sample users.

3.4   Factor Analysis

The KMO test (0.89) and Bartlett's Sphericity test (Chi-squared = 662.37, p-value < 0.05) confirm a correlation among variables, and the Cronbach Alpha test (0.8968) results in a reliability of the data. The selection of factors considered those with eigenvalues greater than 1.0, with three factors being extracted by Principal Component (PC) after varimax rotation, Table 3.

The Factor Analysis discribe the variability among observed variables and possibly correlated variables in a smaller number of variables denominated factors. We have 13 originals variables divided in 3 factors.

Table 3. Factor analysis of MaaS app assessment for a Cluster, n = 88, with 3 factor extracts by principal components

Factors		Autovalues	VExp[1] (%)	VEAc[2] (%)	Variables (Correlation)
F1	Information system of traffic and transport	6.3	48.51	48.51	PC (0.6399); RTI (0.6126); DF (0.7764); TI (0.8085); AMI (0.8380); ICA (0.6995); UCI (0.7954)
F2	Travel plan	1.44	11.08	59.59	TP (0.7363); JP (0.8006); JF (0.7809); MP (0.7848)
F3	Sharing and accessibility	1.26	9.75	69.34	RS (0.7641); OFFMAP (0.7765)

[1] VExp(%) = Proportion of explained variation (%);
[2] VEAc(%) = Proportion of explained variation agreggate (%)

The first factor (F1) grouped seven PC variables: PC (Passenger capacity), (RTI Real time information), DF (Delay forecast), TI (Traffic information), AMI (Active mobility integration), ICA (Integration car app) and UCI (User Collaborative Integration).

They are a explanatory fatorial analysis that represent the user's connectivity with the traffic and transport information systems, being the basis for decision-making and replanning journeys. The information avaliable easly to the users can help to choose the best way in that moment and to be improve the quality life of the users because the save the travel time and this can be used with others daily activites or stay home. The second factor (F2) grouped TP (Travel planner); JP (Journey planner); JF (Journey fare) and MP (Mode preference). They connected user's travel planning as essential MaaS. The third factor (F3) grouped RS (Route sharing) and OFFMAP (Off-line maps). They infer user's sharing and accessibility of information, Table 3.

4   Conclusions

This paper investigates the adoption of MaaS systems as a way to plan journeys using public passenger transportation in MASP, Brazil. To do so, we conducted a survey with 138 respondents and applied statistical analysis.

Our results indicated that the majority of MaaS users are up to 35 years old, and their main goal is to go to work using the public passenger transport system. Also, it was found that people move on foot to access public passenger transport and sometimes substitute routes made by bus by ridesharing services.

The explanatory factor analysis variables improve passengers real time decision and can reduce the transit time on transportation. This reduction improvement the quality of life because the passengers can enjoy this time in other daily activities. The limitation of this paper is about the number of applications studied. However, it does not invalidade the study proposed and can be made in a future research.

Acknowledgments. This study was financed in part by the Coordenação de Aperfeiçoamento de Pessoal de Nível Superior – Brasil (CAPES). Finance Code 001.

References

1. Empresa Paulista de Planejamento Metropolitano S/A - EMPLASA: Plano de Desenvolvimento Urbano Integrado - RMSP. Technical Report, EMPLASA, São Paulo (2019). http://multimidia.pdui.sp.gov.br/rmsp/docs_pdui/rmsp_docs_pdui_0018_diagnostico_final.pdf
2. Cia do Metropolitano de São Paulo: Pesquisa Origem e Destino 2017 50 Anos - A mobilidade da Região Metropolitana de São Paulo em detalhes. Technical Report, Metrô (2019)
3. Companhia do Metropolitano de São Paulo: relatorio-integrado-2019.pdf. Relatório de Administração Relatório Integrado 2019, Companhia do Metropolitano de São Paulo, São Paulo (2019). http://www.metro.sp.gov.br/metro/institucional/pdf/relatorio-integrado-2019.pdf
4. CPTM: (2020). https://www.cptm.sp.gov.br/a-companhia/Pages/a-companhia.aspx
5. SPTrans: (2020). https://www.sptrans.com.br/sptrans/
6. EMTU: Relatório da Administração 2019.pdf. Relatório de Administração, Empresa Metropolitana de Transportes Urbanos de São Paulo S.A. - EMTU/SP, São Paulo (February 2020). https://emtu.sp.gov.br/EMTU/pdf/Balan
7. International Transport Forum: ITF Transport Outlook 2019. World Bank (2019)
8. Galvão, D.M., de Oliveira, E.M.: Fatores intervenientes no uso de aplicativos de mobilidade urbana (2016). https://bdm.unb.br/bitstream/10483/17045/1/2016_DiogoGalvao_EduardoOliveira_tcc.pdf
9. Silva, G.D., Lima, R., Moreira, I., Kronbauer, A.H.: Mobibus: Mobile Real-Time Monitoring Application for Public Transport. Anais do Workshop sobre Aspectos da Interação Humano-Computador na Web Social (WAIHCWS), pp. 047–058 (September 2018), https://sol.sbc.org.br/index.php/waihcws/article/view/3895, conference Name: Anais do IX Workshop sobre Aspectos da Interação Humano-Computador para a Web Social Publisher: SBC
10. Lima, C.R.A.: Desenvolvimento de um aplicativo direcionado a auxiliar os usuários do onibus escolar univeritário. Universidade Federal do Ceará (2020)
11. Raymundo, H., Reis, J.G.M.D.: Measures for passenger-transport performance evaluation in urban areas. J. Urban Planning Dev. **144**(3), 04018023 (2018)
12. Triola, M.F.: Introdução à estatística, vol. 9. ltc Rio de Janeiro (2005)
13. Lewis, N.D.C.: 100 statistical tests in R: what to choose, how to easily calculate, with over 300 illustrations and examples. Heather Hills Press, Milton (2013)
14. Cortina, J.M.: What is coefficient alpha? An examination of theory and applications. J. Appl. Psychol. **78**(1), 98–104 (1993)
15. J.F. Hair Jr., et al.: Análise Multivariada de Dados. Bookman, 6ª edição edn. (May 2009)
16. Souki, G., Pereira, C.: 1566-1566-1-PB.pdf. Satisfação, Motivação e Comprometimento de Estudantes de Administração: Um Estudo Com Base nos Atributos de uma Instituição de Ensino Superior p. 16 (2004)

17. SEADE: Acesso e uso individual da internet no estado de são paulo (2019). https://www.seade.gov.br/produtos2/midia/2020/07/Cetic_produto01_7ago.pdf
18. IBGE: Pesquisa nacional por amostra de domicílios contínua (2020). https://biblioteca.ibge.gov.br/visualizacao/livros/liv101705_informativo.pdf
19. Giuliano, G., Hanson, S. (eds.): The geography of urban transportation. Guilford Press, New York (2017). OCLC: 996405876
20. Rolnik, R., Klintowitz, D.: Mobilidade na cidade de Sao Paulo. Estudos Avanãçados **25**, 89–108 (2011). http://www.scielo.br/scielo.php?script=sci_arttext&pid=S0103-40142011000100007&nrm=iso
21. Jornal do Comércio: Cresce uso de carros por aplicativo nas periferias do país (2020). https://www.jornaldocomercio.com/_conteudo/cadernos/jc_logistica/2020/09/755318-periferias-do-brasil-aumentaram-o-uso-de-carro-por-app.html

Using Flexible Crossdock Schedules to Face Truck Arrivals Uncertainty

Quentin Fabry[1,2(✉)], Lotte Berghman[2], and Cyril Briand[1]

[1] LAAS-CNRS, Université de Toulouse, UPS, Toulouse, France
{q.fabry,briand}@laas.fr
[2] TBS Business School, 1 Place Alfonse Jourdain, 31000 Toulouse, France
l.berghman@tbs-education.fr

Abstract. This paper discusses the use of robust schedules for facing uncertainty arising in crossdock truck scheduling problems. Groups of permutable operations bring sequential flexibility in the schedule, allowing to deal with late or early truck arrivals as the total order and the starting times can be determined in a reactive manner. We focus on the evaluation of a robust schedule considering both the worst maximal lateness of the trucks and the worst total sojourn time of the pallets. We also show how a robust schedule can be evaluated online, taking into account the actual arrival times of the trucks.

Keywords: Crossdocking · Scheduling · Robustness · Groups of permutable operations

1 Introduction

A crossdock is a logistic platform with a set of doors where trucks from different suppliers can unload their products, which are reorganized inside the crossdock before being reloaded on different trucks, depending on their destination. A truck is assumed to be present on the platform at a specific time-window that specifies its planned arrival and latest departure time. This organisation gives rise to numerous problems that have been classified in [3].

This paper focuses on the particular scheduling problem which aims at determining both the door on which each truck is (un)loaded and the starting times of these activities while respecting the time-windows. We assume the general case where each door can be used for both loading and unloading operations. Pallets of inbound trucks can either be temporarily stored inside the crossdock, or can be immediately transferred to outbound trucks that are already docked. We assume that the assignment of the pallets to the trucks is given and that the workforce and handling capacity allow the correct management of pallets inside the crossdock, avoiding any congestion or delay.

Several objective functions have been considered in literature. Many authors focus on time-related objectives such as makespan, lateness or tardiness minimization (see e.g. [4]). Others try to keep the workload (amount of pallets in

© IFIP International Federation for Information Processing 2021
Published by Springer Nature Switzerland AG 2021
A. Dolgui et al. (Eds.): APMS 2021, IFIP AICT 634, pp. 188–195, 2021.
https://doi.org/10.1007/978-3-030-85914-5_20

stock) as low as possible. In this work, we minimize the maximal lateness and we combine both types of objective functions by minimizing the sum of the sojourn times of the pallets. Indeed, a low sojourn time tends to guarantee a high turnover, which is a common objective for crossdock managers [2].

In practice, a good baseline schedule is no guarantee to be efficient because one has to face many perturbations, which can highly influence the quality and the realized turnover and even make the solution infeasible (with respect to the latest departure times of the trucks). There are numerous uncertainties that can occur in a crossdock, for example because of dock incidents, missing workers and last but not least late arrivals of trucks.

There exist different methods providing robustness to a schedule (see e.g. [6]). A classical one is based on the insertion of idle times able to absorb lateness (see e.g. [5]). By allowing to change the starting times inside the time buffer, the modified solution can stay feasible and efficient. In this work, instead of using temporal flexibility, we choose to use *sequential* flexibility, using *groups* to construct robust schedules. For each door of the crossdock, a sequence of groups of permutable operations (i.e. trucks) is defined but the order of the operations inside a group is undetermined a priori. Avoiding to fix the order inside a group allows to adapt the schedule in a reactive manner, according to the real truck arrival times, while controlling the schedule performance.

This paper first states the considered scheduling problem. Then, assuming a predetermined partition of the trucks into groups, it focuses on the evaluation of a robust schedule. We also explain how, during the execution of the planning, the groups can be advantageously used in a reactive manner depending on the actual arrival times of the trucks.

2   Problem Statement

This paper focuses on the so-called Crossdock Truck Scheduling Problem (CTSP). A set I of inbound trucks and a set O of outbound trucks has to be scheduled on a crossdock having n doors. Each inbound (resp. outbound) truck $i \in I$ ($o \in O$) has a processing time p_i (p_o) assumed proportional to the number of pallets to (un)load, a release date or planned arrival time r_i (r_o) and a due date or agreed latest departure time d_i (d_o). For each truck pair (i, o), w_{io} defines the number of pallets going from truck i to truck o. If $w_{io} > 0$, o cannot be loaded before i begins to be unloaded (start-start precedence constraint). In this case, we say that trucks i and o are *connected*. As trucks might arrive late, interval $\Omega_u = [\underline{r_u}, \overline{r_u}]$ defines the uncertainty domain of the release date of truck u (the probability being assumed uniformly distributed on the interval). We further refer to r as a particular arrival time scenario, i.e. a vector which specifies for each truck u its realized arrival time $r_u \in \Omega_u$. Decision variables s_i and s_o model the starting time of the unloading and loading activities, respectively.

In order to face truck arrival uncertainties, we aim at providing a schedule offering sequential flexibility using the well-known concept of groups of permutable operations [1]. We define a *group* g as a subset of trucks, assigned to the same door, that can be sequenced in any order. We refer to $g(u)$ as the group containing truck u. Groups can be formed from only inbound trucks, only outbound trucks, or a mix of both as far as they are not connected. Indeed, for any pair $\{i, o\}$ of trucks in $I \times O$, if $w_{io} > 0$, i.e. truck i has pallets that need to be loaded on truck o, we assume that $g(i) \neq g(o)$ as these trucks are not permutable (truck i can not be scheduled after truck o as there is a precedence constraint from i to o).

On each door k, the groups are sequenced and form a *group sequence* G_k. G_k is an ordered set of groups, assigned to a same door k. The group sequences of the different doors interact with each other due to the start-start precedence constraints between connected inbound and outbound trucks. We refer to $\mathcal{G} = \{G_1, \dots, G_n\}$ as a complete flexible schedule, which is composed of n group sequences, one for each door. In addition, $\theta_\mathcal{G}$ refers to a total order of the trucks, which is an extension of $\mathcal{G}$ (i.e. $\theta_\mathcal{G}$ contains n total orderings of the trucks assigned to the same door, respecting the group sequences of $\mathcal{G}$).

Given a scenario of the arrival times r and a total order $\theta_\mathcal{G}$, one can compute the sojourn time ψ as follows:

$$\psi(r, \theta_\mathcal{G}) = \sum w_{io}(s_o - s_i) \tag{1}$$

where s_i and s_o are feasible start times under scenario r and given a total order $\theta_\mathcal{G}$. Assuming that the length of a time unit corresponds to the time required to (un)load a single pallet and that $\sum p_i = \sum p_o$, ψ also equals $\sum p_o s_o - \sum p_i s_i$. When r and $\theta_\mathcal{G}$ are known, note that the minimum sojourn time ψ^* can be computed in polynomial time using for instance the simplex algorithm. We will detail in Sect. 3 how we combine the maximum lateness and the total sojourn time in a multi-criteria approach.

Let's consider an example with 2 doors and 5 trucks: $I = \{1, 2\}$ and $O = \{3, 4, 5\}$. The arrival times windows are $\Omega_1 = [\underline{r_1}, \overline{r_1}] = [0, 5]$, $\Omega_2 = [6, 11]$, $\Omega_3 = [0, 5]$, $\Omega_4 = [6, 11]$, and $\Omega_5 = [2, 7]$. The due dates are $d_1 = 15$, $d_2 = 17$, $d_3 = 20$, $d_4 = 15$, and $d_5 = 18$. Trucks 1 and 2 carry 5 and 4 pallets, respectively. Trucks 3, 4, and 5, receive 2, 2, and 5 pallets, respectively, assuming that: $w_{13} = 2$, $w_{14} = 2$, $w_{15} = 1$, $w_{23} = 0$, $w_{24} = 0$, and $w_{25} = 4$ (truck 2 only deserves truck 5). On this example with 2 doors, a flexible schedule $\mathcal{G} = \{G_1, G_2\}$ is considered. $G_1 = \{1\} \prec \{2, 3\}$ (i.e., the group sequence on the first door has two groups: a first group containing only truck *1*, sequenced before a second group composed of trucks *2* and *3*). We assume $G_2 = \{4, 5\}$ (i.e. there is a single group containing trucks *4* and *5* on the second door). The schedule represented in the Gantt diagram of Fig. 1 minimizes the maximum lateness $L_{\max}$, assuming scenario $\underline{r}$ and total order $\theta_\mathcal{G}^1$ (with the additional precedence constraints $2 \prec 3$ and $4 \prec 5$). Blue (red) tasks correspond to inbound (outbound) trucks. The three groups are materialized with green boxes. Truck time-windows are represented with colored bars up and below the tasks. $L_{\max} = -5$ is the smallest maximal lateness that can be obtained. The total sojourn time is $\psi = 48$, which can be improved if we choose other additional precedence constraints.

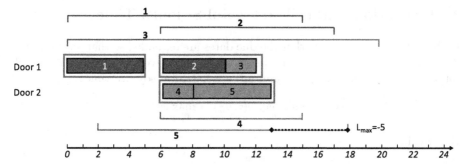

Fig. 1. A schedule minimizing $L_{\max}$ under scenario $\underline{r}$ and total order $\theta_{\mathcal{G}}^1$. (Color figure online)

3 Evaluation of the Worst Lateness

Let us focus first on the lateness. Over all scenarios r and all total orders $\theta_{\mathcal{G}}$, one can compute the worst value of the maximal lateness as

$$\overline{L_{\max}(\mathcal{G})} = \max_{r \in \Omega} \max_{\theta_{\mathcal{G}}} L_{\max}(r, \theta_{\mathcal{G}}). \tag{2}$$

It is obvious that

$$\overline{L_{\max}(\mathcal{G})} = \max_{\theta_{\mathcal{G}}} L_{\max}(\overline{r}, \theta_{\mathcal{G}}) \tag{3}$$

as the lateness can only grow with increasing r. Moreover, considering one particular truck u, the rules defined in [1] allow to determine the particular sequence $\theta_{\mathcal{G}}$ that gives the worst lateness $\overline{L_u}$.

For the above mentioned example, Fig. 2 displays a worst lateness schedule under scenario $\overline{r}$, which is obtained for the total order $\theta_{\mathcal{G}}^2$ imposing $3 \prec 2$ and $5 \prec 4$. The worst lateness $\overline{L_{\max}(\mathcal{G})} = 4$.

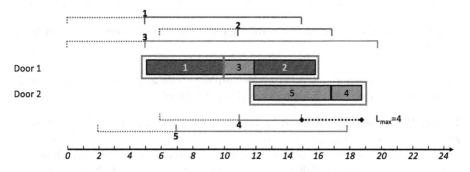

Fig. 2. A schedule giving the worst $L_{\max}$ under scenario $\overline{r}$ and total order $\theta_{\mathcal{G}}^2$.

4   Evaluation of the Worst Total Sojourn Time

In the following, we assume that the due dates are extended so that any scenario $\theta_{\mathcal{G}}$ is time-feasible (i.e., $\tilde{d}_u \leftarrow \max\{d_u; d_u + \overline{L_{\max}}\}$). Over all scenarios r and all total orders $\theta_{\mathcal{G}}$, one can now compute the worst total sojourn time as

$$\overline{\psi(\mathcal{G})} = \max_{r \in \Omega} \max_{\theta_{\mathcal{G}}} \psi(r, \theta_{\mathcal{G}}) = \max_{\theta_{\mathcal{G}}} \psi(\overline{r}, \theta_{\mathcal{G}}). \tag{4}$$

Here again,

$$\overline{\psi(\mathcal{G})} = \max_{\theta_{\mathcal{G}}} \psi(\overline{r}, \theta_{\mathcal{G}}), \tag{5}$$

as any relaxation such that $r \leq \overline{r}$ can only give a better objective value ψ. For our small example, $\overline{L_{\max}}(\mathcal{G}) = 4$ so the new due dates are $\tilde{d}_1 = 15 + 4 = 19$, $\tilde{d}_2 = 17 + 4 = 21$, $\tilde{d}_3 = 20 + 4 = 24$, $\tilde{d}_4 = 15 + 4 = 19$ and $\tilde{d}_5 = 18 + 4 = 22$.

If we come back to our crossdock instance, the schedule depicted in Fig. 2 is also accidentally a worst sojourn time schedule, where $\psi(\mathcal{G}) = \sum p_o s_o - \sum p_i s_i = (2 * 10) + (2 * 17) + (5 * 12) - (5 * 5) - (4 * 12) = \overline{\psi(\mathcal{G})} = 41$. This worst-case schedule can be compared with the schedule presented in Fig. 3, obtained for scenario $\underline{r}$ with total order $\theta_{\mathcal{G}}^3$ defined by $3 \prec 2$ and $4 \prec 5$ and $\psi(\mathcal{G}) = \sum p_o s_o - \sum p_i s_i = (2 * 11) + (2 * 6) + (5 * 13) - (5 * 6) - (4 * 13) = \underline{\psi(\mathcal{G})} = 17$, which is a best sojourn time schedule.

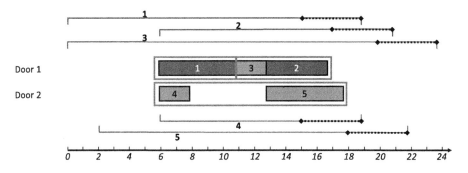

Fig. 3. A schedule giving the best total sojourn time under scenario $\underline{r}$ and total order $\theta_{\mathcal{G}}^3$.

Theorem 1. *Given a general crossdock problem with a flexible schedule $\mathcal{G}$, finding a total order $\theta_{\mathcal{G}}$ that minimizes $\psi(\mathcal{G})$ is NP-Hard.*

Proof. We reduce the single machine scheduling problem $1|r_j| \sum C_j$, which is known to be NP-Hard, to our problem.

We consider a single machine scheduling problem were the operations are indexed $1, \ldots, n$ and we define p_j^s as the processing time and r_j^s as the release date of the operation indexed j. Let us construct a crossdock problem instance with 2 doors, n inbound trucks indexed i such that $p_i = p_i^s - 1$ and $r_i = r_i^s$, for $i = 1, \ldots, n$ and n outbound trucks indexed o such that $p_o = p_o^s$ and $r_o = r_o^s$, for $o = 1, \ldots, n$. We assume that the $n = \sum p_o - \sum p_i$ pallets are the initial stock that is available in the crossdock. We assume that inbound truck indexed i delivers its p_i pallets to outbound truck indexed $o = i$ (i.e., $w_{io} = p_i = p_o - 1$ if $o = i$ else $w_{io} = 0$). Moreover, each outbound truck indexed o receives exactly 1 pallet from the initial stock. The flexible schedule $\mathcal{G} = \{G_1, G_2\}$ is such that G_1 contains one group in which we can find all inbound trucks, while G_2 contains one group in which we can find all outbound trucks. The sojourn time can be expressed as

$$\psi(\mathcal{G}) = \sum_o (s_o - t_0) + \sum_i \sum_o w_{io}(s_o - s_i). \qquad (6)$$

The former term corresponds to the cost of the pallets transferred directly from the stock to the outbound trucks where t_0 defines the beginning of the schedule. The latter is the cost of the pallets moved from inbound to outbound trucks. Let us observe that, for any feasible schedule of the outbound trucks on the second door, it is always possible to build up a similar schedule on the first door for the inbound trucks by defining $s_i = s_o$ if $i = o$ (because $p_i < p_o$ and $r_i = r_o$). Therefore, $\psi(\mathcal{G})$ reduces to $\sum_o (s_o - t_0)$, which equals $\sum_o C_o - K$ where $K = \sum_o (p_o + t_0)$. Hence, minimizing ψ is equivalent to solving a $1|r_j|\sum C_j$ problem on the second door. $\qquad \square$

From Theorem 1, it results that finding the total order that gives the best or the worst sojourn time is also NP-Hard (as the sub-problem is itself NP-hard). For this reason, we will focus now on upper bound of $\psi(\mathcal{G})$ that can be computed in polynomial time.

To obtain a trivial upper bound on the sojourn time, all inbound trucks i can be scheduled at $s_i = \overline{r_i}$ and all outbound trucks o at $s_o = \tilde{d}_o - p_o$. Such a schedule is not necessary feasible because several trucks may be (un)loaded at the same time on the same door and/or the group sequences might not be respected. Nevertheless, since one can ensure that $s_i \geq \overline{r_i}$ and $s_o \leq \tilde{d}_o - p_o$ in any schedule, an upper bound on the sojourn time is obtained. For the example that was presented earlier, the value would be $\sum p_o s_o - \sum p_i s_i = \sum p_o(\tilde{d}_o - p_o) - \sum p_i \overline{r_i} = (2 * (24 - 2)) + (2 * (19 - 2)) + (5 * (22 - 5)) - (5 * 5) - (4 * 11) = 94$. A tighter upper bound can be calculated by imposing sequences inside each group. The incoming trucks are sequenced by non-decreasing $\overline{r_i}$ and scheduled as early as possible. The outgoing trucks are sequenced by non-decreasing latest departure time $\tilde{d}_o$ and scheduled as late as possible. Note that the resulting schedule might still be infeasible as there can be capacity violations between adjacent groups.

Figure 4 illustrates that sequencing the trucks inside the groups and scheduling them according to the previous rule enforces the total order $\theta_{\mathcal{G}}^1$ (already used for the best lateness). This schedule shows an upper bound of $\sum p_o s_o - \sum p_i s_i = (2 * 22) + (2 * 15) + (5 * 17) - (5 * 5) - (4 * 11) = 90$ for $\psi(\mathcal{G})$, which is better than the trivial bound of 94.

5 Online Evaluation of $\Theta_{\mathcal{G}}$

The previous worst-case evaluations of the lateness and the sojourn time are very pessimistic. Assuming a particular online sequencing rule $\mathcal{R}$ for sequencing

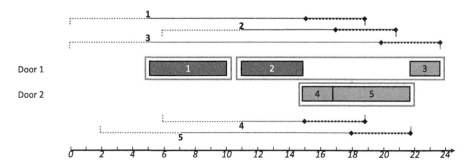

Fig. 4. A schedule giving an upper-bound total sojourn time under scenario $\underline{r}$ and total order $\theta_{\mathcal{G}}^{1}$.

the trucks in a group under scenario r, one can instead try to evaluate the expected value of the maximal lateness and the total sojourn time. A Monte-Carlo method can be used for this purpose. Figure 5 illustrates this idea for scenario $r = \{1, 9, 0, 11, 4\}$ and the online scheduling rule FIFO (inside each group, the trucks are scheduled as soon as they become available). We obtain $L_{\max}(\mathcal{G}) = 1$ and $\psi(\mathcal{G}) = (2 * 6) + (2 * 14) + (5 * 9) - (5 * 1) - (4 * 9) = 44$.

Note that the previous defined bounds assume an optimal schedule for a given sequence of the trucks inside the group. But this might not be respected by a particular online scheduling rule $\mathcal{R}$. Here we find for example $\psi(\mathcal{G}) = 44 \geq \overline{\psi(\mathcal{G})} = 41$.

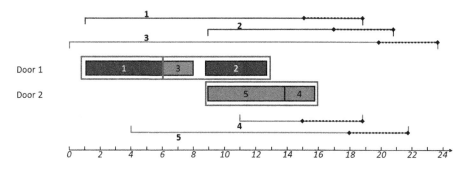

Fig. 5. A online schedule obtained with scenario $r = \{1, 9, 0, 11, 4\}$ and rule FIFO.

6   Conclusion

In this article, we presented some first performance measures to quantify the quality of a flexible schedule on a crossdock defined by a set of group sequences, one for each door. We are able to compute some bounds on the objective value for both the worst maximal lateness and the worst total sojourn time. Future research will concentrate on tightening these bounds, for example by taking into account the start-start precedence constraints that exist between inbound and outbound trucks. Assessing the quality of a flexible schedule is essential to be able to develop algorithms that construct good quality group sequences.

References

1. Artigues, C., Billaut, J.C., Esswein, C.: Maximization of solution flexibility for robust shop scheduling. Eur. J. Oper. Res. **165**, 314–328 (2005)
2. Berghman, L., Briand, C., Leus, R., Lopez, P.: The truck scheduling problem at crossdocking terminals: Exclusive versus mixed mode. In: ICORES 2015, pp. 247–253 (2015)
3. Boysen, N., Fliedner, M.: Cross dock scheduling: classification, literature review and research agenda. Omega **38**, 413–422 (2010)
4. Ladier, A.L., Alpan, G.: Crossdock truck scheduling with time windows: earliness, tardiness and storage policies. J. Intell. Manuf. **29**, 569–583 (2018)
5. Lambrechts, O., Demeulemeester, E., Herroelen, W.: Time slack-based techniques for robust project scheduling subject to resource uncertainty. Ann. Oper. Res. **186**, 443–464 (2011)
6. Xi, X., Changchun, L., Yuan, W., Loo Hay, L.: Two-stage conflict robust optimization models for cross-dock truck scheduling problem under uncertainty. Transp. Res. Part E Logistics Transp. Rev. **144**, 102123 (2020)

Maintenance Improvement and Lifecycle Management

Asset Management, Industry 4.0 and Maintenance in Electrical Energy Distribution

Sam Amelete[1(✉)], Raynald Vaillancourt[1,2], Georges Abdul-Nour[1(✉)],
and François Gauthier[1]

[1] Université du Québec à Trois-Rivières, Trois-Rivières G8Z 4M3, Canada
{sam.amelete,georges.abdulnour}@uqtr.ca
[2] Hydro-Québec Distribution, Montreal H5B 1H7, Canada

Abstract. This article presents the effects of Industry 4.0 (I4.0) combined with Asset Management (AM) in improving the life cycle of complex systems in Electrical Energy Distribution (EED). The boom in smart networks leaves companies in this sector no choice but to move forward I4.0. The contribution of I4.0 to the progress of AM in maintenance in EED will therefore be demonstrated by a case study using simulation. The case study will concern the benefits of using Advanced Metering Infrastructure (AMI), the heart of smart grids, at Hydro-Québec Distribution (HQD), the primary supply authority in Quebec. The HQD network includes 4.3 million clients, on a territory of approximately 250,000 km2 and 680,000 overhead transformers. The results are conclusive: the number of outages will drop by 7% annually and maintenance costs will fall by at least 5% per year.

Keywords: Asset Management · Maintenance · Industry 4.0 · Smart grid · Advanced Metering Infrastructure

1 Introduction

These days, maintenance is considered an integral part of the key processes that make a company competitive and allow it to endure [1]. AM (Asset Management), which involves a balance between costs, opportunities and risks in relation to the desired performance of assets with the goal of achieving the organization's objectives, is indispensable [2]. The new revolution, known as Industry 4.0 (I4.0) is also required with the current advent of new technologies and the major challenges of the moment, which are due especially to the growing complexity of equipment. With the arrival of new sources of private energy (solar, wind, etc.), climate change, attention to social-environmental protection and safety, the EED (Electrical Energy Distribution) sector is perfectly placed in the context stated above. Globalization, labour shortages, the need for even greater network availability and the aging of facilities are other factors that contribute to the need for this transition to excellence in maintenance in EED. It is from this perspective that a good number of companies in this sector are analyzing the possibility of utilizing AM and Industry 4.0 to integrate, optimize and improve their management processes for the life

A. Dolgui et al. (Eds.): APMS 2021, IFIP AICT 634, pp. 199–208, 2021.
https://doi.org/10.1007/978-3-030-85914-5_21

cycle management of complex systems. The objective will be to demonstrate the efficiency of combining AM and I4.0 in life cycle management of complex systems in EED companies. Many authors have focused only either on the use of one or a few technologies as part of smart grids, or on AM in EED. This article therefore makes it possible to link technologies in the current context of I4.0 with AM, then show the benefits of such a connection in life cycle management of complex systems in EED. This link will first be made through a literature review of AM in EED, I4.0 and technological advances in EED. Secondly, a case study at Hydro-Québec Distribution (HQD), the EED company in Quebec, on the use of AMI (Advanced Metering Infrastructure) coupled with the development of customer voltage and consumption monitoring algorithms for the low voltage (LV) overhead network will be outlined. In this case study, maintenance without I4.0 is compared to maintenance with I4.0 through a simulation of discrete events to reveal the potential benefit of moving to I4.0.

2 Literature Review

This section describes the state of the art on the application of AM and I4.0 in life cycle management of complex systems in EED to gather the necessary information for this article.

2.1 Asset Management

The work of Shah et al. (2017) reveals that AM is a mix between the fields of engineering and management that must be based on reliable, relevant and timely information while taking into account strategic business objectives [3]. This relation with information processing was confirmed by Khuntia et al. (2016), who link AM and data management [4]. These same authors also list the different techniques, methods and philosophies that comprise AM. They especially evoke in the EED field RCM (Reliability Centred Maintenance), CBM (Condition Based Maintenance), TBM (Time Based Maintenance), RBM (Risk Based Maintenance), and LCCA (Life Cycle Cost Analysis).

2.2 Industry 4.0 and Maintenance

Based on the literature review, the most widespread and general definition of I4.0 is the one in which Industry 4.0 would be a collective term, a revolution, grouping technologies and value chain organization concepts [1, 5]. Just as for AM, data processing is essential in I4.0. Bengtsson et al. (2018) observe that the new challenge for engineers is data processing in the current fourth industrial revolution [6]. Maintenance systems in the current framework must be sustainable, agile and interoperable. It is essential that these systems also possess the ability to manage disparate data in real time thanks particularly to I4.0 tools such as e-maintenance, smart sensors, IOT, Big Data and augmented reality. These tools are associated with AM best practices such as CBM and LCCA. Smart predictive maintenance, which is simply the improvement of CBM, is a key element in the new industrial revolution [7, 8]. Dąbrowski et al. (2018) emphasize that smart predictive maintenance makes it possible to predict the risk of failure in real time while taking into account the RUL (Remaining Useful Life) and relying on efficient data collection [7]. Wang (2016) continues along the same lines and adds that this type of maintenance uses the tools of I4.0 [CPS (Cyber Physical Systems), IOT (Internet Of Things), Big Data and Data Mining, IOS (Internet Of Service) or Cloud Computing] to detect signs of failure, predict the future behaviour of an asset and thereby optimize operation of the asset [5]. Nonetheless, Bengtsson et al. (2018) recall that the basic concepts and techniques of maintenance (lubrication, cleaning, inspection, etc.) should not be neglected in the current context of the fourth industrial revolution [6]. They propose combining the old maintenance methods with the new emerging technologies of Industry 4.0 for a more efficient maintenance process.

2.3 Link Between AM and I4.0

In general, AM includes acquisition, operation, maintenance and decommission. I4.0 allows to be proactive in context of AM. One of the links that can be established between AM and I4.0 is that AM encompasses the various maintenance policies [4, 9], while I4.0 makes it possible to move toward predictive maintenance and, thus, to maximize an asset's productivity time and life span [7]. This section is summarized in Fig. 1; the table below is taken from Dąbrowski et al. (2018) [7].

AM includes maintenance policies			Destination with 4.0
Maintenance	**corrective**	**predetermined**	**based on condition**	**predictive**

Maintenance	corrective	predetermined	based on condition	predictive
Characteristics	Performed after failure	Performed at predefined intervals	Performed after observing certain conditions on an asset	Completed on the most profitable date after the asset's RUL forecast
Requirements	Competent staff, spare parts available, quick reactions	Deep knowledge of asset life, accurate staff planning and spare parts supply	Monitoring equipment/systems, IT infrastructure, competent staff	Surveillance systems, IT infrastructure, data, models and algorithms
Advantages	Maximizing asset life, no planning costs	Minimizes asset downtime, fewer wear-and-tear failures, high level of planning	Maximizes the productivity time of assets, maximizes the life of an asset	Maximizes asset productivity time, maximizes asset life, high level of planning
Disadvantages	Significant costs related to failure, costs due to unplanned outages	Waste of the RUL (Remaining Useful Life) of the asset, planning is expensive, it does not prevent random failures, requires intensive work	High investment in monitoring and prognostic equipment	High investment in monitoring, prognostic and diagnostic equipment, emerging technology

Fig. 1. Link between AM and I4.0

3 Case Study: Use of AMI

3.1 General Information on AMI

In general, I4.0 makes it possible, in almost real time, to collect and analyze a large volume of data and develop models for predictive maintenance. The EED-specific framework is that the data to collect comes from AMI that measure consumption at customer premises. AMI are considered the backbone of smart grid [10, 11]. Compared to a traditional grid where only the electrical flow circulates, this new type of grid disseminates not only the electrical flow but also the bidirectional information flow between EED companies and clients through AMI [11, 12]. HQD's benefit is that AMI is already installed and, therefore, no installation costs are incurred (Fig. 2).

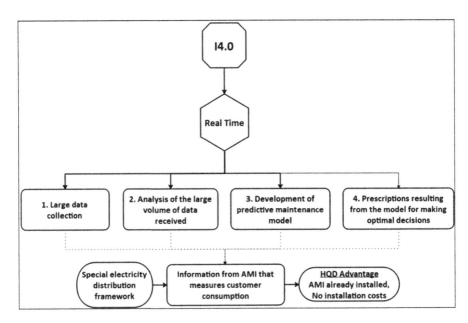

Fig. 2. HQD advantage with regard to evolution to 4.0

In the 2010s, HQD replaced electrical meters used to measure the consumption of all its customers with AMI. This infrastructure could make it possible to detect the deterioration of a transformer (Fig. 3). Damage to a transformer after lightening passes can also be detected by AMI (Fig. 4). They can also serve in identifying an overloaded transformer (Fig. 5) and customer/transformer mismatch (Fig. 6).

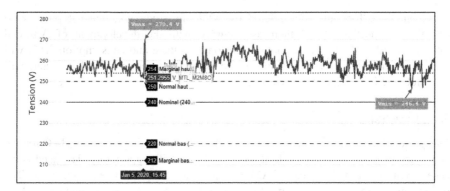

Fig. 3. Detection of a degraded transformer with AMI

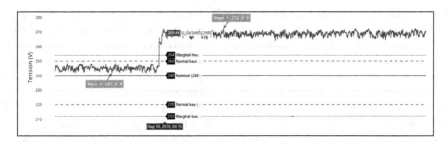

Fig. 4. Detection of a transformer damaged by lightning with AMI

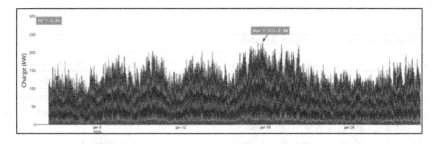

Fig. 5. Detection of an overloaded transformer with AMI

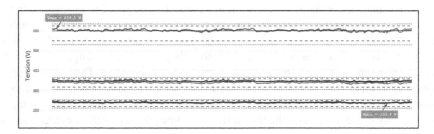

Fig. 6. Detection of customer/transformer mismatch

Given these functionalities offered by AMI, the study will make it possible to establish the profitability of their use coupled with the development of Artificial Intelligence (AI) algorithms to monitor customer voltage and consumption. This will help to identify the problems listed above before outages and breakages and will constitute the I4.0 maintenance case.

3.2   Case Study

The project that consists in demonstrating the benefits of implementing I4.0 for the HQD electrical grid was the result of need combined with opportunity. The need is the necessity in the current context of AM to migrate toward predictive maintenance. The opportunity is that the data permitting this migration are available thanks to AMI installed at customer premises.

As explained above, it consists in comparing maintenance without I4.0 to maintenance I4.0 by simulating a concrete example. The simulation consists in replacing an existing system by a simpler computer model with similar behaviour. The existing system is HQD's overhead low voltage (LV) distribution system. It was selected because it is more convenient to estimate the parameters to consider such as the number of customers interrupted (CI) following an outage. The computer models were created on the Rockwell Arena simulation software. Maintenance without I4.0 is represented by an initial model illustrating the current LV overhead network, with the presence of AMI only. The maintenance 4.0 model integrates the AI algorithms discussed above. Outages as well as customers interrupted, repair time based on the type of day when the outage occurred and the costs resulting from these outages are taken into account. The two models are compared to reveal which is most beneficial as well as the scale of the benefits.

3.3   Building the Simulation Model

Historical data from 2015 to 2019 provided by HQD were used as the basis for developing the models. The period from 2020 to 2024 is the predictive part of the models. The data has been fitted to statistical distributions. Given a data non-disclosure agreement with HQD, we cannot give further details on the distributions used, model logic and what-if scenarios.

The effect of maintenance 4.0 was considered on LV cables, fuses and transformers. Maintenance with I4.0 would make it possible to reduce a certain number of outages on fuses and to convert a certain number of outages on transformers and LV cables into planned outages. AI algorithms would make it possible to identify transformer overload and to replace it preventatively (which would result in a planned outage) before failure occurred. A few irregularities in LV cables due to overload could also be resolved in planned interruptions before they result in breakages. Fuses very often blow because of transformer overload and prevent an outage. They can therefore blow several times and each time be replaced as a corrective measure before it becomes clear that these repetitive breakages on the fuses originate from the transformer's overload. By detecting earlier, the transformer overload, these repetitive outages on the fuses can be avoided.

3.4 Steady State and Validation

As simulation models are finite horizon, the steady state is implemented from the beginning of the simulation. The main outcomes (number of outages, number of CI, costs) are incremented every year. The number of replications was set at 30. With these 30 replications, the percentage of error (half width interval) in the outcomes was cumulatively less than 1% at the end of 2019 (Table 1). The models were configured to roll from 2015 to 2024. The period from 2015 to 2019 made it possible to verify that the program indeed behaves like HQD's actual LV overhead network. The Real/Simulated relationship is presented in Table 2 for the cumulative outcome values from 2015 to 2019. We note that it is very close to 1 for the number of outages and the number of customers interrupted. Regarding costs, the values and distributions selected were estimated based on equipment samples. These estimates are supposedly representative of reality, as are the costs resulting from the models.

Table 1. Percentage of error in quantitative outcome

Quantitative outcome	Error (half width)/Average (%)
Total number of outages	0%
Total CI	0.001%
Costs	0.116%

Table 2. Real/Simulated relationship

Quantitative outcome	Real/Simulated relationship
Outages	0.982
Customers interrupted	1.016
Costs	The values and distributions selected were estimated based on equipment samples that are representative of reality

3.5 Results

The main outcomes quantified were the number of outages, the number of customers interrupted and maintenance costs. Figure 7, Fig. 8, Fig. 9 present these outcomes for maintenance without I4.0 and maintenance with I4.0. For the figures, the y-axes are not filled in and the results are presented as a percentage, still in the context of the non-disclosure of data.

The simulation shows that with I4.0, outages would be reduced by an average of 7% per year (Fig. 7). The number of customers interrupted also fell by an average of 7% annually (Fig. 8), which is because the number of outages and customers interrupted are correlated [1 outage corresponds to a triangular distribution of parameters 7.5 (minimum), 7.7 (equiprobable), and 8.1 (maximum) of customers interrupted].

Costs would be reduced by 5% per year on average with I4.0 (Fig. 9). In fact, for LV cables and transformers, with I4.0, replacement of the equipment for which failure can be predicted should be planned. Maintenance would therefore be performed on a regular basis and would make it possible to avoid costs related to overtime for corrective maintenance. Regarding fuses, a proportion of outages would be totally avoided with I4.0. Maintenance activities that could result in this proportion of outages would therefore be avoided along with the related costs.

Fig. 7. Comparison between maintenance without and with I4.0 in term of outages

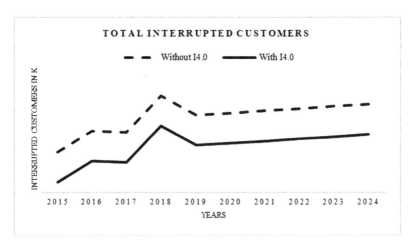

Fig. 8. Comparison between maintenance without and with I4.0 in term of customers interrupted

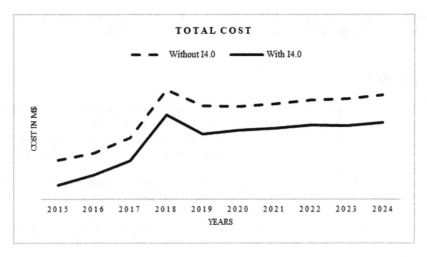

Fig. 9. Comparison between maintenance without and with I4.0 in monetary term

3.6 Discussion

The scenario presented in this paper is conservative but the reductions determined, although appearing to be quite low in percentage, represent thousands of failures avoided, tens of thousands of customers who will be able to benefit from greater continuity of service, and a decrease of maintenance costs in order of millions of dollars CAD.

The case of maintenance I4.0 focused on fuses, transformers and LV cables in the study. Furthermore, the database used takes into account only the primary volumes of outages on equipment and their causes. If the effect of I4.0 on other equipment and volumes beyond the primary ones had been considered, a greater benefits would have been found. Furthermore, the benefits resulting from detecting customer/transformer mismatch, transformers not connected to at least one client could be explored in a later study. A next step resulting from this analysis would be to develop the AI algorithms required considering the potential benefits.

4 Conclusion

Firstly, the literature review reveals the link between AM and I4.0. AM includes the various maintenance policies and I4.0 will make it possible to move toward predictive maintenance. Data collection was one of the biggest tasks for the case study. Through the simulation, the relevance and benefits of matching I4.0 with AM in the EED sector were demonstrated for customer satisfaction, resource optimization and in monetary terms. I4.0 and AM therefore become indispensable for improving life cycle management of complex systems in EED. To the best of our knowledge, this study is the first to show the profitability of using I4.0 with AMI for an electrical grid.

Funding. This research was funded by HQ, and by the NSERC, Natural Sciences and Engineering Council of Research of Canada Grant: CRSNG-RDCPJ-530543-18.

References

1. Al-Najjar, B., Algabroun, H., Jonsson, M.: Maintenance 4.0 to fulfil the demands of Industry 4.0 and factory of the future. Int. J. Eng. Res. Appl. **8**(11), 20–31 (2018)
2. Nieto, D., Amatti, J.C., Mombello, E.: Review of asset management in distribution systems of electric energy–implications in the national context and Latin America. CIRED-Open Access Proc. J. **2017**(1), 2879–2882 (2017)
3. Shah, R., McMann, O., Borthwick, F.: Challenges and prospects of applying asset management principles to highway maintenance: a case study of the UK. Transp. Res. Part A: Policy Pract. **97**, 231–243 (2017)
4. Khuntia, S.R., et al.: A literature survey on asset management in electrical power [transmission and distribution] system. Int. Trans. Electr. Energy Syst. **26**(10), 2123–2133 (2016)
5. Wang, K.: Intelligent predictive maintenance (IPdM) system–Industry 4.0 scenario. WIT Trans. Eng. Sci. **113**, 259–268 (2016)
6. Bengtsson, M., Lundström, G.: On the importance of combining "the new" with "the old" – one important prerequisite for maintenance in Industry 4.0. Procedia Manuf. **25**, 118–125 (2018)
7. Dąbrowski, K., Skrzypek, K.: The predictive maintenance concept in the maintenance department of the "Industry 4.0" production enterprise. Found. Manage. **10**(1), 283–292 (2018)
8. Bokrantz, J., et al.: Smart maintenance: a research agenda for industrial maintenance management. Int. J. Prod. Econ. **224,** 107547 (2020)
9. Germán, M.O., et al.: Power asset management: methods and experiences in Colombian power system. In: 2014 IEEE PES Transmission & Distribution Conference and Exposition-Latin America (PES T&D-LA). IEEE (2014)
10. Živic, N.S., Ur-Rehman, O., Ruland, C.: Evolution of smart metering systems. In: 2015 23rd Telecommunications Forum Telfor (TELFOR). IEEE (2015)
11. Sulaiman, S., Jeyanthy, P.A., Devaraj, D.: Smart meter data analysis issues: a data analytics perspective. In: 2019 IEEE International Conference on Intelligent Techniques in Control, Optimization and Signal Processing (INCOS). IEEE (2019)
12. Anita, J.M., Raina, R.: Review on smart grid communication technologies. In: 2019 International Conference on Computational Intelligence and Knowledge Economy (ICCIKE). IEEE (2019)

Perspectives on the Future of Maintenance Engineering Education

Jon Bokrantz[(⊠)] and Anders Skoogh

Department of Industrial and Materials Science, Division of Production Systems,
Chalmers University of Technology, 41296 Gothenburg, Sweden
jon.bokrantz@chalmers.se

Abstract. In this article, we aim to remedy the effects of skill-biased technological change within maintenance engineering and enable productivity gains
from novel digital technologies such as Artificial Intelligence. We do this by
outlining the critical role of education and the need for renewal and increased
access to higher education within maintenance, followed by reviewing the literature on maintenance engineering education over the past two decades (2000–
2020). In our systematic literature review, we identify nine key themes that have
occupied maintenance researchers in their educational efforts, e.g. design and
development of curricula, programs, and courses; identification of competence
requirements and learning characteristics; and new educational formats such as
gamification and innovative laboratory sessions using novel digital technologies.
Following our review, we propose research- and policy-oriented recommendations for the future of maintenance engineering education.

Keywords: Maintenance · Engineering · Education · Digitization ·
Manufacturing

1 Introduction

The role of maintenance functions within manufacturing plants has changed significantly over the past decades; from undesired cost centers to enablers of resilient and
sustainable production systems. This evolution is fueled by rapid technological change.
Today, novel digital technologies such as Artificial Intelligence (AI), Internet of Things
(IoT), and Additive Manufacturing (AM) are increasingly introduced to the production
process (what to maintain) as well as the maintenance process (how to maintain) [1].

However, economic theories of technological change predict that harnessing the
value of novel technologies requires complementary intangible investments. That is,
before the promises of astonishing new technologies such as AI can blossom, firms
must make large, time-consuming, and often neglected investments in complementary
intangibles [2]. In the economics of digitization, this logic is often expressed as a
bottleneck proposition: digital abundance leads to bottlenecks whenever essential
complements cannot be digitized. No matter how much other inputs are increased, the
absence of any essential complement will act as the weakest link and constrain growth.
The digital winners will therefore be those with as many of the right complements in
place as possible [3].

© IFIP International Federation for Information Processing 2021
Published by Springer Nature Switzerland AG 2021
A. Dolgui et al. (Eds.): APMS 2021, IFIP AICT 634, pp. 209–216, 2021.
https://doi.org/10.1007/978-3-030-85914-5_22

One essential complement to novel digital technologies that cannot be digitized is human skills [2]. This implies that if maintenance workers do not acquire the essential skills to execute new tasks and more complex versions of existing tasks enabled by novel digital technologies, no productivity gains will materialize. To relieve this skills bottleneck, one obvious part of the solution is education. The implicit solution framework is a race between technology and education: growth in demand from more-educated maintenance workers from skill-biased technological change versus growth in supply of more-educated maintenance workers from schooling [4].

Higher education (i.e. universities) plays a key role in this framework, where the need is two-fold: (1) *renew higher education* and (2) *increase access to higher education*. These two needs focusses on producing the right kind of maintenance workers that are complemented rather than substituted by novel digital technologies. However, this is already an uphill battle as it starts from low levels of education among maintenance workers and limited access to higher education [5]. But with the right roadmap for accelerating and renewing higher education in maintenance engineering, universities can increase the preparedness among manufacturing firms in realizing the benefits of novel digital technologies.

The aim of this paper is to stimulate this development of higher education, and we therefore review the existing literature on maintenance engineering education from the past two decades. We contribute to the maintenance discipline by providing an overview of research on maintenance engineering education as well as identifying the key themes that have occupied researchers in their educational efforts. Specifically, we present descriptive findings from a total of 25 articles and uncover nine key themes that reflect the body of knowledge provided by the literature sample. Based on the insights from the review, we propose several recommendations for the future of maintenance engineering education that encompasses both research and policy.

2   Review Methodology

Existing research on maintenance engineering education is scarce. For example, Kans and Metso [6] claim that their structured literature review only revealed four relevant articles between 1997–2011. We therefore designed a Systematic Literature Review (SLR) process focusing on uncovering a wider net of plausibly relevant articles, intending to achieve a broad and representative but not necessarily comprehensive set of articles. The SLR process was designed as a four-step approach (Define, Retrieve, Select, Synthesize), with each step explained in the following sections.

Step 1: Define. In the first step, we defined the required characteristics of literature to be included in our review [7]. We specified a set of inclusion/exclusion criteria [8] within four main categories. (1) *Unit of analysis* was specified to be at the level of an article. (2) *Sources of data* were specified as either journal, conference, book chapter, or thesis, and we accepted any type of study (e.g. conceptual, empirical, review). This allowed us to capture a wide net of potentially relevant articles. Note however that since we focus on scientific literature, our review does not cover sources of data such as public reports or official standards (e.g. CEN - EN 15628). We defined the time window of the review as 2000–2020 since the early 2000s are recognized as the starting point for accelerated interest in digitization within maintenance. (3) *Theoretical domain* was specified as production maintenance, i.e. maintenance of production equipment within the manufacturing industry. (4) *Study context* was specified as higher education where the intended delivering body of education is universities, but the intended target audience could be either university students or industry professionals. Since we focus on higher education, we refer to maintenance as an engineering discipline; typically covered by programs such as mechanical or automation engineering and focused on knowledge situated in the professional practice of maintenance. Still, as a professional practice, maintenance also includes non-engineering topics (e.g. management).

Step 2: Retrieve. The second step consisted of retrieving a baseline sample of potentially relevant literature [7]. As previous similar reviews only uncovered a small number of articles [6], we deployed a two-step procedure. Firstly, we used the following search string in the Scopus database: "(manufacturing OR production) AND maintenance AND engineering AND education". We delimited the search to only relevant disciplines, followed by downloading all articles that were deemed relevant based on title, abstract, and/or keywords. Secondly, we searched for additional articles through tracking references-of-references from the Scopus sample. We did this to avoid overlooking articles that were not indexed in Scopus or remained undetected by our search string. The baseline sample consisted of a total of 51 articles.

Step 3: Select. Using the baseline sample, the third step consisted of selecting pertinent literature by applying the inclusion/exclusion criteria [7]. Firstly, we reviewed the title, abstract, and keywords and classified each article as either "included" or "excluded". We erred in the direction of inclusion for articles that did not clearly meet our definitions of primary studies [8] but marked them as "borderline" cases. At this stage, 15 articles were excluded and 10 articles were marked as borderline. Thereafter, we read the full text of all included and borderline articles. Here we excluded the articles that did not fulfill all of our criteria. For example, we excluded articles that did not fulfill our theoretical domain (e.g. education of aerospace maintenance) or study context (e.g. firm-specific educational programs or a sole focus on on-job training). We also excluded implicit duplicates, i.e. articles by the same authors that covered the same content across multiple publication outlets. A total of 11 articles were excluded at this stage, resulting in a final sample of 25 articles.

Step 4: Synthesize. In the final step, we synthesized the literature [7] by means of two analyses. (1) *Descriptive analysis* focused on providing an overview of the 25 articles included in the review. We analyzed: year of publication, article type, country of affiliation, and target audience. The following classification of article type was used: C = Conference; J = Journal; B = Book chapter, T = Thesis (MSc or PhD). The target audience was classified as either U = University education, P = Professional education, or both (P & U). (2) *Thematic analysis* focused on uncovering the main themes within the body of knowledge provided by the literature sample. Based on reading the full text of all articles, we deployed an inductive and iterative coding approach to identify the themes [8]. The themes were finally used as a classification scheme for all articles, where one article could cover more than one theme.

3 Findings

We present our findings in two sections, reflecting the two types of analyses. The descriptive findings are presented first (Sect. 3.1), followed by the thematic findings (Sect. 3.2). The main thematic findings are summarized in Table 1.

3.1 Descriptive Findings

Four main descriptive findings summarize the articles included in our review. Firstly, articles on maintenance engineering education have been published at a low but consistent pace over the past two decades; 25 articles across 20 years yield an average of 1,25 articles each year. Secondly, the vast majority of articles are published in conference proceedings (C, 72%). We only identified four journal articles (J, 16%) and the rest were book chapters or theses (B & T, 12%). Two of the journal articles are published in generic engineering educational journals and two are published in the same domain-specific journal: Journal of Quality in Maintenance Engineering. Thirdly, there is a focus on both target groups, reflected in that roughly half (U, 52%) of all articles focus on university education and the rest on either professional education or both (P, P & U, 48%). Fourthly, the majority of all articles are published by European authors (72%), especially from the Nordic countries (Sweden, Finland, Norway with 32%). The other countries of affiliation are the US, Australia, Greece, UK, Italy, Slovakia, Spain, Netherlands, Venezuela, Colombia, Ireland, Austria, and Bulgaria. However, it should be noted that our review did not include non-English articles (e.g. Chinese, Korean).

3.2 Thematic Findings

The nine inductively generated themes are listed in Table 1 along with summaries of their thematic content and associated references. The intention is to summarize the body of knowledge provided by the literature for each theme, not to outline the substantive findings from each of the articles within each theme.

Table 1. Summary of thematic findings.

Theme and definition	Thematic content	References
1. Review of educations: existing maintenance engineering educations (e.g. courses and programs)	Overview of existing (past or present) courses and programs in maintenance engineering education, e.g. describing and comparing courses nationally and globally	[6, 9–11]
2. Competence requirements: knowledge, skills, abilities, and other characteristics of maintenance engineering professionals	Competence requirements for professional maintenance engineers; individual skills, bundles of skills, and categorization of skills using educational frameworks (e.g. the CDIO syllabus)	[6, 10, 12–14]

(continued)

Table 1. (*continued*)

Theme and definition	Thematic content	References
3. Learner characteristics: personal, academic, social, and cognitive aspects that influence why, how, and what maintenance engineering students learn	Unique learning characteristics of maintenance engineering students that need to be considered in educational design, e.g. time and space constraints, prior knowledge and skills, and digital literacy of adult learners	[10–12, 15–17]
4. Curricula design: topics and learning objectives relevant for inclusion in maintenance engineering education	Curricula used in existing education or proposals of curricula for future education, e.g. curriculum based on EFNMS requirements and general guidelines for curriculum for modern engineering education	[10, 13, 15–19]
5. Course and program design: design of individual courses and aggregate programs for maintenance engineering education	Design and/or delivery of courses and programs for maintenance engineering education, e.g. MSc courses with a specified structure of content, teaching and learning activities, and assessment	[10, 16, 20–22]
6. Laboratory sessions: learning environments where students can observe, practice, and experiment with maintenance topics, individually or in groups	Laboratory sessions for maintenance engineering education, e.g. remote condition monitoring and maintenance laboratory, techniques for predictive maintenance, and sensor diagnostics	[14, 23–25]
7. Online learning: maintenance engineering education delivered in online learning environments	Online learning environments for maintenance education, e.g. e-Learning systems for vocational education, web-based modules for condition monitoring, and provision of online study materials for asynchronous learning	[10, 15, 17, 18, 22, 26, 27]
8. Gamification: applications of elements of game playing in maintenance engineering education	Learning environments that include game content and game play, e.g. teaching the pitfalls and ambiguities of OEE or strategic challenges with maintenance of rolling stock	[28, 29]
9. AR and VR: applications of AR and VR systems in maintenance engineering education	Experimental learning environments using AR and VR to enable interaction with real (or very close to real) situations in maintenance engineering, e.g. occupational hazards during maintenance execution	[30, 31]

In addition to uncovering and elaborating on the content of the nine themes (Table 1), we also observed five patterns across the themes. Firstly, most of the themes are covered in articles that span the entire review period, suggesting them to be relevant for maintenance engineering education. Also, each theme is covered by a minimum of two articles (i.e. at least 4% of the literature sample). Secondly, "Course program and design" seemed to be an important theme in the first decade, but not the second (6 articles up until 2010; zero articles after 2010). This might be indicative of the shorter life-cycle and rapid evolvement of modern maintenance engineering. Thirdly, and similarly, articles covering "Online learning" also received more emphasis in the first decade of our review (7 articles up until 2013; zero articles after 2013). However, online learning has recently increased in importance due to the COVID-19 pandemic, and we predict that this will soon be reflected in the publication landscape. Fourthly, more recent themes include "Gamification", "AR and VR", as well as "Laboratory sessions" using novel digital technologies (7 articles published since 2015). Fifth and finally, we observe that maintenance researchers have been occupied with presenting ideas, concepts, methods, and tools for how to *renew higher education*, but that there is no or at least very little attention or concrete proposals for how to *increase access to higher education*.

4   Conclusions and Recommendations for the Future

The ultimate goal is to produce the right kind of maintenance workers that are complemented rather than substituted by technology [2]. From our systematic literature review of 25 articles published between 2000–2020, we have identified nine key themes that have occupied maintenance researchers in their educational efforts. Based on the insights from our review, we propose a set of recommendations for the future in terms of two general research suggestions and two general policy suggestions.

Research on Skills. Future maintenance workers need to interface with new technologies such as AI algorithms in novel decision-making processes. However, the potential productivity gains from such process improvement require that maintenance workers possess two forms of complementary skills: domain-specific skills (accumulated through prior learning within the maintenance domain) and vintage-specific skills (accumulated through familiarity of tasks with new technology) [32]. Still, we do not know exactly which skills that are complementarities and which are substitutes, and we do not know exactly how individual and/or bundles of skills interface differently with specific technologies. We therefore call for more research on skills.

Research on Education. As we gain more knowledge into what skills that should be the locus of education, we still face the hurdle of implementation as we lack a body of knowledge on effective maintenance engineering education. Therefore, we call for more research on education - developing explanatory and predictive knowledge on what constitutes effective maintenance engineering education, as well as prescriptive knowledge on evidence-based design of maintenance engineering education.

Renew Education. The race against technology will not be won simply by increasing educational spending whilst holding current educational practices constant, because traditional education is designed for producing traditional skills. Therefore, we call for renewing maintenance engineering education by identifying the right modern skillsets for maintenance workers, translating them into achievable learning objectives, and implementing them using teaching and learning methods that fit a digital age.

Increase Access to Education. Traditional maintenance engineering education has focused on specialized courses, programs, and degrees. Therefore, we call for increasing access to higher education by means of novel forms of individualized education (e.g. module-based online learning and open educational resources) as well as novel forms of interdisciplinary education (e.g. case-based analytics projects with teams of mechanical engineering students and data science students).

References

1. Bokrantz, J., Skoogh, A., Berlin, C., Wuest, T., Stahre, J.: Smart maintenance: an empirically grounded conceptualization. Int. J. Prod. Econ. **223**, 107534 (2020)
2. Brynjolfsson, E., Rock, D., Syverson, C.: The productivity J-curve: how intangibles complement general purpose technologies. Am. Econ. J. Macroecon. **13**(1), 333–372 (2021)
3. Benzell, S.G., Brynjolfsson, E.: Digital abundance and scarce genius: implications for wages, interest rates, and growth 2019. National Bureau of Economic Research (2019)
4. Goldin, C.D., Katz, L.F.: The Race between Education and Technology, Harvard University Press, Cambridge (2009)
5. Alsyouf, I.: Maintenance practices in Swedish industries: survey results. Int. J. Prod. Econ. **121**(1), 212–223 (2009)
6. Kans, M., Metso, L.: Maintenance education in engineering programs on bachelor and master level: evidence from Finland and Sweden. In: Liyanage, J.P., Amadi-Echendu, J., Mathew, J. (eds.) Engineering Assets and Public Infrastructures in the Age of Digitalization. LNME, pp. 465–474. Springer, Cham (2020). https://doi.org/10.1007/978-3-030-48021-9_52
7. Durach, C.F., Kembro, J., Wieland, A.: A new paradigm for systematic literature reviews in supply chain management. J. Supply Chain Manage. **53**(4), 67–85 (2017)
8. Aguinis, H., Ramani, R.S., Alabduljader, N.: Best-practice recommendations for producers, evaluators, and users of methodological literature reviews. Organ. Res. Meth. 1094428120943281 (2020)
9. Hines, J.W.: Maintenance and reliability education. In: Emerson Process Management–CSI Workshop on Reliability Based Maintenance, Nashville, TN (2001)
10. Nerland, A.S.: Competence within Maintenance, Master's thesis Thesis, Norweigian University of Science and Technology (2010)
11. Starr, A., Bevis, K.: The role of education in industrial maintenance: the pathway to a sustainable future. In: Engineering Asset Lifecycle Management, pp. 539–542. Springer (2010). https://doi.org/10.1007/978-0-85729-320-6_61
12. Costello, O., Kent, M.D., Kopacek, P.: Integrating education into maintenance operations: an Irish case study. IFAC-PapersOnLine **52**(25), 415–420 (2019)
13. Kans, M.: Maintenance knowledge requirements for engineering education: a curriculum for the modern engineer. In: International Conference on Maintenance Engineering, IncoME-IV 2019, University of Manchester Middle East Centre Dubai UAE, 24–25 April 2019 (2019)

14. Kans, M., Campos, J., Håkansson, L.: A remote laboratory for maintenance 4.0 training and education. IFAC-PapersOnLine, **53**(3), 101–106 (2020)
15. Emmanouilidis, C., Papathanassiou, N., Pistofidis, P., Labib, A.: Maintenance management E-training: what we learn from the users. IFAC Proc. Volumes **43**(3), 36–41 (2010)
16. Macchi, M., Ierace, S.: Education in industrial maintenance management: feedback from an Italian experience. In: Engineering Asset Lifecycle Management, pp. 531–538. Springer (2010). https://doi.org/10.1007/978-0-85729-320-6_60
17. Papathanassiou, N., Pistofidis, P., Emmanouilidis, C.: Competencies development and self-assessment in maintenance management E-training. Eur. J. Eng. Educ. **38**(5), 497–511 (2013)
18. Stuchly, V., Cubonova, N.: Education of Maintenance Professionals–Experiences and Trends in Slovakia (2011)
19. Khan, S.: Research study from industry-university collaboration on "No Fault Found" Events. J. Qual. Maintenance Eng. (2015)
20. Al-Abdeli, Y., Bullen, F.: A problem based/experiential learning approach to teaching maintenance engineering. In: Proceedings of the 4th ASEE/AaeE Global Colloquium on Engineering Education (2005)
21. Shrivastav, O.P.: Industrial maintenance: a discipline in its own right, world transactions on engineering and technology. Education **4**(1), 107–110 (2005)
22. Beebe, R.: Experience with education in maintenance and reliability engineering by off campus learning. In: Engineering Asset Management, pp. 883–892. Springer (2006). https://doi.org/10.1007/978-1-84996-178-3_20
23. Upadhyaya, B., Hines, J., McClanahan, J., Johansen, N.: Development of a maintenance engineering laboratory. In: Proceedings of the 2002 American Society for Engineering Education Annual Conference & Exposition, Montreal, Canada (2002)
24. Antonino-Daviu, J., Dunai, L., Climente-Alarcon, V.: Design of innovative laboratory sessions for electric motors predictive maintenance teaching. In: IECON 2017–43rd Annual Conference of the IEEE Industrial Electronics Society (2017)
25. Keseev, V.P.: Diagnostic and maintenance education course for PLC based automatic machines. Int. J. Educ. Learn Syst. **4** (2019)
26. Upadhyaya, B., Woo, H.: Web-Based Development and Delivery of Course Material on Maintenance Engineering (2003)
27. Emmanouilidis, C., Spais, V.: E-Training in maintenance. In: E-Maintenance, pp. 475–506. Springer (2010). https://doi.org/10.1007/978-1-84996-205-6_15
28. Martinetti, A., Puig, J.E.P., Alink, C.O., Thalen, J., van Dongen, L.A.M.: Gamification in teaching maintenance engineering: a dutch experience in the rolling stock management learning. In: 3nd International Conference on Higher Education Advance. HEAd (2017)
29. Bengtsson, M.: Using a game-based learning approach in teaching overall equipment effectiveness. J. Qual. Maintenance Eng. (2019)
30. Landa, H.M.: Problems Analysis and Solutions for the Establishment of Augmented Reality Technology in Maintenance and Education (2015)
31. Velosa, J.D., Cobo, L., Castillo, F., Castillo, C.: Methodological Proposal for Use of Virtual Reality VR and Augmented Reality AR in the Formation of Professional Skills in Industrial Maintenance and Industrial Safety, in Online Engineering & Internet of Things. Springer, pp. 987–1000 (2018). https://doi.org/10.1007/978-3-319-64352-6_92
32. Choudhury, P., Starr, E., Agarwal, R.: Machine Learning and Human Capital: Experimental Evidence on Productivity Complementarities, Harvard Business School (2018)

Wear and Tear: A Data Driven Analysis of the Operating Condition of Lubricant Oils

Roney Malaguti[1,3]($^{(\boxtimes)}$) , Nuno Lourenço[2] , and Cristovão Silva[3]

[1] Stratio Automotive - R&D Department, Rua Pedro Nunes - Quinta da Nora, Ed.D, 3030 - 199 Coimbra, Portugal
roney@stratioautomotive.com
[2] Department of Informatics Engineering,
University of Coimbra, CISUC, Coimbra, Portugal
naml@dei.uc.pt
[3] Department of Mechanical Engineering, University of Coimbra, CEMMPRE, Coimbra, Portugal
cristovao.silva@dem.uc.pt

Abstract. Intelligent lubricating oil analysis is a procedure in condition-based maintenance (CBM) of diesel vehicle fleets. Together with diagnostic and failure prediction processes, it composes a data-driven vehicle maintenance structure that helps a fleet manager making decisions on a particular breakdown. The monitoring or controlof lubricating oils in diesel engines can be carried out in different ways and following different methodologies. However, the list of studies related to automatic lubricant analysis as methods for determining the degradation rate of automotive diesel engines is short. In this paper we present an intelligent data analysis from 5 different vehicles to evaluate whether the variables collected make it possible to determine the operating condition of lubricants. The results presented show that the selected variables have the potential to determine the operating condition, and that they are highly related with the lubricant condition.We also evaluate the inclusion of new variables engineered from raw data for a better determination of the operating condition. One of such variables is the kinematic viscosity which we show to have a relevant role in characterizing the lubricant condition. Moreover, 3 of the 4 variables that explaining 90% of the variance in the original data resulted from our feature engineering.

Keywords: Condition-based maintenance (CBM) · Lubricating oils · Diesel vehicle · Intelligent data analysis

1 Introduction

Fleets of vehicles are critical elements for the operations of companies acting in the transportation sector. Thus, identifying vehicles breakdown signatures

© IFIP International Federation for Information Processing 2021
Published by Springer Nature Switzerland AG 2021
A. Dolgui et al. (Eds.): APMS 2021, IFIP AICT 634, pp. 217–225, 2021.
https://doi.org/10.1007/978-3-030-85914-5_23

and building models to predict them before they occur is of major importance and has been an object of study for practitioners involved in the maintenance area [10]. Based on maintenance techniques and methodologies used in failure prediction, modern industries are increasingly using lube oil testing as a crucial factor in maintaining the condition of vehicles [8]. In recent years, efforts have been invested in the development and research of diagnostic and failure prediction systems based on lubricant testing, with the aim of providing early warning of machine failure and to extend the operational life of lubricating oil, avoiding unnecessary oil change costs, waste, or environmental pollution [5,16]. Following this growing body of research in the maintenance field, with a focus on diesel engine lubricants, we developed a series of analysis on data acquired from five vehicles used in passenger transportation of different brands and models to determine performance patterns of these variables, identify anomalies in vehicle behavior and showing that the selected parameters can be used to develop a failure prediction model for vehicle lubrication systems. The paper is subdivided into four sections. Section two is dedicated to a literature survey, in the third section there is an evaluation and modeling of the lubricant data from the vehicles and finally the fourth section contains results and discussion.

2   Literature Review

Condition-Based Maintenance (CBM) is a strategy that monitors the current condition of an asset, helping to decide when a given maintenance operation is required, considering the evolution pattern of certain indicators. Checking these indicators on a machine can include non-intrusive measurements for example: visual inspection, analysis at performance data of the vehicles, and scheduled tests like temperature and vibration analysis [15]. Condition data can be collected at certain intervals or continuously (embedded internal sensors). Some studies present maintenance decision guidelines for improving CBM using detailed analysis of used oil data as a source of information to determine whether the fluid in the system is healthy and suitable for further service, in addition to observing the condition of the equipment through this analysis [8]. Case studies present models for monitoring the condition of diesel engine oil in urban buses, which, by monitoring the evolution of its degradation, aim to implement a predictive maintenance policy or a CBM [10]. Based on lubrication condition monitoring (LCM), the intervals for oil replacement can be increased, which directly implies an increase in availability and a reduction in the costs associated with maintenance [10]. [16] presents a detailed approach to recent research trends in the development of LCM-based approaches applied for maintenance decision support and applications in equipment diagnosis and prognosis. This study reviews and classifies LCM tests and parameters into several categories, which include physicochemical, elemental, contamination, and additive analyses. These studies show that building data-driven models accurately identify the state of wear and tear in a component or system, and make the condition-based maintenance methodology more effective and reliable. Furthermore the study of lubricants can determine the rate of equipment degradation, and the results of lubricant analysis to determine the behavior of wear levels as a function of operating time and operating typology are important tools for developing a predictive maintenance methodology [10]. [9] presents the physicochemical tests in the analysis of oils that are used for the evaluation of their condition and reports that the interpretation of waste oil analysis is very complex because the individual analyses are interdependent. For this reason it is necessary to know the whole oil analysis and make conclusions based on results of individual analyses. According to [5], the analysis of oil aging or degradation have continually evolved to provide a more accurate diagnosis of the remaining life of lubricants or any latent or impending failure in the equipment or processes in which they are being used. To analyze lubricating oils, it is necessary to collect samples during and after operation, and to take into consideration the parameters that will determine the quality of the lubricant and the condition of the equipment [13]. According to [7], the main parameters related to oil degradation are: oxidation, nitration, viscosity, depletion of antioxidant additives, anti-wear, TAN, TBN and RUL. Another important parameter besides those mentioned above is the so-called Oil Stress Factor, which has been used as an estimator of the potential stress suffered by the oil and allows some correlation with its possible degradation, considering the relationship between the specific power per displacement, the oil change period and the oil sump volume [7]. Another important variable is the oil viscosity considering perfect operating conditions which represents the fluidity of the oil at given temperature. In this sense the more viscous oils are thicker, while the less viscous ones are more fluid. [14] explains that the influence of operating conditions on the wear of both the equipment and the lubricants occurs because, due to many short trips and including a cold start, automotive engines often run without reaching their nominal temperature. The relationship between oil temperature and viscosity is known to have a strong effect on engine friction. The Oil stress factor (OSF) is a method for quantifying the stress under which engine oil is placed and allows for the prediction of oil degradation as a function of engine conditions. For this study, 2 different ways will be used to determine OSF to verify the relationship between them and determine the most appropriate for the problem at hand: Oil_z: described in [4] and OSFv3 described in [11] According to [3], in the maintenance of internal combustion engines, different lubricant analysis techniques are used to determine the condition of the oil and the system. A rapid method of analysing the condition of the lubricant is the so-called oil slick test, which allow to estimate the degradation of the lubricant and the presence of contaminants and it was used in this study to provide the prediction model labels. Figure 1 presents an example of an oil slick test. The central zone of the spot is identified, characterized by its dark and uniform intensity, and the intermediate or diffusion zone of the slick that indicates the degree of dispersion of the carbon particles and presence of contaminants. With these parameters defined, information about the dispersion and detergency conditions of a lubricant can be obtained by making an oil stain on filter paper. After applying the oil drop to the test paper, it is possible to see

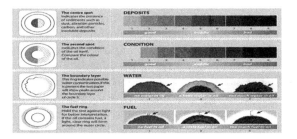

Fig. 1. Example of an oil slick text

an image with up to 4 circles based on the chromatographic effect. Although the slick test provides results on a scale of 0 to 9 for solid particle contamination and for condition. We convert this scale to a binary problem: 0 indicates that the oil is good for operating conditions, and 1 indicates that the oil is not good for operating conditions.

3   Data Analysis

The five vehicles considered in this study have a set of sensors which combined with an acquisition hardware, developed by Stratio Automotive [1], were used to collect the required data. The collected variables are: Engine Oil Temperature (°C), Coolant Temperature (°C), Engine Oil Pressure (mbar), Vehicle speed (km/h) and Engine speed (rpm). Missing value analysis helps to address several concerns caused by incomplete data, since they can lead to misleading interpretations. A descriptive analysis was initially performed on the collected variables to check the percentage of missing values and we observed a negligible percentage (inferior to 5%).

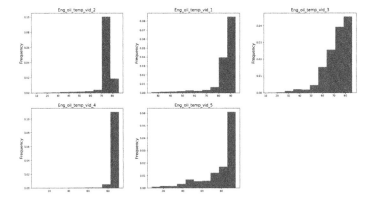

Fig. 2. A histogram grouped into frequency of values

A visual analysis of the variables behaviour allowed to determine that the behavior of the variables was similar among the selected cars despite being of different brands, models and years of manufacture (see Fig. 2). From the analysis of the histograms it can be seen that the data is asymmetrical. The asymmetry indicates that the data may not be normally distributed, but indicates the range of values at which these parameters work most of the time and confirms the limits and optimal operating values. To Confirm confirm whether there was a strong or weak relationship between the distribution of values over the months and the vehicles, we applied use the Kolmogorov-Smirnov test (K-S test). This test confirmed that there is no plausible difference in the data distribution to creating a failures alerts.

Principal Component Analysis (PCA) is a mathematical procedure for converting a set of observations of possibly correlated variables into a set of values of linearly uncorrelated variables called principal components [12]. The Fig. 3 show the PCA analysis from the one vehicle data and determine the lubricant's operating condition (0) or not (1) based on the two most important variables identified (Engine oil temperature x kinematic viscosity). From the analysis of the Fig. 3(a), we can identifier clear zones of differentiation between labels 0 and 1, it is possible to visualize in the zone between −4 and −2 of the x-axis the non-operational condition of the lubricant. However, attention should be paid to overlapping zones when developing future models. It is worth noting that the PCA analysis was performed for all vehicles and the results were cross-sectional, with no plausible distinction between models and brands that would justify changing the variables. Another important point that is drawn from the PCA analysis is the cumulative variance of the parameters, which determines the loss of information with the simplification of variables. According to Fig. 3(b), the blue bars show the percent variance explained by each principal component and the red line shows the cumulative sum. From the graph, we can read the percentage of the variance in the data explained as we add the principal components. So the first principal component explains 35% of the variance in the data set, the first 2 principal components explain 63%, and so on. This chart

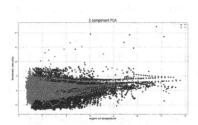

(a) PCA analysis for two principal components

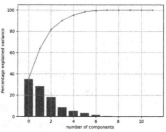

(b) the cumulative explained variance ratio as a function of the number of components

Fig. 3. PCA analysis (Color figure online)

shows that we need only 4 (Engine oil temperature, kinematic viscosity, dynamic viscosity and Oil_z) of the 9 principal components to explain 90% of the variance in the original data. A correlation analysis was performed to better understand the relationships among variables. In statistics, dependence or association is any statistical relationship, causal or otherwise, between two random variables or bivariate data (see Fig. 4).

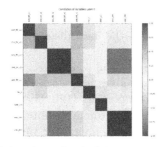

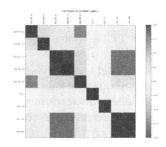

(a) Correlation for the lubricant operation condition (Label 0)

(b) Correlation for the non-operational condition of the lubricant (Label 1)

Fig. 4. Variables correlation

In this way we can see, when analyzing the correlation graphs of the variables, several types of relationships, whether they indicate a positive operating condition or a negative operating condition: 1. Oil_z in relation to all the other variables, has correlation values for label 0, something that is almost not identified for Label 1. This information determines that the calculated variable oil_z is an important and decisive variable for determining the oil's non-operating condition, since it is related to all the variables selected for solving the problem. 2. Oil pressure in relation to oil and liquid temperature, decreases its correlation value when it transitions from label 0 to label 1. This information indicates that the control for the relation of the amount of oil necessary for complete lubrication of the engine, according to its operating temperature, is no longer fully functioning and may not be sufficient. 3. Oil pressure versus engine speed increases its correlation value when it transitions from label 0 to label 1. This information determines that the engine needs to rotate faster to try to meet the lubrication demand. 4. The viscosities in relation to the engine speed decrease their correlation values when transiting from label 0 to label 1. This information determines that the film required for optimal engine lubrication at that speed is no longer being achieved. 5. Oil pressure versus viscosities increase their correlation values when transitioning from label 0 to label 1. This information determines the need for greater lubricant pressure to meet lubrication needs, since oil degradation causes it to lose its properties, viscosity being one of the most important oil properties.

We are also interested in looking into which variables may or may not be relevant as input to develop a model(see Fig. 5). Thus, we can extract from this

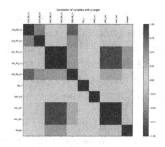

Fig. 5. Correlation between the input variables with the output variable.

correlation graph that the variables oil temperature and liquid temperature have a high correlation value with the target, which is identified because the operating temperatures are directly linked to the calculations made by the Centralina for the engine's lubrication needs, and the higher the engine's operating temperature, the lower the kinematic viscosity and the worse the oil's lubrication power. Another important point to mention is that due to the high temperature relationship, there is consequently a correlation value of the kinematic and dynamic viscosity with the target, even if to a lesser extent. These viscosity correlation values are due to the lubricant properties, and viscosity control is one of the most important factors in determining the lubricant's operating condition.

4   Conclusion

An important component of engine maintenance is to establish the most cost-effective oil change and overhaul intervals in terms of cost, wear, and failure diagnosis efficiency. From the present study, some conclusions can be drawn and could be subdivided into: **Response time:** it is undeniable that lubricant analysis is of utmost importance to determine the wear of the equipment and present better thresholds for equipment replacement. according to [2], real-time data analysis techniques are capable of high-throughput analysis with typical analysis times of less than two minutes compared to laboratory analyses that face both large sample volumes and the constraint of fast turnaround times; **Evaluation parameters:** It is common knowledge in the analyses performed, the influence of temperature on the viscosity of lubricating oils, however as already mentioned in other parts of this object of study, this despite being an important parameter is not the only one that should be analyzed, [6] concludes in his study that to obtain a complete picture of the changes occurring in the oil, it is advisable to interpret the kinematic viscosity values together with the dynamic viscosity, as well as the degree of oxidation and acidity; **Analysis performed:** Through the PCA analysis, it was confirmed that the selected variables can determine the answer to the stated problem, but it is necessary to have at least 4 variables so that the variance of the data is not lost. The kinematic viscosity variable proved to be preponderant for characterizing the lubricant condition or not, and 3 of the 4 variables that explaining 90% of the variance in the original data were new calculated variables, proving that necessary calculate other variables based on the original data to the improvement of the analysis. In addition, the correlation analysis identified relationships that confirm the theory described in this study and consequently pave the way for the development of a model for identifying the operating conditions of lubricants in diesel vehicles.

Acknowledgments. This work is partially funded by national funds through the FCT - Foundation for Science and Technology, I.P., within the scope of the project CISUC - UID/CEC/00326/2020 and by European Social Fund, through the Regional Operational Program Centro 2020 and by national funds through FCT - Fundação para a Ciência e a Tecnologia, under the project UIDB/00285/2020.

References

1. Homepage - stratio. https://stratioautomotive.com/. Accessed 19 Mar 2021
2. Beauvir, M.: Lubricating oil analysis according to ASTM D5185 using the Thermo Scientific iCAP 7400 ICP-OES, p. 3
3. Delgado Ortiz, J., Saldivia Saldivia, F., Fygueroa Salgado, S.: Sistema para la determinación de la degradación del lubricante basado en el tratamiento digital de manchas de aceite de motores diesel. Revista UIS Ingenierías **13**(1), 55–61 (2014)
4. Lee, P.M., et al.: The degradation of lubricants in gasoline engines: development of a test procedure to evaluate engine oil degradation and its consequences for rheology. Tribol. Interf. Eng. Ser. **48**, 593–602 (2005)
5. Lopez, P., Mabe, J., Miró, G., Etxeberria, L.: Low cost photonic sensor for in-line oil quality monitoring: methodological development process towards uncertainty mitigation. Sensors (Switzerland) **18**(7), 2015 (2018)
6. Loska, A.: The kinetics of changes in kinematic viscosity of engine oils under similar operating conditions. Eksploatacja i Niezawodnosc **19**(2), 268–278 (2017)
7. Macián-Martínez, V., Tormos-Martínez, B., Gómez-Estrada, Y.A., Bermúdez-Tamarit, V.: Revisión del proceso de la degradación en los aceites lubricantes en motores de gas natural comprimido y diesel. Dyna (Spain) **88**(1), 49–58 (2013)
8. Muchiri, P.P.N., Adika, C.O., Wakiru, J.M.: Development of Maintenance Decision Guidelines from Used Oil Data of a Thermal Powerplant. **15**(2), 63–71 (2018)
9. Perić, S., Nedić, B., Grkić, A.: Applicative monitoring of vehicles engine oil. Tribol. Ind. **36**(3), 308–315 (2014)
10. Raposo, H., Farinha, J.T., Fonseca, I., Ferreira, L.A.: Condition monitoring with prediction based on diesel engine oil analysis: a case study for urban buses. Actuators **8**(1), 1–15 (2019)
11. Ribeiro, M.F., et al.: Universidade Federal do Triângulo Mineiro **53**(9), 1689–1699 (2013)
12. Shahariar, G.M.H., et al.: Optimisation of driving-parameters and emissions of a diesel-vehicle using principal component analysis (PCA), December 2020
13. Sharma, B.C., Gandhi, O.P.: Performance evaluation and analysis of lubricating oil using parameter profile approach. Ind. Lubr. Tribol. **60**(3), 131–137 (2008)
14. Tauzia, X., Maiboom, A., Karaky, H., Chesse, P.: Experimental analysis of the influence of coolant and oil temperature on combustion and emissions in an automotive diesel engine. Int. J. Engine Res. **20**(2), 247–260 (2019)

15. Vališ, D., Žák, L., Pokora, O.: Failure prediction of diesel engine based on occurrence of selected wear particles in oil. Eng. Fail. Anal. **56**, 501–511 (2015)
16. Wakiru, J.M., Pintelon, L., Muchiri, P.N., Chemweno, P.K.: A review on lubricant condition monitoring information analysis for maintenance decision support. Mech. Syst. Sig. Process. **118**, 108–132 (2019)

A Periodic Inventory Model for Perishable Items with General Lifetime

Fatma Ben Khalifa[1(✉)], Imen Safra[2(✉)], Chaaben Kouki[3(✉)], and Zied Jemai[1,4(✉)]

[1] ENIT, UR OASIS, Tunis, Tunisia
fatma.benkhalifa@enit.utm.tn
[2] ENIT, LR-ACS, Tunis, Tunisia
imen.safra@centraliens.net
[3] School of Management, ESSCA, Angers, France
chaaben.kouki@essca.fr
[4] Centralesupelec, University Paris Saclay, Gif-sur-Yvette, France
zied.jemai@centralesupelec.fr

Abstract. We study a perishable inventory system controlled by a (T, S) periodic review order up to level policy. Items have a general lifetime distribution and the lead time is assumed to be constant. The demands arrive according to a Poisson process with rate λ. The customer is impatient. If he is not served, he will leave the queuing systems. Using the approximate solution of the steady-state probabilities, we are able to obtain the cost components' analytical expression. Next, we compare the analytical results of our model with the simulation results. Finally, we perform a sensitivity analysis to evaluate the effect of the lifetime variation and cost parameters on the optimal cost and stock level S. Our model is an extension of an exponential distribution case. With the general lifetime distribution, we are able to have total flexibility for setting the lifetime variability. This approximation is closer to reality, especially in random environment conditions. Obtained results, from the analytical approximation model, are close to those of the optimal policy with an average accuracy of 7%.

Keywords: Perishable items · General lifetime · Periodic review

1 Introduction

Nowadays, the management of perishable products such as food, blood, and pharmaceutical products, has become one of the major global issues in terms of cost optimization. A new study done by the Food and Agriculture Organization (FAO) indicates that 13.8% of the total produced food in the world is lost [1]. Product perishability is also one of the critical problems in the healthcare field, especially that most of the pharmaceutical goods and all blood products have a limited lifetime. The use of an outdated product in this field puts human life at risk, which makes the problem very serious. The AABB members estimate that the total number of outdated blood components, in blood centers and hospitals in 2013, was 932,000 units. In fact, 4.64% of all processed blood components are perished this year [2].

© IFIP International Federation for Information Processing 2021
Published by Springer Nature Switzerland AG 2021
A. Dolgui et al. (Eds.): APMS 2021, IFIP AICT 634, pp. 226–234, 2021.
https://doi.org/10.1007/978-3-030-85914-5_24

In today's competitive global market, it is mandatory for companies managing perishable products to reduce these losses in order to remain competitive in their industrial fields. The root cause for this intriguing problem can be explained by the stochastic nature of demand, the limitation and the variability of lifetime, and the high customer service requirement. Due to the importance of this issue, perishable inventory has received significant attention from researchers and the scientific community [3, 4].

In the absence of an optimal policy to manage this type of goods, our challenge is to find an analytical approximation that considers the real faced constraints. By doing so, we will be able to make a balance between satisfying customer and decreasing product perishability. So, the question is: How to deal with perishable products when facing several constraints and get an analytical approach sufficiently close to the real system that can evaluate the system performance before making a decision.

This work tackles the above-described problem by investigating the case of a perishable periodic inventory model with general lifetime distribution and proposing an analytical solution to the steady-state probabilities and the cost components. This model can be considered more realistic reflecting the stochastic nature of the lifetime and the demand. The main contribution of this paper is the extension of the analytical approximation given by Kouki [5] to the model in which the lifetime has a general distribution. In addition, since most blood platelets are managed by periodic inventory control, our model can be used as an alternative to existing models, where blood life is typically assumed to be either fixed or exponentially distributed with an average of time units.

The remainder of the paper is organized as follows. Section 2 introduces the relevant literature review of perishable inventory management. Section 3 presents the proposed inventory model. In Sect. 4, we compare the obtained analytical results to the simulation results and we provide a sensitivity analysis to evaluate the impact of different parameters (lifetime variability, Lead time, ...) on the inventory average and the operating cost. Finally, Sect. 5 draws conclusions and suggests potential further research directions.

2   Literature Review

Perishable inventory management is becoming increasingly complex. Products are becoming perishable due to various factors such as product characteristics, nature of demand, and changing customer expectations. Due to the importance of this problem, researchers are focusing on the optimal policy identification.

The literature concerning perishable inventory systems can be classified into various classes depending on whether the inventory is controlled continuously or periodically, products' lifetime is assumed to be constant or random, the lead time is positive or instantaneous, and whether demand is deterministic or stochastic. Nahmias [6] classifies perishable inventory management in two basic categories: Periodic or Continuous Review. Under the continuous review system, the inventory level is known and tracked continuously, requiring more resources and investment. This case is not detailed in this work. We refer readers to [3].

However, the periodic review is inexpensive since inventory evaluation takes place at specific times. These models can be classified according to the lifetime characteristics: fixed and random lifetime. For more details, Nahmias [6] and Goyal [7] presented an interesting review of perishable inventory management based on this classification.

Considering the fixed lifetime models', the first analysis of optimal policies was given by Van Zyl (1964) [6]. But until now, the adoption of the classic periodic replenishment policy for perishable items with a fixed shelf life, a deterministic lead time, and fixed order costs is very difficult to found [8].

But the assumption of a deterministic lifetime is not realistic especially when this type of goods can be deteriorated at any moment in the period of its lifetime due to random perturbation factors such as temperature, humidity, lightness, and packaging location. Actually, disregarding the stochastic nature of the lifetime can be a source of losses and costs. Kouki [5] gave a numerical investigation and showed that the ignorance of randomness of lifetime leads to higher costs.

The stochastic aspect can be illustrated by several probability distributions: Binomial, Uniform, Normal, Exponential, and General. Most works that deal with random lifetime use the exponential distribution, and the majority of these models were found under a continuous review policy [5, 8]. Under the periodic review, the first model that examined a perishable good with zero lead time and random lifetime, was given by Vaughan [9], where the lifetime had a Gamma distribution. Kouki [10] analyzed a periodic review inventory control system of a perishable product having random lifetime with exponential distribution. To cover more cases, Kouki [8] considers that item lifetimes follow an Erlang distribution. Another probability distribution model that covers most cases is the general distribution. It considers Exponential distribution, Gamma distribution, Normal Distribution, etc. The only one who used this distribution was Nahmias [11]. He assumed that successive deliveries would outdate in the same order of their arrival in inventory and showed that the structure of the optimal policy is the same as in the case where the lifetime is deterministic. This model considered that the lead time is zero, which is incoherent with reality [11].

The literature review of perishable inventory management is very rich, but the case of a periodic review with general lifetimes and positive lead times has not been investigated yet. The focus of this research will be the presentation of an analytical approximation model that is close to the optimal policy with acceptable accuracy.

3   Model Description

In the absence of the optimal policy to manage perishable products, we propose an approximate model with a periodic review (T, S) policy. The demand arrives following a Poisson distribution with rate λ and customers are impatient. The lifetime of each product has a general distribution F with means m. Each time an order is triggered, it arrives in stock after a constant lead time $L \leq T$. In this section, we describe the approach made to get the expression of the total cost performance $Z(T, S)$. First, we detail the steps made to get the steady-state probabilities P. Then, we calculate the different cost components. Finally, we present the total cost.

To compute the steady-state probabilities $P(i)$, of the inventory level i, $i = 0, \ldots S$, at $nt + L, n = 1, 2, \ldots$, we rely on the transient probabilities from state i to state j during t. This transition occurs either through a demand arrival or a perished product. So, to calculate these probabilities, we use the demand rate λ and the rate at which items perish, which we denote by $\gamma(n)$. Given that, there are n items in the stock. Movaghar [12] showed that for an $./M/1 + G$ queue:

$$\gamma(n) = \frac{n\Phi(n-1)}{\Phi(n)} - \lambda \tag{1}$$

where $\Phi(n) = \int_0^\infty \left(\int_0^x (1 - F(y)) dy \right)^n e^{-\lambda x} dx$.

In this case, we are interested in calculating the transient probability from the state i to the state j during t time such that $nt + L \le t < (n+1)t + L$. Regarding our model the inventory items' i can be modeled as an $./M/1 + G$ queue whose service rate is $\frac{1}{\lambda}$, whereas the "$+G$" represents the remaining lifetime, which follows the distribution F.

It should be noted that the actual lifetime for a given cycle T is, of course, different from the lifetime given by the distribution F because it may happen that, for a given cycle, some items remain in the stock when an order is received. So, the inventory age is constituted by multiple age categories. In fact, there are items whose lifetime is different from those having an age given by F. In our model, it is assumed that the remaining lifetime for any cycle T is always the same, and it is given by F. This is true if the lifetime follows an exponential distribution that has a memoryless property. For any other lifetime distribution, our model approximates the distribution of the true remaining lifetime by F.

The first step to get the transition probability from i to j is to write the Kolmogorov's Eqs. 2:

$$p'_{i,j}(t) = \begin{cases} -(\lambda + \gamma(i))p_{i,j}(t), i = j \\ -(\lambda + \gamma(j))p_{i,j}(t) + - (\lambda + \gamma(j+1))p_{i,j+1}(t), j < i \le S \end{cases} \tag{2}$$

Using the Laplace transform, we obtain

$$\begin{cases} (z + \lambda + \gamma(i))p_{i,j}(z) = 0, i = j \\ (z + \lambda + \gamma(j))p_{i,j}(z) = (\lambda + \gamma(j+1))p_{i,j+1}(z), j < i \le S \end{cases} \tag{3}$$

We can show by induction that the solution of the above equations is:

$$p_{i,j}(z) = \frac{1}{\lambda + \gamma(j)} \prod_{k=j}^{i} \frac{\lambda + \gamma(k)}{z + \lambda + \gamma(k)} \tag{4}$$

and the inverse of Laplace transform of the above equation gives the transition probability from any state i to j and time $t, nT + L \le t < (n+1)T + L, n = 1, 2, \ldots$

$$p_{i,j}(t) = \left(\prod_{n=j+1}^{i} (\lambda + \gamma(n)) \right) \sum_{k=j}^{i} \left((-1)^{i-j} e^{-t(\lambda + \gamma(k))} \prod_{n=j,n\neq k}^{i} \frac{1}{\gamma(k) - \gamma(n)} \right) \quad (5)$$

We can now find the steady-state probability P using the relation:

$$P = P \times A \times B \quad (6)$$

where $A = p_{i,j}(L)_{0 \leq i \leq S, 0 \leq j \leq S}$ and $B = p_{i,j}(T - L)_{0 \leq i \leq S, 0 \leq j \leq S}$

Now we are ready to derive the cost components. The inventory average is given by:

$$
\begin{aligned}
E(I) &= \frac{1}{T} \sum_{i=1}^{S} \sum_{j=1}^{i} P(i) \int_{0}^{T} j p_{i,j}(t) dt \\
&= \frac{1}{T} \sum_{i=1}^{S} \sum_{j=1}^{i} \sum_{k=j}^{i} \left(jP(i) \prod_{n=j+1}^{i} (\lambda + \gamma(n)) \right) \left(\frac{(-1)^{i-j}(1 - e^{-T(\lambda+\gamma(k))})}{\lambda + \gamma(k)} \prod_{n=j,n\neq k}^{i} \frac{1}{\gamma(k) - \gamma(n)} \right)
\end{aligned}
\quad (7)
$$

Similarly, the expected outdated quantity is:

$$
\begin{aligned}
E(O) &= \frac{1}{T} \sum_{i=1}^{S} \sum_{j=1}^{i} P(i) \int_{0}^{T} \gamma(j) p_{i,j}(t) dt \\
&= \frac{1}{T} \sum_{i=1}^{S} \sum_{j=1}^{i} \sum_{k=j}^{i} \left(\gamma(j)P(i) \prod_{n=j+1}^{i} (\lambda + \gamma(n)) \right) \left(\frac{(-1)^{i-j}(1 - e^{-T(\lambda+\gamma(k))})}{\lambda + \gamma(k)} \prod_{n=j,n\neq k}^{i} \frac{1}{\gamma(k) - \gamma(n)} \right),
\end{aligned}
\quad (8)
$$

and finally, the expected lost sales can be written as:

$$
\begin{aligned}
E(S) &= \frac{\lambda P(0)}{T} + \frac{\lambda}{T} \sum_{i=1}^{S} \sum_{j=1}^{i} P(i)(\lambda + \gamma(1)) \int_{0}^{T} (T - t) p_{i,j}(t) dt \\
&= \frac{\lambda P(0)}{T} + \frac{\lambda}{T} \sum_{i=1}^{S} \left(P(i)(\lambda + \gamma(1)) \prod_{n=2}^{i} (\lambda + \gamma(n)) \right) \sum_{k=1}^{i} \left(\frac{(-1)^{i-1}(-1 + e^{-T(\lambda+\gamma(k))} + T(\lambda+\gamma(k)))}{[\lambda + \gamma(k)]^2} \prod_{n=1,n\neq k}^{i} \frac{1}{\gamma(k) - \gamma(n)} \right)
\end{aligned}
\quad (9)
$$

The total cost is:

$$Z(T, S) = \frac{K}{T} + hE(I) + wE(O) + bE(S) + c(\lambda + E(O) - E(S)) \quad (10)$$

Where K is the unit ordering cost, h is the holding cost per unit time, w is the outdated cost, b is the lost sales cost, and c is the purchasing cost.

4   Numerical Results

In this section, we conduct an extensive numerical study to identify the accuracy of our model's numerical results compared to the obtained simulation results using the simulation software Arena. In the second part, we conduct a sensitivity analysis to evaluate how the lifetime variability of perishable items affects the optimal cost and the system's performance. We also show the impact of the different cost parameters on the optimal total cost.

4.1   Comparison with the Simulation Model

In our numerical analysis, we assume that the lifetime follows a Gamma distribution with mean 3. The scale and shape parameters are given respectively from the intervals below: [2, 5, 10, 20, 50, 100, 150, 200, 300, 500, 1000, 2000, 5000] and [2, 5, 10, 20, 50, 100, 150, 200, 300, 500, 1000, 2000, 5000]. The demand rate is $\lambda = 2$, and the lead time is assumed to be constant, $L = 1$. 2500 MATLAB scenarios are done under different parameters settings: the unit ordering cost per order K belongs to the interval: [5,10,50,100], the unit holding cost per unit h is fixed to 1, the outdated cost W and the purchasing cost c are respectively equal to 5 or 10, the lost sales' cost b could be 50 or 100.

For the simulation model, we consider that the replication length is 10 000 units of time. This number is enough to get a representative result. After getting the two results, a comparative analysis of the obtained numerical results with simulation results is made to identify the accuracy between the two models. We consider that the gap % is the percentage of deviation between the analytical result given by our model TCa and simulation results TCs. The accuracy of the total cost is evaluated using the Eq. 11:

$$gap\% = 100 * \frac{TCs - TCa}{TCs} \tag{11}$$

Our model is exact when the lifetime follows an exponential distribution (alpha = 3 and beta = 1). The gap indicates that the optimal solutions obtained by both methods (MATLAB and Arena) are the same. The Table 1 presents the results of the proposed model and the simulation one for the 24 instances in the case of an exponential distribution.

Table 1. Comparison of the proposed model with the (T, S) simulation model – case of the exponential distribution

Instance	Cost Parameters					Proposed Model			Simulation model		
						T*	S*	Tca	T*sim	S*sim	TCs
	K	c	h	w	b						
1	5	5	1	5	50	0.5	10	62.503	0.5	10	62.503
2	5	5	1	10	50	0.5	9	70.624	0.5	9	70.624
3	5	10	1	5	50	0.5	9	94.516	0.5	9	94.516
4	5	5	1	10	100	0.5	11	76.440	0.5	11	76.440
5	5	5	1	5	100	0.5	11	66.781	0.5	11	66.781
6	5	10	1	10	100	0.5	10	109.981	0.5	10	109.981
7	10	5	1	5	50	1	13	69.873	1	13	69.873
8	10	5	1	10	50	1	12	79.896	1	12	79.896
9	10	10	1	5	50	1	12	103.602	1	12	103.602
10	10	5	1	10	100	0.5	11	86.440	0.5	11	86.440
11	10	5	1	5	100	1	15	75.258	1	15	75.258
12	10	10	1	10	100	0.5	10	119.981	0.5	10	119.981
13	50	5	1	5	50	2	20	100.783	2	20	100.783
14	50	5	1	10	50	1.5	15	113.058	1.5	15	113.058
15	50	10	1	5	50	1.5	15	136.401	1.5	15	136.401
16	50	5	1	10	100	1.5	18	122.773	1.5	18	122.773
17	50	5	1	5	100	1.5	19	107.783	1.5	19	107.783
18	50	10	1	10	100	1.5	17	160.801	1.5	17	160.801
19	100	5	1	5	50	2.5	24	124.263	2.5	24	124.263
20	100	5	1	10	50	2	19	139.841	2	19	139.841
21	100	10	1	5	50	2.5	21	162.645	2.5	21	162.645
22	100	5	1	10	100	2	23	152.050	2	23	152.050
23	100	5	1	5	100	2	24	134.132	2	24	134.132
24	100	10	1	10	100	2	21	192.314	2	21	192.314

Hence, we can conclude that our model is accurate, and guarantees global optimality in the case of an exponential distribution.

For the other cases, the mean gap between the simulation and the MATLAB result is 7%. Our obtained numerical results also indicate that in some conditions ($T \leq 1.5$, $S \leq 13$), the gap is equal to zero. Still, in some other situations, the analytical solution obtained by MATLAB is very close to that of the optimal solution obtained by Arena. For example, in the case of $T \leq 2$, the mean of gaps is 1%. The root cause of this gap can be explained by the approximation that we have done in our model. In reality, the remaining lifetime of articles is not the same. Our model doesn't consider the lifetime spent in the system, which represents the inventory age and the remaining lifetime. If $T \geq 2$, the risk of having different inventory age of product is even higher. To conclude, the smaller T is, the more the risk of having a different inventory age decrease. For the overall items, this risk can be reduced by having T < 2.

4.2 Sensitivity Analysis

In this section, we conduct a sensitivity analysis to evaluate the effect of the lifetime variability and the cost parameters on the optimal stock level and the optimal total cost.

We start by analyzing the impact of the lifetime variability, which is presented by a ratio CV. CV is defined as the ratio between the standard deviation and the expected value of the lifetime

$$CV = \frac{\sqrt{Alpha * Beta^2}}{Alpha * Beta} \tag{12}$$

Impact of the CV
We observe that the optimal cost increases with increasing lifetime variability. For the optimal stock level and the optimal period, we observe that the sensitivity level to CV is the highest when CV is above 0.007. They are stable when CV is between 0.01 and 0.06. For a CV value higher than 0.07, S* and T* decrease with CV. This can be explained that the higher of CV value is, the more the risk of perishability of the products increases, and the shorter the article's lifetime becomes, as shown in Fig. 1.

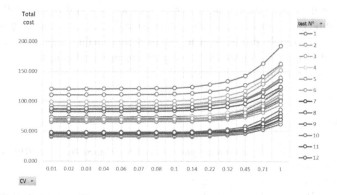

Fig. 1. Sensitivity analysis

Impact of Different Parameters
The main objective here is to evaluate the effect of the variation of the different parameters on the cost performance of our model. Firstly, considering the outdating cost, we have concluded that the higher the expiration/outdating cost is, the higher the total cost is. For the ordering cost K, it's obvious that the total cost increases with K, although the gap between the calculated total cost and simulation decreases. Next, we analyze the evolution of the total cost compared to the lost sales cost. As expected, the accuracy of the gap and the optimal cost increases with the lost-sales. This can be explained by the fact that to reduce the number of lost sales, the decision-makers have to buy more items. This will lead to more perished products and higher total cost. Finally, we analyze the behavior of the total cost with the purchasing cost. We conclude that the gap decreases when C increases, but the total cost behaves the same.

By using this model, the management team of an industrial perishable products unit can define the period and the inventory level that lead to the optimal cost based on the value of the different cost parameters. They can also choose the supplier using the impact of the ordering cost K in the total cost. The analysis of the effect of the different parameters variations to the total cost shows that the decision should be made after an analysis phase of all the cases that could appear (cost variations, lifetime variations, environment variations...). The use of this model can help decision makers to get the optimal solution.

5 Conclusion

In this paper, we consider a (T, S) perishable inventory system with lost sales. The lifetime of the product follows a general life distribution. Using the steady-state probabilities, we first derived the different analytical expressions of the total cost components. Next, we develop a MATLAB program that allows us to define the total optimal operating cost in a well-defined case. Finally, we conduct a numerical study to compare our analytical results with the simulation results. This allow us to conclude that our model is quite close to the real model with a mean accuracy gap of 7%.

This model could be extended considering (S,s) policy or a (T,S) multi-echelon model since in many sectors, the supply chain are more integrated, especially after the appearance of the industry 4.0. It is more likely to find inventory management systems that deal with perishable products in a multi-echelon chain rather than in a mono-echelon model. So, extending this work to periodic multi-echelon model would be a very interesting direction for future research.

References

1. English, A.: Food and Agriculture Organization of the United Nations, 2019. The state of food and agriculture (2019)
2. 2013 AABB Blood Survey Report, n.d. 88.
3. Bakker, M., Riezebos, J., Teunter, R.H.: Review of inventory systems with deterioration since 2001. Eur. J. Oper. Res. **221**, 275–284 (2012)
4. Beliën, J., Forcé, H.: Supply chain management of blood products: a literature review. Eur. J. Oper. Res. **217**, 1–16 (2012)
5. Kouki, C., Jemai, Z., Sahin, E., Dallery, Y.: Analysis of a periodic review inventory control system with perishables having random lifetime. Int. J. Prod. Res. **52**, 283–298 (2014)
6. Nahmias, S.: Perishable inventory theory: a review. Oper. Res. **30**, 680–708 (1982)
7. Goyal, S.K., Giri, B.C.: Recent trends in modeling of deteriorating inventory. Eur. J. Oper. Res. **134**, 1–16 (2001)
8. Kouki, C., Jouini, O.: On the effect of lifetime variability on the performance of inventory systems. Int. J. Prod. Econ. **167**, 23–34 (2015)
9. Vaughan, T.S.: A model of the perishable inventory system with reference to consumer-realized product expiration. J. Oper. Res. Soc. **45**(5), 519–528 (1994)
10. Kouki, C., Sahin, E., Jemaı, Z., Dallery, Y.: Assessing the impact of perishability and the use of time temperature technologies on inventory management. Int. J. Prod. Econ. **143**, 72–85 (2013)
11. Nahmias, S.: Higher-order approximations for the perishable-inventory problem. Oper. Res. **25**, 630–640 (1977)
12. Movaghar, A.: On queueing with customer impatience until the beginning of service. Queu. Syst. **29**(1998), 337–350 (1998)

Efficient Maintenance Planning: The MATISA Company Case Study

Jean-Robert Compérat[1(✉)], Vincent Cliville[2(✉)],
and Lamia Berrah[2(✉)]

[1] IREGE Laboratory, Savoie Mont Blanc University, 74-Annecy, France
jean-robert.comperat@univ-smb.fr
[2] LISTIC Laboratory, Savoie Mont Blanc University, 74-Annecy, France
{vincent.cliville,lamia.berrahl}@univ-smb.fr

Abstract. More and more equipment manufacturers are contracting with customers for maintenance planning (MP) of their equipment; this maintenance being either corrective, preventive or predictive. Due to the costs involved, customers are increasingly asking for a business case justifying the maintenance plan. This paper describes a study conducted with the MATISA Company, a track construction and renewal train manufacturer, and the business case for the equipment MP put forward to a customer. The concept developed consists of a method enabling the Company to provide a systematic explanation of the adopted maintenance strategy based on a joint cost-availability analysis regarding the 'critical' components. We begin by presenting MATISA practice, followed by a brief review of equipment maintenance principles. We then present the MATISA business case, and conclude with some remarks about the prospects for the method adopted and its generalizability from this experimental study.

Keywords: Maintenance · Efficient maintenance planning · Cost · Availability

1 Context Introduction

Founded in 1945, the MATISA Company supplies specialised trains and machines to build, renew, maintain and measure railway tracks. Over time and given the tonnage involved, tracks are subject to deformation due to slipping, infiltration or transformation of the ballast. When the deformation becomes excessive, it is necessary to reduce or even stop rail traffic. Railway companies thus have to regularly maintain their tracks using a ballast tamping machine (BTM).

The process comprises levelling and lining the track (detail A in Fig. 1), adding and compacting some new ballast to reposition the track correctly. The compacting operation entails transmitting vibrations to the ballast by means of several pickaxes dipping into the ballast (detail B in Fig. 1). This tamping, depending on the parameters defined, (number of insertions, tightening time depth) enables the track geometry to be processed at a speed of up to 1200 m/h.

A. Dolgui et al. (Eds.): APMS 2021, IFIP AICT 634, pp. 235–243, 2021.
https://doi.org/10.1007/978-3-030-85914-5_25

After the operation, the ballast is compacted enough (detail C in Fig. 1), to allow trains to travel over it without deformation of the track. This equipment is subjected to strong mechanical constraints sometimes due to heterogeneity of the ballast, so they need frequent maintenance.

Fig. 1. Ballast tamping machine in operation

Four years ago, one of MATISA's customers signed a supply contract for 14 BTMs including MP in a context of high equipment availability and high costs. For the first time a review clause was added regarding the MP cost. MATISA was thus faced with a new problem: "how do we justify our MP proposal?" In this instance a project called Efficient Maintenance Planning (EMP), was launched connecting two laboratories of the University of Savoie Mont-Blanc. The idea was to use data from actual use of the BTM, and process it to produce a reliability model for the computation of maintenance costs.

The aim of the study is the development of a method enabling the MATISA company to construct a MP business case according to cost and availability objectives. This method systematically computes costs and availability for each possible maintenance type to choose the most appropriate one. This paper summarises the method and is organised as follows. In Sect. 2 we briefly review the three types of maintenance principles, as well as essential computation approaches. Section 3 covers the MATISA case study. The method developed is presented, including three steps: critical component identification, processing of reliability data and maintenance costs, and availability computation. We conclude with some remarks about the method adopted.

2 Maintenance Basics

In the Reliability-Availability-Maintainability-Safety (RAMS) approach, the purpose of maintenance is to ensure equipment reliability, availability and safety to produce profitable products or services [1]. In this sense, the European Norm characterises maintenance as: *"Together with all technical, administrative and management staff, during the lifecycle of a property, to maintain or reinstate a given condition so it performs its required function"* [2]. Ensuring a good level of maintenance involves both the designer and user of the equipment: the designer must build reliable and maintainable equipment, and the user must use and maintain it correctly. These two aspects are connected in the maintenance plan which must be prepared before using the equipment [3]. This maintenance plan is applied and thus adapted by the user [4]. On the one hand, it enables the maintenance service to be defined, the type of maintenance to be carried out and the associated schedule, and on the other hand, the operational aspects of the maintenance activity. Operational aspects are usually carried out well by companies due to their knowledge of supplier equipment and skilled maintenance teams [5]. Maintenance choice is not so clear because it depends on equipment technology, the user's company objectives, the economic context and equipment behaviour, according to the RAMS approach [6].

Traditionally, companies choose the type of maintenance based on RAMS objectives. They must make trade-offs between several types of maintenance defined as: improvement, preventive, predictive and corrective [7]. In the maintenance planning definition only the last three types are considered.

- Preventive maintenance consists of avoiding operational failure by return to a state of functioning 'as good as new', thus increasing production capacity and reducing the probability of failure rendering it unable to produce [8].
- Predictive maintenance occurs when maintenance operations are launched according to the actual condition of the equipment, most often provided by sensors and analysis techniques based on artificial intelligence [9].
- Corrective maintenance consists of addressing equipment failure to return it to the 'as good as new' state of functioning [10].

When equipment is complex, involving hundreds of components based on different technologies with multiple interrelationships, several types of maintenance are often used for the different parts of the equipment. The correct choice of maintenance ensures equipment safety thanks to standards or dedicated tools such as failure trees, criticality analysis [11] or specific instructions such as those provided by standards [12]. When the choice remains over, objectives of reliability and availability can be considered through compromise [13, 14]. The literature review shows that a key purpose of maintenance planning involves reliability optimization [15]. However, availability, which combines reliability, maintainability and logistics is also very important. Moreover, availability-based maintenance introduces the aspect of cost in maintenance choice [16] and more precisely the direct maintenance costs and the indirect costs generated by equipment failure [17]. We have adopted this approach, which relies on a cost computation model linking reliability behaviour and economic data [18], in our study.

3 Proposed Computation Method

The proposed model is described based on the EMP study. In a first step the BTM components are ranked according to the cost of replacement parts. Then the failure of the costliest components replaced is processed to identify their reliability behaviour. The possible maintenance types are explored with the BTM designer, and the associated costs are computed from an estimate of the economic data. Finally, the different maintenance types are compared and recommendations are given. Provision of recommendations to the user is not considered in this study.

3.1 Choice of the Critical Components

Data can be collected from the information systems (IS) of the different stakeholders such as the customer, the MATISA After Sales subsidiary and MATISA headquarters. Knowing that the IS were not interoperable, human processing must also be done. The first file extracted from the Enterprise Resources Planning (ERP) database presents the date, reference number, equipment concerned, quantity, and cost of the consumed part for each component. Some information was missing such as the type of maintenance trigger, component consumption type (preventive vs corrective) and location of the component on the equipment (the same component may be present in different parts of the equipment) and the operating duration of the replaced component (or for components involved in movement of the equipment, the distance travelled).

We selected the first equipment delivered to the customer as having the longest lifetime. To reduce manual recovery of information, we carried out a cost Pareto analysis of the replaced parts where 11% of the 245 references replaced represent 80% of the costs. Ultimately, the pickaxe was chosen, which represents 8% of the cost with 19 replacements.

3.2 Cost Model

A maintenance policy is established to manage each component using common procedures such as the preventive maintenance interval or predictive maintenance. Therefore, the exact definition of the maintenance type should follow a predefined framework. Knowing that for pickaxes, the possible maintenance types are corrective, preventive and predictive (based on human inspection which has so far appeared to be easier and more efficient than an instrumentation) MATISA has chosen predictive maintenance. For the sake of comparison, the different maintenance types are expressed using the same unit of *euros per hour*.

Corrective maintenance consists of replacing the broken pickaxe(s) with new one(s) as soon as possible, until the equipment is back at the maintenance station. On average the response time before the *Time to Repair* is 4 h. Thus, the reduction in speed of the BTM due to the reduction in the number of pickaxes involves a production loss of about 20%. So the corrective maintenance cost is the following:

$$C_{Corr.} = C_{Int.} + 0.2PL + DC \tag{1}$$

where $C_{Int.}$ is the cost of the part and the manpower to replace the part and the administrative procedure, PL is the cost of the total production losses and DC are the damage costs due to the failure. This cost corresponds to a *Mean Time Between Failure (MTBF)* of the equipment, so the cost per hour is the following:

$$C_{Corr./hr} = \frac{C_{Int.} + 0.2 \times PL + DC}{MTBF} \tag{2}$$

Preventive maintenance consists of replacing the pickaxes according to a given interval T for a part corresponding to the reliability function $R(T)$. In fact, it remains a part of corrective maintenance because the failure function $F(T) > 0$. In this case a proportion of $R(T)$ components are replaced in a preventive way, avoiding production losses and damage costs. The T interval must be coherent with the maintenance planning which allows the maintenance team to carry out preventive intervention, daily, weekly, monthly, quarterly and yearly. Note that these interventions can be undertaken during the day knowing the equipment is used only at night between 10 pm to 6 am. So, the preventive maintenance cost is the following:

$$C_{Prev.}(T) = C_{Int.} \times R(T) + C_{Corr.} \times F(T) \tag{3}$$

This cost corresponds to a mean duration computed from the mean used time $m(T) = \int_0^T R(t)dt$ for the corrective part given by $F(T)$ and the T interval for the preventive part given by $R(T)$. So, the cost per hour is the following:

$$C_{Prev./hr}(T) = \frac{C_{Int.} \times R(T) + C_{Corr.} \times F(T)}{m(T) \times R(T) + MTBF \times F(T)} \tag{4}$$

Clearly, the preventive cost depends on the T interval and there exists a value T^* which optimizes this cost as shown in Fig. 3.

Predictive maintenance consists of regularly inspecting the pickaxes in the maintenance station before the nightly work of the equipment. Our assumption is that the skill of the maintenance team enables the avoidance of 95% of pickaxe failures, so 5% of corrective maintenance remains. A more refined model could be used if this assumption is not accurate. So, the preventive maintenance cost is the following:

$$C_{Pred.} = (C_{Int.} + C_{Insp.}) \times 95\% + C_{Corr.} \times 5\% \tag{5}$$

where $C_{Insp.}$ is the mean cost of the inspection of a pickaxe. This cost corresponds to a mean duration of the $MTBF - d$ where d is the wasted time between the preventive intervention and the avoided failure.

$$C_{Pred./hr} = \frac{\left(C_{Int.} + C_{Insp.}\right) \times 95\% + C_{Corr.} \times 5\%}{\left(MTBF - d\right) \times 95\% + MTBF \times 5\%} \tag{6}$$

3.3 Cost-Availability Analysis

Let us now consider the reliability data for the computation of $F(T)$, $R(T)$, $MTBF$, $m(T)$; the economic data $C_{Int.}$, PL, DC, $C_{Insp.}$ and d are given by the user. Faced with this unusual demand for the equipment history, the user agrees to only supply the date of the pickaxe change, so 19 corresponding TBF are deduced, supposing that all of the replacements correspond to failures. The reliability data are then considered to be complete. If user data were more precise, some preventive intervention could be identified. In this case the data processing should be adapted to take into account censored data.

Using only one Weibull model, as shown in Fig. 2a, is not satisfactory due to the non-linearity of the data. Therefore, a more complex Weibull model is proposed to distinguish the two clouds of points in Fig. 2b. So, the pickaxe behaviour is modelled by:

- An initial model corresponding to the blue cloud where $\beta = 1.04$, $\eta = 629\ hrs$, $\gamma = 0\ hr$. It means that the earliest failures with $\beta = 1.04$ are time independent, so knowing the pickaxe function, they are extrinsic failures due for instance to incorrect use. This point has been confirmed by the MATISA team. For these failures no maintenance is necessary.
- A second model corresponding to the brown points where: $\beta = 4.76$, $\eta = 1019\ hrs$, $\gamma = 1950\ hrs$ with. $MTBF = 2906\ hrs$. It means that the failure rate is rapidly increasing in a phenomenon of accelerated wear $\beta = 4.76$, after a period without failures $\gamma = 1950\ hrs$. So, maintenance is required after the 0 failure period.

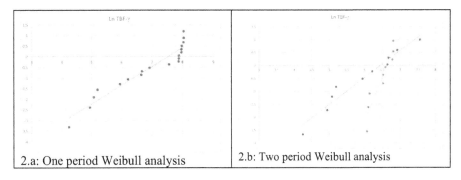

| 2.a: One period Weibull analysis | 2.b: Two period Weibull analysis |

Fig. 2. Weibull regression models for the pickaxe component

Consequently, for the maintenance type recommendation, only the second part of the pickaxe life is considered.

The economic data are known only by the user who does not want to disclose them. However, the MATISA expert has a high degree of skill in this area so he provided an estimate of this data with $C_{Int.} = 3490€$, $PL = 240000€$, $DC = 3000€$, $C_{Insp.} = 1000€$ and $d = 80$ hrs. By applying (2), (4) and (6) the maintenance costs are:

$$C_{Corr./hr} = \frac{3490 + 0.2 \times 240000 + 3000}{2906} = 6.36€ / hr$$

$$C_{Prev./hr} (T^* = 2200) = \frac{3490 \times 99.88\% + 54490 \times 0.12\%}{2200 \times 99.88\% + 2177 \times 0.12\%} = 1.59€ / hr$$

$$C_{Pred./hr} = \frac{(3490 + 1000) \times 95\% + 6.36 \times 5\%}{(2906 - 80) \times 95\% + 2906 \times 5\%} = 1.42€ / hr$$

We note that theoretical optimal T interval is $T^* = 2320$. Given the organisational constraints, preventive maintenance will occur every nine months corresponding to about $T^* = 2200$ as shown in Fig. 3.

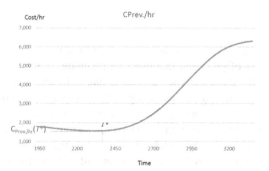

Fig. 3. Preventive maintenance cost evolution according to T

From this cost computation it appears that predictive maintenance is better, with a cost advantage of about 14% compared to preventive maintenance. Corrective maintenance is much more expensive and must be avoided. Before making this choice the user has to check whether the unavailability of the machine is not too high. Table 1 below gives the corresponding unavailability of the machine due to pickaxes according to the type of maintenance. We underscore that corrective maintenance gives the worst result with a high level of unavailability. Preventive maintenance is much better than predictive, but both ensure a low level of unavailability which is consistent with the user requirement.

Table 1. Unavailability associated with each type of maintenance.

Type of maintenance	Unavailability (Unav.) *Unav.*
Corrective	$Unav. = \frac{0,2 \times 4 \times 16}{2906} = 0,440\%$
Preventive	$Unav. = \frac{0,2 \times 4 \times 16 \times 0,12\%}{2200 \times 99,88\% + 2906 \times 0,12\%} = 0,001\%$
Predictive	$Unav. = \frac{0,2 \times 4 \times 16}{2813} \times 5\% = 0,022\%$

Therefore, at the conclusion of this analysis, the recommendation remains the same as initially, i.e., undertaking predictive maintenance prior to nightly equipment use. However, if the availability criterion becomes very important for the user, preventive maintenance could be a better alternative. The difference this time, is that the MATISA company can explain the choice to its customer. Certainly, a robustness analysis should complete this study, namely by investigating the production loss value or the reliability model which have substantial effects on the cost computation.

We note that the question of the interoperability of the IS will be a key factor in generalising this analysis to the entire set of critical components. Thus, a Product Breakdown Structure (PBS) code to define the location of each component on the equipment is required for correct information processing.

4 Conclusion

This article presents a real maintenance case study in a context where users ask suppliers for justification of proposed maintenance planning. A method including critical component selection, potential types of maintenance identification, reliability behaviour modelling and maintenance cost computing is proposed. It allows the partners to share knowledge about equipment, be confident, justify and possibly adjust and improve the current maintenance regime. Two conclusions can be considered. The first concerns the MATISA company which can generalize the method to the entire set of critical components and integrate the processing of data in its future interoperable maintenance information system, after opting to manage the PBS code in the equipment's master data. Beyond the MATISA context, such a method could be applied to any complex equipment if both technical and economic data are available. The second one is more relevant in the academic context. It concerns the updating of reliability data (with increasing use of the equipment, the number of failures will increase and the reliability model may change, affecting the maintenance recommendation). Introducing real-time reliability and cost analysis could be of interest to both the equipment manufacturer and the user.

References

1. Jardine, A.K.S., Tsang, A.H.C.: Maintenance, Replacement and Reliability: Theory and Applications. Taylor and Francis CRC Press, Boca Raton (2005)

2. Comité Européen de Normalisation: EN 13306: MAINTENANCE - MAINTENANCE TERMINOLOGY (2013)
3. Palmer, R.D.: PE MBA: CMRP. Maintenance Planning and Scheduling Handbook. Fourth Edition. McGraw-Hill Education, New-York (2019)
4. Kelly, A.: Strategic Maintenance Planning. Butterworth-Heinemann (2006)
5. Sullivan, G.P., Pugh, R., Melendez, A.P., Hunt, W.D.: Operations & maintenance best practices: a guide to achieving operational efficiency. US Dep Energy. Fed Energy Manag Progr. (2010). https://doi.org/10.2172/1034595
6. Wang, H.: A survey of maintenance policies of deteriorating systems. Eur. J. Oper. Res. **139** (3), 469–48 (2002)
7. Moubray, J.: Reliability-Centered Maintenance, 2nd edn. Industrial Press Inc., New-York (1997)
8. Fumagalli, L., Macchi, M., Giacomin, A.: Orchestration of preventive maintenance interventions. IFAC-Papers On Line (2017)
9. Mobley, R.K.: An introduction to predictive maintenance. Butterworth-Heinemann (2002)
10. Erkoyuncu, J.A., Khan, S., López Eiroa, A., Butler, N., Rushton, K.: Perspectives on trading cost and availability for corrective maintenance at the equipment type level. Reliab. Eng. Syst. Saf. **168**, 53–56 (2017)
11. American National Standard: ANSI/AIAA S-102.2.4: Capability-Based Product Failure Mode - Effects and Criticality Analysis (FMECA) Requirements (2015)
12. Comité Européen de Normalisation: EN 50126. Railway application - The specification and demonstration of Reliability, Availability, Maintainability and Safety (RAMS). Part 1: Basic requirements and generic process. http://clc.am/qvkB4g
13. Dekker, R.: Application of maintenance optimization models: a review and analysis Reliab. Eng. Syst. Safety **51**, 229–240 (1996)
14. Darghouth, M.N., Ait-Kadi, D., Chelbi, A.: Joint optimization of design, warranty and price for products sold with maintenance service contracts. Reliability Eng. Syst. Safety Syst. **165**, 197–208 (2017)
15. Sherif, Y.S., Smith, M.L.: Optimal maintenance models for systems subject to failure - a review. Naval Res. Logist. Quart. **28**, 47–74 (1981)
16. Bohlin, M., Wärja, M.: Maintenance optimization with duration-dependent costs. Ann. Oper. Res. **224**, 1–23 (2015). https://doi-org.camphrier-1.grenet.fr/10.1007/s10479-012-1179-1
17. Lyonnet, P.: La Maintenance: mathématiques et méthodes. 4ème édition. Editions TEC et DOC (2000)
18. Boucly, F.: Le management de la maintenance: évolution et mutation. AFNOR Editions (2008)

Understanding Schedule Progress Using Earned Value and Earned Schedule Techniques at Path-Level

Christian Capone$^{(\boxtimes)}$ and Timur Narbaev$^{(\boxtimes)}$

Kazakh-British Technical University, Tole Bi Street 59, Almaty, Kazakhstan
c_capone@ise.ac, t.narbaev@kbtu.kz

Abstract. Project monitoring and control is one of the core processes of effective production planning and scheduling. As part of this process, earned value management (EVM) is used to measure and forecast the duration and cost of production projects and activities. Using the EVM-based earned schedule (ES) value, the schedule variance (SV(t)) metric is calculated. This metric is further used to analyze the schedule progress. Based on this, potential schedule delays and slack times are calculated on both project-level and path-level. However, commonly in practice, they are derived from SV(t) values on the project-level. Moreover, the research on an individual path level or comparison of SV(t) on the project-level with the ones of the path-level is limited. This study proposes such a comparative analysis. The findings reveal misleading results regarding the project-level schedule analysis outcomes due to inconsistency in the computations from both path- and project-levels. For example, when the project-level analysis suggests a schedule delay the path-level analysis shows the project has no delay. Using a hypothetical production project, this study demonstrates how and when such inconsistent outcomes may arise. This study pioneers such concepts as "false positives" and "false negatives". Based on its findings, the study discloses prospects for future research in this area.

Keywords: Production scheduling · Earned value management · Schedule network analysis · Misleading outcomes

1 Introduction

Project monitoring and control is one of the core processes of effective production planning and scheduling. It helps to analyze the schedule progress and cost performance in ongoing projects, upon which duration or budget deviations from the original project plan can be measured [1]. Not well-defined scope, poor risk management, and ineffective monitoring and control are the main reasons why projects continue to fail [2]. The underperforming organizations in project management have a project success rate of 32%, and as a consequence, 9.9% of the project budget is wasted due to poor project performance [3]. As part of the monitoring and control process, earned value management (EVM) measures and forecasts the duration and cost outcomes of production projects and activities [4]. EVM consists of tracking the project's progress by

© IFIP International Federation for Information Processing 2021
Published by Springer Nature Switzerland AG 2021
A. Dolgui et al. (Eds.): APMS 2021, IFIP AICT 634, pp. 244–251, 2021.
https://doi.org/10.1007/978-3-030-85914-5_26

contrasting the work's scope and actual costs to the project schedule and budget defined in the original plan [5–7].

However, some studies demonstrated that the EVM technique might lead to inconsistent results regarding the schedule progress analysis [8–10]. Inconsistency occurs when comparing the results derived from project-level analysis versus path-level analysis. This study presents and analyzes such inconsistencies and pioneers the concept of "false positive" or "false negative." For example, when the project-level analysis suggests a schedule delay, the path-level analysis shows the project has, in fact, no delay ("false positive"). Consequently, if not prevented, such inconsistency may lead to misleading estimates of duration in ongoing projects.

The purpose of this paper is to present how and when the EVM technique shows the above inconsistencies as to the schedule progress analysis. Using a hypothetical production project, the study shows that such inconsistency occurs when comparing the project-level results with ones of the individual path-level.

2 Theoretical Background

Table 1 summarizes the key concepts used in this paper. EVM schedule analysis is founded on two metrics, earned value (EV) and planned value (PV). EV is the budgeted cost of the work done and therefore earned. EV is then compared to PV, the budgeted cost of the work planned, to obtain the schedule variance (SV):

$$SV = EV - PV \tag{1}$$

If SV is positive, then according to Eq. (1), the amount of work earned (EV) is exceeding the amount of work planned (PV), and therefore the project is ahead of its schedule. On the contrary, if SV is negative, the project is behind its schedule [11, 12].

It is noted that SV, as per Eq. (1), raises one concern. SV is not directly connected to the schedule, and indeed its dimension is in monetary units and not in time units. Furthermore, assessing the project schedule progress using this indicator leads to unreliable conclusions [13, 14].

An attempt to overcome this deficiency of SV was proposed by the Earned Schedule (ES) technique [13]. The ES metric is equal to time when the PV was supposed to be equal to EV and therefore is a better indication of the schedule progress. Then, ES can be compared with Actual Time (AT) to obtain Schedule Variance, SV(t):

$$SV(t) = ES - AT \tag{2}$$

If SV(t) is positive, then the project is ahead of its schedule. Instead, if SV(t) is negative, the project is behind its schedule.

After our reflections, it becomes clear that Eq. (2) is inaccurate because ES does not consider how the tasks are distributed in relation to their predecessors and successors (project topology). The inaccuracy becomes important when the project has a predominant number of parallel activities over sequential activities [15].

This is the reason why Lipke is suggesting to use SV on critical path only when project has parallel activities (i.e. multiple paths).

Table 1. Glossary of the key concepts.

Abbreviation	Meaning
EVM	Earned value management
EV	Earned value
PV	Planned value
SV	Schedule variance
ES	Earned schedule
AT	Actual time
SV(t)	Schedule variance from earned schedule
CPM	Critical path method
FP	Fan-in path
CP	Critical path

Project topology can be described using the Critical Path Method (CPM), in which the project's tasks can be represented by an oriented graph (network) [16]. The longest path, named the critical path, is the one that characterizes the project in terms of its duration. Any delay of the activities on the critical path (critical activities) causes a project delay. Instead, the non-critical paths have a certain degree of slack, i.e., they can be delayed without delaying the project. The total path slack is defined as the time when the path can be delayed without delaying the project [17, 18].

3 Methodology

Equations (1) and (2) are defined and calculated at the project-level, and therefore, they cannot consider the project topology. Instead, when Eqs. (1) and (2) are calculated at path-level, an indication of the project performance in critical activities separated from the project performance in non-critical activities is provided. Consequently, path-level calculations give more information on what is happening in the critical path and to which extent the critical path can be affected by non-critical activities.

Figure 1 shows the tasks, their durations, and dependencies of a fictional production project with 7 activities. An example of such a production project can be an assembly line construction: the critical activities concern the installation of a conveyor belt. The project has a duration of 14 weeks. The other non critical activities are in the fan-in paths (FP). FP is the partial path constituted by non-critical activities merging into a critical path and it do not contain any critical activity. In FP1 fan-in path, we have the conveyor belt's power line installation and testing. The power line installation cannot start before week 5, should end before week 10 but requires only 3 weeks of work (therefore, have 2 weeks of slack). There is just one activity in FP2 fan-in path: the production plant's legal authorities' signatures. This activity requires 2 weeks of work, should start not earlier than week 4 and should end before week 12 (hence its slack is 5 weeks).

Figure 1 represents the critical activities which resemble the critical path (CP1). FP1 is the FP represented by activities B-C. It is merging into the critical path A-E-F-G and having a slack of 2 weeks. FP2 is the FP represented by activity D, merging into the critical path A-E-F-G and having a slack of 5 weeks. In Fig. 1 it is also recorded the project baseline, including the planned budget for each activity and each week (represented by the figures in the cell). PV and cumulative Planned Values (CumPV) are calculated both at project-level (in figures, column "Level" with the value of "Project") and at path-level (in figures, column "Level" with the value of "CP1" for the critical path, "FP1" and "FP2" or the fan-in paths).

Level	Activity	Duration	Predecessors	WEEKS 1	2	3	4	5	6	7	8	9	10	11	12	13	14
CP1	A	4	-	20	10	5	30										
FP1	B	2	A					20	10								
FP1	C	1	B							40							
FP2	D	2	A					40	30								
CP1	E	5	A					30	30	20	20	30					
CP1	F	2	C, E										10	10			
CP1	G	3	D, F												20	30	20
Project			PV	20	10	5	30	90	70	60	20	30	10	10	20	30	20
Project			CumPV	20	30	35	65	155	225	285	305	335	345	355	375	405	425
CP1			PV	20	10	5	30	30	30	20	20	30	10	10	20	30	20
CP1			CumPV	20	30	35	65	95	125	145	165	195	205	215	235	265	285
FP1			PV	0	0	0	0	20	10	40	0	0	0	0	0	0	0
FP1			CumPV	0	0	0	0	20	30	70	70	70	70	70	70	70	70
FP2			PV	0	0	0	0	40	30	0	0	0	0	0	0	0	0
FP2			CumPV	0	0	0	0	40	70	70	70	70	70	70	70	70	70

Fig. 1. Project baseline

The authors will discuss two different possible project executions in the next section, and EVM/ES metrics will be calculated using both the classical approach (at project-level) and our proposed methodology (at path-level).

4   Results and Findings

Figure 2 and Fig. 3 presents two different possible scenarios of the project execution. ES, EV, and SV(t) are calculated for each of the 2 scenarios, both at the path-level and at project-level. For both scenarios, the study analyzes the circumstance in which SV(t) detects a "false positive."

4.1   Scenario 1: Non-critical Fan-In Path Delayed Less Than Its Slack

Figure 2 shows the project- and path-level's EV, ES, and SV(t) when the critical path (activities A-E-F-G) is not delayed (and therefore, the project duration is aligned with the project baseline). There is a delay in a non-critical activity (activity D), on FP2, for an amount less than the path total slack (the slack is 5 weeks, the delay of activity D is 2 weeks).

Level	Activity	WEEKS													
		1	2	3	4	5	6	7	8	9	10	11	12	13	14
CP1	A	20	10	5	30										
FP1	B					20	10								
FP1	C							40							
FP2	D					20	15	15	20						
CP1	E					30	30	20	20	30					
CP1	F										10	10			
CP1	G												20	30	20
Project	PV	20	10	5	30	90	70	60	20	30	10	10	20	30	20
Project	CumPV	20	30	35	65	155	225	285	305	335	345	355	375	405	425
Project	EV	20	30	35	65	135	190	265	305	335	345	355	375	405	425
Project	ES	1,00	2,00	3,00	4,00	4,78	5,50	6,67	8,00	9,00	10,00	11,00	12,00	13,00	14,00
Project	SV(t)	0,00	0,00	0,00	0,00	-0,22	-0,50	-0,33	0,00	0,00	0,00	0,00	0,00	0,00	0,00
CP1	PV	20	10	5	30	30	30	20	20	30	10	10	20	30	20
CP1	CumPV	20	30	35	65	95	125	145	165	195	205	215	235	265	285
CP1	EV	20	30	35	65	95	125	145	165	195	205	215	235	265	285
CP1	ES	1,00	2,00	3,00	4,00	5,00	6,00	7,00	8,00	9,00	10,00	11,00	12,00	13,00	14,00
CP1	SV(t)	0,00	0,00	0,00	0,00	0,00	0,00	0,00	0,00	0,00	0,00	0,00	0,00	0,00	0,00
FP1	PV	0	0	0	0	20	10	40	0	0	0	0	0	0	0
FP1	CumPV	0	0	0	0	20	30	70	70	70	70	70	70	70	70
FP1	EV	0	0	0	0	20	30	70	70	70	70	70	70	70	70
FP1	ES					5,00	6,00	7,00							
FP1	SV(t)					0,00	0,00	0,00							
FP2	PV	0	0	0	0	40	30	0	0	0	0	0	0	0	0
FP2	CumPV	0	0	0	0	40	70	70	70	70	70	70	70	70	70
FP2	EV	0	0	0	0	20	35	50	70	70	70	70	70	70	70
FP2	ES					4,50	4,88	5,33	8,00						
FP2	SV(t)					-0,50	-1,13	-1,67	0,00						

Fig. 2. Scenario 1. Critical Path (CP1) is executed according to the baseline. Activity D, which belongs to FP1, is behind schedule but within its total path slack.

The project-level ES values show that the project has a delay in weeks 5, 6, and 7, with the corresponding SV(t) values being negative. However, the project-level results are misleading since they generate a "false positive." Indeed, the project is not experiencing any delay.

Contrary to this, the SV(t) values at the critical path-level capture the correct project schedule status (no delay). For the critical path CP1, SV(t) is equal to 0 from week 1 to week 14, and therefore no delay is identified. For FP1, SV(t) is also equal to 0 (no delay). For FP2, SV(t) at FP2 level shows that the delay is less than the FP2 total slack, which suggests no delay at the project-level. Hence, project managers should take no corrective measures, even though Eq. (2) at the project-level suggests this.

4.2 Scenario 2: Non-critical Fan-In Path Delayed More Than Its Slack

Figure 3 shows the project's EV, ES, and SV(t) when it experiences a delay in non-critical activities B and C, on FP1, for an amount that is more than the path total slack (the total path slack is 2 weeks, the delay of activities B and C is 3 weeks).

		WEEKS													
Level	Activity	1	2	3	4	5	6	7	8	9	10	11	12	13	14
CP1	A	20	10	5	30										
FP1	B					10	10	10							
FP1	C							10	10	20					
FP2	D					40	30								
CP1	E					30	30	20	20	30					
CP1	F											10	10		
CP1	G													40	30
Project	PV	20	10	5	30	90	70	60	20	30	10	10	20	30	20
Project	CumPV	20	30	35	65	155	225	285	305	335	345	355	375	405	425
Project	EV	20	30	35	65	145	215	245	275	315	335	345	355	395	425
Project	ES	1,00	2,00	3,00	4,00	4,89	5,86	6,33	6,83	8,33	9,00	10,00	11,00	12,67	14,00
Project	SV(t)	0,00	0,00	0,00	0,00	-0,11	-0,14	-0,67	-1,17	-0,67	-1,00	-1,00	-1,00	-0,33	0,00
CP1	PV	20	10	5	30	30	30	20	20	30	10	10	20	30	20
CP1	CumPV	20	30	35	65	95	125	145	165	195	205	215	235	265	285
CP1	EV	20	30	35	65	95	125	145	165	195	195	205	215	255	285
CP1	ES	1,00	2,00	3,00	4,00	5,00	6,00	7,00	8,00	9,00	9,00	10,00	11,00	12,67	14,00
CP1	SV(t)	0,00	0,00	0,00	0,00	0,00	0,00	0,00	0,00	0,00	-1,00	-1,00	-1,00	-0,33	0,00
FP1	PV	0	0	0	0	20	10	40	0	0	0	0	0	0	0
FP1	CumPV	0	0	0	0	20	30	70	70	70	70	70	70	70	70
FP1	EV	0	0	0	0	10	20	30	40	50	70	70	70	70	70
FP1	ES					4,50	5,00	6,00	6,25	6,50	7,00				
FP1	SV(t)					-0,50	-1,00	-1,00	-1,75	-2,50	-3,00				
FP2	PV	0	0	0	0	40	30	0	0	0	0	0	0	0	0
FP2	CumPV	0	0	0	0	40	70	70	70	70	70	70	70	70	70
FP2	EV	0	0	0	0	40	70	70	70	70	70	70	70	70	70
FP2	ES					5,00	6,00								
FP2	SV(t)					0,00	0,00								

Fig. 3. Case 2. Non-critical activities B and C (from FP1) are behind the schedule more than the path slack. There is an impact on the critical path (CP1).

The project-level ES values show that the project has a delay in weeks from 5 to 9, with the corresponding SV(t) values being negative. However, also in this case, the project-level results are misleading since they generate a "false positive." The project is not experiencing any delay during weeks 5–9 but only after week 10, when the cumulative delay in FP1 exceeds its slack. SV(t) values at the critical path-level capture this status: no delay during weeks 5–9, but from week 10. Therefore, project managers are suggested by SV(t) at the project-level to activate countermeasures to put in track the project from week 5, while this is needed only from week 10.

5 Conclusions

It is critical to have reliable project monitoring metrics to control the production project duration during its execution. Such metrics also help introduce timely corrective actions (i.e., when the project is not adhering to the baseline) and estimate project outcomes (i.e., if the project final duration needs to be computed). The EVM approach with its EV, PV, and ES metrics has been used in project management practice to perform such actions. Even though EVM is a widely adopted tool in practice, it has some limitations. It might lead to inconsistent results as to the schedule progress analysis.

This paper demonstrates this inconsistency when comparing the results derived from project-level analysis versus path-level analysis. In terms of duration analysis, the ES and SV(t) metrics calculated at the project-level could not discern what happens on the path-level. Using a hypothetical production project's schedule, this study introduced 2 possible execution scenarios to demonstrate these inconsistent outcomes. The metrics at the project-level gave contradictory results compared to the metrics at the path-level.

Scenario 1 was the case when the project has had a delay in its non-critical activities. Nevertheless, this delay was absorbed by the fan-in path slack. The metrics computed at the project-level detected this delay, while in fact the project was not behind its schedule ("false positive"). Scenario 2 was the case when the project had a delay in its non-critical activities. However, this delay was not totally absorbed by the fan-in path slack. The metrics computed at the project-level showed this delay by the amount of time that did not reflect the project's actual duration.

This study revealed the reason for such inconsistent outcomes. Inconsistency was originated because the project was assessed at the project-level and not at the path-level. Also, the fan-in paths were monitored closely to detect the slack usage and assess any impact on the critical path.

Therefore, to monitor the schedule progress in ongoing projects based on the actual schedule status, the authors suggest analyzing ES and SV(t) at the path-level and not only at the project-level. It is also essential to consider the slacks in fan-in paths.

Future research is suggested in this area. First, other schedule outcome scenarios should be analyzed. Second, the impact of the path-level schedule analysis on the duration estimation should be analyzed. Third, empirical analysis with multiple project data should be conducted to foresee the research and practical generalizations.

Practitioners in the industry can use the proposed approach for more realistic schedule analysis and duration management in their ongoing projects. The project schedule must be analyzed not only on the aggregated project-level, but also on the individual path-levels. Then, the results of such separate assessments should be compared. Only after this, appropriate corrective actions for more informed schedule management should be taken.

Acknowledgment. This research was funded by the Science Committee of the Ministry of Education and Science of the Republic of Kazakhstan (Grant No. AP09259049).

References

1. De Marco, A., Narbaev, T.: Earned value-based performance monitoring of facility construction projects. J. Facil. Manag. **11** (2013). https://doi.org/10.1108/147259613113 01475
2. Harrin, E.: Why Do Some Projects Fail? (And Some Succeed?). ITNOW **60**, 54–55 (2018). https://doi.org/10.1093/ITNOW/BWY107
3. Project Management Institute: Success in Disruptive Times. Pulse of the Profession. Project Management Institute, Newtown Square, PA (2018)
4. Humphreys, G.: Project Management Using Earned Value. Humphreys & Associates, Inc. (2018)
5. Przywara, D., Rak, A.: Monitoring of time and cost variances of schedule using simple earned value method indicators. Appl. Sci. **11**, 1357 (2021). https://doi.org/10.3390/APP11041357
6. Anbari, F.T.: Earned value project management method and extensions. Proj. Manag. J. **34**, 12–23 (2003). https://doi.org/10.1109/EMR.2004.25113
7. Narbaev, T., De Marco, A.: An earned Schedule-based regression model to improve cost estimate at completion. Int. J. Proj. Manage. **32**, 1007–1018 (2014). https://doi.org/10.1016/j.ijproman.2013.12.005
8. Lipke, W.: Examining project duration forecasting reliability. PM World J. **3**, 1–10 (2014)
9. Vanhoucke, M.: Measuring Schedule Adherence. Meas. News. 21–26 (2013)
10. Lipke, W., Zwikael, O., Henderson, K., Anbari, F.: Prediction of project outcome. The application of statistical methods to earned value management and earned schedule performance indexes. Int. J. Proj. Manag. **27**, 400–407 (2009). https://doi.org/10.1016/j.ijproman.2008.02.009
11. Project Management Institute: Practice Standard for Earned Value Management. Project Management Institute, Newtown Square, PA (2011)
12. De Marco, A., Narbaev, T., Rafele, C., Cagliano, A.C.: Integrating risk in project cost forecasting. In: Proceedings of the 22nd Summer School Francesco Turco, pp. 117–122. AIDI - Italian Association of Industrial Operations Professors, Bergamo (2017)
13. Lipke, W.H.: Schedule is different. Meas. News. **2**, 31–34 (2003)
14. Vandevoorde, S., Vanhoucke, M.: A comparison of different project duration forecasting methods using earned value metrics. Int. J. Proj. Manag. **24**, 289–302 (2006). https://doi.org/10.1016/j.ijproman.2005.10.004
15. Lipke, W.: Speculations on project duration forecasting. Meas. News. **3**, 4–7 (2012)
16. Soroush, H.M.: The most critical path in a PERT network. J. Oper. Res. Soc. **45**, 287 (1994). https://doi.org/10.2307/2584163
17. Lu, M., Li, H.: Resource-activity critical-path method for construction planning. J. Constr. Eng. Manag. **129**, 412–420 (2003). https://doi.org/10.1061/(ASCE)0733-9364(2003)129:4 (412)
18. Vanhoucke, M.: The critical path method. In: Project Management with Dynamic Scheduling, pp. 37–56. Springer, Berlin Heidelberg (2012). https://doi.org/10.1007/978-3-642-40438-2_3

Health Indicator Modeling and Association Rule Mining for Stoppages Prediction in a Refinery Plant

Giovanni Mazzuto⬤, Sara Antomarioni$^{(\boxtimes)}$⬤,
Filippo Emanuele Ciarapica⬤, and Maurizio Bevilacqua⬤

Department of Industrial Engineering and Mathematical Science,
Università Politecnica Delle Marche, Ancona, Italy
{ g.mazzuto, s.antomarioni, f.ciarapica,
m.bevilacqua}@univpm.it

Abstract. Predictive maintenance practices represent a relevant feature for improving the useful life of the systems and decreasing costs. Hence, the modelling of the Health Indicator is a useful support in order to define the Remaining Useful Life of a system. In this work, an approach for the Health Indicator modeling of an oil refinery sub-plant is proposed; in addition, the Association Rule Mining is applied, in order to identify the components frequently requiring a work order prior to a stoppage of the plant: in this way, the Remaining Useful Life determined via the Health Indicator is used to inspect such components and, possibly, avoid the stoppage.

Keywords: Predictive maintenance · Health indicator · Association rule

1 Introduction and Background

The emerging Industry 4.0 technologies nowadays provide reliable and accessible smart systems that enable the spreading of predictive maintenance (PdM) practices [1]. The importance of PdM is testified by its ability in improving the useful life of the machine and in decreasing the maintenance costs [2]. The approach at the basis of the development of a reliable PdM system regards the collection and analysis of large amount of data, belonging to relevant time frames [3] as well as the definition of an indicator of system's health [4]. Assessing an appropriate Health Indicator (HI) allows the understanding of the deviation from the regular operating performance of the system in terms of its Remaining Useful Life (RUL). HI definition supports in increasing the knowledge of the system by focusing the analysis on the most relevant information sources. In this sense, having a precise HI enables the possibility of predicting the RUL of a system confidently [5] and is thus the main focus of many researches (e.g., [6, 7]). Recent literary contributions focused on the development of a HI using several different techniques. For instance, some focused on the development of multi-objective models to derive the health of the system for fault diagnostics and prognostics [8], while other implemented artificial neural networks and K-means clustering [9] and genetic algorithms [10]. Even in terms of application areas, there is a

© IFIP International Federation for Information Processing 2021
Published by Springer Nature Switzerland AG 2021
A. Dolgui et al. (Eds.): APMS 2021, IFIP AICT 634, pp. 252–260, 2021.
https://doi.org/10.1007/978-3-030-85914-5_27

certain heterogeneity: in some works, the focus is posed on semiconductor equipment [11], other focus on the vibration analysis of wind turbines [12]. HIs can indeed be applied for the definition of the remaining useful life of mechanical machinery, as testified by several works (e.g., [13, 14]). Given these assumptions, this work proposes an approach to model the health indicator for a sub-plant of an oil refinery and identify the component causing the performance loss. Predictive maintenance interventions on specific components are performed to avoid system stoppage, prioritizing them through implementing the Association Rule Mining (ARM). Indeed, the Association Rules (ARs) among component failures before the occurrence of a plant stoppage are used as a guide to determine, with a certain probability level, which are the components that caused the HI worsening. In this way, the ARs help identify relationships within a dataset when they are not immediately identifiable [15]. In recent literature, ARM is applied to different fields, ranging from the behavior description [16] to the sub-assemblies production scheduling [17]. In a predictive maintenance perspective, ARM has already been applied to detect the relationships among component failures [18]. Despite the valuable implementations proposed, among the others, by the named authors, there is a lack of research in terms of joint application of HIs definition and ARM.

2 Methodology

In the following, the proposed procedure to define the Health Indicator is described. The procedure is general so that it can be applied to various equipment as long as sensor readings are available. The input dataset contains the readings of one or more system sensors. For simplicity of explanation a single sensor is considered. Seven fundamental steps are performed in order to model the HI:

1. Standardization of the signals (S_s) from system sensors and partitioning of the initial dataset into training and testing sets.
2. Modelling of the Health Indicator (HI): the mean time between two stoppages represents the life duration of the system. The objective at the basis of the HI is creating a degradation profile considering that at the beginning of the HI the reliability of the system is equal to 1 (hence, maximum) while, at the moment of the stoppage, it is minimum (hence, equal to 0). The behavior of the HI is described by Eqs. (1)–(3), being $DUR_{i,m}$ the time between two stoppages of category m considering the i-th machine, $TI_{i,m}'$ indicates the remaining hours before the stoppage, while $TI_{i,m}``$ is the normalized value.

$$TI_m' = [DUR_m - 1 \quad DUR_m - 2 \quad \cdots \quad 0] \tag{1}$$

$$TI_m(t)'' = \frac{TI_m(t)'}{DUR_m} \tag{2}$$

$$HI_m(t) = TI_m(t)'' + \left(1 - TI_m(t=1)''\right) \tag{3}$$

Equation 3 is such that the first value of $HI_{i,m}$ is equal to 1. In particular, $HI_{i,m}$ represents an initial HI for the considered machine and stoppage.

Once HIs have been calculated for each machine and stoppage, through a linear interpolation, HIs and S_s can be correlated in order to find the transformation coefficient (Eq. 4) able to translate the information from the measures space to the HI space.

$$HI_{total} = b \cdot S_{s,total} \tag{4}$$

HI_{total} represents the array composed of all the determined HIs ($HI_{total} = [HI_{1,m} HI_{2,m}...HI_{n,m}]$) and, at the same way, $S_{s,total}$ is the arrey composed of all the standardised signals ($S_{s,total} = [S_{s,1} S_{s,2}...S_{s,n}]$). The parameter b can be in the form of an array if more than one sensor readings are available. In the present paper, it is a scalar since just one sensor readings are available.

Once the transformation "b" has been identified, the transformed HI* is calculat-edfor each machine and stoppage according to Eq. 5:

$$HI_{i,m}^* = b \cdot S_{s,i} \tag{5}$$

3. Once all the transformed $HI_{i,m}^*$ have been calculated, a non-linear interpolation has been performed to correlate the $HI_{i,m}^*$ with time (in form of Eq. 6).

$$HI_{i,m}^* = f_{i,m}(t_{s,i}) \tag{6}$$

In particular, function f() can be chosen in the same form for all the stoppage categories or differently to define different profile for different categories. At this point, function f () is stored to be used in the K-NN algorithm. Thus, the system training is completed.

4. During the testing phase, the testing signal is transformed as well, using the weights b determined at step 3. Even the duration of the standardized testing signals ($S_{s(test)}$) is assessed ($t_{s(test)}^*$) and the functions $f(t_{s(test)}^*)$ are evaluated for all the $S_{s(test)}$.

5. $HI_{j,m,test}^* = f(t_{s(j,test)}^*)$ and $HI_{i,m}^* = f(t_s^*)$ are compared through the KNN algorithm in order to identify the closest similarity profile. K-nearest neighbours (KNN) algorithm is a machine learning technique applicable for solving regression and classification problems. The main idea at its basis is that the closer an instance is to a data point, the more similar they will be considered by the KNN [19]. Reference functions $-HI_{i,m}^* = f_{i,m}(t_{s,i})$ - are considered as models to be compared to newly defined ones - $HI_{test}^* = f(t_{s(test)}^*)$. The distances d_{ij} (e.g., Euclidean distance) among $HI_{j,m,test}^*$ and $HI_{i,m}^*$ are used to calculate the similarity weights between the testing and the training. The similarity weight sw_{ij} is determined as reported in Eq. 7. Then, the weights are ranked in descending order and, finally, determine the number of similar units (Eq. 8). Specifically, k refers to the number of function to be selected for the comparison, while N is the number of training units.

$$sw_{ij} = exp\left(-d_{ij}^{2}\right) \tag{7}$$

$$SU = min(k, N) \tag{8}$$

6. Starting from the KNN results, the Weibull distribution is fitted considering the k-similar profiles and the median is determined.
7. Subtracting the $t_{s(test)}^{*}$ from the median determined at step 6, the RUL is assessed.

Eventually, the proposed approach requires the extraction of the ARs describing the relationships between component failures and plant stoppages. In this way, when a deviation in the operating performance is detected, the estimated RUL is used to inspect the components likely to be the ones causing the stoppage, so that their normal functioning can be reset and, possibly, the actual stoppage avoided.

Mining the Association Rules from a dataset implies the extraction of non-trivial attribute-values associations which are not immediately detectable due to the dimensions of such dataset [20]. Consider a set of Boolean data $D = \{d_1, d_2, \ldots d_m\}$ named items and a set of transactions $T = \{t_1, t_2, \ldots t_k\}$; a transaction t_i is a subset of items. An Association Rule $a \rightarrow b$ is an implication among two itemsets (a and b) taken from D, whose intersection is null (a $\cap$ b = Ø). In order to evaluate the goodness of a rule, different metrics can be used, such as the support (Supp) and the confidence (Conf):

- $Supp(a, b) = \frac{\#(a,b)}{\#(T)}$: it measures the number of transaction containing both a and b over the totality of transactions.
- $Conf(a \rightarrow b) = \frac{supp(a,b)}{supp(a)}$: it measures the conditional probability of the occurrence of b, given the fact that a occurred.

For the purposes of this work, an ARs $a \rightarrow b$ is the implication relating the component requiring a work order (a) and the stoppage (b). So, the $Supp(a, b)$ expresses the joint probability of having a failure on a component and a stoppage, while the $Conf(a \rightarrow b)$ represents the probability of having a stoppage given the fact that the component a failed. In this work the FP-growth [21] is applied to perform the ARM.

When the health indicator highlights the risk of a stoppage, the components are inspected to control their functioning, sorting them by decreasing confidence value. If a failure or a malfunctioning is detected on the first component, it is replaced, else the following one is inspected; depending on the maintenance policy adopted by the company, the inspection can involve all the components included in the ARs, can stop when the first failure is detected or can involve the ARs until a certain threshold.

3 Application

The refinery considered for the case study is located in Italy. It has a processing capacity of 85,000 barrel/day. The sub-plant taken into consideration in this application is the Topping unit. Data refer to a three-year time interval. Specifically, the mass-flow across the plant is collected hourly for each day. Three categories of stoppages or flow deceleration are identified by the company: Non-Significant (NS), if the reduction of the daily mass flow is between 20% and 50%; Slowdown (SLD), if the reduction of the daily mass flow is between 50% and 90%; Shutdown (SHD), if the reduction of the daily mass flow is between 90% and 100%. The dataset containing these data is structured as reported in Table 1: the first column indicates the date of the acquisition; the following twenty-four columns report the hourly mean value of the mass flow registered across the plant, while the last column indicates the kind of stoppage occurred during the day (if any). The mass-flow measures are also used to train and test the proposed approach. In all, 1095 rows and 24 columns are standardized and used to this end. The algorithm is carried out on an approach evaluation Intel® Core™ i7-6700HQ CPU @ 2.60 GHz, using Matlab 2019©. Once the dataset is standardized, steps 1–5 of the proposed approach are carried out. Figure 1 displays the HI profiles obtained through the algorithm in pink for the three stoppage category, while in black the current trend. Evidently, the latter cannot be considered as an anticipator of the NS stoppage, but is far more similar to the SHD one, given its trend. Hence, the through steps 6 and 7, of the proposed algorithm, the RUL can be determined and the relationships among the component failures and SHD stoppages can be enquired.

Table 1. Excerpt of the mass flow dataset indicating the sub-plant, the date of the acquisition, the hourly measurements and the stoppage category.

Date	v01	v02	v03	...	v22	v23	v24	Stoppage
01/01	411.5	409.6	407.56	...	407.22	407.37	407.56	–
02/01	409.49	410.8	408.03	...	378.41	374.27	372.32	NS
03/01	375.83	376.23	373.42	...	409.72	408.86	409.16	–

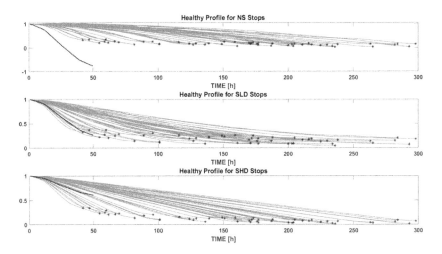

Fig. 1. The HIs comparison.

A second dataset, i.e., the work order list, is taken into account in order to identify the components requiring a maintenance intervention on a specific day (Table 2). This dataset is integrated with the one reported in Table 1 in order to be able to mine the association rules.

Table 2. Work Order (WO) dataset detailed by sub-plant, date and component.

Sub-plant	WO date	Component
Topping	10/06	Valve
Topping	17/11	Controller
Topping	04/02	Drainer
Topping	24/10	Valve

The relationships among component failures and stoppage category are derived through the Association Rule Mining. Specifically, the interest is identifying the work orders historically preceding the stoppages in order to use them as guidelines to understand which failure might cause the stoppage and intervene. The ARM, in this application, is executed using the well-known data analytics platform RapidMiner, that is widely applicable due to its graphical interface. In all, 120 rules have been identified, setting the minimum support threshold to 0 – in order not to lose any potential relation between components and stoppage category (and vice versa). The minimum confidence, instead, is set to 0.1. The set of ARs in the form $component_i \rightarrow stoppage_j$ is used to identify the components possibly affecting the abnormal functioning of the plant. In the proposed example, it appears that the deviation of the mass flow can be related to a SHD stoppage: 14 rules have been identified, even though only an excerpt is reported (Table 3).

Table 3. ARs relating the WO and the SHD stoppage

Component	Stoppage category	Confidence
Furnace	SHUT_DOWN	0.60
Condensation detector	SHUT_DOWN	0.25
Chiller	SHUT_DOWN	0.25
Chimney	SHUT_DOWN	0.23

This implies that the first component to be checked is the Furnace since, from the actual data of the past events, it requires a work order before the occurrence of a SHD (in other words, the rule Furnace $\rightarrow$ SHUT_DOWN has a confidence of 0.60). The following components to be checked, i.e., Condensation detector and Chiller, are the ones having the second value of confidence. During the inspection, the technician may detect a failure or a malfunctioning. If a failure or a malfunctioning is detected in one or more components, they should be fixed in the attempt to avoid the occurrence of the stoppage. Remarkably, the order of the inspection is relevant in terms of time: indeed, according to the profile of the HI, the RUL is determined and the inspection, as well as the preventive replacing of the components should be carried out within the time limit imposed by the RUL.

4 Discussion and Conclusions

The proposed approach well suits the dynamic environment characterizing the maintenance field. Indeed, it supports the definition of the RUL of a system and, accordingly, defines the roadmap to inspect the possible cause of the performance losses. In this way, it is possible to fix the malfunctioning promptly, so that the stoppage of the system can be avoided or, at least, the flow can be restored shortly. One of the main advantages of the proposed approach, is the fact that part of the analysis is carried out offline (e.g., training and testing of the proposed datasets, association rule mining) while its application can be run online, during the functioning of the system. The datasets on which the analysis is based can be updated without any impact on the approach implementation. In the proposed example, a single sensor is considered. However, the approach is easily extendable to case studies receiving data from more sensors since the proposed algorithm is general. The accuracy of the proposed approach strictly depends on the quality of the collected data. Before starting the implementation of the algorithm, some preliminary activities on data are required: indeed, it is necessary to clean data from inconsistencies, replace the missing values, eliminate disturbances in the sensor system and eventually, filter to limit the boundaries of the study. In this way it is ensured that the starting database is solid, so that the results are reliable too. As shown in Table 4, the prediction error varies with the percentage of the validation data considered: selecting the 70% of the dataset allows the minimum prediction error, if compared to the 50% and 90% cases. These outcomes, however, are not generalizable since they are strictly related to the specific case study, the sampling time and the initial prediction instant.

Table 4. Prediction error ranges and percentiles varying the validation data percentage for Shutdown stoppages

Validation data	Upper	75%	Median	25%	Lower
50%	7.2	5.16	4.22	3.31	1.69
70%	−1.91	−2.03	−2.24	−2.25	−2.43
90%	−2.3	−2.49	−2.79	−3	−3.49

It should be considered that the data used in this study are usually collected in contexts such as process industries and refineries. In fact, they are used to establish the normal operation of plants and some basic maintenance activities. They are not the result of complex reprocessing or acquisition performed specifically for this purpose.

Few reworkings have been performed (e.g., standardization and filtering). The algorithm is therefore based on the data available to the organization. The algorithm provides promising results in terms of prediction and in reasonable times, being it also able to use data stored for other purposes and thus requiring a minimum effort in terms of data collection. From the company's perspective, knowing in advance the type of intervention to be made to avoid stoppages or to intervene promptly represents a considerable benefit. Indeed, the costs related to such stops are saved. In this work, the goodness of the algorithm is verified at theoretical level through simulations. Further development of this work regard a real evaluation of the actual advantages.

References

1. Ran, Y., Zhou, X., Lin, P., Wen, Y., Deng, R.: A Survey of Predictive Maintenance: Systems, Purposes and Approaches. http://arxiv.org/abs/1912.07383. Accessed 17 Mar 2021
2. Selcuk, S.: Predictive maintenance, its implementation and latest trends. Proc. Inst. Mech. Eng. Part B J. Eng. Manuf. **231**, 1670–1679 (2017). https://doi.org/10.1177/0954405415601640
3. Bevilacqua, M., Ciarapica, F.E., Mazzuto, G.: Fuzzy cognitive maps for adverse drug event risk management. Saf. Sci. **102**, 194–210 (2018). https://doi.org/10.1016/j.ssci.2017.10.022
4. Sotiris, V.A., Tse, P.W., Pecht, M.G.: Anomaly detection through a bayesian support vector machine. IEEE Trans. Reliab. **59**, 277–286 (2010). https://doi.org/10.1109/TR.2010.2048740
5. Yang, H., Sun, Z., Jiang, G., Zhao, F., Mei, X.: Remaining useful life prediction for machinery by establishing scaled-corrected health indicators. Meas. J. Int. Meas. Confed. **163**, 108035 (2020)https://doi.org/10.1016/j.measurement.2020.108035
6. Guo, L., Lei, Y., Li, N., Yan, T., Li, N.: Machinery health indicator construction based on convolutional neural networks considering trend burr. Neurocomputing **292**, 142–150 (2018). https://doi.org/10.1016/j.neucom.2018.02.083
7. Lei, Y., Li, N., Lin, J.: A new method based on stochastic process models for machine remaining useful life prediction. IEEE Trans. Instrum. Meas. **65**, 2671–2684 (2016). https://doi.org/10.1109/TIM.2016.2601004
8. Baraldi, P., Bonfanti, G., Zio, E.: Differential evolution-based multi-objective optimization for the definition of a health indicator for fault diagnostics and prognostics. Mech. Syst. Sign. Process. **102**, 382–400 (2018). https://doi.org/10.1016/j.ymssp.2017.09.013
9. Amihai, I., et al.: Modeling machine health using gated recurrent units with entity embeddings and K-means clustering. In: Proceedings - IEEE 16th International Conference on Industrial Informatics, INDIN 2018, pp. 212–217. Institute of Electrical and Electronics Engineers Inc. (2018)
10. Laloix, T., Iung, B., Voisin, A., Romagne, E.: Parameter identification of health indicator aggregation for decision-making in predictive maintenance: Application to machine tool. CIRP Ann. **68**, 483–486 (2019). https://doi.org/10.1016/j.cirp.2019.03.020
11. Luo, M., Xu, Z., Chan, H.L., Alavi, M.: Online predictive maintenance approach for semiconductor equipment. In: IECON Proceedings (Industrial Electronics Conference), pp. 3662–3667 (2013)
12. Gerber, T., Martin, N., Mailhes, C.: Time-Frequency Tracking of Spectral Structures Estimated by a Data-Driven Method. https://doi.org/10.1109/TIE.2015.2458781

13. Calabrese, F., Regattieri, A., Botti, L., Mora, C., Galizia, F.G.: Unsupervised fault detection and prediction of remaining useful life for online prognostic health management of mechanical systems. Appl. Sci. **10**, 4120 (2020). https://doi.org/10.3390/app10124120

14. Lei, Y., Li, N., Gontarz, S., Lin, J., Radkowski, S., Dybala, J.: A model-based method for remaining useful life prediction of machinery. IEEE Trans. Reliab. **65**, 1314–1326 (2016). https://doi.org/10.1109/TR.2016.2570568

15. Buddhakulsomsiri, J., Siradeghyan, Y., Zakarian, A., Li, X.: Association rule-generation algorithm for mining automotive warranty data. Int. J. Prod. Res. (2006). https://doi.org/10.1080/00207540600564633

16. Rygielski, C., Wang, J.C., Yen, D.C.: Data mining techniques for customer relationship management. Technol. Soc. **24**, 483–502 (2002). https://doi.org/10.1016/S0160-791X(02)00038-6

17. Agard, B., Kusiak, A.: Data mining for subassembly selection. J. Manuf. Sci. Eng. Trans. ASME. **126**, 627–631 (2004). https://doi.org/10.1115/1.1763182

18. Antomarioni, S., Pisacane, O., Potena, D., Bevilacqua, M., Ciarapica, F.E., Diamantini, C.: A predictive association rule-based maintenance policy to minimize the probability of breakages: application to an oil refinery. Int. J. Adv. Manuf. Technol. **105**(9), 3661–3675 (2019). https://doi.org/10.1007/s00170-019-03822-y

19. Dudani, S.A.: The distance-weighted k-nearest-neighbor rule. IEEE Trans. Syst. Man Cybern. **SMC-6**, 325–327 (1976). https://doi.org/10.1109/TSMC.1976.5408784

20. Fayyad, U.M., Irani, K.B.: Multi-interval discretization of continuos-valued attributes for classification learning. In: Proceedings of the 13th International Joint Conference on Artificial Intelligence (1993). https://doi.org/10.1109/TKDE.2011.181

21. Han, J., Pei, J., Yin, Y.: Mining frequent patterns without candidate generation. SIGMOD Rec. (ACM Spec. Interes. Gr. Manag. Data). **29**, 1–12 (2000). https://doi.org/10.1145/335191.335372

Productivity Improvement in Manufacturing Systems Through TPM, OEE and Collaboration Between Maintenance and Production: A Case Study

Rui Costa[1][✉] and Isabel Lopes[2]

[1] Department of Production and Systems, School of Engineering,
University of Minho - Campus de Azurém, 4800-058 Guimarães, Portugal
[2] School of Engineering, ALGORITMI Research Centre,
University of Minho - Campus de Azurém, 4800-058 Guimarães, Portugal
ilopes@dsp.uminho.pt

Abstract. The following paper describes a project where Total Productive Maintenance (TPM) methodology was used in order to improve an automotive industry production line availability and quality. After performing a diagnosis, major flaws were revealed about maintenance and production communication, as well as missing information about the production of defects and maintenance interventions. It was necessary to solve these problems before being able to analyse production inefficiencies, define and implement improvement actions. This project showed the significant impact on costs and quality that can be achieved using TPM, OEE and collaboration between production and maintenance. But beyond that, it showed that despite the industry 4.0 being on the agenda, there is a low use of communication technologies and, therefore, significant gains can still be achieved through basic analysis of recorded data if they are properly organized and standardized. It appears that special attention must be paid to the collection of data, to ensure its proper use for decision making.

Keywords: Collaboration · Data management · OEE · Quality management · TPM

1 Introduction

Nowadays, to become competitive and market leaders, manufacturing companies seek to adopt behaviour patterns and rules that guarantee a good performance of their production systems, as well as to embrace innovation [1]. High quality, low cost and small lead time are the three main client demands, that can be met through methods and tools provided by Lean Manufacturing. Nonetheless for achieving these goals, it is imperative to have control over every expense generated by the company [2]. Maintenance department is usually seen as non-value adding in a company, however, there is a clear need for reducing costs related to equipment status, keeping it in optimal conditions for preventing catastrophic ruptures to production flow. Total Productive Maintenance

Total Productive Maintenance (TPM) is a maintenance methodology that a company to maintain equipment in perfect conditions. The methodology objective is to maximize general equipment effectiveness, improving the Overall Equipment Effectiveness (OEE) indicator, through direct collaboration of every department [3]. The OEE indicator considers produced quantities, number of defects, planned and unplanned stop times, allowing manager to know the factors that need improvement and to make internal and external benchmarking [4]. The desired output for production is only tangible through high equipment availability influenced by equipment reliability and maintainability [5].

Managers are focused in highlighting existing or potential maintenance related problems, in order to improve performance and minimize maintenance operational cost. Systems used for data collection that allow the use of prediction techniques may help to discover useful rules that allow locating critical issues that will have substantial impact on improving all maintenance processes [6]. Although these techniques are appropriate to deal with a large amount of data, the quality of data is crucial for a fast and adequate feeding of the prediction system. During normal plant activity, large quantities of data are produced and are not always considered "clean", or proper to be used. Usually the records include noisy, missing and inconsistent data, making this the first barrier to be solved before going for more advanced data prediction systems that industry 4.0 has to offer [7].

This paper describes a project that aimed to improve the performance of a production line that manufactures Exhaust Gas Recirculation (EGR) valves that composes an EGR module in modern combustion vehicles. The EGR valve is responsible for controlling the mixed amount of combustion expelled gases with fresh air, reducing the amount of greenhouse gas emissions. Given the huge amount of EGR valves needed to feed vehicle manufacturers around the world, errors should be avoided to be able to fulfil placed order quantities.

The project was undergone by a team composed by quality engineers, process and maintenance technicians. It started by the identification of the causes of inefficiency and flaws using OEE and the TPM pillars as diagnosis tools. Then, taking advantage of the collaboration between team members, improvement actions were defined and implemented.

The present paper is organized as follows. In Section 2, the diagnosis of the studied production line is depicted, revealing the prime failures of its low performance. Section 3 describes the improving actions implemented to the production line in order to correct the flaws identified. In Sect. 5, the results of those improvements are presented and conclusions from the study are drawn.

2 Diagnosis

2.1 Data Registration Process

During the diagnosis phase, some limitations to the analysis due to the method used in the production line to register information related to production activities were immediately identified:

1. No distinction between different types of stops: During normal production time, different reasons may lead to the equipment stoppage, resulting in an overall temporary stop of the line production activities. Equipment stops can either due to equipment breakdown (ex: failure of mechanical or electrical components), or due to a production part quality issue that forced the equipment to stop in order to correct the issue. The non-differentiation of these stops, since all stops are registered as "breakdown", and the lack of details about actual equipment breakdowns do not allow future analyses regarding where to invest the company's time and resources in order to make improvements in that equipment.
2. Wrong quantification of quality defects: During a normal production shift, information that is documented regarding quality defects does not refer any detail about the stage of the process where they were produced or what caused them. The lack of detailed and normalized information does not allow the team to use quality tools like Pareto diagrams with the scope of identifying and solving those quality problems.
3. Maintenance interventions information: The fact that maintenance technicians do not register all interventions performed on the production line equipment, and the fact that the ones that were registered are not normalized, not allowing for future detailed analyses, becomes one more step-back to the production line managers to decide in what improvement actions to invest.

2.2 Analysis Based on OEE

By analysing the OEE indicator of the production line, it was possible to find out the factors that most contribute to the low value of OEE. Figure 1 shows the behaviour of both OEE and its constituting factors. From April 2019 to December 2019, the average value of the OEE was 54,90%. In that same period of analysis, the availability factor had the worst result, with an average of 60,75%, followed by quality factor with 90% and performance factor with 94%.

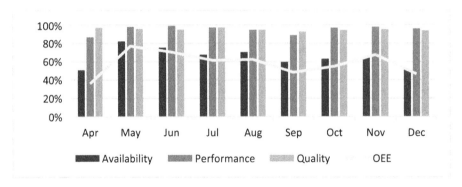

Fig. 1. OEE behaviour from April 2019 to Dec 2019

After deducing that the availability factor was the main responsible for the low value of OEE, the analysis was focused on the inefficiencies related to this factor. Figure 2 identifies through an accumulated bar chart, the sum of inefficiencies registered in the production line. All reported inefficiencies are quantified as wasted time and the chart exhibits the percentage compared to the production time.

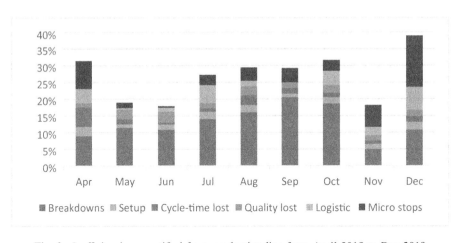

Fig. 2. Inefficiencies quantified from production line from April 2019 to Dec 2019

The chart of Fig. 2 shows that the biggest inefficiency is "breakdowns". As it was explained in Sect. 2.1, the "breakdowns" inefficiency must be interpreted as "equipment stops" motivated by failures or by product quality issues.

Since the registration method used by the company did not provide enough information for the team to study the existing problems, a new one that allows for more detail about defects production and equipment stops was implemented. This method relies on an input form that categorizes and differentiates the type of stops and defects so that the operators can register the information without mistakes and with the necessary details during normal production activity. The detail provided allows the engineers to understand what the main motives of defects are, and the respective causes. After two months of records with this new method, it was possible to build Table 1.

Table 1. Quantity: stops vs production defects

Average time stopped	Time stopped	N° Stops	Equipment	N° defects	% Defects
143,46	5164	36	OB128	658	57,87%
47,38	1042,5	22	OB100	175	15,39%
43	430	10	OB131	63	5,54%
37,33	560	15	OB130	35	3,08%
21,5	129	6	OB127	88	7,74%
158,96	3179	20	OB129	86	7,56%

Through Table 1, it is possible to conclude that the equipment which produces the highest number of defects is also the one which stops the most, suggesting that those stops aimed solving those problematic quality defects.

Given the fact that the data retrieved during these two months had enough detail to determine the main reasons of defects in production by applying quality tools, it was possible to find their root-cause and consequently proceed to improvements. Two main categories of defects were uncovered. The first one was a leakage detected in the leakage test and the second is detected at the final stage of the process, at the hysteresis test. The first category occurs when the valve is not able to restrain the air stream to a certain desired volume. The team used an Ishikawa diagram in order to find the source of error and, after carefully testing all parameters, it was unveiled that a small misalignment of the valve regulating membrane, the flap, caused an undesired leak. This leak occurred due to a gap in the flap caused by the degradation of the tool that adapts and secures the valve in the machine during the welding stage. The second category was unveiled during the hysteresis test that consists in simulating the valves normal field behaviour, exposing it to routine stress while in normal operation. The team found that this defect is the result of two problems, both due to wrong inner component angles. The gas mixture is controlled by a small electric motor that is attached to the valve. The two components that are responsible to connect the motor to the valve, in order to transfer the energy, are usually welded in a wrong and non-functional angular position, causing the valve to fail in the test. After carefully testing the welding equipment, the team unveiled that the equipment components responsible to stabilize those two components during the welding process were heavily damaged and worn out, causing unwanted gaps.

2.3   Analysis Based on TPM Pillars

Pillar	Observation
Autonomous maintenance	The presence of dust, debris, and obsolete components in the production line are indicators that this pillar is not present. Therefore, autonomous maintenance plans are needed
Planned maintenance	Maintenance plans for the equipment of the production lines are defined, but they are not fulfilled
Focused improvement	Equipment improvements meant to solve momentary problems to resume production activity as soon as possible and are not part of a continuous improvement approach
Quality maintenance	During the performed quality analysis, a problem with a measuring system was identified. A gage R&R study led to the conclusion that this system was not able to evaluate production parts. This fact suggests that this pillar is not well embed in the company
Office TPM	Communication between logistics and maintenance is not the finest. The fact that maintenance technicians do not have any in- formation about spare parts stock, suggests that improvements within this pillar are needed
Training	Both pillars are well present, they represent the base beliefs of the company, and their presence is remarkable due to the heavy attention given to the workers
Safety, health and environment	

Maintenance team efficiency is also noticeably low. Maintenance interventions take a long time to complete due to low availability of technicians and tools, and lack of knowledge. Given the fact that this type of industry is highly automated, the need for maintenance technicians specialized in automation is clear. One other problem detected was the lack of support to the production line, with only one specialized technician working in central shift, not even providing support to the night shift. Due to the high number of maintenance calls, almost no time is left for technicians to register the actions or changes made during that maintenance intervention.

The company uses a software to manage and monitor its plant maintenance activities and controlling its expenses, however, due to some inefficiencies with the software, it becomes poorly used by the maintenance technicians. The software is slow to run, requiring a lot of data entries to register a maintenance intervention and around 8 min necessary to fulfil the registration of a single intervention.

3   Implementation of Improvement Actions

3.1   Autonomous Maintenance

Since many equipment breakdowns or quality issues were related to detrimental pro-duction environments, there was an obvious need for improving that environment. Together, with the tacit knowledge of both maintenance technicians and equipment suppliers, an autonomous plan was created. The maintenance actions that comprise the plan are performed by the operators at the beginning of every shift. The aim of this maintenance plan is to reduce the chance of error or problems with production, via cleaning, lubricating and adjusting the necessary parts.

3.2 Quality Improvements

In order to mitigate the quality problems in production, some improvements were made to the production line equipment. The problems were solved by developing and creating new tools to replace the older degraded ones, eliminating gaps that previously existed. The leak detected during the leakage test was eliminated by the replacement of the tool used to secure the valves position during the welding operation, assuring a good quality and continuous production.

New measurement systems were developed to adopt a new evaluation method to judge the productions output quality, reducing the variability compared to the older measurement systems, allowing for a more controlled production process.

3.3 Maintenance Management and Data Gathering

The maintenance team was enhanced with the addition of an automation specialist, covering all three production shifts, becoming therefore more available. The lack of tools was also eliminated by investing in a maintenance tool car for every technician, eliminating waiting times for the tools to be available.

The implementation of a mobile maintenance management system was probably the biggest improvement of all, regarding maintenance organization and communication. The system also allowed for a better communication between technicians of different labouring shifts. This newly implemented mobile registration system allowed the maintenance technicians to both register and access information about equipment as well as consulting information about spare parts at the warehouse in a much faster and efficient way with the use of QR codes that connect the technician directly to the equipment profile. This improvement also reduced the time required to register a maintenance intervention, enhancing the maintenance technician's availability. Since the information can be accurately registered, KPI calculation can now be trusted by the engineers, allowing the identification of effective improvement actions.

4 Results

The improvement actions implemented in the project described in this paper brought significant upgrades to the production line. The new method of registration provided a structured data base to be used for studying problems and finding solutions. During the months of January and February 2020, information was registered using the new data record method, allowing for the definition of improvement actions, implemented throughout the months of March and April 2020. In the following six months (May to October 2020), the availability factor increased about 11%, compared to the previous nine months, from an average of 61%, to an average of 72%. Regarding quality, after the implementation period from March to April 2020, the following two months registered 4500€ saved in the production of defects. The company uses a KPI known as "scrap vs sales" which measures the value of scrap produced compared to the value of sales for that month. For the same period of analyses mentioned earlier, this KPI went from 3,4% to 2,4%.

5 Conclusions

In this project, the diagnosis phase allowed, through an analysis based on the factors and inefficiencies associated with the OEE and based on the TPM pillars, to prioritize improvement actions. The collaboration between production and maintenance and the redefinition of data records were key factors in achieving the portrayed improvements.

A perfect synchronization between production and maintenance is desirable to obtain the maximum value from the assets. The need for standardized and organized records of information is also irrefutable, whether concerning defects on production or maintenance interventions. It is only possible to implement a predictive maintenance system, for instance, if this standardization is achieved, becoming the first step into industry 4.0. Therefore, the same way as Training is a pillar of TPM, it seems to be necessary to consider a new pillar designated by "Communication and data management" in order to enhance TPM implementation in today's digital manufacturing environments.

A fast and effective communication between maintenance and production, maintenance and logistics and between shifts can bring significant gains. Good data management makes it easier to highlight inefficiencies and their causes, constituting a driver for continuous improvement. Since the time spent in manufacturing plant to collect and access data and information should be reduced, given the fact that it is a non-value adding activity, implementing available technologies such as mobile devices, is a key for a successful implementation of TPM in companies. However, this should be accompanied by a reorganization and standardization of data records for allowing appropriate analysis. Thus, the development and implementation of ontologies in the maintenance domain is required.

References

1. Huang, S.H., et al.: Manufacturing productivity improvement using effectiveness metrics and simulation analysis. Int. J. Qual. Reliability Manage. **17**(9), 1003–1016 (2003)
2. Hall, R.W.: Lean and the Toyota Production System **20**(3), 22–27 (2004)
3. Rajput, H.S., Jayaswal, P.: A Total Productive Maintenance (TPM) Approach to Improve Overall Equipment Efficiency **2**(6), 4383–4386 (2012)
4. Ahuja, I.P.S., Khamba, J.S.: Total productive maintenance: Literature review and directions. Int. J. Qual. Reliability Manage. **25**(7), 709–756 (2008)
5. Vashisth, D.S., Kumar, R.: Analysis of a redundant system with common cause failures. Int. J. Eng. Sci. Technol. **3**(12), 8247–8254 (2011)
6. Bastos, P., Lopes, I., Pires, L.: A maintenance prediction system using data mining techniques. In: Proceedings of the World Congress on Engineering, vol. III, London (2012)
7. Bastos, P., Lopes, I., Pires, L.: Application of data mining in a maintenance system for failure prediction. In: Steenbergen, R., Van Gelder, P.H.A.J.M., Miraglia, S., Vrouwenvelder, T. (eds.) Safety, Reliability and Risk Analysis: Beyond the Horizon, pp. 933–940. Taylor and Francis Group, London, UK (2014)

Stochastic Dynamic Programming for Earliness-Tardiness Single Machine Scheduling with Maintenance Considerations

Sabri Abderrazzak[1,2]([✉]), Allaoui Hamid[1], and Souissi Omar[2]

[1] Univ. Artois, EA 3926, Laboratoire de Génie Informatique et d'Automatique de l'Artois (LGI2A), Béthune, France
`abderrazzak.sabri@univ-artois.fr`
[2] Institut national des postes et télécommunications, Rabat, Morocco

Abstract. We study in this paper the problem of simultaneously scheduling resumable jobs and preventive maintenance on a single machine to minimize the earliness-tardiness cost. The machine is subject to random breakdowns according to Erlang distribution and minimal repair is considered. The age of the machine defines its probability of breakdown and performing preventive maintenance renews the age of the machine to zero, however the preventive maintenance operations cost valuable time that can increase the overall earliness-tardiness cost. A stochastic dynamic programming solving approach is presented for solving this problem with illustrated meaning to its algorithm.

Keywords: Preventive maintenance · Dynamic programming · Production scheduling

1 Introduction

In all industrial contexts, production is the main function of the system and the essential source of value, and should ideally be continuously active, and as every order have to be delivered on a prefixed due date, the optimal sequence in which orders should be fed to the machine is often not obvious, the earliness-tardiness model is one of many used to optimize this process, it aims at finishing orders following a just-in-time performance strategy, as quick response to customer's orders and respecting their delivery dates is key to success in the manufacturing business, however finishing jobs too early increases the stocking and warehousing costs and further lowers the profit margin, this strategy has been adopted by many big companies (Apple, McDonald's, Toyota ..) and was proven to be successful at lowering the cost of goods while keeping the customers satisfied.

However, production systems are not ideal and tend to fail regularly due to over usage or equipment failure, so while it is already not evident to schedule production jobs, the randomness of failure events adds another layer of difficulty

© IFIP International Federation for Information Processing 2021
Published by Springer Nature Switzerland AG 2021
A. Dolgui et al. (Eds.): APMS 2021, IFIP AICT 634, pp. 269–276, 2021.
https://doi.org/10.1007/978-3-030-85914-5_29

to the task of production scheduling. To assert a certain level of control over the random aspect of breakdowns, preventive maintenance PM is performed, and while it does not exclude the possibility of failure, it fairly reduces the increasing risk of machine breakdown. However, performing preventive maintenance costs valuable time that could be used for production, while not performing it presents the machine to the increasing risk of failure, hence the trade-off.

The literature around this problem is extensive, especially in the areas of operational research and production systems, however, the majority of these papers considers that the machines are available at all times, and no maintenance is needed, and since this is often not true as we explained industrial machines tend to fail regularly, we in this paper treat the case of scheduling N jobs on a single machine considering the possibility of machine failure.

2   State of the Art

Among the first attempts to solve the problem of single machine scheduling with common due date and earliness-tardiness penalties, [1] studied the general case where the due date is not prefixed and is to determine. The method proposed by authors consists of assigning the optimal due date as well as the optimal feasible sequence of jobs that minimize the sum of earliness tardiness penalties and cost of due date assignment, more in depth, for a set of N jobs all available at time zero, and C_j being the completion time of a job j, the goal is to determine a due date D^* and a feasible sequence σ^*, that minimize the objective function

$$f(d, \sigma) = \sum_{j=1}^{n} \alpha \, E_j + \beta \, T_j$$

with $E_j = max(d - C_j, 0)$ and $T_j = max(C_j - d, 0)$ denoting respectively the earliness and tardiness of job j, and α, β being the respective cost coefficients of earliness and tardiness.

A huge interest in the scheduling with due date assignment sparked after the work of [1], different generalizations of the problem were proposed, such as replacing the common due date with common due window [1], the consideration of due date tolerance [4], ... etc. For a more detailed review of these works, we refer the readers to the survey of [2].

On a less generalized level, we are most interested in the case where the common due date is predetermined. In such a problem, the objective is to determine the optimal feasible sequence σ^* for which the simplified function

$$f(d, \sigma) = \sum_{j=1}^{n} \alpha \, E_j + \beta \, T_j$$

is minimized. [5] proposed an enumerating algorithm to solve the variant of the problem where ($\alpha = \beta = 1$), later to that [6] proposed dynamic programming algorithm that solves the problem in pseudo polynomial time,[7] also proposed a DP algorithm with pseudo-polynomial run time as well as a branch-and-bound method based on a Lagrangian lower-and-upper bounds. For the variants where

α_j and β_j are constants ($\alpha_j=\alpha$, $\beta_j=\beta$), [8] proposed a branching procedure, however his method only work for small sized instances. The case of ($\alpha_j \neq \beta_j$) was only solved with the help of approximation methods, like the work of [9] where a meta-heuristic was used to obtain approximate solutions.

All works above assume that the machine is available at all times, however, the problem of job scheduling where the machine is subject to failure and breakdowns is very lightly studied in the literature. [10] was among the earliest and few efforts aimed in this direction as authors studied the case where the machine is subject to external shocks following a non-homogeneous Poisson process, [11] considers stochastic model for breakdowns. A more elaborated effort was made by [12] where they considered that breakdowns follow an Erlang distribution and presented a stochastic dynamic programming algorithm for preventive maintenance scheduling that minimizes earliness-tardiness costs. [14] presented a model that solves the job scheduling based on periodic preventive maintenance performance, and in a very similar fashion, [13] also uses a periodic maintenance scheduling to solve the problem. [18] also defines a periodic planning for preventive maintenance where the interval for PM is dynamically updated while scheduling the jobs. [16] proposed a mixed-integer linear programming model to simultaneously schedule the production and maintenance tasks, optimizing the earliness-tardiness costs as well as a wide range of objectives (preventive maintenance costs, idle-time costs, components and assembly costs ..). [17] successfully integrated production and preventive maintenance in a single mathematical model to simultaneously schedule both activities while optimizing the due-date meeting and machine availability. Following the recent trends in the scientific literature, [19] and [20] used the deep Q-Learning algorithm to learn an optimal policy to jointly schedule production jobs and maintenance operations.

3   Problem Statement

The problem of job scheduling with preventive maintenance has been solved using dynamic programming for non-resumable jobs, we in this paper consider the resumable case, where in the event of breakdown, the progress made so far on the job is not lost, and the machine can resume working on it after repair from the last progress point.

This paper divides problem to two steps, first we assume that the machine is available at all times, and solve the job scheduling with common due date using a dynamic programming algorithm, where for an input of N jobs and their respective processing time, we expect as output a sequence of the jobs for which the earliness tardiness cost is minimal, then we further elaborate the solution considering the element of preventive maintenance and breakdowns, using a stochastic dynamic programming model, that take as input the solution of the first step, and prior to the execution of each job, we decide optimally whether to perform preventive maintenance or not.

let C_{ET} be the cost function for a sequence of jobs S and a due date D:

$$C_{ET}(S, D) = \sum_{j \epsilon S}(\alpha_j\, E_j + \beta_j\, T_j)$$

3.1 Deterministic Dynamic Program

Here, we are concerned with the total 'weighted earliness-tardiness (WET)' in which the jobs have different weights w_j but a common due date that is loose; $\alpha_j = \beta_j = w_j$ and $d_j = d$. The approach is solved to optimality via DP and is based on the work of [15]. The procedure is pseudo-polynomial.

As before, call the set of early jobs E and the set of tardy job T. The efficiency of the algorithm depends crucially on the third Property mentioned in [15], namely, the fact that all jobs in either subset E or T must be ordered in decreasing 'weighted shortest processing time (WSPT)' order measured (in absolute value) from time D as the origin. The proof of this assertion is evident when one considers each subset by itself with time measured away from D.

Based on this property one starts by re-arranging the jobs in WSPT. This constitutes the list of the jobs from which selection shall be made. If job k is selected for placement on the machine it must be true that all preceding jobs 1 through $k-1$ must have been placed on the m/c either in E or in T. This leads to the definition of the "stages" as progressing from 1 to n; stage k involves the first k jobs in the list. Let $W_k \subseteq N$ denote the set of the first k jobs in the list, where N denotes the set of all jobs $W_k = 1, ..., k$.

At stage k the total occupancy of the machine must be $P(W_k) = \sum_{i=1}^{k} p_i$, observe that the total processing time of any subset of jobs is constant independent of their sequence, and independent of whether or not they straddle d, though we know that in an optimal sequence, no job will straddle d, but some job in E must end at d and some job in T must start at d, assuming that no α_j or β_j is equal to 0.

Let e denote the sum of the processing times of the subset of jobs in W_k that are early (in set E, to the left of D). Alternatively, we could have selected t as the sum of the processing times of the subset of jobs in W_k that are Tardy (in set T, to the right of D); but we shall stick with e. Then the tardy jobs (in set T, to the right of D) complete at time $P_k - e$;

Shift the origin to d and measure all times from d in either direction. Job k is either in E or in T. If it is in E then it is placed first (farthest from d) and its completion time shall be $(e - p_k)$; and its cost is $w_k\,(e - p_k)$. If it is placed in T then it is placed last (again, farthest from D) and its completion time shall be $(P(W_k) - e)$; and its cost is $w_k\,(P_k - e)$.

Let $f_k(e)$ denote the minimal cost to schedule the set S_k composed of jobs 1 through k when the jobs in $E \subseteq S_k$ occupy time e. Then we are led to the extremal equation,

$$f_k(e) = \min \begin{cases} a_k(e - p_k) + f_{k-1}(e - p_k), & \text{if job } k \text{ is placed} \\ & \text{in } E,\, e \geq p_k \\ b_k \cdot (P(W_k) - e) + f_{k-1}(e) & \text{if job } k \text{ is placed} \\ & \text{in } T,\, P_k - e \geq p_k \end{cases}$$

$$0 \leq e \leq P(W_k)$$

which is initiated at $f\varnothing(.) = 0$

and terminated when $f_n(e)$ is evaluated for all feasible e and the minimum is determined. Observe that in the determination of $f_k(e)$ either of the two options may be infeasible, in which case the corresponding value f would be put ∞ to prohibit its adoption.

The Algorithm

Initiate the DP iterations with: $f_0(e) = 0$, for $e = 0, 1, 2, ..., \sum_{j=1}^{n} p_j$ and terminate it when the minimum cost schedule is found at $f_n(0)$. By the WSPT order there is one set $S_k = 1, ..., k$. At stage k one enumerates over the values of e, which ranges from 0 to $P(W_k)$ Therefore the complexity of the DP procedure is seen to be $O(n \sum_{j=1}^{n} p_j)$; it is pseudo-polynomial.

3.2 Stochastic Dynamic Program

After solving the first part, we now consider the possibility of machine breakdown, we consider that breakdown events occur following the Erlang distribution for which the density function is defined as:

$$f(x; k, \lambda) = \frac{\lambda^k x^{k-1} e^{-\lambda x}}{(k-1)!} \quad \text{for } x, \lambda \geq 0,$$

For a given job in the optimal sequence given by part 1 starting at time t, and for which the processing time is p_j, we define the probability of a breakdown event happening during its execution by : $P(t) = \int_0^t f(x)dx$. We also define a_j, the age of the machine before executing the job j (Fig. 1),

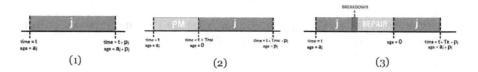

Fig. 1. PM is performed (1); PM is not performed and : no breakdowns occur (2), a breakdown occurs (3)

Now before executing job j, we have to choose between two decisions:

1. Perform preventive maintenance, which takes T_{PM} amount of time, and reduces the probability of breakdown to zero as we maintain the machine to as-new condition, it also resets the age of the machine to zero,

2. Do not perform preventive maintenance and proceeds directly to the treating of job j, this leads to two possible outcomes:
    - The machine does not breakdown, which happens with probability $1 - p(a_j)$, the job j is finished at time $t + p_j$, and the age of the machine at the end of job j is $a_j + p_j$
    - A breakdown event occurs, which happens with probability $p(a_j)$, a repair operation of duration T_R is necessary, the progress made before the breakdown is not lost and the machine will resume the job after repair from the last progress point. The job finishes at time $t + T_R + p_j$. The repair is minimal, which means the machine is repaired just enough to start operating again, and it does not affect its age. The age at end of execution is $a_j + p_j$.

The Formulation
To solve this problem, we formulate a dynamic programming algorithm for instances where $(\alpha_j = \beta_j = 1)$, $(\alpha_j = \beta_j)$ and $(\alpha_j = \alpha, \beta_j = \beta)$.

First, we order the optimal sequence from part 1 in reverse from n to 1, and then for every stage of the DP, we evaluate the cost of both decisions.

For the case of $d_j = 1$, it is simple to see that the cost of stage j is $C_{ET}(t + T_{PM} + p_j)$, however for the case of $d_j = 0$ where the machine has two possible scenarios, the total cost at time t is either $C_{ET}(t + p_j)$ in case no breakdown happened, or $C_{ET}(t + p_j + T_R)$ in the scenario where a breakdown occurs, both outcomes happen with respective probabilities $1 - p(a_j)$ and $p(a_j)$, so to estimate the expected cost of the decision $d_j = 0$, we calculate the weighted cost of both cases.

The state of the dynamic programming model at any stage is given by the time and the age of the machine, and let $f_n(t, a)$ be the expected cost of stages $j, j + 1, \ldots, n$ when considered at time t with age a. As we start the iterations on the stages backwards, the base case for our model stands at $j = n$, for that we give:

$$f_n(t, a) = \min_{d_j = 0,1} \left\{ C_{ET} \times p(a_j) + C_{ET} \times \overline{p(a_j)} \right\}$$

After stage n, for any $1 \leq j < n$, the cost of stage j when considered at time t with age a is given by the recursive formula:

$$f_j(t, a_j) = \min_{d_j = 0,1} \left\{ \begin{matrix} C_{ET}(t_1) \times p(a_j) + C_{ET}(t_2) \times \overline{p(a_j)} + f_{j+1}(t_1, a_{j+1}).p(a_j) \\ + f_{j+1}(t_2, a_{j+1}).\overline{p(a_j)} \end{matrix} \right\}$$

with:

- $\overline{p(a_j)} = 1 - p(a_j)$
- $t_1 = t + T_R + p_j$
- $t_2 = t + T_{PM} \times d_j + p_j$
- $a_{j+1} = a_j \times (1 - d_j) + p_j$

It is obvious that in an optimal solution, the start time of the first job is less than D, and considering that the age of the machine is zero ($a_1 = 0$) at the start of the sequence, we calculate the variable intervals for each stage knowing that the start time of the sequence is in the $(0, D)$ interval

$$T_{\max} = D + \sum_{j=1}^{n} p_j + max(T_{PM}, T_R), \; a_{\max} = \sum_{j=1}^{n} p_j : \text{For stage 1.}$$

$$T_{\max} = T_{\max} - p_{j-1} - max(T_{PM}, T_R), \; a_{\max} = a_{\max} - p_{j-1} : \text{For stage } j\epsilon[2, n]$$

The problem is solved when we reach $j = 1$, we can get the optimal sequence of preventive maintenance decisions as well as the start time of the first job in the sequence by finding the minimal value of cost in stage n, then climb back up the table to stage 1 to formulate the decision tree.

4   Conclusion

In this paper we have studied the problem of job scheduling with preventive maintenance on a single machine using stochastic dynamic programming to minimize the earliness tardiness cost relative to a common due date, this problem is particularly understudied in the industrial production research community, whereas production units with scheduling systems that do not factor maintenance and breakdowns in the planning procedure suffer from uncertainty in delivery dates, and are hugely under-performing. The two-steps algorithm that we propose to solve the problem consist of initially solving the problem of scheduling n jobs with no breakdowns considered, the solution obtained from this step is then used as an input to the second phase where we consider breakdowns following the Erlang distribution and solve the problem of preventive maintenance planning for the sequence obtained in the first step. The final output is a decision tree that defines the optimal decisions based on how the stochastic event of breakdowns play out in time. In future works, since the method we present schedules the jobs and maintenance tasks on a single machine only, we are most interested in generalizing the existing model to a job-shop use case. In addition, dynamic programming is computationally expensive and is only efficient for small numbers of jobs, therefore we also consider exploring the use of recent advances in artificial intelligence to solve this problem with lower computational cost.

Acknowledgment. This work is a part of the ELSAT2020 project. The ELSAT2020 project is cofinanced by the European Union with the European Regional Development Fund, the French state and the Hauts de France Region Council.

References

1. Seidmann, A., Panwalkar, S.S., Smith, M.L.: Optimal assignment of due-dates for a single processor scheduling problem. Int. J. Prod. Res. **19**(4), 393–399 (1981)

2. Gordon, V., Proth, J.-M., Chu, C.: A survey of the state-of-the-art of common due date assignment and scheduling research. Eur. J. Oper. Res. **139**(1), 1–25 (2002)

3. Liman, S.D., Panwalkar, S.S., Thongmee, S.: Common due window size and location determination in a single machine scheduling problem. J. Oper. Res. Soc. **49**(9), 1007–1010 (1998)

4. Cheng, T.C.E., Gupta, M.C.: Survey of scheduling research involving due date determination decisions. Eur. J. Oper. Res. **38**(2), 156–166 (1989)

5. Bagchi, U., Sullivan, R.S., Chang, Y.-L.: Minimizing mean absolute deviation of completion times about a common due date. Naval Res. Logistics Q. **33**(2), 227–240 (1986)

6. Hall, N.G., Posner, M.E.: Earliness-tardiness scheduling problems, i: weighted deviation of completion times about a common due date. Oper. Res. **39**(5), 836–846 (1991)

7. Hoogeveen, J.A., van de Velde, S.L.: Earliness-tardiness scheduling around almost equal due dates. INFORMS J. Comput. **9**(1), 92–99 (1997)

8. Bagchi, U., Sullivan, R.S., Chang, Y.-L.: Minimizing mean squared deviation of completion times about a common due date. Manage. Sci. **33**(7), 894–906 (1987)

9. James, R.J.W.: Using tabu search to solve the common due date early/tardy machine scheduling problem. Comput. Oper. Res. **24**(3), 199–208 (1997)

10. Pinedo, M.L., Ross, S.M.: Scheduling jobs subject to nonhomogeneous Poisson shocks. Manage. Sci. **26**(12), 1250–1257 (1980)

11. Birge, J., et al.: Single-machine scheduling subject to stochastic breakdowns. Naval Res. Logistics (NRL) **37**(5), 661–677 (1990)

12. Allaoui, H., et al.: Scheduling n jobs and preventive maintenance in a single machine subject to breakdowns to minimize the expected total earliness and tardiness costs. IFAC Proc. **41**(2), 15843–15848 (2008)

13. Benmansour, R., et al.: Minimizing the weighted sum of maximum earliness and maximum tardiness costs on a single machine with periodic preventive maintenance. Comput. Oper. Res. **47**, 106–113 (2014)

14. Todosijievic, R., et al.: Optimizing the periodic maintenance problem using General Variable neighbourhood search." ROADEF-15ème congrès annuel de la Société française de recherche opérationnelle et d'aide à la décision (2014)

15. Alidaee, B.: Schedule of n jobs on two identical machines to minimize weighted mean flow time. Comput. Ind. Eng. **24**(1), 53–55 (1993)

16. Chansombat, S., Pongcharoen, P., Hicks, C.: A mixed-integer linear programming model for integrated production and preventive maintenance scheduling in the capital goods industry. Int. J. Prod. Res. **57**(1), 61–82 (2019)

17. Kolus, A., El-Khalifa, A., Al-Turki, U. M., Duffuaa, S.O.: An integrated mathematical model for production scheduling and preventive maintenance planning. Int. J. Qual. Reliab. Manage. (2020)

18. Ye, H., Wang, X., Liu, K.: Adaptive preventive maintenance for flow shop scheduling with resumable processing. IEEE Trans. Autom. Sci. Eng. **18**(1), 106–113 (2020)

19. Yang, H., Li, W., Wang, B.: Joint optimization of preventive maintenance and production scheduling for multi-state production systems based on reinforcement learning. Reliab. Eng. Syst. Saf. **214**, 107713 (2021)

20. Huang, J., Chang, Q., Arinez, J.: Deep reinforcement learning based preventive maintenance policy for serial production lines. Expert Syst. Appl. **160**, 113701 (2020)

An Assessment of Order Release Models in Hybrid MTO-MTS Flow Shop with Bottleneck

Federica Costa[1]([⊠]), Kaustav Kundu[2],
and Alberto Portioli-Staudacher[1]

[1] Department of Management, Economics and Industrial Engineering,
Politecnico di Milano, Milan, Italy
`federica.costa@polimi.it`
[2] National University of Singapore, Singapore, Singapore

Abstract. The traditional configurations of market response, make-to-order (MTO) and make-to-stock (MTS), are no more suitable in today's competitive context, forcing companies to a transition towards hybrid solutions. Unfortunately, this has been neglected, in particular at the operational level where the Order Review and Release issue counts only two related articles but restricted to job shops. Therefore, researchers are moving towards flow shop configuration, particularly addressing the issue of bottleneck. Literature links this topic to the Theory of Constraints by Goldratt and Cox [14], from which Drum Buffer Rope (DBR) has been designed as a production planning and control tool. The objective of this paper has been defined as verifying how the decision on the release model changes considering the designed hybrid flow shop model. Simulation results are not clearly in favor of one over the other, since besides severity, there is another important factor to consider: the choice of control at dispatching level, and its connected trade-offs. In particular, implementing this control with bottleneck-based rule is effective for MTO performances, especially in case of high severity. Instead, when control at dispatching is absent, the workload control as release rule is preferred, leading also to the best lead times for low severity.

Keywords: MTO · MTS · Order review and release · Bottleneck

1 Introduction

In the current competitive environment, manufacturers deal with mega trends as growing product customization and internationalization of their businesses that ultimately cause shorter product life cycle, the explosion in the number of product families and growing sources of variability [1]. In order to serve the market, firms traditionally choose between make-to-stock (MTS) and make-to-order (MTO) strategies. MTS was typically chosen in low variety context, where products can be standardized, and the focus was on anticipating demand to keep an appropriate level of finished goods stocks. Instead, production within MTO systems is directly triggered by customers' demand,

© IFIP International Federation for Information Processing 2021
Published by Springer Nature Switzerland AG 2021
A. Dolgui et al. (Eds.): APMS 2021, IFIP AICT 634, pp. 277–287, 2021.
https://doi.org/10.1007/978-3-030-85914-5_30

hence the focus is put on assuring short delivery times to clients who can choose among a wide range of families.

However, current context and its business implications force companies to adopt, more and more, a MTO strategy [2–5]. Actually, for some industries this is not sufficient, making necessary the transition towards a hybrid MTO/MTS production mode [6]. This organizational mode is beneficial for those contexts in which product variability and unpredictability of demand would make inefficient to set up manufacturing activities based on traditional frameworks [7].

Many researches argue the importance of production planning and control mechanism for high-variability MTO context, therefore it is immediate to claim that this statement is valid also for this hybrid scenario, which introduces new and different sources of variability [8]. Despite the relevance of the topic, few are the research effort in the hybrid field, since traditional operations management literature categorizes manufacturing systems as either MTO or MTS [9, 10].

From the previous research, it is revealed that hybrid environment is studied in job shops, not in flow shops. Apart from the load based rules, potential of Drum Buffer Rope (DBR) as production planning and control tool, especially when bottleneck-severity is high is investigated in flow shops [11, 12]. Given these premises, the paper intends to investigate and fill the gap in terms of order release within hybrid flow shop with bottleneck, and adding the recent literature findings on capacity constrained resources.

The article is organized as follows: a theoretical background about the applicability of the Workload Control in hybrid environment followed by the research question is provided in Sect. 2. Simulation model and methodology are discussed in Sect. 3. The results and conclusions are depicted in Sect. 4 along with implications and future research.

2   Literature Review

This section aims at identifying and summarizing the main publications. In hybrid environment, production tries to leverage on the point of strength of both MTS and MTO, assuring shorter delivery lead times compared to pure configurations reaching the required level of product variety. This organizational mode is beneficial for those contexts in which product variability and unpredictability of demand would make inefficient to set up manufacturing activities based on traditional frameworks [7].

Load based rules such as Workload Control (WLC), particularly "Order Review and Release" is proved to be beneficial in MTS and MTO companies but there are very few works in the hybrid MTO-MTS hybrid environment [7, 10]. For details, please refer to Eivazy et al. [10].

Since the reference article by Eivazy et al. [10] explores specifically the semi-conductor industry and leaves flow shop without any consideration, the paper intends to enlarge the original study, generalizing the model and addressing the problem in this alternative configuration. The change of perspective in terms of shop floor characteristics makes necessary the deepening of a second stream of literature, specifically addressed towards flow shop with bottlenecks.

Bottlenecks are defined as those portions of a production system which are not able to process any additional job without the use of capacity adjustments. Therefore, they constitute a limit for the output rate, and they have to be carefully considered since companies cannot afford any waste of time for these resources [13]. The management of capacity-constrained resources, in literature, is associated with the Theory of Constraints (TOC) by Goldratt and Cox [14]. In recent years, DBR, a new production planning and control tool adopting the principles of TOC, emerged. The most interesting aspects of recent literature on bottlenecks and DBR are included in four articles by Thürer M., who addressed different thematic: the drum schedule improvement [15], the bottleneck shiftiness [12, 16] and the comparison with other release rule [11].

Constant Work-in-Process (CONWIP) is basically an extension of DBR, since here the control is set at the last station of the shop floor, regardless the position of the bottleneck. The model has been introduced by Spearman et al. [17] as an alternative to Kanban system, which would allow systems to be more robust, flexible and easier to set up. Actually, Framinan et al. [18], in their literature review, recognized that different authors proposed their own conceptualizations, however the most important element was common among all of them: a system which keeps the maximum amount of work-in-process at a constant level.

The implementation of CONWIP is usually associated with the use of cards, which must be attached to a job to be realized in the shop floor without separating them until the end of the last processing stage [19].

Operation management literature recognizes different decision that managers should face when setting up a system based on constant work-in-process [17, 20]: 1. The production quota, 2. The maximum amount of work. 3. The capacity shortage trigger. 4. How to forecast the backlog list. 5. Number of cards operating in the system. 6. How to sequence the jobs in the system.

Researchers clearly specify that these aspects have to be contextualized in a hierarchical planning procedure [21]. In particular, the first five elements of the list could belong to the tactical level, while the last one to the control level.

Given the findings on DBR and the severity factor on one side, and the reference research based on workload on the other, the objective has been defined as verifying how the decision on the release model changes in hybrid MTO-MTS flow shop. Therefore, the research question has been formulated considering observations of the reviewed literature as:

"In the hybrid flow shop model, is Workload Control able to outperform bottleneck-based approach?"

To answer the research question, a simulation model is built and different scenarios are run.

3   Simulation Model and Methodology

The simulation model has been implemented through Python programming language and some of its dedicated modules. The structure follows the one of the reference study [10] (see Fig. 1), thus it is constituted by a release module and a dispatching module.

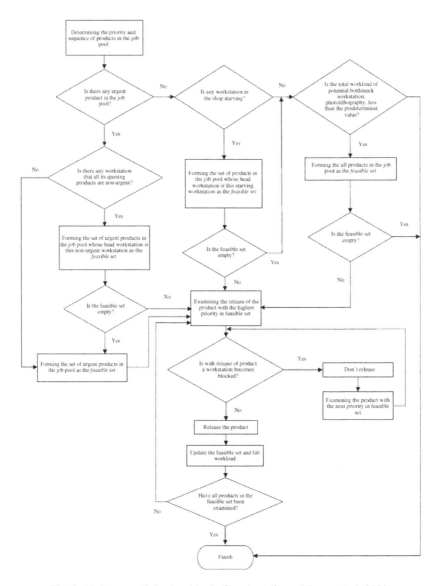

Fig. 1. Release-module algorithm's flowchart, from (Eivazy et al. 2009)

It tests the following release models:

1) DBR: which controls the number of jobs released but not yet completed at the bottleneck station. Orders can enter the shop floor only if the number of jobs are lower than the "buffer limit", and this evaluation is carried out whenever a job is added to the pre-shop pool (PSP) or an operation is completed at the bottleneck station.

2) CONWIP: the structure is similar to DBR, but the controlled station is the last one. Therefore, evaluation of release is based on the arrival at the PSP or when the job leaves the department.

3) Workload Control Continuous (WL-CON): it does not allow the release of a job if its contribution to the workload of stations make one of them to not fit a threshold, called norm. The evaluation of release is activated whenever a job arrives at the PSP or whenever an operation is completed.

4) Immediate Release (IM): it represents the absence of a controlled release.

Among the PSP-sequencing and dispatching rules proposed in the analysed literature, the ones able to identify urgent jobs given a set of orders have been selected. This is necessary to apply the prioritization principle proposed in the reference model: urgent MTO, urgent MTS, non-urgent MTO, and non-urgent MTS. Three alternatives have been selected:

- Critical Ratio (CR): it is the same rule applied by Eivazy et al. [10], hence it already fits the hybrid context. The information on due dates and predicted cycle time are drawn from pre-simulation runs.
- Modified Planned Release Date (MODPRD) and Modified Planned Bottleneck Start Time (MODPBST): they are, respectively, the PSP-sequencing and dispatching rules proposed for the drum schedule improvement. They have been conceived for the MTO context, therefore some modifications were necessary. Concerning the MTO jobs, the measure to establish the urgency remains the same of the literature, instead, for MTS it is applied the one of Critical Ratio, based on WIP and its planned values (taken from pre-simulation runs).
- First in First out (FIFO): which represents the absence of prioritization mechanism.

Models and rules have been tested in a flow shop configuration constituted by 5 stations as in previous studies [4, 22, 23], in which only one could be the bottleneck in the same simulation scenario. Referring to the previous research [15], the first station (Position 1) is considered to be the bottleneck position. Besides the common simulation entities that could be found in similar publications, another one has been added: the warehouse. This object store MTS jobs that have just been processed at the corresponding machine. This is important to realize the logic of MTS: customers withdraw products kept in the Finished Good Warehouse, and this triggers a replenishment mechanism that flow upstream till the PSP.

The processing time setting values are drawn from a statistical distribution taken from the literature, while in the base case a deterministic "total processing time" is established. MTO and MTS jobs differ for the variance of their distribution (lower for MTS, since more standardized), while their means are equal. Two levels of bottleneck severity have been selected, as to account for the following conditions: high and low [11].

Another aspect for the design of the model concerned the identification of the relative weight of MTS and MTO on the overall capacity managed by the system. Therefore, we set 480 min as the daily available time and 30 min as the average processing time of a job, the maximum daily capacity to 16 jobs. However, the value corresponds to the maximum utilization of machines, thus the value has been lowered to 15 jobs, as to account for a minimum degree of spare capacity. Once these values have been identified, another factor, called "MTS Weight", established the weight of MTS on these 15 jobs. These computations were fundamental for establishing: the arrival rate of MTO and the mean of the normal distribution constituting the demand of MTS products.

Finally, preliminary runs of simulations have been necessary for the setting of due date's parameters, predicted cycle times of both MTO and MTS and values for norms, buffer limit and total WIP. Parameters of the simulation model and the experimental setting are represented in Table 1.

Table 1. Design of experiment

Shop configuration studied	Pure flow shop
Number of machines	5
Capacity of each stage	480 time unit
Arrival rate distribution	Exponential
Processing time distribution MTO	Truncated log-normal Mean 30, variance 900 Minimum 0, maximum 360
Processing time distribution MTS	Truncated Log-normal Mean 30, variance 40 Minimum 0, maximum 360
Jobs contractual due date	Uniform [α, β]
ORR model	WL-Continuous, DBR, CONWIP, IM
Sequencing rule	FIFO, CR, MODPRD
Dispatching rule	FIFO, CR, MODPBST
Rule levels (Norms, Buffer Limit, Total WIP)	6-levels for each rule WLC-Norms: 72, 90, 120, 150, 420, 540 DBR-Buffer Limit: 2, 4, 6, 10, 15, 35 CONWIP-Total WIP: 10, 15, 20, 30, 60, 70
Bottleneck position	Position 1
Bottleneck severity	0.65, 0.80
MTS weight	30% of 15 jobs

It is important to notice that not all combinations between sequencing and dispatching factors have been included in the experiment. It is more likely that a company adopts a unique logic for these prioritization aspects, therefore the selected levels respect this observation (in all the document, the first acronym stands for sequencing, the second for dispatching):

1. FIFO – FIFO
2. FIFO – CR
3. CR – CR
4. FIFO – MODPBST
5. MODPRD – MODPBST

The response variables monitored are: MTO Gross Throughput Time (GTT), that is the overall lead time, from arrival at the PSP to the completion; the MTO Shop Floor Time (SFT) that is the time from the release to the completion; the tardiness, composed by percentage of tardy jobs, mean tardiness and standard deviation of lateness; and the production achievement, that is the performance of interest for MTS jobs, and it is defined as the average values of the percentage of the daily customer demand that the company is able to satisfy. Each scenario is replicated 10 times and the average value for each performance measure is used for analysis. Paired t-test is performed whenever there is significant difference in results.

4 Results and Conclusions

The analysis of results has been conducted following the concept of scenario defined by the levels of: bottleneck position, severity and MTS weight. We firstly reported a preliminary investigation aimed at understanding whether the scenario-factors produce results in line with the literature and with the design phase. Expectations are generally respected. However, CONWIP shows better performances when the bottleneck is positioned at the first station, in contrast to findings in Thürer et al. [18], but in line with previous researches [15]. This deviation is reasonable considering the impact of dispatching rules, since in prior studies it is shown how this may lead to different conclusions; the fact that this simulation uses different parameter setting could affect results.

The core of the analysis focused on the control of the time-performance curves (defined as GTT versus SFT) of the different release rules and on their relative positioning varying scenarios factors. As found also in previous studies, the PSP-sequencing does not add relevant benefit to time performances. Therefore, it is not considered in the main analysis. But it can be observed that to select the proper release rule, the choice of the dispatching is a very significant one to consider, given different levels of severity. In contexts characterized by high severity (0.80), MODPBST is the best performing rule, and especially in combinations with the DBR rule, especially at shorter shop floor time (Fig. 2).

On the other hand, if FIFO rule is applied under high severity, WLC is the most appropriate release rule (Fig. 3). The difference between Fig. 2 and Fig. 3 is explained by the Immediate Release point. Immediate Release is obtained at much lower shop floor time with MODPBST rule than with FIFO rule. This justifies MODPBST performs better than FIFO dispatching rule.

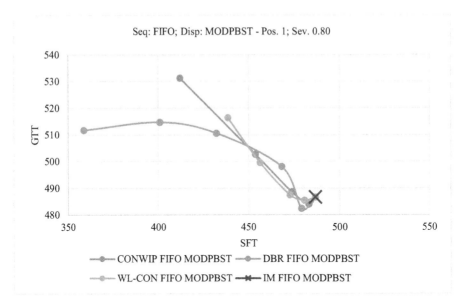

Fig. 2. Performance curve comparison in case of high severity and MODPBST dispatching.

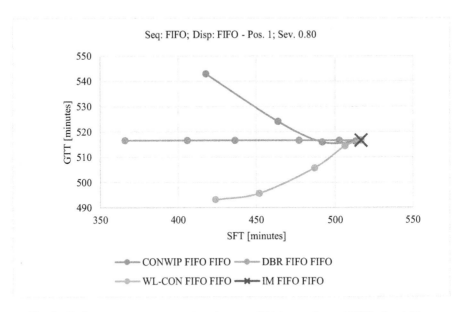

Fig. 3. Performance curve comparison in case of high severity and FIFO dispatching.

At severity level 0.65, WLC is still the best choice compared to the other possibilities with FIFO dispatching. It seems that WLC does not require additional control at dispatching in order to obtain the best performance. A plausible justification comes from the balancing capabilities of WLC that effectively manage the differences between the two typologies of orders. The last rule considered, CR, is completely outperformed by others: probably due to fact that the rule exploits static information on cycle times and also to its inner inefficient effects.

Once the best values for the time performances of MTO (the most important measure) have been found, for sake of completeness, the analysis continues investigating the trade-offs for the other dimension of interest that could be identified choosing between different dispatching rules (i.e. tardiness and production achievement).

It is shown how MODPBST, as in literature, guarantees the best performances in terms of tardiness and percentage tardy, while FIFO worsens these values. Contrarily, looking at production achievement of MTS, FIFO is the most performing rule, since it does not implement an explicit system of prioritization of MTO over MTS.

Given the observations on this part of simulation results, it can be said that the categorical dominance of one compared to the other cannot be stated. Not only the decision of the proper release rule depends on the severity level, as found in the pure MTO context, but also it has to be considered whether a control at dispatching level is implemented. In fact, it influences tradeoffs which decision makers have to carefully analyze in terms of time, tardiness and production achievement.

4.1 Implications and Future Research

From a practical point of view, the research highlights the main trade-offs that managers have to face in this type of hybrid MTO-MTS production system. In case of high severity, managers have to take into account that choosing MODPBST as dispatching leads to the best performance in terms of MTO lead times and tardiness, which implies higher control cost and lower capability of meeting daily demands of MTS product. Instead, in case of low severity, MODPBST loses its better positioning in terms of MTO lead time. When choosing FIFO as dispatching, thus Workload Control at release level, specular performances for the mentioned indicators are observed at different severity levels.

The results presented in this paper depend on the validation made during the design of the simulation model and its parameters. The research is the first attempt to conceptualize this context through the presented model, therefore future researches are needed to test the worthiness of results. Other possible streams for future efforts may include: different positions of the bottleneck, different values for the MTS weight, different values for the bottleneck severity, the study of environmental factors (e.g. machine failure); testing periodic release models; the deepening of the relation between CONWIP and DBR; and finally, the study of the production achievement performance and the CR dispatching rule.

References

1. Francas, D., Löhndorf, N., Minner, S.: Machine and labor flexibility in manufacturing networks. Int. J. Prod. Econ. **131**(1), 165–174 (2011)
2. Kingsman, B., Hendry, L., Mercer, A., De Souza, A.: Responding to customer enquiries in make-to-order companies problems and solutions. Int. J. Prod. Econ. **46–47**, 219–231 (1996)
3. Kingsman, B., Hendry, L.: The relative contributions of input and output controls on the performance of a workload control system in make-to-order companies. Prod. Plan. Control **13**(7), 579–590 (2002)
4. Kundu, K., Land, M.J., Portioli-Staudacher, A., Bokhorst, J.A.: Order review and release in make-to-order flow shops: analysis and design of new methods. Flex. Serv. Manuf. J., 1–33 (2020).https://doi.org/10.1007/s10696-020-09392-6
5. Rossini, M., Audino, F., Costa, F., Cifone, F.D., Kundu, K., Portioli-Staudacher, A.: Extending lean frontiers: a Kaizen case study in an Italian MTO manufacturing company. Int. J. Adv. Manuf. Technol. **104**(5–8), 1869–1888 (2019). https://doi.org/10.1007/s00170-019-03990-x
6. Eivazy, H., Rabbani, M.: A novel production control model for manufacturing systems with pure MTS, pure MTO, and hybrid MTS-MTO products. In: 2009 International Conference on Computers and Industrial Engineering, CIE 2009 (2009)
7. Fernandes, N.O., Gomes, M., Carmo-Silva, S.: Workload control and order release in combined MTO-MTS production. Rom. Rev. Prec. Mech. Opt. Mechatron. **43**, 33–39 (2013)
8. Małachowski, B., Korytkowski, P.: Competence-based performance model of multi-skilled workers. Comput. Ind. Eng. **91**, 165–177 (2016)
9. Soman, C.A., Van Donk, D.P., Gaalman, G.: Combined make-to-order and make-to-stock in a food production system. Int. J. Prod. Econ. **90**(2), 223–235 (2004)
10. Eivazy, H., Rabbani, M., Ebadian, M.: A developed production control and scheduling model in the semiconductor manufacturing systems with hybrid make-to-stock/make-to-order products. Int. J. Adv. Manuf. Tech. **45**(9), 968–986 (2009)
11. Thürer, M., Stevenson, M., Silva, C., Qu, T.: Drum-buffer-rope and workload control in high-variety flow and job shops with bottlenecks: an assessment by simulation. Int. J. Prod. Econ. **188**, 116–127 (2017)
12. Thürer, M., Stevenson, M.: Bottleneck-oriented order release with shifting bottlenecks: an assessment by simulation. Int. J. Prod. Econ. **197**, 275–282 (2018)
13. Ashcroft, S.H.: Applying the principles of optimized production technology in a small manufacturing company. Eng. Cost. Prod. Econ. **17**(1–4), 79–88 (1989)
14. Goldratt, E.M., Cox, J.: The Goal: A Process of Ongoing Improvement. North River Press, Croton-on-Hudson, NY (1984)
15. Thürer, M., Stevenson, M.: On the beat of the drum: improving the flow shop performance of the Drum–Buffer–Rope scheduling mechanism. Int. J. Prod. Res. **56**(9), 3294–3305 (2018)
16. Thürer, M., Qu, T., Stevenson, M., Li, C.D., Huang, G.Q.: Deconstructing bottleneck shiftiness: the impact of bottleneck position on order release control in pure flow shops. Prod. Plan. Control **28**(15), 1223–1235 (2017)
17. Spearman, M.L., Woodruff, D.L., Hopp, W.J.: CONWIP: a pull alternative to Kanban. Int. J. Prod. Res. **28**(5), 879–894 (1990)
18. Framinan, J.M., González, P.L., Ruiz-Usano, R.: The CONWIP production control system: review and research issues. Prod. Plan. Control **14**(3), 255–265 (2003)

19. Hopp, W., Spearman, M.: Basic factory dynamics. In: Factory Physics: Foundations of Manufacturing Management (1996)
20. Herer, Y.T., Masin, M.: Mathematical programming formulation of CONWIP based production lines; and relationships to MRP. Int. J. Prod. Res. **35**(4), 1067–1076 (1997)
21. Spearman, M.L., Hopp, W.J., Woodruff, D.L.: A hierarchical control architecture for Constant Work-in-Process (CONWIP) production systems. J. Manuf. Opers. Manag. **2**, 147–171 (1989)
22. Portioli-Staudacher, A., Costa, F., Thürer, M.: The use of labour flexibility for output control in workload controlled flow shops: a simulation analysis. Int. J. Ind. Eng. Comput. **11**(3), 429–442 (2020)
23. Kundu, K., Rossini, M., Portioli-Staudacher, A.: Analysing the impact of uncertainty reduction on WLC methods in MTO flow shops. Prod. Manuf. Res. **6**(1), 328–344 (2018)

Additive Manufacturing and Mass Customization

Impact of Failure Rate Uncertainties on the Implementation of Additive Manufacturing in Spare Parts Supply Chains

Mirco Peron[1(✉)], Nils Knofius[2], Rob Basten[3], and Fabio Sgarbossa[1]

[1] Department of Mechanical and Industrial Engineering, Norwegian University of Science and Technology, S P Andersens V 3, 7031 Trondheim, Norway
mirco.peron@ntnu.no
[2] Fieldmade AS, Torvet 6, 2000 Lillestrøm, Norway
[3] School of Industrial Engineering, Eindhoven University of Technology, PO Box 513, 5600 MB Eindhoven, The Netherlands

Abstract. The world of spare parts may be revolutionized by the advent of additive manufacturing (AM). Thanks to the possibility to manufacture spare parts on-demand, AM has attracted great attention in the last years as a substitute of conventional manufacturing techniques (CM). However, both researchers and practitioners point out two main limitations that might hinder the transition from CM to AM for the manufacturing of spare parts: AM parts' high production costs and uncertain failure rate. While the former limitation will most likely be overcome in the near future, the latter remains an open issue, so far uninvestigated. We therefore aim to investigate the effect of uncertain failure rate estimates on the optimal inventory level and on the total costs of spare parts management. To do so, we adapt a periodic inventory management policy available in the literature to include failure rate uncertainties and perform a parametrical analysis to investigate their impact varying the mean values of the failure rate, the lead times, and the unitary backorder and production costs. From the results it emerged that the effects of the failure rate uncertainties on the optimal inventory level and on the total costs of spare parts management increases exponentially, leading to a divergence up to 250% for both.

Keywords: Failure rate uncertainty · Spare parts · Additive manufacturing

1 Introduction

Spare parts management represents a crucial aspect in nowadays society where highly available production systems are required. However, efficient spare parts management is often challenging, due to, e.g., intermittent demands (difficult to forecast both in terms of quantity and frequency), strong dependency on suppliers, long procurement lead times, and high downtime costs [1, 2].

Recently, Additive Manufacturing (AM) has emerged as a way to overcome these challenges: AM enables the manufacturing of parts in an economic and fast fashion, in addition to the possibility to manufacture spare parts close to the point of use [3]. By manufacturing spare parts on-demand, AM can reduce the high inventory levels

A. Dolgui et al. (Eds.): APMS 2021, IFIP AICT 634, pp. 291–299, 2021.
https://doi.org/10.1007/978-3-030-85914-5_31

necessary to cope with intermittent demand and to avoid the risk of incurring high downtime costs, while, especially when in-sourced, it can decrease the dependency on suppliers. Moreover, AM can positively affect also the environmental footprint by reducing the resource consumption (the amount of raw material required in the supply chain is reduced, as well as the need wasteful and polluting manufacturing processes) and the emissions of air pollutant from transportation (spare parts can be manufactured close to the point of use) [4].

Consequently, driven by the potential benefits of lower inventory levels, overall costs and environmental footprint, researchers and practitioners have started investigating the suitability of AM in the spare parts management field, evaluating under which conditions (e.g., demand, backorder costs, lead times, etc.) AM was economically beneficial, including also considerations about the possibility to produce spare parts directly on the point of use [5–8]. However, these results highly rely on the assumptions and on the parameters considered, especially on the consideration of different mechanical properties between AM and conventional manufacturing (CM) parts. Westerweel et al., for example, adopting a lifecycle cost analysis where different designing costs and potential benefits associated with AM parts were also considered, confirmed the high impact of mechanical properties differences on the profitability of AM as manufacturing technique [7]. Mechanical properties like tensile and fatigue strength, in fact, determine when the failure of a part will occur (and hence its failure rate): under the same working conditions, the higher the mechanical properties, the later in time the part will fail. Whereas in the pioneering works the mechanical properties of AM and CM parts were considered identical, it has recently become common practice to consider AM parts characterized by lower mechanical properties (and hence by higher failure rates) than CM counterparts [9]. However, although the assumption of lower mechanical properties held true in the past when AM techniques started being investigated, the use of post-process operations (e.g., polishing, Hot Isostatic Pressing, and Annealing) has recently shown to lead to mechanical properties equal or even higher than those of CM parts [10–12]. This was confirmed by Sgarbossa et al., who, investigating the scenarios for which the use of AM for spare parts management would result economically beneficial over CM, deployed an interdisciplinary approach in which they derived AM mechanical properties with material science techniques for different AM techniques and post-processing combinations [13].

From the analysis of these works, it emerges that a current characteristic feature of AM parts is the mechanical properties uncertainties, which might hinder their use. Westerweel et al., for example, stated that *"a current limitation of AM technology is that there is often uncertainty concerning the mechanical properties of such parts"* [7]. Similarly, Knofius et al. reported that together with high unit cost *"low and uncertain reliabilities of printed parts often rule out the use of AM"* [9]. The uncertainty in the mechanical properties corresponds in turn to the uncertainty in the failure rates, which represents, however, an overlooked issue.

The effects of failure rate uncertainties have only recently started being investigated for CM parts. Specifically, van Wingerden et al. evaluated their impact on the holding costs and on the number of backorders [14]. However, dealing with AM, despite failure rate uncertainties even higher than those of the CM parts (due to the limited knowledge of these techniques) and their assumed importance, no one has addressed this problem yet to the best of our knowledge. It thus remains unclear to which extent failure rate uncertainties impact the benefits of AM in spare parts supply chains. This work represents a first step and will investigate the effects of failure rate uncertainties on the total cost and the optimal inventory policy. To model the failure rate uncertainty, we considered the failure rate not to be known precisely but to be normally distributed with a certain mean value (λ) and with a standard deviation σ. The effects of these uncertainties on the optimal inventory level and the total costs of spare parts management were then determined through a parametrical analysis considering more 7,500 scenarios derived from practice, and the results are reported in Sect. 3. Details about the methodology used can instead be found in Sect. 2.

It is worth mentioning that the main goal of this work is that of rendering clear to the scientific community the great errors that would be committed by neglecting the failure rate uncertainties.

2 Method

To understand how the failure rate uncertainties can impact the optimal inventory level and the total costs of spare parts management, we carried out a parametrical analysis where 7,500 different scenarios were developed. Specifically, first we developed the benchmark solution where we assumed the failure rate to be known. Here, the optimal inventory level and the total costs of spare parts management were determined considering the periodic review model with Poisson distributed demand also used by Sgarbossa et al. [13]. It is worth mentioning that this model holds true only when we are in the "random failures" area of the bathtub curve [15]. The total costs C_{tot} has been measured according to Eq. 1, and it is defined as the sum of holding costs C_h, backorder costs C_b and production costs C_p, which are in turn defined in Eqs. 2, 3 and 4, respectively.

$$C_{tot} = C_h + C_b + C_p; \tag{1}$$

$$C_h = h \cdot c_p \cdot \sum_{y=0}^{S-1} (S - y) \cdot P_{\lambda, T+L, y}; \tag{2}$$

$$C_b = c_b \cdot \sum_{y=S+1}^{\infty} (y - S) \cdot P_{\lambda, T+L, y}; \tag{3}$$

$$C_p = \lambda \cdot c_p, \tag{4}$$

where S is the order-up-to-level, y is the stochastic demand (i.e., the number of failures in the period $T + L$), L is the lead time, T is the review period, h is the holding cost rate, c_p and c_b are the unitary production and backorder costs, respectively, λ is the failure rate and $P_{\lambda, T+L, y}$ is the probability of having y failures over the period $T + L$ given the failure rate λ.

The optimal inventory level S^* is the order-up-to-level that minimizes the total costs.

Second, we adapted the formulas to take into consideration the failure rate uncertainties. Specifically, we considered the uncertainty in the failure rate to follow a normal distribution, leading to the holding costs C_h, backorder costs C_b and production costs C_p to be now modelled according to Eqs. 5, 6 and 7, respectively.

$$C_h = h \cdot c_p \cdot \int_0^\infty f(x) \cdot \sum_{y=0}^{S-1} (S - y) \cdot P_{x,T+L,y} dx; \qquad (5)$$

$$C_b = c_b \cdot \int_0^\infty f(x) \cdot \sum_{y=S+1}^\infty (y - S) \cdot P_{x,T+L,y} dx; \qquad (6)$$

$$C_p = c_p \cdot \int_0^\infty f(x) \cdot x dx, \qquad (7)$$

where x is a random variable following a normal distribution N with mean λ and standard deviation σ. The associated probability density function is expressed by $f(x)$.

Then, we carried out the parametrical analysis considering 7,500 different scenarios using data obtained from discussions with experts in the field and from the literature [8, 9, 13]. Specifically, we aimed to cover different spare parts supply chain scenarios. We considered three values of the unitary backorder cost c_b in order to cover three possible situations (i.e., low, medium and high costs related to production losses), nine values of the cost ratio $\frac{c_b}{c_p}$ (from now on we will refer to this simply as *cost ratio*) to cover different part sizes and materials (big and metallic parts are covered considering low cost ratios, while small and plastic parts are considered with high cost ratios), five values of failure rate λ to consider different part consumptions, five values of the lead time L to include both in-source and out-source AM production (0.2 week, which corresponds to one working day, and 0.6 week, which corresponds to three working days reflect the in-source production, while 1, 1.5 and 2 weeks reflect the out-source production), and ten values of uncertainties in the failure rate, expressed through the standard deviation σ. Specifically, the values of the failure rate were chosen considering the suggestions of Knofius et al. [9]. They reported, in fact, that AM is perceived valuable in low-volume applications, i.e., "*on scenarios where the combination of failure rate and installed base size causes 1 to 7 demands per year*". Based on this, we considered in our work scenarios where the spare parts demand ranges from 4 parts per year to 1 part every 3 years. The different values considered for the analysis are reported in Table 1.

Table 1. Parameters adopted in the parametrical analysis.

Parameters	Value(s)	Unit
Unitary backorder cost (c_b)	5,000; 25,000; 50,000;	€/week
λ	0.005; 0.01; 0.02; 0.04; 0.08	1/weeks
L	0.2; 0.6; 1; 1.5; 2	Weeks
Cost ratio $\left(\frac{c_b}{c_p}\right)$	20; 40; 60; 80; 100; 120; 140; 160; 180; 200	-
Standard deviation (σ)	5; 10; 15; 20; 25; 30; 35; 40; 45; 50	%

Another input parameter is the holding rate h which was assumed constant and equal to 0.58% of the production cost on a weekly basis (it is common practice to consider it equal 30% of the production cost on a yearly basis [16]). It is worth mentioning that the standard deviation is given as percentage of the mean value (i.e., λ), and we consider that the order for AM can be placed every L periods, meaning that $T = L$.

Finally, we considered the effects of failure rate uncertainties on the optimal inventory level and on the total costs as difference with the benchmark solution. Specifically, the effects of failure rate uncertainties on the optimal inventory level were considered through the parameter ΔS^* (Eq. 8), while those on the total costs through the parameter ΔC_{tot} (Eq. 9).

$$\Delta S^* = S^*_{uncertainty} - S^*_{benchmark}; \tag{8}$$

$$\Delta C_{tot} = \frac{C_{tot,uncertainty} - C_{tot,benchmark}}{C_{tot,benchmark}} \cdot 100, \tag{9}$$

$S^*_{uncertainty}$ and $S^*_{benchmark}$ represent the optimal inventory level and $C_{tot,uncertainty}$ and $C_{tot,benchmark}$ the total costs with uncertain failure rate and known failure rate, respectively. The parameter ΔC_{tot} is expressed in percentages.

3 Results and Discussions

The results of the parametrical analysis were then used as inputs in a main effects analysis to understand the importance of the various parameters on ΔS^* and ΔC_{tot}, and the results are reported in Fig. 1 and Fig. 2, respectively.

From the main effects plot it is interesting to see that the unitary backorder cost c_b affects neither ΔS^* nor ΔC_{tot}, but what matters (in terms of costs) is the ratio $\frac{c_b}{c_p}$. This can be explained mathematically. Starting from the latter, considering Eq. 9, if we introduce in the formula the ratio $\frac{c_b}{c_p}$ (by simply dividing Eq. 9 by c_p) and if we render it explicit, we obtain the following:

$$
\begin{aligned}
&\Delta C_{tot} \\
&= \frac{\left(h \cdot \int_0^\infty f(x) \cdot \sum_{y=0}^{S-1}(S-y) \cdot P_{x,T+L,y}dx + \frac{c_b}{c_p} \cdot \int_0^\infty f(x) \cdot \sum_{y=S+1}^{\infty}(y-S) \cdot P_{x,T+L,y}dx + c_p \cdot \int_0^\infty f(x) \cdot xdx \right)}{\left(h \cdot \sum_{y=0}^{S-1}(S-y) \cdot P_{\lambda,T+L,y} + \frac{c_b}{c_p} \cdot \sum_{y=S+1}^{\infty}(y-S) \cdot P_{\lambda,T+L,y} + \lambda \right)} \\
&\quad - \frac{\left(h \cdot \sum_{y=0}^{S-1}(S-y) \cdot P_{\lambda,T+L,y} + \frac{c_b}{c_p} \cdot \sum_{y=S+1}^{\infty}(y-S) \cdot P_{\lambda,T+L,y} + \lambda \right)}{\left(h \cdot \sum_{y=0}^{S-1}(S-y) \cdot P_{\lambda,T+L,y} + \frac{c_b}{c_p} \cdot \sum_{y=S+1}^{\infty}(y-S) \cdot P_{\lambda,T+L,y} + \lambda \right)}
\end{aligned}
\tag{10}
$$

It can be seen that ΔC_{tot} does not depend on the unitary backorder cost c_b, hence explaining the results reported in the main effects plot. Moreover, since the optimal inventory level S^* is the order-up-to-level that minimizes the total costs, if these do not depend on the unitary backorder cost c_b, then neither the ΔS^*. It is worth mentioning

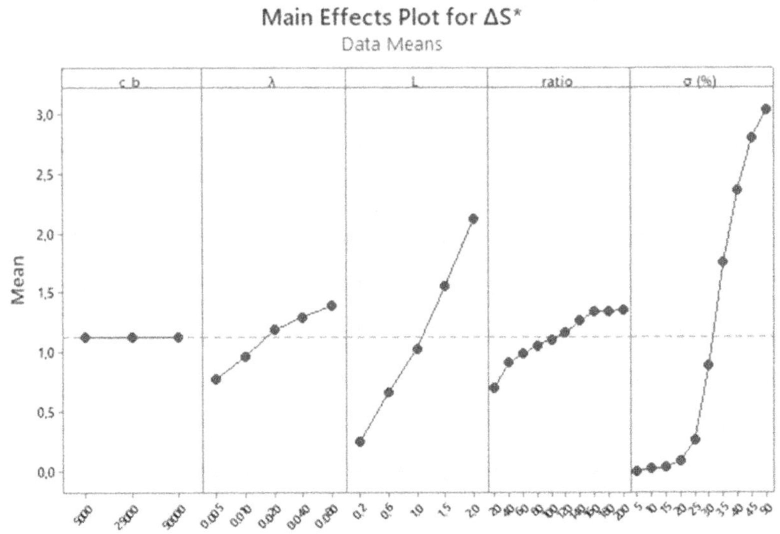

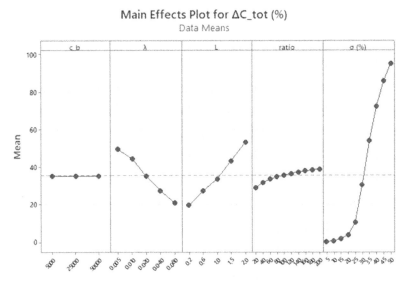

Fig. 1. Main effects plot for ΔS^*, where c_b is the unitary backorder cost, λ the failure rate, L the lead time, $\frac{c_b}{c_p}$ the cost ratio (i.e., the ratio between the unitary backorder costs and the unitary production costs), and σ the standard deviation.

Fig. 2. Main effects plot for ΔC_{tot}, where c_b is the unitary backorder cost, λ the failure rate, L the lead time, $\frac{c_b}{c_p}$ the cost ratio (i.e., the ratio between the unitary backorder costs and the unitary production costs), and σ the standard deviation.

that this holds true only in this case since we consider the differences and the relative differences for the optimal inventory levels and for the total costs, respectively: if we had considered the absolute values this would have not held true.

The main observation, however, is the fact that the failure rate uncertainties (σ) affect both ΔS^* and ΔC_{tot}, and that their effect increases exponentially. Specifically, the effect remains contained on both ΔS^* and ΔC_{tot} for $\sigma < 20\%$, for then diverging. Indeed, with $\sigma > 20\%$, 97% of the times the optimal inventory level is higher than that of the benchmark solution, while the percentage variation in the total costs ΔC_{tot} varies from 4% to 242% (ΔC_{tot} is always lower than 7% when $\sigma < 20\%$). Specifically, the lower variations occur when the lead times are low and the failure rates are high, while the higher variations when the lead times are high and the failure rates are low.

From this, it emerges the need to keep the failure rate uncertainties as low as possible in order to minimize the mistakes that would be made otherwise by neglecting it in the spare parts management. To do so, it is fundamental that researchers and practitioners in the material science field focus on two different and concurrent aspects, i.e. (i) a mechanistic knowledge of the failure behavior of AM parts and (ii) an improved monitoring of the AM manufacturing processes. The former, achievable through an experimental and theoretical understanding of the behavior of AM components, would in fact allow practitioners and researchers to be able to accurately determine the microstructure of a specific part just by knowing the process parameters used and then to relate it to a precise estimation of the mechanical properties (and hence of the failure rate) thanks to a plethora of experimental data (data-driven approach) [12]. The second aspect, then, would favor a more precise determination of the failure rate by carrying out in-situ observations during the manufacturing of the parts: by knowing the shape and heat distribution of the melt pool it is in fact possible to predict the presence of defects within the parts, and hence to estimate the mechanical properties (and hence of the failure rate) thanks to the knowledge developed in aspect (i) [17].

4   Conclusions and Future Research

In this work we aim to understand the impact of failure rate uncertainties on the optimal inventory level and on the total costs of spare parts management. This represents in fact a very important issue that has however been overlooked by researchers and practitioners despite its well-known importance. Researchers and practitioners, in fact, have focused on understanding under which conditions (failure rates, production and backorder costs, lead times, locations of the facilities, etc.) the transition from CM to AM for producing spare parts is beneficial, but they have completely overlooked the failure rate uncertainties despite their well-known importance for the final suitability of AM. In this work we have hence addressed this topic, with the principal purpose of render clear to the scientific community the great errors that would be committed by neglecting the failure rate uncertainties.

To do so, we modify a periodic review model to consider failure rate uncertainties and we carried out a parametrical analysis considering 7,500 different scenarios. From the results it emerged that the failure rate uncertainties (σ) has an exponentially increasing effect both on the optimal inventory level and on the total costs (evaluated through ΔS^* and ΔC_{tot}, respectively). This confirms the assumption reported in the literature that mechanical properties uncertainties (and hence failure rate uncertainties) are a major hold back on the switch from CM to AM for the manufacturing of spare parts. Only minor failure rate uncertainties are thus acceptable to build efficient spare parts supply chains with AM, and from our analyses a limit of 20% seems to be sufficient. In fact, from our finding, almost 97% of the times that $\Delta S^* > 0$ σ was greater than 20%. Similarly, the impact on the total costs is limited when $\sigma \leq 20\%$ (the percentage variation in the total costs ΔT_c is always lower than 7%). However, further analyses are needed to confirm the validity of 20% as limit.

Based on these results, it should emerge clearly the importance of including the failure rate uncertainties in the spare parts management analysis, and practitioners can use the modified periodic model reported in Eqs. 5–7 to determine the order-up-to-level that considers their values of the failure rate uncertainties. Moreover, based on these results, we aim to point out the need for researchers and practitioners in material science to reduce the uncertainty in the failure rate, and this can be achieved through a combined approach that aims to increase both the knowledge of the failure behavior of AM parts and the monitoring operations of the AM manufacturing processes. This represents a fundamental step for exploiting the full benefits of AM for spare parts management since it will break down one of the two main barriers limiting its use.

Moreover, managers need to be assisted in the decision of the best sourcing option (CM or AM). Although we discussed in Sect. 1 that something has already started moving, much still needs to be done. This will represent the main focus of our future research activities, where we will focus on the development of a robust DSS able to handle the failure rate uncertainties to ensure the correct decision about sourcing options, so whether a spare part should be produced using AM or CM, and this work represents a crucial milestone of our future research activities, without which we could not go ahead. It is in fact fundamental to understand the correct impact of the failure rate uncertainties to be able to develop such a robust DSS.

References

1. Huiskonen, J.: Maintenance spare parts logistics: special characteristics and strategic choices. Int. J. Prod. Econ. **71**(1–3), 125–133 (2001)
2. Roda, I., Arena, S., Macchi, M., Orrù, P.F.: Total cost of ownership driven methodology for predictive maintenance implementation in industrial plants. In: Ameri, F., Stecke, K.E., von Cieminski, G., Kiritsis, D. (eds.) APMS 2019. IAICT, vol. 566, pp. 315–322. Springer, Cham (2019). https://doi.org/10.1007/978-3-030-30000-5_40
3. Walter, M., Holmström, J., Yrjölä, H.: Rapid manufacturing and its impact on supply chain management. In proceedings of the logistics research network annual conference, 9–10 (2004)
4. Peng, T., Kellens, K., Tang, R., Chen, C., Chen, G.: Sustainability of additive manufacturing: an overview on its energy demand and environmental impact. Addit. Manuf. **21**, 694–704 (2018)
5. Song, J.S., Zhang, Y.: Stock or print? Impact of 3-D printing on spare parts logistics. Manage. Sci. **66**(9), 3860–3878 (2020)

6. Liu, P., Huang, S.H., Mokasdar, A., Zhou, H., Hou, L.: The impact of additive manufacturing in the aircraft spare parts supply chain: supply chain operation reference (Scor) model based analysis. Prod. Plan. Control **25**(13–14), 1169–1181 (2014)
7. Westerweel, B., Basten, R.J., van Houtum, G.J.: Traditional or additive manufacturing? Assessing component design options through lifecycle cost analysis. Eur. J. Oper. Res. **270** (2), 570–585 (2018)
8. Westerweel, B., Basten, R., den Boer, J., van Houtum, G.J.: Printing spare parts at remote locations: fulfilling the promise of additive manufacturing. Prod. Oper. Manage. **30**, 1615–1632 (2018)
9. Knofius, N., van der Heijden, M.C., Sleptchenko, A., Zijm, W.H.M.: Improving effectiveness of spare parts supply by additive manufacturing as dual sourcing option. OR Spectrum **43**(1), 189–221 (2020). https://doi.org/10.1007/s00291-020-00608-7
10. Liu, S., Shin, Y.C.: Additive manufacturing of Ti6Al4V alloy: a review. Mater. Des. **164**, 107552 (2019)
11. Beretta, S., Romano, S.: A comparison of fatigue strength sensitivity to defects for materials manufactured by AM or traditional processes. Int. J. Fatigue **94**, 178–191 (2017)
12. Peron, M., Torgersen, J., Ferro, P., Berto, F.: Fracture behaviour of notched as-built EBM parts: characterization and interplay between defects and notch strengthening behaviour. Theoret. Appl. Fract. Mech. **98**, 178–185 (2018)
13. Sgarbossa, F., Peron, M., Lolli, F., Balugani, E.: Conventional or additive manufacturing for spare parts management: an extensive comparison for Poisson demand. Int. J. Prod. Econ. **233**, 107993 (2021)
14. Van Wingerden, E., Tan, T., Van Houtum, G.J.: Spare parts management under double demand uncertainty. BETA publicatie: working papers (2017)
15. Ohring, M.: Engineering Materials Science. Elsevier (1995)
16. Azzi, A., Battini, D., Faccio, M., Persona, A., Sgarbossa, F.: Inventory holding costs measurement: a multi-case study. Int. J. Logistics Manage. **25**, 109–132 (2014)
17. Egan, D.S., Dowling, D.P.: Influence of process parameters on the correlation between in-situ process monitoring data and the mechanical properties of Ti-6Al-4V non-stochastic cellular structures. Addit. Manuf. **30**, 100890 (2019)

Mass Customization: Customizing for the Human Aspect of Operations Management

Håkon Lund(✉) ⓘ, Stine Sonen Tveit ⓘ, and Lars Skjelstad ⓘ

SINTEF Digital, S.P. Andersens veg 3, Trondheim, Norway
{haakon.lund,stine.tveit,lars.skjelstad}@sintef.no

Abstract. There is a tendency that the consumer market is getting more and more individualized as an effect of people craving customized products, and producers seeing this as an opportunity for earning more money on a product or service customized to a customer's specific needs. This customization increases the complexity tied to the product, not necessarily for the consumer, but typically for the producer. As the complexity of products are moved closer to the producer, the job of producing and/or assembling the end-product gets more complicated. For instance, a higher degree of flexibility will be needed, if compared to traditional mass production where one typically produces in bulk. This will again demand more from the organization and its employees in form of more responsive systems, machines, processes, and not least employees. In this paper we suggest a self-assessment form to measure the individual job satisfaction at the shopfloor and take one step in the direction of customizing the daily work of employees in mass customizing companies.

Keywords: Mass customization · Job design · Job satisfaction · Job coordination

1 Introduction

The core of any business model is to increase the value of a product through value creating activities. Today, end-customers are getting more comfortable buying online and specifying what they want with individualized products. The digital revolution is changing almost every industry and their business model, making the world more custom. The advances in manufacturing technologies and information systems have made it possible for companies to rapidly develop and manufacture products to meet customers specific needs economically viable [1].

Mass Customization (MC) as a business strategy puts the customer in center of operations, seeking to exploit the fact that every customer wants individual fitted offerings. MC can be defined as the ability to manufacture a high volume of product options for a large market that demands customization, without substantial tradeoffs in cost, delivery, and quality [2]. This business strategy has slowly replaced or, in some cases, supplemented mass production in the industry [3]. MC has gained increased focus over the past years and companies in various manufacturing industries such as

© IFIP International Federation for Information Processing 2021
Published by Springer Nature Switzerland AG 2021
A. Dolgui et al. (Eds.): APMS 2021, IFIP AICT 634, pp. 300–308, 2021.
https://doi.org/10.1007/978-3-030-85914-5_32

electronics, furniture, jewelry, clothing, pharmaceuticals, food and beverages, etc. are focusing on how to meet the market demands with individual needs and wishes efficiently. According to Pine [4], principles for MC include speed, information, on-demand operations, dispatching, no finished goods inventory, digitalization/automatization, and modularization. If applied right in a manufacturing company, customers will experience the joy of numerous choices alongside prices and delivery times that can be expected from a mass producer. Three core capabilities are identified for mass customizers [5]; First, to design a solution space (SSD) that always hold offerings of interest to the customer. It is not a goal to make everything for everybody, but to be able to constantly update the product portfolio to reflect customers ever changing needs within the line of business the company is in. The second core capability is often denoted choice navigation (CN) and addresses how to help the customer to identify the exact right product from all possibilities without experiencing fatigue or mass confusion during the process. Often this is solved with the introduction of product configurators. The third capability is robust processes (RP), which points at the company's ability to fulfill orders rapidly and in any sequence they might appear. This last capability covers both technical and human aspects of the processes.

A key factor that facilitates MC is the way the work is organized within the company [6]. People are vital to the process. Viability depends on sufficient operator skill to handle increasingly complex shop floor tasks that stem from customizing products at a high speed. Only with the help of skilled people, both on the production line and in the design and engineering processes, will digital technologies enable MC to be economically feasible. MC companies operates with short delivery time and operators often have a sense-of-urgency towards delivering the product in good condition and at the right time.

Literature indicates that people with a high level of motivation and satisfaction at work often translate these positive experiences into a productive workforce [7]. In the same way MC companies understands the end-customers need for individualized products, one should also consider the need to distinguish according to operators' preferences at shopfloor level. Often in a production line the complexity of the activity may vary, and therefore in some workstations the work conditions are manageable for some, however, for others these activities and conditions give a greater strain on the operator. Short planning horizons might further add pressure to some employees. Let's also recognize that in i.e., manufacturing of modules, entirely different situations can be found, where small batch production of variants might dominate the scene.

The purpose of this research is to gain a greater insight into how job satisfaction criteria are met at the shopfloor in MC companies, and to form a basis for designing work-packages on an individual level. By developing a self-assessment form for this, companies can better understand how to optimize and customize, not only for end-customers, but also the everyday work of the operators.

The remainder of the paper is structured as follows; First, relevant work on the topic of job satisfaction is presented. Next, the research approach and context are described. Then, we present a self-assessment form for understanding and adjusting work conditions at shop-level in manufacturing companies. This includes a consideration of how MC is related to job satisfaction. Finally, the work is concluded, and limitations and future work is described.

2 Job Design

"Imagine designing the role of a police officer. Illustrative work design decisions include the following: Which activities should be grouped together to form a meaningful job? Which decisions should be made by officers and which by their supervisors? Should individual jobs be grouped together into a team? Can one build in routine tasks amid complex ones to ensure officers are not overwhelmed by demands? These decisions about the content and organization of officers' tasks, activities, relationships, and responsibilities will affect outcomes at multiple levels, including individual officers, such as how engaged they feel or their level of strain; the wider organization, such as whether the police service achieves its targets; and society, such as how effectively crime is detected and prevented." – elaborated by Parker and Sharon, [8].

Interest in the topic of job design, also called work design, arose as a response to the wide-scale adoption of scientific management principles in the design of early industrial jobs. The general thought was to design work systems with standardized operations and highly simplified work so that people could be just as interchangeable as standardized machine parts. A problem with this approach was that most people did not find the routinely, repetitive jobs motivating. This led the researcher Frederick Herzberg to specify that, to motivate employees to do good work, jobs should be enriched rather than simplified [9, 10]. This is when job design emerged from studies of alienating and meaningless jobs, where psychological research on the subject has motivation at its core [11]. At an individual level, job rotation, job enlargement, and job enrichment emerged as motivational countermoves to simplified jobs, where job enrichment is said to be the most important as an effect of its emphasis on increasing employees' autonomy [8]. The correlation between job design and job satisfaction has been researched. The results of studies confirms that there is a significant relationship between job design and job satisfaction [12, 13]. Additionally poor job design will undoubtedly bring about dissatisfaction [14]. Another study suggests that jobs which are interesting, motivating, and meaningful often supply employees with a high level of satisfaction, which translates into a productive workforce that can meet business goals [7].

Job design is defined as the system of arrangements and procedures for organizing work, including the set of activities that are undertaken to develop, produce, and deliver a product [15]. Work consists of five core job characteristics: Job variety, job autonomy, job feedback, job significance and lastly job identity [16]. For more in-depth literature on the topic of the five dimensions see [8]. Following beneath is a closer look at the core job characteristics through the dominant motivational model of job design, the job characteristics model (JCM) (Fig. 1):

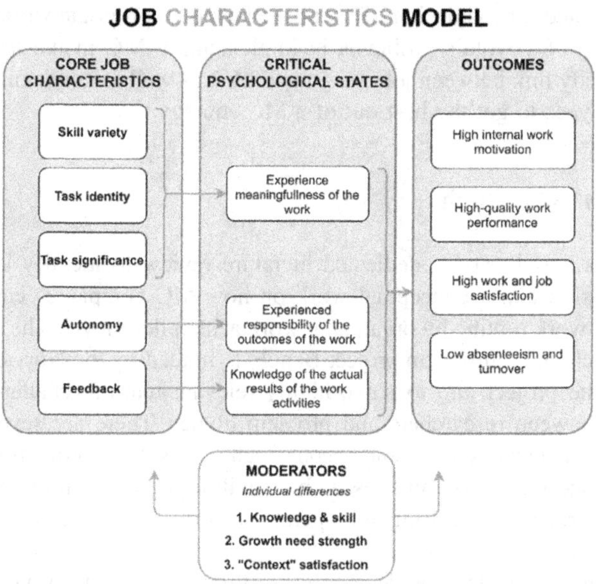

JOB CHARACTERISTICS MODEL

Fig. 1. The Job characteristics model, this recreation is based on the work of Oldham & Hackman [16]

Skill Variety: Refers to the range of abilities needed to perform a job. Monotony is not what most people look for in their dream job; conversely, employees want to be able to enlist various skills throughout their employment to avoid getting bored. Employee motivation will increase if your team members are using a variety of diverse skills in their positions, rather than one set skill repeatedly.

Task Identity: Means the extent to which a job involves completing an identifiable piece of work from start to finish, with a visible outcome. Motivated employees will be more likely to complete tasks if they identify with them and have seen them through from start to finish.

Task Significance: The extent to which a job is important to and impacts others within and outside of the organization is known as task significance. When employees feel that their work is significant to their organization, they are motivated to do well, and this will lead to increased employee productivity.

Autonomy: Measures each employee's level of freedom and ability to schedule tasks. Employees like to be able to make decisions and have flexibility in their roles.

Feedback: Refers to the degree to which an employee receives direct feedback on their performance. A team needs feedback to motivate employees in the long term.

Job content is a continuous process and should not be a single event that produces lasting structural changes in the design of work [17]. Campion [11] found that a group of highly trained, disciplined, and motivated workers were a key resource for the success of the MC-strategy in the National Bicycle Industrial Company. Oldham,

Hackman [16] cited for job design, remarks the lack of appropriate workforce skills, as the major cause of Toyota's problems in implementing MC in the late 1980s. This implies an already link between job design and MC, as well as confirming the need for satisfied employees to get the best out of a MC strategy.

3   Research Approach

The research is based upon a dedicated literature review to identify key aspects for optimal job design and a conceptual work on how MC companies can optimise the operators daily work routine by organizing work at shopfloor level. The study is part of the joint research and innovation project BeneFIT, funded by the Norwegian Research Council, and the project aim to solve highly relevant real-life challenges through a collaboration between researchers and problem holder. There are several employees with different competences, tasks and needs which makes the coordination on shopfloor level complex and throughout this research we will introduce a preliminary system for assessment criteria for optimising for operators within manufacturers with MC as a business strategy.

The first conceptual step, the development of the assessment form described in this paper, will be followed by another paper on results and findings from the self-assessment. The planned research design of the self-assessment results will include empirical data collected from approx. 100 operators in five different MC manufacturers. Through case studies within the manufacturers, it will be detected how the operators handle the enormous solution space daily, such as how inspired, comfortable, and motivated the work is perceived. Respondents of the suggested assessment form will be selected based on relevant competence and therefore represent operators at shopfloor and middle management.

4   Results and Discussion

Several researchers have previously suggested a link between MC and job design and describe it as challenging to succeed with MC as a business strategy without job satisfaction among operators [11, 16]. When comparing the MC Principles with the Job Characteristics, it is quickly revealed that there are several correlations between the two. For instance, a MC company with a large product-portfolio, and no finished goods inventory, needs to have high speed in production to meet customer demands towards delivery time. Which again would demand highly specialized operators who most likely would experience a high degree of fluctuating workload. Or rather, a workforce with a high degree of skill variety. Task significance can also be said to higher than in traditional mass producers where they have inventory of finished products, whereas every produced product will go to a specific customer, and not to an inventory where it may lay for a long period of time before it finally, and hopefully, finds its way to the end-customer. Another correlation is the information principle matched with the job characteristic feedback, there will be no feedback without information (Fig. 2).

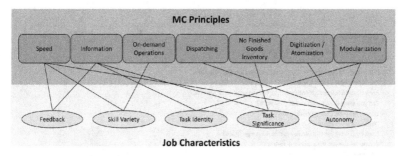

Fig. 2. Examples of correlation between MC principles and job characteristics.

This match between the principles and the characteristics makes us believe that MC companies are arranged for, or at least, has a good starting point for achieving a high degree of job satisfaction. However, this is only an assumption at this point, therefore we want to assess this through an assessment form.

When something is assessed at shopfloor level, for example with regards to ergonomics, it is often done for the 'average person'. However, for optimal results and solutions from such assessments there is a need to distinguish the individuals. The same challenges arise when studying the different value-creating activities. The work in a factory is composed of many different activities and types of work. For some, there are activities that are too challenging/time-pressured/physically heavy, and therefore the job becomes a place filled of stress and lack of control, while for others, the same activity is perceived motivating and satisfying. The goal of using this form is simply to get a greater insight into job satisfaction on an individual level. Which again will be crucial to be able to customize for a higher degree of satisfaction at the shopfloor, and therefore contribute to a higher productivity. Which is key resource for the success of the MC-strategy [18]. To meet the customers varying demands, with respect to volume and type of individual needs, operators in a MC company may have to move work-stations several times a day due to short-term demand. Once the needed amount of a component is produced, further movement may be necessary. Such a situation where operators need to orient on the instant need of the factory to face new order mixes never seen before can be demanding and have great strain on some, while not on others. By customizing it is possible to evenly balance the activities so everyone will have more of the activities themselves find motivating to gain a more productive workforce [7].

This research propose a form which is based on the five job design dimensions: variety, autonomy, feedback, significance, and identity. Through the eyes of job design, we will assess work with regards to the five dimensions (Fig. 3).

Self-assessment form: Job satisfaction

	Questions	Yes			No	Satisfied?		Comments?
		Day	Week	Month		Yes	No	
Skill variety	Does your work consist of varying tasks?							
	Do you feel montony?							
	Is the range of abilities needed to perform your job challenging?							
	Do you ever get bored at work?							
Task identity	Are you completing an identifyable part of the product or function?							
	Can you see a visual outcome of your work?							
	Do you feel you pass on work to early?							
	Does your work contain too much responsibility?							
Task Significance	Does your work contain elements that feels significant?							
	Do you find any of your tasks insignifcant?							
	meaningful?							
	Is your work important for the end customer?							
	Is your internal customer satisfied with your delivery?							
Autonomy	Do you have any freedom in your work to make own decisions?							
	Is it elements you can't decide/influence?							
	Can you influence on job-rotation?							
	Would you prefer more desicion-support?							
Feedback	Do you get significant feedback?							
	Is the feedback structured and constructive?							
	Does the feedback motivate you?							
	Does the team reflect on feedback together?							

Fig. 3. A minimized version of the form on job satisfaction.

When using the proposed question-form for the first time, it is important to have a common understanding of how it is supposed to be answered, even tough is seems simple and straightforward. This should preferably be presented for everyone in advance. When one does the assessment on a personal level, it should reflect the persons individual preferences and when possible, explain the thoughts behind the reasoning, in the comment section. This way the scientist, production management and/or other employees can get a better understanding of what entails a satisfactory job environment for the individual. The results from this form could ultimately be a supplement to the competence-matrix which is used by the production management when organizing and coordinating the operators. The results may also help managers by shedding light on which workstations include the heaviest or most unmotivating activities, which again could be candidates for automation, or to ensure a fair distribution of work tasks among the operators.

How often this assessment tool should be used will vary from company to company based on the situation. This is also supported through the recommendations from Sinha and Van de Van [12], who points out that organizations should be redesigned constantly and consistently to meet the changing need of workers as well as changes in the work environment.

When one does the assessment on a personal level, it should reflect the persons individual preferences and explain the reasoning behind the scores noted in the form. This way the production management and/or other employees can get a better understanding of what entails a satisfactory job environment for the individual. This process would ultimately create a fine meshed overview of the employee's satisfaction at every single process, which again could be a tool for the production management when organizing and coordinating the operators. Such a tool may also help managers by shedding light on which workstations includes the heaviest or most unmotivating activities to ensure a fair distribution of work tasks to achieve a high degree og satisfaction among operators.

5 Conclusion

The large variety found in operations within a MC company, such as one-of-a-kind manufacturing and assembly on one hand, and batch production of standardized modules on the other, constitutes an interesting arena for job-assessment, since operators are multi-skilled and have experience from different job situations.

The proposed assessment form for job satisfaction on an individual level raises the possibility of customizing the coordination and workload of the human capital at shopfloor level. This has the possibility of raising job satisfaction individually but also as a whole, and therefore contributing to a more efficient production. However, the effect of more individualized coordination at the shop floor may oppose other wanted effects or routines. One could for example experience that job-rotation would be limited as an effect of the customization, and therefore it is a possibility that it could lead to a more specialized workforce. Nevertheless, we do believe that it could also do the opposite if the implementation and continuous use is done with sufficient involvement from both employees and managers.

Another potential use is with regards to hiring new operators. When the assessment is done, one would have an overview of all the current operators, what tasks is the least liked, and therefore one could more easily locate the type of person which would fit the need on the shopfloor to the highest degree. From an automation viewpoint one could also assess what processes and tasks are best to automatize or digitize, with regards to satisfaction of the operators.

With regards to future work, one should evaluate the content of the assessment form and perhaps split it into several forms, personal and objective assessment. Then the assessment tool must move into an in-depth testing phase and exchange of experiences at the shopfloor.

References

1. Liu, G., Shah, R., Schroeder, R.G.: Linking work design to mass customization: a sociotechnical systems perspective. Decis. Sci. **37**(4), 519–545 (2006)
2. McCarthy, I.P.: Special issue editorial: the what, why and how of mass customization. Prod. Plan. Control **15**(4), 347–351 (2004)
3. Hart, C.W.: Mass customization: conceptual underpinnings, opportunities and limits. Int. J. Serv. Ind. Manage. **6**, 36–45 (1995)
4. Pine, B.J.: Lecture notes, from seminar on Mass Customization at Røros (2016)
5. Salvador, F., De Holan, P.M., Piller, F.: Cracking the code of mass customization. MIT Sloan Manag. Rev. **50**(3), 71–78 (2009)
6. Pine, B.J., Victor, B., Boynton, A.C.: Making mass customization work. Harv. Bus. Rev. **71**(5), 108–111 (1993)
7. Schermerhorn, J.R., et al.: Organizational Behaviour. Langara College (2006)

8. Parker, S.K.: Beyond motivation: Job and work design for development, health, ambidexterity, and more. Ann. Rev. Psychol. **65**, 661–691 (2014)
9. Herzberg, F.: The Managerial Choice: To be Efficient and to be Human. Irwin Professional Publishing (1976)
10. Herzberg, F.I.: Work and the Nature of Man (1966)
11. Campion, M.A.: Interdisciplinary approaches to job design: a constructive replication with extensions. J. Appl. Psychol. **73**(3), 467 (1988)
12. Oghojafor, B.A., Adebakin, M.A.: Assessment of job design and job satisfaction among doctors and nurses in Lagos, Nigeria hospitals. Afr. J. Bus. Manage. **6**(48), 11702–11706 (2012)
13. Michaels, C.E., Spector, P.E.: Causes of employee turnover: a test of the Mobley, Griffeth, Hand, and Meglino model. J. Appl. Psychol. **67**(1), 53 (1982)
14. Taylor, R.: Evaluating an instrument designed to assess job satisfaction of airline passenger service staff. Res. Pract. Hum. Resour. Manag. **12**(1), 172–183 (2004)
15. Sinha, K.K., Van de Ven, A.H.: Designing work within and between organizations. Organ. Sci. **16**(4), 389–408 (2005)
16. Oldham, G.R., Hackman, J.R., Pearce, J.L.: Conditions under which employees respond positively to enriched work. J. Appl. Psychol. **61**(4), 395 (1976)
17. Berg, J.M., Wrzesniewski, A., Dutton, J.E.: Perceiving and responding to challenges in job crafting at different ranks: when proactivity requires adaptivity. J. Organ. Behav. **31**(2–3), 158–186 (2010)
18. Kotha, S.: From mass production to mass customization: the case of the National Industrial Bicycle Company of Japan. Eur. Manag. J. **14**(5), 442–450 (1996)

Impacts of Additive Manufacturing on Supply Chains: An Empirical Investigation

Albraa A. Noorwali[1,2(✉)], M. Zied Babai[2], and Yves Ducq[1]

[1] University of Bordeaux, CNRS, IMS, UMR 5218, 33405 Talence, France
albraa.noorwali@kedgebs.com, yves.ducq@u-bordeaux.fr
[2] Kedge Business School, 680 cours de la Libération, 33405 Talence, France
mohamed-zied.babai@kedgebs.com

Abstract. Over the last decade, Additive Manufacturing has received an increased attention as many manufacturing companies have increasingly adopted new technologies to capture new opportunities. This research identifies the impacts of Additive Manufacturing (AM) on the supply chain when compared to the case of conventional manufacturing. Through an empirical investigation conducted with 17 multinational companies in the manufacturing sector, the impacts of AM are analysed by focusing on post-processing operations, lead times, cost implications and the use of the make-to-order & make-to-stock strategies. The empirical investigation reveals two major benefits of AM, namely: the ability to produce complex parts and the reduction of inventory levels. However, the empirical results were mixed for some other impacts of AM. In fact, although many experts agreed on the general benefits of AM, a significant number did not see much difference from the conventional methods. We also provide empirical evidence that, under AM, lead-times do not reduce as opposite to what is reported in the literature, which might be due to the extra time required for quality checks and post-processing.

Keywords: Additive manufacturing · Supply chain · Conventional manufacturing · Empirical investigation

1 Introduction

Nowadays, the global supply chain continues to be disrupted by new technologies, especially in the manufacturing sector and logistics operations [1]. Three dimensions printing using Additive Manufacturing (AM) is one of the technologies that is expected to revolutionize how things are manufactured [1]. AM is commonly defined as the process of joining different materials to come up with a 3D model, which is usually done layer upon layer [2]. The Additive manufacturing process starts with the development of a 3D model by the use of computer-Aided Design software [2]. The 3D model contains all the specifications and essential details of the product. The creation of a 3D project requires some basic essential ingredients including feed materials, the digital model, and the 3D printer as shown in Fig. 1.

A. Dolgui et al. (Eds.): APMS 2021, IFIP AICT 634, pp. 309–318, 2021.
https://doi.org/10.1007/978-3-030-85914-5_33

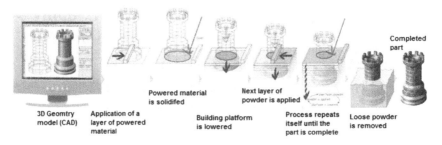

Powered material is solidifed

Next layer of powder is applied

Completed part

3D Geomtry model (CAD)

Application of a layer of powered material

Building platform is lowered

Process repeats itself until the part is complete

Loose powder is removed

Fig. 1. Additive manufacturing process. Source [7].

The academic literature shows that, by using AM, many companies have experienced increased agility and flexibility, which allows for better use of resources and materials, which results in low cost of production [3]. Besides, manufacturers of customized products experience high flexibility with competitive production costs and high added value. It has also been linked to other benefits such as the reduction of carbon emissions due to the reduction of transportation activities, which is a key issue, being advocated by the United Nations in a bid to protect and conserve the environment [4]. However, AM is also linked to some drawbacks, including the requirements for post-processing and slow build rates. The popularization and relevance of additive manufacturing in modern companies have increased the academic interest to understand its implications and benefits on the supply chain [4]. However, it should be noted that most of the existing empirical studies have only focused on few levels and processes of the supply chain, mainly the production and inventory management. To bridge this gap in the literature constitutes one of the objectives of our paper.

This work aims to empirically investigate the impacts of AM on supply chains. This will contribute to the existing literature by extending the scope of the analysis to include the impacts on all levels and processes of the supply chain, from the procurement to the relationship with customers, including the design and prototyping stage. Note also that our empirical investigation is conducted with a good sample of multinational companies having an experience with AM. Also, the research will be help to answer more questions in supply chain such as the contexts where AM is more applicable in the supply chain, which is important for the organizations' decision making.

This study is organized as follows. After presenting the context and objectives of the paper in this introductory section, we present in Sect. 2 a theoretical analysis that provides a broader area of knowledge on the impact of AM on the supply chain. Section 3 is dedicated to the empirical investigation, which discusses the research methodology and the empirical findings of the study. We close the paper in Sect. 4 with some conclusions and avenues for future research.

2   Theoretical Analysis

The AM technologies have a very disruptive impact on the global supply chain. In this section, based on our review of the literature, we identify the impacts of AM on four dimensions of the supply chain, namely: the procurement, the production and operations, the transportation and inventory, and the manufacturer/customer relationship.

2.1   Impact on Procurement

In any supply chain, a strong relationship between the manufacturer and the suppliers of raw materials is very essential. In AM, unavailability of raw materials might result in long unproductivity given that suppliers of the AM raw materials are very limited [5]. Therefore, the manufacturers have to carefully select and establish strong relationships with the suppliers unlike in conventional manufacturing where there are a higher number of suppliers of raw materials. The AM technology in the supply chain helps to lower the supply risk. This is because 3DP allows a product to be produced using a single raw material or a mixture of different materials, which eliminates the need for the manufacturer to source costly components and sub-assemblies.

2.2   Impact on Production and Operations

Unlike conventional production, which focuses on mass production, the AM technology could drive the transition to mass customization tailoring the products to each of the customer's requirements [5]. This means that customers are able to be involved in the design and production activities, which can change priorities of cost and profit management and hence making the supply chain more agile and flexible according to the different market changes. Given that the AM technology is highly flexible, the technology is able to produce a wide range of different outputs easily, quickly and cheaply. Therefore, the AM technology plays a very essential role in the creation of innovative processes for the production and testing of prototypes or updating product designs [5]. The technology is also applicable in direct product manufacturing especially for products with the need for customizability and complexity but with low production volumes [1]. Therefore, due to the additive nature of the technology, product designers and manufacturers are not tied to traditional constraints such as design for manufacturing. Instead, the technology allows many products to be redesigned. Finally, AM is strongly correlated with the product complexity. In fact, the more complex the product is in terms of shape and design features, the more beneficial AM will be over conventional manufacturing methods and the more cost saving can be achieved. Under the conventional manufacturing methods, the production process time and cost will increase with the design complexity. Conversely, production time and costs under AM should not be much impacted by the level of design complexity neither the flexibility of production.

2.3   Impacts on Transportation and Inventory

The movement of different products across the globe is being replaced by the movement of the 3D files while the physical inventories of the finished products are being replaced by digital inventories. By using the 3DP, the raw materials are used in the final manufacturing of the product and by producing on-demand, which means that there are fewer finished goods to be stocked or transported. This allows for warehousing and logistics to be rationalized as well as reduced logistical costs and positive environmental effects [7]. The inventory of the raw materials used is also cheaper and safer compared to conventional manufacturing. Due to the precision of the technology, AM products should be lighter and potentially more compact than an equivalent part conventionally manufactured, which leads to a reduction of the transportation and inventory holding costs. It is also worth pointing out that in relation with the complexity of products, integrating the parts of a product in a single piece could also reduce the need for the upstream transportation to source numerous parts. This results in reduced logistics cost, simplifying the management of logistical flows and positive environmental impacts as well as the reduction of disruptions along the supply chain. Integrating the parts in a single piece could also decrease the raw materials and WIP inventories, which means a potential for reduced holding costs.

Through reshoring, AM could play a key role in reducing demand for the global transportation whereby the physical flow will be replaced with the transfer of digital files [8]. Also, as noted above, inventories could then be affected due to the increased use of on-demand production possibilities of AM and this will have great and long-lasting impacts on the supply chains as well as the supply chain management.

2.4   Impact on Manufacturer/Customer Relationship

The AM shifts the production of goods closer to the final consumer and enhances the build-to-order approaches that have a positive impact on the manufacturer-customer relationship [7]. By using the AM, customers become part of the manufacturing processes whereby they can design and transfer ready-to-print files to the manufacturer and hence become a core creator, which promotes faster turnover [9]. According to Chekurov et al. [5], the technology has increased the role of the customer in the process as they have been given control over the design and production in collaboration with the manufacturer a relationship referred to as prosumers [5]. Overall, AM transforms the way the final consumer is reached more efficiently and effectively, further strengthening the customer-manufacturer relationship.

To validate some of the findings of the theoretical analysis for the impacts of AM on the supply chain, an empirical investigation should be conducted with a sample of manufacturing companies. The following section presents the research methodology used to provide empirical evidence of some impacts and limitations of AM.

3   Empirical Investigation

The main objectives of the empirical investigations are:

- To empirically validate or refute some impacts of AM that are identified in the theoretical analysis;
- To focus on the main interrogations and unclarities related to AM

3.1 Target Audience and Research Participants

Given that the findings of the research will depend on the composition of the participants to the study, a great care was given to the selection of the target audience. The first step aimed to identify the target audience involving potential experts from different industries with expertise in AM and supply chain management. We have obtained their contacts from different sources, mainly the University alumni database, and the LinkedIn network. By analyzing their credentials, we have assessed whether they were sufficiently qualified to take part in the survey as experts. An invitation letter was then sent to the potential participants including a short explanation of the aim of the study. Finally, a panel of experts from 17 multinational companies agreed to take part in the study. The list of companies includes Safran, Alstom, Michelin, Mercedes-Benz, Siemens, Ford, Schlumberger, BMW, Total, AM Polymers GmbH, and American Additive Manufacturing.

3.2 Research Process

First, the study used a critical literature review to investigate different manufacturing companies and suppliers that have used the 3DP technology. The literature review was important as it helped to identify the present knowledge research gaps in this area of study. The study's empirical investigation began from the theoretical foundation and then moved into the main research data whereby both qualitative and quantitative data were collected from different case studies through questionnaires. The questionnaire sent to the participants is composed of 61 questions, which were divided into 8 subsections whereby the questions are sought to capture and address: (1) Preliminary information of the company; (2) Workforce of the company; (3) Pros & Cons of AM; (4) Post processing operations; (5) Quality; (6) Lead Time & operations duration; (7) Cost impacts; (8) Make To Order (MTO) versus Make To Stock (MTS) and low volumes versus high volumes.

4 Findings and Discussions

4.1 Context of the Use of AM

We first analyzed the type of materials (plastic and metal) used by the companies in AM manufacturing. The empirical research shows that the majority (84.62%) of the manufacturing companies use both plastics and metals. In addition, we sought to determine whether for the companies, AM production is done in-house or through outsourcing. The empirical results show that 41% of the companies use both the in-house and outsourcing, 18% of the companies only outsource the AM products while 41% uses in-house production.

4.2   Pros and Cons of the Use of AM

The companies were asked about the benefits of AM in their supply chain. The confirmed benefits and the percentage of companies, reported in Fig. 2, are: Produce complex parts (76%), Cost beneficial on low volumes (82%), Parts consolidation (52%), and Great Design & Prototyping (70%). The refuted benefits include; Reduced number of suppliers (17%) and a reduced need for transportation (35%) and less material waste (50%). These findings are in line with the findings by Chan et al. [9] who state that 3DP enhances the capability to produce components that are more complex at a low cost and allows for a great design and prototyping.

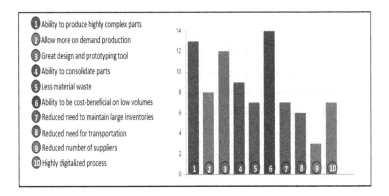

Fig. 2. Benefits of AM

This research is also sought to identify the disadvantages of using AM from the perspectives of the considered companies, as shown in the Fig. 3. The main cons validated by the empirical investigation include: the important capital expenditures required to develop AM, confirmed by 47% of the companies, the extended quality checks, the need for a specific workforce and some thermal or structural issues such as the risk for distortions and stresses during the cooling phase, which were confirmed by 47% of the companies as well. The less validated cons include: the risk for supply shortage (17%) and the long manufacturing time on large volumes (17%).

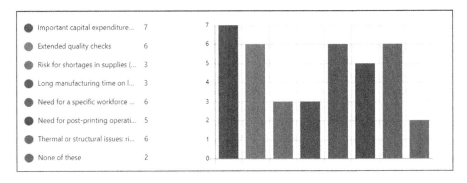

Fig. 3. Cons of AM

4.3   Post-processing Operations

The companies were also asked about the post-processing operations as impacted by AM. The results show that 70% of the companies need to perform post-processing operations and out of the 70%, 66% outsource some post-processing operations, which allow them to focus on the core competencies. These results are in line with some of the reasons why organizations use the dual sourcing whereby organizations achieve a competitive advantage when they combine their core competencies and abilities with those of their customers, suppliers and other external resources [10]. As shown in Fig. 4, the empirical results also reveal that the duration of the post-processing phase greatly depends on the product while 62% reported that production when using AM was below 40% of production time. This finding supports the suggestions by Chan et al. [9] who stated that 3D printing provides an opportunity for manufactures to reduce lead-time production.

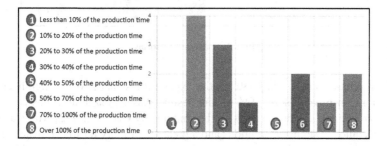

Fig. 4.   Post-processing operations

4.4   Lead Times of Different Phases

Here we compare the lead times of different phases in AM to those of the conventional manufacturing method. In general, 70% of the companies stated that AM reduced overall product development time (entire process) while 30% stated that there was no change. However, in the design phase, the majority of the experts 41% stated that it remained the same, 29% said that it was longer while 29% stated that it was shorter.

For prototyping, 92% of the experts stated that it was shorter. This supports the research by Chan et al. [9] who stated that AM allows for rapid prototyping by the use of CAD.

The majority of the respondents, 46%, stated that the production time using AM was shorter than that of the conventional production, which is in line with the findings of Kunovjanek and Reiner [6] which shows that 3DP technology plays a crucial role in reducing the production lead-time due to less assembly times required and less delivery times between processes.

For post-processing, 30% of the respondents stated that it was longer compared to conventional manufacturing while 70% stated that it was similar. For the control phase, 70% stated that it was similar while 30% stated that it was longer. This might be due to the fact that extra time is needed for quality checks and post-processing.

4.5 Cost Implications

In terms of cost implications, the empirical results show that 62% of the respondents stated that production cost is significantly reduced by 30% or more when using AM. This agrees with Kunovjanek et al. [6] who stated that production lead times when using 3DP is reduced significantly which contributes to production costs but disagrees with Sirichakwal and Conner, [11] who stated that the 3DP technology may not have an edge over the conventional technology in terms of the cost of production (Fig. 5).

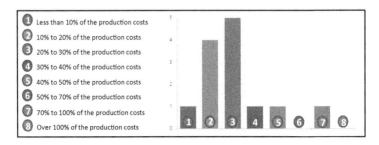

Fig. 5. Cost implications

The results also show that 53% of the experts think that AM has significant cost implications on procurement, 59% on the design phase, 71% think it has cost implications on inventory. This agrees with the findings by Gao et al. [12] who stated that AM offers quick customized solutions and a great opportunity for MTO, which reduces the cost on inventory and procurement. In the design phase and production, Chan et al. [9] note that AM reduces the costs by improving the efficiency as well as shortening the development time. However, the majority of the respondents (59%) did confirm this, which concurs with the findings by Chan et al. [9] who states that cost of production when using AM is also lower because it takes place with minimum labor and labor cost. However, this depends on the cost incurred in different phases of the supply chain whereby some design and development phases are relatively costly compared to the production cost.

5 MTO vs. MTS and Low Volumes vs. High Volumes

The empirical results show that 53% of the respondents stated that they were using the MTO strategy with AM, 20% are using MTS while 27% are using both strategies.

54% of the respondents agreed that AM is relevant in an MTS vs MTO strategy while 46% disagreed. These mixed results are in line with the findings by Nickels [13] who stated that in the future, manufacturers will be able to produce AM spare parts on demand especially in decentralized locations whereby the order penetration will be through MTO. On the other hand, even though Ryan et al. [14] questions the usability of AM in MTS due to the lack of customization, Olhager [15] states that with long production times, MTS becomes more appropriate than MTO as it can help to have products ready to ship.

The majority of the respondents (62%) disagreed that AM is only interesting on low volumes while only 38% agreed. These findings however contradict the suggestions by Potstada and Zybura [16] who states that AM in MTS is most appropriate for small scale products especially with the current printers and [13] who states that AM in MTO is mainly applicable for low volumes by use of specialized equipment.

6 Conclusion

This research has theoretically and empirically identified some of the most significant impacts of additive manufacturing on the supply chain, including the procurement, the production & operations, the transportation & inventory and the manufacturer-to-manufacturer relationship. The study significantly contributes to the limited literature on the link between AM and all supply chain processes and it is a response to the existing calls for further research. The review of the literature reveals that there is a great potential for AM, which is expected to reduce the production time, reduce costs, and allow for easier customization. However, the majority of the studies dealing with the impacts of AM on supply chains have ignored the fact that the impacts can be different at different levels and processes of the supply chain. Therefore, we have conducted an empirical investigation with a panel of experts in major manufacturing companies to give their insights on how AM impacts different levels/processes of the supply chain. The empirical results have revealed two major impacts of AM: the ability to produce complex parts and the reduction of the inventory levels.

The research has generated important valuable insights to the AM research. However, it should be noted that the results have also portrayed many mixed results with regard to the cost implications, the post-processing operations, and the lead times. This, therefore, leads to the suggestion that AM has only enabled the transition but the conventional manufacturing will not be entirely phased out. AM should in the mean-time complement conventional manufacturing. However, the empirical investigation has been based on a limited sample size, which may limit the generalization of the findings. Hence, it is recommended that more research should be conducted using larger empirical samples and other methods such as simulation models or relativity analysis and regression to better validate the current study's findings.

It is worth pointing out that the findings of the empirical investigation provide evidence of the impact of AM on the supply chain performance. The companies' sample considered in the empirical investigation in this paper is rich enough (multi-national companies with different sizes and proposing different types of products) to be representative for general contexts. However, it is obvious that the generalisability of the findings cannot be confirmed due to the limited size of the sample of considered companies, which may represent a limitation of this research work. Hence, extending the analysis by considering a bigger sample of companies would be an interesting avenue for further research contributing to the generalisability of this article's findings.

References

1. Mellor, S., Hao, L., Zhang, D.: Additive manufacturing: a framework for implementation. Int. J. Prod. Econ. **149**, 194–201 (2014)
2. Khajavi, S.H., Partanen, J., Holmström, J.: Additive manufacturing in the spare parts supply chain. Comput. Ind. **65**(1), 50–63 (2014)
3. Delic, M., Eyers, D.R.: The effect of additive manufacturing adoption on supply chain flexibility and performance: an empirical analysis from the automotive industry. Int. J. Prod. Econ. **228**, 107689 (2020)
4. Huang, R., et al.: Energy and emissions saving potential of additive manufacturing: the case of lightweight aircraft components. J. Clean. Prod. **135**, 1559–1570 (2016)
5. Chekurov, S., Metsä-Kortelainen, S., Salmi, M., Roda, I., Jussila, A.: The perceived value of additively manufactured digital spare parts in the industry: an empirical investigation. Int. J. Prod. Econ. **205**, 87–97 (2018)
6. Kunovjanek, M., Knofius, N., Reiner, G. Additive manufacturing and supply chains–a systematic review. Prod. Plan. Control, 1–21 (2020)
7. Zijm, H., Knofius, N., van der Heijden, M.: Additive manufacturing and its impact on the supply chain. In: Zijm, H., Klumpp, M., Regattieri, A., Heragu, S. (eds.) Operations, Logistics and Supply Chain Management. LNL, pp. 521–543. Springer, Cham (2019). https://doi.org/10.1007/978-3-319-92447-2_23
8. Hedenstierna, C.P.T., Disney, S.M., Eyers, D.R., Holmström, J., Syntetos, A.A., Wang, X.: Economies of collaboration in build-to-model operations. J. Oper. Manag. **65**(8), 753–773 (2019)
9. Chan, H.K., Griffin, J., Lim, J.J., Zeng, F., Chiu, A.S.: The impact of 3D printing technology on the supply chain: manufacturing and legal perspectives. Int. J. Prod. Econ. **205**, 156–162 (2018)
10. Oettmeier, K., Hofmann, E.: Impact of additive manufacturing technology adoption on supply chain management processes and components. J. Manuf. Technol. Manage. **27**, 968–977 (2016)
11. Sirichakwal, I., Conner, B.: Implications of additive manufacturing for spare parts inventory. 3D Printing Addit. Manuf. **3**(1), 56–63 (2016)
12. Gao, W., et al.: The status, challenges, and future of additive manufacturing in engineering. Comput. Aided Des. **69**, 65–89 (2015)
13. Nickels, L.: AM and aerospace: an ideal combination. Met. Powder Rep. **70**(6), 300–303 (2015)
14. Ryan, M.J., Eyers, D.R., Potter, A.T., Purvis, L., Gosling, J.: 3D printing the future: scenarios for supply chains reviewed. Int. J. Phys. Distrib. Logist. Manage. **47**, 992–1014 (2017)
15. Olhager, J.: Strategic positioning of the order penetration point. Int. J. Prod. Econ. **85**(3), 319–329 (2003)
16. Potstada, M., Zybura, J.: The role of context in science fiction prototyping: the digital industrial revolution. Technol. Forecast. Soc. Chang. **84**, 101–114 (2014)
17. EOS Homepage. https://www.eos.info/additive_manufacturing/for_technology_interested. Last Accessed 16 Jul 2021

A Knowledge-Based Approach for Decision Support System in Additive Manufacturing

Qussay Jarrar$^{(\boxtimes)}$, Farouk Belkadi$^{(\boxtimes)}$, and Alain Bernard$^{(\boxtimes)}$

Ecole Centrale de Nantes, Laboratory of Digital Sciences of Nantes,
LS2N UMR 6004, Nantes, France
{qussay.jarrar,farouk.belkadi,alain.bernard}@ls2n.fr

Abstract. The large amount and different types of data and knowledge generated within the Additive Manufacturing (AM) value chain are highly challenging in terms of management and organization. Understanding the interconnections between all these immaterial corpuses is important for decision making and process optimization issues. Moreover, AM has more parameters than conventional manufacturing processes, and many of these parameters are difficult to assess and monitor. Therefore, it becomes important to develop computer-based solutions that are able to aid the decision maker and to support the management of all information along the AM value chain. In this paper, a knowledge-based decision support framework using ontological models and mechanisms is proposed for the above objective. Cost estimation is conducted as an application of the proposed framework.

Keywords: Knowledge-based approach · Decision support system · Automatic cost estimation · Additive manufacturing

1 Introduction

Even though the history of Additive Manufacturing (AM) technology is relatively short, it has shown expeditiously growing interest in various domains and significant improvement on the quality of the produced parts as well as the efficiency of the related processes [1]. Despite of these benefits and opportunities, many issues and challenges such as traceability, accuracy, and parameters' inconsistency still need to be solved [2]. With the growing complexity of AM process due to multiple interconnections between heterogeneous parameters, changing one parameter could affect multiple criteria of the produced parts [3]. Even for expert users, it is difficult to select the suitable values of process parameters for successful AM building results [4]. Moreover, different types of data generated along the product transformation cycle are creating new opportunities for knowledge discovery [5]. So, understanding these data and knowledge definition and correlation is essential for decision making and optimization from the earliest stages of AM process.

In this topic, it becomes important to develop the right architecture of decision-making system that correctly uses and manages all this corpus of information [6], while paying particular attention to the key performance indicators and process parameters management [7]. Thus, the main objective of this paper is to propose a knowledge-

© IFIP International Federation for Information Processing 2021
Published by Springer Nature Switzerland AG 2021
A. Dolgui et al. (Eds.): APMS 2021, IFIP AICT 634, pp. 319–327, 2021.
https://doi.org/10.1007/978-3-030-85914-5_34

based system (KBS), using an AM dedicated ontology, to support the expert decision along the AM value chain. Section 2 presents a literature review on KBS and decision-aid systems for AM. Section 3 proposes the main foundations of the proposed KBS. Then, an application of this framework to support the decision making in cost estimation is presented in Sect. 4.

2   Knowledge-Based Decision Support Solutions for AM

Decision Support Systems (DSS) have proven an important role to support the experts in various fields related to AM value chain. For instance, process planning support aims to identify and adjust all parameters necessary to optimize the build and post-processing steps [8]. Even though, the decision process is still complicated in terms of data management due to huge amount of data and heterogeneity of knowledge. The use of Artificial Intelligence (AI) leads to improvement of DSS through better exploitation of expert knowledge (rule inferences) as well as smart data mining and machine learning [9]. KBS are kind of computer systems that imitate human reasoning for problem-solving by reusing previous experiences and inferring business rules [10]. These systems are currently coupled with Knowledge Management (KM) practices to capture and formalize tacit knowledge [11]. This kind of system consists of three main components; Inference engine, User Interface, and Knowledge Base (KB) [12]. In this type of approaches, knowledge modeling is a critical issue to satisfy the consistency of the KB. With regard, ontology is one of the most effective tools to formalize the domain knowledge, while supporting the automatic reasoning and information retrieval based on business rules [13, 14].

Lately, attempts have been made to develop a knowledge base in a form of ontology as a decision support for AM. Some works have contributed to propose a knowledge base that formalize Design for AM (DfAM) knowledge to be retrieved and reused to support the designers in process planning, [15, 16]. For instance, Kim et al. [15] use Ontology Web Language OWL to categorize DFAM knowledge into: Part design, Process planning, and Manufacturing features. SQWRL queries are applied to formalize design rules and retrieve DFAM knowledge to be reused for solving new problems. Using the same mechanisms, Hagedorn et al. [16] aim to support innovative design in AM, by capturing information related to various fabrication capabilities of AM, and their application in past innovation solutions. Samely, Liu et al. [4] propose a KB that uses previous process planning cases and manufacturing rules. Eddy et al. [14] introduce Rules-Based algorithm to select the best process plan as a combination of feasible processes allowing the lowest total cost of the resulted AM part.

In summary, most of the developed approaches are specific and dedicated to solve particular aspects of AM process, so they need high labor intensive to operate in general context. In previous work, Sanfilippo et al. [10] propose an ontology as a generic reference model with the ambition to represent all main characteristics of AM value chain. The proposed knowledge-based approach is realized as a part of this research work by extending the scope to the preparation and post-processing steps, and taking into account the link between customer specification and process characteristics, for effective cost estimation at the earliest stage of the AM project.

3   The Proposed KBS Framework

The computational ontology proposed by [10] is developed in OWL by means of Protégé tool, and uses the concepts of "template" and "reusable case" as generic containers to structure and reuse useful knowledge for decision-aid perspective. Templates can be seen as a semantic dictionary that organizes the collection of specific types of AM data and knowledge. A "case" is used for the traceability of a given AM project (successful or failed) through the instantiation of a collection of templates.

For instance, the template of machine will be used to create library of existing machine families by defining the main attributes for each category. The first instantiation permits the declaration of a given reference of machine (or process, product, material, etc.) with interval of possible values for the predefined parameters (Ex. Machine XX has heating temperature between 300 and 500°). Then, the creation of reusable case is achieved by combining a set of templates with exact parameters values (ex. Case project ZZ uses the processes PP to transform the material MM in the machine XX with the parameters heating temperature 450°, material density is 4.4 g/cm^3, etc. It results on the product AA with characteristics: surface roughness: 5–18 μm).

Relaying on that conceptual framework, first the ontology has been enriched with high level of granularity and details axioms covering a wider range of control, and post processes, among others. Five types of templates are initially distinguished: Product, machine, feature, material, and process. Then, templates contents have been updated and other types are added to cover project characteristics, customer specifications, and finally, cost model as an example of decision-aid perspective.

By doing so, the proposed KB is structured and formalized around five layers as shown in Fig. 1. The first layer forms the generic knowledge model representing all AM related concepts (i.e. process, Machine, Material, resource, etc.), and their relationships, following the meta-model proposed in [10] based on the Descriptive Ontology for Linguistic and Cognitive Engineering (DOLCE).

The second layer includes the meta-definition of the different types of templates as well as the semantic definition of case as concepts connected through constraints and the relation HasTemplate. Concretely, Project template allows the description of main categories of projects through their classification by customer activity sector, result type (study, prototype, realization, etc.), complexity, etc. Product template classifies the main families of products according to some invariants (i.e. category of size, form of the support, generic shape, etc.). Feature template completes the product template by classifying main elementary geometric shapes, so that a product can be identified as a combination of elementary shapes and other free forms with specific dimensions. Process Template classifies possible standard processes connected to the AM value chain (support optimization, build, control, post-process, etc.), and identify for every type of process the main parameters to be adjusted in and the constraints to be respected (compatible resources and materials, etc.). Material template helps to distinguish all material types based on their physical properties, as well as compatibility and treatment constraints. Finally, Machine template describes the nominal characteristics of existing AM machines and related equipment (manufacture name, max. build dimensions, temperature range, etc.).

Based on these definitions, the real basic templates are defined in the fourth layer as individuals of the types of templates defined in layer 2, with range of values for every parameter. The fifth layer contains the second instantiation where a collection of templates conducts to a specific reusable case. The exact values of these individuals are automatically extracted from the database. This latest contains all the necessary data collected from customer specification, 3D models and other technical documents. By means, the ontology contains only useful information while the real data is still stored in the database to avoid redundancy. Finally, the third layer gathers the needed business rules and similarity constraints to support the decision-making process through linking the current project data with similar cases, on one side, and the generation of new knowledge by inference, on the other side.

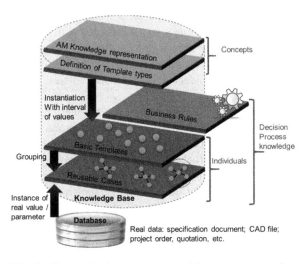

Fig. 1. Knowledge base structure and layer interconnection

In practice, the execution of decision support starts with the analysis of the customer requirements and additional specifications. New knowledge could be defined and parameters values refined through the application of some business rules. Then, the related templates are identified and business rules are again used to classify the new project in the right category (project complexity, product size, etc.) Based on that, similar cases are searched and the right decision model is identified for application. The results are saved in the database after validation of the expert. However, if similar cases or templates are not found, the enrichment process of the knowledge base is trigged in collaboration with industrial experts to identify new rules and/or cases. The next section illustrates the execution of the decision-aid mechanism for cost assessment, as an important step to help expert for defining cost quotations.

4   Framework Application: (Cost Estimation DSS)

Cost is one of the major performance indicators for the AM manufacturer to be competitive. Its estimation is a challenging task that requires a vast amount of manufacturing knowledge about the whole process in several cases, part of this knowledge is not available in the beginning of the project and the expert should base his quotation on his own expertise with different hypothesizes [17]. Therefore, the proposed solution aims to provide a support for the cost estimation of AM products to help expert when answering specific client demands or to answer call for tenders. For the decision model, the proposed approach is based on Activity-Based Costing (ABC) method for providing appropriate cost structure of the final cost for metal and laser-based Powder Bed Fusion (PBF). The model helps identifying the main cost drivers within AM value chain and their correlations with the available inputs and parameters at early stages when receiving customer specifications. The ABC model is prepared in a form of mathematical equations, coupling the total cost of each activity with the related cost-center resources (machines, labor, tools, etc.).

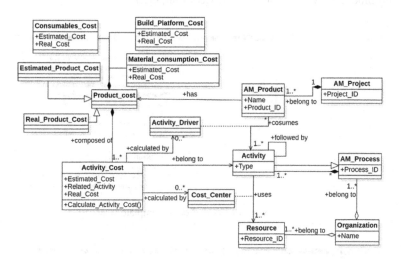

Fig. 2. ABC meta-model

Figure 2 illustrates the ABC meta-model for the integration of their useful knowledge as a specific template in the knowledge repository (ontology). For the simplicity of reading, UML graphical language is used. The mathematical equations are integrated as constraints and business rules, while the requested parameters to evaluate these equations are available in different templates to support their automatic evaluation. By means, the global equation of the cost model is given bellow. The detailed parameters are out of the scope of this paper because of the page size restrictions.

> Final Product cost = Total material cost + Build Platform cost + $\sum$Activity cost + consumable costs

For the sake of example, we assume that we want to estimate the cost of fabricating a specific part using Titanium Ti64 material, and manufactured on an EOS290 DMLS (Direct Metal Laser Sintering) machine (example from [18]). In this example only AM process and machine templates are illustrated due to the paper size limitation, and only the costs related to build job, machine setup, and machine output activities are estimated. At first, the required basic templates for the DMLS process are selected from the ontology. Then, the machine type and the resource needed for this process are coupled (machine operator with its cost rate which is equal to 110 euro/hour) as shown in Fig. 3. Figure 4 shows the characteristics of this machine type including the cost rate for running this machine as a cost center rate for build job activity. However, the estimation of build time obtained from several software packages exist for estimating the build time like (Materialise-Magics, EOSprint, etc.).

Fig. 3. Individual of AM process template (DMLS)

Fig. 4. Individual of machine type (EOSM290)

Based on the values stored in the templates, the cost for build job, machine setup, and machine output activities are inferred using the SWRL rules in the ontology and built-in reasoner Pellet that represent the cost estimation equations for these activities, as show in the two rules below R1 and R2. The mapping with the identified templates conducts to the categorization of the project as medium complexity for massive product with medium size. The supporting strategy is standard category.

```
R1:  ProcessTemplate(?x)  ^  hasBuildDurationInHour(?x,
?y)  ^  specifiesMachineType(?x,  ?z)  ^  hasCostRateEu-
roPerHour(?z, ?a) ^ swrlb:multiply(?I, ?y, ?a) -> has-
BuildingCostInEuro(?x, ?I)


R2: ProcessTemplate(?x) ^ specifiesMachineType(?x, ?y)
^ hasMachineSetupDurationInHour(?y, ?z) ^ hasMachine-
OutputDurationInHour(?y,    ?a)    ^    hasActorBusiness-
Role(?x,   ?t)   ^   hasCostRateEuroPerHour(?t,   ?i)   ^
swrlb:multiply(?u, ?z, ?i) ^ swrlb:multiply(?p, ?a,
?i) -> hasMachineSetupCostInEuro(?x, ?u) ^ hasMachine-
OutputCostInEuro(?x, ?p)
```

5   Conclusion and Future Work

The main goal of the proposed knowledge-based framework is to improve the performance of additive manufacturing value chain, by supporting data sharing and tracing along AM value chain, and support the experts' decision making in different cases of AM field. This work details the methodological framework in terms of the conceptual approach, and framework layer's structure. Ontology has been used to constitute the knowledge base with its ability to capture heterogeneous knowledge, along with rule-based approach in a form of SWRL in the ontology to integrate the amount of knowledge provided by experts (know-how, decisions, etc.) in order to deduce new knowledge. One application of this framework is exposed to support the decision making in cost estimation which aims to aid the manufacturing products cost estimation. Using Activity-Based Costing (ABC) method for providing appropriate cost structure of the final cost, identifying the main cost drivers within AM process chain and their correlations to the available inputs and parameters at early stages, considering customer specifications, and product characteristics.

The project is currently under progress. At one hand, the approach needs to be complemented with other techniques beside the rule-based approach such as similarity measures, in order to foster the use of this framework in real world setting. On the other hand, the implementation of this framework in software application requests the creation of specific connectors and parsers to automatically extract data from documents and 3D models. Moreover, future work will be important to define other decision-making scenarios focusing on qualitative performance indicators.

Acknowledgement. The presented results were conducted within the French national project "SOFIA" (SOlution pour la Fabrication Industrielle Additive métallique). This project has received the support from the French Public Investment Bank (Bpifrance) and the French National Center for Scientific Research (CNRS). The authors would like to thank all industrial and academic partners for their involvement in this research.

References

1. Negi, S., Dhiman, S., Sharma, R.K.: Basics, applications and future of additive manufacturing technologies: a review. J. Manuf. Technol. Res. **5**(1/2), 75 (2013)
2. Al-Meslemi, Y., Anwer, N., Mathieu, L.: Modeling key characteristics in the value chain of additive manufacturing. Procedia CIRP **70**, 90–95 (2018)
3. Wang, Y., Zhong, R.Y., Xu, X.: A decision support system for additive manufacturing process selection using a hybrid multiple criteria decision-making method. Rapid Prototyping J. **24**(9), 1544–1553 (2018)
4. Liu, X., Rosen, D.W.: Ontology based knowledge modeling and reuse approach of supporting process planning in layer-based additive manufacturing. In: 2010 International Conference on Manufacturing Automation, pp. 261–266 (2010)
5. Witherell, P.: Emerging Datasets and Analytics Opportunities in Metals Additive Manufacturing. In: Direct Digital manufacturing Conference (2018)
6. Kim, D.B., Witherell, P., Lipman, R., Feng, S.C.: Streamlining the additive manufacturing digital spectrum: a systems approach. Addit. Manuf. **5**, 20–30 (2015)
7. Belkadi, F., Vidal, L.M., Bernard, A., Pei, E., Sanfilippo, E.M.: Towards an unified additive manufacturing product-process model for digital chain management purpose. Procedia CIRP **70**, 428–433 (2018)
8. Gibson, I., Rosen, D., Stucker, B., Khorasani, M.: Additive Manufacturing Technologies, vol. 17, p. 195. Springer, New York (2014)
9. Merkert, J., Mueller, M., Hubl, M.: A Survey of the Application of Machine Learning in Decision Support Systems. ECIS Completed Research Papers, Paper 133 (2015)
10. Sanfilippo, E.M., Belkadi, F., Bernard, A.: Ontology-based knowledge representation for additive manufacturing. Comput. Ind. **109**, 182–194 (2019)
11. Li, B.M., Xie, S.Q., Xu, X.: Recent development of knowledge-based systems, methods and tools for one-of-a-kind production. Knowl.-Based Syst. **24**(7), 1108–1119 (2011)
12. Ghazy, M.M.: Development of an additive manufacturing decision support system (AMDSS). Newcastle University. NE1 7RU, United Kingdom. PhD thesis (2012).
13. Meski, O., Belkadi, F., Laroche, F., Ritou, M., Furet, B.: A generic knowledge management approach towards the development of a decision support system. Int. J. Prod. Res. 1–18 (2020). https://doi.org/10.1080/00207543.2020.1821930
14. Eddy, D., Krishnamurty, S., Grosse, I., Perham, M., Wileden, J., Ameri, F.: Knowledge management with an intelligent tool for additive manufacturing. In: Proceedings of ASEM International Design Engineering Technical Conferences and Computers and Information in Engineering Conference, vol. 57045, p. V01AT02A023 (2015)
15. Kim, S., Rosen, D. W., Witherell, P., Ko, H.: A design for additive manufacturing ontology to support manufacturability analysis. J. Comput. Inf. Sci. Eng. **19**(4), 1–10 (2019). https://doi.org/10.1115/1.4043531
16. Hagedorn, T.J., Krishnamurty, S., Grosse, I.R.: A knowledge-based method for innovative design for additive manufacturing supported by modular ontologies. J. Comput. Inf. Sci. Eng. **18**(2), 1–12 (2018). https://doi.org/10.1115/1.4039455

17. Kadir, A.Z.A., Yusof, Y., Wahab, M.S.: Additive manufacturing cost estimation models—a classification review. Int. J. Adv. Manuf. Technol. **107**(9), 4033–4053 (2020)
18. Barclift, M., Joshi, S., Simpson, T., Dickman, C.: Cost modeling and depreciation for reused powder feedstocks in powder bed fusion additive manufacturing. In: Solid Free Fabers Symposium, pp. 2007–2028 (2016)

A Bibliometric Analysis Approach to Review Mass Customization Scientific Production

Danijela Ciric[✉] ⓘ, Bojan Lalic ⓘ, Uglješa Marjanovic ⓘ,
Milena Savkovic ⓘ, and Slavko Rakic ⓘ

Faculty of Technical Sciences, University of Novi Sad, 21000 Novi Sad, Serbia
danijela.ciric@uns.ac.rs

Abstract. Mass customization is an important manufacturing concept aimed at integrating product varieties to provide customized services and products based on individual needs. This concept has emerged in the 1980s as demand for product variety increased, and the research in this area has been present for the last three decades. This article aims to study the scientific production around mass customization through metadata analysis of all articles indexed in the bibliographic database Web of Science. The science mapping and bibliometric analysis was conducted using the "bibliometrix" R Package. Also, a graphical analysis of the bibliographic data was performed using VOSviewer software. This study identified the most relevant sources, authors, and countries active and influential through a five-stage workflow consisting of study design, data collection, data analysis, data visualization, and data interpretation. Keyword analysis revealed the related emerging research topics. Co-citation and co-occurrence analysis was performed to underline research streams.

Keywords: Bibliometric analysis · Bibliometrix · Mass customization

1 Introduction

In the last few decades, the manufacturing sector has been undergoing constant changes and technological advancement, keeping manufacturing companies in a continuous state of disruption [1]. Individual needs and customer requirements have become a priority for companies to gain a competitive advantage [2]. Mass customization concept has emerged in the 1980s as demand for product variety increased [3], and it has been identified as a competitive strategy by an increasing number of companies [4]. This is an important manufacturing concept aimed at integrating product varieties to provide customized services and products based on individual needs. Research in this area has been present for the last three decades.

Many authors have used bibliometric analysis to identify aspects of science that receive the most contributions from authors, journals, organizations, and countries, and the collaborative networks among them [5, 7–11]. Bibliometric studies have become an emergent discipline, given the importance posed on the assessment of scientific production. The bibliometric studies help researchers understand and analyze the research structure, the extent of the topic, emergent trends, and its evolution over time [5, 6]. The objective of this bibliometric analyzes is to analyze the scientific production

© IFIP International Federation for Information Processing 2021
Published by Springer Nature Switzerland AG 2021
A. Dolgui et al. (Eds.): APMS 2021, IFIP AICT 634, pp. 328–338, 2021.
https://doi.org/10.1007/978-3-030-85914-5_35

around mass customization through bibliographic data analysis of all articles indexed in the Web of Science containing "mass customization" in the title or authors keywords with the aim identify the most relevant sources, authors, countries active and influential in this field with the emergent trends and evolution over time. This study is targeted to a broad and diverse audience from various research fields like engineering, operations research, management science, business economics, etc. The science mapping and bibliometric analysis was conducted using "bibliometrix" R Package tool [12] while the graphical analysis of the bibliographic data was done using VOSviewer software [13].

The paper's remainder is structured as follows. Section 2 describes the research workflow. Section 3 presents research results and findings, followed by a conclusion with limitations and suggestions for further research in Sect. 4.

2   Research Workflow

This research is conducted following a standard workflow consisting of five stages [14]:

(1) Study design - In the first stage, the research objective was identified and based on that the study design was structured. The objective was to review mass customization scientific production and its intellectual and conceptual structure; (2) Data collection - In the second stage, bibliographic data were retrieved from the online bibliographic database Clarivate Analytics Web of Science. The search was restricted to Web of Science as it is the most important database of scientific articles whose metrics are widely used in academic assessment. After that, data converting and loading was performed to adjust it into a suitable format for the "bibliometrix" tool. All indexed articles that contain "mass customization" in the title or authors keywords were included. Only publications in English were included and all document types except articles were excluded. The following search string were used: *(((TI = (mass customization OR mass-customization OR mass customisation OR mass-customisation)) OR (AK = (mass customization OR mass-customization OR mass customisation OR mass-customisation)))) AND LANGUAGE: (English) AND DOCUMENT TYPES: (Article);* (3) Data analysis – In the third stage, descriptive analysis and network extraction were performed using the "bibliometrix" R package tool for quantitative research in bibliometrics and scientometrics [12]. Firstly, annual scientific production, the most productive countries and authors, and co-authorship among countries were analyzed. After that, the most relevant publishing sources and highly cited articles, and keyword occurrences were analyzed; (4) Data visualization – In the fourth stage, a visual analysis of the bibliographic data was done using VOSviewer software [13], specifically co-citation and keyword co-occurrences analysis; (5) Interpretation – In the fifth stage, the findings were described.

3 Research Results and Description of Findings

The final sample consisted of 802 articles published in 268 sources (journals and conference proceedings) during the timespan 1996:2021. These articles were (co)authored by 1630 people, out of which there were 97 single-authored documents and 705 multi-authored documents, with the average number of authors per document 2.03. Articles are concentrated around main research areas: engineering, operations research management sciences, computer sciences, and business economics. Web of Sciences assigns indexed articles to one or more research areas. The 802 articles in our sample were assigned to 53 research areas. The top five research areas are shown in Table 1.

Table 1. Top five research areas assigned to articles in the sample

Research areas	# Articles	% of 801
Engineering	478	59.601%
Operations research management science	252	31.421%
Computer science	198	24.688%
Business economics	182	22.693%
Automation control systems	42	5.237%

Figure 1 graphically represents the tendencies in publications on mass customization from 1996 to April 2021. When analyzing the annual scientific production, it could be seen that the number of articles published per year had a stable growth from 1996 to 2004. Multiple periods were identified until 2019 with different and decreasing growth rates. The decreasing growth rate could signalize that research in this field is consolidating. From 2019 to 2020, the number of articles published grew rapidly again. It must be noted that Fig. 1 doesn't present all data for 2021 but only until May of that year.

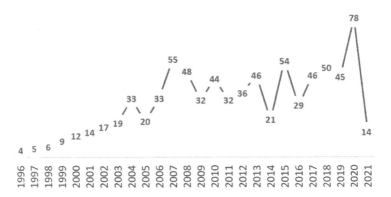

Fig. 1. Number of articles published per year

3.1 Most Productive Countries and Authors

Table 2 shows the top ten most productive countries with the total citations (TC) per country and average citations per article (AC). It could be observed that China is the country whose authors have published most articles, and the USA is second. When analyzing the number of total citations per country, the situation is reversed, with an average citation of 18.09 per article for the USA and 13.94 for China. It is important to highlight that England has the highest average citations per article (23.67) among the leading countries, which can be used as a proxy for scientific importance or article quality. When analyzing the funding sources in articles, it was identified that the National Natural Science Foundation of China NSFC is the funding agency with the highest occurrence in articles (76 articles). It could be noted that China is highly influential and dedicated to research in this field. Table 3 shows the most productive authors in mass customization research. This classification is based on the number of publications and the author's h-index, which is calculated for this bibliographic collection. When comparing the number of articles produced with the production year start and the h-index for this bibliographic collection, it could be seen that Zhang M and Huang GQ are the two most influential authors. Forza C is the most productive author with 21 articles. According to co-authorship analysis among countries (Fig. 2), the most intensive collaboration exists among the USA, China, and England.

Table 2. Top ten most productive countries

Country	# Articles	TC	AC	Country	# Articles	TC	AC
China	259	1715	13.94	South Korea	40	130	6.19
USA	191	1495	18.01	Canada	34	238	11.90
England	57	497	23.67	Brazil	33	92	5.41
France	43	408	19.43	Denmark	29	211	17.58
Italy	43	282	11.28	Germany	27	88	5.87

Table 3. Top ten most productive authors

Authors	No. of articles	H-index	Total citations	Production year start
Forza C	21	10	249	2002
Jiao JX	17	1	16	1997
Trentin A	17	11	256	2007
Tseng MM	17	2	6	1997
Zhang M	14	8	337	2005
Huang GQ	11	4	339	2007
Salvador F	11	2	27	2002
Hvam L	10	6	86	2007
Liu WH	9	6	75	2013

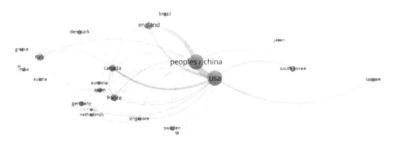

Fig. 2. Co-authorship analysis among countries (source: extracted from VOSviewer software)

3.2 Most Relevant Sources

In Table 4, the top ten most relevant journals publishing articles related to mass customization are presented. The most relevant source is the International Journal of Production Research, with 60 articles published. This is a prominent journal that publishes leading research on manufacturing and production engineering, followed by the Journal of Intelligent Manufacturing, with 34 articles published, representing a unique international journal for developers of intelligent manufacturing systems. The International Journal of Production Economics, with 32 articles published, focuses on topics treating the interface between engineering and management. When analyzing the article annual occurrences growth, the International Journal of Production Economics is on the rise in previous years, as opposed to the International Journal of Production Research and the Journal of Intelligent Manufacturing, which are declining since 2010. When comparing the average citation per article, h-index for this bibliographic collection, and the number of articles published, the International Journal of Production Economics is the most influential.

3.3 Most Influential Articles

H-index for this bibliographic collection consisting of 802 articles related to mass customization is 68, with a total of times cited 21,795. Table 5 shows the most influential articles in mass customization research from 1996 to April 2021. This table was constructed based on the number of total citations per article. Among the ten most cited articles in this research area, there is just one article published in a journal from the ten most productive journals (Table 4). Although the most productive journals are mainly in industrial engineering, production, operational, and manufacturing research, among the ten most influential articles are the ones that are mostly published in journals oriented towards management sciences.

Table 4. Top ten most relevant sources

Sources	# Articles	Impact factor	H-index	TC
International Journal of Production Research	60	4.577	15	581
Journal of Intelligent Manufacturing	34	4.311	13	369
International Journal of Production Economics	32	5.134	12	419
International Journal of Advanced Manufacturing Technology	28	2.633	5	82
Production Planning and Control	27	3.605	8	132
International Journal of Computer Integrated Manufacturing	20	2.861	7	114
Computers in Industry	19	3.954	7	184
IEEE Transactions on Engineering Management	18	2.784	5	118
International Journal of Operations and Production Management	18	4.619	7	231
Computers and Industrial Engineering	17	4.135	6	97

3.4   Main Keywords and Keyword Co-occurrences

This section provides an overview of both main keywords (measured by the keyword frequency) and keyword co-occurrences. Keyword analysis helps identify research trends [15]. Table 6 shows the ten most used keywords and keyword-plus (automatically generated from the titles) in the mass customization articles. It could be identified that multiple periods exist with distinct growth rates for "mass customization" word occurrences when we observed word growth through annual occurrences. When analyzing other main keywords through annual occurrences, more or less the flat growth rate could be identified.

In Fig. 3 keyword co-occurrences are presented through seven separated clusters identified through Vosviewer. Cluster nodes are connected with the links. The red cluster includes "mass customization" as the dominant keyword and "design", "modularity", "system", "variety", "optimization" "product configuration" as other most important keywords, including many other keywords like "product family", "product family design", "product platform", "platform design", "family design", etc. In the second, green, cluster, the most important keywords are "model", "product", "innovation", "quality", including other keywords like "information", "choice", "customer", "satisfaction", and others. The blue cluster includes "impact", "performance" and "integration" and "strategy" as most important keywords, followed by "manufacturing practices", "quality management", "customer", "capability", "perspective", etc. "Mass customisation," "management", "postponement", "strategy" are the main keywords in the yellow cluster. The purple cluster consisted of the following main keywords: "supply chain," "customization", "mass production", "complexity" and "big data". Other words in this cluster are "sustainability", "industry 4.0", "internet of things", etc. The sixth (light blue) cluster contains "product development", "technology", "3d printing", "additive manufacturing", "flexibility", etc., and the seventh (orange) cluster included keywords like: "logistics service supply chain", "allocation" and "scheduling."

Table 5. Top 10 highly cited articles

Author (year)	Title	Source	TC	AC
De Silveira et al. (2001)	Mass customization: literature review and research directions	International Journal of Production Economics	629	29.95
Von Hippel and Katz (2002)	Shifting innovation to users via toolkits	Management Science	488	24.40
Feitzinger and Lee (1997)	Mass customization at Hewlett-Packard: the power of postponement	Harvard Business Review	442	17.68
Schafer et al. (2001)	E-commerce recommendation applications	Data Mining and Knowledge Discovery	421	20.05
Huffman and Kahn (1998)	Variety for sale: mass customization or mass confusion?	Journal of Retailing	406	16.92
Von Hippel (1998)	Economics of product development by users: the impact of "sticky" local information	Management Science	403	16.79
Duray et al. (2000)	Approaches to mass customization: configurations and empirical validation	Journal of Operations Management	382	17.36
Gilmore and Pine (1997)	The four faces of mass customization	Harvard Business Review	346	13.84
Franke et al. (2010)	The "i designed it myself" Effect in mass customization	Management science	307	25.58
Zhong et al. (2013)	RFID-enabled real-time manufacturing execution system for mass-customization production	Robotics and Computer Integrated Manufacturing	261	29

3.5 Co-citation Analysis

VOSviewer software was used to conduct co-citations analyses. Figure 4 shows that five clusters were identified concerning co-citation analysis based on cited sources. Three clusters in which the highest co-citation intensity was identified were furthered analyzed. The red cluster includes the following main sources: International Journal of Production Research, International Journal of Production Economics, Journal of Intelligent Manufacturing, Computers in Industry, etc. As it could be seen, this cluster covers almost all journals from the list of most productive journals in mass customization research (Table 4.) The blue cluster includes the following main sources:

Table 6. Main keywords

Author keywords	Occurrences	Keyword-plus	Occurrences
Mass customization	297	Design	121
Mass customisation	90	Mass customization	75
product configuration	19	Impact	57
3d printing	15	Management	55
Additive manufacturing	15	Model	49
Mass production	14	Performance	38
Supply chain management	14	Systems	36
Modularity	12	Variety	35
Product design	10	Product	29
Product platform	10	System	28

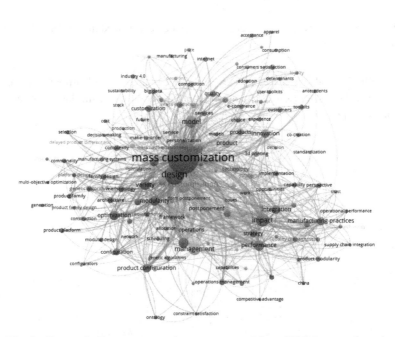

Fig. 3. Keywords Co-occurrences (source: extracted from VOSviewer software)

Journal of Operations Management, Harward Business Review, Management Sciences, Production and Operations Management, Strategic Management Journal, etc. The green cluster contains the following main sources: Journal of Marketing, Journal of Marketing Research, Journal of Consumer Research, and Journal of Product Innovation Management. The blue and the green cluster are more oriented towards management sciences and marketing research.

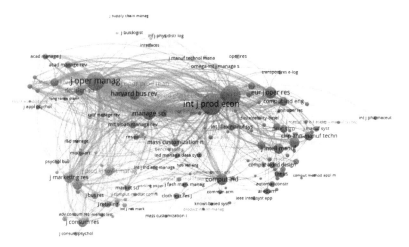

Fig. 4. Co-citation analysis based on cited sources (source: extracted from VOSviewer software) (Color figure online)

Regarding local cited references, co-citation analysis identified four clusters (Fig. 5). The largest red cluster included many nodes, where the largest refers to Da Silveria et al. [4].

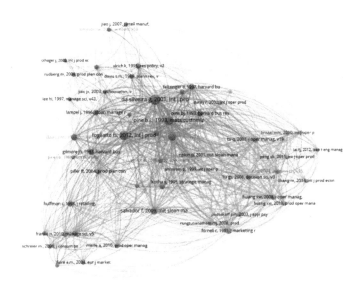

Fig. 5. Co-citation analysis based on cited references (source: extracted from VOSviewer software) (Color figure online)

4   Conclusion

Accumulation of papers, analysis of bibliographic data to determine the structure of research, and tendencies in the evolution of a particular topic, are becoming more complicated as the production of articles grows. Thus, the knowledge base is increasingly difficult to analyze objectively. Bibliometric analysis is becoming very valuable and helpful in conducting objective and reproducible science mapping and research structure analysis in all research areas. Using the "bibliometrix" R Package tool and VOSviewer software, the bibliometric analysis of the bibliographic data was performed on a sample of 802 articles related to muss customization published between 1996 to April 2021. The mass customization literature comprises research predominantly in industrial engineering, engineering manufacturing, and operations research, with the International Journal of Production Economics as the journal with the highest impact and increasing productivity in this topic. Annual scientific production had a stable growth from 1996 to 2004. After that, the decreasing growth rate could signalize that research is consolidating. Though, it must be noted that the number of articles published grew rapidly again in 2020. We identified a high concentration of articles in the most productive countries (the USA and China), whose authors collaborate intensively on this topic. The extensive amount and variety of data allowed us to identify the keyword occurrence and co-citations networks and reveal the related emerging research topics and research streams.

The limitations of this research should be also highlighted. Namely, this research is strictly limited to bibliographic data and analysis that could be extracted using the "bibliometrix" R Package tool and VOSviewer software. The content analyzes of the articles from the sample was not performed. Findings presented in this study can assist future research in this or related research areas in order to overcome these limitations. Future research could answer some of the following questions: Is there an evolution of the mass customization tendency through the years for the research areas? Are there any particular types of products or industries for which mass customization is especially relevant or especially successful? Are there any marked differences between articles from the different "journal clusters"?

References

1. Ciric, D., Lolic, T., Gracanin, D., Stefanovic, D., Lalic, B.: The application of ICT solutions in manufacturing companies in Serbia. In: Lalic, B., Majstorovic, V., Marjanovic, U., von Cieminski, G., Romero, D. (eds.) APMS 2020. IAICT, vol. 592, pp. 122–129. Springer, Cham (2020). https://doi.org/10.1007/978-3-030-57997-5_15
2. Zawadzki, P., Żywicki, K.: Smart product design and production control for effective mass customization in the industry 4.0 concept. Manage. Prod. Eng. Rev. 7(3), 105–112 (2016). https://doi.org/10.1515/mper-2016-0030
3. Pine II, B.: Mass Customization: The New Frontier in Business Competition. Harvard Business School Press, Boston (1993)
4. Da Silveira, G., Borenstein, D., Fogliatto, H.S.: Mass customization: literature review and research directions. Int. J. Prod. Econ. 72(49), 1–13 (2001)

5. Merediz-solà, I., Bariviera, A.F.: Research in international business and finance a bibliometric analysis of bitcoin scientific production. Res. Int. Bus. Financ. **50**, 294–305 (2019)

6. Mongeon, P., Paul-Hus, A.: The journal coverage of Web of Science and Scopus. Scientometrics **106**(1), 213–228 (2015)

7. Ellegaard, O., Wallin, J.A.: The bibliometric analysis of scholarly production: how great is the impact? Scientometrics **105**(3), 1809–1831 (2015)

8. Echchakoui, S., Barka, N.: Industry 4.0 and its impact in plastics industry: a literature review. J. Ind. Inf. Integr. **20**, 100172 (2020)

9. Jin, R., Yuan, H., Chen, Q.: Resources, conservation & recycling science mapping approach to assisting the review of construction and demolition waste management research published between 2009 and 2018. Resour. Conserv. Recycl. **140**, 175–188 (2019)

10. Alon, I., Anderson, J., Munim, Z.H., Ho, A.: A review of the internationalization of Chinese enterprises. Asia Pac. J. Manage. **35**(3), 573–605 (2018). https://doi.org/10.1007/s10490-018-9597-5

11. Bashir, M.F., Komal, B.B., Bashir, M.A.: Analysis of environmental taxes publications: a bibliometric and systematic literature review. Environ. Sci. Pollut. Res. **28**, 20700–20716 (2021)

12. Aria, M., Cuccurullo, C.: Bibliometrix: an R-tool for comprehensive science mapping analysis. J. Informet. **11**(4), 959–975 (2017)

13. Jan, N., Ludo, V.E.: Software survey: VOSviewer, a computer program for bibliometric mapping. Scientometrics **84**(2), 523–538 (2010)

14. Zupic, I., Catez, T.: Bibliometric methods in management and organization. Organ. Res. Meth. **18**(3), 429–472 (2015)

15. Strozzi, F., Colicchia, C., Creazza, A., Noè, C.: Literature review on the 'smart factory' concept using bibliometric tools. Int. J. Prod. Res. **22**(55), 6572–6591 (2017)

Frameworks and Conceptual Modelling for Systems and Services Efficiency

Framework of the Architecture of the Communication Process Within Industry 4.0 Oriented Production System

Marek Fertsch⬀, Michał Fertsch⬀, and Agnieszka Stachowiak⁽⬀⁾⬀

Poznan University of Technology, 60-965 Poznan, Poland
{marek.fertsch,agnieszka.stachowiak}@put.poznan.pl

Abstract. Implementation of the Industry 4.0 concept requires changes on many levels. Implementation of technical solutions (ICT technologies, automation, robotization, AI) entails changes in the organization of processes, as well as in management and communication patterns. The article presents the concept of the IT system architecture supporting communication between the production planner and the production system in the enterprise. The aim was to develop a solution supporting and improving communication between a man and a machine. This area is important for the effectiveness, completeness and quality of information flow and the quality of decisions made on the basis of interpreted feedback. The solution presented in the article was developed as part of the study work on the preparation of the concept of reorganization of the company's production system during the preparation for the implementation of the Industry 4.0 concept. The analyzed enterprise manufactures single large-size machines. The technologies used include casting, machining and assembly. The analyzed production unit was the machining department, as it was selected as a pilot department for the implementation of Industry 4.0. The developed solution will be exemplary and will be the best practice to be used at the next stages of the implementation of Industry 4.0 in the enterprise.

Keywords: Production planning · Man-machine communication · Industry 4.0

1 Introduction

1.1 Industry 4.0

Industry 4.0 is the term broadly referred to, for some companies still something to strive form, for the others the step already taken on the path to Industry 5.0 and further future developments. Interest of both academic and business environments, cognitive and utilitarian aspects of the concept, result in growing number of publications in the field. The dynamics of the growth is distinctive and presented in the Fig. 1a. The concept is multidisciplinary which brings representatives of many disciplines to discussing various aspects of Industry 4.0, as presented in the Fig. 1b.

The publications originating from 2011 – year in which the Industrie 4.0 program was announced in Germany - refer to definitions (Culot et al. 2020; Nosalska et al. 2019; Piccarozzi et al. 2018), scopes (Piccarozzi et al. 2018; Vaidya et al. 2018), pillars

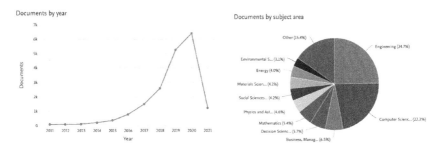

Fig. 1. a. Publications on Industry 4.0 (Scopus database, extracted 26 March 2021). b. Disciplines referred to in publications on Industry 4.0 (Scopus database, extracted 26 March 2021)

(Bai et al. 2020), tools (Frank et al. 2019; Dalenogare et al. 2018; Chiarello et al. 2018) that can be used to upgrade a company to Industry 4.0 level, benefits (Tupa et al. 2017; Davies et al. 2017), difficulties and challenges connected with Industry 4.0 implementation (Thames et al. 2017; Masood et al. 2020), case studies, literature surveys and comparative studies (Pacchini et al. 2019; Davies et al. 2017; Strandhagen et al. 2017; Grieco et al. 2017). Industry 4.0 as broadly defined set of methods, techniques and tools implemented to increase manufacturing efficiency has for ten years been in the center of attention. Development of methods and tools enabling digitization (Bai et al. 2020), Internet of Things (Bai et al. 2020; Frank et al. 2019), Big Data Analysis (Chiarello et al. 2018), Cloud Computing (Thames et al. 2017), augmented reality (Tupa et al. 2017), additive manufacturing (Davies et al. 2017) opened new fields for scientific research. Consequently, interest of academic society is stimulated by interest of business environment all over the world and actively contributes to dissemination of the concept worldwide, proven by numerous reports by independent and governments institutions (Grieco et al. 2017; Schumacher et al. 2016). Countries and regions develop their original, yet Industry 4.0 based, programs stimulating entrepreneurs and economies (Piccarozzi et al. 2018; Dalenogare et al. 2018; Davies et al. 2017) to improve their performance. Benchmarks and best practices published all over the world confirm universality of the concept – it can be implemented in many sectors of industry – and its positive impact on individual companies and entire economies. Recognition of potential benefits inspired one of large Polish companies to initiate processes striving for its adjustment to Industry 4.0 requirements.

1.2   Experience of Polish Companies in Implementation of Industry 4.0

According to Global Entrepreneurship Monitor (GEM) Poland has been included in the efficiency economies with the aspirations to join the group of innovation-oriented countries in recent years. Polish companies to be competitive need to follow the trends and solution recognized worldwide. However, the study conducted by Siemens and Millward Brown on Smart Industry in 2016 (Siemens 2016) showed that only 25%

representatives of Polish production companies were familiar with the concept of Smart Industry. At the same time, a significantly higher number of people declared that their organizations used technologies and solutions characteristic for smart factories. This proved, that there is a gap in knowledge on modern management and industry concepts.

The study conducted by Siemens and Millward Brown on Smart Industry in 2017 (Siemens 2017) proved some progress, showing large interest in innovativeness. The results of the survey show that the technologies that give the greatest competitive advantage are the automation and robotization of production. The most commonly used solution supporting innovativeness was automation with the use of individual machines - in 48.6% of companies have already been implemented, and 10.4% of enterprises had plans for implementation. In turn, the robotization of the entire production line took place in 14.3%, and is planned in 3.6% of companies.

The survey Smart Industry 2018 (Siemens 2018) was conducted on a nationwide sample of 200 companies from the industrial or production sector with the number of employees up to 249 employees, conducting production activity in Poland, i.e. having a production plant or plants operating in Poland. The analysis of the results takes into account the specificity of the heavy and light industry sector.

Smart Industry 2018 Report concludes that 60% of entrepreneurs have not heard of the Industry 4.0 concept. However, this is not synonymous with the non-use of modern technologies by these companies. It has already been proved by findings from previous reports 2016 and 2017.

2 Theoretical Background

2.1 Production System in Industry 4.0 Context

The elements that constitute the production system in the conditions of Industry 4.0 can be roughly divided based on their nature into four interrelated groups (layers). Brief characteristics of the layers covers the nature of elements and processes performed within them: 1) physical layer - it is made up of production and auxiliary machines and devices, implementing and supporting physical processes of material transformation: production processes. The term 'supporting' used above should be understood in a narrow sense - as the implementation of physical processes ensuring the continuity and proper course of the basic process, which is transformation of work objects (materials) in terms of shape, size, appearance, physical or chemical composition or properties. These processes are the so-called auxiliary and service processes and include transport and storage in the production process, production quality control, replacement of tools and workshop aids, and maintenance; 2) IT layer - devices (computers) and software controlling elements of the physical layer and creating a virtual copy of physical reality and supporting people in collecting and visualizing information relevant to decision-making. The task of this layer is also to make some decisions (in predefined scope, based on functionalities available); 3) Social layer - people working in the production system, both on operational and managerial level, communicating and cooperating with its various layers; 4) Communication layer - Internet ensuring the flow of information between individual layers and their elements.

The layers are not isolated, they make an open system of elements cooperating in achieving the predefined goal (production task) and link to environment with material and information flow. In Industry 4.0 context the physical layer will be strongly related or even integrated with IT layer as it will consist of cyber-physical systems. Cyber-physical systems operation control, according to the views dominating in the literature on the subject, will be based on the technology of embedded systems. These are special-purpose computer systems that are an integral part of the hardware they operate. Each embedded system is based on a microprocessor (or microcontroller) programmed to perform a limited number of tasks. The challenge seems to be integration of social and communication layer so that the production system benefited from synergy.

2.2   Integrated Physical and IT Layer Structure and Functions

According to the literature on the subject, the CPS layer will cover five levels, as presented in the Fig. 2:

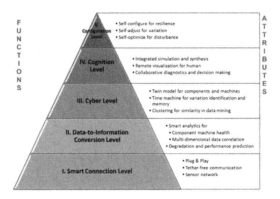

Fig. 2. 5C architecture for implementation of cyber-physical system Source (Lee et al. 2015).

The architecture presented covers mostly IT structure issues but it links them to physical layer through implemented technical solutions, mostly located at level I (smart connection level), data interpretation schemes, located at levels II and III, the upper levels are linked to social and communication layers as they support decisions making (level IV) and resilience of the system (V): Smart Connection level - it consists of data collecting devices - sensors (sensors) installed on machines and devices whose task is to capture signals from the surrounding environment, recognize and record them, and a network that amplifies the signals and transmits them over long distances, further processing using digital techniques and computers and remembering it. Data-to-information Conversion level - this level consists of a set of programs collecting and processing data collected by the layer of data collecting devices. These programs can be located on one central computer, on several computers or in the "cloud". The tasks of this level are: diagnosing the condition of machines, devices and work environment, predicting failures of machines and devices and environmental hazards and their potential impact on the operation of the system, analysis of collected data in terms of searching for their temporal, spatial and causal relationships for the needs of system and environment diagnostics.

Some of the tasks of this level can also be performed by embedded systems, which are elements of the physical layer. The division of tasks in terms of transforming data into information between the elements of the physical layer and the IT layer is not clearly defined. It is difficult to indicate the criteria for this division. It seems that the main criterion should be to maximize the operational reliability of the entire production system. **Cyber level** - consists of a set of programs collecting and processing information collected by the layer transforming data into information. The tasks of this level are: modeling the behavior of machines, devices, changes in resource availability over time, analysis of the distribution (statistics) of events, activities, system states in time to forecast their frequency and duration, grouping of collected information for similarity for analysis using Big Data Analysis techniques. **Cognition level** - the level that recognizes (diagnoses) the operation of the system - consists of a set of programs collecting and processing information collected by the layer that analyzes information. It also organizes communication in the system by controlling the flow of data and information between individual layers. The tasks of this level are: preparation of information and data visualization for the needs of computer-human communication, simulation and information integration for resource demand forecasting, organization of cooperation in the field of joint (human-computer system) assessment of the situation and joint decision-making. **Configuration level** – the highest level that stabilizes the system providing resilient control, supervisory control and actions. The level is based on self-learning mechanisms and auto-regulations and its tasks are: Self-configuration, Self-adjustment, Self-optimization.

The structure is internally linked and related with other layers, which requires multi-level communication. The framework of communication schemes and architecture for the communication processes not only enabling but supporting the communication developed for a large machining industry company is presented in the next chapters of the paper.

3   Problem Definition

The problem to be solved is designing interface (communication scheme) between man and machine to support information flow and decision making process in complex environment striving for increased automation and digitization of processes. The information flow in the analyzed production department is based on the blueprints system. The production planner fills in the relevant documents, analyzes the situation and makes appropriate decisions based on the reports from the workstation service. The approach is based on manual approach, planner's knowledge and experience.

In Industry 4.0 environment such approach is insufficient and inefficient. Communication needs to be improved and potential of IT support, imminent element of Industry 4.0 concept, should be exploited. The problem was defined for a specific production environment, as a part of a dedicated project striving for adjusting the production system to Industry 4.0 level.

Yet, we believe that communication process and its improvement are problems that many companies face, disregarding their technical and technological advancement, automation and robotization level. Hence, though referred to the specific company, the problem is universal in nature.

4 Problem Solution

4.1 Structure of Communication Process

For the problem defined in the Sect. 3 the following solution framework was designed. The proposed communication is based on availability of database extracting data from sensors and covering three data sets (S, P, D):

S - a set of workstations within a given production unit.

The elements of the set s_i, i = {1,...,n} are divided into groups distinguished according to: **Group size** - this parameter is identified by the number of workstations of a given type in the production unit: Location - this parameter is distinguished by the location of a given station in the production process in a given production unit, it is possible to classify the station into three groups in terms of significance: 1) initial, stations performing initial operations in the processes performed in a given unit, 2) intermediate, positions that perform intermediate (middle) operations in the processes performed in a given unit, final, stations carrying out finishing operations in the processes performed in a given unit, **Availability** - this parameter is determined in relation to the planning horizon, on the basis of the load plan for a given workstation from the workstation system, each time unit is assigned the status: 1) available, 2) busy, 3) damaged, based on reports.

P - a set of items performed in a given production unit in a given planning horizon. The elements of the set p_j, j = {1, m} are divided into categories according to the following criteria: 1) advancement - it is defined as the relation of the planned start-up date to the current date, according to this criterion it is possible to classify a given subject into the following groups: pending - the launch date is a future date in relation to the current date; delayed - the launch date is the one that has already passed; in progress - split into three categories: a) in progress as planned - in the 'information' part, the execution of at least one technological operation has been registered, the date of completion of the last registered completed operation corresponds to that planned in the MES, b) in progress and pending - in the 'information' part, the execution of at least one technological operation has been registered, the deadline, the planned date of launching the next scheduled operation has already expired, c) in progress, in processing - in the 'information' part, the start of any technological operation is registered, there is no information about its completion, the planned completion date has not yet expired, d) in progress, interrupted in the 'information' part, the start of any technological operation is registered, there is no information about its completion, the planned completion date of the registered operation has already expired; e) completed - split into two categories: completed as planned - in the 'information' part, the execution of the last technological operation was recorded, the date of execution of this operation is earlier or equal to the planned completion date, completed delayed - in the 'information' part, the execution of the last technological operation has been registered, the date of performing this operation is later than the planned completion date, 2) importance - this category determines the significance of a given assortment item from the point of view of the production process carried out in a given production unit, according to this criterion it is possible to classify a given item into the following groups (including a given assortment item in a specific group is done using the expert method): a) key, b) significant, c) supplementary; 3) quantity - this category can be referred to as the planned quantity of a given item of assortment ratio to the quantity available after a given operation, according to this criterion, it is possible to classify a given item into the following groups: a) launched according to the plan - if the quantity included in a given operation corresponds to the planned quantity, b) completed according to the plan - if the quantity completing a given operation corresponds to the quantity planned, c) insufficient - if the quantity that starts or ends a given operation is smaller than the quantity planned.

D - a set of data assigned to a given set of positions and the set of objects performed on it in a given planning horizon. Each data saved in this set has two versions: 1) planned value - imported from the MES system, 2) actual value - saved as information from sensors or embedded systems installed on the workstations.

Data $d_{(i,\ 1)}$ where $i = \{1,\ldots, N\}$ and $1 = \{1,\ldots, P\}$ relating to workstations are of the following scope: availability of the position, the date of launching a given operation on the workstation, completion date of a given operation on the workstation. The suggested structure of the process is dedicated to the specific problem defined in the Sect. 3, nevertheless we designed it to be as universal and flexible as possible to enable its implementation in any production systems which deals with similar problems.

4.2 Communication Process Realization

Communication between a production planner and the systems is based on continuous interactions. The system produces the following reports: 1) damaged positions and available positions, each report is prepared according to the categories of initial, intermediate and final positions; 2) completed items divided into the categories of scheduled completion and delayed completed, the reported items are divided into the categories of key, material and supplementary items, 3) items waiting to be launched with a breakdown into the categories of pending and pending delayed, the reported items are divided into categories of key, significant and supplementary items, 4) report on the number of completed assortment items from the insufficient category, broken down into the categories of key, significant and supplementary items.

The system collects data from embedded systems, sensors and sensors on an ongoing basis. The incoming data is continuously used to update the reports. After each update, two versions of reports - the one before the update and the one after the update are compared by the experimental system. If the differences between the reports are considered significant, the information about it, together with the version of the report, is provided to the production planner after updating. In addition to this information, the scheduler also has access to all subsequent versions of the reports.

The set of reports generated by the system has been supplemented with a mechanism for comparing and tracking the compliance of the production flow between the planned, and the actual flow. The concept of the applied mechanism was based on the method of analyzing the process capability. It is a computational procedure for assessing whether the process is running correctly and meets the requirements. A modified capability index model was used. The indicator used to track the compliance of the production flow between the planned amount and the actual flow was built on the basis of the process capability index C_p used in the process capability analysis method. In the original version, this indicator is a measure of the precision of the process. It measures the width of the actual process scatter relative to the width of the tolerance field. Data from control charts are used in the process capability analysis. Control limits are the numerical values within which the process is to run. These are usually the minimum (lower limit) and maximum (upper limit) allowable values of certain process parameters. The boundaries are defined at the design stage of the process.

In the applied solution, the lower and upper limits of the process were adopted arbitrarily. The value of the lower control limit was assumed to be $S_l = 0$. The value of the upper control limit was assumed to be $S_u = 1$. The production system was divided into three channels: 1) initial channel including positions qualified as initial, 2) an indirect channel including positions classified as intermediate, 3) end channel including positions qualified as ending.

For each of the distinguished channels, it was assumed that a separate control chart was developed and that the proposed U_f flow uniformity index was calculated separately.

The values of the analyzed process will be marked on the control card at the beginning and end of the technological operation. These values will be adopted depending on whether the commencement or completion of a given technological operation at a specific position took place as planned, was delayed or was faster than planned: a) in the case when the commencement or termination of a given operation took place on the scheduled date, the process value x = 0.5 entered on the control card, b) if the start or end of a given operation was delayed compared to the scheduled date, the process value x = 1 + α entered on the control card, where α is the delay value; c) in the case when the commencement or completion of a given technological operation took place before the scheduled date, the process value x = 1 entered on the control card.

The flow uniformity index U_f is calculated at the end of each shift for each channel separately according to the formula similar to the coefficient C_p.

$$U_f = 1/3\delta \tag{1}$$

where:
U_f - flow uniformity index.
T = 1 - tolerance range, the difference between the upper and lower control limit.
δ - standard deviation.

With the adopted method of determining the value of the process applied on the control card, in a situation when all technological operations are started and completed on time, the U_f coefficient takes the value of zero. The value of the coefficient decreases in the case of earlier commencement or termination of technological operations, and it decreases significantly in the case of delays.

After collecting a specific set of empirical data, the authors intend to check whether the specific U_f value can be assigned to specific states of the production process.

It is possible to modify the structure or the flow of the communication process to adjust and adapt it to the specific conditions of any other company dealing with the communication problem in manufacturing process.

5   Conclusion

Work on the development of the communication scheme presented in this article is in progress. The analysis of the production system led to an update of the system concept. It turned out that due to the specific quality requirements of some of the elements produced in the production system, the data on the course of their production process must be extended, stored in separate files and made available to external stakeholders on request. It was decided that this data would come from the communication system between the production planner and the production system, and collected, stored and made available by the IT system operating at the level of the entire enterprise. This requires designing an interface between the communication system between the production planner and the production system and the information system operating at the enterprise level.

The developed solution was pre-evaluated during the presentation for the company. Basic assumptions were presented and explained, conclusions were discussed and as a result some improvements to initial idea were introduced (they are included in the conceptual solution presented in the paper). The implementation is on-going and after it is completed the system will be evaluated with the set of qualitative and quantitative measures including: cohesion rate (information flow vs material flow), muda size (for time, errors, and activity mudas), cost of information flow (prior to implementation and after that). The results of evaluation will be the basis for improvement, we assume periodic evaluation to control growing maturity of the solution.

The team of automation and IT specialists operating in the company is currently working on the concept of selecting embedded systems and sensors, connecting them into a network and selecting software. The expected results from the communication system implementation will consist in qualitative and quantitative improvement of information flow expressed by: number of errors, number of unnecessary actions and decisions taken, lead-time for information flow and material flow, flexibility of manufacturing system and the cost of information flow. The evaluation measures for evaluation of the system were selected to identify the expected benefits and enable continuous improvement of the solution.

Acknowledgment. The research was financed from Faculty of Engineering Management project fund nr 0812/SBAD/4185.

References

Bai, C., Dallasega, P., Orzes, G., Sarkis, J.: Industry 4.0 technologies assessment: a sustainability perspective. Int. J. Prod. Econ. **229**, 107776 (2020)

Chiarello, F., Trivelli, L., Bonaccorsi, A., Fantoni, G.: Extracting and mapping industry 4.0 technologies using Wikipedia. Comput. Ind. **100**, 244–257 (2018). https://doi.org/10.1016/j.compind.2018.04.006

Culot, G., Nassimbeni, G., Orzes, G., Sartor, M.: Behind the definition of Industry 4.0: analysis and open questions. Int. J. Prod. Econ. **226**, 107617 (2020)

Dalenogare, L.S., Benitez, G.B., Ayala, N.F., Frank, A.G.: The expected contribution of Industry 4.0 technologies for industrial performance. Int. J. Prod. Econ. **204**, 383–394 (2018)

Davies, R., Coole, T., Smith, A.: Review of Socio-technical Considerations to Ensure Successful Implementation of Industry 4.0. Procedia Manuf. **11**, 1288–1295 (2017)

Frank, A.G., Dalenogare, L.S., Ayala, N.F.: Industry 4.0 technologies: Implementation patterns in manufacturing companies. Int. J. Prod. Econ. **210**, 15–26 (2019)

Grieco, A., et al.: An Industry 4.0 case study in fashion manufacturing. Proc. Manuf. **11**, 871–877 (2017)

Lee, J., Bagheri, B., Kao, H.-A.: A Cyber-Physical Systems architecture for Industry 4.0-based manufacturing systems. Manuf. Lett. **3**, 18–23 (2015)

Masood, T., Sonntag, T.: Industry 4.0: adoption challenges and benefits for SMEs. Comput. Ind. **121**, 103261 (2020)

Nosalska, K., Piątek, Z.M., Mazurek, G., Rządca, R.: Industry 40: coherent definition framework with technological and organizational interdependencies. J. Manuf. Technol. Manage. **31**(5), 837–862 (2019)

Pacchini, A.P.T., Lucato, W.C., Facchini, F., Mummolo, G.: The degree of readiness for the implementation of Industry 4.0. Comput. Ind. **113**, 103125 (2019)

Piccarozzi, M., Aquilani, B., Gatti, C.: Industry 40 in management studies: a systematic literature review. Sustainability **10**(10), 3821 (2018)

Schumacher, A., Erol, S., Sihn, W.: A Maturity Model for Assessing Industry 4.0 Readiness and Maturity of Manufacturing Enterprises, Procedia CIRP, Vol. 52, 161–166 (2016)

Siemens report on Smart Industry (2016). https://assets.new.siemens.com/siemens/assets/api/uuid:f923a16c-496d-45ce-976b-98b351371789/Raport-Smart-Industry-Polska-2016.pdf. Accessed 15 Mar 2021

Siemens report on Smart Industry (2017). https://assets.new.siemens.com/siemens/assets/api/uuid:1718b566-6758-4660-92ab-fc6109c677e8/2raport-smart-industry-polska-2017.pdf. Accessed 15 Mar 2021

Siemens report on Smart Industry (2018). https://assets.new.siemens.com/siemens/assets/api/uuid:5ab60cd0-cc54-49a3-a564-9ab13e971ea4/smart-industry-polska-2018-raport.pdf. Accessed 15 Mar 2021

Strandhagen, J.W., Alfnes, E., Strandhagen, J.O., Vallandingham, L.R.: The fit of Industry 4.0 applications in manufacturing logistics: a multiple case study. Adv. Manuf. **5**(4), 344–358 (2017). https://doi.org/10.1007/s40436-017-0200-y

Thames, L., Schaefer, D.: Industry 4.0: an overview of key benefits, technologies, and challenges. In: Thames, L., Schaefer, D. (eds.) Cybersecurity for Industry 4.0. SSAM, pp. 1–33. Springer, Cham (2017). https://doi.org/10.1007/978-3-319-50660-9_1

Tupa, J., Simota, J., Steiner, F.: Aspects of risk management implementation for industry 4.0. Proc. Manuf. **11**, 1223–1230 (2017)

Vaidya, S., Ambad, A.P., Bhosle, S.: Industry 4.0 – a glimpse. Procedia Manuf. **20**, 233–238 (2018)

A Fuzzy Accident Risk Analysis Approach for a Concurrent Engineering Platform

Mahmoud Shahrokhi[1]([✉]) [iD] and Alain Bernard[2]

[1] University of Kurdistan, Sanandaj, Iran
m.shahrokhi@uok.ac.ir
[2] Centrale Nantes (LS2N, UMR CNRS 6004), Nantes, France
Alain.bernard@ec-nantes.fr

Abstract. This paper uses the fuzzy theory basics to assess accident risk that may damage a target (e.g., humans, assets, or the environment). Converting a target's position to a membership degree in a fuzzy danger zone (FDZ) helps calculate risk indices. Using FDZs normalizes the effects of different kinds of hazards, similarly visualizes them, and distinguishes the impact of a threat on various types of targets. This paper presents a related mathematical formulation. The proposed approach evaluates the accident risks by simulating industrial activities in CAD, virtual reality, and augmented reality when using a concurrent engineering platform. This approach can calculate the risk index during a human task simulation and through real-time human interaction with a virtual machine during safety analysis and training. The results also are credible to activate alarm systems according to the operator's limbs place during work. The model provides a normalized and similar scale for various risks (e.g., biological, chemical, and physical hazards) and computes the effect of danger on different target types.

Keywords: Risk analysis · Concurrent engineering · Fuzzy logic · Virtual reality · Augmented reality

1 Introduction

Using the three digital prototypes in CAD, virtual reality, and augmented reality creates realistic visualizations, renderings, and animations of the complex systems. It plays an essential role in concurrent engineering platforms, where various disciplines use these models to predict industrial systems' behavior before constructing and employing them. The conventional risk analyses approaches are inconvenient for using these models to perform quantitative risk analyses. This research develops a fuzzy approach for doing risk analysis in a concurrent engineering context by using geometric shapes for facilitating collaboration and sharing risks information by visualizing the risk entities and preventing inconsistencies.

A. Dolgui et al. (Eds.): APMS 2021, IFIP AICT 634, pp. 351–360, 2021.
https://doi.org/10.1007/978-3-030-85914-5_37

2 Background

Dangers are the potential of things or situations to cause harm, and "risk" is an indicator for evaluating their importance by aggregating the severity and the likelihood of their possible consequences [1, 2]. A danger creates hazards (e.g., a toxic substance that makes a toxification hazard). A danger zone (DZ) is a hypothetical area where the threat can potentially cause harm [3]. The hazard magnitude denotes the parameters to explain the potential of the hazard for harming the target. It is the value of physicals (e.g., speed and temperature), chemical (e.g., the amount and density of one or several hazardous materials), biological or conceptual parameters (e.g., the probability or risk of an accident). Figure 1 shows the hazard magnitude variation around a hypothetical hazard object indicated by a red star. The horizontal axis (x-axis) represents the locations around the danger source, and the vertical axis shows the intensity of the danger in its neighborhoods. The dashed line in this figure shows the hazard magnitude variation as a mathematical function of the one-dimensional geometric coordinates. In this figure, the traditional danger zone is shown with a red line and includes every point where the assumed intensity of the danger is more than an acceptable level ($\underline{H}$).

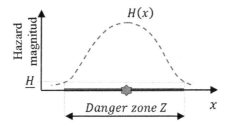

Fig. 1. Representation of a mono-dimensional DZ, as a classic set of points

Some examples of hazard amplitude are the intensity of hazardous radiation around a radioactive material, the high-temperature air around a fire source, the explosion blast wave, or the toxic gas concentration during a poisonous gas leak. It can even be an understanding of the concept of collision risk around a dangerous moving object.

In this way, a conventional DZ is a crisp (classic) set of points in the workplace, illustrated as follows:

$$Z = \{x | H(x) > \underline{H}\} \qquad x \in X \tag{1}$$

3 The Literature Review

This chapter introduces the basic concepts and a review of previous applications of 3D models in risk analysis.

Bernard and Hasan considered a danger zone as one of the workplace entities, characterized by its name and origin [4]. Hasan and et al. considered DZ one of the system's safety modeling entities described by its name, nature, size, and source [5]. Pouliquen and et al. use it for estimating the severity of danger, in real-time, in the virtual reality context for a sheet-pressing operation [6]. In recent years, very little research has been done on risk analysis in 3D using the concept of a danger zone. Alba and et al. proposed a distributed real-time anti-collision approach that uses hazardous areas to create the ability to prevent collisions with other objects on the robot, based on accurate 3D simulation of a manufacturing cell [7]. Yi-Hao and Yet-Pole construct a three-dimensional fire risk analysis technique for common building fires by simulating the thermal radiation hazards [8]. Cao and et al. studied flame propagation behaviors in explosion venting and the quantitative relationship of the maximum flame front length, and they calculated the variation of the temperature field in explosion venting [9].

4   The Proposed Model

According to fuzzy set theory, not only can an object be inside or outside a set, but it can also have a degree of membership.

By assigning membership between 0 and 1 to each point, Shahrokhi and Bernard introduce a "fuzzy space" to distribute risk around a hazard factor [10]. It explains how each location has a degree of belonging to the fuzzy danger set. Shahrokhi and Bernard measured instantaneous risk indices for each body part for simulation sequences by measuring body parts' membership in a Gaussian FDZ [11].

4.1   The Proposed Model Description

This paper proposes a mathematical risk analysis model using the concept of a fuzzy danger zone to consider several types of targets with a different values. The effects of hazards vary on the different types of targets.

The proposed model is developed based on the following assumptions:

1. There is a dangerous source that produces a hazard.
2. A hazard barrier reduces some part of the hazard magnitude.
3. There are several types of targets.
4. The hazard has different effects on different kinds of targets.
5. There is a danger zone for each type of target.
6. Each target has a target protective barrier that reduces the danger for the target.
7. The exposure time is known and limited.
8. The exposure mode is known and similar for all target types.
9. The targets are immovable during the exposure time.
10. The hazard and target attributes are constant and unchanged over the exposure time.

4.2   The Proposed Model Formulation

The model uses the following symbols:

k	Target type index ($k \in K$)
J_k	Set of targets of type k
φ_k^h	The portion of the reduced hazard magnitude by the hazard safety barrier for the target type k
φ_j^k	A fuzzy hedge describing the ability of the protective target barrier to reduce the magnitude of the hazard for the target t_j^k
t_j^k	Target j, (jth target) of target type k, ($k \in K, j \in J_k$)
$x_{t_j^k}$	Coordinates of the jth target of target type k
X	Workplace universe of discourse
$H(x)$	The magnitude of the hazard in point x
H_j^l	Maximum acceptable level of the hazard for target j
H_j^h	Minimum mortal (destructive) level of the hazard for target j
$\tilde{Z}^k$	Fuzzy danger zone produced by the hazard for the target type k
$\mu_{\tilde{Z}^k}^H(H(x))$	The membership degree FDZ (Hazard severity), in point x, according to the hazard amplitude for target type k
$\mu_{\tilde{Z}_j^k}\left(x_{t_j^k}\right)$	Membership degree of presence of protected target j in the fuzzy danger zone $\tilde{Z}^k$, according to the target position (final hazard severity)
$d\left(\mu_{\tilde{Z}_j^k}\right)$	Target damage, the vulnerability function of the target of type k, which calculates the expected percentage target damage, based on $\mu_{\tilde{Z}_j^k}$
$W_{t_j^k}$	The value of the target t_j^k
$D_{t_j^k}\left(x_{t_j^k}\right)$	The value of damage (loss of the value) of the target t_j^k caused by accident, based on the target place

By using fuzzy sets notifications, an FDZ is an ordinary fuzzy set such as $\tilde{Z}$, defined by its domain (x) and membership function $\mu_{\tilde{Z}}(x)$ as [12]:

$$\tilde{Z} = \int_X \frac{\mu_{\tilde{Z}}(x)}{x} \tag{2}$$

In this way, the value of the membership function $\mu_{\tilde{Z}}(x)$ is a continuous function that indicates the degree of membership of point x in a fuzzy set $\tilde{Z}$, which can take any value between 0 and 1, as follows:

$$\mu_{\tilde{Z}} : x \rightarrow [0, 1] \qquad x \in X \tag{3}$$

In the above formula, X is the universe of discourse of variable x. The classic DZ is a $\alpha - cut$ of the FDZ, as follows:

$$DZ = \left\{ x \mid \mu_{\tilde{Z}}(x) > \alpha, x \in X \right\} \tag{4}$$

Figure 2 shows how increasing the value of α from α_1 (Fig. 8a) to α_2 (Fig. 8b) leads to a decrease in the recognized area of the danger zone.

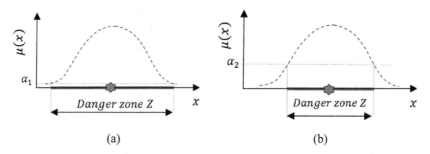

(a)   (b)

Fig. 2. A demonstration of a mono-dimensional DZ, as an α-cuts of an FDZ

By considering attributes of the hazard and the target, $\mu_{\tilde{Z}}^H(H)$ assigns a danger membership degree to each hazard magnitude, for each target type k, as follows:

$$\mu_{\tilde{Z}^k}^H : H(x) \rightarrow [0,1] \qquad \forall H(x) \in \mathbb{R}^+ \tag{5}$$

Figure 3 shows a schematic diagram of the general form of the relationship between the degree of membership in the FDZ for target type k and the magnitude of the hazard.

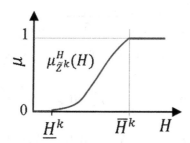

Fig. 3. The relationship between the hazard magnitude and the membership degree of the FDZ for a specific target type

For example, Table 1 illustrates the physiological tolerance time for various carbon dioxide concentrations (percent by Volume (% V/):

Table 1. Physiological tolerance time for different carbon dioxide concentration

The concentration of Carbon Dioxide in Air (% V/V) ($H(x)$)	Maximum exposure limit (minutes)
0.5	Undefined
1.0	Undefined
2.0	480
1.5	60
3.0	20
4.0	10
5.0	7
6.0	5
7.0	Less than 3

Figure 4 may present the relationship between the concentration of carbon dioxide in the air and the degree of membership in the FDZ for 10 min' exposure of target type k:

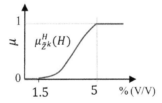

Fig. 4. The degree of membership in the FDZ for the exemplified scenario

By changing the variable $\mu_{\tilde{Z}_j^k}\left(x_{t_j^k}\right) = \mu_{\tilde{Z}^k}^H(H(x_{t_j^k}))$, the result will be:

$$\mu_{\tilde{Z}_j^k} : \left(x_{t_j^k} \in X\right) \rightarrow [0,1] \qquad \forall j \in J \tag{6}$$

Thus the following fuzzy set defines FDZ for the target t_j^k:

$$\tilde{Z}_j^k = \left\{(x,\mu)|x \in X, \mu = \mu_{\tilde{Z}_j^k}(x)\right\} \qquad \forall k \in K, j \in J_k \tag{7}$$

For example, Fig. 5 shows an FDZ that assigns a membership degree to each point's coordinates in mono-dimensional space.

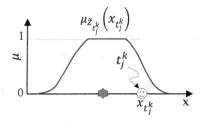

Fig. 5. A demonstration of a fuzzy mono-dimensional DZ

Assigning 0 membership to a point means that the hazard magnitude is equal to or less than the maximum hazard acceptable level. Setting 1 to a place indicates that the danger for the target in that place is equal to or greater than a fatal or destructive threshold level. The effect of protective barriers describes their power to neutralize the danger as the proportion of reduction of the danger amplitude (φ). The values 0 and 1 for φ indicate an unprotected and a fully protected target, respectively. The values between 0 and 1 concern a protective barrier that diminishes some part of the hazard. Therefore, the FDZ for a protected target is defined as follows:

$$\mu_{\tilde{Z}_j^k}\left(x_{t_j^k}\right) = \begin{cases} 0, & \left(1-\varphi_j^k\right)H\left(x_{t_j^k}\right) \leq \underline{H}_j^k \\ h_j\left((1-\varphi_k^h)H\left(x_{t_j^k}\right)\right), & \underline{H}_j^k < \left(1-\varphi_j^k\right)H\left(x_{t_j^k}\right) \leq \bar{H}_j^k \\ 1, & \left(1-\varphi_j^k\right)H\left(x_{t_j^k}\right) \geq \bar{H}_j^k \end{cases} \tag{8}$$

Where $h_j(H)$ maps the hazard magnitude (or other hazard attributes) to its harmfulness for the protected target on a scale between 0 and 1.

If it would be possible to define target vulnerability function $d\left(\mu_{\tilde{Z}^k}\right)$ for calculating the expected damage, based on $\mu_{\tilde{Z}_j^k}$, then, by defining function D as follows, we can directly estimate the target damage based on the target location:

$$D_{t_j^k}\left(x_{t_j^k}\right) = d\left(\varphi_j^k\left(\mu_{\tilde{Z}_j^k}\left(x_{t_j^k}\right)\right)\right) \qquad x_{t_j^k} \in X \tag{9}$$

Where φ_j^k apply the effect of the target barrier on the fuzzy danger zone.

4.3   Numerical Example

Here, an accident scenario is presented in a one-dimensional workplace space to illustrate the model application. The objective is to assess the degree of inhalation damage of 4 targets of two types exposed to the toxic cloud of carbon dioxide for 10 min. Before the exposure, the ventilation system reduces 15% of the leaked gas concentration ($\varphi_k^h = 0.15$). The following table presents the CO_2 concentration in different workplace locations before and after ventilation operation (Table 2).

Table 2. Reduction of the CO_2 concentration by using the hazard barrier, in the exemplified scenario

Coordinates of the place (x)	$H(x)$ (percent by Volume)	
	Immediately after the accident	After air ventilation
4	8.05	7
5	6.9	6
8	5.75	5

Suppose two different types of targets exposing to high CO_2 concentrations. Table 3 illustrates the accident analysis process and results according to the exemplified scenario.

Table 3. The accident analysis process and results, according to the exemplified scenario

Target	Target type	Target value (\$)	Target place	Hazard magnitude	Hazard severity	The target safety barrier effect of	Final hazard severity	Target vulnerability function (%)		Target damage
t_j^k	k	$W_{t_j^k}$	$x_{t_j^k}$	$H(x)$	$\mu_{\tilde{Z}^k}^H(H)$	$\varphi_j^k(\mu)$	$\mu_{\tilde{Z}_j^k}(x_{t_j^k})$	$d\left(\mu_{\tilde{Z}_j^k}\right)$	(%)	Monetary unit
t_1^1	1	10^6	4	7	1	$(\mu)^{1.2}$	1	$100\mu_{\tilde{Z}_1^1}$	100	10^6
t_2^1		10^8	5	6	0.9	$(\mu)^{1.4}$	0.86	$100\mu_{\tilde{Z}_2^1}$	86	8.6×10^7
t_1^2	2	10^6	5	6	0.9	$(\mu)^2$	0.81	$70\mu_{\tilde{Z}_j^k}$	56.7	5.67×10^5
t_1^2		10^7	8	5	0.7	$(\mu)^{1.5}$	0.59	$70\mu_{\tilde{Z}_j^k}$	41.3	4.13×10^6

5 Discussion and Limitations

This paper aims to integrate risk analysis into a 3D design platform based on using geometric profiles to illustrate the spatial risk distribution. Using an FDZ in a CAD model visualizes the normalizing effects of different kinds of hazards. For example, while simulating a toxic spill accident, each FDZ gives a typical picture of a gradual decrease in the mass concentration as the cloud moves away from the epicenter of the evaporation, which can be compared with created FDZ from an explosion accident, at another point, at the same time. It can be applied to calculate the risk index during a human task simulation and through real-time human interaction with a virtual machine during safety analysis and training. The results also are credible to activate alarm systems according to the operator's limbs place during work. The use of fuzzy danger zone has the following advantages:

1. Visualize a representative danger zone in 3D platforms and calculate the membership degree in an FDZ as a hazard index using computerized calculation methods during a simulation.
2. Create a normalized and similar scale for various risks (e.g., biological, chemical, and physical hazards).
3. Compute the effect of danger on different types of targets.
4. Calculate a momentary risk index for each specific target (e.g., different human limbs) according to their type and location.

Also, the following limits the "application of the model."

1. The model lacks validation.
2. Using this approach requires developing more complex risk analysis applications.
3. Model development requires a lot of data on the nature of risk, the effect of distance on reducing it, and the effect of risk on the various types of targets expressed by mathematical formulas.
4. The model ignores the effect of the time mode of exposure of the target to the danger.
5. The model assumes that the risk factor and a goal location remain constant during the exposure.
6. The model applies to hazards whose severity depends on the target distance from them.

More efforts are necessary to integrate complementary risk analysis methods such as FMEA and fault trees into CAD platforms. Supposing a linear effect of barrier on the hazard magnitude assumes that it neutralizes a part of the hazard. Using a more realistic function for the actual impact of the safety measures improves the model. This approach is only applicable to dangers with known spatial effects. The model supposes that danger zone attributes and the target location are fixed and recognized during the exposure. Further research can discuss combining the probability and fuzzy danger zone concepts and combining several FDZs.

6 Conclusion

This paper provides an overview of definitions of a DZ as an essential risk analysis concept. It supports applying the fuzzy set theory for modeling DZs as a meter of spatial danger variation. It presents a mathematical model to calculate a real-time risk index during three-dimensional simulations of activities. Using this approach helps perform the risk and design analyses concurrently and improves multidisciplinary communication. Future research may consider the effects of multiple dangers, variations of the target exposure time and place.

References

1. Jo, Y.D., Parkd, K.S.: Dynamic management of human error to reduce total risk. J. Loss Prev. Process Ind. **16**(4), 313–321 (2003)
2. Polet, P., Vanderhaegen, F., Amalberti, R.: Modelling border-line tolerated conditions of use (BTCU) and associated risks. Saf. Sci. **41**(2–3), 111–136 (2003)
3. Gallego, L.E., et al.: Lightning risk assessment using fuzzy logic. J. Electrostat. **60**(2–4), 233–239 (2004)
4. Bernard, A., Hasan, R.: Working Situation Model for Safety Integration during Design Phase. CIRP Ann. Manuf. Technol. **51**(1), 119–122 (2002)
5. Hasan, R., Bernard, A., Ciccotelli, J., Martin, P.: Integrating safety into the design process: elements and concepts relative to the working situation. Saf. Sci. **41**, 155–179 (2003)
6. Pouliquen, M., Bernard, A., Marsot, J., Chodorge, L.: Virtual hands and virtual reality multimodal platform to design safer industrial systems. Comput. Ind. **58**, 46–56 (2007)
7. Alba, F., Indri, M., Romanelli, F.: A real time distributed approach to collision avoidance for industrial manipulators. In Proceedings of the 2014 IEEE Emerging Technology and Factory Automation (ETFA), pp. 1–8 (2014)
8. Yi-Hao, H., Yet-Pole, I.: Development of a 3D risk analysis technique for fire disaster and its application on accident simulation of a public site. J. Loss Prev. Process Ind. **69**, 104349 (2021)
9. Cao, W., et al.: Explosion venting hazards of temperature effects and pressure characteristics for premixed hydrogen-air mixtures in a spherical container. Fuel **290**, 120034 (2021)
10. Shahrokhi, M., Bernard, A.: A fuzzy approach for definition of dangerous zone in industrial systems. In: IEEE International Conference on Systems, Man and Cybernetics, vol. 7, pp. 6318–6324 (2004)
11. Shahrokhi, M., Bernard, A.: Modelling of the occupational hazards entities in a general model of products processes and resources. Revue International d'ingénierie numérique **2**(1–2), 113–128 (2006)
12. Zimmermann, H.J.: Fuzzy Set Theory—and its Applications. Springer, New York (2011). https://doi.org/10.1007/978-94-010-0646-0

Service Capability Ontology

David Görzig[1(✉)] and Thomas Bauernhansl[1,2]

[1] Fraunhofer IPA, Nobelstr. 12, 70569 Stuttgart, Germany
dvg@ipa.fraunhofer.de
[2] Institute of Industrial Manufacturing and Management (IFF),
University of Stuttgart, Stuttgart, Germany

Abstract. Digitization is transforming previously physical products into holistic product-service systems which open up opportunities for new business models. But to achieve an excellent customer experience with them, a use case-specific configuration of the extensive product-service systems is necessary. One possible approach for the efficient implementation is to modularize the systems. In digital product-service systems, these modules require a holistic view that includes physical and digital resources as well as processes and people. The construct of capability might be a suitable framework to define such modules purpose-based and to manage the configuration. However, capabilities are not sufficiently defined in the literature and are, therefore, hardly ever used in practice. The aim of this paper is to create a common understanding of the term capability in the context of product-service systems with the help of an ontology.

Keywords: Product-service systems · Digitization · Capabilities

1 Introduction

For several years now, digitization has been extensively changing industries. With a simplified access to information, the focus of business models is shifting from products towards customized services that maximize customer experience and open up new sources of revenue for mechanical engineering. [1] However, due to their deep integration into customer processes, the resulting product-service systems are much more extensive and dynamic. With each new business relationship, providers need to reconfigure the product-service systems to customer requirements. In order to manage the required changes efficiently, service-based business models could be designed modularly. In addition to software, such a module should include also physical resources such as people and machines as well as processes. Capabilities can provide a starting point for this by encapsulating enterprise components as a purpose-driven system [2]. Although capabilities are becoming increasingly important, there is no uniform definition of the term in the literature [3]. Thus, capabilities are not applicable in business practice today. The aim of this paper is to present an approach for the flexible design and adaption of service-based, digital business models with the help of capabilities. Therefore, a common understanding of capabilities by means of an ontology is needed. As a framework for this paper, the Knowledge Engineering Methodology of Noy and McGuinness has been selected. [4] Accordingly, the domain

A. Dolgui et al. (Eds.): APMS 2021, IFIP AICT 634, pp. 361–368, 2021.
https://doi.org/10.1007/978-3-030-85914-5_38

digital product-service systems is determined in Sect. 2. In Sect. 3, existing capabilities definitions are examined and important components of capabilities are derived. In Sect. 4, classes for service capabilities are defined and assigned relations.

2   Domain of Digital Product-Service Systems

Starting point of digital product-service systems is the development towards smart and worldwide connected products that enable new data-driven business models [1]. Digitization thus adds an information-based service component to previously purely physical products and creates product-service systems. However, services are fundamentally different in their nature from physical products. Services can be defined as the application of resources through deeds, processes, and performances for the benefit of others or oneself [5]. They are much broader in scope and more dynamic than physical products. To better understand the resulting changes in business models and to derive what is necessary for their modular description, a deeper examination of service-based business model components is necessary. According to Gassmann, a business model consists of the four views "who", "what", "how" and "value" [6].

First step is the analysis of the "who". A service is a cooperative process in which value is created through consistent orientation and adaptation to a specific context of use. [7] The term cooperative indicates the emergence of ecosystems. These contain a task-oriented and in consequence short-term joint value creation of provider, customer und additional partners via common institutional logics. Technically, the required rapid adaption of the ecosystem to a specific task and context is based on the application of platforms that provide standards for cross-company collaboration [8]. In summary, the question of "who" becomes far more short-term and encompasses actors, context, their common goal and how they interact. The second question focuses on what is the value proposition. Customers no longer purchase goods but rather solutions to problems in their individual context. Physical goods are just tools or distribution mechanisms for a service. Companies are not exchanging outputs anymore but performance. Providing the appropriate resources embedded in processes is the key to generate performance. [8] As customers become part of the value chain, their resource base rapidly changes. In addition, new technologies such as smart sensors, interfaces and platforms need to be taken into account. Thus, the "how" includes the resources of the actors and the processes in which they are applied. A particularly important issue is the transfer of value. By shifting to services, value is measured in a new way. Instead of focusing on pure output, the focus is on performance, which leads to an improved customer experience. It is no longer charged per product, but per customer benefit in pay-per-x models. For this purpose, it is necessary to be able to measure the customer benefit.

3   State of the Art in Capabilities Research

Following the identification of the relevant properties of digital service systems, the concept of capability is examined from five different perspectives. Based on this, the relevant elements of a capability are derived.

3.1   Concept of Capability in Common Language and Philosophy

According to the Oxford English Dictionary, the term capability can be defined as the ability to do something [9]. To be capable originates from the Latin word capabilis which means to be susceptible to something [10]. The FrameNet project offers a semantic description of the capability concept [11]. It defines capabilities as the preconditions that an entity has to meet in order to participate in an event. Further features for the characterization of capabilities are external circumstances, the degree and frequency of fulfillment of the preconditions, the status of the capability, the explanations for the existence of the capability, the relevant features and roles of the entity as well as the temporal determination of the event. Historically, Aristotle analyzed the concept in his ninth book of Metaphysics [12]. He refers to capabilities as the principle for measurably changing something else or oneself. Thus, they form the starting point of a causal chain. The basis for the emergence of capabilities are the characteristics of their carriers which produce certain effects under certain external circumstances. It can be distinguished between an active capability – being able to change something – and a passive capability – being able to be changed. While Aristotle focuses on the process of change and its results, FrameNet concentrates on the properties of the entities. Both approaches complement each other well and show overlaps in the consideration of boundary conditions.

3.2   Capabilities in Military

In the field of military planning, capabilities are applied as a reaction to the increasingly dynamic threat situation. By helping to overcome the need to consider fixed scenarios and instead focus on the objectives, they increase the flexibility of the armed forces in unexpected situations [13]. Capabilities are defined as the ability to achieve a desired operational effect in a specified context for a certain time frame during a mission [14]. The operational effect represents the target state that has to be achieved to successfully encounter a threat and complete a mission [15]. The previously defined context includes the entire spectrum of possible situations and is described by scenarios, conditions, locations and threats. [13] The time frame defines how quickly capabilities should be ready and how long they should be sustained. Capabilities are generated by combining building blocks such as personnel, material, training, infrastructure, and management into an interlocking system. [14] The building blocks differ by country.

3.3   Capabilities in Information Systems

Capabilities in enterprise architecture (EA) are based on military capabilities. EA defines capabilities as the ability and capacity of a company to achieve a specific purpose or outcome in a certain context. Ability refers to the available individual competencies to achieve a goal. Capacity refers to the availability of resources such as people, money and tools. [16] Capabilities describe what a company does to create customer value [17]. Therefore, they encapsulate resources, roles, processes, context and information. Moreover, capabilities are described as non-redundant, stable over time, hierarchical and combinable [3]. The CaaS project identifies three groups of capability elements [16]. Enterprise and capability modeling contains business goals, KPI, processes and resources in order to develop generic solutions that can be reconfigured according to the context. Secondly, the context represents the situations in which the solutions are used. Capability delivery patterns are the third area. They describe best practice solutions for achieving business goals in a defined context.

The Capability Maturity Model Integration (CMMI) presents another way of applying capabilities [18]. CMMI is a framework that supports the development of software and products. For this purpose, it has five maturity levels that contain several predefined process areas. The progress in each process areas is tracked based on specific goals with the help of the four capability levels incomplete, performed, managed and defined. In contrast to the other approaches presented, CMMI is much more specific and focused on development processes.

3.4   Strategic Business Planning

The concept of organizational capability is deeply rooted in the resource-based view of strategic business planning. The aim of this concept is to explain competitive advantages [19]. Organizational capabilities enable an organization to repeatedly perform an activity according to an intended and specific purpose [20]. They represent a tool for organizations to configure their resources [21]. Organizational capabilities can be divided into operational and dynamic capabilities. Operational capabilities enable an organization to solve current operative problems without change [20]. Therefore, they encapsulate routines and resources company-specific [21]. Routines are activities that are executed in a reproducible and reliable manner [20]. Resources are everything to which a company has direct or indirect access. They are divided in tangible (machines, tools, …) and intangible (knowledge, leadership, skill, brands, …) resources [21]. Dynamic capabilities enable a company to change its operational capabilities [20]. Through these capabilities, companies can integrate, build and reconfigure internal and external competencies to adapt themselves to a rapidly changing environment. This results in innovative competitive advantages [22].

3.5   Manufacturing

Operations management uses capabilities to plan manufacturing systems in an automated manner. Contributions in this field of research usually use the term skill. These are elementary, solution-neutral functionalities of resources which are described by parameters and which are independent of hardware and operating principles [23]. By linking several skills so-called composite capabilities are created [24]. The BaSys project adds the goal to the capability definition in order to trigger an effect in the physical or virtual world. This effect is described as the change of property values of objects by the resource [25]. Composite capabilities can be described by different components. At their core, they consist of a sequence of elementary skills that are steered by a control flow. The overall composite capability system communicates with its environment via input and output parameters and uses transformation functions to convert them into an understandable form for the elementary capabilities. Templates allow the elementary capabilities to be assigned to resources. Mechanical connections describe physical and spatial relationships [23].

Further capability types in operations management are the machine and the process capability in quality management. A machine capability describes the ability of a machine to continuously produce a certain product quality. Process capability extends the term to the entire manufacturing process.

3.6   Discussion of the Relevant Capability Classes

All presented disciplines use capabilities in slightly different ways. However, there are great similarities in the definitions. Capabilities are hierarchical, stable over time, and non-overlapping. As illustrated in Table 1, they have very similar building blocks.

Table 1. Elements of capabilities

Approach	Purpose	Effect (Change)	Resources act./pass	Process	Context	Time	Inter-faces
3.1 FrameNet	-	-	x / -	x	x	x	-
3.1 Aristotle	x	x (x)	x / x	-	x	-	-
3.2 Military cap.	x	x (x)	x / x	x	x	x	x
3.3 EA cap.	x	x	x / -	x	x	-	x
3.3 CMMI	x	-	- / -	x	-	-	-
3.4 Res.-based view	x	x	x / -	x	-	-	-
3.5 Manufacturing	-	x (x)	x / x	x	-	-	x
3.5 Machine cap.	-	x	x / -	x	-	-	-

First element of most capabilities is the purpose. This is a superior goal to be achieved through the application of one or more capabilities. In military, for example, a mission is accomplished with the help of capabilities. In strategic planning, competitive advantages are generated. The purpose is achieved by attaining effects. An effect is a measurable change of the target object. Aristotle describes e.g. the healing of a patient with the help of a doctor's capabilities. In manufacturing, the properties of an object are changed. To achieve the effect, resources are applied in processes. Resources are tangible and intangible assets that are limited. A distinction can be made between active resources, which create change, and passive resources, which are changed. The changes are carried out in a specific context and time period. The context includes everything the provider of the capability cannot influence like the place or external conditions. The basis for the correct execution of a capability is the provision of the required information through interfaces. In the further course, capabilities will be defined as the ability of a system of resources to change itself or another system of resources in a defined context and timeframe in order to achieve a superior objective.

4   Structure of a Service Capability Model

In their basic definition, services and capabilities are very similar. While services are about the use of resources for the benefit of oneself or someone else, capabilities focus on changing the resource base of oneself or someone else for a higher objective. Due to the high degree of congruence, it seems possible to apply capabilities as a framework for the description of services and the business models associated with them. Due to the hierarchical structure and long-term orientation of capabilities, business models can be built up modularly. To map the capability components to the requirements of services as well as to uncover gaps, the classification according to Gassmann is applied again [6].

In order to assign service-based business model and possible capabilities, the question of "who" is asked first. Capabilities are deployed between at least two actors. The first actor uses its resource system to change the resource system of the second actor. Characteristic features to describe the who are the underlying purpose as well as the interfaces between the actors provided for its realization. Furthermore, the context and time frame of the change need to be mapped. The context consists of different context elements, each of which can be described by a measured value. The what is the starting point for the modularization of business models. By using the construct effect, capabilities allow the purpose to be decomposed into solution-neutral building blocks. An effect can be achieved through different capabilities. Effects can be described as measurable and repeatable changes of a resource base in a specific context and time frame. A maturity level for each effect can be tracked. The how includes the specific solution and is described by the resources applied in processes. Resources might be people, software, hardware, information, materials, energy, infrastructure or intangible assets. Resources are described by their names, properties, interfaces, and capacity. Ultimately, however, the specific properties of these resources are responsible for the execution of processes and thus for the application of a capability. Each property is applicable through one or more interfaces that might be physical, digital or a human-machine interface. Adjustments to effects are initially made by replacing full capabilities. If no suitable capability is available in the ecosystem, the resources and processes of existing capabilities can be adapted. The result is a new capability with a lower maturity level. The last field is the description of values. So far, capabilities are not associated with costs and a benefit in the literature. Because capabilities define a resource system in a purpose-oriented way. This is generally possible. During the execution of processes, costs are incurred that are offset by the benefits to the benefiting actor. These benefits are also the key performance indicator for the billing of pay-per-x business models. Alternatively, single effects may be used. Figure 1 summarizes the characteristics of capabilities in an ontology. It shows the most important elements of capabilities and assigns them to the areas of a business model. By proceeding step-by-step through the four phases, it becomes possible to identify the relevant capabilities of a provider and to determine the adjustments that may be necessary.

For the practical use of capabilities, it is advantageous to be able to express capabilities in a sentence. Based on the analysis, the following form can be used: *Who* (active actor) wants to change *what* (resources of beneficiary actor) from *whom* (beneficiary actor) with what *effect* and *purpose* in which *context* and in which *time frame*.

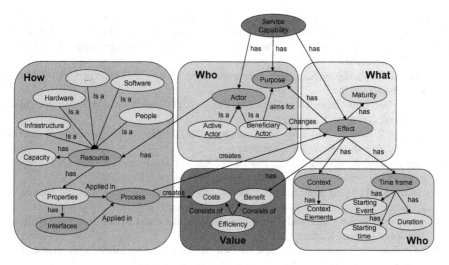

Fig. 1. Service capability ontology

5 Summary and Outlook

The aim of this paper is to analyze the term capability in a cross-domain view and to derive a uniform understanding for its use in the area of service description. For this purpose, the domains of general usage, military, business informatics, economics and manufacturing were examined. From this basis, classes were derived and a model was developed. Modeling an ontology is an interactive process. The goal of this paper is to generate a first draft that can be further refined in subsequent steps. In the further elaboration of the model, a system for automated matching of capabilities and customer requirements will be brought into practical use. Moreover, the capability model will be further refined by mapping the capability base of individual companies.

References

1. Goerzig, D., Bauernhansl, T.: Enterprise architectures for the digital transformation in small and medium-sized enterprises. Procedia CIRP **67**, 540–545 (2018)
2. Goerzig, D., Karcher, S., Bauernhansl, T.: Capability-based planning of digital innovations in small-and medium-sized enterprises. In: 2019 IEEE 21st Conference on Business Informatics (CBI), pp. 495–503 IEEE (2019)
3. Wißotzki, M.: Exploring the nature of capability research. In: El-Sheikh, E., Zimmermann, A., Jain, L.C. (eds.) Emerging Trends in the Evolution of Service-Oriented and Enterprise Architectures. ISRL, vol. 111, pp. 179–200. Springer, Cham (2016). https://doi.org/10.1007/978-3-319-40564-3_10
4. Noy, N.F.: McGuinness DL Ontology development 101: A guide to creating your first ontology. Technical report
5. Vargo, S.L., Lusch, R.F.: Evolving to a new dominant logic for marketing. J. Mark. **68**, 1–17 (2004)

6. Gassmann, O., Frankenberger, K., Csik, M.: Geschäftsmodelle entwickeln: 55 innovative Konzepte mit dem St. Galler Business Model Navigator, 1. Aufl. Hanser, München (2013)
7. Böhmann, T., Leimeister, J.M., Möslein, K.: Service-systems-engineering. Wirtschaftsinf **56**, 83–90 (2014)
8. Lusch, R.F., Nambisan, S.: Service innovation: a service-dominant logic perspective. MIS Q. **39**, 155–175 (2015)
9. Oxford University Press. Definition of capability (2021). https://www.lexico.com/definition/capability. Accessed 5 Jan 2021
10. Merriam-Webster. Definition of capability (2021). https://www.merriam-webster.com/dictionary/capable. Accessed 5 Jan 2021
11. Ruppenhofer, J., Ellsworth, M., Petruck, M.R.L., et al.: FrameNet Data (2021). https://framenet.icsi.berkeley.edu/fndrupal/frameIndex. Accessed 5 Jan 2021
12. Jansen, L.: Tun und Können: Ein systematischer Kommentar zu Aristoteles Theorie der Vermögen im neunten Buch der Metaphysik. Springer, Wiesbaden (2016)
13. Air Force Materiel Command: Capabilities-Based Assessment (CBA) Handbook. Office of Aerospace Studies, Kirtland (2014)
14. Australian Government, Department of Defense: Defence Capability Development Handbook, Canberra (2012)
15. US DoD: JCIDS Manual: Manual for the Operation of the Joint Capabilities Integration and Development System (2018)
16. Bērziša, S., et al.: Capability driven development: an approach to designing digital enterprises. Bus. Inf. Syst. Eng. **57**(1), 15–25 (2015). https://doi.org/10.1007/s12599-014-0362-0
17. Homann, U.: A Business-Oriented Foundation for Service Orientation. Microsoft (2006)
18. Software Engineering Institute: CMMI für Entwicklung Version 1.3. Carnegie Mellon University, Hanscom (2011)
19. Müller-Stewens, G., Lechner, C.: Strategisches Management: Wie strategische Initiativen zum Wandel führen. Schäffer-Poeschel, Stuttgart (2011)
20. Helfat, C.E., Winter, S.G.: Untangling dynamic and operational capabilities: strategy for the (N)ever-changing world. Strat. Mgmt. J. **32**, 1243–1250 (2011). https://doi.org/10.1002/smj.955
21. Wu, S., Melnyk, S., Barbara, F.: Operational capabilities: the secret ingredient. Decis. Sci. **41**, 721–754 (2010)
22. Teece, D.J., Pisano, G., Shuen, A.: Dynamic capabilities and strategic management. Strateg. Manag. J. **18**, 509–533 (1997)
23. Hammerstingl, V.: Steigerung der Rekonfigurationsfähigkeit von Montageanlagen durch Cyber-physische Feldgeräte. Dissertation, Technischen Universität (2019)
24. Geschäftsstelle Plattform Industrie 4.0: Describing Capabilities of Industrie 4.0 Components. Bundesministerium für Wirtschaft und Energie (BMWi), Berlin (2020)
25. Perzylo, A., Grothoff, J., Lucio, L., Weser, M., et al.: Capability-based semantic interoperability of manufacturing resources: a BaSys 4.0 perspective. IFAC-PapersOnLine **52**, 1590–1596 (2019)

Guideline to Develop Smart Service Business Models for Small and Medium Sized Enterprises

Mike Freitag[1]([✉]), Christian Schiller[1], and Oliver Hämmerle[2]

[1] Fraunhofer IAO, Nobelstraße 12, 70569 Stuttgart, Germany
Mike.Freitag@iao.fraunhofer.de
[2] Institut Für Arbeitswirtschaft Und Technologiemanagement IAT,
Universität Stuttgart, Nobelstraße 12, 70569 Stuttgart, Germany

Abstract. The shift from product-oriented to service-oriented business requires a rethink, especially in traditional companies in the mechanical and plant engineering industry. This guideline for the development of Smart Services business models is intended to illustrate the complexity and thus improve their handling, supporting the planning and modelling of a Smart Service. The focus of this paper is to introduce a step-by-step model to develop business models for small and medium sized enterprises in the manufacturing industry and on the selection of suitable service business model patterns. Therefor it will show alternative service business model patterns and at the end to select the right one. This is an important process before starting smart service engineering.

Keywords: Smart service · Service business model · Service lifecycle management · Service engineering · SME

1 Introduction

This guideline describes a step-by-step development of Smart Services, especially in manufacturing sector. The term "Smart Services" refers to data-based, individually configurable service offerings consisting of services, digital services and products that are organized and provided via integrated platforms [1]. The product systems of SME are basically stable, but the service systems offer potential for improvement. So, the focus of this paper is on the development of smart service business models and not on the development of business models for a product service system or on development of an engineering process for product-service systems [2, 3].

It is becoming increasingly important to offer suitable Smart Services to complement the products of manufacturing enterprises. Therefor an integrated development and subsequent management of these Smart Services is of central importance. Figure 1 illustrates the essential elements of this guideline for the development of Smart Services on the basis of the 3 phases:

- Service Design Thinking [4–6],
- Service Business Model [7] and
- Smart Service Engineering [8].

A. Dolgui et al. (Eds.): APMS 2021, IFIP AICT 634, pp. 369–375, 2021.
https://doi.org/10.1007/978-3-030-85914-5_39

When a Smart Service is developed, both the three phases and the sub-processes in these phases can be repeated iteratively. Each of these three phases is already iteratively in progress. Especially in Design Thinking and Smart Service Engineering, the iterative approach is a core element of the process model. The development of alternatives also plays an important role in business modeling. In the approach presented in this paper, the possibilities of iteration are limited (dark arrows) due to small and medium-sized companies.

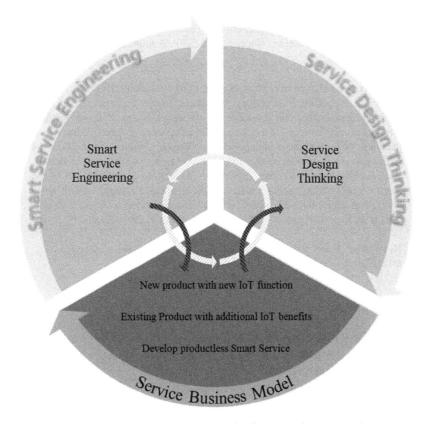

Fig. 1. The essential components in the development of Smart Services [1]

The design thinking process refers to Plattner et al. [4] and thus includes the 6 phases: understanding, observing, defining a position, finding ideas, developing a prototype and testing. These phases form the first development step of the smart service with the associated business model.

The further phases service business model development and smart service engineering form the main part of this paper and are described below in more detail below.

2 Develop New Business Models

In particular small and medium-sized companies (SMEs) often focus too much exclusively on technical aspects, right up to the management level. But, in addition to the technical potential, newly developed smart services must also exploit the economic added value they offer. This requires an appropriate and innovative business model. A business model depicts all the players involved, their respective roles and contributions to value creation, the benefits for customers and other players, and the sources of revenue resulting from the business activities. In part, it is also described as a management hypothesis about what customers want, how they want it, and how a company can fulfill the wants and make money in the process [8]. In this context, business models refer to the fundamental logic in a company and describe how a business functions and how company activities and elements interact [9]. An important element of business models is the central importance of customer orientation. Business models define the benefits for customers, how these benefits are delivered, and how a company generates revenue [10].

The mechanisms described must also be taken into account when developing new smart service concepts in mechanical and plant engineering, such as in electroplating technology. In order to develop a business model systematically, it is first necessary to select a suitable business model scheme. In recent years, various procedures and methods have become established in (smart) service engineering to support business model development. These include the Service Business Model Canvas (SBMC) according to Zolnowski [11], the Business Model Canvas (BMC) according to Osterwalder and Pigneur [12] or the Service Dominant Architecture (SDA) according to Warg et al. [13]. Due to its easy-to-understand structure, the BMC according to Osterwalder and Pigneur [12] has become established, especially for start-ups and smaller companies. It also has the advantage that a completed BMC can be further developed into an SBMC at any time if needed and if sufficient data is available. A developed business model is an important component and forms the basis for the complete service engineering process [14].

In order to structure the process towards a business model and thus simplify it, especially for SMEs, a four-step approach was developed and applied in a company from the electroplating industry. The approach is designed to develop the essential aspects of a business model step by step. This also enables SMEs with limited human and financial resources to systematically address this topic.

In the approach described below, it does not matter whether the final business model ends up being represented by the Service Business Model Canvas, the Business Model Canvas, the Service Dominant Architecture, or by a completely different scheme.

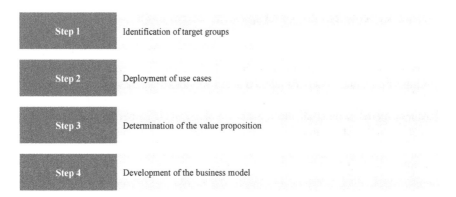

Fig. 2. The four-stage model for developing a smart service business model

Stage 1. The first step is to define the primary customer target group. An important question here is; who in particular will be addressed by the new smart service and the corresponding business model? According to Osterwalder and Pigneur [12], differentiation of the target groups is necessary if their needs require and justify an individual offer, if they are reached via different distribution channels, if they require different types of payment, if they have significantly different profitability or if they are willing to pay for different aspects of an offer. In electroplating, for example, a distinction can be made between in-house and contract electroplating or between small, medium and large companies, depending on the service concept. Further target group definitions can be made with regard to the liquidity of the respective company or in the differentiation between "makers" and "out-sourcers" (make-or-buy decision).

Stage 2. In the second step, a concrete use case will be developed for the previously defined target group. It must be explained how the service is to be provided, how frequently it is expected to be provided, and what the goals of this business are. In addition, the Unique Selling Point (USP) of the business model idea should be clarified and defined.

Stage 3. The third step is to determine the specific value proposition of the business model idea. It is to clarify what benefits the new or enhanced smart service will provide to the customer and which customer problems can be solved in specific terms. For this step, it makes sense to get a comprehensive picture of the customer in advance and not to develop without taking their actual needs into account.

Stage 4. In the fourth step, the business model is completed. According to Freitag & Hämmerle [15] the following three options have to be considered when developing business models for smart services:

- Existing product with additional IoT benefits,
- New product with new IoT function and
- Develop productless Smart Services.

Finally, in step 4, the core aspects of the business model developed in steps 1 to 3 are brought together and logically linked with a suitable method like the Service Business Model Canvas or the Business Model Canvas. In addition, a viable price and cost structure must now be developed.

The business model is the foundation of a proper service engineering process [16] and for the subsequent further development of the smart service.

3   Agile Service Engineering

As shown by Moro et al. [3], there are many approaches and guidelines to the design of product-service systems, such as Muto et al. [2]. As announced in Sect. 1, the focus of this paper is on smart service, where are also many different ways of management. A small selection of these is briefly described below.

In their framework, Zheng et al. [17] propose an integration of value networks, service ecology thinking, and ICTs and offer future perspectives and possible guidelines for the transformation of industry and the further development of new service-based business models.

DIN SPEC 33543 [18] describes a process model for the agile, flexible and rapid development of digital service systems in an industrial context. Starting from the concrete development of a service as a performance result, the process model considers the holistic design of digital service systems. Updated methods from service engineering as well as suitable methods from related areas such as business analytics and software development are presented to help companies structure the development process for their own needs and carry it out in a customer-oriented, efficient and successful manner.

Jussen et al. [19] also present a smart service engineering approach for industrial smart services. The focus here is on the individual steps in service development and the connections and iterations of the single elements of the smart service - based on a case study. The model delivers high speed and quality in project implementation by combining agile working methods and focus on customer centricity.

For the suitability for small and medium size enterprises, it seems reasonable to choose a process model based on these approaches. One possibility to do this is described in the 20-page guideline of Freitag und Hämmerle [20]. This guideline for development of smart services is also based on the Service Lifecycle Management [21–23].

The entire process is therefore not focused on the smart service alone, but aims at the smart service as a holistic solution. This means that the levels of business model management and network management are also taken into account.

4   Summary

The shift from product-oriented to service-oriented business requires a rethink, especially in traditional companies in the manufacturing industry. The three different main phases Design Thinking, Service Business Models and Service Engineering are important to develop a Smart Service. Here in the paper the focus is on the Service Business Models for small and medium size enterprises. A four-step model for developing a smart service business model is presented. In the final, fourth step, three different options for a smart business model patterns for small and medium-sized enterprises were presented, so the right one can be selected for the chosen use case. Based on the chosen business model pattern, the Smart Service in the manufacturing industry will be developed.

Acknowledgements. This work has been partly funded by the German Federal Ministry of Education and Research (BMBF) through the Project "SmARtPlaS" (No. 02K18D112), the project "DigiLab NPO – Digitallabor für Non-Profit-Organisationen 4.0" (No. 02L18A230). The authors wish to acknowledge the Commission, the Ministry and all the project partners for their contribution.

References

1. Freitag, M., Wiesner, S.: Smart service lifecycle management: a framework and use case. In: Moon, I., Lee, G.M., Park, J., Kiritsis, D., von Cieminski, G. (eds.) APMS 2018. IAICT, vol. 536, pp. 97–104. Springer, Cham (2018). https://doi.org/10.1007/978-3-319-99707-0_13
2. Muto, K., Kimita, K., Shimomura, Y.: A guideline for product-service-systems design process. Procedia CIRP **30**, 60–65 (2015)
3. Moro, S., Cauchick-Miguel, P.A., Mendes, G.D.S.: Product-service systems benefits and barriers: an overview of literature review papers. Int. J. Ind. Eng. Manage. **11**(1), 61–70 (2020)
4. Plattner, H., Meinel, C., Weinberg, U.: Design-Thinking - Understand-Improve-Apply. Springer, Heidelberg (2009)
5. Brenner, W., Uebernickel, F., Thomas, A.: Design thinking as mindset, process, and toolbox. In: Brenner, W., Uebernickel, F. (eds.) Design Thinking for Innovation, pp. 3–21. Springer, Cham (2016). https://doi.org/10.1007/978-3-319-26100-3_1
6. Schallmo, D.R.A.: Design Thinking erfolgreich anwenden. So entwickeln Sie in 7 Phasen kundenorientierte Produkte und Dienstleistungen, Springer Gabler, Wiesbaden (2017). https://doi.org/10.1007/978-3-658-12523-3
7. Wirtz, B.W., Schilke, O., Ullrich, S.: Strategic development of business models: implications of the Web 2.0 for creating value on the internet. Long Range Plann. **43**(2–3), 272–290 (2010).
8. Teece, D.J.: Business models, business strategy and innovation. Long Range Plann. **43**, (2–3), 172–194 (2010)
9. Stähler, P.: Geschäftsmodell als Analyseeinheit für Strategie (2015). Accessed 7 Apr 2021
10. Rüger, M., Fischer, D., Nägele, R.: Strategieorientierte Geschäftsmodellentwicklung. In: Bullinger, H.-J., Bauer, W., Rüger, M. (eds.) Geschäftsmodell-Innovationen richtig umsetzen: Vom Technologiemarkt zum Markterfolg, pp. 18–31. Fraunhofer IAO, Stuttgart (2018)
11. Zolnowski, A.: Analysis and Design of Service Business Models. Dissertation, Universität Hamburg (2015)
12. Osterwalder, A., Pigneur, Y.: Business Model Generation – A Handbook for Visionaries Game Changers and Challengers. Wiley, New Jersey (2010)

13. Warg, M., Weiß, P., Engel, R., Zolnowski, A.: Service dominant architecture based on S-D logic for mastering digital transformation: the case of an insurance company. In: Russo-Spena, T., Mele, C. (eds.) What's ahead in Service Research? New Perspectives for Business and Society, Proceedings. RESER, University of Naples (2016)

14. Burger, T.: Testen in der Dienstleistungsentwicklung. Stuttgarter Beiträge zum Testen in der Dienstleistungsentwicklung: Band I. Fraunhofer Verlag, Stuttgart (2014)

15. Freitag, M., Hämmerle, O.: Agile guideline for development of smart services in manufacturing enterprises with support of artificial intelligence. In: Lalic, B., Majstorovic, V., Marjanovic, U., von Cieminski, G., Romero, D. (eds.) APMS 2020. IAICT, vol. 591, pp. 645–652. Springer, Cham (2020). https://doi.org/10.1007/978-3-030-57993-7_73

16. Burger, T.: Testen in der Dienstleistungsentwicklung: Ergebnisse einer qualitativen Erhebung bei Anbietern produktbegleitender Dienstleistungen. Fraunhofer Verlag, Stuttgart (2014)

17. Zheng, M., Ming, X., Wang, L., Yin, D., Zhang, X.: Status review and future perspectives on the framework of smart product service ecosystem. Procedia CIRP **64**, 181–186 (2017)

18. DIN SPEC 33453: Entwicklung digitaler Dienstleistungssysteme. Project: Design Thinking for Industrial Services (DETHIS). Beuth Verlag GmbH, Berlin (2019)

19. Jussen, P., Kuntz, J., Senderek, R., Moser, B.: Smart service engineering. Procedia CIRP **83**, 384–388 (2019)

20. Freitag, M., Hämmerle, O.: Die Entwicklung von Smart Services im Maschinen- und Anlagenbau. Ein Leitfaden Fraunhofer Verlag, Stuttgart (2021)

21. Freitag, M., Kremer, D., Hirsch, M., Zelm, M.: An approach to standardise a service life cycle management. In: Zelm, M., Sinderen, M.v., Pires, L.F., Doumeingts, G. (eds.) Enterprise Interoperability, pp. 115–126. Wiley, Chichester (2013)

22. Freitag, M.: Ein konfigurierbares Vorgehensmodell für die exportorientierte Entwicklung von technischen Dienstleistungen. Dissertation, Universität Stuttgart, Fraunhofer Verlag, Stuttgart (2014)

23. Freitag, M., Hämmerle, O.: Smart service lifecycle management. Wt werkstattstechnik Online **106**(H 7/8), 477–482 (2016)

Conceptual Approach to Product Development Process Based on Supply Chain Concepts

Joanine Facioli Urnau[1,2], Alda Yoshi Uemura Reche[1],
Arthur Beltrame Canciglieri[1], Osiris Canciglieri Junior[1(✉)],
and Anderson Luis Szejka[1]

[1] Industrial and Systems Engineering Graduate Program (PPGEPS), Polytechnic School, Pontifícia Universidade Católica Do Paraná (PUCPR), Curitiba, Paraná CEP: 80215-901, Brazil
{osiris.canciglieri,anderson.szejka}@pucpr.br

[2] Boticário Indústria de Cosméticos, Boticário Group, Av. Rui Barbosa, 4110. Afonso Pena, São José dos Pinhais, PR CEP: 83065-260, Brazil

Abstract. There is currently a trend in the Product Development Process (PDP) and Supply Chain (SC) to make this relationship closer and more fluid, presenting a difficulty due to the complexity involved. The complexity of innovation projects can be even more demanding, especially due to the need to launch them in shorter and more assertive terms in the current context of industry 4.0, in which global networks are emphasized in the exchange of information. Given this context, this article aims to conduct a systematic review of the literature exploring the relationship between the PDP and SC. In this way, it was possible to propose a new approach contemplating the conception of the product development process combined with the concepts of the supply chain, such as support for the design and conception of product packaging from an industry in the cosmetics sector. As a result, it was possible to contribute to the existing gap between the integration of these two research areas.

Keywords: New product development · Supply chain · Industry 4.0 · Supply chain concepts · PDP · SC

1 Introduction

Currently, the complexity of the operations of the industries and the speed of changes required by consumers, demand that companies have and seek even more agility and assertiveness in what will be offered. In addition to this context, we have industry 4.0, known as the fourth stage of industrialization, production needs to adapt to the constant fluctuations in demand between products, it is necessary to optimize production based on the communication of Internet tools of things and improving the human-machine interface (HMI) [1].

Based on this context, it is necessary that the Product Development Process (PDP) and Supply Chain (SC), narrow and update constantly so that this relationship is more and more synchronized and that innovations occur more efficient. Considering the strategic nature of SC's design feels almost forced to integrate it into the development

A. Dolgui et al. (Eds.): APMS 2021, IFIP AICT 634, pp. 376–384, 2021.
https://doi.org/10.1007/978-3-030-85914-5_40

of products and processes [2, 8, 12, 18, 23, 25]. Although it is widely accepted that product design decisions and their associated supply chain are interrelated, it is unclear how they interact with each other [3]. The integration and relationship of these large areas, therefore, presents difficulties in sharing/exchanging information and losses in the process. Although this problem has been improved by applying the concepts of industry 4.0 in the use of technology to have full access to all necessary information, the gains and the importance of this alignment between PDP and SC are still unclear. It is from this context that the present work aims to search in the literature the methods and approaches that cover the integration between SC and PDP.

This relationship adds a wide range of processes, whether internal or external, to be coordinated correctly and effectively. Thus, companies need to view the innovation process as a collaborative process, in which a supply chain plays an essential role for success. In this way, a supply chain integration with the management structure, in which each entity can have visibility of other parts of the supply chain, allows the potential for a better production decision (support for product innovation or focus on quality) and, therefore cost savings and reduced response time.

2   Systematic Literature Review

The Systematic Review explored works related to the integration of the new product development process and the Supply Chain through the CAPES/MEC Research Portal Platform (Coordination for the Improvement of Higher Education Personnel). This database was chosen because it is one of the most complete available to search for publications, and for that, keywords and their correlates were used that serve the large areas (PDP and SC) crossed together, reaching a total of 23,522 articles. As a refinement, the cleaning and selection of this total were carried out, considering only the articles published in the first quartile (Q1) according to the *Scimago Journal Ranking - 2020* resulting in 138 articles. From this, a more complete analysis of each work was carried out, also using inclusion and exclusion criteria, resulting in 17 most relevant research/articles found in the literature with their contributions and limitations as described in Table 1. Subsequently, these articles were selected based on titles and abstracts, going to 480 works, which were again carried out based on inclusion criteria (Address both subjects as main, be written in English, peer-reviewed, with SJR close to or greater than 1 and JCR greater than 1) and to remove duplicate articles. As a result of this process, 138 works were analyzed more deeply, resulting in 17 most relevant articles, which were read in full, allowing to bring their contributions and as described in Table 1.

Table 1. The most relevant research works founded in the literature review.

Author/Year	Contributions	Limitations
Nihtilä, Jukka [4]	Provides information about the complex process of cross-functional integration at the beginning of NPDP	It neglected the integration between R&D and other commercial functions other than production. Lack of knowledge about the end customer, supply and marketing
Appelqvist et al. [5]	The Article deals a lot with the term reengineering and focuses on the supply chain without changing the PDP. It identifies the lack of companies to recognize their business situation and act accordingly	Focuses a lot on the systems modelling and development of a Platform, in addition to the lack of application cases to evaluate the effects
Blackhurst et al. [6]	It features modelling of mathematical functions performed within the SC, which allows the user to model decisions and using the results to assist in SC reengineering decisions and product and process design decisions	Tested on sampling, without being applied to a wide variety of PP and SC, which can be a problem the applicability of the large-scale approach due to a large number of variables and the uncertainty of the operation
Van Hoek and Chapman [7]	The article reinforces the need to consider SC stakeholders and their alignment in advance so that product availability is guaranteed on the launch date	It only presents areas for future research and does not go into any depth
Ellram et al. [21]	It identifies that there are no works that deal with the 3 dimensions (Supply chain, product and process) - 3DCE. It proposes some ways of working together to meet the needs of the client	Lack of modelling that allows total understanding and intrinsic needs
Seuring [9]	It brings a framework of the product-matrix relationship with an alternative approach, which analyzes the content of the decision together with the perspective of the process captured in the five Ps of the SC strategy	Only one of the five applied cases cover all phases of the product's life cycle and brings a more focus on the post-market
Pero et al. [10]	It brings stronger evidence that the performance of SC depends heavily on the alignment of the NPD-SCM. Affirms that modularity does not necessarily reduce the complexity of the configuration	It does not address the issue of the need for internal alignment and product characteristics and their alignment impacts
Droge et al. [11]	The article integrates SC with a company's product strategy, bringing a positive link between product and process modularity and service performance	The work limits the sample size, being very small and can lead to the error of accepting or rejecting the sample, in addition to being limited to a single sector

(continued)

Table 1. (*continued*)

Author/Year	Contributions	Limitations
Baud-Lavigne et al. [22]	It brings a more focused study on standardization, which is the correlation between the level of standardization and the gain to SC, with demand being a key parameter	It was not able to model the problem considering both the standardization and the allocation of the product, and the solution is highly complex
Madenas et al. [13]	Provides publications in the information flow area in SC and provides a comprehensive review of representable articles for each phase of the product life cycle	Focused on systems to integrate fields and not necessarily how to do that
Chiu and Okudan [14]	The Method helps to better understand the impact of different levels of modularity and determine which product architecture to apply according to market situations, from the initial stages of the project	The model does not analyze management criteria and the method considers only the assembly project (DFA) and the supply chain project (DFSC)
Morita et al. [15]	Normative model, in which the company implements initiatives to strengthen the SC process, to ensure a match between the product's characteristics and the SC process, increasing competitiveness	Model is not a derivative of observations of the real behaviour of the company, in addition to using the assumption of stable and unchanged demand
Pashaei and Olhager [16]	The Article shows the type of design of SC corresponds to the type of design of the product	The Article fails to bring a holistic view of the integration of SC and PD
Zimmermann [17]	It presents a model that synthesizes the main practices identified to improve innovation performance, involving actors internal and external to the organization, such as the SC	It is a systematic review with a new model that is unclear and without application focusing on innovation
Khan et al. [24]	The article states that companies can create competitive capabilities by integrating product design with SC through management	It does not investigate how opportunities and challenges change over time. In addition to not investigating its similarities and differences in different sectors
Tolonen et al. [19]	The NPD process must manage pure product development activities and SC capacity building activities. This requires alignment and cooperation between the NPD and SC processes	Design par excellence (DFX) was left out of the analysis to keep the focus on the SCCC, in addition to being an empirical analysis of a single company
Primus and Stavrulaki [20]	It brings about Interdependence between PD and CS, focusing on the compatibility between PD variables and their SC, how they affect the effectiveness of NPIs and the quantitative benefits of alignment decisions	The Article made the alignment between several products of the same line, and generations of the same product, going beyond the launch, besides not addressing the potential causes of misalignment and the transversal approach

3   Content Analysis

From the Systematic Review, it was possible to better understand the gap concerning the integration of the supply chain since the initial phases of the PDP, requiring the development of an approach that would treat the process holistically from pre-development to production and product availability. This is a preliminary conceptual approach to product development based on supply chain concepts, called Supply product development (SPD) as illustrated in Fig. 1.

This context presents in the two large boxes, in which the first presents the PDP process composed of its macrophases (Pre-Development, Development and Post-Development), steps and phases, and the second box presents the supply chain area and what is included. Both have an arrow that feeds back into the process, as the lessons learned from projects and supply carried out, whether successful or unsuccessful, must be available in the data to prevent them from recurring.

The PDP Box brings a greater highlight to the Development macrophases highlighted in yellow in the figure, which is composed of its five phases (training project, conceptual project, detailed project, product preparation and launch). The box that represents the SC, on the other hand, brings the processes inserted within it (suppliers, industry and distribution, retail and customer), and unlike the PDP, the SC does not have well-defined steps and macrophases. In addition, this is based on no operation support.

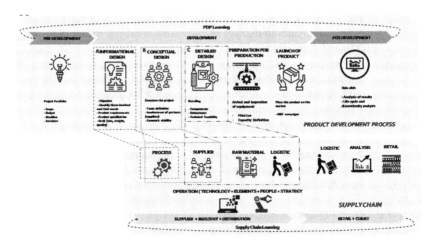

Fig. 1. Research context.

Regarding the PDP, Pre-Development is applied to all types of Innovation projects and is the moment when the scope of the project is discussed, aiming at the objective to be achieved within a stipulated budget. At this stage, it is important to understand the desires that the consumer expects from the product, ensuring the strategic orientation of development. For this proposed approach, this step is maintained, in comparison with other existing methods, however, it brings the inclusion of supply chain representatives in the discussions, to reduce uncertainty and eliminate eventual mapped problems of the project, such as distribution issues, lead production time and complexity, even if on a macro basis, based on market demand.

Moving on to the Development of macrophase, it consists of 5 phases. The first, the informational project, uses information received from the previous step and translates these into technical characteristics according to the target audience. At this stage, the presence of representatives from SC already assists in the prospecting of suppliers, based on the level of service, technical knowledge, commitment and existing warehouses. The second phase (conceptual design) is the time for more detailed definitions, related to the creation, representation and selection of solutions for product design, in addition to the definition of the team and supplier involvement. In this, the representatives of SC, evaluate and assist in the creation of the sketches, in addition to the inclusion of suppliers, already duly evaluated, with the product options available in the portfolio of each or in the manufacturing of new moulds in order to meet the requirements listed. The third stage, known as detailed design, generated the product specifications, as a definition of the raw material and material of the product and its components, including the accepted tolerances, presenting a control plane and a prototype.

Details related to packaging, storage and transport are also pre-defined, which makes the presence of SC necessary, as well as an analysis of operations (planning, suppliers, engineering and logistics), to generate market, aesthetic and economic evaluations. In the preparation of the product, known as the fourth phase, the Pilot Lot is carried out, which generates the integration of the product with the production process (production and maintenance) and SC is already more present in other existing models. The fifth phase is the product launch that involves the implementation of the launching plan (marketing) and the operations plan (production), with the initial production monitored, and it is the moment that planning efforts are proven in scheming the production and the arrival of all inputs, packaging and equipment, guaranteeing production and supply.

As shown in Fig. 2, the first 3 phases are evident, with the dots showing where the PDP interfaces with the supply chain related to them are. Highlight A, in Fig. 2, brings the interface of the informational design, with the process part and the highlight B, of the conceptual design, interconnected to the process and to the supplier in a more evident and decisive way. Highlight C, on the other hand, features the detailed project, making it more integrated with the suppliers, raw materials and logistics, since it is the moment when specification decisions are made, the process at the supplier is analyzed and also the logistics part of manufacturing and availability to the customer.

The last post-development macrophase, which is also not the focus of this approach, but is important because it considers production at scale itself, and makes the assessment of the acceptance of the target audience before the launch and the total life cycle of the product. With well-planned planning, good results should be made available for this macrophase just to be managed. Figure 2 illustrates the proposal for a new approach to the Product Development Process based on the Supply Chain perspective focusing on the product packaging. This approach brings the insertion of the Supply Chain in the product development process.

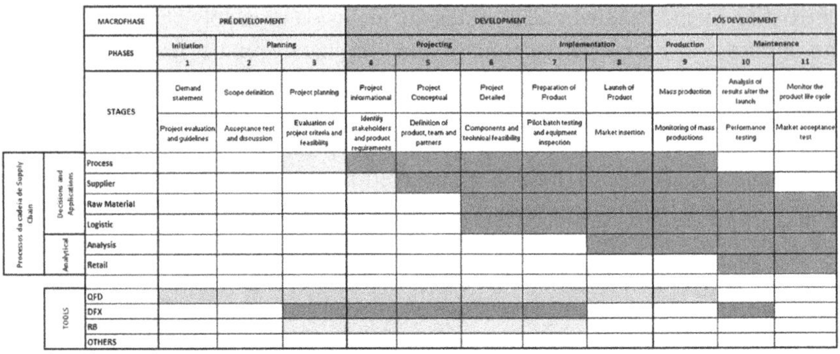

Fig. 2. Proposed approach (SPD).

4 Final Discussion

This study presented in this paper has mapped in the literature the integration of PDP and SC. Based on a systematic review, 138 relevant articles were identified after refinement, 17 of them were classified as the most important for the research exploration. It was possible to identify existing contributions and limitations in the relevant research works, which highlighted the gap in the literature of the lack of an approach that treats the Supply Chain (SC) together in the Product Development Process (PDP) in a holistic way. For the proposed approach, the whole context behind the subject was exposed, showing how the PDP could be arranged within organizations, with more predefined macrophases and steps, and how the SC can be classified and correlated with it, given its complexity.

The approach proposes the insertion of representatives of SC in the last stage of pre-development, even if it is more superficially, and being of extreme need from the beginning of the Development until the end of the PDP. This interaction helps to reduce time, costs and gains in quality and agility.

Changing the PDP considering the SC can be quantified by the time of the product development cycle, which tends to decrease, reducing design errors, avoiding rework, increasing the final quality of the product (different teams working from the same point of view) and assertiveness in decision points.

The approach, already being applied in the PDP process of a company with a focus on packaging (jar of body moisturizer), so that the authors could evaluate its effectiveness and efficiency. There is also a cultural change in the PDP process development teams, considering the limitations of the supply chain, going beyond the needs of the product considering the production restrictions.

In summary, this study sought to identify what was the most suitable way for integrating the PDP with the SC, entering a gap on how this occurred holistically, and based on this observation, proposing a new approach for the integration of the two great areas, as well as to propose future studies with the application of this to stimulate and verify the same process in the more complex products development. It is believed that the application can be extended to other industries such as automotive and pharmaceuticals, however, we may have other specific limitations in each field.

Acknowledgement. The authors especially thank the financial support of Pontifícia Universidade Católica do Paraná (PUCPR) - Polytechnic School – Industrial and Systems Engineering Graduate Program (PPGEPS), by the Coordenação de Aperfeiçoamento de Pessoal de Nível Superior – Brazil (CAPES) and by the National Council for Scientific and Technological Development (CNPq).

References

1. Kafermann, H., Lukas, W.D., Wahlster, W.: Industrie 4.0 Mit dem Internet der Dinge auf dem Weg zur 4. In: Industrially Revolution (2011)
2. Fine, C.H.: Clockspeed-based strategies for supply chain design. Prod. Oper. Manag. **9**(3), 213–221 (2000)
3. Zhang, X., Huang, G.Q., Rungtusanatham, M.J.: Simultaneous configuration of platform products and manufacturing supply chains. Int. J. Prod. Res. **46**(21), 6137–6162 (2008). https://doi.org/10.1080/00207540701324150
4. Van Hoek, R., Chapman, P.: How to move supply chain beyond cleaning up after new product development. Supply Chain Manag. Int. J. **12**(4), 597–626 (2007). https://doi.org/10.1108/13598540710759745
5. Nihtilä, J.: R&D–production integration in the early phases of new product development projects. J. Eng. Tech. Manage. **16**(1), 55–81 (1999). https://doi.org/10.1016/S0923-4748(98)00028-9
6. Appelqvist, P., Lehtonen, J., Kokkonen, J.: Modelling in product and supply chain design: literature survey and case study. J. Manuf. Technol. Manag. **15**(7), 675–686 (2004). https://doi.org/10.1108/17410380410555916
7. Blackhurst, J., Wu, T., O'grady, P.: PCDM: a decision support modeling methodology for supply chain, product and process design decisions. J. Oper. Manag. **23**, 325–343 (2005). https://doi.org/10.1016/j.jom.2004.05.009
8. Teixeira, G.F.G., Canciglieri Junior, O.: How to make strategic planning for corporate sustainability? J. Cleaner Prod. **230**, 1421–1431 (2019). https://doi.org/10.1016/j.jclepro.2019.05.063
9. Ellram, L.M., Tate, W.L., Carter, C.R.: Product-process-supply chain: an integrative approach to three-dimensional concurrent engineering. Int. J. Phys. Distrib. Logist. Manag. **37**(4), 305–330 (2007). https://doi.org/10.1108/09600030710752523
10. Seuring, S.: The product-relationship-matrix as framework for strategic supply chain design based on operations theory. Int. J. Prod. Econ. **120**(1), 221–232 (2009). https://doi.org/10.1016/j.ijpe.2008.07.021
11. Pero, M., Abdelkafi, N., Sianesi, A., Blecker, T.: A framework for the alignment of new product development and supply chains. Supply Chain Manag. Int. J. **15**(2), 115–128 (2010). https://doi.org/10.1108/13598541011028723
12. Uemura Reche, A.Y., Canciglieri Junior, O., Estorilio, C.C.A., Rudek, M.: Integrated product development process and green supply chain management: contributions, limitations and applications. J. Clean. Prod. **249**, 119429 (2020). https://doi.org/10.1016/j.jclepro.2019.119429
13. Baud-Lavigne, B., Agard, B., Penz, B.: Mutual impacts of product standardization and supply chain design. Int. J. Prod. Econ. **135**(1), 50–60 (2012). https://doi.org/10.1016/j.ijpe.2010.09.024

14. Madenas, N., Tiwari, A., Turner, C.J., Woodward, J.: Information flow in supply chain management: a review across the product lifecycle. CIRP J. Manuf. Sci. Technol. **7**(7), 335–346 (2014). https://doi.org/10.1016/j.cirpj.2014.07.002
15. Chiu, M.-C., Okudan, G.: An investigation on the impact of product modularity level on supply chain performance metrics: an industrial case study. J. Intell. Manuf. **25**(1), 129–145 (2012). https://doi.org/10.1007/s10845-012-0680-3
16. Morita, M., Machuca, J.A.D., Flynn, E. J., Pérez, J.L.: Aligning product characteristics and the supply chain process – a normative perspective. Int. J. Prod. Econ. **161**(C), 228–241 (2015). https://doi.org/10.1016/j.ijpe.2014.09.024
17. Zimmermann, R., Df Ferreira, L.M., Carrizo Moreira, A.: The influence of supply chain on the innovation process: a systematic literature review. Supply Chain Manag. Int. J. **21**(3), 289–304 (2015). https://doi.org/10.1108/SCM-07-2015-0266
18. Urnau, J.F., Canciglieri Junior, O.: Discussion of new product development process based on the supply chain in the context of Industry 4.0. In: 2nd Integrating Social Responsibility and Sustainable Development (2021). ISBN 978-3-030-59974-4
19. Tolonen, A., Haapasalo, H., Harkonen, J., Verrollot, J.: Supply chain capability creation – the creation of the supply chain readiness for a new product during product development process. Int. J. Prod. Econ. **194**, 237–245 (2017). https://doi.org/10.1016/j.ijpe.2017.09.007
20. Primus, D.J., Stavrulaki, E.: A product centric examination of PD/SC alignment decisions at the nexus of product development and supply chains. Int. J. Logistics Manag. **28**(2), 634–655 (2017). https://doi.org/10.1108/IJLM-04-2016-0112
21. Van Hoek, R., Chapman, P.: From tinkering around the edge to enhancing revenue growth: supply chain-new product development. Supply Chain Manag. Int. J. **11**(5), 385–389 (2006). https://doi.org/10.1108/13598540610682390
22. Droge, C., Vickery, S.K., Jacobs, M.A.: Does supply chain integration mediate the relationships between product/process strategy and service performance? An empirical study. Int. J. Prod. Econ. **137**(2), 250–262 (2012). https://doi.org/10.1016/j.ijpe.2012.02.005
23. Uemura Reche, A.Y., Canciglieri, O., Estorilio, C.C.A., Rudek, M.: Green supply chain management and the contribution to product development process. In: Leal Filho, W., Borges de Brito, P.R., Frankenberger, F. (eds.) International Business, Trade and Institutional Sustainability. WSS, pp. 781–793. Springer, Cham (2020). https://doi.org/10.1007/978-3-030-26759-9_46
24. Khan, O., Stolte, T., Creazza, A., Lee Hansen, Z.N.: Integrating product design into the supply chain. Cogent Eng. (2016). https://doi.org/10.1080/23311916.2016.1210478
25. Uemura Reche, A.Y., Canciglieri Junior, O., Rudek, M.: The importance green supply chain management approach in the integrated product development process. In: Integrating Social Responsibility and Sustainable Development - Addressing Challenges and Creating Opportunities (2021). ISBN 978-3-030-59974-4

**Optimization of Production
and Transportation Systems**

Interactive Design Optimization
of Layout Problems

Xiaoxiao Song[1]([⊠])[iD], Emilie Poirson[1][iD], Yannick Ravaut[2], and Fouad Bennis[1]

[1] Laboratoire des Sciences du Numérique de Nantes (LS2N), ECN, UMR 6004,
44321 Nantes, France
{Xiaoxiao.song,Emilie.poirson,Fouad.bennis}@ec-nantes.fr
[2] Thales Communications, 49300 Cholet, France
yannick.ravaut@thalesgroup.com

Abstract. Layout optimization plays an important role in the field of industrial engineering. The layout problem presented here involves the real and virtual rectangular components. The real components can be the devices or buildings depending on the application. The space of accessibility associated with the real component is virtual, which allows the user to access the real component in reality, such as facility maintenance. However, most of the layout problems are NP hard. The great complexity of layout problems increase the difficulty in finding a feasible layout design in a reasonable time. To resolve these problems, we propose a hybrid constructive placing strategy which makes the search of feasible designs easier. The multi-objective application presented in this study demonstrates the effectiveness and portability of the method. Since the number of optimal layout designs can be very large, a cluster approach is followed to group all similar solutions. First, the notion of pairwise similarity indicator is introduced to analyze the similarity among the optimized layout designs. Second, the visualization of the hierarchical clustering of similarity matrix is customized. Then for each design, the user can interact with it by locally modifying the position or rotation of the component. The interactivity helps the user evaluate performance of the designs and preferable results are typically achieved.

Keywords: Layout problem · Hybrid constructive placing strategy · Interactive design

1 Introduction

The layout problems (LPs) concern placing a given number of components with known dimensions in a given number of containers. The component can be the equipment, device, cabinet or building, work-space depending on the application. The innovative formulation of LP came out in [1], which introduces the

Supported by China Scholarship Council.

A. Dolgui et al. (Eds.): APMS 2021, IFIP AICT 634, pp. 387–395, 2021.
https://doi.org/10.1007/978-3-030-85914-5_41

virtual component to resolve the problem of accessibility in the practical applications. Solving a multi-objective LP consists of finding several solutions that optimizes the objectives and respects a set of constraints. Generally, each placement problem presents non-overlap and non-protrusion constraints. These constraints express the fact that there is no overlap between real components and each component must stay inside the container.

Various methods have been developed to solve optimization problems. Constructive heuristic and meta-heuristic methods that can provide sub-optimal solutions have been developed to solve multi-objective LPs. Constructive heuristic procedures build a layout from scratch by successively selecting and placing facilities until a completed layout is obtained [4]. The efficiency of Simulated Annealing (SA) in solving complex combinatorial problems making it interesting for extension to multi-objective optimization [10]. In addition, it is worth noting that more and more researchers now work on hybrid methods by combining different optimization strategies [3,5,7,8].

LPs are generally considered as optimization problems and most search algorithms are developed for global optimization. However, LPs are not like other mathematics optimization problems, the complexity of the design space, and the discontinuities in the search space that make it hard to optimize analytically. In addition, in practical applications, the needs of users cannot be expressed as simple mathematical expressions. The great complexity of layout problems increase the difficulty in finding a feasible layout design in a reasonable time. Motivated by previous works [2], we propose an efficient SA based algorithm coupled with a constructive placing strategy, which makes it easier to search feasible designs in multi-objective LPs. First, using SA based optimization to determine the placement order of components. Second, to explore the feasible space and guarantee constraints, a constructive placing strategy is applied to benefit overlap between virtual components while keeping the maximal free space and respect non-overlap constraint where real components cannot overlap with others. In the experiment study, it proves the efficiency and portability of the algorithm.

Since multi-objective optimization usually solves objectives simultaneously. Therefore there is no single optimal solution but a set of compromised solutions, widely known as Pareto optimal set. However, there may be similarities within the design set. In [1], the author distinguishes two configurations geometrically. For example, the design i differs from the design j if one of the components of the layout has been moved from at least a certain distance. In fact, it can filter very similar designs. But a more precise method is to evaluate the similarity globally rather than comparing between one of the components. In order to find the ideal solution without making the user tired, a similarity indicator is proposed for each pair of Pareto optimal design and a hierarchical clustering [9] is performed. By visualizing the hierarchical similarity, the user could select the most appropriate solution.

A hybrid constructive placing strategy is developed to solve the LP considering the virtual and real components. Subsequently, the detailed similarity description and visualization tool is introduced. Finally, conclusion and future work are given.

2   Hybrid Constructive Placing Strategy

For the hybrid optimization, we need to determine the placing order and the placing strategy. Suppose we have 8 real components, the permutations of placing order are 8!. Exploring all possibilities is time consuming. So we use SA algorithm to optimize the order of placing components into the container. The constructive placing strategy is based on the difference process to update these *empty maximal spaces* (EMSs) [6]. EMSs represent the list of largest rectangle empty space in the container. In the LP, there are real components $C_i = \{x_i, y_i, w_i, h_i\}$, $i \in n$, n is the number of components and a list of associate n_i virtual components $v_{ij} = \{x_{v_{ij}}, y_{v_{ij}}, w_{v_{ij}}, h_{v_{ij}}\}, j \in n_i$ (see Fig. 1). The virtual components can be considered as a set of rectangles that are defined in the local frame of real component and can be deduced by the relatives coordinates to the associates real component. If there is rotation, the coordinates and size will update in the corresponding local frame as shown in Fig. 1(b).

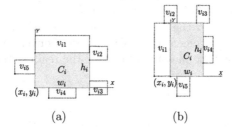

(a)   (b)

Fig. 1. Component representation: (a) Before rotation, (b) After rotation.

Considering the non-overlap constraint, we use two EMSs lists to track the empty space generation where current real components, real and virtual components are placed, named S, S' respectively. The space in S' is used to place new real components and guarantees non-overlap of real components, while the space in S is used to place new virtual components and benefits overlap between virtual components. In the following sections, we describe the main idea of the constructive placing strategy and the application.

2.1   Placing Convention

The placement of component is determined by respecting a placement convention. Without loss of universality, there are three predefined convention options that guarantee non-overlap and non-protrusion constraints:

- Wall convention: Place the real components along the boundary of the empty space. Measure the real components and then the associated virtual components where the components being placed fit.

– Center convention: Place the virtual components along the boundary of the empty space. Measure the virtual components and then the associated real components where the components being placed fit.
– Random convention: Place components randomly along the boundary of the empty space. Mix the first two conventions mentioned above.

2.2   Space Generation

The EMS is a rectangle like and defined by its bottom left vertices, width and height along x-axis and y-axis where $s = [x_s, y_s, w_s, h_s]$. A space generation example of wall convention is shown in Fig. 2. At beginning, there is no component inside the container, the empty space $s_0 = [0, 0, W, H]$ in S and S' is initialized to the size of the container. After placing the real component C_1, new empty spaces are generated. So we update S and S' as $\{s_1, s_2\}$. A slicing tree illustrates the space generation in Fig. 2(c), (d). If there is a virtual component attached to the real component, for example v_{11}, the placement of v_{11} will generate new empty spaces $\{s_3, s_2\}$ in S'. With these two lists, we can track the empty spaces generated by the placed components during the placing procedure. Figure 3 illustrates a placement example of center convention. In this case, the virtual components will be measured first and the real components are followed later.

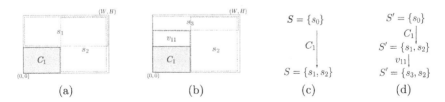

Fig. 2. Example of wall convention: (a) Space generation after placing C_1, (b) Space generation after placing v_{11}, (c) Slicing tree of S, (d) Slicing tree of S'.

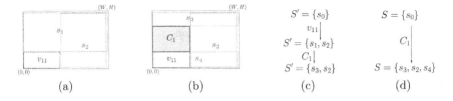

Fig. 3. Example of center convention: (a) Space generation after placing v_{11}, (b) Space generation after placing C_1, (c) Slicing tree of S', (d) Slicing tree of S.

2.3   Placing Strategy

To place the component properly, first enumerate all permutations of the space in S and S'. Then apply the placing convention to determine the configuration of the components. The constructive placing strategy is formulated as follows:

1. Initialize the empty space in S and S' to the container space.
2. Place the new component sequentially according to the placing order. If the pair of space $(s', s), s' \in S', s \in S$ satisfies the size requirement for the component, then go through 4-way orientations of the component to find all the feasible configurations. By default, the placement of the component always closes to the boundary of the selected empty space $min(s', s)$ or $max(s', s)$ and generates new empty spaces with less margin. If there is feasible configuration, record the temporary configuration of component. If one component has several feasible placements, the one with maximal free space after placing the component will be selected as the prior choice.
3. Update S and S'. Repeat placing new components until a complete layout is finished. Otherwise, marked the placing order as unfeasible.

2.4   Application

To evaluate the performance of the hybrid optimization algorithm, we select different experiments including single-container LP and multi-container LP. The configuration of the component is determined successively by constructive placement according to the optimized order. During the optimization process, the non-dominated solutions will be kept in the external archive.

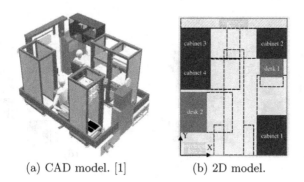

(a) CAD model. [1]   (b) 2D model.

Fig. 4. Model of single-container LP. (Color figure online)

Single-container LP is a shelter proposed in [1] (see Fig. 4(a)) minimizes the difference of center of gravity that indicated by the blue and red points(objective 1) while maximizes the distance among cabinets and electrical box(objective 2). The simplified model is shown in Fig. 4(b) which formulates by rectangles with

mass (real components) and dotted rectangles without mass (virtual components). For example the space of accessibility of desk allows the user sit down.
If the virtual components are considered in optimization, then the components
density increases until 90%. The high density of the LP makes it harder to find
the feasible solutions. However, the proposed hybrid optimization takes less than
5 min to finish 400 iterations and 4 solutions are Pareto optimal designs. The
Pareto front is shown in Fig. 5(a) and the corresponding layout designs are displayed in Fig. 6(a) to (d). The previous optimal solution based on interactive
modular optimization that presented in [1] is shown in Fig. 6(e) which is dominated by solution (b) and (c). The hybrid constructive placing strategy splits
the space to evaluate the non-overlap constraint and the obtained high-quality
results prove the optimization efficiency.

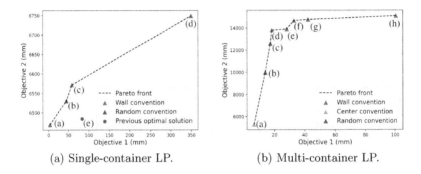

(a) Single-container LP.   (b) Multi-container LP.

Fig. 5. Display of Pareto front.

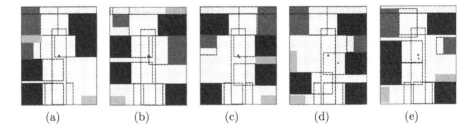

(a)   (b)   (c)   (d)   (e)

Fig. 6. Display of Pareto-optimal designs of single-container LP.

The innovative optimization method is also extended to solve multi-container
LPs by mixing container loading and component placing. In general, the implementation in multi-container LP is quite straight forward by taking the space
of different containers as the initial empty space in S and S'. We conduct the
proposed method to optimize the center of gravity along the x-axis(objective 1)

and separate the components(objective 2) on a two containers LP. The obtained Pareto front after 400 iterations is shown in Fig. 5(b) and the corresponding layout designs are displayed in Fig. 7. All designs satisfy non-overlap and non-protrusion constraints and have different configurations. The computation complexity remains in the same level as in the single-container LP because of the same number of components. Experimental results show the portability of the proposed algorithm.

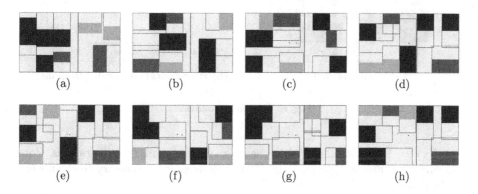

(a)   (b)   (c)   (d)

(e)   (f)   (g)   (h)

Fig. 7. Display of Pareto-optimal designs of multi-container LP.

3   Interactive Design

In the real-world LPs, there are subjective requirements, for example the components should be accessible from the entry, which is not easy to be integrated into the problem formulation. However, by displaying the obtained Pareto front, the user can use his expertise to interact and explore the design space by manipulating locally the configuration of some components, and find the design that satisfies all the requirements. In other words, the user plays a major role in the selection of the ideal result of the application. For the optimized solutions, there may be similarities within the design set. Therefore, we define a similarity indicator to evaluate the similarity of the design, which helps the user distinguish between layout design. A similarity indicator represents how closely the current layout design resembles the others.

To calculate the similarity indicator, first, permute all the layout designs that belongs to Pareto optimal set. For each pair, calculate an element-wise, in other word, pixel by pixel difference. Then, calculate the percentage of the same elements among all elements. The value of indicator is in the range of 0 to 1. The larger the indicator is, the more closely the layout designs are. The similarity matrix is formulated by the symmetrical matrix where the lower/upper triangular part containing the similarity indicator of each paired designs. The similarity matrix of the multi-container LP is represented in Fig. 8(a). By comparison, it turns out that optimal designs of Fig. 7(d), Fig. 7(e) and Fig. 7(h); Fig. 7(f) and

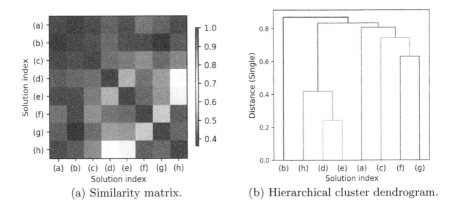

(a) Similarity matrix.   (b) Hierarchical cluster dendrogram.

Fig. 8. Similarity analysis.

Fig. 7(g) has higher similarity value because of some similar configurations. Considering the different type of similar layout designs, it is necessary to cluster the optimal set.

For the similarity matrix, we apply the hierarchy cluster algorithm [9] to build nested clusters by merging similar solutions successively. At each iteration, a distance matrix of clusters is maintained. When only one cluster remains, the algorithm stops, and this cluster becomes the root. The hierarchical similarity relation is shown in Fig. 8(b). For example, optimal designs of Fig. 7(d) and Fig. 7(e) with highest similarity are grouped into the cluster 1 and the design in Fig. 7(h) with smaller similarity value is grouped with the cluster 1 as the cluster 2. The visualization tool can provide the hierarchy similarity information of the designs and help the user select the preferable solutions quickly.

4   Conclusion and Future Work

The proposed hybrid constructive algorithm is the first attempt to search directly the feasible space of multi-objective LPs that formulated by the rectangular real and virtual components. In the practical applications, the conventional optimization usually takes a couple of hours or days to solve the problem which is computationally expensive. By contrast, the hybridization of SA and constructive placing strategy takes less computational efforts to find the high-quality layout designs even if the density of the problem is quite high. The user can therefore select the final design according to the preference which guarantees the interaction in time. What's more, it can be easily adopted to multi-container LP which involves the assignment and placement of components. The experimental results prove the effectiveness and portability of the proposed algorithm. Moreover, a indicator that can provide similarity information is defined, based on the position and rotation of all components.. From a practical point of view, similarity analysis is very important and useful for users to distinguish layout designs and then make the final decision by choosing one of these optimal designs.

Actually, the proposed algorithm is based on the difference process of rectangular empty spaces, it could be interesting to extend the algorithm to other applications, for example the LP with free-form components, where the update of the empty spaces should also adapt to the shape of the component. Furthermore, the accessibility of the optimal designs should be taken into account during the optimization process. For example in Fig. 7(c), some virtual components are blocked such that the related real component is not accessible. Afterwards, the complex layout problem in three-dimensional space will be considered. Expand the possibility of interaction between virtual reality and optimized spatial layout, which are more suitable for manipulating objects in three-dimensional space.

References

1. Bénabès, J., Poirson, E., Bennis, F., Ravaut, Y.: Interactive modular optimization strategy for layout problems. In: ASME 2011 International Design Engineering Technical Conferences and Computers and Information in Engineering Conference - 37th Design Automation Conference, vol. 5, pp. 553–562 (2011)
2. Gonçalves, J.F., Resende, M.G.: A biased random-key genetic algorithm for the unequal area facility layout problem. Eur. J. Oper. Res. **246**, 86–107 (2015)
3. Guan, C., Zhang, Z., Liu, S., Gong, J.: Multi-objective particle swarm optimization for multi-workshop facility layout problem. J. Manuf. Syst. **53**, 32–48 (2019)
4. Hosseini nasab, H., Fereidouni, S., Ghomi, S., Fakhrzad, M.: Classification of facility layout problems: a review study. Int. J. Adv. Manuf. Technol. **94**, 957–977 (2018)
5. Kropp, I., et al.: A multi-objective approach to water and nutrient efficiency for sustainable agricultural intensification. Agric. Syst. **173**, 289–302 (2019)
6. Lai, K., Chan, J.W.: Developing a simulated annealing algorithm for the cutting stock problem. Comput. Ind. Eng. **32**, 115–127 (1997)
7. Lima, S.J.A., Santos, R.A.R., Alves de Araujo, S., Triguis Schimit, P.H.: Combining genetic algorithm with constructive and refinement heuristics for solving the capacitated vehicle routing problem. In: Nääs, I., et al. (eds.) APMS 2016. IAICT, vol. 488, pp. 113–121. Springer, Cham (2016). https://doi.org/10.1007/978-3-319-51133-7_14
8. Mariem, B., Marc, Z., AFFONSO, R., Masmoudi, F., Haddar, M.: A methodology for solving facility layout problem considering barriers – genetic algorithm coupled with A* search. J. Intell. Manuf. **31**, 615–640 (2019)
9. Müllner, D.: Modern hierarchical, agglomerative clustering algorithms. ArXiv arXiv:1109.2378 (2011)
10. Pllana, S., Memeti, S., Kolodziej, J.: Customizing pareto simulated annealing for multi-objective optimization of control cabinet layout. In: 2019 22nd International Conference on Control Systems and Computer Science, pp. 78–85 (2019)

A Fast and Efficient Fluid Relaxation Algorithm for Large-Scale Re-entrant Flexible Job Shop Scheduling

Linshan Ding, Zailin Guan$^{(\boxtimes)}$, and Zhengmin Zhang

Huazhong University of Science and Technology, Wuhan, China
d201980276@hust.edu.cn

Abstract. In this paper, we study a large-scale re-entrant flexible job shop scheduling problem (FJSP) with the objective of makespan minimization. In the proposed problem, machine quantities, job types, and processes of jobs are known in advance. At least one machine is available for each process. The large production demand for each type of jobs leads to a large-scale manufacture feature in this problem. To address the problem, we first establish a fluid model for the large-scale re-entrant FJSP. Then, we design a priority update rule to improve the assignment of jobs and machines. We finally propose a fast and efficient fluid relaxation algorithm (FRA) to solve the large-scale re-entrant FJSP through the relaxation fluid optimal solution. Numerical results show that the FRA is asymptotically optimal with the increase of the problem scale. The scale of problems has little effect on the FRA's solving speed. Therefore, we conclude the FRA is suitable for solving the large-scale re-entrant FJSP.

Keywords: Flexible job shop scheduling · Fluid model · Fluid relaxation · Re-entrant flows · Large scale optimization

1 Introduction

The flexible job shop scheduling problem (FJSP) is an extension of the job shop scheduling problem [1]. It breaks through the constraint of resource uniqueness. FJSPs have a set of available machines for each process and the solution space of FJSP is further expanded. Thus, we consider it as a more complex NP-hard problem [2]. We study a large-scale re-entrant flexible job shop scheduling problem (FJSP). In the large-scale re-entrant FJSP, each process has an available machine set, each process routing may have re-entrant flows, different processes of the same job can be processed on the same machine, and the demand for each type of job is large. The large production demand for each type of jobs leads to a large-scale manufacture feature in this problem. Compared with FJSPs, the large-scale re-entrant FJSP has many identical copies of the fixed set of jobs, which increases the number of jobs to be scheduled. The increasing number of jobs results in the huge exponentially solution space which increases the complexity of scheduling. Hence, the large-scale re-entrant FJSP is more complex than FJSP with same job types. There are the large-scale re-entrant FJSP in actual

© IFIP International Federation for Information Processing 2021
Published by Springer Nature Switzerland AG 2021
A. Dolgui et al. (Eds.): APMS 2021, IFIP AICT 634, pp. 396–404, 2021.
https://doi.org/10.1007/978-3-030-85914-5_42

production, such as semiconductor manufacturing lines [3]. Therefore, it is important to study an efficient solution algorithm for actual production.

In recent years, researchers have done a lot of research for large-scale job shop scheduling by the fluid approach. For instance, Bertsimas and Gamarnik (1999) propose a fluid relaxation algorithm that replaces discrete jobs with continuous fluid flow to solve the large-scale job shop scheduling and packet routing problem [4]. Boudoukh et al. (2001) propose a simulated fluid solution heuristic algorithm that approximated the job shop scheduling problem to a continuous deterministic scheduling problem [5]. Dai and Weiss (2002) propose a fluid heuristic online scheduling algorithm based on bottleneck machine safety inventory. However, the safety inventory calculation is cumbersome, which is not conducive to practical application. The inventory formation and inventory clearance take a long time, which increases the makespan [6]. Nazarathy and Weiss (2010) propose a simple heuristic method to solve a large-scale job shop scheduling problem with the processing time randomly generated. Numerical results show that the proposed heuristic method is asymptotic optimality with the increase of the number of jobs [7].

Some scholars propose some fluid approaches by constructing the fluid solution tracking formula to solve the large-scale job shop scheduling problems. Bertsimas and Sethuraman (2002) construct the fluid solution tracking formula by combining the fluid relaxation approach with fair queuing in communication networks. They propose a fluid synchronization algorithm based on the fluid solution tracking formula [8]. Gu et al. (2017) construct a virtual scheduling formula which as the benchmark to determine the processing priority of each job on each machine. Based on the virtual scheduling formula, they propose a tracking virtual scheduling algorithm to solve the general job shop scheduling problem [9]. Gu et al. (2018) study the large-scale random job shop scheduling problem with a generally similar number of jobs. The objective of this problem is to minimize the maximum completion time. They propose a strategy to solve the random job shop scheduling problem by tracking the fluid schedule [10].

Up to now, scholars have done a lot of research on large-scale re-entrant job shop scheduling. However, no research has been found on large-scale re-entrant FJSPs. Thus, we establish a fluid model and propose an efficient fluid relaxation algorithm for the large-scale re-entrant FJSP.

The remaining parts of this paper are as follows: In Sect. 2, we establish a fluid model to describe our problem. In Sect. 3, we design the priority updating rule and propose a fluid relaxation algorithm to solve the large-scale re-entrant FJSP. In Sect. 4, we verify the performance of the fluid relaxation algorithm on several artificial benchmark problems. The conclusion is presented in Sect. 5.

2 The Proposed Fluid Model

We establish a fluid model for solving the large-scale re-entrant flexible job shop scheduling problem. In our model, processes of different types of jobs are divided into different classes $k = \{1, 2, 3 \ldots K\}$. We use Z_{krj} to indicate whether the jth process of the rth type of job is represented as class k (value 1 for yes, 0 for no). We assume the job is composed of fluid. We use continuous fluid flow instead of discrete jobs. Thus, the number of jobs is not required to be an integer in the fluid model. Within unit time, the machine can allocate its processing time (the real number between 0 and 1) to different classes. Each machine has a fixed proportion of processing time to deal with each class. The output of our model is the proportion of time allocated to each class by each machine. The notations we used are introduced follows:

Indexes:
i: Machines, $(i = 1, 2, 3 \ldots I)$.
r(r'):   Job types, $(r = 1, 2, 3 \ldots R)$.
j(j'):   Processes, $(j = 1, 2, 3 \ldots J_r, \forall r \in \{1, 2, 3 \ldots R\})$
(k'):   Classes, $k = 1, 2, 3 \ldots K$, $K = \sum_{r=1}^{R} J_r$.

Input data:
N_r: The total number of rth type of job.
M_I: Set of machines, $M_I = \{1, 2 \ldots I\}$.
t_{ik}:   Processing time of class k on machine i.
L_K: Set of classes, $L_K = \{1, 2 \ldots K\}$.
M_k: Set of available machines for class k.
K_i: Set of available classes for machine i.

Decision variables:
u_{ik}:   The proportion of processing time allocated to class k by machine i.

Notations:
Z_{krj}:   Binary variable, $Z_{krj} = 1$ if the jth process of the rth type of job is represented as class k, $\sum_r^R \sum_j^{J_r} Z_{krj} = 1 \ \forall k \in L_K$.
t_{ik}:   Processing time of class k on machine i.
e_{ik}:   Processing rate of class k on machine i, $e_{ik} = 1/t_{ik}$.
$p_{kk'}$:   Binary variable, take value 1 if class k' is the tight post-process of class k.
T_k: Completion time of class k.
c_{ik}:   Binary variable, $c_{ik} = 1$ if class k is available for machine i.
E_k: Total processing rate of class k, $E_k = \sum_{i=1}^{I} e_{ik} u_{ik}$.
$Q_k(t)$:   The actual number of class k at time t.
$Q_k^+(t)$:   The actual total number of class k which at time t has not yet completed processing.
$Q_{ik}^+(t)$:   The actual total number of class k which at time t has not yet completed the process by machine i.
$q_k(t)$:   The fluid number of class k at time t.
$q_k^+(t)$:   The total fluid number of class k which at time t has not yet completed processing.
$q_{ik}^+(t)$:   The total fluid number of class k which at time t has not yet completed the process by machine i.

The fluid model satisfies the following equations:

$$Q_k(0) = \sum_{r=1}^{R} N_r Z_{kr1} \quad \forall k \in L_K \tag{1}$$

$$q_k(0) = Q_k(0) \quad \forall k \in L_K \tag{2}$$

$$q_k(t) = q_k(0) - tE_k + t \sum_{k' \in L_k} E_{k'} p_{k'k} \quad \forall k, k' \in L_K \tag{3}$$

Equation (1) represents the actual number of each class in time 0. Equation (2) means the fluid number of each class in time 0. Equation (3) represents the fluid number of each class in time t.

$$Q_k^+(0) = \sum_{r=1}^{R} \sum_{j=1}^{J_r} Z_{krj} N_r \quad \forall k \in L_K \tag{4}$$

$$q_k^+(0) = Q_k^+(0) \quad \forall k \in L_K \tag{5}$$

$$q_k^+(t) = q_k^+(0) - tE_k \quad \forall k \in L_K \tag{6}$$

Equation (4) means the actual total number of each class which has not yet completed processing in time 0. Equation (5) represents the total fluid number of each class that has not yet completed processing in time 0. Equation (6) represents the total fluid number of each class in time t.

$$q_{ik}^+(0) = q_k^+(0) \frac{e_{ik} u_{ik}}{\sum_{i=1}^{I} e_{ik} u_{ik}} \quad \forall i \in M_I, k \in L_K \tag{7}$$

$$q_{ik}^+(t) = q_{ik}^+(0) - t e_{ik} u_{ik} \quad \forall i \in M_I, k \in L_K \tag{8}$$

$$T_k = \frac{q_k^+(0)}{E_k} \quad \forall k \in L_K \tag{9}$$

In Eq. (7), the total fluid number of class k which has not yet completed the process by machine i at the initial time is given. Equation (8) represents the total fluid number of class k which has not yet completed the process by machine i at time t. Equation (9) means the completion time of each class in the fluid model.

$$\sum_{r=1}^{R} \sum_{j=1}^{J_r} Z_{krj} = 1 \quad \forall k \in L_K \tag{10}$$

$$\sum_{k=1}^{K} u_{ik} \leq 1 \quad \forall i \in M_I \tag{11}$$

$$0 \leq u_{ik} \leq c_{ik} \quad \forall i \in M_I, k \in L_K \tag{12}$$

$$E_k \le \sum\nolimits_{k'=1}^{K} E_{k'} p_{k'k} \quad \forall k, k' \in L_K : q_k(0) = 0 \tag{13}$$

Equation (10) means that each process of each type of job can only be represented by one class. Constraints (11) show that the machine utilization is less than 100%. Constraint (12) represents the range of decision variables. Constraint (13) indicates that the processing rate is less than or equal to the arrival rate if the initial fluid number of class k equal to zero, which guarantees the solution is feasible.

The objective is to minimize the maximum completion time of all classes, as indicated in Eq. (14).

$$C_{max} = min(max\{T_1, \ldots T_K\}) \tag{14}$$

3   The Priority Update Rule and the Fluid Relaxation Algorithm

We can obtain the proportion of time allocated to each class by each machine using the fluid model. However, we do not specify the machine assignment for each job and the processing sequence of jobs on each machine in detail. Therefore, we propose a priority updating rule based on the fluid model to guide the machine selection and job processing sequence.

3.1   The Priority Update Rule

We define the priority of class k at time t as Eq. (15).

$$F_k = \frac{Q_k^+(t) - q_k^+(t)}{Q_k^+(0)} \quad \forall k \in L_K \tag{15}$$

We use F_k value to represent the priority of class k. We select the class with the maximum F_k value at each decision point. It means we select the job to process which has the maximum F_k value at the decision time. We have to allocate an available machine for each chosen class. Thus, we define Eq. (16) to represent the priority of each available machine to each class at time t.

$$B_{ik} = \frac{Q_{ik}^+(t) - q_{ik}^+(t)}{q_{ik}^+(0)} \quad \forall k \in L_K, i \in M_I \tag{16}$$

We choose an available machine which has the highest B_{ik} to process the job according to F_k.

In each decision time, we select a class k that has the maximum F_k value first (if different classes have the same F_k value, we select a class from them randomly). Then we select an available idle machine that has the maximum B_{ik} value to process the class k (if different machines have the same B_{ik} value, we select a machine from them randomly). Finally, we complete the job selection and machine assignment in manufacturing.

3.2   The Fluid Relaxation Algorithm

We propose a fluid relaxation algorithm (FRA) to solve the large-scale re-entrant flexible job shop scheduling problem. We first solve the fluid model with the CPLEX to obtain the optimal maximum completion time C_{max} (the lower bound value) and the proportion of time allocated to each class by each machine in the fluid model. Then we propose a fluid relaxation algorithm based on the priority update rule.

The detailed steps of the algorithm are as follows:

Step1: Solve the fluid model with the CPLEX to obtain all u_{ik}.

Step2: We assume that the current time is represented by TIME_NOW, the next idle time of machine i represented by TIME_NEXT (i). Then all the machines are idling in the initial time (TIME_NOW = 0).

Step3: Generate the set of M_{now} which includes all the machines which are idling and have available jobs at time TIME_NOW.

Step4: Generate the available class set K_{now},
$\forall i \in M_{now}, if\ k \in K_i\ and\ Q_k(now - time) > 0, then\ k \in K_{now}$. If $K_{now} = \varnothing$, end the algorithm and output the solution.

Step5: Select the class k from a set K_{now} which has the maximum F_k value, then select the machine i from set $M_{now} \cap M_k$ which has the maximum B_{ik} value to process class k.

Step6: Update the value of TIME_NEXT (i), Q_k, Q_k^+, F_k and B_{ik}. Update the set M_{now}. If $M_{now} \neq \varnothing$, go to step 4.

Step7: Update the value of TIME_NOW. TIME_NOW $= min_{i \in M_I}TIME\_NEXT(i)$, go to step3.

The asymptotic optimality of FRA:

Theorem 1. Consider a flexible job shop scheduling problem with R job types and I machines. The FRA produces a schedule with makespan time C_{FRA} such that:

$$C_{max} \leq C_{FRA} \leq C_{max} + (R+2)t_{max}J_{max} \qquad (17)$$

In Eq. (17), C_{max} is the lower bound provided by the fluid model, t_{max} is the maximum processing time over all processes in all machines. J_{max} is the maximum number of processes of any job type. The proof of Theorem 1 is similar as the Theorem 4 which proposed by Dai and Weiss [6].

In our problem, $(R+2)t_{max}J_{max}$ is a constant in a finite range. The FRA satisfies the following Eq. (18) as the total number of jobs goes to infinity.

$$\frac{C_{FRA}}{C_{max}} \approx 1 \qquad (18)$$

From Eq. (18), we see that the FRA is asymptotically optimal as the number of jobs increases.

4 Computational Experiments and Results

To verify the superiority of the proposed fluid relaxation algorithm, we develop a numerical experiment for the large-scale re-entrant FJSP. The algorithm is implemented on a PC with Inter (R) Core (TM) I5-9300 CPU @ 2.40 GHz 2.40 GHz and 8 GB RAM. We construct an artificial example with 3 job types and 10 machines. We initialize the set of available machines for each process randomly. The processing time of all processes obeys the uniform random distribution U (1, 5). In Table 1, we provide the available machines and the processing time of each process. "-" indicates the machine is not available for this process.

Table 1. Processing times.

Job	Process	M1	M2	M3	M4	M5	M6	M7	M8	M9	M10
R1	O11	3.3	-	4.1	-	2.2	4	1.5	1.2	-	3.9
	O12	-	-	2.5	-	3.7	-	1.5	3	4.3	1.5
	O13	-	-	4.2	-	-	4.7	1.4	-	-	4.5
	O14	-	-	-	2.1	-	5	-	3.9	2.9	-
	O15	-	3.4	-	-	-	1.6	-	-	3.9	-
R2	O21	4.9	-	3.5	-	-	-	-	4	4.1	3.7
	O22	3.8	-	-	4.6	-	2.8	-	1.9	4.7	-
	O23	-	3.6	3.7	-	3.7	-	-	2.2	2.1	-
	O24	1.1	-	1.4	-	1.5	-	-		1.7	1.3
	O25	4.9	2.3	-	-	1.1	1.5	1.5	1.4	-	-
R3	O31	-	2.2	1.4	-	3.8	1.4	4.9	3.2	2.6	-
	O32	3.1	2.8	1.3	-	-	-	-	2.7	-	3.4
	O33	1.9	-	2.8	-	-	2.8	-	1.1	-	3.7
	O34	-	2	-	-	4	-	3.2	-	-	2.6
	O35	-	1.1	-	4.5	-	-	4	-	2.1	3.7

In Table 2, we calculate the results of FRA solving the re-entrant FJSP with different problem scales. The problem scale is denoted by the total number of jobs multiply the total number of machines (n × m). C_{max} is the lower bound value of the problem which we obtain with CPLEX. C_{FCFS} is the results which we obtain with the First Come First Serve policy (FCFS). GAP represents the proximity of the FRA solution to C_{max}. We get the GAP value through the following Eq. (19).

$$\text{GAP} = \frac{C_{FRA} - C_{max}}{C_{max}} \times 100\% \qquad (19)$$

The GAP gradually decreases with the increase of problem scale, indicating that FRA is asymptotically optimal with the increase of the number for various jobs. The CPU time of FRA within 4 s for all instances and the increments in CPU time is small as problem scale increases. The results show that the fluid relaxation algorithm

Table 2. Results obtained by FRA.

Instance	R1	R2	R3	n × m	C_{max}	C_{FRA}	C_{FCFS}	GAP	Computing time (s)
1	6	8	10	24 × 10	21.2	24.6	37.8	16.03%	0.81
2	12	16	20	48 × 10	42.4	47.1	74.8	11.08%	0.96
3	24	32	40	96 × 10	84.9	89.6	144	5.53%	1.05
4	48	64	80	192 × 10	169.9	175.6	285.2	3.35%	0.73
5	96	128	160	384 × 10	339.9	348.1	545.8	2.41%	1.24
6	192	256	320	768 × 10	679.9	691.7	1147.3	1.73%	1.74
7	384	512	640	1536 × 10	1359.8	1378.3	2290.1	1.36%	2.36
8	768	1024	1280	3072 × 10	2719.7	2755.9	4487.5	1.33%	3.44

(FRA) can solve the problem efficiently and quickly, the problem scale has little effect on the solving speed. The FRA is suitable for solving the large-scale re-entrant FJSP.

The FCFS policy is a traditional dispatching rule in semiconductor manufacturing [11]. The following Fig. 1 compares the FRA and the FCFS policy in eight instances. Note that the FRA outperforms the FCFS policy in all instances. The results indicate that the FRA has the potential to improve the productivity in semiconductor manufacturing.

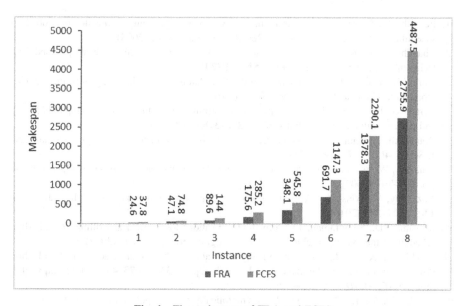

Fig. 1. The makespan of FRA and FCFS

5   Conclusion

In this paper, we study a large-scale re-entrant FJSP with machine numbers, job types, and processes of job are known and fixed. Moreover, the demand quantity for each type of jobs is a large value. We present a fluid relaxation algorithm (FRA) and a priority update rule based on the fluid model to solve the large-scale re-entrant FJSP. We construct a large-scale re-entrant FJSP with 3 job types and 10 machines to evaluate the proposed algorithm. Numerical results show that the fluid relaxation algorithm is asymptotically optimal with the increase of the number of various jobs. Moreover, the problem scale has little effect on the solving speed of the FRA. The FRA outperforms the FCFS policy in all instances which indicates the FRA has the potential to improve the productivity in semiconductor manufacturing. Furthermore, the low computation times make the FRA practical for implementation.

However, we do not consider the set-up time and machine failure in the fluid model which effects the productivity in semiconductor manufacturing. In future research, we can incorporate set-up time and machine failure in the fluid model or as an additional step in the FRA.

Acknowledgement. This work was supported by the National Key R&D Program of China (Grant No. 2018YFB1702700), the Youth Program of National Natural Science Foundation of China (Grant No. 51905196), and the National Natural Science Foundation of China under Grants No.71620107002.

References

1. Pezzella, F., Morganti, G., Ciaschetti, G.: A genetic algorithm for the flexible job-shop scheduling problem. Comput. Oper. Res. **35**(10), 3202–3212 (2008)
2. Chaudhry, I.A., Khan, A.A.: A research survey: review of flexible job shop scheduling techniques. Int. T Oper. Res. **23**(3), 551–591 (2016)
3. Kim, S.H., Lee, Y.H.: Synchronized production planning and scheduling in semiconductor fabrication. Comput. Ind. Eng. **96**, 72–85 (2016)
4. Bertsimas, D., Gamarnik, D.: Asymptotically optimal algorithms for job shop scheduling and packet routing. J. Algorithms **33**(2), 296–318 (1999)
5. Boudoukh, T., Penn, M., Weiss, G.: Scheduling jobshops with some identical or similar jobs. J. Sched. **4**(4), 177–199 (2001)
6. Dai, J.G., Weiss, G.: A fluid heuristic for minimizing makespan in job shops. Oper. Res. **50**(4), 692–707 (2002)
7. Nazarathy, Y., Weiss, G.: A fluid approach to large volume job shop scheduling. J. Sched. **13**(5), 509–529 (2010)
8. Bertsimas, D., Sethuraman, J.: From fluid relaxations to practical algorithms for job shop scheduling: the makespan objective. Math. Program. **92**(1), 61–102 (2002)
9. Gu, M., Lu, X., Gu, J.: An asymptotically optimal algorithm for large-scale mixed job shop scheduling to minimize the makespan. J. Comb. Optim. **33**(2), 473–495 (2015). https://doi.org/10.1007/s10878-015-9974-7
10. Gu, J., Gu, M., Lu, X., Zhang, Y.: Asymptotically optimal policy for stochastic job shop scheduling problem to minimize makespan. J. Comb. Optim. **36**(1), 142–161 (2018)
11. Siebert, M., et al.: Lot targeting and lot dispatching decision policies for semiconductor manufacturing: optimisation under uncertainty with simulation validation. Int. J. Prod. Res. **56**(1–2), 629–641 (2018)

Identification of Superior Improvement Trajectories for Production Lines via Simulation-Based Optimization with Reinforcement Learning

Günther Schuh[1], Andreas Gützlaff[1], Matthias Schmidhuber[1],
Jan Maetschke[1(✉)], Max Barkhausen[2], and Narendiran Sivanesan[2]

[1] Laboratory for Machine Tools and Production Engineering (WZL),
RWTH Aachen University, Campus-Boulevard 30, Aachen, Germany
j.maetschke@wzl.rwth-aachen.de
[2] 654 Manhattan Avenue, Brooklyn, NY 11222, USA

Abstract. An increasing variety of products contributes to the challenge of efficient manufacturing on production lines, e.g. in the Fast Moving Consumer Goods (FMCG) sector. Due to the complexity and multitude of adjustment levers, the identification of economic actions for improvement is challenging. Reinforcement learning offers a way to deal with such complex problems with little problem-specific adaptation. This paper presents a method for decision support for economic productivity improvement of production lines. A combination of discrete event simulation and reinforcement learning is used to identify efficient, sequential trajectories of improvements. The approach is validated with a fill-and-pack line of the FMCG industry.

Keywords: Manufacturing system · Production line · Machine learning · Simulation

1 Introduction

Manufacturing companies are facing customer demand for high quality products in a large number of variants. The resulting small batch sizes and frequent product changes lower the average Overall Equipment Effectiveness (OEE) [1] especially for companies that manufacture at high speed on production lines, such as the Fast Moving Consumer Good (FMCG) industry [2, 3]. Moreover, some companies allocate products in production networks back to western countries with high automation available due to a higher standard of digitalization [4]. This leads to consolidation and hence to increased planned utilization of production lines. As a result, the demands on the productivity and stability of production lines are increasing. Thus a growing focus on increasing the OEE can be observed within the industry sector leading to raising attention in research as well [5, 6].

The configuration of the production system, consisting of several machines, buffers, conveyors, etc., has a fundamental influence on its productivity and stability, and therefore on the OEE and ultimately on the production costs [7]. Improving such systems is a complex problem, the complexity of which increases dramatically with the number of machines. The buffer allocation subproblem alone is an NP-hard problem [8, 9].

To meet this challenge, Discrete Simulation-Based Optimization (DSBO) is widely used in the industry to improve the configuration of production lines because most real-world problems cannot be solved analytically due to their stochastic nature [8, 10]. However, studies show that companies need more help in conducting simulation studies, interpreting the results and deriving feasible step-by-step actions from them [11, 12].

Additionally, the identification of effective adjustment levers to improve brownfield production lines is challenging because the restraining element of the system shifts dynamically, due to the mutual dependencies of the systems elements. Because of this, and because different actions incur different costs, the identification and prioritization of efficient actions for improvement only make sense by considering the overall system behavior and costs, not only by focusing on the bottleneck-orientated OEE [5, 13, 14].

In the context of Cyber Production Management Systems (CPMS) [15], giving decision support in such complex but well-defined optimization problems, artificial intelligence (AI) methods, especially reinforcement learning (RL), are receiving more and more attention [16, 17]. The motivation for applying RL is that the RL agent learns to react efficiently to the dynamics of the environment, without any prior knowledge of the system dynamics [18].

This paper presents a method for improving the productivity of production lines efficiently using RL. The aim is not to find an optimal configuration but to discover trajectories of sequential improvements, which could be interpreted and implemented step by step and thus create the basis for practical decision support.

This paper is structured as follows: In Sect. 2, the advantages of using RL for optimizing production lines are presented. In Sect. 3, a comprehensive literature review on the state of the art is presented and the challenges of improving production lines are described. In Sect. 4, the methodology and experimental setup considering a fill-and-pack line of a FMCG manufacturer are described. The findings are discussed in Sect. 5.

2   Chances of Optimizing Production Lines Using RL

Discrete-event simulations (DES) are suitable for the evaluation of complex, stochastic systems, where a closed-form mathematical model is hard to find. Although simulation is not an optimization technique on its own, it can be combined with complementary optimization to improve real-world systems effectively by integrating in metaheuristics [19]. Instead of using the simulation as a black box solution, it is advisable to closely integrate optimization with simulation, statistically extract information from existing simulation runs to guide the parameter-search [10, 20]. Thus, metaheuristics may need to be adapted to the specific characteristics of the problem [20, 21]. The same applies to specific mathematical models.

For this reason, more and more approaches use AI for optimization in combination with simulation [12]. What makes RL an attractive solution candidate is that it does not require holistic a-prioiri knowledge of the problem or a dedicated mathematical model of the target production setup. RL is model-free in the sense that the RL agent learns about its environment simply by interacting with it [19].

RL can be understood as learning from a sequence of interactions between an *agent* and its *environment*, where the agent learns how to behave in order to achieve a goal [18]. The default formal framework to model RL problems is the Markov Decision Processes (MDP), a sequential decision process modeled by a state space, an action space, and transition probabilities between states and rewards [18, 19].

In an MDP, the agent acts based on observations of the *states* of the environment – in our case, these are the observations returned by the DES. The *rewards* received by the agent are the basis for evaluating these choices. The agent learns a *policy*, which may be understood as a function from state observations to actions. The agent's objective is to maximize the future cumulative discounted reward received over a sequence of actions [18].

Below, we will explain how improving a production line sequentially can be modeled as an MDP. This said, several challenges for the simulation-based optimization of production lines exist, which will be discussed in the following section.

3 State of the Art

The improvement of production lines has been the subject of research for decades. Due to the large number of publications, only the most relevant and recent approaches are listed here. For more detailed references, the reader is advised to refer to [8, 12, 22, 23]. The approaches can be roughly divided into analytical or mathematical models and simulation-based approaches [23]. Even though analytical approaches usually cannot cover the complexity of real use cases [8, 10, 19], there are a variety of specific analytical models for subproblems [24, 25]. Especially the optimization of buffer allocation has received much attention from researchers [22], such as in [9, 26]. There are further approaches, which solve other specific subproblems. For example, [25] designs an algorithm for the optimization of split and merge production and [27, 28] focus on downtime reductions (affected by Mean-Time-to-Repair).

However, since the combination of several small actions on different machines is expected to yield higher efficiency gains than major improvement on single machines [29], an isolated consideration of subproblems is therefore of limited benefit. [8, 13, 14] also argue, that due to the complex dependencies, optimization is only possible by considering the entire system and not by focusing on improvement actions on the bottleneck. At the same time, after a certain point, optimizing cycle times is more economical than further improving the availability of all machines [14].

[2, 30] explicitly consider fill-and-pack lines in the FMCG industry. However, they do not present an optimization approach, but rather simulation case studies. On the other hand, they underline the potential of optimizing such lines and show the need for a combined consideration of improvement costs and increased productivity.

[13, 23] show that without considering the overall system, prioritizing improvement activities such as maintenance activities is not advisable and that this is not adequately addressed in the literature. None of the approaches listed systematically considers improvement trajectories, i.e. a sequence of independently realizable actions to

improve a production system. Rather, they focuses on finding an (near-) optimal overall solution rather than looking at the path to get there, i.e. the improvement trajectories.

[12] gives an overview of DSBO approaches in manufacturing in general and shows that machine learning approaches for optimizing production systems are getting more and more attention in research. [10] sees the need for further research combining statistical learning in combination with DSBO. [16] predicts a vast increase in the importance of automated decisions based on AI in production management.

4 Methodology and Experimental Setup

The methodology to identify superior improvement trajectories for production lines via DSBO with RL consists of three steps. First, we describe the used DES. Second, we introduce the MDP formulation to apply RL in order to optimize the simulation. Finally, we address the algorithm used to learn this MDP.

The underlying research hypothesis is that by making available observations $X(s)$ on the status of the production line, and by supplying the agent with the profit of an action (reward R_a), the agent is able to learn policies which lead to efficient improvement trajectories for production lines.

The overall goal is to discover *interpretable and implementable* trajectories of parameter changes, including those affecting availability and cycle time, starting from the status quo of the production line and leading to increased productivity efficiently. This is measured by the profit resulting from the additional products produced and the costs of the necessary improvement actions. Hence, the goal is not only finding (near-) optimal parameter sets, which could be harder to interpret and unrealistic to implement in a real-world setting.

4.1 Discrete Event Simulation (DES)

We consider a simplified fill-and-pack-line of the FMCG industry, consisting of four machines (blower, filler, case packer, shrinker) linearly linked by accumulative conveyors. The third machine, the case packer, combines six of the produced goods with one tray (packaging material) from a case erector (see Fig. 1).

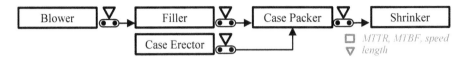

Fig. 1. Modelled production line with five machines and four conveyors

The failure probabilities of the machines are described with Mean-Time-To-Repair (MTTR) and Mean-Time-Between-Failures (MTBF), using an Erlang distribution [31]. The cycle times of the machines are given in pieces/min. The second machine, the filler, represents the bottleneck in terms of cycle time. The speed of the conveyors is not changed, but it is always higher than the surrounding machines. Due to the constant size of the products, the buffer size is determined by the length of the conveyor. Therefore, 19 parameters of four different types ($5\times$ MMTR, MTBF, speed and $4\times$ length, see Fig. 1) result in the state $s \in S$ (see Sect. 4.2).

The simulation logs the time that each machine stands still due to its own failure (failure time), as well as the time that a machine is blocked due to a downstream failure (blockage time). In addition, the blockage time of the conveyors is logged. These 14 times are added to the observation vector $X(s)$ and are thus seen by the agent (see Sect. 4.2). Each run of the simulation is 500 min.

For each adjustment of a parameter resp. each improvement measure, machine-specific costs are incurred. These costs are based on assumptions, which depend on the application-specific context, as in [14]. To calculate the earnings from an improvement measure, the quantity of additional goods produced is set in relation to the speed of the bottleneck machine, as proposed by [1]. An increase of this relation is equated with correspondingly positive earnings. The profit for the company is the difference between the earnings from the increased output and the costs for the corresponding improvement action. This profit forms the reward R_a (see Sect. 4.2). For a reinforcement learning agent, this reward function incentivizes profit maximizing behavior.

The simulation environment used is a customized version of the DES ManPy based on SimPy [32].

4.2 Framework for Reinforcement Learning: Formulation of MDP

The standard formal framework for reinforcement learning problems is a MDP, as mentioned above [18]. An MDP is a 4-tuple (S, A_s, P_a, R_a), where S is a set of states called the *state space*, A_s is a set of actions in the state $s \in S$ called the *action space*, P_a is the *probability* that at time t action $a \in A_s$ in state $s \in S$ will lead to state s' at time $t+1$, R_a is the immediate or expected *reward* received for transitioning from state $s \in S$ to state s' by taking the action $a \in A_s$. Importantly, an MDP is characterized by the Markov property, meaning that transition probabilities between states and states, and between state-action pairs and rewards, depend only on the present state, but not on past states.

In this case, the set of states is a subset of $\mathbb{R}^{20}$ where the first 19 entries are observations from the line simulation (see Sect. 4.1) and the last entry is the time step given by an integer. Each state s yields an observation vector $X(s)$ composed of the 19 parameters, the failure and blockage time for each element, the costs of the last improvement action, and an integer entry, which counts the steps of the optimization procedure. The action space is parametrized by a discrete and a continuous parameter, where the first represents which machine and which parameter to manipulate next, and the latter represents the delta to the current parameter of the machine currently being optimized. State transitions are governed by the stochastic simulation and the deterministic cost function for the improvement actions resp. parameter changes. The reward is the change in profit output by the simulation (as defined in Sect. 4.1) in going from state $s \in S$ to state $s' \in S$ via action $a \in A_s$. The resulting MDP has the Markov property for the obvious reason that the results of a simulation run, and hence the reward and next state, are only affected by properties of the simulation and the present configuration, but not on any configurations of previous simulation runs.

An episode, i.e. a possible improvement trajectory, consists of five improvement opportunities. That is, the agent is allowed to change five parameters in sequence, choosing both the parameter to change next, and the delta.

4.3   Training the Agent

There are multiple ways to learn a successful policy, i.e. a probability distribution over action given state observations; see [18] for an introduction. An important class of methods, which proved to be very successful by using *deep neural networks*, are so-called *policy gradients* [33]. The goal of policy gradient methods is to learn a probability distribution over actions, given a state observation $X(S)$, such that future discounted rewards are maximized. In order to choose an action given a state observation (in our case, an action changing the configuration of the production line) at a step in time t, the agent samples from a probability distribution parametrized by the outputs of the neural network. Policy gradient methods all have in common that the agent learns to optimize future expected rewards at each step, in formulae, $E[G_t|s, \pi] = E[R_t + \gamma * G_{t+1}|s, \pi]$, where G_t is the total future reward received by the agent from time t on, and $\gamma \epsilon [0; 1]$ is a discount factor for future rewards. We set $\gamma = 0.9$. In practice, this means that at $t = 0$, present and future rewards $r_0..r_4$ are discounted at rates $< 1, 0.9, 0.81, 0.72, 0.65 >$. Unlike in a continuous MPD, in a finite-horizon MDP like ours, the expected value of total future rewards for the agent is finite even if the $\gamma = 1$, i.e. even if no discount is applied to future rewards. But as is often the case, we have found that, by applying a significant discount to future rewards and hence by incentivizing more greedy behavior, convergence is achieved much more quickly.

In this setup, we use *Proximal Policy Optimization (PPO)*, a class of algorithms developed at OpenAI, which yields state-of-the-art results for a wide range of problems. The main motivation for using PPO as opposed to classical Policy Gradient methods lies in the fact that the latter are very sensitive to choices of step size, whereas PPO adapts the step size by taking into account the Kullback-Leibler divergence of the previous policy and the updated policy [34].

5   Application and Key Findings

Performing the described methodology with the set-up outlined, it can be observed, that the reward over the training episodes increases on average, i.e. the agent learned optimizing the reward and thus the production line considering the complex dependencies and the assumed costs without any prior knowledge of the system (s. Fig. 2a). It can be further stated that the presentation of the observations of the line (blockage times) to the agent accelerates the learning and improves the achieved reward.

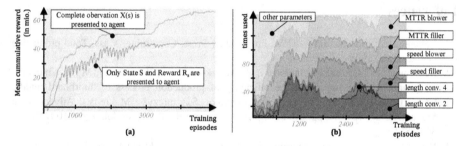

Fig. 2. Cumulative Reward (left) and changed parameters (right) over training episodes

Figure 2b shows that in the beginning, parameters are changed randomly (note that parameters are combined as *other*), but as the training progresses, a few parameters (shown on the very right of Fig. 2b) are selected significantly more often, as these are the most successful in terms of increasing productivity for the modelled production line. The most successful trajectory found consists of adjustments to reduce the MTTR of the filler, the reduction of MTTR of the blower, the increase of the speed of the filler, the adjustment of the conveyor 2 and the speed of the blower. This trajectory earns a reward of 64.3 Mio. €.

The advantage of this approach is that several trajectories with different combinations of parameters but comparable rewards were found. These interpretable improvement trajectories can thus be used for step-by-step decision support in the optimization process of production lines to prioritize alternative improvement actions and their combination. In this way, the use of DSBO becomes more easy for the user to interpret and thus more practical.

6   Conclusion and Further Research

In this paper, a methodology for identifying alternative improvement trajectories for production lines with RL has been presented. An RL agent with policy gradient method was able to learn policies from a DES and generate alternative trajectories without a-priori knowledge. Thus, a practical and interpretable assistance for the prioritization of improvement actions is presented. The promising results motivate further research. A fixed budget for an optimization could be specified and given to the agent as another constraint. Additionally production knowledge in the form of heuristics could be added to the RL agent to further improve the quality of trajectories or reduce computational effort. An extension of the validation to a larger industrial use case in combination with the comparison with other optimization methods like [8] is intended.

Acknowledgment. The authors would like to thank the German Research Foundation DFG for funding this work within the Cluster of Excellence "Internet of Production" (Project ID: 390621612).

References

1. Nakajima, S.: Introduction to TPM. Productivity Press, Cambridge, Mass, Total productive maintenance (1988)
2. Bartkowiak, T., Ciszak, O., Jablonski, P., Myszkowski, A., Wisniewski, M.: A simulative study approach for improving the efficiency of production process of floorboard middle layer. In: Hamrol, A., Ciszak, O., Legutko, S., Jurczyk, M. (eds.) Advances in Manufacturing. LNME, pp. 13–22. Springer, Cham (2018). https://doi.org/10.1007/978-3-319-68619-6_2
3. Bech, S., Brunoe, T.D., Nielsen, K., Andersen, A.-L.: Product and Process Variety Management: Case study in the Food Industry. Procedia CIRP (2019)
4. Butollo, F.: Digitalization and the geographies of production: Towards reshoring or global fragmentation? Competition & Change (2020)
5. Andersson, C., Bellgran, M.: On the complexity of using performance measures: Enhancing sustained production improvement capability by combining OEE and productivity. J. Manuf. Syst. **35**, 144–154 (2015)
6. Del Carmen Ng Corrales, L., Lambán, M.P., Hernandez Korner, M.E., Royo, J.: Overall equipment effectiveness: systematic literature review and overview of different approaches. Applied Sciences (2020)
7. Koren, Y., Hu, S.J., Weber, T.W.: Impact of Manufacturing System Configuration on Performance. CIRP Annals (1998)
8. Yegul, M.F., Erenay, F.S., Striepe, S., Yavuz, M.: Improving configuration of complex production lines via simulation-based optimization. Computers & Industrial Engineering (2017)
9. Xi, S., Chen, Q., MacGregor Smith, J., Mao, N., Yu, A., Zhang, H.: A new method for solving buffer allocation problem in large unbalanced production lines. Int. J. Prod. Res. **58**, 6846–6867 (2020)
10. Rabe, M., Deininger, M., Juan, A.A.: Speeding up computational times in simheuristics combining genetic algorithms with discrete-Event simulation. Simulation Modelling Practice and Theory (2020)
11. Karlsson, I.: An interactive decision support system using simulation-based optimization and knowledge extraction. Dissertation Series. Doctoral thesis, monograph, University of Skövde (2018). http://urn.kb.se/resolve?urn=urn:nbn:se:his:diva-16369
12. Trigueiro de Sousa Junior, W., Barra Montevechi, J.A., Carvalho Miranda, R. de, Teberga Campos, A.: Discrete simulation-based optimization methods for industrial engineering problems: a systematic literature review. Computers & Industrial Engineering (2019)
13. Ylipää, T., Skoogh, A., Bokrantz, J., Gopalakrishnan, M.: Identification of maintenance improvement potential using OEE assessment. Int. J. Productivity Perf. Mgmt. **1**, 126–143 (2017). https://doi.org/10.1108/IJPPM-01-2016-0028
14. Wu, K., Zheng, M., Shen, Y.: A generalization of the Theory of Constraints: Choosing the optimal improvement option with consideration of variability and costs. IISE Trans. **3**, 276–287 (2020). https://doi.org/10.1080/24725854.2019.1632503
15. Burggraf, P., Wagner, J., Koke, B.: Artificial Intelligence in Production Management: A Review of the Current State of Affairs and Research Trends in Academia. IEEE, Piscataway (2018)
16. Burggräf, P., Wagner, J., Koke, B., Bamberg, M.: Performance assessment methodology for AI-supported decision-making in production management. Procedia CIRP (2020)
17. Gosavi, A.: Solving markov decision processes via simulation. In: Handbook of Simulation Optimization, vol. 216 (2014)

18. Sutton, R.S., Barto, A.: Reinforcement Learning. An Introduction. Adaptive Computation and Machine Learning. The MIT Press, Cambridge, MA (2018)
19. Gosavi, A.: Simulation-Based Optimization. Parametric Optimization Techniques and Reinforcement Learning. Springer, New York **55** (2015)
20. Juan, A.A., Faulin, J., Grasman, S.E., Rabe, M., Figueira, G.: A review of simheuristics: Extending metaheuristics to deal with stochastic combinatorial optimization problems. Operations Research Perspectives (2015)
21. Hubscher-Younger, T., Mosterman, P.J., DeLand, S., Orqueda, O., Eastman, D.: Integrating discrete-event and time-based models with optimization for resource allocation. IEEE (2012)
22. Tempelmeier, H.: Practical considerations in the optimization of flow production systems. Int. J. Prod. Res. **1**, 149–170 (2003). https://doi.org/10.1080/00207540210161641
23. Bergeron, D., Jamali, M.A., Yamamoto, H.: Modelling and analysis of manufacturing systems: a review of existing models. IJPD (2010)
24. Nourelfath, M., Nahas, N., Ait-Kadi, D.: Optimal design of series production lines with unreliable machines and finite buffers. J. Qual. Maintenance Eng. **2**, 121–138 (2005). https://doi.org/10.1108/13552510510601348
25. Liu, Y., Li, J.: Split and merge production systems: performance analysis and structural properties. IIE Trans. **6**, 422–434 (2010). https://doi.org/10.1080/07408170903394348
26. Spinellis, D.D., Papadopoulos, C.T.: A simulated annealing approach for buffer allocation in reliable production lines. Annals of Operations Research (2000)
27. Zhang, M., Matta, A.: Models and algorithms for throughput improvement problem of serial production lines via downtime reduction. IISE Trans. **11**, 1189–1203 (2020). https://doi.org/10.1080/24725854.2019.1700431
28. Filho, M.G., Utiyama, M.H.R.: Comparing the effect of different strategies of continuous improvement programmes on repair time to reduce lead time. Int. J. Adv. Manuf. Technol. **87**(1–4), 315–327 (2016). https://doi.org/10.1007/s00170-016-8483-x
29. Godinho Filho, M., Utiyama, M.H.R.: Comparing different strategies for the allocation of improvement programmes in a flow shop environment. Int. J. Adv. Manuf. Technol. **77**(5–8), 1365–1385 (2014). https://doi.org/10.1007/s00170-014-6553-5
30. Jasiulewicz-Kaczmarek, M., Bartkowiak, T.: Improving the performance of a filling line based on simulation. IOP Conf. Ser.: Mater. Sci. Eng. **145**, 042024 (2016). https://doi.org/10.1088/1757-899X/145/4/042024
31. Harrington, B.:Breakdowns Happen. How to Factor Downtime into your Simulation. Whitepaper (2014)
32. Dagkakis, G., Heavey, C., Robin, S., Perrin, J.: ManPy: an open-source layer of DES manufacturing objects implemented in simPy. IEEE, Piscataway, NJ (2013)
33. Sutton, R.S., McAllester, D., Singh, S., Mansour, Y.: Policy Gradient Methods for Reinforcement Learning with Function Approximation. MIT Press, Cambridge (1999)
34. Schulman, J., Wolski, F., Dhariwal, P., Radford, A., Klimov, O.: Proximal Policy Optimization Algorithms (2017). https://arxiv.org/pdf/1707.06347

Straight and U-Shaped Assembly Lines in Industry 4.0 Era: Factors Influencing Their Implementation

Marco Simonetto[(✉)] and Fabio Sgarbossa

Department of Mechanical and Industrial Engineering, Norwegian University of Science and Technology, S P Andersens V 3, 7031 Trondheim, Norway
marco.simonetto@ntnu.com

Abstract. The increasing of products variety is moving companies in rethinking the configuration of their Assembly Systems (ASs). An AS is where the products are being configured in their different variants and its configuration needs to be chosen in order to handle such high variety. Two of the most common AS configurations are the straight-line and the U-shaped line. In this paper we want to first determine and define, through a narrative literature research, which are the factors that are relevant in order to compare these two AS configurations. Additionally, with the advent of Industry 4.0 (I4.0) technologies it is possible that these new technologies have an impact on these factors. For this reason, first, we investigated how I4.0 technologies impact these factors and then we saw how the choice of the AS configuration, between straight-t line and U-shaped line, change based on the impact of the technologies. The seven factors here defined open the opportunity for future research challenges.

Keywords: Assembly system · Configuration · Straight-line · U-shaped line · Industry 4.0

1 Introduction

An AS configuration is a sequence of several workstations organized in a certain way in order to assemble different parts to final products. The assembly process consists of a sequence of typically ordered tasks which cannot be subdivided and should be completed at its assigned workstation [1]. The two AS configurations more used are the straight-lines and the U-shaped lines [2, 3], Fig. 1. A straight-line configuration is represented by a sequence of workstations in a line. Simply rearranging the straight-line into a U-shaped it is possible to obtain the U-shaped line. In both cases, there can be a human worker in each workstation or there can be single workers managing more workstations [4, 5]. However, in U-shaped lines, it is easier for human workers to move from one workstation to another since they can move across both sides of the line, allowing more flexibility and degrees of freedom in the number of workers that can be assigned in these configurations with respect of the straight-line configurations.

Traditionally, a straight-line is suitable for mass-production of standardized products [6]. Because of the growing demand for customized products, in the last few years,

© IFIP International Federation for Information Processing 2021
Published by Springer Nature Switzerland AG 2021
A. Dolgui et al. (Eds.): APMS 2021, IFIP AICT 634, pp. 414–422, 2021.
https://doi.org/10.1007/978-3-030-85914-5_44

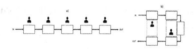

Fig. 1. Straight-line configuration (a) and U-shaped line configuration (b).

the products' variety is increased [7]. The U-shaped line is an example of layout that can handle this increase of variety [8]. However, recently also straight-lines are gained more importance in low volume production of customized products [9]. This can complicate the decision process of which layout configuration to choose. Moreover, the introduction of I4.0 technologies in these configurations can have an impact in this decision.

Industry 4.0 emerges from the synergy of the availability of innovative technologies and the demand by consumers for high quality and customized products and it aims at connecting resources, services, and humans in real-time throughout the production in order to attain an advanced level of operational effectiveness and productivity, as well as a higher level of automatization [10]. Its economic impact is supposed to be huge [11]. It holds the promise of increased flexibility, better quality, and improved productivity [12]. Industry 4.0 technologies are starting to be an integrated part of the AS creating a new generation of AS, the so-called Assembly System 4.0 (AS4.0) [13]. The technologies that can be adopted from AS4.0 can be grouped into Collaborative Robots, Augmented Reality (AR), Internet of Things (IoTs), and Cloud Computing and Data Analysis [13].

In literature is it possible to find some qualitative guidelines about when to choose an AS configuration respect to another [14] and a work that gives an idea of factors that can be considered is the one of [8]. The factors that [8] used are the number of tasks, network density, and the cycle time. However, these are not the only factors that need to be taken into consideration to compare straight-line and U-shaped line. Therefore, we are going to look through a narrative literature review, at which are other factors that need to be taken into consideration when one wants to compare the two configurations.

This research is done in order to answer the following research questions:

1. Which are the factors that have to be considered in order to compare the two AS configurations straight-line and U-shaped line?
2. How Industry 4.0 technologies impact on these factors?

The research wants to help companies that are facing the problem of the increase in product variety, or that are simply thinking in changing their AS configuration, in understanding which are the factors that they need to know in order to be able to compare the two AS configurations. This to facilitate their decision process. The implementation of the right Industry 4.0 technologies can give further help to companies to reach their production performance but can also influence the factors. Therefore, it is important to know if and how the technologies are going to impact on the factors. The remainder of this paper is structured as follows. In Sect. 2 we explained the methodology applied in the paper. In Sect. 3, we answered at the first research question. In Sect. 4, we answered at the second research question and finally, Sect. 5 concludes the work.

2   Methodology

In this paper, to answer at our two research questions, we conducted a narrative literature review. The keywords that we used for the research of the papers are presented in Table 1. We used the Scopus database, searching only result in English as language without limits in the document type and in the year of publications of the papers.

Table 1. The two groups of keywords used in the research

First group of keywords	Assembly*, Assembly system, Line*, Straight line, U shape, U shape*
Second group of keywords	Augmented reality, Cloud computing, Collaborative robo*, Data analysi*, Internet of thing, Assembly*, Assembly time, Quality, * time, Products quality, Products variety

These keywords were used as a single keyword or, most of the time, as a combination of two, or more, words thanks to the operator "AND". For example, one combined research can be: "Assembly*" AND "Collaborative robo*".

3   Factor Influencing the Configuration Selection

In this section with an inductive approach, we derived the relevant factors that a company has to know when it has to decide which is the best configuration for their AS between straight-line and U-shaped line. Here below there is the list of identified factors followed by an analysis of the selected papers which helped us to derived them.

Cycle Time: indicates the time elapsed between completions of two consequent units.

Number of Tasks: it is the number of different activities that each operator must do in each workstation and is a measure used to indicate the problem size for combinatorial problems such as the SALB (Simple assembly line balancing) and UALB (U-shaped assembly line balancing) problems.

Network Density: calculating network density entails dividing the number of actual precedence relationships by the theoretical maximum number of relationships that could exist for a problem of that size. Extreme network density values of 0.0 and 1.0 correspond to flexible and rigid assembly sequences, respectively [8].

Products Variety: is the number of different products that are assembled in an assembly line.

Volumes Variety: is the difference between the quantity to produce of a product one day and the quantity to produce of the same product the following day.

Quality: is the quality of the final assemble products that come out from the assembly line.

Complexity of Tasks: is the complexity of each task of the assembly process.

Following the definitions here above introduced, the papers found by the literature are here presented in order to better explain the different factors.

In straight-line it is not easy as in U-shaped line to adapt to changes in cycle time. This because of the high potential of rebalancing the U-shaped line with a new cycle time and the reallocation of workers [6]. The productivity in straight-line is lower than the one of U-shaped line when network density is high. Indeed, when the network density is low is better to use straight-lines [8]. Straight-lines can guarantee less flexibility in manufacturing volumes respect to U-shaped lines since in U-shaped lines you can increase or decrease the number of operators on the line [15] and the quality of final assembled products is usually better in U-shape lines [2]. The quality in U-shaped is higher thanks to the improved visibility and communication between operators on the line, which facilitates problem-solving and quality improvement [16]. In U-shaped lines usually, a human worker does more tasks than one in a straight-line. As operator responsibilities expand to include more assembly tasks, operators are used more efficiently when using a straight-line configuration [8]. This because more are the different assembly tasks that one human worker must remember and higher will be his mental workload. When a human worker has to walk from a workstation to another one to do his work, the things to keep in mind are not only the time lost by the worker to walk and his physical strain but there is also the possible congestion that can be generate in the line by all the workers that have to move [4, 8]. This congestion can be more problematic in the U-shaped line due to the limited space within the line generating a lost in performance. The walking time of human workers not only influence the physical demand of workers and the congestion of the lines but adding it at the processing time significantly increases the number of workers that are requested in order to execute the assembly tasks [17]. U-shaped lines are a good choice when the workers have to do repetitive actions and avoid keeping wrong postures during the execution of their activities [18]. Moreover, the U-shape lines are more flexible than the straight-lines, balancing by reducing the precedence relations thanks also to the multiskilled workers that perform various tasks in different workstations along the assembly line [19]. U-shaped workers are required to possess more skills than on straight-lines [20].

In order to decide if a configuration is better than another one companies need Key Performance Indicators (KPIs) or objective functions to measure (e.g. costs, flexibility, ergonomics, productivity). Therefore, companies need first to understand how these functions are going to be influenced by the factors and then how to do multi objectives analysis. It will be important to define one or more objective functions and see how these factors impact the decision of the AS configuration. Future works can be indeed related to the definition of these objective functions. Moreover, sensitivity analyses can help to see how the variations of the different factors can change the final decision of which configuration to choose.

4   The Impact of Industry 4.0 Technologies

In this section we are going to investigate the literature to understand how the I4.0 technologies impact the factors defined in the previous section. Collaborative robots do not only improve the performance of the assembly lines [21], but they can also help the human workers in reducing potential occupational risks like awkward postures, mental workload and repetitive actions [22]. This means better ergonomic conditions in the assembly lines. Moreover, collaborative robots can reduce the surface used and so decrease the distances traveled by the human workers [23]. The main improvements that AR can give to assembly operations are the errors reduction and time efficiency. However, researchers have different opinions about these two improvements [24, 25]. There are different opinions also in terms of usability of AR technology. [26] showed how for the participants of their experiments were easier to use paper instructions instead of the AR instructions displayed through Head-mounted display. In [24], experiment's participants instead, in terms of cognitive load, usability and performance, preferred the AR-based instruction than the paper ones. IoT technologies can help companies with the management of the different variants and of the different volumes of products to produce since the consumers can change their orders until the last second and different consumers have different requests [27]. The data collected from the IoT technologies can be analyzed thanks to Data analysis techniques, like machine learning algorithms, and together with the Cloud Computing, that can store data, manage data, and share data and information, the quality of the final products can be guaranteed reducing also the time to do the inspection of the products [28]. These technologies cannot only increase the quality of the final products but can also decrease the amount of scrap parts in a real industrial scenario, consequently saving valuable resources such as energy and raw materials [29] increasing the efficiency of the systems [30].

In Table 2 we can see which are the I4.0 technologies applied in the AS and we summarized the effect of each technology in each factor.

From Table 2 one interesting result that we can see is that there is a technology, AR, that have "Decreases/Increases" as result. This result means that is not well known yet the real impact of this technology with respect to the cycle time. In fact, at the moment the research with this technology regarding this factor are showing different results. This can be related for example to the experience of the human workers in using the technology or on how the AR instructions are designed and presented to the human workers.

Based on the results of Table 2 we created Table 3. Table 3 gives the idea of how the choice of the configuration can change based on the decrease or increase of the factors. In Table 3 we also did the column, based on the review of the literature in the previous section, of the case in which there is no I4.0 technology in the AS.0. This column helps to see that an I4.0 technology can open the opportunity to move to another configuration with respect to the case without technology.

Table 2. Impact of the I4.0 technologies on the factors.

Factor	Industry 4.0 technology			
	Collaborative robot	Augmented reality	IoT technologies	Cloud computing and data analysis
Cycle time	Decreases	Decreases/ Increases	Decreases	Decreases
Number of tasks	/	/	/	/
Network density	/	/	/	/
Products variety	Increases	Increases	Increases	Increases
Volumes variety	Increases	/	Increases	Increases
Quality	Increases	Increases	Increases	Increases
Complexity of tasks	Decreases	Decreases	Decreases	Decreases

Table 3. How the choice of the AS configuration change based on the impact of a I4.0 technology on a factor (U = U-shaped; S = Straight-line; / = not found in literature).

Factor		Without I4.0 technology	Industry 4.0 technology			
			Collaborative robot	Augmented reality	IoT technologies	Cloud computing and data analysis
Cycle time	Low	S	S	/	S	S
	Medium	U/S	U		U	U
	High	U				
Number of tasks	Low	U	/	/	/	/
	Medium	U/S				
	High	S				
Network density	Low	S	/	/	/	/
	Medium	U/S				
	High	U				
Products variety	Low	S	S	S	S	S
	Medium	U/S				
	High	U	U	U	U	U
Volumes variety	Low	S	/	S	S	S
	Medium	U/S				
	High	U		U	U	U
Quality	Low	S	S	S	S	S
	Medium	U/S				
	High	U	U	U	U	U
Complexity of tasks	Low	S	S	S	S	S
	Medium	U/S				
	High	U	U	U	U	U

From Table 3 we can see that, for example, when the quality of the final products increases thanks to the collaborative robots from low to medium, the choice of the configuration of the AS can go to the straight-line configuration instead of the U-shaped line configuration. Indeed, the increase in quality thanks to the collaborative robot gives the opportunity to use the straight-line configuration that usually, without the technology, guarantees a lower quality with respect to the U-shaped line configuration. Of course, it is not only the focus on one factor that defines the choice of the configuration of the AS4.0. Therefore, the combined behavior of these factors with regard to the choice of the configuration can be a matter of interesting future research. Moreover, it will be interesting to do a deeper investigation of the literature to see what it is possible to find about the cases that in Table 3 are now presenting the "/". Especially for all the technologies in the case of the factor "Number of tasks", for the technology "Cloud computing and Data Analysis" for the factor "Network density" and for the technology "Collaborative robot" for the factor "Volumes variety".

5 Conclusion

In this paper, we first determined, based on the literature, the factors that a company has to know when it is time to decide which is the best AS configuration to adopt between the straight-line and the U-shaped line and second we saw how the Industry 4.0 technologies, that can be adopted in these AS configurations, impact in these factors. Being this an exploratory research, our conclusions need to be support by some quantitative results. This is the reason why this work will be used as a starting point for the creation of a mathematical model that will help us validate the assumptions made here.

References

1. Battini, D., Faccio, M., Persona, A., Sgarbossa, F.: Balancing–sequencing procedure for a mixed model assembly system in case of finite buffer capacity. Int. J. Adv. Manuf. Technol. **44**(3–4), 345–359 (2009)
2. Rabbani, M., Moghaddam, M., Manavizadeh, N.: Balancing of mixed-model two-sided assembly lines with multiple U-shaped layout. Int. J. Adv. Manuf. Technol. **59**(9–12), 1191–1210 (2012)
3. Mukund Nilakantan, J., Ponnambalam, S.G.: Robotic U-shaped assembly line balancing using particle swarm optimization. Eng. Optim. **48**(2), 231–252 (2016)
4. Calzavara, M., Faccio, M., Persona, A., Zennaro, I.: Walking worker vs fixed worker assembly considering the impact of components exposure on assembly time and energy expenditure. Int. J. Adv. Manuf. Technol. **112**(9), 2971–2988 (2021)
5. Chen, Q., Liao, S., Wu, Z., Yi, S.: Comparative analysis of the performance of a novel U-shaped 'chasing-overtaking' production line. Int. J. Prod. Res. **54**(12), 3677–3690 (2016)
6. Erel, E., Sabuncuoglu, I., Aksu, B.A.: Balancing of U-type assembly systems using simulated annealing. Int. J. Prod. Res. **39**(13), 3003–3015 (2001)

7. Battaïa, O., Otto, A., Sgarbossa, F., Pesch, E.: Future trends in management and operation of assembly systems: from customized assembly systems to cyber-physical systems. Omega **78**, 1–4 (2018)
8. Aase, G.R., Olson, J.R., Schniederjans, M.J.: U-shaped assembly line layouts and their impact on labor productivity: an experimental study. Eur. J. Oper. Res. **156**(3), 698–711 (2004). https://doi.org/10.1016/S0377-2217(03)00148-6
9. Boysen, N., Fliedner, M., Scholl, A.: A classification of assembly line balancing problems. Eur. J. Oper. Res. **183**(2), 674–693 (2007)
10. Thames, L., Schaefer, D.: Software-defined cloud manufacturing for industry 4.0. Procedia cirp. **52**, 12–17 (2016)
11. Kagermann, H., Helbig, J., Hellinger, A., Wahlster, W.: Recommendations for implementing the strategic initiative INDUSTRIE 4.0: securing the future of German manufacturing industry; final report of the Industrie 4.0 working group. Forschungsunion (2013)
12. Zhong, R.Y., Xu, X., Klotz, E., Newman, S.T.: Intelligent manufacturing in the context of industry 4.0: a review. Engineering **3**(5), 616–630 (2017)
13. Cohen, Y., Naseraldin, H., Chaudhuri, A., Pilati, F.: Assembly systems in industry 4.0 era: a road map to understand assembly 4.0. Int. J. Adv. Manuf. Technol. **105**(9), 4037–4054 (2019). https://doi.org/10.1007/s00170-019-04203-1
14. Battini, D., Faccio, M., Persona, A., Sgarbossa, F.: New methodological framework to improve productivity and ergonomics in assembly system design. Int. J. Ind. Ergon. **41**(1), 30–42 (2011)
15. Şahin, M., Kellegöz, T.: Increasing production rate in U-type assembly lines with sequence-dependent set-up times. Eng. Optim. **49**(8), 1401–1419 (2017)
16. Guerriero, F., Miltenburg, J.: The stochastic U-line balancing problem. Naval Res. Logist. (NRL) **50**(1), 31–57 (2003)
17. Sirovetnukul, R., Chutima, P.: The impact of walking time on U-shaped assembly line worker allocation problems. Eng. J. **14**(2), 53–78 (2010)
18. Zhang, Z., Tang, Q., Ruiz, R., Zhang, L.: Ergonomic risk and cycle time minimization for the U-shaped worker assignment assembly line balancing problem: a multi-objective approach. Comput. Oper. Res. **118**, 104905 (2020)
19. Tiacci, L.: The assembly line simulator project: modeling U-shaped, un-paced, mixed model assembly lines. XIX Summer School Impianti Industriali, The role of industrial engineering in a global sustainable economy, Senigallia (AN–ITA) (2014)
20. Hwang, R., Katayama, H.: A multi-decision genetic approach for workload balancing of mixed-model U-shaped assembly line systems. Int. J. Prod. Res. **47**(14), 3797–3822 (2009)
21. Bloss, R.: Collaborative robots are rapidly providing major improvements in productivity, safety, programing ease, portability and cost while addressing many new applications. Ind. Robot Int. J. (2016)
22. Mateus, J.C., Claeys, D., Limère, V., Cottyn, J., Aghezzaf, E.-H.: A structured methodology for the design of a human-robot collaborative assembly workplace. Int. J. Adv. Manuf. Technol. **102**(5–8), 2663–2681 (2019). https://doi.org/10.1007/s00170-019-03356-3
23. Gil-Vilda, F., Sune, A., Yagüe-Fabra, J.A., Crespo, C., Serrano, H.: Integration of a collaborative robot in a U-shaped production line: a real case study. Procedia Manuf. **13**, 109–115 (2017)
24. Lampen, E., Teuber, J., Gaisbauer, F., Bär, T., Pfeiffe, T., Wachsmuth, S.: Combining simulation and augmented reality methods for enhanced worker assistance in manual assembly. Procedia CIRP **81**, 588 (2019)
25. Longo, F., Nicoletti, L., Padovano, A.: Smart operators in industry 4.0: a human-centered approach to enhance operators' capabilities and competencies within the new smart factory context. Comput. Ind. Eng. **113**, 144–159 (2017)

26. Büttner, S., Funk, M., Sand, O., Röcker, C.: Using head-mounted displays and in-situ projection for assistive systems: a comparison. In: Proceedings of the 9th ACM international conference on pervasive technologies related to assistive environments, pp. 1–8 (2016)
27. Thramboulidis, K., Kontou, I., Vachtsevanou, D.C.: Towards an IoT-based framework for evolvable assembly systems. IFAC-PapersOnLine **51**(11), 182–187 (2018)
28. Schmitt, J., Bönig, J., Borggräfe, T., Beitinger, G., Deuse, J.: Predictive model-based quality inspection using machine learning and edge cloud computing. Adv. Eng. Inf. **45**, 101101 (2020)
29. Coupek, D., Lechler, A., Verl, A.: Cloud-based control strategy: downstream defect reduction in the production of electric motors. IEEE Trans. Ind. Appl. **53**(6), 5348–5353 (2017)
30. Carvajal Soto, J.A., Tavakolizadeh, F., Gyulai, D.: An online machine learning framework for early detection of product failures in an industry 4.0 context. Int. J. Comput. Integr. Manuf. **32**(4–5), 452–465 (2019)

Optimization of Supply Chain Agility and Reconfigurability

An Approach to Assess Risks Related to Information System in Supply Chain

Selmen Boubaker[✉], Samuel Dumondelle,
and Parisa Dolatineghabadi

Capgemini Engineering, Nantes, France
Selmen.boubaker@altran.com

Abstract. On one hand, no one can deny the importance of the information system in today's industrial and logistic activities. The progress in IT tools and systems allowed to process real-time data giving the opportunity to enhance considerably the management of production and transportation operations. On the other hand, supply chain digitalization is a sensitive process that can generate increased risks for the companies' activities. Therefore, such risks should be identified and managed. In this study, we follow Failure Mode, Effects, and Criticality Analysis (FMECA) approach to assess the risk linked to the information system of supply chains. We also present the methodology and choices adopted to apply this study in an aeronautical supply chain case.

Keywords: Supply chain digitalisation · Information reliability · Information risk analysis · FEMCA

1 Introduction

Many industries have started their transition to the Industry of the Future (Industry 4.0) with the ambition of deploying a more agile, autonomous, environmentally responsible, and productive organisation. Big Data, Internet of Things (IoT) and artificial intelligence are taking place at all levels of the value chain to enable the automation of information and production flows. However, despite the considerable advances observed in recent years in the industry, the supply chain (SC) seems to lag behind the deployment of these technologies, which comes also with additional risks affecting its overall activities. Many authors highlighted the importance of virtualization and IT systems to enhance the values in supply chain activity. However, this will only be possible with the presence of reliable and secure information systems [1–4]. Indeed, if many IT risks have always existed in the economy, those related to SC are becoming more and more important with consequent impacts. We note the WannaCry cyber-attack on Renault, which in May 2017, which caused production interruption in several plants. "What is certain is that the IT networks of major manufacturers are now closely connected to those of their suppliers, to enable just-in-time stock management" [5]. This attack also affected around a hundred countries [6].

Current studies related to risks in SC are mainly conducted from logistics, economics, management or safety/health perspectives [7]. Although we find in the literature, the studies related to information flows and their risks, they are oriented towards

A. Dolgui et al. (Eds.): APMS 2021, IFIP AICT 634, pp. 425–434, 2021.
https://doi.org/10.1007/978-3-030-85914-5_46

IT flows and information systems, and therefore do not cover all information flows. Other studies are more specific to the Security of Information Systems in SC [8].

In this study, we focus on assessing the risks associated with information flows of SC in order to present preventive measures to enhance the information's flow reliability. An FMECA approach is used in order to identify and assess risks and then present preventive measures. A case from the aeronautical sector is studied relying on supply chain experts' experience and opinions.

This paper is organized as follows. In Sect. 2, we present the literature review on risk analysis methods in SC and other industry sectors. In Sect. 2, we describe the adopted FMECA methodology for this study. In Sect. 3, we scrutinize different steps followed and results obtained. Finally, we present conclusion and perspectives for further researches.

2   Literature Review

Nowadays, industries are moving toward modern's network connections thanks to the new technological infrastructures. Supply chain is not excluded from this trend. These changes require new secure and mobile services. Therefore, it is necessary to move to connected IP systems, which are secure, reliable and efficient [9]. One way to make a system reliable and efficient is to identify well risk. In this section, first, we present the main concepts linked to the risk assessment and management. Second, we study risk analysis methods used in the literature and industry.

2.1   The Concepts of Reliability, Safety and Risk

In order to succeed in the transition toward supply chain 4.0, supply chain information systems must be reliable and secure. Reliability, according to the Cambridge dictionary, is "how accurate or able to be trusted someone or something is considered to be» [10]. According to ISO, it is the "Ability of an entity to perform a required function, under given conditions, during a given time interval" [11]. The concept of safety is more diverse. Safety according to [12] is "the probability, that no catastrophic accidents will occur during system operation, over a specified period of time". These two concepts, Reliability and Safety, together with Availability and Maintainability are the four key concepts of Dependability. "Dependability is the science of failures. It covers the concepts of reliability, availability, maintainability and safety" [13]. However, in order to control dependability, we need to assess and control risks. Risk is defined as the danger, or the possibility of danger, defeat, or loss. According to ISO, a risk is "a combination of the probability of a damage and its gravity" [11].

2.2   Risk Analysis Methods

There are several commonly used risk analysis methods. In the study presented in [14], we find a comprehensive classification approach to determine their choice of use.

We chose the FMECA, a method that allows both, to anticipate risks, and, to capitalize on feedbacks. It permits to identify all potential failures and failure modes, evaluate risks and prioritize actions to be taken. Moreover, FMECA is the most widespread method in the industry, and the most versatile [15].

It should be noted that numerous methods and tools have been developed for analyzing information system risks. The Operationally Critical Threat, Asset, and Vulnerability Evaluation (OCTAVE method used in [16] allows to define a risk-based strategic assessment and planning technique for security. OCTAVE is a self-directed approach, meaning that people from an organization assume responsibility for setting the organization's security strategy. However, OCTAVE is complex to deploy, considering that the main users for this method could be from small companies with limited resources. The French Information Security Club developed the Harmonized Method of Risk Analysis method (MEHARI). "MEHARI's general approach consists in analyzing security issues: what are the feared scenarios? and in the prior classification of IS entities according to three basic security criteria (confidentiality, integrity, availability). These issues express the dysfunctions that have a direct impact on the company's activity. Then, audits identify the vulnerabilities of the IS. And finally, the actual risk analysis is done". [17] uses The Threat Assessment & Remediation Analysis (TARA). The greatest strength of TARA also represents its greatest weakness. It only focuses on the greatest risk and less impacting risks are ignored. [18] presents the OWASP Software Assurance Maturity Model. OWASP only focuses on some subsets of threats in very specific environment. These methods must be managed by dedicated structures such as IT departments.

Although FMECA is widely used for process flows, few works in the literature are relating to information flows [19]. The information flow is present in these works as a component of which we give relatively little importance, the analysis focuses only on material flows. In our study, we focus on analyzing risks linked to the information flow using an FMECA analysis presented in the following section. This choice is also taken up in [20] for their study on the reliability of data in a management information system. FMECA approach is a tool that allows detecting the possible critical points and propose improvements. This approach has been used in different sectors including Supply Chain. The application of this approach in farming and food supply chain has resulted in proposing improvements in the traceability system focusing on the most severe situations from a systems criticality point of view [21].

3   Methodology: FMECA Analysis

An FMECA analysis is carried out in a multidisciplinary participatory mode. The method takes place in five major stages. We adopt the same definitions of elements presented in [22]:

1. Preparation where we define the working group, the scope of the analysis, and the procedure to be followed.
2. Functional analysis, which aims to list all the phases of the process in order to identify the potential causes of malfunctioning and to prepare the study of failures.
3. Failure identification and rational study of failure modes.
4. Failure evaluation and criticality study and failure hierarchy.
5. Actions to be identified to search for solutions.

In the following paragraphs, we present details of these steps and choices taken for our study.

3.1   Preparation: To Define the Working Group, the Scope of the Study

Working Group: an expert of quality management with significant experience in managing the deployment of FMEA in the industry was chosen as a moderator to guarantee the method, manage and ensure the follow-up of the analysis. A multidisciplinary working group of seven members was selected for their skills and their significant experience in SC, particularly in aeronautics sector. These participants have professional experiences from five to twenty years, acquired in the industry, and mainly within aeronautical industrials such as AIRBUS, STELIA, and SPIRIT. Their functions in the procurement, planning or logistics departments have enabled them to use and master information tools as well as business procedures. During their experiences, the participants were able to observe, as actors or observers, various malfunctions of all kinds and with various consequences, observed at various levels of SC. The working group had prior awareness of the FMECA method.

The Scope Studied: flows of information in an aeronautical supply chain is defined as the scope of this study. We study all IT tools used such as enterprise resource planning (ERP) and other information flows such as e-mails, EDI, and customer/supplier portals. Manuscripts, as physical information sources, are still widely used in industry. Only some flows were not taken into consideration, such as e-mails and faxes. Phone communications were considered as a secondary, informal means of communication rather than a formal information flow. Moreover, as these flows are not limited to the analyzed entity, but also to its environment, including suppliers and customers, the study covers internal and external information flows. This study cannot cover entirely all companies, because "FMECA is based on an inductive search for causes" [20]. This implies the use of factual data with evaluations of criteria to be individualized for each company. The aim of this analysis is to present a base for studies, not only for aeronautical companies and aeronautical suppliers, but also for all other manufacturing industries.

During this preparation stage, we chose tools to be used for our study. We adopt the standard model of the risk matrix presented in [23]. However, for this study, columns that are not relevant to the monitoring of actions were not used: the pilot of the action, the dated objective, the validation of the action, etc. Other columns were added in order to facilitate data filtering. For the criteria grids and ratings, there are no imposed models. However, some proposed models can be found in the literature. A scale of 1 to 4 with 4 criteria for a hospital supply chain was used in [19]. A scale of one to five with five criteria for a study on management information systems in the textile industry was chosen in [24]. [20] used a more complex grid with a scale of one to ten with ten criteria, close to the FMEA 4th Edition at Caterpillar [25]. We choose a scale of one to ten to rate severity, frequency and detectability on a scale of one to ten, choosing only four criteria: one, three, six and ten to have a significant difference in criticality.

3.2 Functional Analysis: Preparing a Functional Breakdown and Preparing the Failure Study

A group of consultants with significant experiences in the aeronautical supply chain carried out mapping (see Fig. 1), starting with a representation of the macro and semi-macro physical flows. Maps are completed later by adding the information flow.

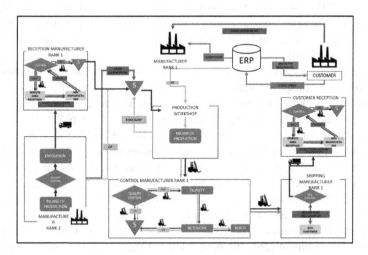

Fig. 1. Extract from the upstream flow map

Based on the items and information flows identified in the maps, we have broken down this process into activities in a Value Stream Mapping (VSM). Each activity is detailed: who is responsible for it, what is the nature and medium of the information exchanged. These VSMs obtained will be served as a basis for building the FMECA in the next step.

3.3 Preparation of the FMECA Grid

We integrated each line of the VSM obtained previously into the FMECA grid, then after analyzing the nature of each flow and each action, only lines corresponding to the information flow were kept.

We note that some line groupings have been created. Indeed, some tasks/actions are repeated throughout the SC. Grouping these tasks results in a more visible table, but above all, when modifying or updating the information added, we have to ensure that the information is consistent at all stages. Five groupings, called Blocks, were created: Block Co for control, Block Re for Reception, Block SP for Production Monitoring and Block Tra for Transfer (between workshops or stations).

3.4   Identification: Identify Failures and Make a Rational Study of Failure Modes

Ishikawa Analysis

To begin the analysis, we have determined, based on consultants' experience, what could be the most impactful and frequent problem along with the SC information flow. By its nature, ERP (including SAP) is the system that we find throughout the SC in industry, with external links with suppliers and customers. We have excluded the telephone, e-mail, and fax. In fact, they are only used to support the use of the ERP and generally in an informal way.

The problem identified is "The information transmitted by the ERP is deficient (No information, Incomplete information, Incorrect information etc....)".

We use the Ishikawa method to determine the different possible causes of the problem. During a brainstorming session, the working group listed the different potential failures that can disrupt the information flow of an ERP in a global way. So starting from the effect, we identify the possible causes of this problem, then define the causal chain by the five whys method. For each effect, we studied the possible direct causes. For each direct cause, we examine the possible secondary causes. The process consists of asking questions up to five times in order to determine the root cause.

The next step is discernment, where only relevant causes are kept. These causes are classified into five families of possible causes: Materials, Machines, Methods, Manpower, and Environment [26]. We have added Management as possible sources of a problem. In our study, we have determined that information is the primary material. Therefore, all causes related to the information transmission are in the category of the first subject. For the hardware, we take all the causes related to computers (computers and software), and networks (computer and electrical or computer, electrical, etc.). Using this analysis, we find all causes linked to the settings and operator modes linked to the workforce failures. For those linked to the environment, we find causes linked to the work environment as well as external disturbances. For the management, we identify mostly causes linked to hierarchical decision-making (Fig. 2).

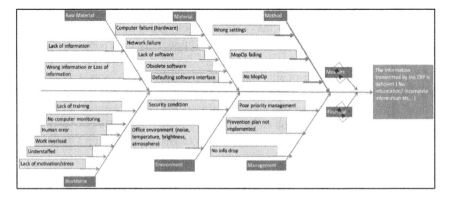

Fig. 2. Ishikawa analysis for the information flow of the supply chain

Identification of Failure Modes

There are five categories of generic failure modes [22]: 1) Loss of function, 2) Untimely operation, 3) Unable to start, 4) Unable to stop, 5) Degraded operation.

In our study, we identify three failure modes: loss of function, inconvenient operation and degraded operation. In precise technical terms, for loss of function: Information not transmitted, information not processed, operation not carried out. For degraded operation: incomplete information, poor transcription of information, poorly performed operation.

In the FMECA grid, for each existing line, taken from the VSMs, we must analyze all the potential failure modes. For this research, we use the generic modes, the precise terms but also the "generic" analysis carried out with the Ishikawa method on the ERP information flow. For each line, the group asks the question: How can this not work? For example, if the function is "calculation of the part requirement", the responses were "calculation of the requirement does not work (Loss of function)" and "calculation of the requirement does not work properly, we are obliged to launch a command manually (Degraded operation)".

Search for Causes of Failure

For each failure mode, for each line of the VSM concerned by an information flow, we define the potential causes. We use data and causes already determined by the Ishikawa of the generic ERP information flow when this risk analysis is transposable. The experience of each member of the working group allows us to identify/recognize potential causes (Table 1).

Study of the Effects

In this step, we look for the effect that has the greatest impact on the company. Shorted by its importance, we look for the effect on the customer/human safety (physical risk, environmental risk). Then, we investigate the effect on customers (delay in delivery). Then, we distinguish the major effect on the company or the process (line stoppage, stoppage with disruption of production), the minor effect on the company or the process (stoppage without disruption of the line), and the case of no significant effect. We note that for the lines resulting from the Ishikawa analysis, the causes indicated are the root causes. For the other lines, the causes noted are the primary causes (Table 1).

Table 1. Extract from the FMECA table

Process activities	Process sub-activities	Failure modes	Causes	Effects	Means of detection
Release of parts requirements	Calculation of net requirement (MRP)	Degraded operation (manual control)	Parameter error	Order delay	Auto control
Release of parts requirements	Calculation of net requirement (MRP)	Information not transmitted	Computer problem	No command	Auto control
Release of parts requirements	Calculation of net requirement (MRP)	Loss of function	Parameter error	No command	SAP transaction or excel export
Release of parts requirements	Calculation of net requirement (MRP)	Loss of function	Computer problem	No command	Minimum stock alert for VMI

Survey of Existing Detection Means

For each failure mode, we search for existing detection means, which are of a technological nature (ERP alert, printer alert, etc.) or human (self-checking, visual control).

Evaluating Identified Failures and Studying Their Criticality

It is now a question of quantifying the risks. To do this, the FMECA method defines quantification criteria to which a score will be assigned.

- The frequency of occurrence (F): it indicates how often cause of the failure will occur.
- The gravity (G) or severity (S): that is the evaluation of the importance of the effects of the failure on people and/or the installation.
- The risk of non-detection (ND), often paradoxically called detection (D): the probability that the cause and the mode has occurred and the failure will reach the user.

Figure 3 presents the rating criteria grids adopted corresponding to (G), (F) and (D).

G=Gravity:

10	With chain stop	Stopped for more than 1 week
6	With breakage without stopping the chain resolved with external intervention	Stopped for more than 1 day
3	With non-stop chain breakage solved internally	Stopped for more than 1 hour
1	No risk of breakage	Stop less than 5 minutes

CRITICAL = G x F x D

If severity or frequency= 10, mandatory action

If criticality > 100, mandatory action

F=Frequency:

10	Appears almost certainly	At least once a day
6	Appears regularly	At least once a week
3	Appears rarely	At least once a month
1	Never appears	Once or twice a year

D=Detectability:

10	Undetectable	No means of detection	No probability of detection
6	detectable by self-checking	Random / uncertain detection	A detection system is in place but is not infallible
3	Fault reported by the machine without automatic stop	Probable detection	Human detection
1	Fault reported by the machine with automatic stop	Certain / automated automated (100%)	The detection system is foolproof

Fig. 3. Rating criteria grids

3.5 Corrective Actions: Identification of Preventive Actions, Palliative/Curative Actions, Corrective Actions

For each failure, actions are proposed to reduce criticality. These actions may relate to severity, frequency or detectability. Thus, for an action that acts on the cause of a failure, we expect an improvement in the frequency of this failure after the action has been implemented. A better means of detection should decrease detectability.

We can note that gravity is a little bit improved by actions. Indeed, generally, the actions that improve gravity are either design-related (in the case of a product) or require significant investments. In our study, it is the multiplication of networks and back-up systems. We can consider that an effective action must improve the factor by one level. Thus, it takes two detective actions to decrease the detectability from ten to three (with our evaluation grid). For each action, a new valuation must be carried out taking into account the expected effects of these actions. The objective is to reduce these criticalities below the defined threshold, 100 in our study.

4 Conclusions and Perspectives

No one can deny the importance of the information system for supply chain activities. Therefore, it is essential to assess and manage increasing risks linked to information flows in the supply chain. In this paper, we present a FMECA approach allowing the assessment of risks associated with the information system of supply chains. As a result, 368 risks were identified. Thirty risks have a criticality of 360 (gravity *detectability*frequency), 145 have a criticality more than 180 and 221 have a criticality more than 100. Concerning causes of failures, 181 are related to the working force and 109 to materials (computer networks and software). Out of 368 proposals to mitigate risks, 149 are related to staff training/awareness and 81 are hardware-related, of which 45 can be addressed by an Information Security Management System (ISMS). However, 130 (out of 149) proposals related to training/awareness could be transformed into technological actions (IOT or AI). As a conclusion, it is noticeable that human error is still one of the major risks associated with the flow of information in SC. Despite the work that companies are doing to raise awareness among their employees, these actions are still limited and the solution can be to automate more data entry activities and to integrate more advanced data entry control systems.

This work can be a basis for further researches aiming to evaluate and enhance the supply chain information system's reliability.

References

1. Dobrovnik, M., Herold, D.M., Fürst, E., Kummer, S.: Blockchain for and in logistics: what to adopt and where to start. Logistics **2**, 18 (2018). https://doi.org/10.3390/logistics2030018
2. Francisco, K., Swanson, D.: The supply chain has no clothes: technology adoption of blockchain for supply chain transparency. Logistics **2**, 2 (2018). https://doi.org/10.3390/logistics2010002
3. Prause, G.: Smart contracts for smart supply chains. IFAC-PapersOnLine **52**, 2501–2506 (2019). https://doi.org/10.1016/j.ifacol.2019.11.582
4. Banerjee, A.: Chapter Three - Blockchain technology: supply chain insights from ERP. In: Raj, P., Deka, G.C. (eds.) Advances in Computers, pp. 69–98. Elsevier (2018)
5. Renault, un mois et demi après WannaCry. In: Les Echos. (2017). https://www.lesechos.fr/2017/06/renault-un-mois-et-demi-apres-wannacry-156961. Accessed 4 Feb 2021
6. Cyberattaque mondiale : Renault-Nissan dans l'œil du cyclone. Le Monde.fr (2017)
7. Tapiero, C.S.: Analyse des risques et prise de décision dans la chaîne d'approvisionnement. Revue francaise de gestion **186**, 163–182 (2008)
8. Ruel, S., Ouabouch, L.: Paradoxe du système d'information dans la supply chain : vecteur de performance ou facteur de risques ? (2015)
9. Boiko, A., Shendryk, V., Boiko, O.: Information systems for supply chain management: uncertainties, risks and cyber security. Procedia Comput. Sci. **149**, 65–70 (2019). https://doi.org/10.1016/j.procs.2019.01.108

10. Cambridge Dictionary|English Dictionary, Translations & Thesaurus. https://dictionary.cambridge.org/. Accessed 17 Mar 2021
11. ISO.Org (1999) ISO/CEI Guide 51:1999(fr). https://www.iso.org/obp/ui/#iso:std:iso-iec:guide:51:ed-2:v1:fr. Accessed 14 Feb 2021
12. Mulazzani, M.: Reliability versus safety. IFAC Proc. Volumes **18**, 141–146 (1985)
13. Avizienis, A., Laprie, J., Randell, B.: Fundamental Concepts of Dependability (2001)
14. Mazouni, M.H.: Pour une meilleure approche du management des risques: de la modélisation ontologique du processus accidentel au système interactif d'aide à la décision, vol. 239 (2009)
15. Thoppil, N.M., Vasu, V., Rao, C.S.P.: Failure mode identification and prioritization using FMECA: a study on computer numerical control lathe for predictive maintenance. J. Fail. Anal. Prev. **19**(4), 1153–1157 (2019). https://doi.org/10.1007/s11668-019-00717-8
16. Caralli, R., Stevens, J.F., Young, L.R., Wilson, W.R.: Introducing OCTAVE Allegro: Improving the Information Security Risk Assessment Process. 951038 Bytes (2007). https://doi.org/10.1184/R1/6574790.V1
17. Wynn, J., et al.: Threat Assessment & Remediation Analysis (TARA): Methodology Description Version 1.0 (2011)
18. Chandra, P.: Software assurance maturity model. A guide to building security into software development v1 0, OWASP Project (2008)
19. Kahla–Touil, I.B.: Gestion des risques et aide à la décision dans la chaîne logistique hospitalière : cas des blocs opératoires du CHU Sahloul. Ph.D. thesis, Ecole Centrale de Lille; Institut Supérieur de Gestion de Sousse (2011)
20. Bironneau, L., Martin, D., Parisse, G.: (PDF) Fiabiliser les données d'un système d'information de gestion par la méthode AMDEC : principes et études de cas. In: ResearchGate (2010). https://www.researchgate.net/publication/282059106_Fiabiliser_les_donnees_d'un_systeme_d'information_de_gestion_par_la_methode_AMDEC_principes_et_etudes_de_cas. Accessed 29 Jan 2021
21. Bertolini, M., Bevilacqua, M., Massini, R.: FMECA approach to product traceability in the food industry. Food Control **17**, 137–145 (2006). https://doi.org/10.1016/j.foodcont.2004.09.013
22. Rapinel, J.-B., Sebti, H.: Préparation de l'AMDEC - Groupe de travail - Compétence. http://amdec.fmeca.free.fr/preparationAMDEC31.html. Accessed 29 Jan 2021
23. AIAG A (FMEA) Failure Mode & Effects Analysis|AIAG. https://www.aiag.org/quality/automotive-core-tools/fmea. Accessed 28 Jan 2021
24. Mansour, S.: La place de l'Analyse des Modes de Défaillance, de leurs Effets et de leur Criticité (AMDEC) dans l'industrie. In: 3rd International Conference on Innovation and Engineering Management (IEM-2015), pp. 6. Sousse (2015)
25. FMEA Quick Reference Guide. CATERPILLAR (2008)
26. Saizy-Callaert, S., Causse, R., Thébault, A., Chouaïd, C.: Failure mode, effects and criticality analysis (FMECA) as a means of improving the hospital drug prescribing process. Int. J. Risk Saf. Med. **15**, 193–202 (2002)

Supplier Selection by Using the Goal Programming Approach

Mahmoud Shahrokhi[1](✉) , Zahra Sobhani[1], and Alain Bernard[2]

[1] University of Kurdistan, Sanandaj, Iran
m.shahrokhi@uok.ac.ir
[2] Centrale Nantes (LS2N UMR CNRS 6004), Nantes, France
Alain.bernard@ec-nantes.fr

Abstract. Supplier selection problems have been considered widely in litera-ture; however, considering the availability and reliability of the products pro-vided by suppliers has been investigated less. In this regard, the presented work addresses a supplier selection problem in which the reliability of the parts is one of their main factors for supplier selection. This paper develops a multiobjective mathematical goal programming model to allocate the system's components orders to the suppliers. The model minimizes the system construction costs and maximizes the probability of working the system in nominal and half capacity. The similarity of the ordered components affects their delivery lead times and prices. The model determines the optimal solution for an industrial system composed of 4 parts. The proposed approach includes using the reliability block diagram to develop the Markov chain model. A multiobjective binary nonlinear mathematical program uses the Markov model to select the optimal components suppliers. Solving the model by goal programming approach provides the possibility of reflecting the decision-maker opinion relative to the construction cost's importance compared to system availability.

Keywords: Reliability block diagram (RBD) · Goal programming · Concurrent engineering · Markov chain

1 Introduction

This paper presents a multiobjective approach to determine the components suppliers for making the feedwater system (FWS) of heat-recovery steam-generator boilers used in combined cycle power plants. A nonlinear binary goal programming model uses the Markov chain results to optimizes total costs, including components price, system construction delays penalty, and the system's availability.

Many kinds of research applied optimization approaches such as integer pro-gramming, mixed integer programming, nonlinear programming, and heuristics to deal with serial-parallel and multistate systems' availability and supplier selection in supply chains. Levitin et al. determined the optimal versions of components and redundancy of different subsystems in multistate series-parallel systems [1]. Rui and et al. improved design configuration by developing a reliability optimization algorithm [2]. Yi and et al. view a reliability optimization problem by selecting components reliability among

© IFIP International Federation for Information Processing 2021
Published by Springer Nature Switzerland AG 2021
A. Dolgui et al. (Eds.): APMS 2021, IFIP AICT 634, pp. 435–444, 2021.
https://doi.org/10.1007/978-3-030-85914-5_47

different alternative levels when the system's overall performance is a function of each part's failure rate [3]. Montoro-Cazorla et al. studied a system subjected to shocks governed by a Poisson process, and the internal failures and the inspection times exponentially distributed [4]. Ge et al. developed an optimization model to determine critical components' reliability in a serial system [5]. Carpitella et al. developed a mathematical model for calculating a k-out-of-n system's stationary availability using the Markov chain model [6]. Chambari et al. proposed a bi-objective simulation-based and a customized NSGA-II optimization algorithm for a redundancy allocation problem [7]. Es-Sadqi et al. attempted to find the optimal system configuration that maximizes the availability and minimizes the investment cost. They evaluated the genetic algorithm and the constraint programming performance and proposed a new optimization method based on forwarding checking as a solver [8]. Sawik investigated a multi-period supplier selection problem in a supply chain with disruption and delay risks and then proposed a dynamic portfolio approach. This approach helps decision-makers decide on the suppliers of finished products, but it does not discuss the availability of the ordered parts [9]. Chen et al. developed a model to consider supplier selection and project scheduling simultaneously. They studied multiple concurrent projects that were independent operationally but with similar suppliers, when these projects' activities began as their needed resources became available. Then, this model was solved using a mathematical programming-based heuristic [10]. Bodaghi et al. introduced a weighted fuzzy multiobjective model to address supplier selection, customer order scheduling, and order quantity allocation in supply chains. They considered the reliability of on-time delivery of customer orders and evaluated the flexibility of suppliers [11]. Yoon et al. incorporated supplier selection with risk mitigation policies and utilized multiobjective optimization-based simulation for their model [12]. They showed that the use of upstream and downstream strategies simultaneously leads to better results. Cui et al. investigated sustainable supplier selection in deferent multitier supply chain structures and combined fuzzy set theory, stepwise weight assessment ratio analysis, plus a Bayesian network to propose their model [13].

The previous researches did not consider the life cycle cost, reliability, and availability of the system simultaneously. This paper attempts to consider more real wolds parameters by developing a multiobjective mathematical goal programming model for assigning system component orders to the suppliers. This model minimizes system construction costs and maximizes the likelihood of the system operating at nominal and half-load capacity, while the similarity of the ordered components leads to change their delivery time and price. Using the proposed approach to select the components supplier of a typical industrial system illustrates the model application for an industrial system. The following sections explain this model and solve it for a numerical example and discuss the results.

2 The Proposed Model

The discussed problem concerns selecting the suppliers for critical components of FWS (Fig. 1).

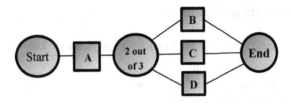

Fig. 1. Studied series-parallel system

Component B, C, and D are feedwater pumps. Each of them provides 50% of the nominal system capacity, and component A is the instrumentation device that controls the overall system parameters. Several suppliers offer different qualities (i.e., failure and repair rates), prices, and delivery lead times. The availability of the system depends on the reliability and reparability of its components. Also, suppliers offer incremental quantity discounts; however, large orders result in higher delivery lead time. During the system exploitation phase, the system may be in one of three states, according to the failure of its components: working at nominal capacity (NC), half capacity (HC), and shutdown (SD). NC occurs when A and at least two out of B, C, and D are working. HC occurs when A and only one out of B, C, and D are working. SD results from failure of A or all B, C, and D. Figure 2 illustrates the Markov model of all possible states for this system. In this figure, oval, trapezoid, and rectangular forms represent NC, HC, and SD. Operation of components B, C, and D are identical, and ordering one of them to supplier j, delivery lead time, and the price will be L_{Bj} and C_{Bj}, respectively. By ordering two components among these components to supplier j, the unit price and delivery lead time of each of them will be C'_{Bj} and L'_{Bj}, respectively. Finally, by ordering all these three components to supplier j, price and delivery time values will be C''_{Bj} and L''_{Bj}, respectively. Assembling B, C, D should begin after A, and simultaneous assembly of B, C, D does not change their assembly times. Times and costs of assembling processes are deterministic and known and independent from the quality of the components. Deterministic weighting factors express the goals' importance.

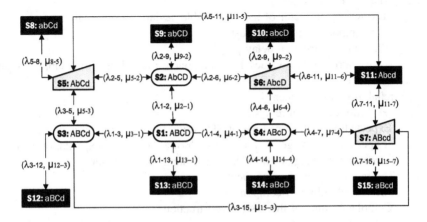

Fig. 2. The system's Markov model diagram

3 The Mathematical Model

The model indices, parameters, and decision variables are as follows:

$i = A, B, C, D$: The components

$j = 1, 2, ..., J$: The components' suppliers

$k = 1, 2, ..., K$: The assembly process

$l = 1, 2, ..., L$: The system states

$m = 1, 2, 3$: The goals

C_{Aj} = Purchasing price of A from supplier j

C_{Bj} = Unit price of B, C, or D from supplier j when purchasing separately

C'_{Bj} = Unit price of purchasing two of B, C, and D from supplier j

C''_{Bj} = Unit price of purchasing similar B, C, and D from supplier j

R_{ij} = reliability of component i offered by supplier j

R = Minimum requested system's reliability

T = System construction completion deadline

B = The maximum available budget for purchasing components

n = Number of components (n = 4)

C^D = Daily delay penalty for system construction

L_{Aj} = Delivery lead time of component A from the supplier j

L_{Bj} = Delivery lead time of ordering one of B, C, or D from the supplier j

L'_{Bj} = Delivery lead time of ordering two similar components among B, C, or D to supplier j

L''_{Bj} = Delivery lead time of ordering all components B, C, and D to supplier j

F_{Ak} = Time of process k for assembling component A

F_{Bk} = The time of process k for assembling each of components B, C or d

K_A = Set of required processes for assembling component A

K_B = Required assembly processes on components B, C, and D

μ_{ij} = The rate of repair of component i, offered by supplier j

λ_{ij} = The rate of failure of component i, offered by supplier j

b_m = The value of goal m

w_m = The weighting factor of the undesirable deviation from goal m

A_1 = The components purchase cost

A_2 = The total construction delay penalty

y_{ij} = Binary variable with values 1, if component i is ordered from supplier j, and zero otherwise.

R_i = reliability of component i

R_e = reliability of the entire system

P_0 = Expected percentage of time of SD during the system exploitation phase

P_{50} = Expected percentage of time of HC during the system exploitation phase

S_l = Expected percentage of time that the system spends in state l

μ_i = The rate of repair of component i

λ_i = The rate of failure of component i

T^c = Completion time of the system construction

T^i_c = Completion time of assembling component i

T^B = The time of delivery of all components B, C, and D
d_m^+, d_m^- = Positive and negative deviations from goal m

Equations (1) to (35) show the objective function and constraints of the model.

$$Min\, Z = w_1 d_1^+ + w_2 d_2^+ + w_3 d_3^+ \tag{1}$$

$$\text{Subjected to :} \tag{2}$$
$$A_1 = \sum_{j=1}^{3} y_{Bj} y_{Cj} y_{Dj} (3C''_{Bj})$$

$$+ \sum_{j=1}^{3} \left(y_{Bj} y_{Cj} (1 - y_{Dj}) + y_{Bj} y_{Dj} (1 - y_{Cj}) \right.$$
$$+ y_{Cj} y_{Dj} (1 - y_{Bj}) \right) \times \left(2C'_{Bj} \right)$$
$$+ \sum_{j=1}^{3} \left(y_{Bj} (1 - y_{Cj}) (1 - y_{Dj}) \right.$$
$$+ y_{Cj} (1 - y_{Bj}) (1 - y_{Dj}) + y_{Dj} (1 - y_{Bj}) (1 - y_{Cj}) \right)$$
$$\times C_{Bj} + \sum_{j=1}^{3} y_{Aj} C_{Aj}$$

$$P_0 = S_8 + S_9 + S_{10} + S_{11} + S_{12} + S_{13} + S_{14} + S_{15} \tag{3}$$

$$P_{50} = S_5 + S_6 + S_7 \tag{4}$$

$$P_0 - d_2^+ = b_2 \tag{5}$$

$$P_{50} - d_3^+ = b_3 \tag{6}$$

$$T^A = \sum_{j=1}^{3} y_{Aj} L_{Aj} + \sum_{k \in k_A} F_{Ak} \tag{7}$$

$$T^B = \sum_{j=1}^{3} y_{Bj} y_{Cj} y_{Dj} L''_{Bj} \tag{8}$$

$$+ \left(\sum_{j=1}^{3} \left(y_{Bj} y_{Cj} (1 - y_{Dj}) + y_{Bj} y_{Dj} (1 - y_{Cj}) \right.\right.$$
$$+ y_{Cj} y_{Dj} (1 - y_{Bj}) \right) \times Max \left(L_{Bj}, L'_{Bj} \right) \right)$$
$$+ \left(\sum_{j=1}^{3} \left(y_{Bj} (1 - y_{Cj}) (1 - y_{Dj}) \right.\right.$$
$$+ y_{Cj} (1 - y_{Bj}) (1 - y_{Dj}) + y_{Dj} (1 - y_{Bj}) (1 - y_{Cj}) \right)$$
$$\times Max \left(L_{Bj}, L'_{Bj} \right) \right)$$

$$T^C = \max(T^B, T^A) + \sum_{k \in k_B} F_{Bk} \tag{9}$$

$$A_2 = \max(0, T^c - T)C^D \tag{10}$$

$$A_1 + A_2 - d_1^+ = b_1 \tag{11}$$

$$A_1 \leq B \tag{12}$$

$$\mu_i = \sum_{j=1}^{3} Y_{ij}\mu_{ij} \quad \forall i \tag{13}$$

$$\lambda_i = \sum_{j=1}^{3} Y_{ij}\lambda_{ij} \quad \forall i \tag{14}$$

$$\sum_{j=1}^{3} y_{ij} = 1 \quad \forall i \tag{15}$$

$$y_{ij} \in \{0.1\} \quad \forall i, j \tag{16}$$

$$(\lambda_1 + \lambda_2 + \lambda_3 + \lambda_4)S_1 = \mu_2 S_2 + \mu_4 S_3 + \mu_3 S_4 + \mu_1 S_{13} \tag{17}$$

$$(\lambda_1 + \mu_2 + \lambda_3 + \lambda_4)S_2 = \lambda_2 S_1 + \mu_4 S_5 + \mu_3 S_6 + \mu_1 S_9 \tag{18}$$

$$(\lambda_1 + \mu_4 + \lambda_3 + \lambda_2)S_3 = \lambda_4 S_1 + \mu_2 S_5 + \mu_1 S_{12} + \mu_3 S_7 \tag{19}$$

$$(\lambda_1 + \mu_3 + \lambda_2 + \lambda_4)S_4 = \lambda_3 S_1 + \mu_4 S_7 + \mu_2 S_6 + \mu_1 S_{14} \tag{20}$$

$$(\lambda_1 + \mu_2 + \lambda_3 + \mu_4)S_5 = \lambda_4 S_2 + \lambda_2 S_3 + \mu_3 S_{11} + \mu_1 S_8 \tag{21}$$

$$(\lambda_1 + \mu_2 + \lambda_4 + \mu_3)S_6 = \lambda_3 S_2 + \lambda_2 S_4 + \mu_4 S_{11} + \mu_1 S_{10} \tag{22}$$

$$(\lambda_1 + \mu_3 + \lambda_2 + \mu_4)S_7 = \lambda_4 S_4 + \lambda_3 S_3 + \mu_2 S_{11} + \mu_1 S_{15} \tag{23}$$

$$\mu_1 S_8 = \lambda_1 S_5 \tag{24}$$

$$\mu_1 S_9 = \lambda_1 S_2 \tag{25}$$

$$\mu_1 S_{10} = \lambda_1 S_6 \tag{26}$$

$$(\mu_2 + \mu_3 + \mu_4)S_{11} = \lambda_4 S_6 + \lambda_2 S_7 + \lambda_3 S_5 \tag{27}$$

$$\mu_1 S_{12} = \lambda_1 S_3 \tag{28}$$

$$\mu_1 S_{13} = \lambda_1 S_1 \tag{29}$$

$$\mu_1 S_{14} = \lambda_1 S_4 \tag{30}$$

$$\mu_1 S_{15} = \lambda_1 S_7 \tag{31}$$

$$\sum_{l=1}^{15} S_l = 1 \tag{32}$$

$$R_e = 1 - P_0 \tag{33}$$

$$R_e \geq R \tag{34}$$

$$P_{100} = S_1 + S_2 + S_3 + S_4 \tag{35}$$

The objective function (1) minimizes a weighted summation of deviations from the goals. Equation (2) calculates total purchasing costs according to their suppliers' components' similarity and the offered price. Equations (3) and (4) calculate the SD and HC proportion time, respectively. Equations (5) and (6) calculate deviations from the second and third goals. Equation (7) is the assembly time of component A by adding its delivery lead time and times of its assembly processes. According to their suppliers and order sizes, Eq. (8) calculates the delivery lead time of all B, C, and D. Supposing that larger orders increase delivery lead time, this equation can be written, simplifies this equation by removing the max operators. Constraint (9) calculates the completion time of the system construction project by adding the possible earliest time of starting assembly processes of components B, C, and D, with the time of these processes. The max operator indicates these processes can begin after delivering B, C, and D and completing A's assembly. Equation (10) calculates the construction delay penalty by multiplication the daily delay penalty by the difference between the project's end time and its deadline. Equation (11) calculates the total construction cost by adding the component purchasing price and construction delay penalty. The model ignores the assemblies' processes' costs because they are constant and independent from decision variables. Constraint (12) limits the maximum components' purchasing cost to a pre-defined level. Equations (13) and (14) determine the components' failure and repair rates, respectively, considering their suppliers. Equation (15) indicates that the supplier for each element is unique. Constraint (16) determines the domain of binary variables. Constraints (17) to (32) are Markova processes equilibrium equations, written according to Fig. 2, and ensure that the sum of the input streams to each state, in the long term, is equal to the sum of the output streams and the sum of all times ratio is 1. Constraint (33) calculates the entire system's reliability as the proportion of times it is not shutting down, and Eq. (34) ensures the requested minimum level of system reliability. Constraint (35) calculates the ratio of times that the system will work at nominal capacity states. It facilitates the analyses of the results.

4 Numerical Results

Table 1 presents the problem parameter values, and Table 2 shows the optimal solution. The optimal reliability is 0.99, 0.9, 0.9, and 0.95 for A, B, C, and D, respectively. Component A does not have any redundant components, making component A more critical. The entire system's reliability is about 0.85 (i.e., the system works at NC and HC modes, 55% and 29.7% of the time, respectively) and 0.15% of the times the system is at SD state. Deviation from the second and third goals is very high, resulting

Table 1. The model parameters values

Para.	Value	Para.	Value	Para.	Value
B	1200	n	4	R	0.8
R_{i1}	0.9	R_{i2}	0.95	R_{i3}	0.99
μ_{i1}	0.05	μ_{i2}	0.07	μ_{i3}	0.1
λ_{i1}	0.05	λ_{i2}	0.03	λ_{i3}	0.01
b_1	6100	b_2	0.05	b_3	0.05
w_1	0.01	w_2	200	w_3	40
T	75	C^D	300		

		Supplier (j)	
	1	2	3
Relia-bility	0.9	0.95	0.99
C_{Aj}	200	220	240
C_{Bj}	300	340	380
C'_{Bj}	250	280	320
C''_{Bj}	200	240	280
L_{Aj}	5	7	17
L_{Bj}	6	19	31
L'_{Bj}	8	24	37
L''_{Bj}	12	30	42

Assembly process (k)	1	2	3	4	5
F_{Ak}	3	5	7	4	2
F_{Bk}	6	13	16	5	-

Table 2. The model's optimal solution

Decision variable	Value	Decision variable	Value
A_1	1080	R_1	0.99
A_2	5100	R_2	0.9
R_e	0.847	R_3	0.9
P_{50}	0.297	R_4	0.95
P_0	0.153	Z	31.363
d_1^+	80	T^c	92
d_3^+	0.247	d_2^+	0.103

from the relative importance (i.e., higher weighted factor) of the first goal. Components' purchase price and the project delay penalty are so high that ordering higher reliability components is not justifiable despite a sufficient purchase budget.

5   Discussion

This paper uses goal programming as a multiobjective decision-making approach to optimize the systems' design configuration by considering the system life cycle's parameters. The model objective is achieving a sufficiently low construction cost and increasing the system's availability during its exploitation. These objectives are defined based on the supply chain's criteria and alternatives.

Considering the components' constant failure and repair rates justifies using the exponential distribution function as a memoryless probability distribution. This assumption is required to use the Markov model. Otherwise, system simulation models may create the same results. However, integrating the simulation model in the goal program model will remain a modeling challenge. Using the more appropriate probability distributions (e.g., the Normal distribution function) improves the model's result. The goals' weighting factors express the decision-maker opinion relative to the construction cost's importance compared to system availability. Reducing construction costs is a short-term objective, leads to decreasing the system availability and customer satisfaction.

Varying the goals' weighting factors changes the priorities between the system construction cost and system availability. The model applicability can be improved, by considering uncertainty in the model parameters, such as component repair and failure rates and system costs. Besides, the goal weighting factors may express as fuzzy numbers or linguistic variables. Future research may also model the effect of using similar components on their repair rates and system availability.

6 Conclusions

This paper developed a nonlinear binary goal programming model to select suppliers of an industrial system's components. The model minimizes the system's life cycle cost, including the cost of purchasing price and the construction delay penalty, and maximizes the system's availability concurrently. The numerical results illustrate the effect of the order sizes on the components' prices and delivery lead times. They also show how varying the goals' weighting factors provides a trade-off between short-term (minimizing the system construction cost) and long-term objectives (maximizing the system availability).

References

1. Levitin, G., Lisnianski, A.: Joint redundancy and maintenance optimization for multistate series-parallel systems. Reliab. Eng. Syst. Saf. **64**(1), 33–42 (1999)
2. Rui, P., Xiao, H., Liu, H.: Reliability of multistate systems with a performance sharing group of limited size. Reliab. Eng. Syst. Saf. **166**, 164–170 (2016)
3. Yi, L.Y.: Reliability analysis of multistate systems subject to failure mechanism dependence based on a combination method. Reliab. Eng. Syst. Saf. **166**, 109–123 (2017)
4. Montoro-Cazorla, D., Pérez-Ocón, R.: Constructing a Markov process for modelling a reliability system under multiple failures and replacements. Reliab. Eng. Syst. Saf. **173**, 34–47 (2018)
5. Ge, Q., Peng, H., van Houtum, G.J., Adan, I.: Reliability optimization for series systems under uncertain component failure rates in the design phase. Int. J. Prod. Econ. **196**, 163–175 (2018)
6. Carpitella, S., Certa, A., Izquierdo, J., La Fata, C.M.: k-out-of-n systems: an exact formula for the stationary availability and multiobjective configuration design based on mathematical programming and TOPSIS. J. Comput. Appl. Math. **330**, 1007–1015 (2018)
7. Chambari, A., Azimi, P., Najafi, A.A.: A bi-objective simulation-based optimization algorithm for redundancy allocation problem in series-parallel systems. Expert Syst. Appl. **173**, 114745 (2021)

8. Es-Sadqi, M., Idrissi, A., Benhassine, A.: Some efficient algorithms to deal with redundancy allocation problems. J. Autom. Mobile Robot. Intell. Syst. **14**, 48–57 (2021)

9. Sawik, T.: Selection of a dynamic supply portfolio under delay and disruption risks. Int. J. Prod. Res. **56**, 760–782 (2017)

10. Chen, W., Lei, L., Wang, Z., Teng, M., Liu, J.: Coordinating supplier selection and project scheduling in resource-constrained construction supply chains. Int. J. Prod. Res. **56**, 6512–6526 (2018)

11. Bodaghi, G., Jolai, F., Rabbani, M.: An integrated weighted fuzzy multiobjective model for supplier selection and order scheduling in a supply chain. Int. J. Prod. Res. **56**, 3590–3614 (2017)

12. Yoon, J., Talluri, S., Yildiz, H., Ho, W.: Models for supplier selection and risk mitigation: a holistic approach. Int. J. Prod. Res. **56**, 3636–3661 (2017)

13. Cui, L., Wu, H., Dai, J.: Modelling flexible decisions about sustainable supplier selection in multitier sustainable supply chain management. Int. J. Prod. Res., 1–22 (2021)

Using an Auction-Based System in Cloud Manufacturing for Selecting Manufacturing-as-a-Service Providers

Kelvin Sparr, Damian Drexel[ID], and Ralph Hoch[(✉)][ID]

Research Center Digital Factory, Vorarlberg University of Applied Sciences,
Dornbirn, Austria
{kelvin.sparr,damian.drexel,ralph.hoch}@fhv.at

Abstract. The shift towards mass customization in production and technological advancements lead to new manufacturing paradigms. Such paradigms facilitate the distribution of production to distributed companies, located all around the globe, essentially creating a cloud-based manufacturing platform. In such a system, manufactures may provide their production facilities as services to others – leading to the paradigm of Manufacturing-as-a-Service (MaaS). One major challenge in MaaS is the discovery of manufacturing resources and the distribution of orders to them. We propose an ontology based template matching method to find fitting manufacturing resources. Based on this selection we introduce a multi agent-based auction system for distributing orders and production planning. To illustrate its practical applicability we integrated the proposed approach in an existing cloud manufacturing platform.

Keywords: Manufacturing-as-a-Service · Cloud manufacturing · Ontologies · Auction-based production planning

1 Introduction

The manufacturing industry has been subject to major changes in recent years as technological advancements are becoming increasingly versatile. The digitization of manufacturing processes elevated these processes from mere physical hardware components to complex Cyber Physical System (CPSs) manufacturing systems including pervasive mining of process data as well as IT supported production planning and control approaches.

The digitization of manufacturing enables the distribution of orders to multiple manufacturing facilities or even multiple manufacturers. From this approach, which is in contrast to conventional manufacturing systems, *Cloud Manufacturing (CMfg)* systems emerged. In these systems, production of a single order by a customer may potentially involve distributed manufacturers for each step in the manufacturing process. This is due to the increasing customizability [1] of products, which makes on-site production considering all variations difficult and,

© IFIP International Federation for Information Processing 2021
Published by Springer Nature Switzerland AG 2021
A. Dolgui et al. (Eds.): APMS 2021, IFIP AICT 634, pp. 445–454, 2021.
https://doi.org/10.1007/978-3-030-85914-5_48

hence, the outsourcing of some production steps to third-party manufacturers inevitable. Essentially, one manufacturer uses services of other manufacturers for producing goods – this is known as *Manufacturing-as-a-Service (MaaS)*.

In MaaS manufacturers register their offered manufacturing services at a central cloud platform, allowing other manufacturers to select them based on specific attributes and characteristics such as price or quality. This selection process typically involves manual steps, which can be more prone to error with the increasing number of available manufacturers. Furthermore, distributing workload, i.e., scheduling and production planning, in CMfg is still not solved [2], and most approaches are neither flexible nor can they be automated. To take full advantage of CMfg and MaaS, establishing an automated selection of manufacturing services, taking changing attributes such as price quota into account, is desirable.

In this context, we propose a novel approach for production planning for CMfg and MaaS platforms using an ontology-based template matching algorithm. Our approach allows the automatic extraction of fitting manufacturing services from a knowledge base given a set of required and preferred attributes. For the actual selection of a specific service, we propose using an auction-based approach, which takes constraints, e.g. maximum price, defined by the service providers as well as the customers into consideration. To this end, the overall manufacturing process is split into single manufacturing steps, which are handled individually, allowing for a more flexible distributing system.

The remainder of this paper is organized as follows: First, we provide background information on technologies to make the paper self-contained and give an overview of relevant literature. Second, we describe our proposed solution and its implementation. Building on this section we demonstrate our findings in a feasibility prototype. Finally, we conclude with a discussion and sketch future work.

2   State of the Art

There exists research covering a vast variety of topics regarding distributed manufacturing environments, such as CMfg. In particular, the use of semantic technologies for specifying tasks and the use of multi-agent systems for distributing workload, as the number of resources strongly impacts the complexity [3], have been a research topic for quite some time. Typically, a CMfg platform provides manufacturer services to its users [4] and in this field MASs have been used for service discovery [5] and also as an effective technology for solving issues in scheduling and distributing workload [3].

Bratukhin and Sauter [6] propose two strategies for increasing flexibility in distributed manufacturing systems based on decision-making algorithms. In one of their strategies they propose the utilization of agents for increasing flexibility in manufacturing systems. Ameri and Kulvatunyou [7] combine a reference ontology for supply chains with agents for connecting manufacturing suppliers in order to establish a supply chain for an order. Both approaches, in contrast to our approach, do not consider alternatives and, in particular, constraints of customers when distributing workload. Furthermore, we divide larger processes into single manufacturing steps, which are individually handled and assigned by auctions, for creating a more flexible distribution approach.

Vogel-Heuser et al. [8] present a distributed production system utilizing CPPS and agents as a possible solution for increased flexibility and adaptability. Agents can also compete with each other to achieve the best outcome for themselves [9]. For example in [10] the authors propose a MAS, which is capable of scheduling multi-project instances via auction-based communication. In this decentralized approach of decision-making, project agents try to allocate resources, which are represented by resource agents, by bidding on free time slots in an auction held by an exchange agent. We partly build upon this work and utilize these techniques for selecting a single provider using auctions. However, we also further investigate the utilization of auctions for providing alternatives and, thus, enabling customers to select the best fitting results for their needs.

Semantic technologies, such as ontologies, are commonly used in combination with CMfg [11–13], e.g., to realize scheduling systems [14], and are a means for formally specifying tasks and systems. Obitko and Marik [15] use ontologies with MASs for addressing issues in heterogeneous systems. Kulvatunyou et al. [16] propose a framework to support design and manufacturing tasks in CMfg as well as the distribution of them. In [17] an upper ontology for distributed manufacturing is proposed. Other ontologies for CMfg are, for example, the ManuService ontology [18], the ontology described by Talhi et al. [19], and the multi dimensional information model for manufacturing capabilities [20]. Similarly, Jang et al. [21] use semantic manufacturing capability profiles for discovering manufacturing services. We build upon this previous work and utilize the knowledge representation in ontologies provided by an existing CMfg platform [22] for systematically extracting matching services for given orders and combine them with a MAS for distributing and scheduling workload.

Typically, work with MAS utilize well-established frameworks. One well-known framework is JADE [23], which uses the Foundation for Intelligent Physical Agents (FIPA) [24] standard for communication between agents. A more recent framework is SARL [25], which utilizes a statically typed programming language to create multi-agent systems. We base our implementation on SARL and integrate it with an existing CMfg platform.

3   Manufacturing Resource Selection

In this section we first sketch the data model needed for representing manufacturing resources and products, then we show how fitting resources can be selected given a set of characteristics and demonstrate how auctions may be used to determine service providers. Finally, we present an integration with an existing CMfg platform for demonstrating the practical applicability.

3.1   Representing Resources and Template Matching

Formalizing manufacturing resources and products is essential for a feasible implementation of a MaaS platform. Typically, this is accomplished via a knowledge base that provides flexible data structures. Using *templates* for parts of this data model, in our case manufacturing steps, allows matching against the knowledge base for an automatic selection of fitting service providers.

Our approach builds upon the knowledge representation used in the CMfg platform described in [22]. This platform consists of an upper ontology as well as specifically tailored ontologies. While the upper ontology provides shared concepts, the tailored ontologies focus on specific views on the domain of manufacturing, e.g., configuration of orders, the processes involved in producing an order, or the representation of manufacturing resources. For example, for the manufacturing resources ontology it is sufficient to view the concept *Product* as a single entity, as specified in the upper ontology, while the process related ontology also includes information about the configuration provided by the customer. In this section we do not describe the full ontology but instead only some of the concepts pertinent to the work described in this paper. Figure 1 gives an overview of parts of the ontology concepts relevant to this work.

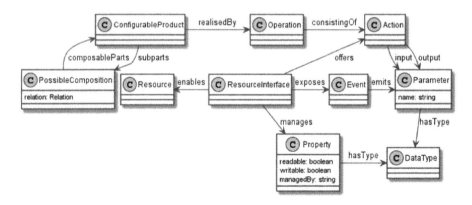

Fig. 1. Simplified classes from the ontology, used in the auction system

Before a product can be manufactured it has to be configured in two ways. First its sub-parts, e.g. what type of bearing should be included, and second, which *Operation* is used to manufacture a specific part, needs configuration. In this paper we specifically address the automation of the second configuration, i.e., assigning specific manufacturing operations, and subsequently service providers, to sub-parts of a product. Technically speaking, each product is represented by an *ConfigurableProduct* in the knowledge base and each *Operation* describes possible sequences of *Actions* for manufacturing the product. In this context, each *Action* describes a single capability of a manufacturing resource. It is defined by its *inputs* and *outputs*, which consist of a *name* and a *type*.

Since both, the manufacturing service providers as well as the products use the same data model concepts, we can automatically derive a *template* for selecting resources. The generation of the template is based on an actual operation connected to a product, i.e., we generalize from a concrete instance to a generic representation. This template decouples the *Operations* from a specific product and enables the automated selection of fitting resources. The previous link between an operation and a product is now represented by the template, which serves as a placeholder, and therefore, it may be necessary to enrich it with additional metadata. Essentially, we identify service providers that may substitute the *Actions* specified in the *Action-* and *OrderTemplates*. Figure 2 illustrates the process of selecting eligible *Actions*, where the second action is eliminated as its structure is not fitting.

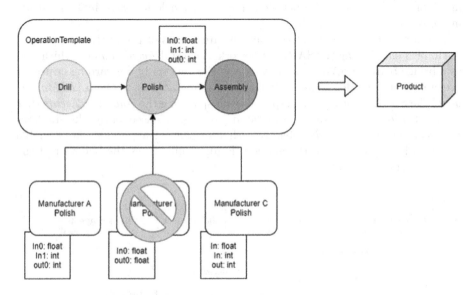

Fig. 2. Selecting fitting resources via template matching

We dynamically create these templates using SPARQL queries. Via this query we are able to filter all fitting structures from the knowledge base and, additionally, filter them by constraints, e.g., price. Each SPARQL query for an *Action-Template* is executed exactly once and returns a list of fitting manufacturing services. An abridged version of the query is shown in Listing 1.1.

Listing 1.1. General structure of a SPARQL-Query for *ActionTemplate* matching.

```
SELECT ?action WHERE {
    ?action rdf:type cidop:Action;
        cidop:input ?in0;
        ...
        cidop:input ?inN;
        cidop:output ?out0;
        ...
```

```
        cidop:output ?outN;
    ?in0 cidop:hasType cidop:integer;
        cidop:name "inputName0" .
            ...
    ?outN cidop:hasType cidop:string;
        cidop:name "outputNameN" .
}
```

3.2 Auction

To automate the resource selection process we propose using a multi-agent auction system, which includes constraints by customers, e.g., preferred price or due date, and manufacturers, e.g. lowest acceptable price. According to these constraints, the auction process identifies appropriate service providers for each individual *Action* of the product, i.e., an auction is held for each *ActionTemplate* in a given *OperationTemplate*.

From a technical perspective, the software agents of the auctioning process are implemented using the SARL framework. A central *AgentHandler*, which acts as a bridge between SARL and Java, starts the auction by forwarding customer preferences and bidder configurations of the manufacturer to the *SARLMainAgent*. The *SARLMainAgent* is responsible for spawning the *AuctionerAgents* that are needed for carrying out the auctioning process. Consequently, the *AuctioneerAgents* spawn the *BidderAgents* each representing a provider for a viable *Action*, which then bid on the auction. Figure 3 illustrates the behavior of the auction system.

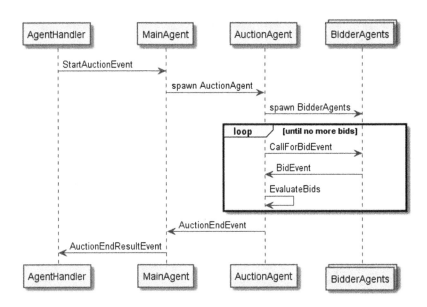

Fig. 3. Course of the auction process

SARL organizes agents in so-called *spaces*. *Spaces* determine which events an agent or any other object subscribed to the *space* may receive. The *MainAgent* exists in the *global space*, to which the *AgentHandler* is also subscribed to. *AuctioneerAgents*, spawned by the *MainAgent*, reside in the *inner context space* of the *MainAgent*. Subsequently, the *BidderAgents* spawned by the *AuctioneerAgents* reside in the *inner context space* of their respective *AuctioneerAgent*. By utilizing these *spaces*, the bid events sent out by the *BidderAgents* can only be received by the corresponding *AuctioneerAgent*, whereas the *AuctioneeerAgents* direct their results to the *MainAgent* via an *AuctionEnd* event. Furthermore, *AuctioneerAgents* and their *BiddingAgents* are spawned in parallel to speed up the auctioning process.

In addition to customer preferences and the bidder configurations by the manufacturers, the auction process depends on the selected auction type, e.g. *English*, *Japanese*, or *Sealed*. After all auctions have been held for each *ActionTemplate* in an *OperationTemplate*, the results of these auctions, specific *Actions*, are aggregated to form a concrete *Operation*. Because a product may consist of multiple sub-products, and each sub-product may require an *Operation*, an aggregation on this level is necessary as well. The *ConfiguredProduct* is then finalized with the aggregated *Operations* and can be forwarded to the respective manufacturing scheduling services in the system. By performing auctions for all production steps of a product, the final order may consist of *Actions* of various manufacturers.

3.3 Integration

To apply the methods for template matching and for selecting the most applicable service provider for a production step, a reusable implementation is necessary. We have chosen to implement the auction and template matching functionalities as single (micro-)services with well-defined interfaces. This enables their reuse in different platforms and scenarios, such as CMfg. To show the practical applicability we integrated our presented services within the existing cloud platform described in [22], as it already utilizes OWL for its knowledge base and uses a (micro-)service infrastructure. Figure 4 gives an overview of its architecture.

Each service communicates via an event based communication system implemented in the cloud platform. As the auction and template matching functionalities are also implemented as services, the integration of them into the platform was trivial. We implemented our services using the Java programming languages and utilized SPARQL queries to perform the template matching against the knowledge base. The auctions themselves are implemented using SARL.

3.4 Discussion

While the system produces the optimal results according to the given parameters, e.g., asked price, work has to be done in order to balance the distribution of orders. For example, if the same manufacturing resource is constantly selected, some kind of penalty may be required for a fairer distribution of resources.

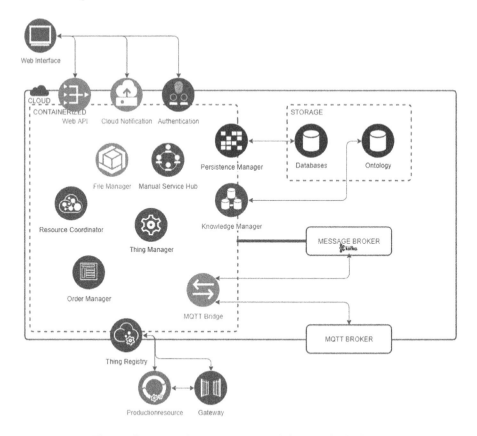

Fig. 4. Conceptual representation of the cloud platform

Consequently, manufacturers with fewer orders and slightly less preferable bids would have a chance to be involved in the production of a product.

The parameters for the auctions are currently fixed for each manufacturing resource. In future work we intend to request such quotas from each service on-demand, which enables the integration of time constraints based on the current workload of a service.

4   Conclusion

With the shift from *Mass Production* to *Mass Customization* the production of goods has to become more flexible. This can be achieved by distributing manufacturing not only to different production plants, but to different companies. A concept supporting the distribution of production is CMfg. In CMfg manufacturers can offer their production capabilities as services creating MaaS. For scheduling production orders in such an environment we use an auction-based approach in combination with an automatic manufacturing service discovery via template matching in ontologies with SPARQL.

We created an auction system consisting of a standalone, coordinating service and multiple agents, where each agent represents a service provider participating in the auction. By doing so, we are able to balance customer needs and those of service providers and identify the optimal manufacturer. Furthermore, we can easily integrate additional requirements and support various types of auctions.

In conclusion, the combination of template matching and agent based auctions offers a dynamic and highly scalable approach to the problem of scheduling in a distributed manufacturing environment. Especially, for systems like CMfg this can be a viable solution, though, further work is required.

Acknowledgment. The Cloud-Manufacturing Platform, data analytics, Digital Twin and IT- and OT-Security efforts are financed by FFG-Project No. 866833 "CIDOP" and FFG-Project No. 864798 "COMBINE".

References

1. Marques, M., Agostinho, C., Zacharewicz, G., Jardim-Gonçalves, R.: Decentralized decision support for intelligent manufacturing in Industry 4.0. J. Ambient Intell. Smart Environ. **9**(3), 299–313 (2017)
2. Sokolov, B., Ivanov, D., Dolgui, A. (eds.): Scheduling in Industry 4.0 and Cloud Manufacturing. ISORMS, vol. 289. Springer, Cham (2020). https://doi.org/10.1007/978-3-030-43177-8
3. Liu, Y., Wang, L., Wang, X.V., Xu, X., Zhang, L.: Scheduling in cloud manufacturing: state-of-the-art and research challenges. Int. J. Prod. Res. **57**(15–16), 4854–4879 (2019)
4. Zhang, L., et al.: Cloud manufacturing: a new manufacturing paradigm. Enterp. Inf. Syst. **8**(2), 167–187 (2014)
5. Guo, L., Wang, S., Kang, L., Cao, Y.: Agent-based manufacturing service discovery method for cloud manufacturing. Int. J. Adv. Manuf. Technol. **81**(9), 2167–2181 (2015). https://doi.org/10.1007/s00170-015-7221-0
6. Bratukhin, A., Sauter, T.: Bridging the gap between centralized and distributed manufacturing execution planning. In: 2010 IEEE 15th Conference on Emerging Technologies and Factory Automation (ETFA 2010), pp. 1–8. IEEE (2010)
7. Ameri, F., Kulvatunyou, B.: Modeling a supply chain reference ontology based on a top-level ontology. In: International Design Engineering Technical Conferences and Computers and Information in Engineering Conference, vol. 59179, p. V001T02A052. American Society of Mechanical Engineers (2019)
8. Vogel-Heuser, B., Diedrich, C., Pantforder, D., Gohner, P.: Coupling heterogeneous production systems by a multi-agent based cyber-physical production system. In: 2014 12th IEEE International Conference on Industrial Informatics (INDIN), pp. 713–719. IEEE, Porto Alegre, July 2014
9. Weiss, G.: Multiagent Systems: A Modern Approach to Distributed Artificial Intelligence. MIT Press, Cambridge (1999)
10. Adhau, S., Mittal, M.L., Mittal, A.: A multi-agent system for distributed multi-project scheduling: an auction-based negotiation approach. Eng. Appl. Artif. Intell. **25**(8), 1738–1751 (2012)
11. Xu, X.: From cloud computing to cloud manufacturing. Robot. Comput. Integr. Manuf. **28**(1), 75–86 (2012)

12. Cai, M., Zhang, W., Zhang, K.: ManuHub: a semantic web system for ontology-based service management in distributed manufacturing environments. IEEE Trans. Syst. Man Cybern. Part A Syst. Hum. **41**(3), 574–582 (2010)
13. Lu, Y., Xu, X., Xu, J.: Development of a hybrid manufacturing cloud. J. Manuf. Syst. **33**(4), 551–566 (2014)
14. Sanko, J., Haav, H.M., Kotkas, V.: Ontology-based customization of a scheduling system for discrete manufacturing. In: DB&IS (Selected Papers), pp. 57–70 (2016)
15. Obitko, M., Marik, V.: Ontologies for multi-agent systems in manufacturing domain. In: Proceedings, 13th International Workshop on Database and Expert Systems Applications, pp. 597–602. IEEE Computer Society, Aix-en-Provence (2002)
16. Kulvatunyou, B., Wysk, R.A., Cho, H., Jones, A.T.: Integration framework of process planning based on resource independent operation summary to support collaborative manufacturing. Int. J. Comput. Integr. Manuf. **17**(5), 377–393 (2004)
17. Ameri, F., Dutta, D.: An upper ontology for manufacturing service description. In: International Design Engineering Technical Conferences and Computers and Information in Engineering Conference, vol. 425, pp. 78, 651–661 (2006)
18. Lu, Y., Wang, H., Xu, X.: ManuService ontology: a product data model for service-oriented business interactions in a cloud manufacturing environment. J. Intell. Manuf. **30**(1), 317–334 (2016). https://doi.org/10.1007/s10845-016-1250-x
19. Talhi, A., Fortineau, V., Huet, J.C., Lamouri, S.: Ontology for cloud manufacturing based product lifecycle management. J. Intell. Manuf. **30**(5), 2171–2192 (2017). https://doi.org/10.1007/s10845-017-1376-5
20. Luo, Y., Zhang, L., Tao, F., Ren, L., Liu, Y., Zhang, Z.: A modeling and description method of multidimensional information for manufacturing capability in cloud manufacturing system. Int. J. Adv. Manuf. Technol. **69**(5–8), 961–975 (2013). https://doi.org/10.1007/s00170-013-5076-9
21. Jang, J., Jeong, B., Kulvatunyou, B., Chang, J., Cho, H.: Discovering and integrating distributed manufacturing services with semantic manufacturing capability profiles. Int. J. Comput. Integr. Manuf. **21**(6), 631–646 (2008)
22. Merz, R., Hoch, R., Drexel, D.: A cloud-based research and learning factory for industrial production. Procedia Manuf. **45**, 215–221 (2020). Learning Factories across the value chain – from innovation to service – The 10th Conference on Learning Factories 2020
23. Bellifemine, F., Poggi, A., Rimassa, G.: JADE - A FIPA-compliant agent framework. In: Proceedings of PAAM, vol. 99, p. 33, London (1999)
24. Poslad, S.: Specifying protocols for multi-agent systems interaction. ACM Trans. Auton. Adapt. Syst. **2**(4), 15–es (2007)
25. Rodriguez, S., Gaud, N., Galland, S.: SARL: a general-purpose agent-oriented programming language. In: 2014 IEEE/WIC/ACM International Joint Conferences on Web Intelligence (WI) and Intelligent Agent Technologies (IAT), pp. 103–110. IEEE, Warsaw, Poland, August 2014

Modularity Metric in Reconfigurable Supply Chain

Slim Zidi[1,2](✉) [iD], Nadia Hamani[2] [iD], and Lyes Kermad[1] [iD]

[1] University of Paris 8, 140 Rue de la Nouvelle, 93100 Montreuil, France
slim.zidi02@etud.univ-paris8.fr
[2] University of Picardie Jules Verne,
48 Rue d'Ostende, 02100 Saint-Quentin, France

Abstract. Confronted with an increasingly uncertain and fluctuating economic environment characterized by a technological evolution driven by industry 4.0 concepts, companies have to adapt their supply chains in order to improve its competitiveness. They must also implement strategies that allows them to deal with these new challenges. Supply chain modularity offers the opportunity to change and reorganize the structure of the supply chain to meet changing market needs. In this paper, we propose a new framework to design a modular supply chain using Design Structure Matrix and a modularity measurement in Reconfigurable Supply Chain. We also show the importance of integrating the direction of flows, i.e. inbound and outbound flows in the calculation of modularity and, in particular, its impact on lead time. Finally, an illustrative example is developed to validate the proposed measurement.

Keywords: Modularity · Assessment · Reconfigurable Supply Chain · Design Structure Matrix

1 Introduction

Manufacturing systems face numerous challenges and changes due to the excessive production capability and economic globalization. Thus, companies start implementing manufacturing and logistics systems that are more flexible and more agile by several actions of reconfiguration. They are also looking for technical and organizational strategies, such as reconfigurability, to improve the design of their supply chains [1]. In fact, reconfigurability can be defined as the ability to change the supply chain structure and functions at the lowest cost. Reconfigurable Supply Chain (RSC) is a supply chain that is flexible to alter its configuration with relatively minor resource requirements and without losing its operational efficiency in response to the changing customer demands and operating environment [2, 3]. RSC, also called the collaborative network, is defined as the process of modifying the structure of the agile supply chain or virtual enterprise. Reconfigurability in supply chain has five characteristics extended from those of Reconfigurable Manufacturing Systems (RMS): modularity, integrability, convertibility, diagnosability and customization [4]. Recently, authors, in [5], have defined the RSC as a network capable of adapting to structural changes by rearranging,

© IFIP International Federation for Information Processing 2021
Published by Springer Nature Switzerland AG 2021
A. Dolgui et al. (Eds.): APMS 2021, IFIP AICT 634, pp. 455–464, 2021.
https://doi.org/10.1007/978-3-030-85914-5_49

reallocating or changing its components in order to quickly adjust its capabilities, structure and functionalities using modularity to respond to market requirements.

Supply chain complexity requires a high degree of independence between the elements of the supply chain in order to reduce the overall lead time and ensure high responsiveness to customer requests. [6] considered modularity as an effect strategy applied to meet the demand for increasing variety in the market. According to [7], modularity is not a binary measure. In other words, the product or system cannot be either modular or integral, but there is a definite degree of modularity. In the literature, the assessment of modularity of products or systems was given great attention. In production systems and product-related architectures, modularity affects productivity, development time and product manufacturing cost [6]. In supply chain, the interactions between modules represent inbound or outbound physical, informational and functional flows. Modularity has also a direct impact on lead time because the control of flows allows improving the performance of the supply chain, especially in terms of time.

The objective of this research work is to propose a modularity measurement in RSC based on a modular design using the DSM matrix.

The paper is organized as follows. In Sect. 2, a definition of supply chain modularity is provided and review papers focusing on a modularity measurement are presented. Section 3 proposes a methodology for modularity design and assessment in RSC. Section 4 shows an illustrative example. Conclusion and perspectives are given in the last section of the paper.

2   Literature Review

2.1   Supply Chain Modularity

[8] defined the supply chain modularity as the degree of non-proximity of the elements of the supply chain. This degree is measured according to four dimensions: geographic proximity, organizational proximity, cultural proximity and electronic proximity. Indeed, modularity in RSC refers to the degree to which all product, process and resource entities at all levels of enterprises of supply network are modular [4].

According to [9], it is not limited to the process and product, but also concerns the supply chain, which allows generating different configurations with a variety of functionalities. [10] showed that modularity has gone beyond the technical dimension (product modularity) to achieve organizational modularity (modularity of the logistics chain). Standardization of interfaces facilitate the flow exchange between modules with the same interface. In addition, it ensures modules independence and facilitates its recombination. For supply chains and processes, interfaces can be in the form of contracts, transaction protocols and operational procedures [9]. A modular supply chain has low geographic, organizational, cultural and electronic proximity.

Several methods were used for designing a modular architecture or system namely Design Structure Matrix (DSM), Modular Function Deployment (MFD), Function Structure Heuristic (FSH), Variant Mode and Effects Analysis (VMEA) and Axiomatic Design (AD). Indeed, each method is deployed according to the application level of modularity (product, process, manufacturing system, supply chain). Each method has advantages and limitations related to its characteristics and implementation aspects. [11] presented a comparative study between three modular design methods to determine which method is the most appropriate to meet a specific objective [12]. For example, the MFD is more suitable for determining design variants and for make-buy decisions [11], which is more management-oriented than engineering-oriented [12]. On the other hand, DA and FSH are more oriented towards modularization of products and their transformation into a set of functional requirements. In this same context, the VMEA is used to describe the impact of product variants in all units of the company while evaluating the cost [13]. For complex systems with too many interactions, DSM is the most appropriate method for a better modular design [11].

A system is considered modular when it consists of a set of independent and autonomous components coupled to each other and having well-defined relationships with their functions. Although the interfaces between the components are standardized and require a low level of coordination, modularity cannot be reduced to the notion of proximity. Several measures were proposed to evaluate the degree of modularity that depends basically on the number of modules and the number of interactions between modules.

2.2   Modularity Assessment

[7] conducted a comparative study of 13 modularity metrics for product and system architecture. These metrics were classified into three essential parameters, namely similarity, combination and coupling. Moreover, [6] proposed a modularity metric to maximize the cohesion degree and minimize the coupling degree.

Several measures were also suggested to evaluate the degree of modularity in RMS. To assess the degree of reconfigurability of RMS, [14–16] used several indicators including modularity. In fact, the essential utilized parameters are the similarity and the degree of independence. [15] applied the formula given by [17] which proposed a modularity index based on the degree of independence between product modules. In the same context, [6] introduced a reconfigurability measure including modularity based on the determination of reconfiguration ease and cohesion. In [16], a measure of modularity in the reconfigurability assessment was also developed based on the degree of module independency and the number of modules that corresponds to the optimum module granularity. Besides, [18] presented an index for modularity system assessment by taking into account five aspects such as machine module relationship, number of shared modules, product module relationship, process plan machine and product family module relationship.

In the supply chain, interactions correspond to physical and information flows whose direction affects considerably the lead-time. Indeed, if the number of inbound flows is high for a module, it means that its lead-time is high and vice versa. In this study, the degree of influence of each module, which allows assigning an importance weight to each module, is integrated.

3   The Proposed Approach

Our approach aims to at designing a modular supply chain and evaluating its degree of modularity, as shown in Fig. 1. Its first step is to break down the supply chain processes into a set of activities. However, the second step consists in identifying the interactions between the determined activities that allow grouping the activities with strong interactions into a module. The third step is to build clusters of activities having strong interactions with the DSM clustering. Then, to evaluate the degree of the supply chain modularity, the fourth step, which consists in determining the degrees of intra- and inter-modules, is applied. Then, the degrees of influence of each module from the number of incoming flows and the number of outgoing flows is calculated in the fifth step in order to better analyze the modules interactions. Based on these parameters, the degree of supply chain modularity is evaluated.

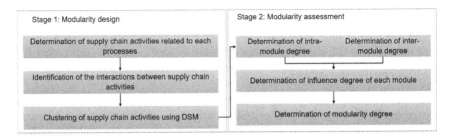

Fig. 1. Proposed methodology of modularity assessment in RSC

3.1   Modularity Design

Supply chain is a set of processes involved in providing products to meet the needs of end-customers. These processes consist of a set of activities that convert inputs into outputs using the necessary resources. The determination of supply chain activities related to each processes gives a more detailed view about flows. Indeed, the modular design of the supply chain is based on analyzing the interaction between supply chain.

These interactions correspond to the physical flows that mainly concern the internal and external transport of materials or products and to the information flows that coordinate all activities. For determining the impact of one activity over the other, the scale proposed by [19] in a range between 0 and 1 is used (Fig. 2).

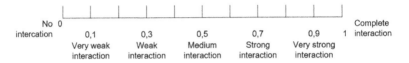

Fig. 2. The scale used for the activities interactions strengths [19]

According to [19], the identification of the intercations consists in making three matrices according to the three types of flows. Then, in order to obtain the final matrix of interactions, the three identified matrices must be aggregated with the following weights: the matrix of information flows, physical flows and functional flows are multiplied respectively by 0,5; 0,3 and 0,2.

The DSM is a matrix that allows reorganizing the system elements that are in the rows and columns of the matrix. Then, the identified interactions placed in the matrix allows grouping the matrix elements by applying clustering algorithms. The main objective of the latter is to reorder the rows and columns so that all marks will be as close to the diagonal as possible or will form a tight cluster with other marks [11]. In our approach, the elements of the DSM matrix correspond to the activities related to the supply chain processes identified in the first step. In order to cluster the activities, increase interactions within modules and decrease interactions between modules, the Euclidean distance is used.

3.2 Modularity Assessment

The measurement of the degree of modularity is based on the numbers of intra-modules and inter-modules interactions [1, 20]. The module with the greatest number of inputs is the module that takes the longest time to function, which indicates that this module will increase the supply chain lead-time [1]. Therefore, the decrease of output numbers will reduce the total time of this module and consequently the lead time of the supply chain. The degree of modularity depends on both the type of interaction (inbound or outbound) of each module and the degree of independence of modules [1]. For this reason, it is important to take into account the degree of influence of the module on the modularity measurement. This degree noted DI of module i is defined as the direction of interactions between the elements of the supply chain, which is the difference between D_i and R_i. Indeed, if the flows are incoming, then the value of will be negative. Otherwise, in the case of outgoing flows, it will be positive. The most influenced module i (the one that receives the most interaction/flows) takes the longer time of execution. Moreover, this module affects the total operating time of the supply chain, i.e. the lead-time that decreases the degree of modularity.

$$M = \frac{Ia + (1 - Ie)}{2} \tag{1}$$

$$Ia = \frac{1}{NM} \sum_{i \in NM} \frac{Ai}{TAi} \tag{2}$$

$$Ie = \frac{1}{NM} \sum_{i \in NM} \frac{Ei}{TEi} PIi \tag{3}$$

$$PIi = \frac{(DIi + X)}{\sum\limits_{i \in NM} (DIi + X)} \tag{4}$$

$$X = Min(|DI1|, |DI2|, ..., |DINM|)$$ (5)

where:

- M is the degree of modularity
- Ia is the degree of intra-relations
- Ie is the degree of inter-relations
- A_i is the number of interactions within the same module
- TA_i is the total of interactions within the same module
- E_i is the number of interactions between modules
- TE_i is the total of interactions between modules
- PI_i is the weight assigned to each module
- D_i is the sum of the rows corresponding to module i
- R_i is the sum of the columns related to module i
- DI_i is the degree of influence of each module
- X is the minimum value of the absolute values of DI_i
- NM is the number of modules

4 Illustrative Example

In this section, the proposed approach is illustrated based on the example taken from [19] representing a multi-echelon supply chain with of a manufacturing organization with its own warehouse and distribution system, composed of 7 processes: plan, source, make, deliver return, warehouse and order process. Two partners are interacting with the company: suppliers and customers. Each process is decomposed into a set of activities to determine the interactions between them. This example is given to reorganize all the activities of the supply chain in order to maximize the intra-modules relationships and minimize the inter-modules relationships using DSM, as shown in Fig. 3 and Fig. 4 [19].

For highly interdependent elements, decision makers can group them into the same functional department by changing the physical layout of the supply chain. Indeed, some activities can be restructured by moving them from one department to another (from one process to another) for better communication and coordination. Although research has shown that the size of the teams must be reduced to ensure effective communication, the results of the modular design have shown that this reconfiguration is more manageable, so that personnel can work in collaboration with personnel from the same module (sub-group).

Each activity has two types of flows: the inbound flows that are necessary for the realization of the activity and the outbound flows of the activity that are necessary for the execution of other activities in relation with it. For example, the flow entries 0.2, 0.5, 0.3 and 0.1 in row X18 represent the information and material needs inputs from the elements X1, X2, X15 and X16. On the other hand, the three entries 0.7, 1 and 1 in the column X18 represent the needs of information and material outputs for the elements X16, X19 and X20 from the element X18.

		X1	X2	X3	X4	X5	X6	X7	X8	X9	X10	X11	X12	X13	X14	X15	X16	X17	X18	X19	X20	X21	X22
Plan: Business Strategy	X1	■	0.2					0.1								0.1							
Plan: Resource Allocation	X2	0.4	■	0.5											0.1								
Plan: Coordination and communication	X3	0.1	0.8	■																			
Source: Delivery scheduling	X4		0.5	0.5	■	0.8	0.9		0.1														
Source: Supplier selection	X5	0.5	0.2		0.9	■		0.7	0.2														
Source: Inv management	X6		0.9		0.8		■				0.5												
Produce: Production design	X7	0.4	0.8			0.2		■	0.1														
Produce: Individual parts of processing	X8		0.8		0.3		0.5	0.1	■		0.5	0.1											
Produce: Sub system coordination	X9		0.8	0.8			0.8	0.3		■		0.8											
Produce: WIP/FG Inv Mgmt	X10		0.8				0.6	0.5			■	0.1	0.3		0.2								
Warehouse: Inventory control	X11	0.8	0.4					0.5				■	0.2	0.2	0.3								
Warehouse: Procurement	X12	0.8	0.4	0.5							0.2	0.8	■		0.1								
Warehouse: Carrier selection	X13	0.5	0.2									0.2	0.5	■	0.1								
Warehouse: Capacity and operation	X14	0.7	0.3									0.9	0.1		■								
Deliver: Distribution channel	X15	1	0.3											0.5		■							
Deliver: Schedule and routing	X16		0.1											0.5			■		0.7				
Order: Quotes	X17	0.2	0.3													0.5	0.1	■					
Order: Processing orders	X18	0.2	0.5													0.3	0.1		■				
Order: Back Orders	X19	0.2	0.5													0.3	0.1	1		■			
Order: Invoice	X20																		1	0.5	■		
Return: Receive and verify	X21	0.5																				■	
Return: Defective rework/ Dispose	X22		0.7																			0.9	■

Fig. 3. The DSM before clustering

		X1	X11	X12	X13	X14	X15	X4	X5	X6	X2	X3	X7	X8	X9	X10	X16	X18	X21	X17	X19	X22	X20
Plan: Business Strategy	X1	■					0.1				0.2		0.1										
Warehouse: Inventory control	X11	0.8	■	0.2	0.2	0.3					0.4					0.5							
Warehouse: Procurement	X12	0.8	0.8	■		0.1					0.4	0.5				0.2							
Warehouse: Carrier selection	X13	0.5	0.2	0.5	■	0.1					0.2												
Warehouse: Capacity and operation	X14	0.7	0.9	0.1		■					0.3												
Deliver: Distribution channel	X15	1			0.5		■																
Source: Delivery scheduling	X4							■	0.8	0.9	0.5	0.5		0.1									
Source: Supplier selection	X5	0.5					0.9		■		0.2		0.7	0.2									
Source: Inv management	X6						0.8			■	0.9					0.5							
Plan: Resource Allocation	X2	0.4				0.1					■	0.5											
Plan: Coordination and communication	X3	0.1									0.8	■											
Produce: Production design	X7	0.4							0.2		0.8		■	0.1									
Produce: Individual parts of processing	X8							0.3		0.5	0.8		0.1	■	0.5	0.1							
Produce: Sub system coordination	X9									0.8	0.8	0.8	0.3		■	0.8							
Produce: WIP/FG Inv Mgmt	X10		0.1	0.3		0.2					0.8		0.6	0.5		■							
Deliver: Schedule and routing	X16				0.5						0.1						■	0.7					
Order: Processing orders	X18	0.2					0.3				0.5						0.1	■					
Return: Receive and verify	X21	0.5									0.5								■				
Order: Quotes	X17	0.2					0.5				0.3						0.1			■			
Order: Back Orders	X19	0.2					0.3				0.5						0.1	1			■		
Return: Defective rework/ Dispose	X22										0.7								0.9			■	
Order: Invoice	X20																	1			0.5		■

Fig. 4. Clustering of activities using DSM [19]

To measure the degree of modularity of this supply chain, the degrees of intra- and inter-modules were calculated based on the numbers of interactions within the modules and between the modules. The degree of influence of each module was also computed in order to assign a weight of importance to each module. The obtained results are shown in Table 1.

Table 1. The obtained results for the 9 modules

	Ri	Di	DIi	DIi + X	PIi	Ai	Ei
Module 1	4.8	3.10	−1.70	4.50	0.08	17	26
Module 2	1	4.10	3.10	9.30	0.17	4	12
Module 3	8.8	2.60	−6.20	0	0	16	33
Module 4	2.2	1.60	−0.60	5.60	0.10	2	9
Module 5	0.9	0.50	−0.40	5.80	0.10	0	2
Module 6	0	1.10	1.10	7.30	0.13	0	4
Module 7	0.5	2.10	1.60	7.80	0.14	0	6
Module 8	0	1.60	1.60	7.80	0.14	0	2
Module 9	0	1.50	1.50	7.70	0.14	0	2

The results were used to calculate the degree of modularity of this supply chain. In this example, the modular design of the supply chain shows, on the one hand, that the degree of intra-modules is low with a value of 0.31 due to the weak values of the weights of the interactions within the modules. On the other hand, the degree of inter-modules is very weak with a value equal to 0.01, which reveals that this clustering using DSM matrix allowed obtaining a high degree of independence between the different modules. Thus, the degree of modularity is 0.64, as demonstrated in Table 2.

Table 2. The calculation of the degree of modularity

	Ai/Tai	Ei/TEi	Ei/(TEi * PIi)	Ia	Ie	M
Module 1	0.56	0.135	0.0109	0.307	0.01004	0.64
Module 2	0.66	0.105	0.0175			
Module 3	0.53	0.171	0			
Module 4	1	0.112	0.01129			
Module 5	0	0.047	0.00495			
Module 6	0	0.095	0.01246			
Module 7	0	0.142	0.01997			
Module 8	0	0.047	0.00666			
Module 9	0	0.047	0.00657			

The results indicate that the supply chain has a high degree of modularity due to the proposed modular decomposition. By considering the degree of influence of the intercations (inbound or outbound flows) it was possible to assign a weight of importance to each degree of inter-modules in order to understand the impact of the module on the lead time of the supply chain. Indeed, with a low number of inbound flows, the lead time was low and vice versa. The proposed measure of modularity shows the impact of the degree of influence of the different modules, especially lead time, on the performance of the supply chain.

5   Conclusion

Modularity is a key factor of RSC that allows reducing lead time by ensuring independence between the modules formed using the DSM matrix. Interactions between supply chain activities correspond to physical, information and functional flows. Therefore, it is important to take into account the direction of the flows, whether incoming or outgoing, to determine its impact on lead time. In this article, an approach of supply chain modularity assessment was introduced. Most of the proposed modularity measures rely on the degree of coupling, the degree of cohesion and the number of modules, especially for modular product architectures.

The main contribution of this approach is that it takes into account the degree of influence of the interactions between modules in order to reduce the lead time of the supply chain. It was concluded that, if the number of incoming flows of a module is high, the lead time of this module will be high and vice versa. It is, therefore, important to increase the degree of intra-module in order to reduce the degree of inter-module and, consequently, the degree of influence of each module. It was also proven that lead time is a fundamental parameter that allows improving the performance of RSC.

The proposed approach has two main limitations. First, the model does not consider the cost of the modular design in the evaluation of the degree of modularity. It is recommended to integrate this parameter to improve the selection of the best modular configuration. Second, conceptually, it is recommended to improve the scale of determination of interactions between activities and to integrate objective criteria to improve clustering and to achieve a highly modular configuration.

For future research work, we may focus on the impact on the six characteristics of RSC on the improvement of the degree of reconfigurability.

References

1. Zidi, S., Hamani, N., Kermad, L.: New metrics for measuring supply chain reconfigurability. J. Intell. Manuf. 1–22 (2021). https://doi.org/10.1007/s10845-021-01798-9
2. Chandra, C., Grabis, J.: Supply Chain Configuration. Springer, New York (2016). https://doi.org/10.1007/978-1-4939-3557-4
3. Ivanov, D., Sokolov, B.: Adaptive Supply Chain Management. Springer, London (2009). https://doi.org/10.1007/978-1-84882-952-7
4. Kelepouris, T., Wong, C.Y., Farid, A.M., Parlikad, A.K., McFarlane, D.C.: Towards a reconfigurable supply network model. In: Intelligent Production Machines and Systems, pp. 481–486. Elsevier (2006)
5. Dolgui, A., Ivanov, D., Sokolov, B.: Reconfigurable supply chain: the X-network. Int. J. Prod. Res. 58, 4138–4163 (2020). https://doi.org/10.1080/00207543.2020.1774679
6. Cheng, X., Wan, C., Qiu, H., Luo, J.: A measure for modularity and comparative analysis of modularity metrics. In: Huang, G.Q., Chien, C.-F., Dou, R. (eds.) Proceeding of the 24th International Conference on Industrial Engineering and Engineering Management 2018, pp. 266–277. Springer, Singapore (2019). https://doi.org/10.1007/978-981-13-3402-3_29
7. Höltta-Otto, K., Chiriac, N.A., Lysy, D., Suk Suh, E.: Comparative analysis of coupling modularity metrics. J. Eng. Des. 23, 790–806 (2012)

8. Voordijk, H., Meijboom, B., de Haan, J.: Modularity in supply chains: a multiple case study in the construction industry. Int. J. Oper. Prod. Manag. **26**, 600–618 (2006). https://doi.org/10.1108/01443570610666966

9. Wolters, M.J.J.: The business of modularity and the modularity of buisiness. Selbstverl, Rotterdam (1999)

10. Bouaissi, A., Allaoui, H., Jean-Christophe, N.: La modularité produit et chaîne logistique dans un contexte collaboratif et durable : revue de littérature et cadre conceptuel. In: Xème Conférence Internationale : Conception et Production Intégrées, Tanger, Morocco (2015)

11. Hölttä, K., Salonen, M.: Comparing three different modularity methods. In: ASME 2003 Design Engineering Technical Conferences: 15th International Conference on Design Theory and Methodology, Chicago, Illinois, USA, 2–6 September 2003 (2003)

12. Okudan Kremer, G.E., Gupta, S.: Analysis of modularity implementation methods from an assembly and variety viewpoints. Int. J. Adv. Manuf. Technol. **66**, 1959–1976 (2013). https://doi.org/10.1007/s00170-012-4473-9

13. Stjepandić, J., Ostrosi, E., Fougères, A.-J., Kurth, M.: Modularity and supporting tools and methods. In: Stjepandić, J., Wognum, N., J.C. Verhagen, W. (eds.) Concurrent Engineering in the 21st Century: Foundations, Developments and Challenges, pp. 389–420. Springer, Cham (2015). https://doi.org/10.1007/978-3-319-13776-6_14

14. Farid, A.M.: Measures of reconfigurability and its key characteristics in intelligent manufacturing systems. J. Intell. Manuf. **28**(2), 353–369 (2014). https://doi.org/10.1007/s10845-014-0983-7

15. Gumasta, K., Kumar Gupta, S., Benyoucef, L., Tiwari, M.K.: Developing a reconfigurability index using multi-attribute utility theory. Int. J. Prod. Res. **49**, 1669–1683 (2011)

16. Wang, G.X., Huang, S.H., Yan, Y., Du, J.J.: Reconfiguration schemes evaluation based on preference ranking of key characteristics of reconfigurable manufacturing systems. Int. J. Adv. Manuf. Technol. **89**(5–8), 2231–2249 (2016). https://doi.org/10.1007/s00170-016-9243-7

17. Hölttä, K., Suh, E.S., de Weck, O.: Tradeoff between modularity and performance for engineered systems and products (2005)

18. Haddou Benderbal, H., Dahane, M., Benyoucef, L.: Modularity assessment in reconfigurable manufacturing system (RMS) design: an archived multi-objective simulated annealing-based approach. Int. J. Adv. Manuf. Technol. **94**(1–4), 729–749 (2017). https://doi.org/10.1007/s00170-017-0803-2

19. Chen, S.-J. (Gary), Huang, E.: A systematic approach for supply chain improvement using design structure matrix. J. Intell. Manuf. **18**, 285–299 (2007). https://doi.org/10.1007/s10845-007-0022-z

20. Zidi, S., Hamani, N., Kermad, L.: Classification of reconfigurability characteris-tics of supply chain. In: 8th Changeable, Agile, Reconfigurable and Virtual Production Conference (CARV), Aalborg City University, Denmark (2021, In press)

Heuristic Algorithm for the Safety Stock Placement Problem

Abderrahim Bendadou[1(✉)], Rim Kalai[1], Zied Jemai[1,2], and Yacine Rekik[3]

[1] LR-OASIS, National Engineering School of Tunis, University of Tunis El Manar,
Tunis, Tunisia
[2] Université Paris-Saclay, CentraleSupélec, Laboratoire Génie Industriel,
3 rue Joliot-Curie, 91190 Gif-sur-Yvette, France
[3] EMLYON Business School, 23 Avenue Guy de Collongue,
69134 Ecully, Lyon, France

Abstract. In this paper, we develop an iterative heuristic algorithm for the NP-hard optimization problem encountered when managing the stock under the Guaranteed Service Model in a multi-echelon supply chain to determine a good solution in a short time. Compared to the Baron solver that was restricted with a maximum time equal to 20000 s, we achieved on average more than 88% reduction in calculation time and about 0.3% cost reduction.

Keywords: Guaranteed service model · All or nothing property · Algorithmic

1 Introduction

Inventory optimization in the multi-echelon supply chain is achieved by allocating adequate safety stock at each stage to cover the uncertainty of customer demand. For this purpose, two models are proposed by researchers: The Stochastic Service Model (SSM) and the Guaranteed Service Model (GSM). The number of investigations dealing with GSM is large and has followed an increasing trend in recent years. To have a comprehensive view on GSM investigations, the reader is referred to the literature review in [1]. Papers dealing with methods for solving the GSM model optimization problem can be classified into two groups: those who worked on exact methods and others who focused on approximate methods. Simpson in [16] was the first to formalize the GSM for the multi-echelon supply chain. He argued that the optimal solution is none other than an extreme point of the polyhedron formed by the linear constraints of the program. This propriety entitled by "all or nothing". Several other investigations study the properties of the optimal solution in some specified cases such as type of the network, different service measures, we refer the reader to visit [2,6–8,13,14,17]. Particularly, the founded properties in some of these investigations enabled researches to develop exact resolution methods. [12] introduces dynamic programming algorithms to

© IFIP International Federation for Information Processing 2021
Published by Springer Nature Switzerland AG 2021
A. Dolgui et al. (Eds.): APMS 2021, IFIP AICT 634, pp. 465–473, 2021.
https://doi.org/10.1007/978-3-030-85914-5_50

determine the optimal extreme point for systems with serial, assembly or distribution network. The investigation of [3], which is the first which extend the GSM model for general multi-echelon supply chains proposes solving the problem by adopting a dynamic programming algorithm. However, the proposed algorithm concerns only the systems with spanning-tree networks. [8] shows that the problem of finding optimal safety stock placement is NP-hard for general acyclic networks, Consequently, she develops a branch and bound algorithm to determine the optimal solution. She also improves the complexity of the algorithm presented by [3]. The authors in [4] develop a dynamic programming approach under the assumption of an arbitrary cost function that does not respect concavity, monotony, continuity, properties. They mainly concentrate on networks with clusters of communality, which are a particular case of general networks. In contrast, in our heuristic algorithm, the demand bound function still maintains its properties (concavity, monotonicity and continuity). The authors in [5] modified the dynamic programming algorithm of [3] for general acyclic network problem, they considered an arbitrary cost function that can be non-concave or non-monotone. [11] show that the safety stock placement problem can be formalized as a mixed integer programming (MIP) by approximating the concave cost function by a piecewise linear function. Then, they structure an iterative algorithm to solve the MIP problem. Resolution techniques based on exact methods require a high computation time and several researchers have attempted to reduce this time either by developing techniques for certain types of networks or by adopting approximate methods for general networks. Therefore, they propose heuristic algorithms that determine in a short time a suboptimal solution. In general, these calculation methods differ from each other because they are generally proposed for specific cases or they are based on specific insights. [15] provide for instance two heuristics algorithms based on the approximation of the objective function: the first one is based on the technique of iterative linear approximation while the second one employs the two-piece linear function as an approximation. Although they are fast, they often do not reach a good quality solution as in [11]. [13] proposed metaheuristic and heuristics methods (Linear Approximation , Simulated Annealing, Threshold Accepting, Tabu Search) to solve the optimization problem. [9] propose a heuristic algorithm based on genetic algorithm. In this study, we present an iterative heuristic algorithm based closely on the propriety of all or nothing for the safety stock placement problem when the supply chain is managed under the GSM model. We show efficiency numerically in terms of computational time and solution quality.

2   Model Description

2.1   Mathematical Formulation

In this section, we briefly discuss the generalization of GSM as introduced by [3] for supply chains with a complex network. To the best of our knowledge, this model applies to all types of networks.

Given a multi-echelon supply chain, let A, E be respectively the set of all existing arcs in the network and the set of all stages. We define by the following expression the maximum replenishment time M_j for stage j:

$$M_j = L_j + max\{M_i \setminus (i,j) \in A\} \qquad (1)$$

Where L_j defines the lead time corresponding to stage j. Both the classical model and the generalized one share following assumptions:

- The lead times of all stages are deterministic.
- The lead times does not depend on the order size.
- External demand arrive stationary from i.i.d. process and occurs at stages facing the end customer.
- The inventory is controlled according to the periodic review base-stock policy with a common review period.
- Each stage is characterized by two times: the inbound service time SI_j which is the time to wait between placing an order and its receipt. The service time S_j that stage j offers to its customers. It is the time to wait between the arrival of an order from a customer and its satisfaction (The service times that stage j offers to its customers are assumed to be equal).

To face the demand variation, each stage j should have a stock during the net replenishment time $\tau_j \in \{1, 2, ..., M_j\}$ where

$$\tau_j = SI_j + L_j - S_j \qquad (2)$$

Under the GSM model, each demand stage i should satisfy all the received orders during the net replenishment time which does not exceed the bound $D_i(\tau_i)$ where D_i is non decreasing concave function with $D(0) = 0$. To ensure 100% of service satisfaction, two conditions should be realized: Fist, each internal stage i should satisfy the internal order it receives from its immediate successors during the net replenishment time and which do not exceed the value $D_i(\tau_i)$. To do that, the order-up-to level B_i associated with stage i should be equal to the demand bound function at the value expressed by the net replenishment time related to stage i:

$$B_i = D_i(\tau_i) \qquad (3)$$

Second, speed up the satisfaction of orders that exceed the bound by extraordinary measures such as (expedition, production overtime, outsourcing). We express the inventory level related to stage i at time t by:

$$I_i(t) = D_i(\tau_i) - \sum_{l=t-\tau_i+1}^{t} d_i(l) \qquad (4)$$

Where $d_i(l)$ is the observed demand at time l at stage i. Referring to μ_i the mean of the demand coming to stage i for one period, we can express the expected safety stock at stage i as:

$$E[I_i(t)] = D_i(\tau_i) - \mu_i \tau_i \qquad (5)$$

Let the unit holding cost at a stage i denoted by h_i, the GSM optimization aims to determine the optimal safety stock location and quantity that minimize the total expected holding cost. Such an optimization should satisfy the following constraints:

- Service times, inbound times, and replenishment times of all stages should be positive.
- All input items must be available before the beginning of the process, for this purpose, for each $(i,j) \in A$, we must assume $SI_j \geqslant S_i$.
- If DS defines the set of stages were the demand take place and SS defines the set of supply stages, $\forall i \in SS$ the inbound service time SI_i should be equal to the time offered by the external supplier which we denote $\underline{SI_i}$, likewise, $\forall i \in DS$, the service time S_i should be equal to time imposed by the end costumer which we denote $\overline{S_i}$.

Consequently, the GSM optimization problem is formulated as follows:

$$
\begin{aligned}
\text{Min} \quad & \sum_{i \in E} h_i \left(D_i(\tau_i) - \mu_i \tau_i \right) \\
\text{(P)} \quad \text{subject to} \quad & \tau_i = SI_i + L_i - S_i && \forall i \in E \\
& SI_i + L_i - S_i \geqslant 0, && \forall i \in E \\
& SI_j \geqslant S_i, && \forall (i,j) \in A \\
& SI_i = \underline{SI_i}, && \forall i \in SS \\
& S_i = \overline{S_i}, && \forall i \in DS \\
& SI_i \geqslant 0, && \forall i \in E
\end{aligned}
$$

As mentioned in the introduction, previous studies showed that the optimal solution of such an optimization problem is an extreme point of the feasible region. Besides, it is proved that problem (P) is NP-hard (Lesnaia [8]). We point out that the above mathematical formulation may be modified slightly when the supply chain is serial. In these systems, a single service time is considered for each stage, more precisely, given a serial system indexed from the most downstream to the most upstream which carries the index N. Each stage has only one upstream, So: $\forall i \in \{1, ..., N\} : SI_i = S_{i+1}$. Under this setting, the optimal solution remains expressed by the extreme point property as we have always a concave minimization under a polyhedron. Therefore, $\forall i \in \{1, ..., N\}$ the optimal service time at the stage i is expressed according to the following relation

$$ S_i^* = S_{i+1}^* + L_i \text{ or } 0 $$

Researchers called this property all or nothing (store or not store), all if $S_i^* = 0$, nothing if $S_i^* = S_{i+1}^* + L_i$ (i.e. $\tau_i^* = 0$). This property is optimal when the system is serial. However, researchers did not talk about this property when the supply chain is with a complex network. We can extend this property for this kind of system by considering this setting, $\forall j \in E$

$$ SI_j = \max\{S_i : (i,j) \in A\} \tag{6} $$

$$ S_j = SI_j + L_j \text{ or } 0 \tag{7} $$

Under this setting, each stage either has the stock that cover the time related to the supplier that takes longer to respond to an order or it does not hold stock. We refer that all solutions inspired by this property are feasible. However, it may not be optimal when the network of the supply chain is complex.

3 Mathematical Results

In this section, we provide some mathematical results that our algorithms adopt. In the following, we remind the reader that when we use the term selected stage (or stages), we indicate that stage holds inventory according to all or nothing property (Eq. 6, 7).

Let us consider a feasible solution inspired by all or nothing property in a multi-echelons supply chain with general network, we express this solution by the set of selected stages that we refer by $\mathcal{Y}$, on the other hand, for each stage i, we consider that $D_i - \mu_i \tau_i$ is non decreasing function. Let B be a subset of stages.

3.1 Notations

$c(i)$	Holding cost incurred at stage i by selecting stages in $\mathcal{Y}$,
$c_B(i)$	New holding cost incurred at stage i by selecting stages in $B \cup \mathcal{Y}$,
C	Total holding cost incurred at the system by selecting stages in $\mathcal{Y}$,
C_B	New total holding cost incurred at the system by selecting stages in $B \cup \mathcal{Y}$,
SI_i, S_i	Are respectively the inbound service time and service time at stage i by selecting stages in $\mathcal{Y}$,
SI_i^B, S_i^B	Are respectively the new inbound service time and service time at stage i by selecting stages in $B \cup \mathcal{Y}$.

Therefore, according to Eq. 6 and 7, if $v \notin B \cup \mathcal{Y}$ then $c(v) = 0$, else

$$c(v) = h_v(D_v(SI_v^B + L_v) - \mu_v(SI_v^B + L_v))$$

Let E_1, E_2 be two subsets of stages belonging to the same echelon (i.e. stages in $E_1 \cup E_2$ are located in the same echelon). We assume that $E_1 \cap \mathcal{Y} = \emptyset$ and $E_2 \cap \mathcal{Y} = \emptyset$. we have the following results:

Lemma 1. *If $E_1 \subseteq E_2$ then:*

- $\forall v \in E_1 \cup \mathcal{Y} : c_{E_2}(v) \leqslant c_{E_1}(v)$.
- $\forall v \in E_2 \setminus E_1 : c_{E_2}(v) > c_{E_1}(v)$
- $\forall v \in E \setminus E_2 \cup \mathcal{Y} : c_{E_2}(v) = c_{E_1}(v)$

Now, we assume that $E_1, E_2, \mathcal{Y}$ are two by two disjoint sets. We define E_3 by $E_3 = E_1 \cup E_2$

Lemma 2. *If $C_{E_1} < C$ then $C_{E_3} < C_{E_2}$*

On the other hand, we denote by E_4 the set of all stages belonging to the same echelon. In addition, we suppose that $E_4 \cap \mathcal{Y} = \emptyset$.

Let us consider the following procedure

Procedure 1

- $V_1 = \emptyset$
- *Add to V_1 each stage $v \in E_4 \setminus V_1$ satisfying $C_{V_1 \cup \{v\}} < C_{V_1}$*

If $V_1 \neq \emptyset$ and V_2 is a subset of V_1 $(V_2 \subset V_1)$ then

Lemma 3. $C_{V_1} < C_{V_2}$

Procedure 1 and Lemma 3 constitutes a substrate idea on which we build the greedy algorithm. More precisely, at each echelon, if the stages are selected according to procedure 1, then we will be sure that no subset of the selected stages can be found under which the total cost is lower. Moreover, we can not select any other stages belonging to the same echelon, because this increases the total cost according to procedure 1.

3.2   The Iterative Heuristic Algorithm

We reveal in this section the heuristic algorithm for the problem (P) based on all or nothing property. It aims to determine on a short time a good solution.

Given a multi-echelon supply chain composed of P echelons and N stages (the arcs between stages belonging to the same echelon are not supposed to be in the associated network). This algorithm requires the satisfaction of the following condition

$$\forall i \in DS : \overline{S}_i < L_i$$

Under this condition, we can know in advance that according to the optimal solution the demand stages will always be considered as stock points (i.e. $\forall i \in DS : \tau_i^* > 0$), and then we can easily build the initial feasible solution. Outside this condition, the algorithm may need an extension to be more efficient.

On the other hand. In order to apply this algorithm, stages must be numbered according to the following way:

- Number the stages belonging to echelon 1 from top to bottom, and continue to number stages belonging to the next echelons with the same way.

Let us consider new notations

F_j = set of all stages belong to echelon j.
O_n = set of selected stages at the iteration n.
e_{ij} = stage that belongs to echelon j and numbered by i.
n_j = number of the existing stages at echelon j.

As a summary, at each iteration, the algorithm apply procedure 1 from echelon 1 to the penultimate echelon. The algorithm stops only if the selected stages are identical to those of the previous iteration.

Algorithm 1: The iterative heuristic algorithm

Initialization :

1. Define the supply chain network.
2. Number the stages as the way described above.
3. Set $O_0 = \phi$ and $O_1 = DS$.

iteration n :

while $O_n \neq O_{n-1}$ do

    for $j = 1$ to $P - 1$ do

        $O_n = O_n \setminus F_j$;

        Let W_n be a different set of O_n;

        while $O_n \neq W_n$ do

            $W_n = O_n$;

            for $i = \sum_{k=1}^{j-1} n_k + 1$ to $\sum_{k=1}^{j} n_k$ do

                if *the total cost reduces by choosing the stage e_{ij}* then

                    $O_n = O_n \cup e_{ij}$;

---

4 Numerical Experiments

This section aims to test the effectiveness of the heuristic algorithm presented below. We code the algorithm and the optimization program by using Mathlab R2015b and AMPL respectively on a personal computer with Intel core i3-4005U processor (1.70 GHz) and 4 GR RAM. The baron solver (version 19.3.22) is adopted to compare the performance of our algorithm in terms of cost and computational time, since it is suitable for non-convex optimization problems [10]. We have set the Maxtime option of the baron solver to 20000 (s). In each test, we generate a random network with random lead times and standard deviations. More precisely, these parameters are chosen randomly in [50, 150], and in [3, 9] respectively. Regarding the holding cost parameters, we consider for each stage i that the value of h_i is equal to the maximum holding cost of its upstream stages plus a random scalar U. Furthermore, for the 60 generated problems, all the supply and customer service times are assumed to be zero while the safety factor is assumed to be equal to 2.

On the other hand, we consider four types of networks: serial, assembly, distribution and general acyclic. We do 15 tests for every type of network starting with a three-stage supply chain, then every time we increase the number of stages until 30.

Table 1 specifies the average, minimum, and maximum values of the CPU time observed by applying the iterative heuristic algorithm for each type of network. Moreover, it is shown in the CPU time gaps column the performance of its computation by comparing with the CPU time reached by the baron solver.

On the other hand, Table 2 shows the algorithm efficiency in terms of cost and quality solution by comparing it with the baron solver. Values with a negative sign mean that the solution obtained by the baron solver is better than

Table 1. The efficiency of the algorithm regarding the CPU Time

Network type	CPU Time (s)			CPU Time Gaps %		
	Mean	Min	Max	Mean	Min	Max
Serial	0.52	0.09	1.48	94.85	64.51	99.99
Assembly	1.03	0.1	2.52	80.03	41.44	96.00
Distribution	0.68	0.09	1.88	91.10	71.7	99.75
General acyclic	0.43	0.03	1.81	86.71	54.83	99.61

Table 2. The efficiency of the algorithm regarding the total cost of detention

Network type	Cost Gaps %		
	Mean	Min	Max
Serial	0.74	0	4.72
Assembly	−0.47	−3.63	7.67
Distribution	0.83	0	8.14
General acyclic	0.24	−6	9.75

that obtained by the algorithm, while those without any sign indicate that the solution obtained by the algorithm is better than the solution obtained by the baron solver.

Particularly, it is observed from Table 1 that for each type of network the average CPU time is always less than 1.5 s while the maximum value is always less than 3s. On the other hand, through this algorithm we achieved more than 80% reduction in the CPU time.

Under the Table 2, it is showed that the algorithm can reach good solutions with a reduction of more than 0.2% and more than 9% in best cases, whereas, under the cases where the baron solver access to good solutions we noted that all the gaps are less than or equal to 6%.

5   Conclusion

We introduce in this study an iterative heuristic algorithm for the NP-hard optimization problem that we face when managing the stock under the guaranteed service model for a multi-echelon supply chain. The algorithm's structure is based closely on the propriety of all or nothing which is not optimal for complex networks. This algorithm has proved its robustness through numerical experiments for any type of network, on the other hand. As a perspective to this work we propose to find an extension when $\underline{S}_i \geqslant L_i$ (i is a demand stage) or to apply it for general cyclic networks.

References

1. Eruguz, A.S., Sahin, E., Jemai, Z., Dallery, Y.: A comprehensive survey of guaranteed-service models for multi-echelon inventory optimization. Int. J. Prod. Econ. **172**, 110–125 (2016)
2. Ghadimi, F., Aouam, T.: Planning capacity and safety stocks in a serial production-distribution system with multiple products. Eur. J. Oper. Res. **289**(2), 533–552 (2021)
3. Graves, S.C., Willems, S.P.: Optimizing strategic safety stock placement in supply chains. Manuf. Serv. Oper. Manage. **2**(1), 68–83 (2000)
4. Humair, S., Willems, S.P.: Optimizing strategic safety stock placement in supply chains with clusters of commonality. Oper. Res. **54**(4), 725–742 (2006)
5. Humair, S., Willems, S.P.: Technical note–optimizing strategic safety stock placement in general acyclic networks. Oper. Res. **59**(3), 781–787 (2011)
6. Inderfurth, K., Minner, S.: Safety stocks in multi-stage inventory systems under different service measures. Eur. J. Oper. Res. **106**(1), 57–73 (1998)
7. Lee, K., Ozsen, L.: Tabu search heuristic for the network design model with lead time and safety stock considerations. Comput. Ind. Eng. **148**, 106717 (2020)
8. Lesnaia, E.: Optimizing safety stock placement in general network supply chains. Ph.D. thesis, Massachusetts Institute of Technology. Operations Research Center (2004)
9. Li, H., Jiang, D.: New model and heuristics for safety stock placement in general acyclic supply chain networks. Comput. Oper. Res. **39**(7), 1333–1344 (2012)
10. Lundell, A., Kronqvist, J.: Polyhedral approximation strategies for nonconvex mixed-integer nonlinear programming in shot. J. Glob. Optim. (2021). https://doi.org/10.1007/s10898-021-01006-1
11. Magnanti, T.L., Max Shen, Z.J., Shu, J., Simchi-Levi, D., Teo, C.P.: Inventory placement in acyclic supply chain networks. Oper. Res. Lett. **34**(2), 228–238 (2006)
12. Minner, S.: Inventory placement in acyclic supply chain networks. Oper. Res. Spektrum **19**(4), 261–271 (1997)
13. Minner, S.: Strategic Safety Stocks in Supply Chains. Springer-Verlag, Heidelberg (2000). https://doi.org/10.1007/978-3-642-58296-7
14. Minner, S.: Strategic safety stocks in reverse logistics supply chains. Int. J. Prod. Econ. **71**(1), 417–428 (2001). Tenth International Symposium on Inventories
15. Shu, J., Karimi, I.: Efficient heuristics for inventory placement in acyclic networks. Comput. Oper. Res. **36**(11), 2899–2904 (2009)
16. Simpson, K.F.: In-process inventories. Oper. Res. **6**(6), 863–873 (1958)
17. Yadegari, E., Alem-Tabriz, A., Zandieh, M.: A memetic algorithm with a novel neighborhood search and modified solution representation for closed-loop supply chain network design. Comput. Ind. Eng. **128**, 418–436 (2019)

Advanced Modelling Approaches

An Empirical Examination of the Consistency Ratio in the Analytic Hierarchy Process (AHP)

Valery Lukinskiy[1]([✉]), Vladislav Lukinskiy[1], Boris Sokolov[2],
and Darya Bazhina[1]

[1] National Research University Higher School of Economics (HSE University),
St. Petersburg, Russia
[2] Saint Petersburg Institute for Informatics and Automation of the Russian
Academy of Sciences, St. Petersburg, Russia

Abstract. Papers related to solving practical problems in all areas of economic activity use the AHP methodology from the 1980s, proposed on the basis of studying a limited number of tangible objects. One possible option to overcome this situation could be a new approach based on probability theory and mathematical statistics. We used information obtained from processing 292 matrices collected between 2014 and 2020 and reflecting expert judgements. We were able to compare a particular expert's judgement with an array of expert judgements from previous studies to refine the computational operations of the AHP. It was found that the probability estimates of the consistency indices for expert judgements differ significantly from the probability estimates for the generated values; e.g., for 6×6 matrices, they differ by a factor of 20. The results of our study do not confirm the need to revise expert judgements if the consistency ratio (C.R.) is greater than 0.10, and confirm the need for more example calculations for tangible objects and for new dependencies to estimate intangible objects based on artificial intelligence models and methods.

Keywords: Expert judgements · Consistency ratio · Tangible objects

1 Introduction

Ivanov and Sokolov [1] emphasize that during the supply chain (SC) planning horizon, different structural elements (decision-makers, processes, products, control variables, constraints, goals, perturbations, and so on) are involved in the decision making for SC planning. Dolgui et al. [2] highlight that different problems need different solutions, and no one technique can be universally applied to the same effect. According to Felice [3], one of the most commonly used multi-criteria decision making methods is the Analytic Hierarchy Process (AHP). Csató [4] notes that in real-world applications the judgements of decision-makers may be inconsistent: for example, alternative A is two times better than alternative B, alternative B is three times better than alternative C, but alternative A is not six times better than alternative C. Sarraf and McGuire [5] note that the consistency ratio (C.R.) is the ratio of the consistency index to the average random index for the same order matrix. A C.R. of 0.10 or less is considered acceptable.

© IFIP International Federation for Information Processing 2021
Published by Springer Nature Switzerland AG 2021
A. Dolgui et al. (Eds.): APMS 2021, IFIP AICT 634, pp. 477–485, 2021.
https://doi.org/10.1007/978-3-030-85914-5_51

In works related to practical tasks (the multi-objective facility layout problem, selection of automated guided vehicles for handling materials, supplier assessment, selection of the most suitable managers for projects, design operations in distribution centres, calculating a supply chain performance index, inventory classification, making sustainable investment decisions, and many others), the value C.R. $\leq$ 0.1 is used to assess matrix consistency [6–20]. Table 1 provides information from some of these sources in more detail.

Table 1. Assessing matrix consistency in works related to solving practical problems.

Reference	Main purpose of the study	Remarks
[8]	The paper proposes a model for supplier assessment	As CR < 0.10, the degree of consistency is satisfactory. If the value is higher, that would indicate that the PCM must be revised
[11]	This paper proposes a tool for the decision-making process of selecting the most suitable managers for projects	If CR is higher than 0.10, then the judgment matrix is inconsistent and judgments should be reviewed and improved
[17]	AHP and VIKOR techniques are used to evaluate the supplier	If CR $\leq$ 0.1, the judgement matrix is acceptable; otherwise, it is considered inconsistent
[20]	The aim of this paper is to provide a framework for sustainable SC development	The value of CR must be lower than 0.10 for an acceptable level of consistency

A number of papers question the need to revise expert opinions if C.R. > 0.1. Falsini et al. [21] outline that in the original version of AHP, indeed, if C.R. is greater than 0.10 the decision maker traditionally should not tolerate the error and should reject the analysed matrix. In a business environment, problems connected to this limitation are clearly identifiable: every iteration of the same step implies a cost in terms of time and money. Ishizaka and Labib [22] note that for all consistency checking, some questions remain: what is the cut-off rule to declare my matrix inconsistent? Should this rule depend on the size of the matrix? The results of Ishizaka and Siraj [23] experimentally invalidate the threshold of C.R. < 0.1 and suggest a much higher threshold of acceptance. Out of 50 AHP participants, 5 did not report their level of inconsistency in the given questionnaire. Out of the remaining 45 participants, only 8 participants passed the widely accepted criterion of C.R. < 0.1. Chao et al. [24] indicate that inconsistency of PCM exists naturally in many sport activities, thus the ranking should depend on the existing matches in spite of the inconsistencies. Abastante et al. [25] declare that the C.R. threshold has to be suggested by the analyst depending on the complexity of the problem. Brunelli [26] emphasizes that not all the facets of pairwise comparison matrices can be fruitfully analyzed by means of randomly generated matrices. This suggests increasing the use of empirical preferences in the study of preference relations. According to Grzybowski and Starczewski [27], expert systems are designed to assist decision-makers and they are not substitutes for them. Expert systems do not have such human capabilities as feelings, responsibility or simply concern about risk. Thus the final decision about the rejection or acceptance of the PCMs should belong to the DMs.

Thus, works related to practical problem solving in all areas of economic activity use C.R. $\leq$ 0.1 to assess matrix consistency [28, 29] in spite of the results of studies on the development of AHP. It should be noted that the value C.R. $\leq$ 0.1 was derived from a study on a limited number of tangible objects. One possible way to overcome this situation is to take a new approach based on probability theory and mathematical statistics.

This paper presents a probabilistic approach for evaluating matrix consistency, which, compared to the deterministic approach, allows establishing quantitative relationships between expert and generated matrices. We used information obtained from processing 292 matrices collected between 2014 and 2020 and reflecting expert judgements. The obtained results do not confirm the need to revise expert judgements if C.R. is greater than 0.10, calls for many more example calculations for tangible objects and a search for new dependencies to estimate intangible objects based on artificial intelligence models and methods.

The rest of the paper is organised as follows. The results of designing a methodology for assessing matrix consistency are presented in Sect. 2. Section 3 provides the directions for future research.

2   Conducting a Probabilistic Assessment of Matrix Consistency

Despite considerable progress in the study and use of the analytic hierarchy process (AHP), some aspects remain under-researched. One of them is the problem of assessing the difference between generated and expert (expert-generated) matrices for tangible and intangible objects.

The choice of a particular criterion value z, equal to a certain value of the consistency ratio C.R., is of fundamental importance, as it affects the rest of the calculation procedure according to the AHP. According to Saaty [28, 29], if the calculated value of C.R. is less than or equal to z, the matrix is considered consistent; in this case, the priority vector w_i and the consistency index C.I. can be used for decision making. If C.R. $> z$, then experts must reconsider some of the judgements in the matrix.

Table 2 shows the statistical characteristics used to determine the parameters of the distribution laws chosen to approximate the C.I. samples of expert and generated matrices. The samples of the first type are a summary of the material presented in various sources (International Journal of Production Research, International Journal of Production Economics, Expert Systems with Applications, European Journal of Operational Research, Decision Support Systems, Omega, and others) and in our own research. We used information obtained from processing 292 matrices collected between 2014 and 2020 and reflecting expert judgements. Samples of the second type were generated on the basis of generated matrices of dimensions $n \times n$ [28, 29].

Table 2. Statistical characteristics and distribution law parameters for expert and generated C.I. samples.

Matrix	Type of sample	Sample size	Statistical characteristics		Distribution law	Parameters of distribution	
			$\bar{x}_i$	σ		m	b_m
3 × 3	1	76	0.050	0.037	Weibull	1.35	0.73
	2	100	0.382	0.517	Weibull	0.73	0.53
4 × 4	1	60	0.160	0.140	Weibull	1.15	0.95
	2	600	0.894	0.620	Weibull	1.45	0.91
5 × 5	1	86	0.445	0.240	Rayleigh	2.00	0.89
	2	600	1.124	0.540	Truncated normal		
6 × 6	1	57	0.561	0.405	Weibull	1.40	0.91
	2	600	1.225	0.450	Normal		
7 × 7	1	13	0.315	0.251	Weibull	1.25	0.93
	2	600	1.354	0.343	Normal		

Analysis of the statistical data in Table 2 shows that most of the distribution functions of the first and second type of samples can be approximated by the Weibull distribution [30].

$$F(x) = 1 - \exp\left[-\left(\frac{b_m \cdot x}{\bar{x}}\right)^m\right], \tag{1}$$

where m and b_m are, respectively, shape and scale parameters, and x is an argument (consistency index C.I.).

The parameters are calculated using a method of moments. One can also use tables [30] where the values m and b_m are listed depending on a coefficient of variation v. For instance, for an expert sample of the first type (3 × 3 matrix) at $v = 0.74$, we will get $m = 1.35$, $b_m = 0.73$. Then the probability of consistency at $z = 0.05$ and, consequently, C.I. = 0.026 will amount to

$$F(C.I. = 0.026) = 1 - \exp\left[-\left(\frac{0.73 \cdot 0.026}{0.050}\right)^{1.35}\right] = 0.237$$

Table 3 shows the results of the $F(C.I.)$ distribution functions calculated for the first and second type samples.

Table 3. Probabilistic assessment of expert F_1(C.I.) and generated F_2(C.I.) matrices.

Matrix	C.I.	C.R. $\leq z$	F_1(C.I.)	F_2(C.I.)	F_1(C.I.)/F_2(C.I.)
3 × 3	0.026*	0.050*	0.237	0.1500	1.58
	0.052	0.100	0.600	0.2300	2.61
	0.100	0.193	0.900	0.350	2.57
4 × 4	0.050	0.056	0.281	0.0140	20.07
	0.072*	0.080*	0.313	0.0230	13.61
	0.100	0.112	0.423	0.0350	12.09
5 × 5	0.110*	0.100*	0.070	0.0270	2.59
	0.200	0.180	0.140	0.0400	3.50
6 × 6	0.125*	0.100*	0.101	0.0052	19.42
	0.200	0.160	0.187	0.0080	23.37
7 × 7	0.135*	0.100*	0.270	0.0002	1350
	0.200	0.149	0.420	0.0004	1050

*Extreme values of C.I. for this sample

An analysis of Table 3 (excluding 7 × 7 matrices due to the small sample size of the first type) shows that.

- probability estimates F_1(C.I.) corresponding to the limit value of C.I. ranged from 0.07 (5 × 5 matrix) to 0.313 (4 × 4 matrix), i.e., more than 31% of the expert matrices are consistent;
- for the generated matrices, the F_2(C.I.) values ranged from 0.15 (3 × 3 matrix) to 0.0052 (6 × 6 matrix), i.e., almost 30 times lower;
- F_1(C.I.)/F_2(C.I.) ratio varies widely from 1.58 (3 × 3 matrix) to 19.42 (6 × 6 matrix).

A possible reason for these contradictions is that the average C.I. of the generated matrices is chosen as the random consistency index R.I., which is generated based on a uniform distribution without observing the transitivity requirements between the row and column judgements. Therefore, making the correct decision regarding the limits of C.R. $\leq$ 0.1 values based on the generated matrices requires additional verification of the tangible matrices.

Let's consider a possible approach to solving this problem by comparing the areas of five geometric figures: a circle, triangle, square, diamond, and rectangle [31]. The priority vectors calculated based on expert opinion (w_i) and actual data on the areas of geometric figures (w_{i_ST}) are shown in Table 4 [31].

We consulted three experts, the results of whose calculations are also shown in Table 4. In addition to these indicators, we calculated the average values of absolute deviations according to the formula.

$$\Delta = \frac{\sum_{i=1}^{n} |w_i - w_{i\_ST}|}{n}, \qquad (2)$$

where w_i is the value of the i-th element of the priority vector obtained by the experts (priorities from comparisons); w_{i_ST} is the value of the i-th element of the priority vector obtained from actual data on the areas of geometric figures (actual relative size).

Table 4. Results of calculations of priority vectors w_i and average values of absolute deviations Δ.

Figures	w_{i_ST}	Priority vector, w_i			
		Saaty [31], C.R. = 0.005	Expert 1, C.R. = 0.036	Expert 2, C.R. = 0.036	Expert 3, C.R. = 0.179
Circle	0.471	0.457	0.485	0.555	0.539
Triangle	0.050	0.049	0.052	0.041	0.030
Square	0.234	0.257	0.233	0.185	0.227
Diamond	0.149	0.150	0.152	0.140	0.143
Rectangle	0.096	0.087	0.078	0.079	0.061
Average deviation, Δ		0.0096	0.0076	0.034	0.027

The following conclusions can be drawn from the analysis of Table 4:

- when C.R. values are equal, the average values of absolute deviations of evaluations of the first and second experts differ by a factor of almost 4.5 ($\Delta = 0.0076$ and $\Delta = 0.034$);
- for the third expert (C.R. = 0.179), the average value of absolute deviation is $\Delta = 0.027$, which is less than the average value of the absolute deviation for the second expert ($\Delta = 0.034$), for whom C.R. = 0.036;
- the value of the absolute deviation of the estimates made by the expert [31] is $\Delta = 0.0096$, which is higher than the value for the first expert ($\Delta = 0.0076$).

To illustrate the proposed approach, let us consider a case where a manufacturing company is predicted to purchase 1,000 units of five component parts, the number of which is proportional to the actual data on the areas of geometric figures w_{i_ST} (Table 4). Given the uncertainty of demand, four experts, whose estimates are proportional to the priority vectors w_i (Table 4), were engaged to clarify the volume of purchases of each of the nomenclatures.

The results of the calculation of the discrepancies of the expert and predicted values are given in Table 5. For example, Table 5 shows that if the procurement was based on the judgement of Expert 1, the total number of shortage and surplus units would be 38 units. Taking into account the €10 penalty for each deficit or surplus unit, the additional cost to the company would be €380. The corresponding calculations for the other experts are shown in Table 5, from which it follows that the forecast variant based on the priority vector of Expert 1 (C.R. = 0.036) is the preferable option.

The paradoxical nature of these results calls for many more example calculations for tangible objects and a search for new dependencies to estimate intangible objects based on artificial intelligence models and methods.

Table 5. Evaluating the results of a product purchase decision.

Component parts	w_{i_ST}	Discrepancies between predicted and expert estimates			
		Saaty [31], C.R. = 0.005	Expert 1, C.R. = 0.036	Expert 2, C.R. = 0.036	Expert 3, C.R. = 0.179
Number 1	471	14	14	84	68
Number 2	50	1	2	9	20
Number 3	234	23	1	49	7
Number 4	149	1	3	9	6
Number 5	96	9	18	17	35
Discrepancies, in units	48	38	168	136
Discrepancies, in euros	480	380	1680	1360

3 Conclusion

A probabilistic approach for evaluating matrix consistency has been proposed, which, compared to the deterministic approach, allows establishing quantitative relationships between expert and generated matrices. Analysis of the results from processing 292 matrices shows that the probabilistic estimates of consistency indices (in the case of expert judgements) differ significantly from the probabilistic estimates of consistency indices for the generated values. For example, for 6×6 matrices, the estimates differ by a factor of 20. The results of our study do not confirm the need to revise expert judgements if C.R. is greater than 0.10.

The main directions for further research are the following:

1. The matrix generation algorithm should be refined with the introduction of artificial intelligence elements, which can be identified from the analysis of tangible object matrices.
2. Collection, systematisation, and statistical analysis of expert judgements should be continued in order to obtain representative samples of matrices. They could then be compared with artificial (generated) matrices, which would provide reliable multi-criteria estimates.

Acknowledgments. The research described in this paper is partially supported by state research 0073–2019–0004.

References

1. Ivanov, D., Sokolov, B.: Structure dynamics control approach to supply chain planning and adaptation. Int. J. Prod. Res. **50**(21), 6133–6149 (2012)
2. Dolgui, A., Ivanov, D., Sokolov, B.: Ripple effect in the supply chain: an analysis and recent literature. Int. J. Prod. Res. **56**(1–2), 414–430 (2018)
3. Felice, F.: Research and applications of AHP/ANP and MCDA for decision making in manufacturing. Int. J. Prod. Res. **50**(17), 4735–4737 (2012)
4. Csató, L.: A characterization of the logarithmic least squares method. Eur. J. Oper. Res. **276**, 212–216 (2019)
5. Sarraf, R., McGuire, M.: Integration and comparison of multi-criteria decision making methods in safe route planner. Expert Syst. Appl. **154**, 113399 (2020)
6. Singh, S., Singh, V.: Three-level AHP-based heuristic approach for a multi-objective facility layout problem. Int. J. Prod. Res. **49**(4), 1105–1125 (2011)
7. Maniya, K., Bhatt, M.: A multi-attribute selection of automated guided vehicle using the AHP/M-GRA technique. Int. J. Prod. Res. **49**(20), 6107–6124 (2011)
8. Dai, J., Blackhurst, J.: A four-phase AHP–QFD approach for supplier assessment: a sustainability perspective. Int. J. Prod. Res. **50**(19), 5474–5490 (2012)
9. Salgado, E., Salomon, V., Mello, C.: Analytic hierarchy prioritisation of new product development activities for electronics manufacturing. Int. J. Prod. Res. **50**(17), 4860–4866 (2012)
10. Azizi, M., Azizpour, M.: A BOCR structure for privatisation effective criteria of Iran newsprint paper industry. Int. J. Prod. Res. **50**(17), 4867–4876 (2012)
11. Varajão, J., Cruz-Cunha, M.: Using AHP and the IPMA competence baseline in the project managers selection process. Int. J. Prod. Res. **51**(11), 3342–3354 (2013)
12. Quezada, L., López-Ospina, H.: A method for designing a strategy map using AHP and linear programming. Int. J. Production Economics **158**, 244–255 (2014)
13. Luthra, S., Mangla, S., Xu, L., Diabat, A.: Using AHP to evaluate barriers in adopting sustainable consumption and production initiatives in a supply chain. Int. J. Prod. Econ. **181**, 342–349 (2016)
14. Vieira, J., Toso, M., Silva, J., Ribeiro, P.: An AHP-based framework for logistics operations in distribution centres. Int. J. Prod. Econ. **187**, 246–259 (2017)
15. D'Inverno, G., Carosi, L., Romano, G., Guerrini, A.: Water pollution in wastewater treatment plants: an efficiency analysis with undesirable output. Eur. J. Oper. Res. **269**, 24–34 (2018)
16. Katiyar, R., Meena, P., Barua, M., Tibrewala, R., Kumar, G.: Impact of sustainability and manufacturing practices on supply chain performance: findings from an emerging economy. Int. J. Prod. Econ. **197**, 303–316 (2018)
17. Awasthi, A., Govindan, A., Gold, S.: Multi-tier sustainable global supplier selection using a fuzzy AHP-VIKOR based approach. Int. J. Prod. Econ. **195**, 106–117 (2018)
18. Ishizaka, A., Lolli, F., Balugani, E., Cavallieri, R., Gamberini, R.: DEASort: assigning items with data envelopment analysis in ABC classes. Int. J. Prod. Econ. **199**, 7–15 (2018)
19. Vega, D., Vieira, J., Toso, E., Faria, R.: A decision on the truckload and less-than-truckload problem: an approach based on MCDA. Int. J. Prod. Econ. **195**, 132–145 (2018)
20. Mastrocinque, E., Ramírez, F., Honrubia-Escribano, A., Pham, D.: An AHP-based multi-criteria model for sustainable supply chain development in the renewable energy sector. Expert Syst. Appl. **150**, 113321 (2020)

21. Falsini, D., Fondi, F., Schiraldi, M.: A logistics provider evaluation and selection methodology based on AHP, DEA and linear programming integration. Int. J. Prod. Res. **50**(17), 4822–4829 (2012)
22. Ishizaka, A., Labib, A.: Review of the main developments in the analytic hierarchy process. Expert Syst. Appl. **38**, 14336–14345 (2011)
23. Ishizaka, A., Siraj, S.: Are multi-criteria decision-making tools useful? An experimental comparative study of three methods. Eur. J. Oper. Res. **264**, 462–471 (2018)
24. Chao, X., Kou, G., Li, T., Pen, Y.: Jie Ke versus AlphaGo: a ranking approach using decision making method for large-scale data with incomplete information. Eur. J. Oper. Res. **265**, 239–247 (2018)
25. Abastante, F., Corrente, S., Greco, S., Ishizaka, A., Lami, I.: A new parsimonious AHP methodology: Assigning priorities to many objects by comparing pairwise few reference objects. Expert Syst. Appl. **127**, 109–120 (2019)
26. Brunelli, M.: A study on the anonymity of pairwise comparisons in group decision making. Eur. J. Oper. Res. **279**, 502–510 (2019)
27. Grzybowski, A., Starczewski, T.: New look at the inconsistency analysis in the pairwise-comparisons-based prioritization problems. Expert Syst. Appl. **159**, 113549 (2020)
28. Saaty, T.: The Analytic Hierarchy Process. McGraw-Hill, New York (1980)
29. Saaty, T.: Fundamentals of Decision Making and Priority Theory with the Analytical Hierarchy Process. RWS Publications, Pittsburgh (1994)
30. Weibull, W.: Fatigue Testing and Analysis of Results. Pergamon Press, Oxford (1961)
31. Saaty, T.: Neurons the decision makers, Part I: The firing function of a single neuron. Neural Netw. **86**, 102–114 (2017)

Performance Indicators in Emergency Operating Theaters: A State of the Art

Gustavo Santamaria-Acevedo[1]([⊠]), Oualid Jouini[1], Benjamin Legros[2],
and Zied Jemai[3]

[1] Laboratoire Genie Industriel, Université Paris-Saclay, CentraleSupélec,
Gif-sur-Yvette, France
gustavo.santamaria@centralesupelec.fr

[2] Laboratoire Métis, EM Normandie, 64 Rue du Ranelagh, 75016 Paris, France

[3] LR-OASIS, National Engineering School of Tunis, University of Tunis El Manar,
Tunis, Tunisia

Abstract. This article aims to provide a review and classification of the current state of the art on the performance metrics used for the operations management in emergency operating theaters. We have classified the metrics into two categories. The first category consists of hospital-centered metrics. They are performance measures that are of interest to the hospital due to their possible impact on the institution's productivity or revenue. The second category consists of patient centered metrics. These metrics take explicitly into consideration the patients' experiences and which have a direct impact on the patients' safety and satisfaction. Having a comprehensive set of performance indicators used in Emergency Operating Theaters will allow surgery chiefs and hospital managers to implement missing indicators and to identify previously unknown quality issues, bottlenecks, and areas for improvement.

Keywords: Non-elective surgeries · Operating rooms · Operations management · Key performance indicators

1 Introduction

Non-elective surgeries, also called informally emergency surgeries, are those that require a fast and punctual evaluation, as well as a very fast intervention, in order to save the patient's life or to avoid negative consequences on the patient's well-being. Non-elective surgical patients can be classified in either trauma patients or non-traumatized surgical patients. The former, are those who have been involved in events in which they have sustained life threatening wounds and injuries that require immediate surgery due to blood loss and damaged organs (e.g. patients involved in car accidents). Non-traumatized emergency surgical patients are those who have not sustained life threatening injuries but who have acute symptoms of a usually short duration disease, and who require surgery in

© IFIP International Federation for Information Processing 2021
Published by Springer Nature Switzerland AG 2021
A. Dolgui et al. (Eds.): APMS 2021, IFIP AICT 634, pp. 486–495, 2021.
https://doi.org/10.1007/978-3-030-85914-5_52

a matter of hours (e.g. patients with gastrointestinal bleeding, or appendicitis) [7,16]. Operating Theaters (OT) that handle non-elective surgeries are complex to manage and to analyze due to the difficulties in predicting the stochastic behavior of the different variables under analysis. While in an elective OT the amount of patients is known beforehand, and their arrivals are deterministic because they are scheduled weeks or even months ahead, the demand in Emergency Operating Theaters (EOT) may prove very difficult to predict, not only in the amount of patients, but also in terms of their time of arrival and the severity of their trauma or condition. This leads to complex problems in terms of assignation and synchronization of the already scarce physical and human resources of the OT, since it is possible that multiple emergency surgery patients arrive within a short time window, generating major challenges for the OT managers. Besides the demand, also the length of stay (LOS) and surgery duration of non-elective patients is much harder to predict, and the methods used to make these predictions in elective cases, do not usually work properly in non-elective surgeries [24].

Although there is a considerable amount of research on the management of operating theaters, most of the literature on the field refers to elective surgeries, and only a small percentage deals with non-elective patients. Cardoen et al. [5] review the literature on operating room planning and scheduling, and distinguish between the literature related to the problem setting or the technical features of the problem, already mentioning that the literature on elective surgeries "is rather vast when compared to the non-elective counterpart". Guerriero and Guido [13] analyze a broader scope of literature on operations research applied to the OTs, and in many cases they found that these approaches either do not consider non-elective surgery at all, or that when they do, they make a considerable amount of assumptions. In fact, they found that only 29% of the papers they reviewed consider any stochasticity. To the best of our knowledge, the only literature review that focuses mostly on non-elective surgeries is the one by [25] who focus specially on the different policies that an OT can use to schedule non-elective patients (dedicated, shared, and hybrid policies), and the trade-offs that occur when adopting one of them over another. Among these trade-offs are the differences in overtime, utilization and waiting times for both elective and non-elective patients.

The primary research question to be explored in this state of the art is to identify which are the key performance indicators in the field of non-elective surgery management. Some performance metrics used in non-elective operating theaters are similar to the ones used in operating theaters that handle exclusively elective patients, but there are several indicators that are more specific of non-elective operating theaters. Among these are the amount of cancelled surgeries, which is an indicator usually used in shared operating theaters; the proportion of patients operated within their maximum time to surgery threshold; the waiting time to surgery, etc. The second question that we address is if the surgery theater policy (dedicated, hybrid, or flexible) influences the performance metrics that are used by the hospital to track its emergency operating theater. The performance metrics of operating theaters can be classified into two categories: hospital-centered indicators and patient-centered indicators. The first category refers to indicators that are not relative to the patient's experience in the hospital, and will be presented in Sect. 2, while the latter refers to the metrics that specifically consider the patients' experience in the hospital and are described in Sect. 3.

To identify the literature that is analyzed in this review we have used the databases *Web of Knowledge*, *Science Direct*, and *Pubmed* to search for articles in fields such as operations research, management science, industrial engineering, applied mathematics, and health care services. Search terms such as non-elective surgery, emergency surgery, emergency operating room, emergency operating theater, urgent surgery, non-elective surgery scheduling, non-elective surgery planning, emergency surgery scheduling, non-elective surgery prediction and non-elective patients prediction. The initial search led to a total of 1836 articles. The abstracts of these 1836 articles were read, which reduced the list of possible articles to 278. These 278 articles were read in detail, and of them 117 were kept. Furthermore, the references in some of the initial articles were included, which led to a total of 139 manuscripts. These were subsequently divided into categories according to the topics that they discuss, and in this case we specifically focused on the ones that used some form of performance metrics, which led to the 26 articles that are referenced in this review.

2   Hospital Centered Metrics

Hospital-centered metrics are those performance measures that are of interest to the hospital due to their possible impact on the institution's productivity or revenue. The hospital-centered measures described by [23] are the throughput (number of surgical cases per time unit), the waiting time of surgeons, the overtime costs, and the makespan. Additionally, some other authors use indicators such as the total completion time, the overtime (in terms of time and not of cost), the number of beds, and the idle time for staff or operating rooms [5,9,14]. In what follows, we describe the most used metrics.

2.1   Operating Room Utilization

The capacity utilization, defined by [23] as the proportion of time spent by the surgery patients in the operating room (OR), compared to the total available OR time, is one of the most commonly used to make managerial decisions regarding the operating rooms. This indicator is used by anesthesiologists and surgery chiefs to determine if the operating theater has space and time for additional patients or if they are close to saturation point, and provides healthcare managers with a glance of how effectively the resources of the hospital are being used. Although intuitively it would be expected to consider a high utilization as desirable, in fact this depends on the OT goals and its different stakeholders, since having a very high utilization may lead to saturation of the OT and hence dangerously high waiting times for emergency surgery patients, and also may lead to staff dissatisfaction.

Anognini et al. [1] analyzed how the amount of operating rooms in the operating theater impacts their utilization rate, in order to recommend a hospital what should be the number of operating rooms open at the daytime and nighttime shifts. Sometimes, the utilization indicator is used to decide about the hospital's strategy on managing non-elective patients. For example, [11] measure the utilization of each operating room during the shifts and use it to compare the results between a flexible and a dedicated policy. By measuring the utilization rate of the ORs in both policies they identified that the dedicated policy generates a larger imbalance across the different rooms, because the utilization of the Dedicated Emergency ORs is lower compared to the elective ORs. Koppka et al. [17] measure the vacancy and time of occupancy for each OR, in order to obtain the utilization and the effective usage of the operating rooms, so they can balance the occupancy of the different operating rooms and avoid having an over-utilization of a specific one. Jittamai and Kangwansura [15] set targets for the OR utilization in order to avoid over-utilization and the subsequent overtimes that this generates. Their target utilization for the operating theater totalized 76 h per day with 6 operating rooms, hence an average of 12 h per OR per day. This means, that the target utilization was 50%, and any OR that surpassed this figure may be generating undesired overtimes and longer waiting times.

2.2   Bed Occupancy

Besides the elements directly involved in the surgical procedures, it is quite important to take into consideration that an operating theater is also composed by the stages before and after the surgical procedure. Hence, additional to the capacity in terms of OR's and their staff, it is very important to consider elements downstream, such as the recovery beds in Post Anesthesia Care Units (PACU) or in the ICU.

Bahou et al. [2] have an indicator that keeps track of the total amount of beds available at the moment, as well as in the wards and in each one of 3 recovery units: the ICU-1 for elective patients with complications, the ICU-2 for emergency patients, and an intermediate recovery unit, that they call HDU (High Dependency Unit). To test the reliability of their solution, they keep track of the maximum amount of patients in recovery beds, in order to analyze how the reduction in the availability of recovery beds affects the amount of cancellations. Combining the tracking of this indicator with a sensitivity analysis, they started to move beds from one section to other, and were able to identify that the HDU was a bottleneck for the operating theater, and that the amount of beds in the wards could be reduced and these beds put in the HDU. Van den Broek et al. [4] also measure the bed occupancy at downstream resources, in order to minimize the variability in the bed occupancy levels. By doing this they can make more accurate predictions of the bed occupancy levels, and hence reduce the waiting times for surgery patients, as well as reducing their average LOS in the post surgical process. Kortbeek et al. [18] also measure the bed occupancy, as well as the maximum and minimum occupancy rates per cycle in order to identify the peaks in demand and be able to balance it and allow a more efficient use of available staff and beds. Having a lower variability in the bed occupancy usually makes the probability of rejecting the patient's admission to go down.

2.3   Overtime

In a surgical environment, overtime may refer to the additional hours after the end of the staff's shift that are required to finish either the surgeries of elective patients that were originally scheduled for a time-frame during the shift and that were postponed because of the inclusion of an emergency patient, or the additional hours after the shift's end that were dedicate to operate an emergency patient that arrived close to the end of the shift.

Overtime is considered a very important performance measure by [11], since the operating theater in their study is supposed to have 8-h shifts, and any time spent by a patient after the end of a shift is considered overtime for the staff. Besides the time itself, they also measure the amount of patients who were still in the system after a shift finishes, since a high number of patients in overtime may be the sign of a systematic failure of the OT, while a reduced amount of patients causing the overtime may be a sign of a schedule going wrong in a specific OR. [20] measure the overtime to compare the performance of their methods in different scenarios, and is one of the key constraints in their model since the hospital has a limited overtime capacity. In [17] the overtime indicator serves the purpose of calculating what they have called *perfect day*, the days in which no overtime occurs in any of the OR's in the operating theater, while treating all surgery patients, both emergency and elective; hence, they calculate the sum of overtime in all the rooms both per day and per month.

2.4   Throughput

Another relevant performance measure for a operating theater is the throughput. This indicator, which is the rate at which patients go through the surgical process per unit of time, is usually measured in patients per day and also patients per year. [19] studied a flexible operating theater in Denmark that handles both emergency and elective patients. Because of the potential impacts that the inclusion of non-elective patients has on their schedule, they need to keep track of the amount of non-elective patients operated per day. The hospital described in [17] usually uses a flexible strategy as well, therefore they have to take into consideration the number of emergency surgeries per week that they handle in order to properly represent the hospital's demand. Additionally, this indicator is useful for the hospital, because on given days, if the throughput of non-elective patients is high and the number of emergency patients is not very high, the hospital will change to a dedicated policy, assigning one of their eight operating rooms to non-elective patients.

3   Patient Centered Indicators

Patient centered metrics are defined by [23] as those that take explicitly into consideration the patients' experiences and which have a direct impact on the patients' safety and satisfaction. They identified two main surgical patient-centered performance measures: the waiting time for patients, which refers to the time spent by the patients before the start of their surgery; and in the case of operating theaters that follow a flexible policy, the amount of cancellations of elective surgeries generated by the inclusion of non-elective patients. A third indicator that affects directly the patient, the LOS, is also described in this section.

3.1   Expected Waiting Time for Surgery

In non-elective patients the waiting time for surgery is the time that passes between the patient's booking for surgery and the moment the patient enters to the OR. The waiting time can be interpreted as the length of stay on a surgery waiting list [5]. Because an extended wait can severely affect the patient's health, and may lead to permanent negative health effects and possibly death, the waiting time for surgery is a very critical indicator when managing non-elective surgery patients.

Because having short waiting times is so important for emergency surgery patients, hospitals and OT managers keep track of this metric in order to determine if patients are being operated within a safe timing, and in case they perceive the waiting times are too long, if they can be minimized and at what cost. For example, the hospital analyzed by [1] kept track of the waiting times to surgery of the emergency surgery patients and considered them to be too long. Hence, they wanted to determine how adding more dedicated operating rooms reduces the amount of time that patients wait, in order to find a good balance between surgical outcomes and investments. Van Essen et al. [10] use this indicator to perform the same analysis, since they want to determine the effect that having additional ORs for emergency surgery has on the waiting time.

For [6] the waiting time until the start of surgery is critical because they classify the patients into emergent and urgent, where urgent patients are considered as those that can be postponed for up to 48 h. Therefore, the hospital has to carefully track this indicator in order to ensure that urgent patients get care in a reasonable time. Additionally, by tracking this performance measure they were able to detect that the BIM's of the hospital were unevenly distributed to an extent in which they were increasing the waiting time for emergency surgery unnecessarily and increasing the risk of complications and even death of the patient.

3.2   Length of Stay

Keeping track of how long a patient stays in the hospital and in specific wards is very important for the patient because this indicator is usually related with the outcome of the surgery, and for the hospital because it is a good measurement of efficiency and quality of healthcare. An important element that characterizes the stochastic behavior of non-elective surgeries is that the LOS in the hospital is much more unpredictable than in the case of elective patients. The LOS, defined as the number of days that a patient spends in a hospital, is counted as the difference in days between the date the patient was discharged from the hospital, and the day they were admitted. Therefore, ambulatory cases are usually excluded from this measurement [21, 22]. Additionally, some hospitals measure the time spent by the patient in each of the services, and refer to this as the LOS in a specific ward.

Even though the LOS in the hospital is unique for each and every patient, in the case of elective patients the LOS is easier to predict because the probability of something unexpected happening with the patient's outcome and recovery is considerably smaller. In the case of non-elective patients, the predicted LOS and release date can be quite different from the actual one, due to unexpected complications in the outcomes of the surgeries, problems in the recovery of the patient, or the need of additional surgical procedures. Most of the articles that measure the LOS of patients, focus on an specific ward or part of the surgical patient flow.

3.3   Cancellations

When a hospital uses a non-dedicated policy to handle non-elective cases, there is the risk of having a higher amount of cancellations and higher levels of overtime. This happens because in a non-dedicated operating theater, non-elective surgeries have to be scheduled with priority over previously scheduled elective surgeries. Therefore, the operating theater faces the risk of having schedule disruptions generated by the arrival of non-elective patients, and it is important for the hospital to know how this phenomenon occurs in order to prepare better for the arrival of emergency patients in the future.

The amount of cancellations generated by the inclusion of emergency surgeries into an elective surgery schedule is considered in several articles. [3] consider the amount of cancellations generated by the inclusion of non-elective patients as one of the indicators to evaluate the performance of a flexible operating theater, [8] also take it into consideration and mention how it can affect the bed utilization. [6] is another article that takes into consideration the cancellations of elective patients as a performance indicator, while [2] and [12] analyze the effect that an increase in demand for emergency surgeries has in the cancellation levels of elective patients in cases in which the operating theater is mixed.

The main objective in [2] while studying a hospital in Western Scotland was to reduce the cancellation rate because achieving this goal could defer the construction of additional facilities which would be extremely expensive. Therefore, they measured the amount of cancellations and how they were distributed throughout the week, in order to be able to identify which were the causes of the scheduling problems. By diverting certain patient specialties to certain days, they were able to flatten the cancellation variability as well as reducing the total amount of cancellations. In [26] one of the performance criteria that was considered to determine the performance of an OR scheduling process was the patient cancellations. Because cancelling a surgery generates a negative impact in the schedule of a operating theater, the cancellation of a surgery is in fact penalized in their optimization model.

4   Conclusions

This paper reviews the most important key performance indicators used for the management of non-elective surgery theaters. It would be interesting to review and classify existing literature in terms of operations research tools and quantitative methodologies used for the optimization and operations management of emergency surgery theaters.

The results of this state of the art reveal that not all the hospitals that perform non-elective surgeries use a broad set of performance indicators, and that there is a considerable potential for improvement both from a hospital-centered and a patient-centered perspective. By implementing a full set of performance indicators, hospitals will be able their performance when treating non-elective surgical patients during their flow throughout the different wards and operating theaters. Additionally, tracking a full set of relevant indicators at the same time instead of a few selected ones, can help hospital managers and practitioners to detect the possible bottlenecks in the patient flows, as well as to identify quality issues in the delivery of the different services. Finally, a careful tracking of performance indicators such as surgery cancellations and the overtime, can be very important in hospitals that follow a shared policy, since they can support hospital managers in decision making processes regarding a change of policy or the opening of additional operating rooms.

The management of non-elective surgeries has proven to be a considerably complex task with several issues. The origin of several of these issues is related with the lack of a standard definition of what a non-elective patient is, and which are their severity or acuteness levels. Therefore, one of the main recommendations of the authors would be to implement a framework such as the TACS proposed by [16], which standardizes how non-elective surgical patients are classified and subsequently scheduled. This would facilitate both internal processes, as well as make it easier for hospitals to refer patients to other institutions, and ensure that patients are getting an adequate treatment with the adequate priority regardless of the hospital where they are being operated.

References

1. Antognini, J., Antognini, J., Khatri, V.: How many operating rooms are needed to manage non-elective surgical cases? a Monte Carlo simulation study. BMC Health Serv. Res. **15**(1), 1–9 (2015)
2. Bahou, N., Fenwick, C., Anderson, G., van der Meer, R., Vassalos, T.: Modeling the critical care pathway for cardiothoracic surgery. Health Care Manage. Sci. **21**(2), 192–203 (2017). https://doi.org/10.1007/s10729-017-9401-y

3. Bovim, T., Christiansen, M., Gullhav, A., Range, T., Hellemo, L.: Stochastic master surgery scheduling. Eur. J. Oper. Res. **285**(2), 695–711 (2020)
4. van den Broek d'Obrenan, A., Ridder, A., Roubos, D., Stougie, L.: Minimizing bed occupancy variance by scheduling patients under uncertainty. Eur. J. Oper. Res. **286**, 336–349 (2020)
5. Cardoen, B., Demeulemeester, E., Beliën, J.: Operating room planning and scheduling: a literature review. Eur. J. Oper. Res. **201**(3), 921–932 (2010)
6. Clavel, D., Xie, X., Mahulea, C., Silva, M.: A three steps approach for surgery planning of elective and urgent patients. IFAC-PapersOnLine **51**(7), 243–250 (2018)
7. Columbus, A., et al.: Critical differences between elective and emergency surgery: identifying domains for quality improvement in emergency general surgery. Surgery **163**(4), 832–838 (2018)
8. Duma, D., Aringhieri, R.: An online optimization approach for the real time management of operating rooms. Oper. Res. Health Care **7**, 40–51 (2015)
9. Erdem, E., Qu, X., Shi, J.: Rescheduling of elective patients upon the arrival of emergency patients. Decis. Support Syst. **54**(1), 551–563 (2012)
10. van Essen, J., Hans, E., Hurink, J., Oversberg, A.: Minimizing the waiting time for emergency surgery. Oper. Res. Health Care **1**(2–3), 34–44 (2012)
11. Ferrand, Y., Magazine, M., Rao, U.: Comparing two operating-room-allocation policies for elective and emergency surgeries. In: Proceedings - Winter Simulation Conference, pp. 2364–2374 (2010)
12. Ghasemkhani, A., Tavakkoli-Moghaddam, R., Hamid, M., Mahmoodjanloo, M.: An improvement in master surgical scheduling using artificial neural network and fuzzy programming approach. In: Lalic, B., Majstorovic, V., Marjanovic, U., von Cieminski, G., Romero, D. (eds.) APMS 2020. IAICT, vol. 592, pp. 254–262. Springer, Cham (2020). https://doi.org/10.1007/978-3-030-57997-5_30
13. Guerriero, F., Guido, R.: Operational research in the management of the operating theatre: a survey. Health Care Manage. Sci. **14**(1), 89–114 (2011)
14. Jebali, A., Hadj Alouane, A., Ladet, P.: Operating rooms scheduling. Int. J. Prod. Econ. **99**(1–2), 52–62 (2006)
15. Jittamai, P., Kangwansura, T.: A hospital admission planning model for operating room allocation under uncertain demand requirements. Int. J. Serv. Oper. Manage. **23**(2), 235–256 (2016)
16. Kluger, Y., et al.: World society of emergency surgery study group initiative on timing of acute care surgery classification (TACS). World J. Emerg. Surg. **8**(1), 1–6 (2013)
17. Koppka, L., Wiesche, L., Schacht, M., Werners, B.: Optimal distribution of operating hours over operating rooms using probabilities. Eur. J. Oper. Res. **267**(3), 1156–1171 (2018)
18. Kortbeek, N., Braaksma, A., Smeenk, F., Bakker, P., Boucherie, R.: Integral resource capacity planning for inpatient care services based on bed census predictions by hour. J. Oper. Res. Soc. **66**(7), 1061–1076 (2015)
19. Kroer, L., Foverskov, K., Vilhelmsen, C., Hansen, A., Larsen, J.: Planning and scheduling operating rooms for elective and emergency surgeries with uncertain duration. Oper. Res. Health Care **19**, 107–119 (2018)
20. Lamiri, M., Xie, X., Zhang, S.: Column generation approach to operating theater planning with elective and emergency patients. IIE Trans. (Inst. Ind. Eng.) **40**(9), 838–852 (2008)
21. NHS, N.H.S.U.K.: Average time spent in hospital (2020). https://www.nhs.uk/Scorecard/Pages/IndicatorFacts.aspx?MetricId=4&OrgType=Hospital

22. OECD: Lenght of hospital stay (2020). https://data.oecd.org/healthcare/length-of-hospital-stay.htm
23. Oh, H., Phua, T., Tong, S., Lim, J.: Assessing the performance of operating rooms: what to measure and why? Proc. Singap. Healthc. **20**(2), 105–109 (2011)
24. Stocker, B., Weiss, H., Weingarten, N., Engelhardt, K., Engoren, M., Posluszny, J.: Predicting length of stay for trauma and emergency general surgery patients. Am. J. Surg. **220**, 757–764 (2020)
25. Van Riet, C., Demeulemeester, E.: Trade-offs in operating room planning for electives and emergencies: a review. Oper. Res. Health Care **7**, 52–69 (2015)
26. Vandenberghe, M., Vuyst, S.D., Aghezzaf, E., Bruneel, H.: Stochastic surgery selection and sequencing under dynamic emergency break-ins. J. Oper. Res. Soc. **72**, 1309–1329 (2020)

Energy Transparency in Compound Feed Production

M. T. Alvela Nieto$^{(\boxtimes)}$ ⓘ, E. G. Nabati ⓘ, and K.-D. Thoben ⓘ

Faculty of Production Engineering, BIK-Institute for Integrated
Product Development, University of Bremen, 28359 Bremen, Germany
malvela@uni-bremen.de

Abstract. The finite nature of energy resources forces animal feed producers to minimize their energy consumption. As a first step towards energy conservation, more transparency over the energy usage in compound feed plants is required. However, current feed processing strategies do not consider the high dynamics in products and process conditions, nor do they augment the operator's energy awareness. Digital support tools, such as virtual and augmented reality, can close the gap between required information (e.g., actual operating conditions) and knowledge of operators. In this paper, first, a methodology for making energy values transparent is presented. Then the state of the art of digital tools and related requirements are discussed, followed by a description of the integration of a digital tool in a case study of a compound feed plant located in northern Germany.

Keywords: Energy · Animal feed · Digital tools

1 Introduction

The production of animal feed is associated with high dynamics and energy-intensive processes [2,13]. Total feed production volumes are projected to expand substantially through 2050 to meet the needs of a growing and increasingly affluent population [6,13]. Given the limited existence of energy resources along with the Co2-reduction plans, the implications for animal feed production merit closer consideration [6]. Yet, most animal feed producers produce on customers' demands and in small batch sizes, making energy protocols challenging. Electricity bills, on the other side, do not disclose how much energy on which product is mainly spent. Today, energy consumption in animal feed production is poorly explored, and energy conservation is still considered as a secondary effect with no specific urgency [12].

The traditionally hidden nature of energy has been observed as one barrier to energy awareness, and making energy information accessible is suggested to empower energy savings [5,9]. Indeed, transparency of the energy usage of a process for creating the desired product (i.e., animal feed) lays the foundation for

© IFIP International Federation for Information Processing 2021
Published by Springer Nature Switzerland AG 2021
A. Dolgui et al. (Eds.): APMS 2021, IFIP AICT 634, pp. 496–503, 2021.
https://doi.org/10.1007/978-3-030-85914-5_53

energy savings [9]. Many suppliers of energy metering equipment may provide some visual solutions. Yet, their software systems do not address the visibility problem in an ideal way. Usually, the software is cost-intensive, which enlarges the restraint of feed producers to invest in such a system. Furthermore, this software mainly incorporates standards and basic guidelines (e.g., ISO 50001), as well as it mainly analyses the energy consumption of a plant with an emphasis on the technical aspect. In particular, a feed processing plant of northern Germany has limited process-specific solutions for assisting operative decisions across changing products and operator skills. At the moment, there is a lack of a support tool based on process data that does not intervene in the ongoing operations but provides appropriate (visual) feedback of the consumed energy of a process from a controlling perspective.

Digital support tools have the potential to make energy consumption visible. Then an operator gains a deeper understanding of the process, and related energy usage [5,9]. When it comes to running operations, a digital tool can also help with operator engagement and memory retention, as well as boosting energy awareness [9]. In the following sections, this paper compiles a methodology for energy transparency in feed processing and includes the state of the art of digital support solutions and related requirements. Then, for a case study of an animal feed producer in northern Germany, the deployment of a digital tool is described.

2   Methodology to Energy Transparency in Compound Feed Production

Metering energy values in a systematic, regular and repetitive way, one speaks of energy monitoring. If the gained energy data are being augmented with output values, e.g., consumption per product produced, and this key figure is used in a controlling way, which represents a tool for generating transparency, energy improvements can be supported [7]. The controlling scope within the field of energy involves, according to [5,7], (1) generation of energetic information related to a process, (2) processing of energy information via controlling instruments within the process, (3) provision of energy information in a comprehensible form to the process operators. Further, two fundamental ways of measuring energy consumption with the above controlling scope can be noted [7]:

- Top-down: Measuring the overall energy consumption (i.e., for a production site by the energy supplier) and subsequent derivation of information for the causative processes.
- Bottom-up: Metering every single consumer along with the derivation of information.

Because of higher and lower energy consumers and the high dynamics of the process conditions in feed processing, the bottom-up approach allows this study more flexibility, agility and consistency. Process parameters are conceived as controlling instruments inside a process, then the bottom-up approach (see

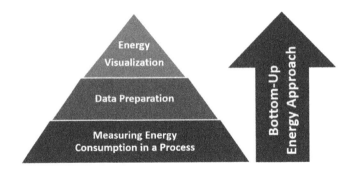

Fig. 1. Proposed approach to energy transparency in compound feed production

Fig. 1) evaluates the consumption of each process in feed production. A foundation of energy controlling in terms of improvements is energy monitoring. Hence, a systematic and regular capture of all relevant energy data of a process is required. Then data preparation is performed for the evaluation of the energy consumption. In this approach, data preparation basically means the generation of comparability and detailed information. The expressiveness and transparency of measured values can be raised by generating appropriate key indicators by associating energy values with the process outputs (product). The use of the specific energy consumption, as the energy consumption per tone of the product, builds a key indicator to the energy. Further, energy figures and resulting information are documented, such that new criteria or targets towards energy strategies can be better and faster understood and reconfigured.

Following the development of energy key figures, a detailed contemplation of the energy values of a product to the control parameters of the process and product specifications is required. Due to the several parameters affecting the energy, visualization instruments must be deployed in order to master the complexity. Energy-saving potentials can be revealed with the help of digital (visual) instruments. Better insights into the operating conditions and related consumed energy, as well as quality standards, enables fine-tuning process configurations without compromising the product quality. Then a fine-tune of process settings is an opportunity for energy savings.

3   Digital Support Tools

3.1   State of the Art

Visualizations like 3D models of equipment, visual representations of key performance indicators, and simulations are some of the possibilities that digital support tools can provide for energy transparency [11]. Using virtual reality (VR) with the aim of visualizing energy-related data, key figures, and energy flows are the most practical applications shown by [11]. As an example, some studies visualize key figures of a hydraulic pump through VR or investigate the energy analytic using VR within the context of digital twins [1].

Visualization methods of process data assisting operator decisions by augmented reality (AR) technology are studied in [8]. As a detailed analysis of data as well as the complexity of technical systems may pose great challenges to workforces, [8] presents different visualization approaches that show context-related information through AR. Some authors in the energy efficiency of buildings investigate visualizations for illustrating energy values. [10] studies visual representations in the form of AR for educating school students about energy consumption. The availability of actual measurements, such as energy usage, indoor and outdoor luminosity or temperature, facilitates the realization of energy-related strategies, as it engages users to save energy [10].

3.2   Requirements of Digital Support Tools for Energy Transparency

Against the existing challenges to energy conservation in feed processing plants, the following requirements for making the consumed energy more transparent and valuable should be considered:

Availability of Data. Data of the process and related consumed energy need to be gathered through sensors, and interfaces to data collections and digital tools must be implemented.

Mitigation of Process Complexity. This paper suggests, first, the creation of energy indicators, linking them to relevant parameters affecting energy values, i.e., tons of product order. Second, other relevant parameters to energy usage, such as process conditions and product specifications, are well-known.

Easy to Use and Mobile. Workforces have to carry the tool easily. The tool should be ergonomic and have enough battery provision. Furthermore, the visualization should be user-friendly, simple to understand, and reachable without much setup.

4   Case Study

A compound feed plant refines agricultural raw materials such as corn, wheat, and soy. Feed mixtures can be up to 50 different components; also, vitamins and enzymes are added [3]. Only in Germany, the total amount of animal feed to be produced is about 23,1 million tons per year: 9.8 million tons for pigs, 6,9 million tons for cattle, and 6.4 million for broilers [4].

The entire feed production line of an animal feed producer was examined concerning energy demands. The compacting (pelleting) process showed the highest share in electrical and thermal energy consumption. Mainly, pelleting combined with short-term conditioning contains high energy values; about 60% of the total energy demand in the plant is used for pelleting. Further, 80% of the products are compacted, as pelleting generates an improved animal digestion performance.

Fig. 2. Pellets after compaction in a press machine (Source: DVT, p.2)

Conditioning is a process of converting mixed mash with heat, water, pressure, and time, to a physical state that is more suitable for compaction. Moreover, the integrated thermal process modifies starch content and improves tastiness. By adding steam, the moisture of mixed mash increases. Because of the gaseous state of the steam, the moisture is homogeneously dispersed in the mixture. Moreover, the steam condenses uniformly on the particle surfaces and provides better lubrication of the pellet, reducing the wear and increasing the production rate. Applying too much heat or water has a negative effect on the quality of the pellet and may lead to the plugging of the press die. In Fig. 2, the feed mixture goes through a die with specific dimensions, openings, and thickness for producing desired pellets as compact cylinders.

4.1   Results and Discussion

The process-related data for the case study of a north Germany's feed producer were already available in electronic form. The data were extensive, including parameter values, energy usage, feed formulations, and quality requirements. First results show that the compound feed has a mean order of about 16 tones of product to be pelleted. Mainly, the energy consumption of pelleting varies from 10 to 15 kWh per tone of pellets. Mostly this consumption is about steam generation, compaction, and subsequent cooling.

   The pelleting process is currently manually operated. Depending on the quality specifications, the parameters of the pelleting process are tuned by hand on the basis of operators' experience. Too much energy is generally consumed with this method of intuition and experience, as operators only control what they can see through their eyes, which is the product quality. Then operators are not aware of the effects of the process settings on the energy consumption, nor can they make critical decisions to conserve energy.

   Figure 3 presents the implemented AR-based digital solution for the particular case study of pelleting. The model of the press machine was built with computer-aided designed software. The main components, such as motors, conditioner, dies, etc., are recreated. The digital tool can be overlaid on the press

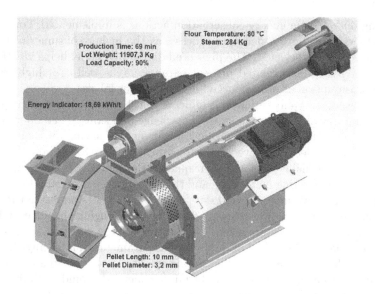

Fig. 3. Digital support tool for a pelleting process

machine for showing actual parameter values of the process (e.g., temperature and steam). As the quality specifications guide the process, a provision of product characteristics, such as lot weight, length, and diameter of the pellets, are displayed in the AR solution. Further information as color energy labels (green, yellow, and red) add insights into the energy performances of each process activity - as conditioning and compacting- by, for instance, comparing actual to mean energy values or energy target values. Values of the pelleting process can be read from a database and visualized into the solution using interfaces. In the plant, the disposal of mobile devices (tablets, smartphones, or glasses) makes it possible to interact and provide visual feedback of the process conditions.

The definition and inclusion of energy figures and process characteristic data in visual form engage operators in interpreting the energy usage (in KWh) per product produced (in ton). As a result, the hidden impacts of manual settings on energy consumption become more visible and reveal energy-saving potentials. Then operators gain a better understanding of the process condition and its correlation to the consumed energy, as they can compare values between orders and quality characteristics using visual information (data). The operating parameters can thus be fine-tuned for energy conservation without affecting the pellet quality.

5   Conclusions

This paper presents an approach for gaining more visibility and control of energy consumption in animal feed production. Then a novel digital support tool for engaging operators in energy-conservation actions is implemented. For the process data visualization, a pelleting process, as the higher consumer of the feed processing plant, is selected. The presented digital 3D model helps identify critical energy figures and related process parameters, as well as it highlights the energy consumption of process activities using color labels.

First discussions and evaluations indicate that the provision of actual process information (data) increases operator knowledge and skills. Then operators can better fine-tune the operating parameters for energy savings without altering the quality of the feed. However, the deployment of the AR solution can only be as good as the available data and their quality. Particularly for older equipment, reading and interpreting meter data and their metrics requires expert knowledge. In addition, massive unstructured data, e.g., product attributes, can make the selection and consistency of relevant data very challenging since feed mixtures have a wide range of components. Further research is required to investigate better the relationships of additional relevant parameters influencing the energy usage in pelleting, such as the fluctuating quality of the raw materials. As an alternative to energy indicators, data-mining methods could optimize and/or forecast process values for energy savings.

Acknowledgments. The authors would like to thank the Federal Ministry for Economic Affairs and Energy (BMWi) and the Project Management Juelich (PtJ) for funding the projects "AI-supported platform for the assistance of production control for improving energy efficiency" - KIPro (funding code 03ET1265A) and "Increasing energy efficiency in production through digitization and AI" - ecoKI (funding code 03EN2047A).

References

1. Abdallah, A., Primas, M., Turcin, I., Traussnigg, U.: The potential of game development platforms for digital twins and virtual labs. In: Lalic, B., Majstorovic, V., Marjanovic, U., von Cieminski, G., Romero, D. (eds.) APMS 2020. IAICT, vol. 592, pp. 117–121. Springer, Cham (2020). https://doi.org/10.1007/978-3-030-57997-5_14
2. Alvela Nieto, M.T., Nabati, E.G., Bode, D., Redecker, M.A., Decker, A., Thoben, K.-D.: Enabling energy efficiency in manufacturing environments through deep learning approaches: lessons learned. In: Ameri, F., Stecke, K.E., von Cieminski, G., Kiritsis, D. (eds.) APMS 2019. IAICT, vol. 567, pp. 567–574. Springer, Cham (2019). https://doi.org/10.1007/978-3-030-29996-5_65
3. DV-Tiernahrung (DVT): Pelletieren von mischutter, p. 2 (2010). https://www.dvtiernahrung.de/fileadmin/redaktion/redaktion/Aktuelles/2009/Einladung_Pelletieren_2010.pdf
4. DV-Tiernahrung (DVT): Mischfutterproduktion 2020: Gutes ergebnis trotz steigender herausforderungen (2020). https://www.dvtiernahrung.de/aktuelles-detail/mischfutterproduktion-2020-gutes-ergebnis-trotz-steigender-herausforderungen
5. Grahl, A., Grohne, C., Ladiges, K., Peters, S. (eds.): Handbuch für betriebliches Energiemanagement: Systematisch Energiekosten senken. Deutsche Energie-Agentur, Berlin, stand: 12/2014 edn. (2014)

6. Haberl, H., et al.: Global bioenergy potentials from agricultural land in 2050: sensitivity to climate change, diets and yields. Biomass Bioenergy **35**(12), 4753–4769 (2011). https://doi.org/10.1016/j.biombioe.2011.04.035

7. Hesselbach, J.: Energie- und klimaeffiziente Produktion: Grundlagen, Leitlinien und Praxisbeispiele (2012)

8. Kalkofen, D., Sandor, C., White, S., Schmalstieg, D.: Visualization techniques for augmented reality. In: Furht, B. (ed.) Handbook of Augmented Reality, pp. 65–98. Springer, New York (2011). https://doi.org/10.1007/978-1-4614-0064-6_3

9. Karlin, B., Zinger, J.F., Ford, R.: The effects of feedback on energy conservation: a meta-analysis. Psychol. Bull. **6**, 1205–1227 (2015). https://doi.org/10.1037/a0039650

10. Mylonas, G., Triantafyllis, C., Amaxilatis, D.: An augmented reality prototype for supporting IoT-based educational activities for energy-efficient school buildings. Electron. Notes Theor. Comput. Sci. **343**, 89–101 (2019). https://doi.org/10.1016/j.entcs.2019.04.012

11. G. Nabati, E., Alvela Nieto, M.T., Decker, A., Thoben, K.-D.: Application of virtual reality technologies for achieving energy efficient manufacturing: literature analysis and findings. In: Lalic, B., Majstorovic, V., Marjanovic, U., von Cieminski, G., Romero, D. (eds.) APMS 2020. IAICT, vol. 591, pp. 479–486. Springer, Cham (2020). https://doi.org/10.1007/978-3-030-57993-7_54

12. Paul, M., et al.: Reconfigurable digitalized and servitized production systems: requirements and challenges. In: Lalic, B., Majstorovic, V., Marjanovic, U., von Cieminski, G., Romero, D. (eds.) APMS 2020. IAICT, vol. 592, pp. 501–508. Springer, Cham (2020). https://doi.org/10.1007/978-3-030-57997-5_58

13. Pelletier, N., et al.: Energy intensity of agriculture and food systems. Annu. Rev. Environ. Resour. **36**(1), 223–246 (2011). https://doi.org/10.1146/annurev-environ-081710-161014

A Framework to Assess Risk of Illicit Trades Using Bayesian Belief Networks

Rashid Anzoom⬩, Rakesh Nagi$^{(\boxtimes)}$⬩, and Chrysafis Vogiatzis⬩

Department of Industrial and Enterprise Systems Engineering,
University of Illinois at Urbana-Champaign, Urbana, IL 61801, USA
{ranzoom2,nagi,chrys}@illinois.edu

Abstract. Recent years have seen the initiatives against illicit trades gain significant traction at both national and global levels. A crucial component in this fight is correct assessment of the risks posed by different trades across different regions. To aid in this cause, we provide a risk prediction framework based on Bayesian Belief Networks. It involves the development of a causal model incorporating variables related to the rise/decline of the illicit trade volume. The influence of these variables are determined by training on available data that are allowed to update over time. Implementation on a sample case study shows relatively low prediction accuracy of our model. Factors constraining its performance are analyzed and possible ways to avert them are discussed. We expect this framework to act as a decision support tool to the policymakers and strengthen them in the fight against illicit trades.

Keywords: Illicit trade · Risk assessment · Bayesian Belief Networks

1 Introduction

The sustained growth and diversification of illicit trades remain a substantial threat worldwide [1]. Recent statistics report the annual turnover of these trades to be in the order of 2.2 trillion US dollars, which corresponds to approximately 8–15% of the global GDP [11]. Efforts to control/disrupt illicit trade are heavily constrained by the scarcity of resources (e.g., workforce, finance), emphasizing the importance of allocating them efficiently. Before planning for disrupting illicit trade, though, we need reasonable estimates of the proliferation risks of different trades in distinct regions of the world.

One could base this estimation process on the available statistics; however, such an approach is risky since data on illicit supply chains are rare and suffer from multiple shortcomings (including incompleteness, unclear boundary specification, low dynamics) [1]. An alternate strategy involves discerning factors that affect the rise or decline of these trades, as well as their degree of influence which we assume to be probabilistic. Available information on these variables will then lead to the estimation of risk. In this paper, we introduce a framework

A. Dolgui et al. (Eds.): APMS 2021, IFIP AICT 634, pp. 504–513, 2021.
https://doi.org/10.1007/978-3-030-85914-5_54

to conduct this assessment in a systematic manner. In particular, we employ Bayesian Belief Networks (BBN) modeling, which is widely known for dealing with probabilistic inference in complex systems [18].

Prior to discussion of the proposed approach, we review previous works related to our research problem. Existing literature on this topic is mostly qualitative in nature: identifying specific and general risk factors for different trades [1]. A few quantitative models have been proposed to predict individual trade risk/volume. For instance, growth of narcotics market was modeled as a function of a small number of variables (e.g., utility, risk, enforcement level, economic status) [2,5]. Researchers have also employed BBN models in some of these works. An expert-driven model is presented at [8] to predict the occurrence of poaching event of rhinos. Data-driven models aimed to predict deforestation, which is related to illegal logging [12,20]. Alternate methodologies used here include artificial neural network and Gaussian process. Apart from these, BBN has also been used to detect activities in illicit trades (e.g., prediction of fraudulent food products) [21]. Using separate prediction models for each trade category might not be convenient for the policymakers. Perhaps with that in mind, The Economist Intelligence Unit [22] developed a country-wise risk index to indicate the prevalence risk of illicit trades. However, the index is linear in nature and defined by expert opinion. Furthermore, it does not distinguish different trade categories and focuses on the regional factors only. Thus, there is need to develop a model that can predict the risk of individual trade categories at different regions as well as provide an aggregated risk score for a particular area or trade. Our framework aims to build a customized model with these features.

The remainder of this paper is organized as follows. Section 2 describes the steps in developing and implementing the framework. Section 3 presents a case study for demonstrating our framework. Our discussion concludes in Sect. 4 through a critical review of the approach and a brief discussion of future avenues.

2   Risk Assessment Framework

The framework to assess the risk of illicit trades consists of five steps as shown in Fig. 1. The following subsections discuss these steps sequentially.

2.1   Identification of Factors Related to Illicit Trades

The discussion on the causes behind the inception and continuation of illicit trades can be found in several places of the literature. Some of the established factors include poor socio-economic conditions, operational risk or lack thereof, the potential return on investment, etc. We divide these factors into two sets: region-specific and trade-specific. The Economist Intelligence Unit (EIU) considered 20 features of the first category to predict regional suitability for illicit trades [22]. The second set, on the other hand, denotes the expected supply chain performance in a business. We propose to incorporate the drivers of the

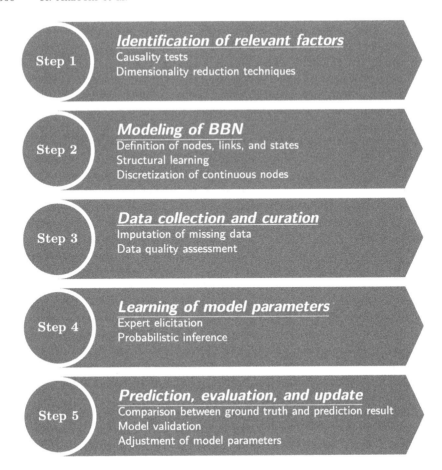

Fig. 1. The five main steps for our illicit trades risk assessment framework.

illicit supply chain in this set (e.g., ease of production/acquisition, storage, concealment and transportation, access to resources, profitability, money laundering, corruption). Beyond this, one can always incorporate additional variables through causality tests, i.e., statistical hypothesis testing. Ordiano [16] recently demonstrated another approach using node embedding and clustering. For customization, it is also possible to filter out some variables through dimensionality reduction techniques (see [23] for details).

2.2 Modeling of a Bayesian Belief Network

Following the selection of variables, we move forward to modeling. Our adopted approach, BBN, is a directed acyclic graphical model of causal relationships based on probability theory [3]. In the constructed graph, nodes denote the variables of interest; while edges represent the causal relationship (dependence) between them. In our case, we can consider five sets of nodes: region-specific factors (A), trade-specific factors (T), trade statistics (S), data reliability (D), and trade risk (R). Trade statistics denote the types of data available regarding illicit trades (e.g., instances reported, transaction volume, number of arrests), while data reliability indicates the confidence in the data at hand. The trade risk is predicted as a probabilistic function of all these variables. In terms of equation, this can be written as follows:

$$P\left(S|A, T, R, D\right) = P(A)P(T)P(R|A, T)P(D)P(S|R, D). \tag{1}$$

In a simpler model, nodes within a set are considered conditionally independent of each other. For a better representation of reality, one can conduct multivariate regression analyses or causality tests among the variables. Given data availability, it is also possible to learn the model structure using several algorithms [19]. Two other salient node attributes in this model are the type and state of nodes. The model supports both discrete and continuous nodes, although the former is preferred. Continuous nodes have to go through discretization by some interval points. The methods for such discretization can be user-specified or algorithmic/data-driven (supervised or unsupervised) [4]. Once we specify all these issues, our model is ready to learn the parameters.

2.3   Data Collection and Curation

As mentioned earlier, the deceptive nature of illicit trades makes it difficult to collect reliable data on them. A discussion on the existing data sources is provided in [1]. Among the five mentioned sources, organizational databases remain the most useful ones for our analysis since they follow a standard format and are regularly updated. Still, it cannot be said that the available statistics accurately represent reality.

This is why it is important to include in our model information regarding the quality and the reliability of the used data. The four major dimensions of data quality are accuracy, completeness, consistency, and timeliness [17]. In the BBN, the set of nodes representing the data reliability aspect represents the state of these quality dimensions. In terms of trade statistics, one can use different types of data as nodes or apply fusion at the information level to obtain an aggregated measure.

2.4   Learning the Model Parameters

In this step, we train our model with the existing dataset to learn the parameters, i.e., to learn the conditional probabilities (CP). While we intend to derive these probabilities straight from the data, it is not unusual for some information to be limited in amount or to be simply unavailable. In such cases, researchers have often used expert opinions for conditional probability elicitation [14]. Considering this, we implement an inference method that is adaptable to such scenarios, including the combination of expert opinion and evidential information, as well as incomplete or small dataset. Further information regarding these algorithms can be found at [7, 13].

2.5   Prediction, Evaluation, and Model Update

Given the parameters and prior probabilities of the variables would provide the risk of a specific trade in a particular region as per Eq. (1). If the ground truth data (actual trade risk/statistic) becomes available, one can compare it with the predicted results through different metrics (e.g., confusion matrix, k-fold cross-validation, spherical payoff) [10].

Most of the databases we use are updated on an annual basis. Incorporating these new pieces of evidence will update the model regularly, improving its adaptability. It is even possible to assign variable weights to cases as well as unlearn previous instances [15].

Finally, should the prediction error become significantly high, it becomes necessary to scrutinize the model. In this case, techniques like sensitivity analysis, cross-validation, and scenario analysis can provide insight regarding the model [6].

3   Case Study

To illustrate the framework introduced in Sect. 2, we present a sample case study to compute the proliferation risk of illicit trades for different countries.

Step 1. We begin with the decision to include 4 trade-specific and 14 region (country)-specific factors influencing illicit trades. The region-specific factors are divided into four categories (trade transparency, supply and demand, governmental policy, and customs environment) as described in [22]). As a consequence, we introduce a node for each of them in the BBN. Two more nodes are introduced to represent the country environment and ease of trade, which influence the node *trade risk*. For data reliability, we only consider one node (completeness) since the age for all data is the same. Finally, we have nodes representing two types of trade statistics (trade volume and number of cases), taking the tally of nodes to 28. He selection of these variables was based on data availability, although information regarding the trade-specific factors was not found. For the sake of model completeness, we assign values to them based on our judgment, e.g., transportation of narcotics is considered to be easy because of its size while transportation of arms is considered difficult.

Step 2. With the selection of the variables complete, we move to build the model. Most of the variables are represented by scores and thus continuous in nature. Availability of data allows a reasonable discretization of continuous nodes. In this model, we employ the equal frequency strategy, which assumes the quartiles as cutpoints. Considering the minimum and maximum possible value of the factors, up to two more cutpoints can be included. The interval between these cut-points represents the states of the discretized nodes. Links between the nodes are assumed to be predetermined, so we do not run any causality test or structural learning. The complete structure of the causal model is visible in Fig. 2. For ease of discernment, the node-sets are color-coded and a legend is provided.

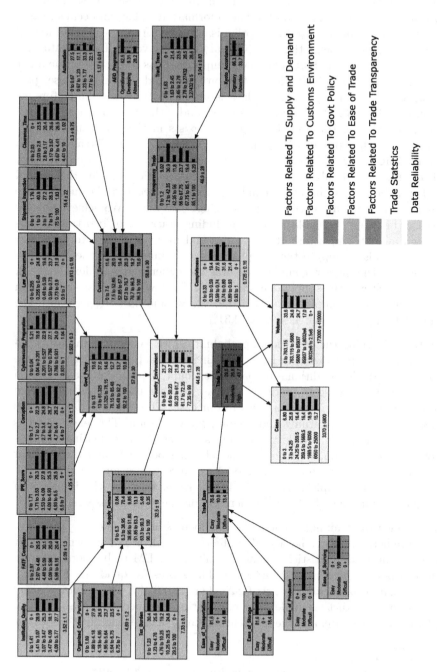

Fig. 2. The BBN model for the case study, built using NETICA.

Step 3. Our next step involves collection and preprocessing of relevant data. Information related to the factors are found on 15 separate databases, the majority of which are listed in [22]. Besides that, information on law enforcement capability, institutional quality, and corruption is extracted from the World Internal Security and Police Index,[1] the GCI (Global Competitiveness Index) database, and the World Economic Forum Global Competitiveness Report.[2] On the other hand, the UNODC (United Nations Office on Drugs and Crime) database[3] provides statistics on illicit trades. No data is found on trade-specific factors, as mentioned earlier. All of the sources used fall under the category of open organizational databases. However, heterogeneity exists in their structure and the volume of data they provide. For example, UNODC provides 27 year-long data regarding drug seizure, while EIU provides tracking competence for only 2 years. Furthermore, each database holds additional information besides the desired ones. For inference of the conditional relationships between the factors, one would need data for all attributes in one single database. We achieve this by collecting the latest available records (including statistics of two trades: narcotics and arms trade) across 160 countries and merging them into a country database. We also compute the completeness and timeliness of the data. The attribute with the highest completeness was the cybersecurity index (95.63%), while the lowest was the supply-demand (45%). The lowest, highest and median tuple (countrywise) completeness was 33%, 92.6%, and 59%, respectively. The overall relationship completeness was 72.31%.

Step 4. For learning the conditional probabilities, we feed this data into NETICA,[4] a software specializing in BBN modeling and analysis. Netica uses three methods to learn the conditional probabilities: count, expectation maximization (EM), and gradient descent method. The last two are used for inferring from an incomplete database, which applies to our case. The available data set was divided into two sets (learning and testing) for validation. The learning set is used to train the model, while the testing set is used for evaluating our prediction. For comparison, we train the model using both EM and the gradient descent method. Once trained, the model assumes values for the conditional probabilities. An example is shown in Fig. 3. Here, we show the influence of tracking capability and the Kyoto Addendum on the trade transparency score.

Step 5. Once the training is complete, our focus shifts to assessing the accuracy of prediction. Since the actual proliferation risk is not known, the test is done on the trade statistics instead. Results show EM to be more accurate (38.46%) than gradient descent (28.85%). The scores for quadratic loss, logarithmic loss, and spherical payoff are 0.825, 3.66, and 0.457. The accuracy is still quite low for a prediction model, but considering the incompleteness of data, simpler model structure, and the inherent difficulty of assessing illicit trades, we

---

[1] http://www.ipsa-police.org/.

[2] http://reports.weforum.org/global-competitiveness-index-2017-2018/.

[3] https://dataunodc.un.org/.

[4] https://www.norsys.com/netica.html.

Track_Trace	Kyoto_Accordance	0 to 1.2	1.2 to 42.35	42.35 to 56	56 to 67.75	67.75 to 85.1	85.1 to 100
0 to 1.63	Signatory	16.667	16.667	16.667	16.667	16.667	16.667
0 to 1.63	Absentee	16.667	16.667	16.667	16.667	16.667	16.667
1.63 to 2.45	Signatory	1.39e-4	1.15e-4	99.999	1.48e-4	1.31e-4	1.38e-4
1.63 to 2.45	Absentee	1.40e-4	99.999	1.30e-4	1.36e-4	1.31e-4	1.40e-4
2.45 to 2.78	Signatory	7.50e-5	71.871	7.34e-5	8.50e-5	28.129	7.56e-5
2.45 to 2.78	Absentee	2.18e-4	99.999	2.13e-4	2.20e-4	1.97e-4	2.20e-4
2.78 to 3.27432	Signatory	4.36e-5	15.829	36.901	42.089	5.182	4.57e-5
2.78 to 3.27432	Absentee	1.35e-4	14.285	71.43	14.284	1.33e-4	1.36e-4
3.27432 to 5	Signatory	3.21e-5	3.431	13.656	27.548	51.899	3.466
3.27432 to 5	Absentee	3.33e-4	33.333	33.333	33.333	3.33e-4	3.33e-4

Fig. 3. Conditional probability of trade transparency score given track and trace performance and Kyoto accordance status (display from NETICA).

consider this value to be reasonable. The omission or imputation of incomplete tuples is expected to improve this accuracy.

Sensitivity analysis measures the degree to which variation in posterior probability distribution of the target node (risk index) is explained by other variables, i.e., how influential different nodes are in predicting risk index [9]. In this case (discrete node), the measure is entropy reduction. Table 1 shows part of our results, listing the individual factors with higher influence. As expected, trade volume and the number of cases have the greatest influence on trade risk. The next two in the list are ease of storage and transportation, which explains the higher spread of narcotics trade over arms in general. The last factor, cybersecurity preparation, is a bit surprising since the transactions are mostly done physically. This might be an issue worth investigating in the future. Once these results are validated, one can predict the risk with greater confidence. We have left the trade risk here as a categorical variable. That said, it is also possible to consider it as an index of continuous nature. The same methodology can be applied for different scales of regions (continent, country, state/district), given, of course, that data for different regions are made available.

Table 1. Sensitivity of trade risk to other node findings.

Node	Mutual info (entropy)	Percent	Variance of belief
Trade volume	0.33	21.3	0.429
Cases	0.082	5.26	0.012
Ease of storage	0.019	1.24	0.004
Ease of transportation	0.019	1.24	0.004
Track and trace	0.009	0.601	0.001
Cybersecurity preparation	0.006	0.419	0.01

4   Conclusion

The ability to predict trade proliferation risk is expected to have great value in the fight against the illicit economy. However, it requires handling a multitude of challenges. This paper discusses the main ideas behind building such a prediction model, and demonstrates the challenges of building one through a case study. The first issue requiring attention is the scarcity and limited availability of data since it has significant impact on the prediction performance. None of the trade-specific factors in the model are clearly defined in the literature. Development of measures for them would be a good idea for future research. For data reliability assessment, timeliness of data merits inclusion. However, the measure of volatility (duration of data validity) in the case of illicit supply chain needs to be set *a priori*. Caution should also be exercised while choosing the method for discretizing continuous variables. In the equal-frequency method, updating the parameters would alter the probability distributions to some extent but the quartiles remain the same, thus affecting the expected value. Finally, if data updated annually become sufficiently available, one should consider detecting dynamics both within and between different variables over time. Dynamic Bayesian networks should be a good choice to carry out this work. These recommendations would be implemented in our future works to overcome the aforementioned limitations and build a workable model with higher prediction accuracy and greater insights.

References

1. Anzoom, R., Nagi, R., Vogiatzis, C.: A review of research in illicit supply-chain networks and new directions to thwart them. IISE Trans. (2021). https://doi.org/10.1080/24725854.2021.1939466
2. Baveja, A., Jamil, M., Kushary, D.: A sequential model for cracking down on street markets for illicit drugs. Socio-Econ. Plan. Sci. **38**(1), 7–41 (2004)
3. Ben-Gal, I.: Bayesian networks. In: Encyclopedia of Statistics in Quality and Reliability, vol. 1. Wiley (2008)
4. Beuzen, T., Marshall, L., Splinter, K.D.: A comparison of methods for discretizing continuous variables in Bayesian networks. Environ. Model. Softw. **108**, 61–66 (2018)
5. Caulkins, J.P., Padman, R.: Interdiction's impact on the structure and behavior of the export-import sector for illicit drugs. Z. Oper. Res. **37**(2), 207–224 (1993)
6. Chen, S.H., Pollino, C.A.: Good practice in Bayesian network modelling. Environ. Model. Softw. **37**, 134–145 (2012)
7. Ji, Z., Xia, Q., Meng, G.: A review of parameter learning methods in Bayesian network. In: Huang, D.-S., Han, K. (eds.) ICIC 2015. LNCS (LNAI), vol. 9227, pp. 3–12. Springer, Cham (2015). https://doi.org/10.1007/978-3-319-22053-6_1
8. Koen, H., de Villiers, J., Roodt, H., de Waal, A.: An expert-driven causal model of the rhino poaching problem. Ecol. Model. **347**, 29–39 (2017)
9. Li, C., Mahadevan, S.: Sensitivity analysis of a Bayesian network. ASCE-ASME J. Risk Uncert. Eng. Syst. Part B Mech. Eng. **4**(1), 011003 (2018)
10. Marcot, B.G.: Metrics for evaluating performance and uncertainty of Bayesian network models. Ecol. Model. **230**, 50–62 (2012)

11. Mashiri, E., Sebele-Mpofu, F.Y.: Illicit trade, economic growth and the role of customs: a literature review. World Customs J. **9**(2), 38–50 (2015)
12. Mayfield, H., Smith, C., Gallagher, M., Hockings, M.: Use of freely available datasets and machine learning methods in predicting deforestation. Environ. Model. Softw. **87**, 17–28 (2017)
13. Mkrtchyan, L., Podofillini, L., Dang, V.N.: Bayesian belief networks for human reliability analysis: a review of applications and gaps. Reliab. Eng. Syst. Saf. **139**, 1–16 (2015)
14. Mkrtchyan, L., Podofillini, L., Dang, V.N.: Methods for building conditional probability tables of Bayesian belief networks from limited judgment: an evaluation for human reliability application. Reliab. Eng. Syst. Saf. **151**, 93–112 (2016)
15. Nielsen, T.D., Jensen, F.V.: Bayesian Networks and Decision Graphs. Springer, New York (2007). https://doi.org/10.1007/978-0-387-68282-2
16. González Ordiano, J.Á., Finn, L., Winterlich, A., Moloney, G., Simske, S.: A method for estimating driving factors of illicit trade using node embeddings and clustering. In: Figueroa Mora, K.M., Anzurez Marín, J., Cerda, J., Carrasco-Ochoa, J.A., Martínez-Trinidad, J.F., Olvera-López, J.A. (eds.) MCPR 2020. LNCS, vol. 12088, pp. 231–241. Springer, Cham (2020). https://doi.org/10.1007/978-3-030-49076-8_22
17. Pipino, L.L., Lee, Y.W., Wang, R.Y.: Data quality assessment. Commun. ACM **45**(4), 211–218 (2002)
18. Pourret, O., Naïm, P., Marcot, B.: Bayesian Networks: A Practical Guide to Applications. Wiley (2008)
19. Scanagatta, M., Salmerón, A., Stella, F.: A survey on Bayesian network structure learning from data. Prog. Artif. Intell. **8**(4), 425–439 (2019). https://doi.org/10.1007/s13748-019-00194-y
20. Silva, A.C., Fonseca, L.M., Körting, T.S., Escada, M.I.S.: A spatio-temporal Bayesian network approach for deforestation prediction in an Amazon rainforest expansion frontier. Spat. Stat. **35**, 100393 (2020)
21. Soon, J.M.: Application of Bayesian network modelling to predict food fraud products from China. Food Control **114**, 107232 (2020)
22. The Economist Intelligence Unit Limited: The global illicit trade environment index (2018)
23. Van Der Maaten, L., Postma, E., Van den Herik, J.: Dimensionality reduction: a comparative review. J. Mach. Learn. Res. **10**(66–71), 13 (2009)

Simulation and Optimization of Systems Performances

Multi-fidelity Simulation-Based Optimisation for Large-Scale Production Release Planning in Wafer Fabs

Zhengmin Zhang[1] , Zailin Guan[1] , Yeming Gong[2]([✉]) ,
and Qian Shen[1]

[1] Huazhong University of Science and Technology, Wuhan, China
hust_zzm@hust.edu.cn
[2] EMLYON Business School, 23 Avenue Guy de Collongue,
69134 Ecully Cedex, France
gong@em-lyon.com

Abstract. This paper focuses on large-scale production release planning problems in wafer fabs. Due to the complexity and dynamic characteristic of production lines, it is useful to develop simulation models to evaluate different production plans and select the optimal one. However, detailed simulation requires large computational costs, especially for large-scale problems. Therefore, we provide a multi-fidelity optimisation with ordinal transformation and optimal sampling (MO2TOS) based on the multiple population evolutionary algorithm to accelerate computational efficiency and address large-scale release planning problems for wafer fabs. In the low-fidelity approximation process of the proposed approach, we employ open queuing theory to estimate cycle times. The experimental results confirm that the low-fidelity model shows a high consistency with the high-fidelity model and the proposed multi-fidelity optimisation method is effective at solving large-scale release planning problems.

Keywords: Queuing theory · Multi-fidelity simulation-based optimisation · Wafer fabs · Production release

1 Introduction

The manufacturing of wafer fabs is a highly complex and time-consuming process because of massive process steps and complex process requirements [1]. Thus, it is difficult to provide an effective production release plan for the production line. In wafer fabs, the production release planning problem seeks an optimal or near-optimal solution to optimise the output and the work-in-process of a production system by determining the release rate of each product type.

Some basic approaches, such as mathematical programming [2, 3], simulation-based optimisation [4, 5], and analytical modelling [1, 6], have been developed to address production release planning problems. Simulation-based optimisation [7, 8] refers to the approaches that search for the optimal solution by using simulation models to directly evaluate the objective values of candidate solutions. Compared with mathematical modelling, this technology can provide accurate estimates of given

© IFIP International Federation for Information Processing 2021
Published by Springer Nature Switzerland AG 2021
A. Dolgui et al. (Eds.): APMS 2021, IFIP AICT 634, pp. 517–525, 2021.
https://doi.org/10.1007/978-3-030-85914-5_55

production plans. Besides, simulation-based optimisation plays an important role in digital twins and has huge advantages in the application of the digital twin platform [9].

However, simulation-based optimisation consumes high computational costs because of its high-precision modelling capability [10]. Real-world production planning problems require considerable computational time to run the entire solution space by the simulation model [11]. Therefore, simulation models are often used to verify the solution quality of mathematical models [12–14]. Some approaches [15–17] address the order release planning problems by iterative simulation and linear programming. Nevertheless, these methods may take a long time to converge if the initial release plan is ineffective or the convergence process is not stable. Therefore, the research question of this paper is: *How to solve large-scale production release planning problems in wafer fabs effectively by simulation-based optimisation?*

This research therefore designs a multi-fidelity optimisation with ordinal transformation and optimal sampling (MO2TOS) based on the multiple population evolutionary algorithm for production release planning problems. The proposed method is developed based on the MO2TOS proposed by Xu et al. [18]. The high-fidelity model is developed using the discrete-event simulation and the low-fidelity model is established as a mathematical expression based on the queuing theory. In the proposed MO2TOS, we provide a multiple population evolutionary algorithm to accelerate the solution space searching and obtain the approximate solution space. Compared with other methods, this proposed method obtains the same optimal solution as MO2TOS when solving large-scale problems, and saves about 90% of computational time.

2   Problem Formulation and Modelling

Consider the following scenario: $k(k = 1...K)$ types of products are produced by $m(m = 1...M)$ workstations of a wafer production line that demand exceeds supply. Product k have $r(r = 1...R_k)$ alternative processing routes, each route has $L_{k,r}$ operations. $M_{k,r,l}$ represents the workstation for the lth operation of product k with processing route r. Products of different types have similar processing flows but not exactly the same. Any processing routes may have re-entrant flows. The demand d_k of product k is known, the optimal release rate and the routing allocation scheme for each product type need to be calculated to increase productivity. We need to find the optimal release plan for different products and obtain the optimal routing allocation plan for each product type with different processing routes. The objective of the problem is to complete the customer's requirements as soon as possible and minimise the maximum work-in-process of workstations in the production line. To maintain balanced production, we put forward the following two assumptions:

1. The release rate of each product in a planning period is stable and changeless.
2. Under any release plan, the product demand capacity cannot exceed the production capacity of the machine. Otherwise, the system cannot reach a steady state and may lead to infinite accumulation of work-in-process.

We provide a mathematical model to describe the proposed problem on the basis of the above assumptions. The objective function are as follows:

$$Min(w1 \cdot makespan + w2 \cdot work\_in\_process) \tag{1}$$

$$makespan = max\, F(k, r, p, L_{k,r}), \forall k, r, p, m \tag{2}$$

$$work\_in\_process = max \left(\frac{\sum_{p=1}^{\lceil F(k,r,p,l) \rceil} \sum_{k=1}^{K} \sum_{r=1}^{R_k} WIP(k, r, p, m)}{\lceil F(k, r, p, l) \rceil} \right), \forall m \tag{3}$$

Subject to:

$$\sum_{p=1}^{\lceil F(k,r,p,l) \rceil} \sum_{r=1}^{R_k} y_{k,r}^p \geq d_k, \forall k, m \tag{4}$$

$$x_{k,r}^p, y_{k,r}^p, F(k, r, p, l), WIP(k, r, p, m) \geq 0, \forall k, r, p, m \tag{5}$$

Equations (1)–(3) represents the objectives of this problem, $w1$ and $w2$ means the weights of two objectives. $F(k, r, p, l)$ means the complete time for the lth operation of product k with processing route r released in period p. $WIP(k, r, p, m)$ is the cumulative work-in-process for product k with processing route r at workstation m in period p, where $WIP(k, p, m) = \sum_{r=1}^{R_k} WIP(k, r, p, m)$. Constraint (4) provides the minimum production quantity for each product. $y_{k,r}^p$ represents the external release material quantity for product k with processing route r in period p. $y_{k,r}^p$, $F(k, r, p, l)$ and $WIP(k, p, m)$ are decision variables linked with $x_{k,r}^p$ (external release material quantity for product k with processing route r in period p). In the proposed mathematical model, we need to derive the relationship between $x_{k,r}^p$ and other decision variables.

3 MO2TOS Based on the Multiple Population Genetic Algorithm

3.1 Low-Fidelity Approximation Based on Queuing Theory

We propose a queuing theory-based low-fidelity approximate method to derive the relationship between $x_{k,r}^p$ and other variables. According to $x_{k,r}^p$, we can approximate the product arrival distribution and calculate the waiting time and the queue length according to queuing theory. Then, $F(k, r, p, l)$ and $WIP(k, p, m)$ can be calculated accordingly, and $y_{k,r}^p$ is obtained according to $x_{k,r}^p$ and $F(k, r, p, L_{k,r})$. Here is a list of the notations we use:

τ_m	The processing time for m in processing any operations
ρ_m^p	The utilisation of workstation m
$P_{k,r,l}$	The processing time of the lth operation of product k with route r
$W(k,r,p,l)$	The waiting time for the lth operation of product k with route r released in period p
λ_m^p	The expected arrival rate for all products at workstation m in period p
$\lambda_m^p(k,r)$	The expected arrival rate for product k at workstation m in period p
$\lambda_{0,m}^p(k,r)$	The external arrival rate for product k at workstation m in period p
$\lambda_{n,m}^p(k,r)$	The arrival rate for product k from workstation n to workstation m in period p

$\lambda_m^p(k,r)$ comprises the external arrival flows and the re-entrant flows. Thus, $\lambda_m^p(k,r)$ can be calculated as:

$$\lambda_{0,m}^p(k,r) = x_{k,r}^p \cdot [M_{k,r,1} = m] \tag{6}$$

$$\lambda_{n,m}^p(k,r) = \sum_{n=1}^{M}\left(\sum_{l=1}^{L_{k,r}-1}\left(x_{k,r}^p \cdot [M_{k,r,l} = n, M_{k,r,l+1} = m]\right)\right), n \neq m \tag{7}$$

Therefore, $\lambda_m^p(k,r)$ can be described as:

$$\lambda_m^p(k,r) = \lambda_{0,m}^p(k,r) + \lambda_{n,m}^p(k,r), \ \forall m,k,r,p \tag{8}$$

λ_m^p is then given by:

$$\lambda_m^p = \sum_{k=1}^{K}\sum_{r=1}^{R_k}\lambda_m^p(k,r), \forall m,p \tag{9}$$

Therefore, the utilisation of workstation m can be provided as:

$$\rho_m^p = \tau_m \cdot \lambda_m^p, \ \forall m,p \tag{10}$$

We refer the approximation method of a GI/G/1 system in Whitt [19] to estimate the expected waiting time of each product lot in any workstations.

$$EW = \frac{\tau\rho\left(C_a^2 + C_s^2\right)g}{2(1-\rho)} \tag{11}$$

Where g is defined as:

$$g\left(\rho, C_a^2, C_s^2\right) = \begin{cases} \exp\left[-\dfrac{2(1-\rho)}{3\rho}\dfrac{\left(1-C_a^2\right)^2}{C_a^2 + C_s^2}\right], & C_a^2 < 1 \\ 1, & C_a^2 \geq 1 \end{cases} \tag{12}$$

τ denotes the service time for a product, ρ means the utilisation of this server, C_a^2 represents the squared coefficient of variation of the arrival interval distribution at this server, while C_s^2 is the squared coefficient of variation for the service-time distribution.

C_a^2 is the variance of the renewal interval divided by the square of its mean, and C_s^2 is the variance of the service time divided by the square of its mean.

In our low-fidelity approximation model, $W(k, r, p, l)$ can be represented by the expected waiting time EW. Accordingly, $F(k, r, p, l)$ can be recorded as:

$$F(k, r, p, l) = P_{k,r,l} + W(k, r, p, l) \tag{13}$$

According to the Little's law:

$$WIP(k, p, j) = W(k, r, p, l) \cdot \lambda_m^p \tag{14}$$

$F(k, r, p, L_{k,r})$ means the makespan of product k released in period p. Because the release rate in each period is the same, we can consider $F(k, r, 1, L_{k,r})$ as the cycle time for product k with processing route r. Thus, $y_{k,r}^p$ can be estimated according to the following formula:

$$y_{k,r}^p = x_{k,r}^p + F(k, r, 1, L_{k,r}) \tag{15}$$

3.2   Framework of MO2TOS Based on the Multiple Population Genetic Algorithm

The steps of MO2TOS based on the multiple population genetic algorithm (MPGA) are exhibited in Fig. 1. Traditional MO2TOS uses the low-fidelity model to estimate all the results of the solution space. Then, it selects high-quality solutions by the ordinal transformation and optimal sampling strategy, and uses the high-fidelity simulation model to calculate these solutions and choose the optimal solution. However, the solution space of large-scale production planning problems may be more than several million. Even if we use the low-fidelity model to run the entire solution space, the computational costs and runtime are not negligible. To reduce computational burden, we design a multiple population evolutionary algorithm to accelerate the solution space search efficiency based on the original MO2TOS. We choose a multiple population evolutionary algorithm because solution spaces of production problems are generally multi-peak, and multiple population evolutionary algorithms are conducive to jumping out of local optimal and accelerating the convergence process.

4   Computational Experiments

We simplify the actual wafer production system and develop some typical wafer production lines to test and estimate the effectiveness of the proposed method. The simplified cases retain the characteristics of batch processing, machine failures and mixed-flow production in actual wafer fabs. First, we develop a small-scale production release planning case to verify the accuracy of the low-fidelity model. We calculate the solution space via the high-fidelity simulation model and the low-fidelity model. Figure 2 plots the output of the solution space after ordinal transformation. According

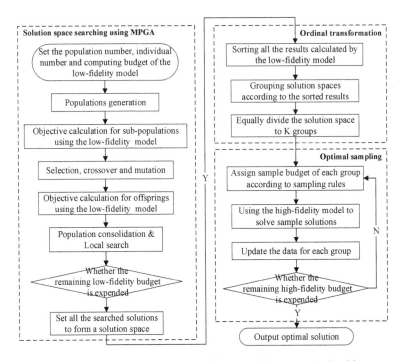

Fig. 1. MO2TOS based on the multiple population genetic algorithm

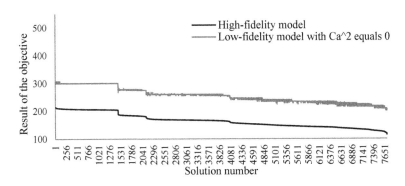

Fig. 2. Output of the solution space after ordinal transformation

to Fig. 2, we find the consistency of the output of the solution space using two models is obvious, which proves the proposed low-fidelity approximation method is feasible. Therefore, the low-fidelity model we proposed in this paper is feasible.

We further develop a large-scale production release planning case and employ the proposed method to solve the case. We first examine the optimisation performance of the proposed multi-population genetic algorithm. Figure **3** shows the convergence curves of the optimal results for the same case when the same low-fidelity budget

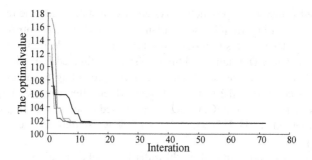

Fig. 3. The convergence curve of the optimal results

(10000) is allocated. From Fig. **3**, we conclude that the proposed algorithm has stable optimisation capability in solution space searching process.

We compare the proposed method with the high-fidelity simulation optimisation (HFSO) method and MO2TOS used by Zhang et al. [4]. HFSO selects specific amount of solutions randomly according to the high-fidelity simulation budget, uses only the high-fidelity model to run all the selected solutions, and searches for the optimal solution according to the results. The MO2TOS method solves the entire solution space by using a low-fidelity model, selects high-fidelity samples using ordinal transformation and optimal sampling, and runs the high-fidelity samples to find the optimal solution. The MO2TOS based on the multi-population genetic algorithm differs from MO2TOS in the first phase. It uses the multi-population genetic algorithm combined with a low-fidelity model to solve the solution space.

Table 1. The optimal results for the large-scale release planning case.

High-fidelity budget	The optimal result			Runtime (s)		
	HFSO	MO^{2}TOS	MO2TOS & MPGA	HFSO	MO^{2}TOS	MO^{2}TOS & MPGA
200	128.048	113.475	*113.292*	425	2221	*358*
400	120.651	113.447	**113.292**	1351	2874	**824**
600	121.166	*113.292*	**113.292**	3028	*3944*	1672
800	124.113	113.292	**113.292**	4908	5503	2785
1000	120.061	113.292	**113.292**	7948	7569	**4906**
1200	117.943	113.292	**113.292**	10244	10348	**7149**

Table **1** provides the optimal results with different methods for the large-scale release planning case. We can conclude: 1. The more fidelity budgets are allocated, the longer the run time is required. 2. Regardless of the amount of high-fidelity budget allocated, HFSO is worse than the compared methods. **3. The method proposed in this paper can find the optimal solution when the high-fidelity budget is only 200, and save about 90% of the computing time than MO2TOS when solving large-scale problems.**

The studied actual wafer production system uses a static lead time release planning model in Manufacturing Requirements Planning (MRP) to develop release plans at present. This model is oversimplified because it considers lead times as workload-independent constants. The static lead time is usually estimated from historical data and experience. This method releases the materials corresponding to the demand of each cycle directly according to the static lead time, which often causes a large amount of work-in-process accumulation. Consider the proposed case as an example, the optimal result of this method is 134.515, which is 18.733% worse than the method proposed in this manuscript.

This method is suitable for real-world wafer fabs that demand exceeds supply. First, managers need to know the demands of multiple planning periods in the future and roughly estimate the upper and lower limits of release rates based on demands. Then, managers can use the proposed low-fidelity estimation method to estimate the revenues of different release plans and obtain the appropriate solution set. Next, they can use the high-fidelity discrete simulation model to run these plans and select the optimal one. This method can greatly reduce computation time and is suitable for large-scale problems. Note that due to some uncertain events or parameters in actual production scenarios, this method may need to update release plans periodically to keep the simulation model consistent with the actual production system.

5   Conclusions

In this research, we present a MO2TOS based on the multi-population evolutionary algorithm to address large-scale production release planning problems in wafer fabs. The low-fidelity estimation model is an open queue approximation model and the high-fidelity simulation model is established based on discrete-event simulation. We test a large-scale case to evaluate the proposed method. The proposed method is compared with the MO2TOS framework proposed by Zhang et al. [4] and the high-fidelity simulation optimisation method. Experiment results show that the proposed method can obtain the same optimal solution as Zhang et al. [4] and save computing time.

In the future, we will consider how to improve the estimation accuracy and speed of the low-fidelity model simultaneously. Moreover, we will study how to let high-fidelity model estimation results feedback to the low-fidelity model and reduce estimation gaps between the low- and the high-fidelity models.

References

1. Chung, S.H., Lai, C.: Job releasing and throughput planning for wafer fabrication under demand fluctuating make-to-stock environment. Int. J. Adv. Manuf. Technol. **31**(3), 316–327 (2006)
2. Asmundsson, J., Rardin, R.L., Uzsoy, R.: Tractable nonlinear production planning models for semiconductor wafer fabrication facilities. IEEE Trans. Semicond. Manuf. **19**(1), 95–111 (2006)

3. Leachman, R.C.: Semiconductor production planning. In: Handbook of Applied Optimisation, pp. 746–762. Oxford University, New York (2001)
4. Zhang, F., Song, J., Dai, Y., Xu, J.: Semiconductor wafer fabrication production planning using multi-fidelity simulation-based optimisation. Int. J. Prod. Res. **58**(21), 6585–6600 (2020)
5. Thuerer, M., Stevenson, M., Land, M., Fredendall, L.: On the combined effect of due date setting, order release, and output control: an assessment by simulation. Int. J. Prod. Res. **57** (6), 1741–1755 (2019)
6. Schneckenreither, M., Haeussler, S., Gerhold, C.: Order release planning with predictive lead times: a machine learning approach. Int. J. Prod. Res. **59**, 3285–3303 (2020)
7. Chen, C., Lee, L.: Stochastic Simulation Optimisation (An Optimal Computing Budget Allocation). Back Matter, pp. 175–227 (2010)
8. Xu, J., Nelson, B., Hong, L.: Industrial strength COMPASS: a comprehensive algorithm and software for optimisation via simulation. ACM Trans. Model. Comput. Simul. **20**(1), 1–29 (2010)
9. Zhang, Z., Guan, Z., Gong, Y., Luo, D., Yue, L.: Improved multi-fidelity simulation-based optimisation: application in a digital twin shop floor. Int. J. Prod. Res. (2020)
10. Asmundsson, J., Rardin, R.L., Turkseven, C.H., Uzsoy, R.: Production planning with resources subject to congestion. Nav. Res. Logist. **56**(2), 142–157 (2009)
11. Fowler, J., Mönch, L.: Modeling and analysis of semiconductor manufacturing. In: Tolk, A., Fowler, J., Shao, G., Yücesan, E. (eds.) Advances in Modeling and Simulation. SFMA, pp. 301–313. Springer, Cham (2017). https://doi.org/10.1007/978-3-319-64182-9_14
12. Bang, J., Kim, Y.: Hierarchical production planning for semiconductor wafer fabrication based on linear programming and discrete-event simulation. IEEE Trans. Autom. Sci. Eng. **7** (2), 326–336 (2010)
13. Kopp, D., Monch, L., Pabst, D., Stehli, M.: Qualification management in wafer fabs: optimisation approach and simulation-based performance assessment. IEEE Trans. Autom. Sci. Eng. **17**(1), 475–489 (2019)
14. Ziarnetzky, T., Kacar, N., Monch, L., Uzsoy, R.: Simulation-based performance assessment of production planning formulations for semiconductor wafer fabrication. In: Winter Simulation Conference, Huntington Beach. IEEE (2015)
15. Missbauer, H.: Order release planning by iterative simulation and linear programming: theoretical foundation and analysis of its shortcomings. Eur. J. Oper. Res. **280**(2), 495–507 (2020)
16. Kim, S.H., Lee, Y.H.: Synchronized production planning and scheduling in semiconductor fabrication. Comput. Ind. Eng. **96**(6), 72–85 (2016)
17. Kim, B., Kim, S.: Extended model for a hybrid production planning approach. Int. J. Prod. Econ. **73**(1), 165–173 (2001)
18. Xu, J., Zhang, S., Huang, E., Chen, C., Lee, L., Celik, N.: MO2TOS: multi-fidelity optimisation with ordinal transformation and optimal sampling. Asia-Pac. J. Oper. Res. **33** (3), 1650017 (2016)
19. Whitt, W.: The queueing network analyser. Bell Labs Techn. J. **62**(9), 2779–2815 (1983)

Toward a Simulation Model for Capacity Analysis of a New Port Terminal

Erik Bergeron$^{(\boxtimes)}$, Léo Gagnon, Jean-François Audy, Pascal Forget, and Amina Lamghari

Université du Québec à Trois-Rivières, 3351 Boulevard des Forges, Trois-Rivières, Canada
{erik.bergeron,leo.gagnon,jean-francois.audy, pascal.forget,amina.lamghari}@uqtr.ca

Abstract. With the current growth of the maritime industry, which is a key element for many supply chains worldwide, ports seek to increase their capacity and performance in order to tackle challenges and opportunities created by the increased demand in the industry. Port expansion is an efficient way to meet this objective, but requires important resources and careful planning. Before undertaking such a major project, it is important for a port to have a firm grasp and understanding of its current capacity as well as the expansion's requirements and limitations in light of its traffic forecasts. This article presents the data analysis realized as part of an expansion project of a Canadian port case. The data analysis is executed in order to feed the first simulation model of its kind in this sector that will jointly consider the logistics operations taking place in the current port and its new terminal. This article addresses the first steps of the model's conception through data analysis as well as solutions to problems encountered. As the study is underway, the preliminary results of the work are presented.

Keywords: Port logistics · Capacity analysis · Systems simulation · Data analytics · Bottlenecks

1 Introduction

For the past years, the shipping industry has been subjected to an increasing pressure to satisfy the growing demand of consumers worldwide. In the supply chain, ports are a central node that enable national and international trade, creates the connections between different transportation systems and joins the many producers and consumers to the markets [1]. The shipping industry is involved in more than 90% of freight transport [2] and the transport of goods by the maritime industry reached 10.7 billion tonnes in 2017, which corresponds to a growth of 411 million tonnes in the last year, of which half is attributable to dry bulk products [3]. Knowing this, ports are faced with the need to optimize their performance in order to meet the growing needs of maritime transport [4].

In order to capitalize on the growing demand from the maritime industry, ports seek to increase their capacity and performance at the operational level. Indeed, several options such as the optimization of port logistics operations and the flow of goods [5] by the integration of new technologies [6] and business processes, the use of inland intermodal terminals [7] and port expansion [8] are solutions explored by port authorities.

Generally, when ports aim to increase their current capacity, expansion projects are favored whenever possible. Expansion projects certainly require significant invest-ments, but they are often straightforward and quickly translate into an increase in capacity once completed. The Canadian port authority involved in this study has begun an expansion project through the upcoming construction of a new terminal adjacent to the current port.

An expansion project of this scope raises several port logistics issues, particularly with regard to the adequate sizing of the individual capacity of the various port logistics resources involved in the movement of goods from their entry to the exit of the port and this, for both the current port and the new terminal. As a logistics platform specializing in the storage and transhipment of a wide variety of non-containerized goods, the Canadian port involved in this study must also consider in its traffic forecasts the significant uncertainties inherent to its portfolio of goods. In this context, it is advisable to study the impact of adding a new terminal on the expected increase in the overall capacity of the port by completing an analysis of the potential bottlenecks that may arise both in the new terminal and in the current port according to the individual capacities of the logistics resources studied and the port authority's forecasts.

The main objective of this project is to identify potential bottlenecks, especially regarding railway transports, following the development of a new terminal for a Canadian port, as well as to determine when these bottlenecks arise and to analyze their extent and impact within the new terminal and the existing port. This project uses simulation as its main tool in order to reproduce the movements of the flow of goods and the use of logistics resources studied within the new terminal and the current port through the analysis of different forecast scenarios. The simulation model developed will not only allow the diagnosis of potential bottlenecks, but must also validate the outcomes of traffic that may pass through the new terminal as well as the current port.

This paper presents the data analysis of the port's railway, maritime, road data and traffic forecast. The steps taken in order to adapt and overcome certain difficulties regarding the data are also exposed. Finally, the structure of the simulation model that will be designed for this study will also be discussed. The paper is organized as follows. Section 2 presents the model development, including the model's boundaries as well as the strategies used to overcome gaps in the port's historical data. Section 3 presents the data analysis and Sect. 4 covers the conclusion and addresses future work.

2 Model Development

The port of this study is a public-owned medium-sized urban port specialized in the storage and multimodal transport of a large variety of non-containerized goods through maritime, road, and railway transportation. The port authority collects data regarding these three transportation modes. Before creating a simulation of the current port and the new terminal to analyse bottlenecks and their impacts, the port's data must first be analysed since this project is data driven. Both the current port's historical data and the port authority's traffic forecasts for the new terminal have their limitations and peculiarities. Working with this data has presented certain challenges and the approach taken for its analysis has been influenced by its constraints.

2.1   System's Boundaries

The system's boundaries refer to the different elements in the system that are taken into account for the project. The main elements of the system are presented in Fig. 1.

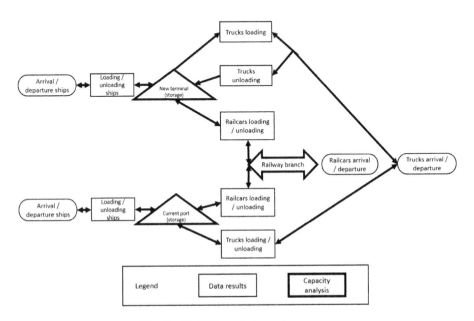

Fig. 1. Model boundaries and processes

Figure 1 includes processes involving maritime, road, rail transport and storage infrastructure. All of these elements are taken into account in the project, but rail transportation is put forward in this study since it is expected by the port authority that the main bottlenecks will be of rail nature and because the railway branch is a shared resource between the current port and the new terminal. As future works in the study, new elements will be addressed and the model will be extended in order to include additional resources and constraints.

Figure 1 can be used to illustrate the flow of goods in four steps in the case of inbound maritime goods that will later leave by road and/or rail. The first step is the goods arrival by vessel at the current port or the new terminal. Then, the goods are unloaded from the vessel and stored in the designated storage infrastructure. When the goods are ready to be sent out, empty trucks and/or railcars enter the port and are loaded. Finally, the loaded trucks and/or railcars exit the port to deliver the goods to the costumer. An important element that is taken into account is the railway branch, which limits the maximal number of railcars that can enter and leave the port in the same convoy. Both the current port and the new terminal share this resource since all railcars enter through the railway branch. The port authority asserted that the maximum length of a convoy is 50 railcars and specified certain intermediate thresholds to be observed to analyse the convoy length during the simulation phase of the project.

2.2   Modeling Strategy

In order to overcome challenges brought by the port authority's historical data, a specific modeling strategy was adopted. Because of gaps and uncertainties in the road and rail data, it was determined that it wouldn't be possible to define accurate seasonality and arrival distributions for the road and rail elements. To overcome this problem, the simulation model uses the maritime data in order to generate the trucks and railcars arrivals. Indeed, it is assumed that the trucks and railcars arrivals are heavily dependent of the vessel arrivals, since the vessels will either restock or destock certain goods in the port. With that in mind, it has been assumed that the trucks and/or railcars transporting goods would start arriving a few days after the arrival of a vessel associated with the specific goods for inbound traffic and the opposite situation for outbound traffic.

3   Data Analysis

In this section are presented the results of the analysis of the port authority's maritime, road and railway data. Most of the data analysed comes from the port's historical data between 2015 and 2019, with the addition of data from 2020 for certain types of new goods that will transit by the new terminal. The data analysis presented in this paper was carried out with the overall objective of the project in view, which will be achieved through a detailed simulation of the current port's and new terminal's logistics operations. For this purpose, two main elements were extracted and analysed from the port authority's data, namely the traffic distribution and the transit time of the three different transportation modes. This study takes into account the current port and the new terminal, but with different levels of detail. The current port is treated as a black box in which all the data from different goods are separated in two families according to an outbound or an inbound traffic, while the new terminal is further investigated through the analysis of nine goods' families. Indeed, the current port being already operational with its current traffic, the main focus is on the new terminal and its resource usage, including shared resources with the current port.

3.1   Traffic Distribution

As stated by the modeling strategy explained in Sect. 2.2, vessel, railcar and truck arrivals all depend on the maritime data. For eight of the nine goods' families of the new terminal, the projected distribution of maritime traffic is based on the historical traffic distribution average for the same goods in the current port between 2015 and 2019. For the ninth goods' family, being a new type of product with no history or relatable goods, it was decided to base its projected distribution on the current port's global average distribution. The resulting maritime traffic distributions are presented in Fig. 2 below.

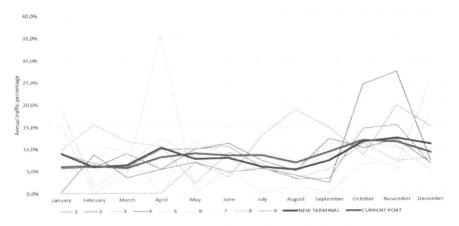

Fig. 2. Current and new terminal maritime traffic distributions

In Fig. 2, the nine slim and faint lines represent the nine goods' families traffic distributions expected during a full year in the new terminal. The "New Terminal", represented by the large dark blue line, is the average of the nine goods' families distributions, while the "Current Port", represented by a the large red line, is the average of all traffic distributions of the current port between 2015 and 2020, exportations and importations combined. It is noted that both the global terminal and current port distributions are similar, with more traffic during spring and fall (around 10%) rather than summer and winter months (around 5%). These seasonal patterns aren't surprising considering that certain goods are related to certain seasons or activities such as agriculture. Finally, it is worth mentioning, that the similarities between the global terminal and the current port average distributions is a normal occurrence since the new terminal will mainly serve goods already existing within the current port.

Even though rail and road traffic will be dependent of the maritime distributions on a macro level, the day to day traffic distributions of these transportation modes remained unknown, which guided the data analysis towards finding the daily arrival distributions of both rail and road transport over a week. Figures 3 and 4 present the results for these traffic distributions.

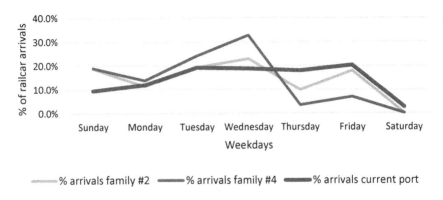

Fig. 3. Weekly distribution of rail transport

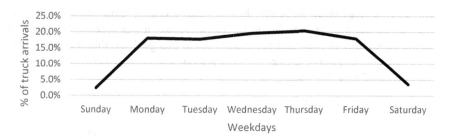

Fig. 4. Weekly distribution of road transport

Figure 3 shows the distributions for the second and fourth goods' families in the new terminal, which are the only families with rail transport in the new terminal, as well as the current weekly rail distribution for the current port, which was obtained through the average of all rail transports of the current port between 2015 and 2019. Figure 4 shows a global weekly distribution for road transport within the current terminal. Indeed, because of the lack of road data, the goods cannot be associated with their matching road transports in the port's historical data, the global distribution presented in Fig. 4 will be applied to the current port as well as the goods' families in the new terminal.

3.2   Scenarios and Maritime Input Parameters

Using the monthly maritime traffic distributions illustrated in Fig. 2, the goal is to generate the arrival of vessels for each family within the model following their respective distributions while maintaining the stochastic context. To this effect, the model will use arrival tables with specific dates that follow the maritime traffic distributions. Each individual arrival table corresponds to a ship arrival scenario, and the number of tables used within the model for each family was determined by selecting the minimum number required to reach the targeted distribution.

The data used in these scenarios is the vessel arrivals during the twelve months of a full year. Specifically, in the arrival tables, for every family, the vessels are set to arrive on the fifteenth day of the month at noon. To add a stochastic element, the simulation model then applies to each vessel arrival within the data an offset of more or less fourteen days in the arrival of the vessels. Thus, the vessel will arrive within the programmed month while randomizing the actual day of the arrival. This approach for generating vessel arrivals randomly during the month was chosen after the analysis of the daily distribution of vessel arrivals in a month showed that the distribution was similar over all days.

As implied so far, each goods' families within the model will have multiple arrival scenarios. The scenarios are run simultaneously during the simulation as control variables in experiments. This enables the model to generate vessel arrivals that tend toward the targeted distributions while maintaining the stochastic context.

In order to reproduce faithfully the maritime traffic distributions without overloading the model with an excessive number of scenarios, it was necessary to determine the minimal number of scenarios required to attain this goal. To this end, an analysis was carried out to observe the arrival distribution results for a number of scenarios varying from 10 to 100, as shown by Fig. 5.

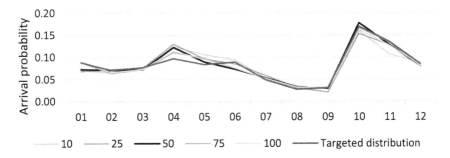

Fig. 5. Vessel distribution for different number of scenarios

After analyzing the data shown in Fig. 5, the decision was made to use 50 scenarios, illustrated by the black line, since it merges satisfactorily with the targeted distribution, illustrated by the red line. Consequently, the maritime arrival tables for each family uses 50 scenarios. An example of an arrival table is shown in Table 1.

Table 1. Boats per month for scenarios (arrival table example)

Scenarios	Month											
	1	2	3	4	5	6	7	8	9	10	11	12
Scenario 1	1	–	–	2	–	–	–	–	1	–	1	–
Scenario 2	1	2	–	–	1	–	–	1	–	–	–	–
⋮	⋮	⋮	⋮	⋮	⋮	⋮	⋮	⋮	⋮	⋮	⋮	⋮
Scenario 50	2	1	–	–	–	–	–	1	–	1	–	–

3.3   Transit Time

The transit time for maritime, rail and road transport were determined by comparing the dates and times between the arrival and departure of every transport mode. In the case of maritime transport, it is assumed that the time between arrival and departure is used for loading and unloading operations with minimal wait time. Taking into account the high costs of berthing a vessel, the hypothesis that the waiting time for maritime operations is minimal is used. In the case of rail and road transports, the port's historical data doesn't contain the required information to distinguish process time from idle time, so the time between arrival and departure of railcars and trucks is seen as the general transit time that contains both idle time and processing time. Table 2 presents the transit times for the goods' families as well as the current port for maritime, rail and road transportation. It is worth pointing out that for transit times of the current port, the data was separated in families 10 and 11 to distinguish operation times associated with inbound and outbound flows of goods.

Table 2. Transit time of maritime, rail and road transport

Goods' families	Direction of flow	Transit time (hours)					
		Maritime		Rail		Road	
		Average	Standard deviation	Average	Standard deviation	Average	Standard deviation
1	OUT	92,2	39,4	N/A	N/A	1,67	2,06
2	IN	101,1	48,8	229,4	272,1	1,54	1,99
3	IN	104,9	56,2	N/A	N/A	1,54	1,99
4	OUT	92,2	39,4	49,0	81,7	N/A	N/A
5	IN	95,7	37,4	N/A	N/A	1,54	1,99
6	IN	89,3	38,8	N/A	N/A	1,54	1,99
7	IN	46,0	42,3	N/A	N/A	N/A	N/A
8	OUT	41,8	10,1	N/A	N/A	1,67	2,06
9	OUT	85,2	47,2	N/A	N/A	1,67	2,06
10	IN	74,7	63,5	38,5	78,9	1,54	1,99
11	OUT	83,3	58,9	63,5	97,9	1,67	2,06

For each of the 9 goods' families of the new terminal as well as for families 10 and 11, representing the current port, the average transit time and the standard deviation were calculated using the current port's historical data between 2015 and 2019. The direction of the flow based on maritime transport was also taken into account for the analysis of all maritime, rail and road transportation. In the case of maritime transport, the high standard deviation is explained by many reasons such as the different types of products grouped in a same goods' family that require different loading and unloading times. Also, the variation in the vessel types and weight within each goods' family leads to significant variations in loading and unloading times. In the case of rail transport, the high deviation is explained by the small amount of data used to calculate the rail statistics presented in Table 2. Indeed, for the second goods' family, few transports of the goods were made between 2017 and 2019, and in the case of the fourth goods' family, the only rail transports made for this family occurred in 2020 and does not offer a large data pool. For these reasons, the high standard deviation was to be expected. In the case of road transport as well as rail transport for the current port, represented by families 10 and 11, the high deviation is explained by the fact that a global average of all transports was used, combining the statistics of many highly different goods, resulting in the high deviations seen in Table 2.

4 Conclusion

This paper presented the first development steps of a simulation model that will reproduce movements of the flow of goods and the use of logistics resources within a new terminal as well as the current port through the analysis of different forecast scenarios. The main goal of this simulation model is to realize the diagnosis of potential bottlenecks and validate the outcomes of traffic that may pass through the new terminal as well as the current port. The first steps presented in this paper take the form of a data analysis of maritime, road and rail transport using the port's historical data and forecasts for their new terminal. A special emphasis is on the port's rail component since the railway branch presented in Fig. 1 is an important shared resource between the current port and the future new terminal, and could become a bottleneck for port logistics operations. The data analysis executed in this paper presents transit times for the inward and outward flow of goods of the current port and 9 families of the new terminal for maritime, road, and rail transport. Certain limitations within the data were addressed through the use of maritime distributions to trigger arrivals of road and rail transports. Although, even with limited data, it was possible to determine weekly arrival distributions that specify the arrival of trucks and railcars for each day of the week.

For future works, the implementation of the model using the Simio simulation software will use the data analysis outcomes overviewed in this paper. The model will also be expanded to include additional constraints and resources involving storage and various thresholds within the port and new terminal. To our knowledge, the simultaneous simulation of both the current port as well as its new expansion with the same model and with both separate and shared resources has never been done in this field. This will allow the Canadian port authority to clearly view the impact of the new terminal on its current operations as well as identify potential bottlenecks and capacity limitations for different forecast scenarios.

References

1. Douaioui, K., Fri, M., Mabrouki, C., Semma, E.A.: Smart port: design and perspectives. Paper Presented at the Proceedings. GOL 2018: 4th IEEE International Conference on Logistics Operations Management, pp. 1–6 (2018)
2. Fruth, M., Teuteberg, F.: Digitization in maritime logistics—what is there and what is missing? Cogent Bus. Manag. 4(1), 1–40 (2017)
3. United Nations Conference on Trade and Development: Review of maritime transport. UNCTAD/RMT/2018. https://unctad.org/en/PublicationsLibrary/rmt2018_en.pdf. Accessed 07 Oct 2019
4. Molavi, A., Lim, G.J., Race, B.: A framework for building a smart port and smart port index. Int. J. Sustain. Transp. 1–13 (2019)
5. Mazouz, A., Naji, L., Lyu, Y.: Container – terminal – gate – system optimization. J. Appl. Bus. Res. 33(3), 605–614 (2017)
6. Rajabi, A., Khodadad Saryazdi, A., Belfkih, A., Duvallet, C.: Towards smart port: an application of AIS data. In: 20th International Conference on High Performance Computing and Communications, 16th International Conference on Smart City and 4th International Conference on Data Science and Systems, pp. 1414–1421 (2019)

7. Reis, V., Almeida, A.: Capacity evaluation of a railway terminal using microsimulation: case study of a freight village in turin. Front. Built Environ. **5** (2019). https://doi.org/10.3389/fbuil.2019.00075
8. Triska, Y., Frazzon, E.M., Silva, V.M.D.: Proposition of a simulation-based method for port capacity assessment and expansion planning. Simul. Model. Pract. Theory **103** (2020). https://doi.org/10.1016/j.simpat.2020.102098

Design of a Physics-Based and Data-Driven Hybrid Model for Predictive Maintenance

Emiliano Traini[✉], Giulia Bruno[✉], and Franco Lombardi[✉]

Politecnico di Torino, Corso Duca degli Abruzzi 24, 10129 Turin, Italy
{emiliano.traini,giulia.bruno,
franco.lombardi}@polito.it

Abstract. The maintenance process is crucial in any system that is prone to failure or degradation, particularly in manufacturing operations. In fact, maintenance costs can reach up to 40% of the cost of production in certain industries. In the era of Industry 4.0, maintenance methods can maximize the use of components predicting the remaining useful life. These methods are identified as Predictive Maintenance and include several innovative technologies, such as IoT for deploying sensors that monitor machines and AI that provides the algorithms to interpret the data collected. The information generated from sensor data allows for more accurate predictions using statistical models that are sensitive to the peculiarities of an individual tool set on a particular machine and used by a certain operator. These models, unlike traditional methods based on physical laws, increase in efficiency as the data increases, and therefore are not efficient or usable when a sufficient bank of data is not available. This work proposes a hybrid model that, being based on both classical physics and data-drive models, demonstrates how it is possible to obtain a prediction method that estimates the state of the tool even in the absence of historical data and that increases its accuracy as such data increases. The proposed model is evaluated by using a public experimental milling dataset.

Keywords: Hybrid model · Predictive Maintenance · Tool condition monitoring · Machine learning · Milling

1 Introduction

Maintenance costs are estimated as a percentage of production costs that vary between 15%, for the manufacturing sector in general, and up to 40% for the metalworking industry [1]. With the proper implementation of Predictive Maintenance (PdM) strategies, these costs can be reduced by up to 30% [2], by automatizing part of monitoring activities, and by optimizing the decision of replacing the resources when strictly necessary. Furthermore, a PdM strategy can reduce the incidence of failures by up to 70%, allowing the productive time of systems to be increased by up to 30% [3]. Another important estimation is that PdM methods based on Machine Learning (ML) algorithms can reduce current maintenance costs by an additional 30%, increasing machine operating life and reducing downtime [4].

A. Dolgui et al. (Eds.): APMS 2021, IFIP AICT 634, pp. 536–543, 2021.
https://doi.org/10.1007/978-3-030-85914-5_57

In the era of Industry 4.0, several technologies, as Internet of Things (IoT) and Artificial Intelligence (AI), enable the real-time data collection required by high-performed PdM methods. In fact, they are based on real-time data collected by a sensors system and Big Data infrastructures. [5] Research has proposed several AI-based methods whose performance grows as the information possessed about the process under observation increases, but they are inoperable with no real-time information.

The performance of physics-based methods depends on (i) the number of variables (sources of variability) considered in the model, (ii) the complexity of the physical laws, and (iii) the estimation quality of few parameters with data offline generated by experiments and inspections. Contrarily, the accuracy of data-driven methods depends on the quantity and quality of historical data, which are difficult to replicate for research analyses [6]. The aim of this work is to propose a hybrid model that takes advantage of the strengths of both methods (physics-based and data-driven) while minimizing the effect of their weaknesses.

The rest of the paper is organized as follows: the second section describes the state of the art, the third one defines the proposed hybrid model, the fourth introduces the milling process case study, and, finally, the last section presents the conclusions and the ideas for future improvements.

2   State of the Art

Starting in 1950, preventive maintenance was introduced in order to limit the effects of a failure, which with the previous approach often led to downtime of the entire production process [7]. The first preventive maintenance methods were based only on time schedules, and for that they are called periodic maintenance. However, these approaches failed to predict abnormal failures and often led to unnecessary interventions.

Differently, it has been estimated that 99% of mechanical failures can be predicted with the help of specific indicators, on this basis was born the Condition Based Maintenance (CBM) [8]. It involves two main processes: diagnostic and prognostic [9]. The improvement of these methods is represented by PdM models, in which measurements on the machine are used in combination with process performance data measured by other devices. The use of such data jointly allows statistical models to analyze historical trends in order to predict the instant when the machine needs an intervention [10].

Prognostics methods can be categorized into data-driven, physics-based and hybrid approaches [11]. Despite the significant recent progress in the Model-Based (MB) and ML hybrid modeling domain, there are various challenges that throttle down the full-fledged growth of hybrid modeling: (i) there is no guidelines for selecting hybrid models, (ii) there are few benchmarks (problems and dataset) for evaluating and comparing hybrid models, (iii) training accurate models with low amount of data or labels, (iv) minimizing data collection costs, (v) solving the complexity due to geometric data formats as CAD files and imbalanced data [12].

3 Proposed Hybrid Model

The proposed method is a hybrid model between physics-based and data-driven approaches, and it aims to exploit the potential of each method.

The first step consists in training the physics-based model and data-driven model individually. In this way, the two methods generate estimations about wear levels (W) or Remaining useful Life (RUL) for each T-th run of a tool, called $W_{PB}(T)$ and $W_{ML}(T)$, respectively.

Then, always with the training set, for each run, the optimal weight $\omega(T)$ is calculated to generate the linear combinations of physics-based and data-driven predictions as stated in the following equation:

$$W = \omega W_{PB} + (1 - \omega) W_{ML}.$$

The weights are defined by choosing as objective to minimize the Root-Mean Square Error (RMSE) and the Root Relative Squared Error (RRSE) of the hybrid predictions (W).

Finally, the trained hybrid model is evaluated on the test set. The estimation of the wear level $W(T)$ during the T-th operation performed with the same tool is a weighted average of physics-based and data driven methods. However, the model estimates a dynamic weight $\omega := \omega(T, P)$ that depends on the number of operations performed by the same tool and on the process parameters P set by the operator.

The details on the two components of the hybrid model are reported in the following.

3.1 Physics-Based Component

Classical mechanics methods concerning the wear of rotating machine tools are based on the non-linear relationship between two main parameters: cutting speed (V_c) and RUL (T). A first equation was proposed by Taylor in 1906 and has the following form: $V_c \cdot T^{1/\beta} = C$ and $C = \alpha \cdot f^{-C/\beta} \cdot d^{-\gamma/\beta}$, where C is the cutting speed with which one minute of life is obtained, d is the depth of cut, f is the feed rate and α, β and γ are empirical constants. $1/\beta$ is an indicator of how much the tool life is affected by changes in cutting speed and empirical data has defined that $1/\beta \in [0.1; 0.15]$ for HS steel tools, $1/\beta \in [0.2; 0.25]$ for carbide tools and $1/\beta \in [0.6; 1]$ for ceramic tools [13].

The physics-based component of the hybrid model (called W_{PB}) is based on the extended Taylor equation for rotary tools, which includes all machining parameters. The equation has the following form: $T = \alpha_0 v_c^{\alpha_1} f^{\alpha_2} d^{\alpha_3} W_{PB}^{\alpha_4}$, where $[T] = [min]$ is the estimation of the useful life of the tool, $[v_c] = [mm/min]$ is the cutting speed, $[f] = [mm/rev]$ is the feed rate, $[d] = [mm]$ is the dept of cut. $[W_{PB}] = [mm]$ is the width of flank wear according to the physics-based method that can be measured in relation to the activity time T, and α_0, α_1, α_2, α_3 and α_4 are empirical constants to be estimated that will be called coefficients, since they represent the coefficients in the multiple regression model. The formula is the following:

$$W_{PB}(T) = e^{[\ln(T) - \ln(\alpha_0) - \alpha_1 \ln(v_c) - \alpha_2 \ln(f) - \alpha_3 \ln(d)]/\alpha_4}$$

The estimation of the coefficients can be done with a multiple linear regression by performing a logarithmic transformation, which can be written in matrix form.

$$Y = \begin{bmatrix} \ln(T_1) \\ \vdots \\ \ln(T_n) \end{bmatrix} = X\alpha = \begin{bmatrix} 1 & \ln(v_{c,1}) & \ln(f_1) & \ln(d_1) & \ln(W_{PB,1}) \\ \vdots & \vdots & \vdots & \vdots & \vdots \\ 1 & \ln(v_{c,n}) & \ln(f_n) & \ln(d_n) & \ln(W_{PB,n}) \end{bmatrix} \begin{bmatrix} \alpha_0 \\ \alpha_1 \\ \alpha_2 \\ \alpha_3 \\ \alpha_4 \end{bmatrix}$$

X is called sensitivity matrix [14] and α contains the coefficients that can be estimated with the method of least squares. The accuracy of the estimation of coefficients depends on the inverse of the matrix $X^T X$, the term on which the optimization criteria are based, as for example the one proposed by [15] that define the minimum data sample to be collected for training the method.

3.2 Data-Driven Component

In parallel, ML methods that can utilize the information contained in sensor measurements can be used to estimate tool wear W_{ML}. The framework used to estimate tool wear from sensor measurements is shown by [16] and [17] and it is based on a multi-step data pre-processing between the data acquisition and monitoring processes.

The first phase of data pre-processing, data cleaning, involves removing values that do not meet certain requirements and are inconsistent with requirements. The second phase is the outlier detection where outliers are the values that deviate strongly from other points in the sample. In the proposed framework, the distinction between searching for outliers within a sensor measurement and between measurements is considered, to recognize extreme signals that indicate process instability. After that, for the sensor measurement, considered as time series, the stationary window selection step is required, which allows the stationary phase of the machine to be selected using the Change Point Detection (CPD) technique.

When data are cleaned, the feature extraction phase follows, and it generates a complex set of predictors. This operation allows to reduce the computational load required by the algorithms to be implemented later and improves the speed of machine learning processes. The features obtained in the previous phase are normalized. Then, in the feature selection step, the large number of features extracted are reduced applying unsupervised methods described in [16].

Finally, a machine learning algorithm is applied to predict the tool wear W_{ML} based on the data preprocessed.

4 Case Study: Milling Process

4.1 The Milling Dataset

The analyses performed in this research work are based on the public Milling dataset, made available by the Prognostic Center of Excellence NASA-PCoE [18]. It contains the values recorded by six sensors throughout the life cycle of 16 tools (cases), under different working conditions identified with 8 scenarios, for a total of 170 machining operations (runs). Each case is characterized by three machining parameters, which follow the recommendations of the tool manufacturer, and by the type of material machined with fixed dimensions (483 mm × 178 mm × 51 mm). Except for the cutting speed, which remains unchanged at 200 m/min, the other variables are dichotomous and in particular: the feed rate has been fixed at 0.25 mm/s or 0.5 mm/s, the depth of cut has been fixed at 0.75 mm or 1.5 mm, while the workpiece materials are cast iron or stainless steel 145.

While the sensors collected data continuously, both during operation and downtime, flank wear measurements (*VB*) were made periodically, removing the insert from the cutter and measuring the distance from the cutting edge to the end of the abrasive wear on the side face of the tool with a special microscope. Given the diversity of machining parameters, cycles with different activity time and number of machining operations were obtained for each tool.

4.2 Comparisons Between Hybrid Model and Single Ones

A comparison of the performance of tool wear prediction on this dataset is provided in [16]. Among different ML algorithms, Neural Network (NN) was the one with the best performance. For this reason, this model was chosen as the data-driven method to be used in the hybrid model.

In Fig. 1, the weights obtained with a training set composed by 10 tools are represented (ω values). In the later runs, the weights reflect the results obtained with the error analysis, in which there is an intermediate linear phase (from run 13 to run 19) in which the Taylor model is more accurate and therefore the weights tend to 1, while in the outer phases the data-driven model based on the NN algorithm prevails.

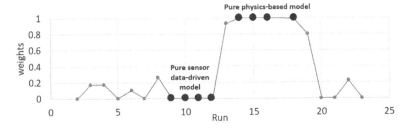

Fig. 1. Weights obtained on the training set.

Figure 2 shows the overall errors of the hybrid model and the single models. In terms of the RMSE, the hybrid model has a similar distribution to the NN model, slightly shifted downward and with one less outlier. While analyzing the distribution of the RRSE, the distribution of the hybrid model has a median value similar to the single models but with much less dispersion. It can be inferred that the hybrid model only slightly improves the overall accuracy of the predictions, while the main advantage of this approach is to obtain a more robust method whose goodness of predictions is less affected by the training data than the single models.

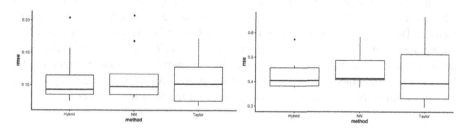

Fig. 2. Hybrid model performance compared to individual model performance.

As shown in Fig. 3, the performance of the hybrid and related single models was analyzed as the size of the training set varied. The error measured with the RRSE metric is always smaller with the hybrid model than with the single models, although the differences are more pronounced with larger training sets. While, analyzing the values of the metric RMSE, it was found that with a training set of small size (composed of 8/14 tools) is more accurate the Taylor model because there are not enough data to train the neural network, which has a much higher error than the physics-based method, and then the hybrid model has intermediate performance between them. While increasing the size of the training set the error of the NN model becomes very similar to that of the Taylor model and consequently the hybrid model obtains better performances than the single models. Moreover, it can be observed that with the hybrid model the increase in accuracy with the increase of the tools used in the training set is greater than that obtained by the single models.

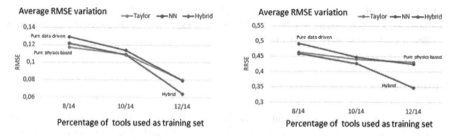

Fig. 3. Performance comparison of models for different training set size

4.3   Discussion of the Results

The results obtained is a primary formulation of a hybrid model applied on a real manufacturing case study, with the aim of monitoring the status of a CNC machine tool through a combination of an NN model with the extended Taylor law. Considering the two approaches applied on the case study, the physics-based methods result the most accurate and robust, in fact, the best overall prediction performance was obtained with the Taylor model. It has the advantage that it can be implemented even in the absence of sensors on board the machine and with few offline measurements to train the model. The main limitation of this method is that it can only be applied to wear phenomena for which a mathematical law describing the trend is known, i.e., only for common wear metrics. The category of data-driven methods based on NN model shows it potential during the last milling runs, i.e., with enough sensor data. This characteristic reflects the ability of such methods to explain high variable trends using the information provided by sensors. Limitations of data-driven methods are the need of installing many sensors on the machines for real-time monitoring, and then the high initial investment.

5   Conclusions and Future Works

The results show that the proposed hybrid approach, defined by the linear combination of a physics-based and a data-driven method, has the best performance than either single method. When single models achieve similar performance, the hybrid approach allows to significantly increase the overall accuracy and specially to obtain much more robust results. In addition, this approach can be used as an unique model to estimate tools that are monitored both offline of along each operation.

With further research, the approach can be validated on other case studies, even on different manufacturing processes and with different wear metrics. In turn, the hybrid model can be extended to predict the RUL of each tool after each run, in term of remaining runs or estimating the remaining time of usage. In addition, it is possible to implement a hybrid approach between a time series method (starting with a simple autoregressive one) and the two used in this work. Other improvements can be done to the hybrid model, such as considering other estimations as input nodes of the NN model.

Acknowledgments. This work has been funded by the Ministero dell'Istruzione, dell'Università e della Ricerca, Grant/Award Number: TESUN-83486178370409, finanziamento dipartimenti di eccellenza CAP. 1694 TIT. 232 ART. 6.

References

1. Agogino, A., Goebel, K.: Milling Data Set, NASA Ames Prognostics Data Repository. BEST lab, UC Berkeley. https://ti.arc.nasa.gov/tech/dash/groups/pcoe/prognostic-data-repository/
2. Heng, A., Zhang, S., Tan, A.C.C., Mathew, J.: Rotating machinery prognostics: state of the art, challenges and opportunities. Mech. Syst. Signal Process. **23**, 724–739 (2009)

3. Dos Santos, A.L.B., Duarte, M., Abrao, A.M., Machado, A.: An optimisation procedure to determine the coefficients of the extended Taylor's equation in machining. Int. J. Mach. Tools Manuf. **39**, 17–31 (1999)
4. Cline, B., Niculescu, R.S., Huffman, D., Deckel, B.: Predictive maintenance applications for machine learning, Orlando, FL, USA. IEEE (2017)
5. An, D., Kim, N.H., Choi, J.: Practical options for selecting data-driven or physics-based prognostics. Reliab. Eng. Syst. Saf. **133**, 223–236 (2015)
6. Johanssona, D., Hägglundb, S., Bushlya, V., Ståhla, J.: Assessment of commonly used tool life models in metal cutting. Procedia Manuf. **11**, 602–609 (2017)
7. Traini, E., Bruno, G., Lombardi, F.: Tool condition monitoring framework for predictive maintenance: a case study on milling process. Int. J. Prod. Res. (2020)
8. Traini, E., Bruno, G., D'Antonio, G., Lombardi, F.: Machine learning framework for predictive maintenance in milling. IFAC-PapersOnLine **52**, 177–182 (2019)
9. Trojan, F., Marçal, R.F.M.: Proposal of maintenance-types classification to clarify maintenance concepts in production and operations management. J. Bus. Econ. **8**, 560–572 (2017)
10. Sullivan, G.P., Pugh, R., Melendez, A.P., Hunt, W.D.: Operations & maintenance best practices - a guide to achieving operational efficiency (release 3.0). Pacific Northwest National Laboratory (2010)
11. Bloch, H.P., Geitner, F.K.: Machinery Failure Analysis and Troubleshooting. Butterworth-Heinemann (2012)
12. Hale, G.: InTech survey: predictive maintenance top technology challenge in 2007. InTech (2007)
13. Daily, J., Peterson, J.: Predictive maintenance: how big data analysis can improve maintenance. In: Richter, K., Walther, J. (eds.) Supply Chain Integration Challenges in Commercial Aerospace, pp. 267–278. Springer, Cham (2017). https://doi.org/10.1007/978-3-319-46155-7_18
14. Arruda, J.R.F., Duarte, M.: Updating rotor-bearing finite element models using experimental frequency response functions. AIAA J. (1993)
15. Xu, L.D., Xu, E.L., Li, L.: Industry 4.0: state of the art and future trends. IJPR **56**, 2941–2962 (2018)
16. Lei, Y.: An improved exponential model for predicting remaining useful life of rolling element bearings. IEEE Trans. Ind. Electron. **62**, 7762–7773 (2015)
17. Liang, Z.: A study of tool life sensitivity to cutting speed. In: ASEE PEER (2002)
18. Liulys, K.: Machine learning application in predictive maintenance. IEEE (2019)
19. Kan, M.S., Tan, A.C.C., Mathew, J.: A review on prognostic techniques for non-stationary and non-linear rotating systems. Mech. Syst. Signal Process. **62–63**, 1–20 (2015)
20. Mobley, R.K.: An Introduction to Predictive Maintenance. Elsevier, Amsterdam (2002)
21. Zhang, Q., Tse, P.W., Wan, X., Xu, G.: Remaining useful life estimation for mechanical systems based on similarity of phase space trajectory. Expert Syst. Appl. **42**, 2353–2360 (2015)
22. Rai, R., Sahu, C.K.: Driven by data or derived through physics? A review of hybrid physics guided machine learning techniques with cyber-physical system (CPS) focus. IEEE Access **8**, 71050–71073 (2020)
23. Lei, Y., Lin, J., He, Z., Zuo, J.: A review on empirical mode decomposition in fault diagnosis of rotating machinery. Mech. Syst. Signal Process. **35**, 108–126 (2013)

Dynamic Bottleneck Starvation Control

Gerd Wagenhaus[1]([⊠]), Niels Gürke[2], Werner Kurt[2],
and Ulf Bergmann[1]

[1] Otto-von-Guericke University, 39106 Magdeburg, Germany
gerd.wagenhaus@ovgu.de
[2] thyssenkrupp Presta Schönebeck GmbH, 39218 Schönebeck, Germany

Abstract. Choosing the most fitting manufacturing principle largely depends on the technical divisibility of jobs and the quantity to be produced. In most cases, a high quantity causes a higher degree of automation. What to do, however, if the production programme is evolving into various product modifications in the long run, thus developing from monolithic flow lines to a quasi-continuous batch production by means of bottleneck machines?

Classic push-controlled routines are failing here, since the batchwise manufacturing in combination with performance-reducing parameters within production systems will cause discontinuous outputs that are difficult to control and, moreover, feature an increased creation of work in process (WIP).

This problem is intensified by a combined influence of necessary setup activities, which often lead to sporadic machine failures. As a matter of fact, this invariably causes a dramatic delay in delivery times, not least because of the extension of the throughput times.

In this paper, we will introduce a manufacturing control that is based on dynamic WIP-oriented bottleneck planning, which will allow to maintain the automatically regulated output optimum by means of a self-controlling system.

Keywords: Production system control · Bottleneck · Solution approach · Practical application · Industrial case

1 Introduction

When customers' call-offs are highly volatile, suppliers are forced to provide flexible manufacturing processes and/or secure supply chains in order to safeguard the readiness for delivery. This is especially difficult to configure and control for complex products. The key to success in this respect is a combination of the lowest possible WIP orientation and the highest possible response capacity, so as to ensure an economical and logistical efficiency combined with high functionality of the supplier systems [1, 2].

As for the operational implementation, it is often organisational, usually WIP-limiting regulations that prove to be essential, which serve as operational routines individually adjusted to the respective production system [3]. Coupled with existing, case-specific boundary conditions, this will invariably lead to individualised manufacturing controls adjusted to the respective capacity of the production system, which depends on both the technological features and the specific customer-supplier-relations [4].

© IFIP International Federation for Information Processing 2021
Published by Springer Nature Switzerland AG 2021
A. Dolgui et al. (Eds.): APMS 2021, IFIP AICT 634, pp. 544–552, 2021.
https://doi.org/10.1007/978-3-030-85914-5_58

The development of such an individually adjusted manufacturing control will be illustrated in the present paper. Our fundamental approach may also provide similar production fields with the means to meet this issue in a systematic and methodically profound way. While the individual solutions arising from that are only transferable in a limited way in their respective versions, the approach for determining the basic functionality usually results in optimised manufacturing control [5–7].

2 Basic Principles

To start with, controlling a system requires the analysis and understanding of its behaviour. One essential model for the systemic description of production processes is the control loop model [cf. 8].

A closed-loop control works in the following way: the control unit transfers information (the control variable) to the system to be controlled (production process), while the result of the manipulation (the process value) is transmitted to the control unit. Since the control process is arbitrarily selectable, control loops are very much suited for describing production systems, especially against the background of utilising runtime-depending control variables.

Besides displaying the typical time response (sequencing rules), another advantage is constituted in the fact that system-inherent parameters are imaged in the control process. Provided that clear customers' call-offs exist, this results in an organisationally worthwhile WIP, for which a changing – but still defined within limits – throughput time can be used as an output basis. This leads to a "sound, super-efficient" WIP which, in most cases, is not an operating point but, as a consequence of interacting parameters, rather a field of operation (setting range) for the optimal correlation of the system's WIP and output [9].

Referring back to Little's Law (or, in modified version, to the Funnel Model), this field of operation can be defined accordingly, with the throughput time of the jobs arising from the relative evaluation of WIP against output. Taking into account the combined interactions of the parameters, this will result in a quasi-stable system behaviour. By definition, this will, in turn, provide a high level of predictability regarding the completion times and, accordingly, on-time delivery, with the production system getting closer to an optimum system behaviour [3, 10, 11].

The complexity of the control unit (here: the manufacturing control method) depends on the type and constitution of the controlled process (here: the production system). Simple and sturdy production systems featuring a high degree of determination or high degree of organisation respectively (i.e. strictly connected flow lines) induce defined, stable performance characteristics which ought to be aspired when faced with the increased complexity of other systems.

According to [3], the following can be stated: Job-shop structures manufacturing a high diversity of products with very different operational sequences mostly require complex scheduling and release methods as well. The fewer variants a production system has to produce, featuring almost identical operational sequences, the simpler it is to design the required scheduling and release method.

Thus, scheduling and release methods should be as simple as possible.

In the present case, three product versions are manufactured in one production system, with the respective operational sequences being identical. Each operation requires the utilisation of several machines of the same type which, every so often, results in time-consuming re-settings due to the product variants. In general, this production system is regarded as a flow shop system with multiple machines, where different lots are produced on individual or shared resources [12].

A rather simple method for job control in such systems is called ConWiP [13]. Here, the material flow is directed in a way that the WIP will be limited during the manufacturing. Similar to a car park, the job release will only be given ("drive in") once the completion of a certain job amount has been signalled ("free space available"), in other words the maximum number of WIP has not been reached. The feedback of the release information is designed here as a global pull, while the jobs are moved from machine to machine in form of a local push [13].

Should there be a bottleneck in the controlled system, this very bottleneck might also work as a signal, i.e. the release will be conducted according to the signalled WIP behind the bottleneck. The benefit is that an automatic bottleneck control is carried out, so that the limiting factor of the production system can be utilised in the best possible way. Analysing the behaviour of the evaluated system will now show that the control process is shortened, making the system more manageable as a whole. Hence, [3] refer to this ConWIP version as "pull-from-the-bottleneck".

All in all, the success of such a scheduling and release method largely depends on the correct determination of the maximum permissible WIP or the limits of variation respectively. The above-described correlation to the performance provides a setting range whose upper and lower thresholds can be determined by using aggregated evaluation methods according to the principles of Little's Law (or the Funnel Model respectively). If the setting range and the parameters are known for their position, they can be used as variable for the controlling of the production system. Acting inside the determined setting range allows for a maximum exploitation of the WIP, thus securing the optimal utilisation of product resources [10, 11].

3 Research Approach and Control Methodology

The control method presented below combines the fundamental bottleneck and WiP-Control mechanisms to form a dynamic bottleneck starvation control method, designed for flow shop systems with multiple machines, where different lots are produced on individual or shared resources (cf. Fig. 1).

As a matter of fact, dynamic schedule rates can be determined for such production systems, with each released WIP showing the systemic availability of the respective bottleneck situation. A defined WIP in front of the bottleneck simplifies the control process, thus increasing the basic output with regard to both quantity and time.

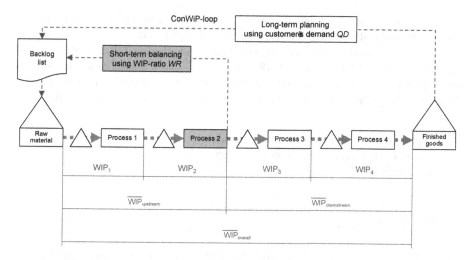

Fig. 1. The basic concept of the dynamic bottleneck starvation control.

Here, the bottleneck process determines the maximum throughput rate THR required to meet the customer's demand QD for the given time t. In other words, for a steady-state system, the throughput rate is equal for each process step i and corresponds to the throughput rate of the bottleneck process:

$$QD(t) = THR \cdot \sum_{i} WC_i \qquad (1)$$

This model-based evaluation makes it easier to determine and monitor the necessary WIP levels within the value stream in front of and directly at the bottleneck by means of averaged figures. There are two crucial values in this respect:

- WIP-ratio at the bottleneck (WR_{BN})

$$WR_{BN} = \frac{WIP_{BN}}{\overline{WIP}_{overall}} \qquad (2)$$

This value is taken for a continuous evaluation of the WIP in order to avoid bottleneck starvation. Additionally, the customers' call-off behaviour will be somewhat shifted via the bottleneck towards the production system, which reduces the response time to fluctuations in the quantity of the individual product variants.

- WIP-ratio upstream the bottleneck (WR_{up})

$$WR_{up} = \frac{\overline{WIP}_{upstream}}{\overline{WIP}_{downstream}} \qquad (3)$$

This value is used for a demand-driven quantity and capacity balancing in order to control the value stream in front of the bottleneck (upstream).

Both values act as an equalization valve in the classical ConWIP control loop. With the help of defined thresholds, a WIP shortage will cause a short-term quantity and capacity balancing of the jobs to be integrated, securing a sufficient WIP in front of the bottleneck. In practice, the determination of these thresholds took place in correlation with

- the present batch size and demand fluctuations,
- the OEM specifications of the delivery service level as well as
- the equipment's failure behavior.

4 Use Case Scenario

In this paper, relevant data and control algorhythm were obtained and verified from a real case study of a company manufacturing system, which is a one of the largest manufacturers of steering system parts. This manufacturing system consists of 6 basic manufacturing technologies and can be characterised as a disconnected flow line with partially shared resources. Three product variants are produced with the same operating sequence in one directed material flow. There were moderate variant shifts in form of quantity fluctuations for the period of evaluation.

The practical planning and control take place according to a weekly production plan based on a monthly master production schedule (MPS). On the one hand, one regularly has to cope with modifications in type or quantity of the manufacturing batch sizes due to a short-term change in customers' call-offs. On the other hand, there is a significant fluctuation of the operational output (expressed via process reliability and machine availability).

In order to ensure the highest possible system utilisation, the bottleneck is scheduled according to the principle "buffer stock before is always full" (identified beforehand as manufacturing technology 3). The installed control loop works entirely independent and is defined as a push system with a limiting WIP.

Downstream the bottleneck, products are undergoing another three processes whose WIP can be regarded as latently available stock because of the high availability of the manufacturing technologies applied there. So, it is used as cumulative control variable.

The available stock was adjusted by means of a specific controlling instrument (cf. Fig. 3), while the fluctuation range between minimum and maximum was determined as a planning parameter for the resource management (see setting range: minimum WIP 72,000 pieces, maximum WIP 88,000 pieces). The entire system behaviour is illustrated by Fig. 2 (given as point cloud).

The illustrated operating points were measured specifically for the case scenario and adjusted as setting range for an intervention logic in order to adjust the production resources in a flexible manner.

- Upper limit:

  - a favourable constellation of the weekly customers' call-offs without any significant machine breakdowns (high OEE-level); When the upper limit was about to get reached, which became apparent by the successive run-up of the WIP downstream the bottleneck, capacity adjustments were initiated with a planning horizon of about 10 working days (change of working shift).

- Lower limit:

  - modifications in products' type and quantity on account of changed weekly customers' call-offs as well as significant machine breakdowns (low OEE-level); When the lower limit was about to get reached, which became apparent by the successive run-out of the WIP upstream the bottleneck, additional production resources were used to (i.e. extra shifts).

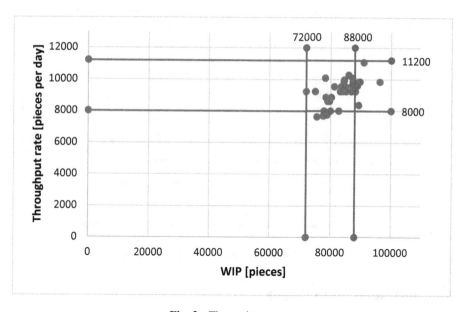

Fig. 2. The setting range.

The planning horizon had to correspond to the reactivity of the production system. This, according to the respective capacity need, allowed for the fact that shifts could be over- or under-staffed in a selective manner, so as to compensate early for possible machine breakdowns, for example.

The following overview of the WIP evaluation introduces a snapshot for the daily check-up of available stock upstream and downstream the bottleneck (cf. Fig. 3).

In it, the WIP-ratio upstream and downstream the bottleneck will be determined as the moving average of the total WIP for each product group in terms of occupied technology, so that changes in product ranges can be made visible in the WIP. Depending on a high and timely booking precision the presented approach is of crucial importance for the control of the entire production system.

As a result of the WIP-oriented control of the system, on-time delivery was kept at any time during the period of evaluation, while the output was raised by about 15% with more or less fixed personnel expenses.

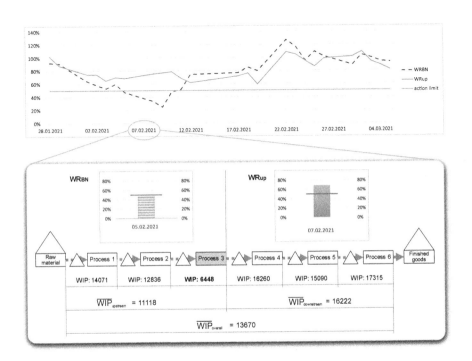

Fig. 3. The developed controlling instrument.

5 Conclusions and Outlook

The application of the introduced control method ensures a quasi-continuous production by means of fixed intervention thresholds. Based on the idea of flow shop systems, it offers the chance for a fast and flexible resource planning and control depending on the customers' call-offs. A quasi-continuous capacity adjustment will be rendered possible, which by recourse to operational regulations and routines will significantly improve the economical situation.

Moreover, with increasing degree of utilisation, the fluctuations of disruptive events could be reduced in the system. As a result, predictive maintenance could be performed (instead of ad-hoc repair with sporadic machine breakdowns) or idle times avoided by automatic releases of subsequent jobs.

Thus, it can be stated that an increased WIP transparency of the entire system combined with clear scheduling and release routines represents a significant step towards operational optimisation.

Further implementations of the introduced control method in more complex systems by the authors illustrate the prerequisites for using.

- a serial manufacturing structure with a directional as well as branched material flow (multistage production process)
- a stable production program over a long period of time (e.g. financial year)
- a manageable amount of product variants (similar product families)

Not suitable are manufacturing structures as a customer-ordered individual production of a high number of very different variants (single part production) with a bidirectional and partly returning material flow.

References

1. Childerhouse, P., Disney, S.M., Towill, D.R.: On the impact of order volatility in the European automotive sector. Int. J. Prod. Econ. **114**(1), 2–13 (2008)
2. Verdouw, C.N., Beulens, A.J.M., Bouwmeester, D., Trienekens, J.H.: Modelling demand-driven chain networks using multiple CODPs. In: Koch, T. (ed.) APMS 2006. ITIFIP, vol. 257, pp. 433–442. Springer, Boston, MA (2008). https://doi.org/10.1007/978-0-387-77249-3_45
3. Hopp, W.J., Spearman, M.L.: Factory Physics: Foundations of Manufacturing Management, 3rd edn. Irwin McGraw-Hill, New York (2008)
4. Bergmann, U., Heinicke, M., Wagenhaus, G.: Methodisch planen - erfolgreich agieren. Industrie-Management Zeitschrift für industrielle Geschäftsprozesse **30**(4), 45–48 (2014)
5. Breithaupt, J.-W., Land, M., Nyhuis, P.: The workload control concept: theory and practical extensions of Load Oriented Order Release. Prod. Plan. Control **13**(7), 625–638 (2002)
6. Fredendall, L.D., Ojha, D., Wayne, P.J.: Concerning the theory of workload control. Eur. J. Oper. Res. **48**(1), 99–111 (2010)
7. Hendry, L., Huang, Y., Stevenson, M.: Workload control: successful implementation taking a contingency-based view of production planning and control. Int. J. Oper. Prod. Manag. **33**(1), 69–103 (2013)
8. Kühnle, H., Bitsch, G.: Foundations & Principles of Distributed Manufacturing: Elements of Manufacturing Networks, Cyber-Physical Production Systems and Smart Automation. Springer, Cham (2015). https://doi.org/10.1007/978-3-319-18078-6
9. Lödding, H.: Handbook of Manufacturing Control: Fundamentals, Description, Configuration. Springer, Heidelberg (2013). https://doi.org/10.1007/978-3-642-24458-2
10. Pound, E.S., Bell, J.H., Spearman, M.L.: Factory Physics for Managers: How Leaders Improve Performance in a Post-lean Six Sigma World. McGraw-Hill Education, New York (2014)
11. Nyhuis, P., Wiendahl, H.-P.: Logistic production operating curves: basic model of the theory of logistic operating curves. CIRP Ann. Manuf. Technol. **55**(1), 441–444 (2006)

12. Yoon, S.-W., Cho, Y.-J., Jeong, S.-J.: Combination effects analysis of bottleneck-load order review/release and the dispatching rule: application to a printed circuit board manufacturing line with multiple bottlenecks. Int. J. Precis. Eng. Manuf. **15**(8), 1725–1732 (2014). https://doi.org/10.1007/s12541-014-0525-4
13. Spearman, M.L., Woodruff, D.L., Hopp, W.J.: CONWIP: a pull alternative to Kanban. Int. J. Prod. Res. **28**(5), 879–894 (1990)

Pricing Models for Data Products
in the Industrial Food Production

Calvin Rix[1]([✉]), Jana Frank[1], Volker Stich[1], and Dennis Urban[2]

[1] Institute for Industrial Management (FIR) at RWTH Aachen University,
Campus-Boulevard 55, 52074 Aachen, Germany
`calvin.rix@fir.rwth-aachen.de`
[2] Lindt & Sprüngli Germany GmbH, Süsterfeldstraße 130,
52072 Aachen, Germany

Abstract. In the food industry, a very large potential of data ecosystems is seen, in which data is understood, exchanged and monetized as an economic asset. However, despite the enormous economic potential, companies in the food industry continue to rely on traditional, product-oriented business models. Existing data in the value chain of industrial food production, e.g., in harvesting, logistics, and production processes, is primarily used for internal optimization and is not monetized in the form of data products. Especially the pricing of data products is a key challenge for data-based business models due to their special characteristics compared to conventional, analog offerings and multiple design options. The goal of this work is therefore to solve this issue by developing a framework that allows the identification of pricing models for data products in the industrial food production. For this purpose, following the procedure of typology formation, essential design parameters and the respective characteristics are derived. Furthermore, three types for pricing models of data products are shown. The results will serve not only stakeholders in the food industry but also manufacturing companies in general as input for an orientation of their data-based business models.

Keywords: Pricing models · Data products · Food production · Typology

1 Introduction

The increasing use of networked machines is generating ever greater volumes of data [1]. In the manufacturing industry the value was 3.5 zettabytes in 2018 and is estimated to grow to 21 zettabytes by 2025 [2]. Against a backdrop of evolving capabilities in the areas of data analytics and storage, as well as artificial intelligence, this data holds continuously growing economic potential [3]. The value of the European data economy, for example, is estimated to grow to 827 billion euros in 2025 [4]. This data is generated across the entire food production value chain: starting with the selection of raw materials, through international transport and production activities, to real-time market analyses [5]. Through intelligent aggregation and processing by data-analytic services, this data can deliver significant added value and become an economic good itself, the so-called data product. As a result value creation is increasingly shifting to

© IFIP International Federation for Information Processing 2021
Published by Springer Nature Switzerland AG 2021
A. Dolgui et al. (Eds.): APMS 2021, IFIP AICT 634, pp. 553–563, 2021.
https://doi.org/10.1007/978-3-030-85914-5_59

data-driven business models that provide unique value to the customer [6]. Nevertheless, the cross-manufacturer use of data in a data economy is still in its infancy [7]. Despite a focus on data monetization of manufacturing companies today, few mechanisms exist to price data products [3]. This can be attributed to characteristics that complicate the choice of a pricing model compared to tangible goods [8]. It is difficult to accurately determine the value of data prior to purchase as the value lies in the derived information, which is intangible and difficult to measure [9]. In addition, data products have a unique cost structure: The fixed costs of building the infrastructure and aggregating the first data product are often substantial ("first copy cost") while the marginal costs of copying and disseminating are negligible [10]. The provisioning costs are composed of the specific value creation process: data extraction, data preparation, information extraction, information provision and information usage [11]. Data products can develop very heterogeneous values for buyers depending on the value creation stage and the specific type [12]. They can be sold directly, as a supplement to existing products and services or as enabler of an entire new value proposition composed of a bundle of services [13].

Due to the above mentioned characteristics and design options, data product pricing is a central challenge of digital business models [14]. Traditional cost- and competition-oriented pricing methods are not sufficient to achieve optimal pricing for data products [15], so that innovative pricing models have become established [8]. Since there can be no universally valid price model for all data products and price models are basically composed of several elements, we addressed the following research question in this paper: *How can pricing models for data products in industrial food production be designed?* Therefore we provide a design framework for the price parameters of data products in the industrial food production. Therefore, we performed a typology formation through workshops with pricing, digitalization and food production experts.

2   State of Research

Since pricing of data products has attracted lot of attention, there has been an increase in recent publications. Nevertheless, research in this area is still in its infancy.

There are publications examining the selection of pricing models as well as the evaluation of prices on data marketplaces [8, 14, 16, 17]. However, these works focus primarily on pure information goods and leaves out data-based service bundles that generate direct added value for the customer. Furthermore, no design factors for the respective data products are shown. Frohmann [15] presents five overarching pillars of pricing models of digital products in his work. The framework provides a precious basis, but refers to digital products in general, whereby the results are on a high level and important design factors for the pricing of the addressed data products in this paper will not be considered. In addition, Buxmann and Lehmann [18] present a model for the pricing of pure software products. Even though many of the design factors can also be applied to this work, it does not cover the entire spectrum of data products due to the focus on pure software products. Liang et al. [8] categorize pricing strategies in terms of different market structures and identify their limitations as part of the Big Data lifecycle. The focus is on setting an appropriate price for the data product. However, as pure digital offers are prioritized, the results are of limited use. In addition, there are scientific approaches that address a systemic overview of design factors of data-based business models and services as well as data marketplaces in particular [3, 19, 20]. In these works, the business models are considered holistically and thus no detailed attention is paid to the respective pricing models.

This shows that even if the current state of research provides building blocks to answer the research question, no framework for the design of pricing models of data products in the industrial food production has been developed yet. Accordingly, there is a research gap not only for the food industry, but also for the entire manufacturing sector.

3 Methodology

Due to the heterogeneous characteristics of data products and diverse design options of pricing models, the method of typology formation is used for designing and building a framework to describe characteristics of data product pricing models within the industrial food production. The development process is based on the well-established approach provided by Welter [21]. With the help of typology an area of investigation can be systematized and thus made comprehensible. Furthermore, it serves to uncover correlations and to support design recommendations [21].

The typification is ideally suited to structure the area of investigation and to offer an application-oriented tool. This includes all relevant characteristics, which are presented holistically as well as the subsequently developed types. When identifying the features as well as their characteristics, the following criteria must be taken into account in order to ensure that the types are meaningful and meet the requirements [22]: First of all, each characteristic must have at least two expressions, whereby an upper limit is not prescribed. In addition, each characteristic must have a certain meaningfulness, which means that there must be a causal and a preferably relationship between the purpose of the examination and the characteristic. Further the differentiability requires that only characteristics that contribute to the differentiation of types are used. The procedure for the formation of the typology is based on a five-step approach (see Fig. 1).

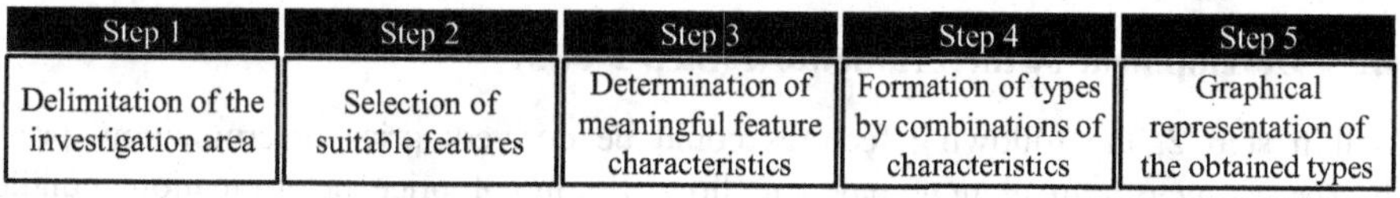

Step 1	Step 2	Step 3	Step 4	Step 5
Delimitation of the investigation area	Selection of suitable features	Determination of meaningful feature characteristics	Formation of types by combinations of characteristics	Graphical representation of the obtained types

Fig. 1. Procedure of the type formation process [21]

In the first step, the definition and appropriate generalization of the given problem takes place, in which primarily the area of investigation is delimited and discussed. Subsequently, the derivation of suitable features (step 2) as well as their characteristics (step 3) takes place. These were derived factually and logically through the experience of the authors and the experts of the EVAREST project team, considering existing literature approaches and requirements from operational practice. This is followed by the identification of typical feature combinations (step 4). Following Grosse-Oetringhaus [22], a combination of progressive and retrograde typing is chosen as an iterative procedure. For this purpose, relevant literature was used as a basis. In addition, consistent combinations of the characteristics were determined according to the configuration theory. Afterwards, the developed combinations were validated by case studies from the food industry. Finally, the results are presented graphically (step 5).

4   Results

The results were developed during the research project EVAREST (see Sect. 6). In the following the steps of typology formation and the achieved results are described.

4.1   Investigation Area (Step 1)

In addition to the delineation of the scope of the study shown in Sect. 1, the retrograde approach requires the consideration of the targeted types in advance. In the literature different approaches can be found that describe and categorize data products.

Tempich [23] defines three different types: Firstly, "Data as a Service", i.e. data are made available by providers and used to generate direct revenue (data * price = revenue). Secondly, "Data as Insights" where data is used to improve product marketing and achieve higher economic results. Thirdly, for "Data-enhanced Products", data enrich physical or virtual products. Hereby, increasing revenue of the enhanced physical product corresponds to the revenue generated by data. Wixom and Ross [24] distinguish data products as follows: "Selling data", "optimize existing products or service" or "improving internal processes". Liozu and Ulaga [13] add "new business models and revenue streams" to these types. Laney [25] defines data products based on economic value which they capture for businesses: "direct exchange with goods, services or monetary resources"; "use to increase income, or reduce risks and expenses". To date, there is no consensus on the definition of data products, so a distinction of data product types has been made using the approach described in Sect. 3.

4.2   Development of the Framework (Step 2 to 3)

Within step 2, the following features could be derived: price determination, price discovery, measurement unit, payment flow, timing of price determination, bundle components, bundling type, degree of integration, differentiation, price dynamic, value creation. The features and feature characteristics (step 3) developed are described below.

Basically, there are three different ways for the *price determination* of data products [12]: cost-based, competition-based and value-based. In the traditional cost-based approach, the supplier costs are calculated and a price is determined for the customer by adding up an amount (cost-plus) [26]. The cost-plus approach is considered ineffective due to the aforementioned cost structure, as the customer's willingness to pay can significantly exceed the costs including the target margin, especially for digital offers and services [15]. Nonetheless, there is widespread use for digital products, due to higher acceptance, simple and quick determination as well as no necessary data regarding demand structures and willingness to pay [12, 27]. In competition-based pricing, expected or observable price levels of the market serve as the main source of pricing [28]. Thus, competition-based approaches have severe limitations due to the lack of data-based offerings, as it requires the existence of an active market where prices can be continuously observed and compared [12]. Basically, cost and competitive situation are important influencing factors for any pricing model, but the isolated use of both methods is neither sufficient to achieve optimal pricing for analog nor intangible assets [15, 27]. It is also necessary to assess the actual value of data products to the customer especially in the industrial sector [27]. Thus, in the value-based approach, the price is no longer based on the provider's internal variables (e.g., costs) or competitive prices, but on the added value that the offered solution generates in the customer's business environment [28]. The added value of the data product is determined on the basis of the benefits that arise over the entire data product lifecycle [29]. Even if value-based pricing is considered to be an superior approach, paradoxically, cost-based and competitive approaches continue to play a dominant role in industrial pricing [30]. One of the main problems in business practice is to gain access to essential data to quantify the value of the offers to the customers [31]. Another aspect is the so-called fixed-pie bias. Even though value-based pricing has the potential for win-win situations, the dominant assumption is that what the company gains, the customer loses and vice versa (zero-sum game) [32].

Price discovery is a key function of marketplaces as it allows suppliers and demanders to set a price at which both agree to the transaction [33]. Firstly, it can be determined by one of the two sides, supplier or demander [20]. In this case, the other side only has the option to accept or reject the offer at this price. Secondly, the price can be determined by the platform provider. Therefore, provider and buyer must accept the determined price to be part of the marketplace [20]. A third option are negotiations between buyers and sellers, which are primarily relevant for goods of higher value [20].

The *measurement unit* of a price model specifies the service the customer pays for [15]. A basic distinction is made between usage-independent and usage-dependent pricing models [15]. In addition to the one-time payment, subscription payments count as usage-independent measurement unit. Usage-dependent pricing models are dependent on the usage phase of the customer. These pricing models are becoming increasingly important, especially for digital goods. The customer pays for the actual use or even the outcome or economic success achieved by the data-based solution [15, 34].

There are three variants for the *payment flow* [15]: single payment, recurring payment and a hybrid combination of both variants.

The *timing of price determination* can be either ex-ante or ex-post the service provision [26]. Ex-ante market pricing is particularly relevant for standardized products and services [15]. Ex-post price determination is based on the actual performance provided by the supplier and is particularly advantageous for individual services [15].

Another elementary part of the pricing model are the *components* that are bundled into the offer [35]. For the considered data products, the data itself, the analytic services used, and the enhanced products and services are the main items to be considered. Furthermore, a holistic data-based solution can also be offered.

Depending on the *bundling type*, three categories are possible [18]: unbundling, mixed bundling and pure bundling. In unbundling, products can only be purchased individually [36]. If the customer can choose whether to purchase the entire bundle or the included products individually, this is termed as mixed bundling. For pure bundling, the products are offered exclusively in the bundle defined by the provider.

Furthermore, the products in the bundle can also be described in terms of their *degree of integration*. The partial services can be independent to each other or have a substitutive or complementary relationship to each other [37].

Price differentiation is based on the optimal exploitation of heterogeneous customers' willingness to pay through different prices [37]. Price differentiation is particularly important for suppliers of purely digital goods, as inexpensive modification greatly facilitates the application [18]. Basically there are three different forms of price differentiation [38]: self-selection, segmentation and willingness to pay. With self-selection, the customer decides for himself which product-price combination he wants to choose [39]. A distinction is made between quantity-based, time-based and performance-based self-selection [40]. In this context, versioning is considered to be very advantageous for digital goods [41]. Often, data product providers offer extensive versions and likewise offerings with reduced functionalities to achieve better market penetration, also for less solvent customers. In segmentation, the provider decides how to differentiate prices on its own criteria [37]. The price can be determined, for example, based on the size of the customer's company, the country or region in which the customer operates [40]. Finally, there is the differentiation that tries to skim off the customer's actual willingness to pay, which, however, is the biggest challenge of the differentiation types [42].

Dynamic pricing is based on adjusting the price over time [18]. For the addressed data products, the penetration and skimming strategy as well as supply & demand and result-orientation are of importance. The penetration strategy has the objective to use low prices in order to maximize market penetration [18]. The skimming strategy aims at skimming off customers with a high willingness to pay with initially high prices and then reducing prices to win further customers. Supply & demand models depend on the buying behavior of market participants [8]. It can be used to balance peak periods with very high demand and to make purchasing more attractive in less busy periods [8]. A strategy that is dynamically oriented towards the achieved result aims to continuously increase the performance for the customer and thus create a positive lock-in effect.

The way in which *value is created* by the data product can be distinguished by three types: product/service sales, barter and achieved performance. A monetary added value can be achieved through the traditional sale of products and services. In addition, bartering plays an essential role for data products [25]. This means the exchange of generated data for added value, like products or better business conditions. The generated and exchanged data represent an indirect value, as it can be resold to interested parties in the ecosystem (e. g. drinking behavior for beverage producer) (see Sect. 4.3). In addition, the monetary added value can also be based on the performance actually achieved for the customer, accounted by a suitable measurement unit [34].

4.3   Pricing Models for Data Product Types (Step 4 to 5)

In the final step, pricing models were derived for the identified data product types and presented graphically by using the developed framework (see Fig. 2).

The first type of data product is the *data product as insight (blue)*. It is composed of raw data and analytical services aggregated into a data product that aims to answer business-critical questions for the customer. The price of this data product is measured by the potential added value that the additional insights bring to a business decision. In addition to basic criteria such as quality and relevance in the business context, the degree of analytical maturity plays a major role for the added value. The value increases from a descriptive data product over a diagnosis to forecasts or even decision support that shows direct guidance for action in the future [43]. Since it is not possible to clearly allocate the added values for the customer, the value can be determined and estimated ex-ante based on of existing value attributes. The price can be paid once or on a subscription basis, e.g. for the purpose of updating the data. In food production data products as insight can add great value to a wide range of areas. In addition to classic price panels, sales forecasts are particularly valuable because they are very volatile and are influenced by various external factors such as weather, seasonality, constantly changing customer needs and political influences. This has a positive impact on inventory management throughout the food production value chain, from retailers to distributors to producers and farmers. Stocks can thus be reduced, and capacity limits improved, thereby reducing the loss due to overcapacity.

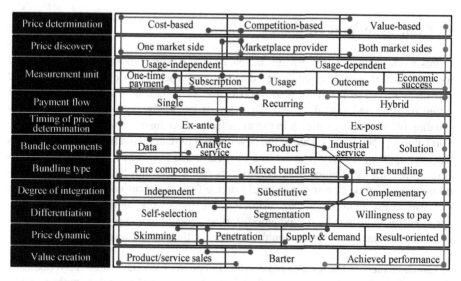

Price determination	Cost-based		Competition-based			Value-based	
Price discovery	One market side		Marketplace provider			Both market sides	
Measurement unit	Usage-independent			Usage-dependent			
	One-time payment	Subscription		Usage	Outcome		Economic success
Payment flow	Single			Recurring		Hybrid	
Timing of price determination	Ex-ante				Ex-post		
Bundle components	Data	Analytic service		Product	Industrial service		Solution
Bundling type	Pure components		Mixed bundling			Pure bundling	
Degree of integration	Independent		Substitutive			Complementary	
Differentiation	Self-selection		Segmentation			Willingness to pay	
Price dynamic	Skimming		Penetration		Supply & demand		Result-oriented
Value creation	Product/service sales		Barter			Achieved performance	

Fig. 2. Typology visualized as a morphological box (Color figure online)

The next type is *data-enhanced product or service (red)*. Compared to conventional products and services, data connectivity enables various special features. In addition to the positive economic factors, such as the possibility of charging higher prices or implementing services more cost-effectively, data connectivity enables innovations for the pricing model. The complementary bundle of services can be billed on a usage basis and even supply & demand models are possible. Furthermore, the data generated can be used to achieve additional value through bartering. Data-based features also allow the customer to select performance levels with little effort, even for hardware products. There are countless implementation possibilities for the food industry. For example Celli Group's smart dispensing systems or Bizerba's innovative weighing technology can be used to directly analyze the consumer behavior in order to optimize inventories, reduce waste or directly measure the success of marketing campaigns for the food manufacturing companies [44, 45].

Data product as performance (green) goes beyond the mere provision of insights and uses prescriptive analytics as part of a holistic solution to generate concrete benefits for the customer. This requires both data analytics and industry-specific expertise. Through a participative business constellation of provider and customer, this data product opens the possibility of implementing performance-oriented pricing models and transferring them into a contractual framework. For this purpose, an interactive price determination with the customer is to be implemented, in which the price is ultimately determined by the result. The timing of the pricing takes place ex-post to be able to use the actual added values achieved and, optimally, to enter a long-term partnership with the customer that is result-oriented and represents a win-win situation. The data generated in the process provides the opportunity to continuously improve the offer and transform it into innovations.

5   Conclusion and Outlook

In this work parameters for pricing models of data product types within the industrial food production were derived. Three data product types were developed, determined and illustrated. The results aim to improve the systematization and classification of future research and extend the existing body of knowledge by specifying the understanding of data product pricing in the manufacturing industry. The research results are also subject to limitations. Due to the new domain of data products, the model requires frequent updating to stay relevant and to incorporate new dimensions and characteristics. Since the creation of the typology was developed with the EVAREST consortium researchers, other researchers could derive further dimensions and characteristics that they deem more significant. Although the framework of the pricing model is specified for industrial food production, further research could reuse the structure for other sectors and an extension could be made for the entire manufacturing industry.

Acknowledgements. The research and development project EVAREST that forms the basis for this report is funded within the scope of the "Smart Data Economy" technology program run by the Federal Ministry for Economic Affairs and Energy and is managed by the DLR project management agency. The authors are responsible for the content of this publication.

References

1. Azkan, C., Iggena, L., Meisel, L., Spiekermann, M., Korte, T., Otto, B.: DEMAND - Perspektiven der Datenwirtschaft. Fraunhofer-Institut für Software- und Systemtechnik ISST, Dortmund (2020)
2. Reinsel, D., Gantz, J., Rydning, J.: The Digitization of the World: From Edge to Core. IDC Corporate USA, Framingham, MA (2018)
3. Fruhwirth, M., Rachinger, M., Prlja, E.: Discovering business models of data marketplaces. In: Bui, T. (ed.) Proceedings of the 53rd Hawaii International Conference on System Sciences, Honolulu, Hawaii, pp. 5738–5747 (2020)
4. Cattaneo, G., Micheletti, G., Glennon, M., La Croce, C., Mitta, C.: The European data market monitoring tool: Key facts & figures, first policy conclusions, data landscape and quantified stories. Publications Office of the European Union, Luxembourg (2020)
5. Ji, G., Hu, L., Tan, K.H.: A study on decision-making of food supply chain based on big data. J. Syst. Sci. Syst. Eng. **26**(2), 183–198 (2017). https://doi.org/10.1007/s11518-016-5320-6
6. Grün, O.: Datenökonomie braucht einen offenen Markt. In: Bär, C., Grädler, T., Mayr, R. (eds.) Digitalisierung im Spannungsfeld von Politik, Wirtschaft, Wissenschaft und Recht: 1. Band: Politik und Wirtschaft, pp. 127–135. Springer, Heidelberg (2018). https://doi.org/10.1007/978-3-662-55720-4_12
7. Spiekermann, M.: Data marketplaces: trends and monetisation of data goods. Intereconomics **54**(4), 208–216 (2019). https://doi.org/10.1007/s10272-019-0826-z
8. Liang, F., Yu, W., An, D., Yang, Q., Fu, X., Zhao, W.: A survey on big data market: pricing, trading and protection. IEEE Access **6**(1), 15132–15154 (2018)
9. Stahl, F., Schomm, F., Vomfell, L., Vossen, G.: Marketplaces for digital data: quo vadis? Comput. Inf. Sci. **10**(4), 22–37 (2017)
10. Shapiro, C., Varian, H.R.: Versioning: the smart way to sell information. Harv. Bus. Rev. **76**(1), 107–115 (1998)
11. BVDW: Data Economy: Datenwertschöpfung und Qualität von Daten. Bundesverband Digitale Wirtschaft (BVDW) e.V., Düsseldorf (2018)
12. Krotova, A., Rusche, C., Spiekermann, M.: Die ökonomische Bewertung von Daten: Verfahren, Beispiele und Anwendungen. Institut der deutschen Wirtschaft, Köln (2019)
13. Liozu, S.M., Ulaga, W.: Monetizing Data: A Practical Roadmap for Framing, Pricing & Selling Your B2B Digital Offers. Value Innoruption Advisors Publishing, Anthem (2018)
14. Stahl, F., Löser, A., Vossen, G.: Preismodelle für Datenmarktplätze. Informatik-Spektrum **38**(2), 133–141 (2013). https://doi.org/10.1007/s00287-013-0751-7
15. Frohmann, F.: Digitales Pricing: Strategische Preisbildung in der digitalen Wirtschaft mit dem 3-Level-Modell. Springer Gabler, Wiesbaden (2018). https://doi.org/10.1007/978-3-658-22573-5
16. Fricker, S.A., Maksimov, Y.V.: Pricing of data products in data marketplaces. In: Ojala, A., Holmström Olsson, H., Werder, K. (eds.) ICSOB 2017. LNBIP, vol. 304, pp. 49–66. Springer, Cham (2017). https://doi.org/10.1007/978-3-319-69191-6_4
17. Cao, T.-D., Pham, T.-V., Vu, Q.-H., Truong, H.-L., Le, D.-H., Dustdar, S.: MARSA. ACM Trans. Internet Technol. **16**(3), 1–21 (2016)
18. Lehmann, S., Buxmann, P.: Preisstrategien von Softwareanbietern. Wirtsch. Inform. **51**(6), 519–529 (2009)
19. Hartmann, P.M., Zaki, M., Feldmann, N., Neely, A.: Capturing value from big data – a taxonomy of data-driven business models used by start-up firms. IJOPM **36**(10), 1382–1406 (2016)

20. Täuscher, K.: Business Models in the Digital Economy: An Empirical Study of Digital Marketplaces. Fraunhofer Center for International Management and Knowledge Economy, Leipzig (2016)
21. Welter, M.: Die Forschungsmethode der Typisierung: Charakteristika, Einsatzbereiche und praktische Anwendung. Wirtschaftswissenschaftliches Studium **35**(2), 113–116 (2006)
22. Grosse-Oetringhaus, W.F.: Fertigungstypologie unter dem Gesichtspunkt der Fertigungsablaufplanung. Duncker & Humblot, Berlin (1974)
23. Tempich, C.: Konzeption und Entwicklung von Data-driven Products/Datenprodukten. In: Haneke, U., Trahasch, S., Zimmer, M., Felden, C. (eds.) Data Science: Grundlagen, Architekturen und Anwendungen, pp. 45–64. Edition TDWI, dpunkt, Heidelberg (2018)
24. Wixom, B., Ross, J.: How to monetize your data. MITSloan Manag. Rev. **58**(3) (2017)
25. Laney, D.B.: Infonomics: How To Monetize, Manage, and Measure Information as an Asset for Competitive Advantage. Taylor & Francis, New York, Abington (2018)
26. Simon, H., Fassnacht, M.: Preismanagement. Springer Fachmedien, Wiesbaden (2016). https://doi.org/10.1007/978-3-658-11871-6
27. Heckman, J.R., Boehmer, E.L., Peters, E.H., Davaloo, M., Kurup, N.G.: A pricing model for data markets. In: University of California Irvine (ed.) iConference Proceedings (2015)
28. Hinterhuber, A.: Customer value-based pricing strategies: why companies resist. J. Bus. Strategy **29**(4), 41–50 (2008)
29. Zechmann, A.: Nutzungsbasierte Datenbewertung: Entwicklung und Anwendung eines Konzepts zur finanziellen Bewertung von Datenvermögenswerten auf Basis des AHP. Dissertation, Universität St. Gallen (2018)
30. Liozu, S.M.: State of value-based-pricing survey: Perceptions, challenges, and impact. J. Revenue Pricing Manag. **16**(1), 18–29 (2017)
31. Töytäri, P., Rajala, R., Alejandro, T.B.: Organizational and institutional barriers to value-based pricing in industrial relationships. Ind. Mark. Manag. **47**, 53–64 (2015)
32. Hinterhuber, A., Liozu, S.M.: Is innovation in pricing your next source of competitive advantage? Bus. Horiz. **57**(3), 413–423 (2014)
33. Bakos, Y.: The emerging role of electronic marketplaces on the Internet. Commun. ACM **41** (8), 35–42 (1998)
34. Stoppel, E., Roth, S.: The conceptualization of pricing schemes: from product-centric to customer-centric value approaches. J. Revenue Pricing Manag. **16**(1), 76–90 (2017)
35. Lehmann, S., Buxmann, P.: Pricing strategies of software vendors. Bus. Inf. Syst. Eng. **1**(6), 452–462 (2009)
36. Olderog, T., Skiera, B.: The benefits of bundling strategies. SBR **52**(2), 137–159 (2000)
37. Diller, H.: Preispolitik, 4th edn. Kohlhammer, Stuttgart (2008)
38. Pigou, A.C.: The Economics of Welfare, 3rd edn. Macmilian, London (1929)
39. Kahin, B., Varian, H.R.: Versioning information goods. In: Kahin, B., Varian, H.R. (eds.) Internet Publishing and Beyond: The Economics of Digital Information and Intellectual Property, pp. 190–202. Publication of the Harvard Information Infrastructure Project. MIT Press, Cambridge (2000)
40. Skiera, B., Spann, M.: Preisdifferenzierung im Internet. In: Schögel, M. (ed.) Roadmap to E-Business, pp. 270–284. Verl. Thexis, St. Gallen (2002)
41. Viswanathan, S., Anandalingam, G.: Pricing strategies for information goods. Sadhana – J. Indian Acad. Sci. **30**(23), 257–274 (2005)
42. Choudhary, V., Ghose, A., Mukhopadhyay, T., Rajan, U.: Personalized pricing and quality differentiation. Manag. Sci. **51**(7), 1120–1130 (2005)

43. Amann, K., Petzold, J., Westerkamp, M.: Prädiktive Analytik. In: Management und Controlling, pp. 251–256. Springer, Wiesbaden (2020). https://doi.org/10.1007/978-3-658-28795-5_8

44. Bizerba: Smart Shelf Lösungen: Vernetzte Smart Shelf Lösungen mit integrierter Wägetechnologie (2020). https://www.bizerba.com/media/themen/security_of_supply/bizerba_insight_smart_shelf_loesungen_de.pdf. Accessed 05 Apr 2021

45. ptc: Celli Group transformiert Nahrungsmittel- und Getränkeindustrie (2020). https://www.ptc.com/de/case-studies/celli. Accessed 16 Apr 2021

AI-Based Approaches for Quality and Performance Improvement of Production Systems

A Neural Network Model for Quality Prediction in the Automotive Industry

Anders Risan, Mohamed Kais Msakni$^{(\boxtimes)}$ ⓘ, and Peter Schütz ⓘ

Department of Industrial Economics and Technology Management,
Norwegian University of Science and Technology, 7491 Trondheim, Norway
andris@stud.ntnu.no, {kais.msakni,peter.schutz}@ntnu.no

Abstract. In this paper, we present a machine learning application for the automotive industry. We study the use of neural networks to predict the location of milled holes in a bumper beam using historical measurement data. The overall goal of the study is to reduce the time needed for quality control procedures as the predictions can supplement manual control measurements. Our preliminary results indicate that the neural network can generally capture the production process variations, but underestimates larger deviations from the specified location.

Keywords: Neural network · Quality control · Machine learning · Manufacturing

1 Introduction

The fourth industrial revolution, commonly referred to as Industry 4.0, marks a new era in global manufacturing, causing a rapid transformation of systems of production, management, and governance [13]. Technological solutions and data processing methods such as the Internet of Things (IoT), Cloud Computing, and Big Data Manufacturing have emerged, allowing a higher degree of connectivity. Together with advances in Artificial Intelligence and new possibilities offered by Machine Learning algorithms, decision-makers can extract valuable information from data and distribute it throughout entire value chains [14]. The technological advances following Industry 4.0 also enable new approaches for quality control by converting the collected data into manufacturing intelligence. Some of these approaches include the ability to perform predictive analysis, real-time quality monitoring, and corrections [16,18].

In this paper, we study the application of a neural network to predict the location of machined holes in a bumper beam based on historical measurement data. The produced bumper beams are measured in fixed intervals to ensure that the produced products satisfy the quality requirements, i. e. that all measurement points are within tolerance limits. In case of discovering a part that

This work was supported by the Research Council of Norway as part of the LeanDigital research project.

violates the tolerance limits, the entire production since the last measurement is scrapped. The goal of using a neural network to predict the quality of the produced products is to address the trade-off between the frequency of carrying out quality control procedures and the risk of waste production. High-fidelity quality predictions would increase the duration of the time interval between physical control measurements, thus reducing downtime in the production system.

The remainder of this paper is organized as follows: In Sect. 2, we provide an overview over applications of machine learning and neural networks in quality prediction. We introduce crash management systems and the bumper beam we develop the neural network for in Sect. 3. Section 4 covers the implementation and the performance of the neural network model. We conclude in Sect. 5.

2   Quality Control and Machine Learning

The purpose of quality control is to ensure that the final product meets the specified quality requirements. This is crucial for the long-term success of any manufacturing company. Despite the complexity of the production system, multi-factor and non-linear interactions between different processes and/or products, a predictive model can be used to predict the end quality of products from the available input data [15]. This information can then be used to improve the production system, e. g. by early calibration of process parameters, resulting in reduced waste production or stabilization of the production process.

The significant amount of data collected from sensors and other monitoring tools has made it possible to apply machine learning in quality control, e. g. predictive maintenance, anomaly detection, monitoring of product quality and machine conditions, as well as process optimization [13,21]. The orientation towards machine learning is, among others, pushed by the limited capacity of classical statistic techniques against complex big data sets. Conversely, machine learning systems tend to improve their performance as the amount of available data grows, making machine learning an adequate tool for extracting valuable information from mass data [1].

Neural networks are among the most widely used models in machine learning. They have been used for a wide range of applications within quality control in manufacturing environments. Notable examples include, amongst others: Karayel [7] highlights the importance for manufacture to predict the surface roughness before machining with a CNC lathe. The prediction can be done using a feedforward multi-layered neural network where the input parameters are cutting depth, cutting speed, and feed rate. The predicted surface roughness is then fed into the control system to obtain the optimal cutting parameters. Tsai et al. [17] develop a supervised feedforward neural network for real-time quality control of the surface roughness in milling cutting operations. Martin et al. [11] propose to automate the quality control process in resistance spot welding. A supervised feedforward neural network is developed to replace a human expert that estimates the quality level of spot welds from ultra sonic oscillograms. In a similar context, Zhao et al. [22] show that the power signal includes useful information to determine the welding nugget states. This information is used by a regression model and feedforward neural network to determine the welding qualities for a real-time detection system. Wang et al. [19] propose a convolutional neural network to automate the process of detecting defects in parts. This quality control process is done by visual inspections and aims at replacing human agents to improve the production efficiency. Wang et al. [20] extend the model for geometrically complex products using cloud-based platform.

In semiconductor manufacturing, virtual metrology is used to avoid the extra cost of physical measurements of wafers. It consists of predicting the wafers properties using machine parameters and sensor data. Due to the high dimentionality of data and complexity of the process, regression models fail to provide good predictions. Thus, machine learning-based methods have been proposed to detect faulty wafers [8]. Maggipinto et al. [10] propose a deep learning-based model, Jia et al. [6] use the group method of data handling-type polynomial neural networks, and Puggini and McLoone [12] develop an extreme learning machine (a particular type of neural networks) for virtual metrology.

The contribution of this paper is to propose a quality prediction model in the automotive industry where products are subject to strict requirements. Unlike most models of the literature, the proposed neural network does not analyze the current product on a real-time basis for validation but instead learns from previously produced and measured products to predict the quality of the following product. By doing so, the production process is smoothed as early adjustments can be anticipated and scrap production is reduced.

3   Quality Prediction for a Bumper Beam

3.1   Crash Management Systems

The main purpose of a car's crash management system is to reduce the impact of a collision; the objective is changing dependent on speed: at low speeds (<15 km/h), the goal is to minimize the cost of repairing the damage. At speeds between 15 and 40 km/h, the main aim is to protect any pedestrians involved in the collision, while the protection of the passengers inside the car is becoming the first priority at higher speeds [4]. Due to its role as an important passive safety system, the crash management system has to satisfy strict requirements regarding deflection and crash stability, set out by legislation, insurance companies, and customers [2]. To ensure that the system has the capability to absorb the maximum amount of crash energy, the different parts are subject to rigorous quality control throughout the production process.

3.2   Description of the Bumper Beam

The front crash management system usually consists of a fascia covering a bumper beam and crash boxes for energy absorbance connecting the bumper beam to the structure of the car [4]. In this study, we focus on the production of the bumper beam.

The bumper beam is produced through stretch forming an extruded aluminium profile before machining holes for mounting the crash boxes and cutting it to length. A total of 20 holes have to be milled, each of which has a narrow tolerance range regarding its location in the beam. In predefined intervals, a beam is taken out of production after the machining process for quality control. During this quality control, the curvature of the beam and the location of the holes are measured. If the measured values violate the specified tolerance limits, the beam is rejected. Figure 1 illustrates different measurement points for the curvature and milled holes. The location of the leftmost hole in Fig. 1, hole HH20, is predicted by the neural network discussed in Sect. 4.

Fig. 1. Measurement points on the beam. The blue rectangles represent the different measurement points of the bend. Hole HH20 is the leftmost hole in the beam. (Color figure online)

Hole HH20 has been selected for analysis for two main reasons: First, it serves as a reference hole for three other holes. As such, any deviation from its dedicated location translates into deviations for the holes referencing HH20. Being able to predict the location of HH20 therefore allows predicting the locations of the other holes. Second, the measure of linear correlation between the holes' historical measurements using the Pearson correlation matrix indicates that the predictive potential of curvature measurements for the location of holes is largest for HH20. The analysis of historical measurement data also shows that the measurements of the Y-coordinate of hole HH20 are very stable. The measurements of the X-coordinate of the same hole, however, are more volatile and vary a lot over time. Thus, we focus our study on predicting the X-coordinate of the future locations of HH20.

We use the available historical measurement data for the entire cluster to train a neural network model for predicting future HH20 locations. The input data is formed by the different measurements that showed high correlations with HH 20. The neural network is used for the approximation of the regression function of the available data, which in this case are homogeneous and continuous. The choice of neural networks is based on their successful application in various domains, especially in manufacturing environments (see Sect. 2). One of the strengths of neural networks is their ability to handle multidimensional and multivariate data while providing high accuracy results [5, 21], as well as to estimate nonlinear functions not known analytically [3].

4   Implementation and Results

4.1   Training, Validation and Test Set

The data available includes 1,255 measurement reports that were collected over three years at specific intervals. These time series data are then divided into two sets. The first 70% of the data forms the first set used for training. The last 30% of the data constitutes the second set used to validate the neural network model. K-fold cross-validation method is applied to reduce the variance in the validation score with respect to the size of the training and validation sets. This generates 878 samples in the training and validation set; a 5-fold split is used, yielding a validation set size of 175 samples. We standardize the input data as the performance of neural networks is sensitive to scale. The standardization of the data is performed on the training, and the same scaler is later used on the testing set. By doing so, there is no information leak between training and testing sets. Also, the performance of the neural network is not affected by the scale between the value of the measurements and the deviations from the nominal values.

4.2   Neural Network Implementation

The neural network is implemented in Python 3.8.6 using the multi-layer perceptron regressor provided by the Scikit-Learn library. We use a neural network with two hidden layers of 20 neurons each and use the default parameters of MLPRegressor of Scikit-Learn. The output layer includes one neuron and converts the flow of the network to the final output. For the weight optimization, however, we use the LBFGS solver, an optimizer in the family of quasi-Newton methods and recommended setting for small datasets for faster converge and better performance.

The goal of the neural network model is to predict the location of hole HH20 based on past bend measurements. We compare the results from three cases that use variations of the available input. The neural networks are trained for each case separately. Case 1 uses 1-lagged measurements, i. e. only the last set of measurements. In Case 2, the neural network is provided with 1-lagged and 2-lagged measurements, i. e. the last two sets of measurements. The last case, Case 3, is fed with 1-lagged, 2-lagged and 3-lagged input data.

4.3   Model Performance

We estimate the neural networks' performance on the testing set by computing the Mean Absolute Error (MAE), the Mean Squared Error (MSE), the Root Mean Squared Error (RMSE), and the coefficient of determination R^2 for the different cases. The results are presented in Table 1.

We see from Table 1 that the prediction quality of the different cases is quite similar, albeit with slightly better performance for Case 3. However, the improvements in the different performance metrics are small, indicating that using more lagged data has limited value for this production process.

Table 1. Performance metrics of the neural network model.

	Case 1	Case 2	Case 3
MAE	0.21	0.21	0.21
MSE	0.08	0.08	0.07
RMSE	0.28	0.28	0.27
R^2	0.09	0.09	0.13

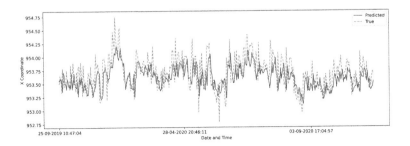

Fig. 2. Performance of case 3, comparing true and predicted location of HH20.

Figure 2 plots the true values of HH20 against the predicted values of HH20 for Case 3. Overall, the neural network manages to track the movements in the time series quite well and predict most of the actual values with sufficient accuracy. However, it tends to smooth predicted values and has difficulties predicting spikes, here values below 953.25 or above 954.25.

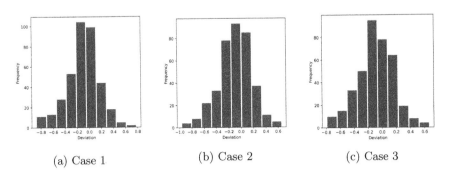

(a) Case 1   (b) Case 2   (c) Case 3

Fig. 3. Residual histogram for all cases of the neural network.

A good prediction should have uncorrelated residuals with zero mean [9]. The descriptive statistics for all models are presented in Table 2, with the corresponding histograms presented in Fig. 3. Again, the different measures and visualization confirm that the prediction quality of the three cases is comparable, with Case 3 performing slightly better. The mean value of Case 1 is positive, whereas the mean values of Case 2 and 3 are negative. This can be attributed to the fact that Case 1 sometimes predicts higher values than the actual values. Cases 2 and 3, on the contrary, are more restrictive and tend to smooth the predicted values. This observation can be confirmed by the *min* and *max* measurements. The mean is close to zero for all cases with a small deviation around it (about 0.27). From both visualization and descriptive statistics, the residuals appear to be close to Gaussian distribution.

Table 2. Descriptive statistics for the residuals.

	Case 1	Case 2	Case 3
Mean	0.10	−0.10	−0.09
Std	0.27	0.27	0.26
Min	−0.88	−0.97	−0.79
25%	−0.23	−0.24	−0.24
50%	0.07	−0.08	−0.08
75%	0.08	0.08	0.09
Max	0.78	0.66	0.67

Overall, the inability to predict any of the spikes can be a challenge for using this neural network to predict the properties of a specific product: if extreme measurements cannot be predicted, the neural network will be overly optimistic regarding the production system's ability to produce parts that are within the specified tolerance limits. It might still be possible though, to use the neural network to detect trends indicating that the production process is no longer stable. Unfortunately, the available measurement data is currently not sufficient for such a study.

5 Conclusion

This paper studies the use of a neural network to predict the location of milled holes in a bumper beam. Three different cases have been analyzed where the neural network is trained on different amounts of historical measurement data. The predicted values match the true locations of the holes on the beam quite well. However, the neural network generally underestimates more extreme deviations from the dedicated position, both in terms of frequency of occurrence and magnitude of deviation.

As a first extension to the work presented in this paper, we will use the neural network for the multivariate case, i.e. to predict the coordinates of multiple holes. An important aspect that needs to be investigated further is also the ability to predict more extreme values to get a more accurate estimation of the probability of producing a beam violating its specifications. A data analysis could help to identify outliers (anomalies) in the production process and thus improve the ability to predict extreme values. Finally, the effect of including other data than measurement data, e.g. alloy or temperature variations in storage, on the quality of the prediction will also be investigated.

References

1. Chollet, F.: Deep Learning with Python. Manning Publications, New York (2017)
2. Davoodi, M.M., Sapuan, S.M., Ahmad, D., Ali, A., Mehdi Jonoobi, A.K.: Mechanical properties of hybrid kenaf/glass reinforced epoxy composite for passenger car bumper beam. Mater. Des. **31**(10), 4927–4932 (2010)
3. Dreyfus, G.: Neural Networks: Methodology and Applications. Springer, Berlin (2005)
4. European Aluminium: Aluminium Automotive Manual. European Aluminium Association, Brussels, Belgium (2015). https://www.european-aluminium.eu/resource-hub/aluminium-automotive-manual/. Accessed 19 Mar 2021
5. Goldstein, M., Uchida, S.: A comparative evaluation of unsupervised anomaly detection algorithms for multivariate data. PLoS ONE **11**(4), e0152173 (2016)
6. Jia, X., Di, Y., Feng, J., Yang, Q., Dai, H., Lee, J.: Adaptive virtual metrology for semiconductor chemical mechanical planarization process using gmdh-type polynomial neural networks. J. Process Control **62**, 44–54 (2018)
7. Karayel, D.: Prediction and control of surface roughness in CNC lathe using artificial neural network. J. Mater. Process. Technol. **209**(7), 3125–3137 (2009)
8. Kim, D., Kang, P., Cho, S., joo Lee, H., Doh, S.: Machine learning-based novelty detection for faulty wafer detection in semiconductor manufacturing. Expert Syst. Appl. **39**(4), 4075–4083 (2012). https://doi.org/10.1016/j.eswa.2011.09.088, https://www.sciencedirect.com/science/article/pii/S0957417411014114
9. Kuhn, M., Johnson, K.: Applied Predictive Modeling, vol. 26. Springer, New York (2013). https://doi.org/10.1007/978-1-4614-6849-3_2
10. Maggipinto, M., Beghi, A., McLoone, S., Susto, G.A.: Deepvm: a deep learning-based approach with automatic feature extraction for 2d input data virtual metrology. J. Process Control **84**, 24–34 (2019)
11. Martin, O., Lopez, M., Martin, F.: Artificial neural networks for quality control by ultrasonic testing in resistance spot welding. J. Mater. Process. Technol. **183**(2–3), 226–233 (2007)
12. Puggini, L., McLoone, S.: Extreme learning machines for virtual metrology and etch rate prediction. In: 2015 26th Irish Signals and Systems Conference (ISSC), pp. 1–6. IEEE (2015)
13. Roblek, V., Meško, M., Krapež, A.: A complex view of industry 4.0. SAGE Open **6**(2), 1–11 (2016)
14. Santos, C., Mehrsai, A., Barros, A., Araújo, M., Ares, E.: Towards Industry 4.0: an overview of European strategic roadmaps. Procedia Manufact. **13**, 972–979 (2017)
15. Schmitt, J., Bönig, J., Borggräfe, T., Beitinger, G., Deuse, J.: Predictive model-based quality inspection using machine learning and edge cloud computing. Adv. Eng. Inf. **45**, 101101 (2020)
16. Tao, F., Qi, Q., Liu, A., Kusiak, A.: Data-driven smart manufacturing. J. Manuf. Syst. **48**(C), 157–169 (2018)
17. Tsai, Y.H., Chen, J.C., Lou, S.J.: An in-process surface recognition system based on neural networks in end milling cutting operations. Int. J. Mach. Tools Manuf. **39**(4), 583–605 (1999)

18. Wan, J., et al.: A manufacturing big data solution for active preventive maintenance. IEEE Trans. Ind. Inf. **13**(4), 2039–2047 (2017)
19. Wang, T., Chen, Y., Qiao, M., Snoussi, H.: A fast and robust convolutional neural network-based defect detection model in product quality control. Int. J. Adv. Manuf. Technol. 3465–3471 (2017). https://doi.org/10.1007/s00170-017-0882-0
20. Wang, Y., Liu, M., Zheng, P., Yang, H., Zou, J.: A smart surface inspection system using faster r-CNN in cloud-edge computing environment. Adv. Eng. Inf. **43**, 101037 (2020)
21. Wuest, T., Weimer, D., Irgens, C., Thoben, K.D.: Machine learning in manufacturing: advantages, challenges, and applications. Prod. Manuf. Res. **4**(1), 23–45 (2016)
22. Zhao, D., Wang, Y., Liang, D., Ivanov, M.: Performances of regression model and artificial neural network in monitoring welding quality based on power signal. J. Mater. Res. Technol. **9**(2), 1231–1240 (2020)

AI and BD in Process Industry: A Literature Review with an Operational Perspective

Rosanna Fornasiero[1]([⊠]) ⓘ, David F. Nettleton[2] ⓘ,
Lorenz Kiebler[3] ⓘ, Alicia Martinez de Yuso[4] ⓘ,
and Chiara Eleonora De Marco[5] ⓘ

[1] CNR-IEIIT, Via Gradenigo, 6, 35100 Padova, Italy
rosanna.fornasiero@ieiit.cnr.it
[2] IRIS Technology Solutions S.L., Ctra. d'Esplugues, 39-41,
08940 Cornellà de Llobregat, Barcelona, Spain
david.nettleton@iris-eng.com
[3] Fraunhofer Institute for Material Flow and Logistics IML,
Joseph-von-Fraunhofer-Str. 2-4, Dortmund, Germany
lorenz.kiebler@iml.fraunhofer.de
[4] Zaragoza Logistics Center, Zaragoza, Spain
amartinez@zlc.edu.es
[5] CiaoTech s.r.l. – PNO Group, Milan, Italy
C.DeMarco@ciaotech.com

Abstract. Among digital technologies, Artificial Intelligence (AI) and Big Data (BD) have proven capability to support different processes, mainly in discrete manufacturing. Despite the fact that a number of AI and BD literature reviews exist, no comprehensive review is available for the Process Industry (i.e. cements, chemical, steel, and mining). This paper aims to provide a comprehensive review of AI and BD literature to gain insights into their evolution supporting operational phases of the Process Industry. Results allow to define the areas where AI/BD are proven to have greater impact and areas with gaps like for example the process control (predictive models) area, machine learning and cyber-physical systems technologies. The sectors lagging behind are Ceramics, Cement and non-ferrous metals. Areas to be studied in the future include the interaction between intelligent systems. humans and the external environment, the implementation of AI for the monitoring and optimization of parameters of different operations, ethical and social impact.

Keywords: Operations management · Artificial Intelligence · Big Data · Process industry

1 Introduction

In the recent years, the great potential of AI/BD has enabled firms to increase their profits and 85% of business leaders believes that these technologies will make their businesses remain competitive. Adoption rates are still quite low, around only 23% adopting some AI/BD technology and a mere 5% having extensively deployed AI/BD solutions and mostly in support functions such as IT and customer service [1]. Nonetheless, 77% of

A. Dolgui et al. (Eds.): APMS 2021, IFIP AICT 634, pp. 576–585, 2021.
https://doi.org/10.1007/978-3-030-85914-5_61

industry managers considered machine learning to be most useful in deploying AI, with smart robotics second (44%), natural language processing third (40%).

Concerning BD, businesses are rapidly growing the volume of their owned digital data, generated from different sources and in different structures, by increasing the amount of users, sensors, processes and other sources. In many cases, BD is a pre-requisite of AI, as it goes beyond traditional database software tools, to enable access, storage, management of large amounts of data to be analysed, interpolated and correlated in AI applications. Important issues for AI are the data collection, access and processes therefore very much in relation with BD handling. Therefore, a high data quality and availability and the implementation of the right algorithms and learning processes, are the biggest challenges for AI [2]. While Process Industry already generates a vast amount of data, it is still facing the challenge of integrating and define data structures and interfaces to create a common access over several processes and locations for usage at operational level by means of AI. In other cases, process industry do not have capability to gather this data available to apply machine learning techniques in a suitable way.

Several papers demonstrate that in discrete manufacturing companies AI/BD technologies can improve performance in terms of efficiency, sustainability, flexibility, agility, robustness and resilience. In the case of the Process industry, the application of AI/BD is lagging behind given the differences in operations (continuous flows can have different problems in terms of monitoring and control with respect to discrete production) and only recently has started to adopt these technologies. The aim of this paper is to conduct a literature review to analyse to what extent AI/BD are used at different operational levels in the process industry to transform data, facilitate real-time decision making using online data and automate decision making. After the presentation of the methodology and the AI/BD taxonomy, the paper proposes a structured analysis of available works in AI/BD fields applied to eight sectors of the Process Industry namely cement, ceramics, chemicals, engineering, minerals and ores, non-ferrous metals, steel, water. As part of the synthesis, on the one hand, the operations which show most important applications of technologies are identified, and on the other, gaps are detected for further study and evaluation.

2   Methodology and AI /BD Taxonomy

The literature review (LR) is recognized as a valid approach and a necessary step for exploring new directions guiding the research toward identifying research gaps and proposing innovative applications with cross-sectorial comparison. A four-step process proposed by [3] was adopted:

1. *Material collection*: based on the research scope, the collection of papers and scientific contributions was carried out by using the search engine of Web of Knowledge and google scholar. A publication search was conducted in terms of structured combination of the key words in title, abstract and keywords taking into consideration technologies as defined in the taxonomy and the process industry

sectors. Since one of the main objectives is to analyse the recent developments of AI and BD, the search was limited to the last 5 years.

2. *Descriptive analysis*: more than 300 papers have collected and analysed by the partners of the project and a preliminary analysis of the formal aspects was used to assess the material in a qualitative way. During the material revision, some references were discarded and other were found of interest and added to our LR. Totally around 200 papers have been kept for categorisation. For reasons of space, in this paper we report only a subset of the most important papers. The full list is available upon request.

3. *Material categorisation*: the collected papers were categorised according to the involved operational dimensions and coded accordingly to obtain a picture of the use of the AI/BD technologies in the eight sectors.

4. *Analysis and results*: during the analysis particular attention have been given to how AI/BD can support processes, establishing which are the most important operations where these technologies can be implemented.

Before to start the LR, a taxonomy has been developed specifically for the AI-CUBE project [4] taking into account current state of the art taxonomies, including the one developed by the EC AI Expert group [5], which has been customized for process industries. In particular, the AI taxonomy has two core categories, "perception and communication" and "cognition and reasoning" and one transversal category "integration and interaction". From these, nine sub-categories are identified, which are summarized and five categories for BD.

Table 1. Taxonomy for AI/BD

Category	Technology	Acronym
AI- Perception and communication	Data understanding and characterization	DUC
	Natural language processing	NLP
	Object and spatial recognition	OSR
	Machine learning	ML
AI- Cognition and reasoning	Intelligent planning	IP
	Expert systems	ES
	Case based reasoning	CBR
AI- Integration and interaction	Intelligent agents	IA
	Cyber-physical systems	CPS
BD –Big Data	Data visualisation	DV
	Data processing	DP
	Data protection	DPR
	Data management	DM
	Computing and storage infrastructure	CSI

3   Results

Steel Sector: There are several examples of ML used for different processes as for example for fatigue property analysis [6] and to predict the tensile strength of steel rods manufactured in an electric arc furnace [7]. ML is also used to enable prediction of systems failure [8] and neural network-based solutions are used for crack prediction to improve the steel-casting process. ES have been developed to analyse the quality of the steel products [9] and for the analysis of metallurgical processes related to continuous casting with a modular system architecture while the DM system is based on the physical and chemical features of steel [10]. NLP is used for entity recognition for the steel product categories; while for OSR, vision-based automatic identification can track without embedding identification codes onto the steel product surfaces [11]. CPS and knowledge-based systems are used to detect functional failure to reduce the time of expertise acquisition and the cost of solving over-generalization and over-fitting problems with a data driven tool to provide fault diagnostics enabling risk-informed decision-making [12].

Engineering Sector: NLP can be integrated in various processes along the value chain, as in the automated mapping of the SC based on text sources for archiving visibility [13] or in the extraction of satisfactory product properties from customer reviews [14] for a customer-centric product customization. ML can be used along the whole process, for example in data driven models for characterising engineering systems [14]. An exemplary field of application for frameworks and systems of intelligent agents can be to address systems engineering problems [15]. In particular, CPS are often used for proactive or predictive maintenance solutions and tools, as described in [16]. Other predictive maintenance solutions can be based on BD like DM and DP, for example by using digital twins [17]. DV for value analysis [18] is also considered.

Ceramics: ML is applied for quality control in the ceramics industry for the detection and classification of defects in the final product in combination with other technologies, like ultrasound sensing [19]. IS using ML (ANN) for the analysis of acoustic emissions and cutting power signals [20] have been applied to predictive maintenance. IP is used for quality control in the manufacturing process, i.e. trajectory planning system solution for glazing spraying using cooperative multi-robots [21] and to optimize experimental conditions to obtain maximum hardness of ceramic samples [22]. Optimization, classification and processing, for example in evaluating rotary ultrasonic machining to select optimum machining parameters can be based on ES [23], while OSR has been applied for Additive Manufacturing technologies for optimization of process, and [24] reported the development of a new feature-based method for identification of geometric features and manufacturing constrains. The development of smart ceramic manufacturing is based on the interconnection assured by with CPS [25] or through IoT based BD analytics [26].

Minerals: [27] main operations in reaching the ore, breaking the ore underground to bring it to the surface and then dressing and smelting it can be supported by AI as a lead technology in decision-making. BD and ML can improve operational efficiency, mine safety, and production workflow [28]. Key operational areas for leveraging from AI are cited as mineral processing and exploration, safety/security, and autonomous vehicles and drillers (SLAM technology). Current issues/problems in the sector include: milling of raw material, mining/extraction, high energy consumption, security and human safety, scheduling/planning, security, automation and remote monitoring.

Cement: Being an energy-intensive sector, innovative approaches based on AI/BD can help to reduce energy consumption and costs in this sector supporting new strategies for optimization of usage. In [29] an AI model (deep learning neural network) learns the dynamics of each of the key industrial assets (cooler, ball mill, vertical mill, preheater, and kiln) and processes from historical sensor data, creating prescriptions by searching for the optimal values of critical control parameters. Moreover, there are some operational phases that need to be supported by AI/BD like kiln, firing, material processing as well as energy consumption optimisation, predictive maintenance, predict process behaviour, supply chain, remote operation.

Non-Ferrous Metals: ML approaches are suggested by [30] for inspecting aluminum structure subjected to temperature changes and by [31] to address the identification of the atoms in the grain boundary regions of the aluminum. In [32], the orthogonal test method and DV are used to observe the effect of multifactor composite action on copper slag to reduce serious environmental problems. ESs are proposed for the analysis of aluminum electrolysis an ES is proposed in [33] for monitoring and emergency decisions of the tank condition of the electrolytic aluminum and for automated inspection system of the spraying parameters splats [34].

Water Sector: It is showed a significant application of digital technologies in the sector. ML is applied in the SC (re)configuring and scheduling and R&D activities for different purposes ranging from energy and resource efficiency in the water distribution systems [35], cost reduction of raw material in water treatment plants, and decision support systems based on artificial neural network application in water and wastewater [36]. IP and IA pursue the sustainability and efficiency in multi-sectoral water allocation [37], the optimization of water infrastructure resilience and performance [38], and the smart utilisation of wastewater storage capacity to prevent flooding. Finally, OSR technologies (e.g. GIS-integrated simulation models) have been developed for the conjunctive use of surface and groundwater and water-constrained agricultural production. As for BD, data collection and BD analytics are applied to monitor water pipeline infrastructure systems [39], DV for wastewater contaminants understanding [40] and DM techniques for hydro informatics purposes [41].

Chemicals: Digital transformation driving major opportunities [42] in the sector. ML application based on artificial neural networks (e.g. neuro-fuzzy) within different control loops are applied for network predictive control regarding energy savings [43]. Most of the studies focused on technologies related to DUC, and ML to predict higher heating values of a biomass [44] and energy use and GHG emissions reduction [45]. BD (mainly DM and DC and SI) are applied for data interoperability supporting computational toxicology and chemical safety evaluation [46] and CSI technologies in development activities of the chemical industry [47, 48].

Figure 1 shows the "heat map" of the references found in the literature search. It can be seen that the "hot" technology category is ML with major applications to the chemical and minerals sectors. It is notable that there are still several areas to be investigated and were the application to the analysed sectors are still limited. DUC, DPR and CSI are still to be investigated with specific focus on these sectors of the process industry, most probably, this is due to the fact that these categories are complementary to other technologies and a transversal approach, sector independent, has been applied till now.

		DUC	NLP	OSR	ML	IP	ES	CBR	IA	CPS	DV	DP	DPR	DM	CSI
Process industry sectors	Cement				4		3	1		1	2	2		1	
	Ceramics			2	4	4	2	1	1	2	1	4		2	
	Chemicals	8		1	10			1		1		2		3	3
	Engineering	1	8		5	1	4	4	4	8	1		1	5	3
	Minerals	2	1	4	14	4	1	1	2	1	1	1	1	3	2
	Non ferrous metals				7		2	1		1	1	3		1	
	Steel		2	5	8		7	1	2	5		2		2	
	Water		1	1	7	1				1	1	2	2	3	

HEAT MAP
> 9 high
4-9 medium
0-3 low

Fig. 1. Heat map of AI/BD for process industry

4 Conclusions

Based on the LR presented shortly in the previous sections, the findings of the paper can be used as a guideline for defining the areas along which to further investigate and where there is a gap to define development paths in the future. In particular:

- *Market analysis and open innovation*: need for forecasting based on intelligent system for customer relationships management and online monitoring and order management systems for the suppliers. Improvements in this area is necessary both for sectors dealing with final consumer (i.e. ceramic) as well as for B2B sectors (i.e. chemical, steel, …) that are "far" from the final market but need to forecast demand of final products to make production planning.
- *Process control and optimisation*: companies in Process Industry need to have support for the real-time integrated control of the different production phases enabling CPS by new way to formalize and treat BD collected along the process from machines, devices etc. to avoid workers to dangerous working conditions. In these sectors with continuous flow of material, it is important to find a way to assure raw material quality control by automatic visual classification and advanced sensing systems with a high precision and timely manner. For what concerns monitoring of inventory level, some areas are related to positioning of the raw material and resources (e.g. internal transport modes) in the warehouse, operators' guide for timely picking and loading activities.
- *Predictive maintenance:* this area is already covered in many sectors but there is the need to further investigate for the development of algorithms based on different types of AI like neural-networks, deep learning etc. taking into account the specificity of the production equipment used in each sector.

- *Research and innovation:* it is necessary to further develop AI/BD technologies supporting management, planning and design of research and innovation. Innovation at product level can be supported by AI/BD for designing, simulating, testing product features. Tools for automatic alignment in the design of product and process is also important. Dealing with the sustainability of the new generation of products is also an important issue and all the data collected with DUC, DP and DM can enable evaluation of energy efficiency and environmental impact.
- *Supply chain:* this area includes all the operational perspectives related to configuration, planning and management of SC. Some important ongoing trends related to Process Industry need to be taken into consideration like industrial symbiosis and value chain integration for circular economy: AI/BD can facilitate the forward flows of the raw materials and primary products, but also manage and integrate it with the reverse flows to the factory, waste management systems, and other value-added activities.

A cross-cutting area of analysis is related to the ethical and social dimension arisen by AI/BD techniques incorporating hybridization of intelligent systems with humans and the role of the AI/BD systems combined with other methods and tools in pandemic situations such as COVID-19 should be studied to define paths to provide new production models to avoid risk propagation.

Acknowledgment. This paper is part of the research in the AI-CUBE Project funded from the European Union's Horizon 2020 research and innovation programme under Grant Agreement N° 958402 (https://www.ai-cube.eu/).

References

1. Ransbotham, S., Kiron, D., Gerbert, P., Reeves, R.: Reshaping business with artificial intelligence. In: MIT Sloan Management Review and The Boston Consulting Group (2017)
2. Wuest, T., Weimer, D., Irgens, C., Thoben, K.-D.: Machine learning in manufacturing: advantages, challenges, and applications. Prod. Manuf. Res. **4**(1), 23–45 (2016)
3. Wang, Y., Li, X., Tsung, F.: Configuration-based smart customization service: a multitask learning approach. IEEE Trans. Autom. Sci. Eng. **17**(4), 2038–2047 (2020)
4. AI-Cube Homepage. https://www.ai-cube.eu/. Accessed 08 Jul 2021
5. Samoili, S., Lopez Cobo, M., Gomez Gutierrez, E., De Prato, G., Martinez-Plumed, F., Delipetrev, B.: AI WATCH. Defining Artificial Intelligence. Publications Office of the European Union, Luxembourg (2020)
6. Zhang, M., Sun, C.N., Zhang, X., Wei, J., Hardacre, D., Li, H.: Predictive models for fatigue property of laser powder bed fusion stainless steel 316L. Mater. Des. **145**, 42–54 (2018)
7. Ruiz, E., Ferreño, D., Cuartas, M., López, A., Arroyo, V., Gutiérrez-Solana, F.: Machine learning algorithms for the prediction of the strength of steel rods: an example of data-driven manufacturing in steelmaking. Int. J. Comput. Integr. Manuf. **33**(9), 880–894 (2020)
8. Karagiorgou, S., Vafeiadis, G., Ntalaperas, D., Lykousas, N., Vergeti, D., Alexandrou, D.: Unveiling trends and predictions in digital factories. In: 15th International Conference on Distributed Computing in Sensor Systems (DCOSS) 2019, pp. 326–332 (2019)
9. Kong, Y., Chen, D., Liu, Q., Long, M.: A prediction model for internal cracks during slab continuous casting. Metals **9**(5), 587–604 (2019)

10. Klinger A., Altendorfer A., Bettinger D., Hughes G.D., Al-Husseini A.A., Gupta D.R.: The new system for control and improvement of technological process at DRI units. Chernye Metally 10 (2017)

11. Kang, L.-W., Chen, Y.-T., Jhong, W.-C., Hsu, C.-Y.: Deep learning-based identification of steel products. In: Pan, J.-S., Ito, A., Tsai, P.-W., Jain, L.C. (eds.) IIH-MSP 2018. SIST, vol. 110, pp. 315–323. Springer, Cham (2019). https://doi.org/10.1007/978-3-030-03748-2_39

12. Fumagalli, L., Cattaneo, L., Roda, I., Macchi, M., Rondi, M.: Data-driven CBM tool for risk-informed decision-making in an electric arc furnace. Int. J. Adv. Manuf. Technol. **105** (1–4), 595–608 (2019). https://doi.org/10.1007/s00170-019-04189-w

13. Wichmann, P., Brintrup, A., Baker, S., Woodall, P., McFarlane, D.: Extracting supply chain maps from news articles using deep neural networks. Int. J. Prod. Res. **58**(17), 5320–5336 (2020)

14. Park, J., Ferguson, M., Law, K.H.: Data driven analytics (Machine Learning) for system characterization, diagnostics and control optimization. In: Smith I., Domer B. (eds.) Advanced Computing Strategies for Engineering, LNCS, vol. 10863, pp. 16–36. Springer, Cham. (2018) https://doi.org/10.1007/978-3-319-91635-4_2

15. Herrera, M., Pérez-Hernández, M., Parlikad, A.K., Izquierdo, J.: Multi-agent systems and complex networks: review and applications in systems engineering. Processes **8**(3), 312–341 (2020)

16. Shcherbakov M.V., Glotov A.V., Cheremisinov S.V.: Proactive and predictive maintenance of cyber-physical systems. In: Kravets, A., Bolshakov, A., Shcherbakov, M. (eds.) Cyber-Physical Systems: Advances in Design & Modelling, pp. 263–278. Springer, Cham (2020). https://doi.org/10.1007/978-3-030-32579-4_21

17. Cheng, D., Zhang, J., Hu, Z., Xu, S., Fang, X.: A digital twin-driven approach for on-line controlling quality of marine diesel engine critical parts. Int. J. Precis. Eng. Manuf. **21**(10), 1821–1841 (2020)

18. Colombo, E.F., Shougarian, N., Sinha, K., Cascini, G., de Weck, O.L.: Value analysis for customizable modular product platforms: theory and case study. Res. Eng. Design **31**(1), 123–140 (2020)

19. Tripathi, G., Anowarul, H., Agarwal, K., Prasad, D.K.: Classification of micro-damage in piezoelectric ceramics using machine learning of ultrasound signals. Sensors **19**(19), 4216 (2019)

20. Nakai, M.E., Aguiar, P.R., Guillardi, H., Bianchi, E.C., Spatti, D.H., D'Addona, D.M.: Evaluation of neural models applied to the estimation of tool wear in the grinding of advanced ceramics. Expert Syst. Appl. **42**(20), 7026–7035 (2015)

21. Qian, Z., QingLong, M., YongQian, X., Gan Lin, G.: The robot intelligent spraying glazing system for sanitary ceramics industry. J. Phys.: Conf. Ser. **1653**, 012028 (2020)

22. Ghayour, H., Abdellahi, M., Bahmanpour, M.: Artificial intelligence and ceramic tools: experimental study, modeling and optimizing. Ceram. Int. **41**(10) Part A, 13470–13479 (2015)

23. Sadegh Amalnik, M.: Expert system approach for optimization of design and manufacturing process for rotary ultrasonic machining. ADMT J. **11**(1), 1–13 (2018)

24. Shi, Y., Zhang, Y., Baek, S., De Backer, W., Harik, R.: Manufacturability analysis for additive manufacturing using a novel feature recognition technique. Comput. Aided Des. Appl. **15**(6), 941–952 (2018)

25. Braccini, A.M., Margherita, E.G.: Exploring organizational sustainability of industry 4.0 under the triple bottom line: the case of a manufacturing company. Sustainability **11**(1), 36 (2019)

26. Faisal, M., Katiyar, V.: Identification of essential requirements of IOT and big data analytics to extend ceramic manufacturing. Int. J. Eng. Sci. Res. Technol. (IJESRT) **5**(12), 919–923 (2016)

27. Key Stages in the Mining Process. https://www.cornwall.gov.uk/environment-and-planning/conservation/world-heritage-site/delving-deeper/mining-processes/key-stages-in-the-mining-process/. Accessed 08 Jul 2021

28. Trends in Modern Mining Technology. https://www.angloamerican.com/futuresmart/stories/our-industry/technology/trends-in-modern-mining-technology

29. AI Powering the future of cement, Cement World. May 2020. https://www.worldcement.com/special-reports/11052020/ai-powering-the-future-of-cement/. Accessed 08 Jul 2021

30. Vitola, J., Pozo, F., Tibaduiza, D.A., Anaya, M.: Distributed piezoelectric sensor system for damage identification in structures subjected to temperature changes. Sensors **17**(6), 1252 (2017)

31. Gomberg, J.A., Medford, A.J., Kalidindi, S.R.: Extracting knowledge from molecular mechanics simulations of grain boundaries using machine learning. Acta Mater. **133**, 100–108 (2017)

32. Lan, W., Wu, A., Yu, P.: Development of a new controlled low strength filling material from the activation of copper slag: influencing factors and mechanism analysis. J. Cleaner Prod. **246**, 119060 (2020).

33. Li, L., Xie, Y., Chen, X., Yue, W., Zeng, Z.: Dynamic uncertain causality graph based on cloud model theory for knowledge representation and reasoning. Int. J. Mach. Learn. Cybern. **11**(8), 1781–1799 (2020). https://doi.org/10.1007/s13042-020-01072-z

34. Mulero, M.A., Zapata, J., Vilar, R., Martínez, V., Gadow, R.: Automated image inspection system to quantify thermal spray splat morphology. Surf. Coat. Technol. **278**, 1–11 (2015)

35. Bagloee, S.A., Asadi, M., Patriksson, M.: Minimization of water pumps' electricity usage: a hybrid approach of regression models with optimization. Expert Syst. Appl. **107**, 222–242 (2018)

36. Hadjimichael, A., Comas, J., Corominas, L.: Do machine learning methods used in data mining enhance the potential of decision support systems? A review for the urban water sector. AI Commun. **29**(6), 747–756 (2016)

37. Zhou, Y., Chang, L.C., Uen, T.S., Guo, S., Xu, C.Y., Chang, F.J.: Prospect for small-hydropower installation settled upon optimal water allocation: an action to stimulate synergies of water-food-energy nexus. Appl. Energy **238**, 668–682 (2019)

38. Facchini, A., Scala, A., Lattanzi, N., Caldarelli, G., Liberatore, G., Dal Maso, L., Nardo, A.: Complexity science for sustainable smart water grids. In: Rossi, F., Piotto, S., Concilio, S. (eds.) WIVACE 2016. CCIS, vol. 708, pp. 26–41. Springer, Cham (2017). https://doi.org/10.1007/978-3-319-57711-1_3

39. Sinha, S., Sears, L.: Collection and compilation of water pipeline field performance data. Pipelines **2017**, 124–135 (2017)

40. Ponce Romero, J.M., Hallett, S.H., Jude, S.: Leveraging big data tools and technologies: addressing the challenges of the water quality sector. Sustainability **9**(12), 2160 (2017)

41. Chen, Y., Han, D.: Big data and hydroinformatics. J. Hydroinf. **18**(4), 599–614 (2016)

42. Piccione, P.M.: Realistic interplays between data science and chemical engineering in the first quarter of the 21st century: Facts and a vision. Chem. Eng. Res. Des. **147**, 668–675 (2019)

43. Kramer, A., Morgado-Dias, F.: Artificial intelligence in process control applications and energy saving: a review and outlook. Greenhouse Gases: Sci. Technol. **10**(6), 1133–1150 (2020)

44. Ighalo, J.O., Adeniyi, A.G., Marques, G.: Application of linear regression algorithm and stochastic gradient descent in a machine-learning environment for predicting biomass higher heating value. Biofuels, Bioprod. Biorefin. **14**(6), 1286–1295 (2020)
45. Makarova, A.S., Jia, X., Kruchina, E.B., Kudryavtseva, E.I., Kukushkin, I.G.: Environmental performance assessment of the chemical industries involved in the responsible care® program: case study of the Russian Federation. J. Clean. Prod. **222**, 971–985 (2019)
46. Watford, S., Edwards, S., Angrish, M., Judson, R. S., Friedman, K.P.: Progress in data interoperability to support computational toxicology and chemical safety evaluation. Toxicol. Appl. Pharmacol. **380**, 114707 (2019).
47. McDonagh, J.L., Swope, W.C., Anderson, R.L., Johnson, M.A., Bray, D.J.: What can digitisation do for formulated product innovation and development? Polym. Int. **70**(3), 248–255 (2020)
48. Pellis, A., Cantone, S., Ebert, C., Gardossi, L.: Evolving biocatalysis to meet bioeconomy challenges and opportunities. New Biotechnol. **40**, 154–169 (2018)

Implementing an Online Scheduling Approach for Production with Multi Agent Proximal Policy Optimization (MAPPO)

Oliver Lohse[✉], Noah Pütz, and Korbinian Hörmann

Digital Manufacturing Technologies Siemens AG, Munich, Germany
{Oliver.Lohse,Noah.Puetz,Korbinian.Hoermann}@siemens.com

Abstract. The manufacturing process relies on a well-coordinated schedule that optimally incorporates all available resources to achieve maximum profit. In the case of machine breakdowns, the created schedule does not contain information on how to proceed further. Manual adjustments to the process order do not guarantee optimal utilization of the available resources, as many interconnections of the manufacturing process are not evident to a human. A reliable method is needed that can react to changing conditions on the shop floor and form well-founded decisions to mitigate negative effects. This paper presents an approach to implement Multi Agent Reinforcement Learning for online scheduling a cell-based manufacturing environment with unpredictable machine breakdowns. The developed "Multi Agent Proximal Policy Optimization"-Algorithm (MAPPO) combines already existing approaches in a novel way, by using the centralized learning and decentralized execution together with an objective function developed for OpenAIs Proximal Policy Optimization algorithm.

Keywords: JSSP · Online scheduling · Multi agent reinforcement learning

1 Introduction

The ongoing development of reinforcement learning methods in combination with data of digitized plants ("Industrie 4.0") yields high potential for the application of data-driven methods in manufacturing processes. Availability, quality and performance, in other words, the overall equipment effectiveness (OEE), can be increased by the analysis of process data [5]. Scheduling based on Reinforcement Learning (RL) is one of the promising examples to increase the performance of a plant. The so-called online-scheduling, also referred to as dynamic scheduling, can decrease the negative effects of sudden machine breakdowns, keeping the performance of the plant at a profitable level [2].

© IFIP International Federation for Information Processing 2021
Published by Springer Nature Switzerland AG 2021
A. Dolgui et al. (Eds.): APMS 2021, IFIP AICT 634, pp. 586–595, 2021.
https://doi.org/10.1007/978-3-030-85914-5_62

Advanced planning and scheduling systems (APS) rely on heuristics and meta-heuristics to determine the best possible sequence of manufacturing jobs. Solving this job shop scheduling problem (JSSP) is time consuming and computationally expensive. When unforeseen disruptions occur, rescheduling cannot occur immediately, resulting in impaired production throughput. This effect is amplified when a production line is converted to matrix production. Here, the production cells are no longer rigidly connected and offer the product many opportunities to pass through production. Due to the high complexity of this optimization task, it is not possible for humans to reroute the products in the best possible way in case of a disruption.

Recent research results in the field of reinforcement learning show that RL is able to incorporate many dependencies, uncertainties and probable future decisions into the decision-making process [11]. Furthermore, it has been shown that multi agent systems are capable of working cooperatively to achieve a common goal [7]. These developments suggest that multi agent reinforcement learning can be used to solve the JSSP. In the paper, the JSSP is formulated as a Markov Decision Process. Building on OpenAI's Proximal Policy Optimization (PPO) [10], a multi agent is developed that is capable of solving the JSSP. The results of the MAPPO are then evaluated using a simple heuristic.

2 State of the Art

2.1 Planning and Scheduling

The main purpose of scheduling is to ensure that the capacities of the manufacturing plant, including machines and human resources, are utilized to the fullest potential. Sudden machine breakdowns, such as broken drill-bits or hydraulic issues, are the main factor of influence on the calculated finishing time of a product. The previously calculated static schedules don't include disruptions. These incidents are commonly known but not well predictable in the manufacturing process. Foresighted planning of production steps that considers these events is impossible. Such failed equipment has a negative impact on time constraints for the following products [9].

Optimal scheduling of all production orders is a classic job shop scheduling problem (JSSP). Advanced planning and scheduling IT-systems resort to heuristics and meta-heuristics to solve the JSSP [3,13]. Thus, an approximated solution is found for the JSSP. However, due to the high complexity of the JSSP, these methods are very time consuming and computationally expensive [13]. They are therefore not suitable for reacting immediately to the changed situation on the shop floor in the event of a disruption.

Approaches to solve the JSSP using RL have already been published. There are approaches where the dispatching rules are determined by a decentralized MARL algorithm [4,8,12]. An agent controls the dispatching rules of a machine or work center. The products have no intelligence in these approaches. Other approaches present a centralized MARL approach in which the products decide independently on which machine they want to be processed [1]. For this purpose, a Deep Q-network is used for each product. The paper shows that a centralized MARL approach can in principle solve the JSSP.

2.2 Proximal Policy Optimization

The "Proximal Policy Optimization" is a policy gradient method for a single agent approach [10]. Policy gradient methods parameterize the policy directly and alter the weights of the parameterization to produce a policy that maximizes the expected return. These methods are fundamental in recent achievements in using reinforcement learning for mastering video games or the game of Go [11]. However, policy gradient algorithms are sensitive to the adjustment of the step size. The step size determines the extent to which the parameters of the neural net are changed during training; if it is too small, the training is unnecessarily protracted; if it is too large, the changes are too strong and do not lead to the optimum policy.

By using the clipped surrogate objective L^{Clip}, the PPO controls the change of the policy during the training. The PPO ensures the necessary sensitive adjustment of the step size for each iteration and additionally prevents excessive fluctuations of the neural net parameters [10].

3   Concept of the MAPPO-Algorithm

The MAPPO algorithm presented is based on the single agent PPO. The PPO, with its agent, describes a single product-agent. In contrast to the single agent PPO, in the MAPPO all product-agents share a centralized critic. The centralized critic evaluates the actions of each individual product-agent in the context of all product-agents. For this purpose, it receives the global state and all actions of time step t as input. The L^{Clip} function of the PPO calculates the parameter Θ, which indicates how strongly the parameters of the neural network of the product-agent must be adjusted, see Fig. 1. For the adjustment of the neural network of the critic, in addition to the global state, the assigned rewards are also needed. Thus, the product-agents maximize the overall reward with respect to their own reward. Comparable to the centralized critic of the MADDPG [6], the critic itself is only needed for training. During execution, each product-agent takes an action based on the available state, which implicitly considers the actions of the other product-agents.

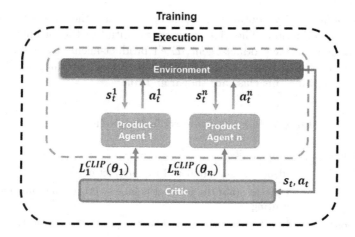

Fig. 1. Overview of the MAPPO-Algorithm approach. During the training all product-agents share a centralized critic. In execution the critic is no longer used and each product-agent makes decisions independently.

4 Implementation of the MAPPO in a Production Environment

4.1 Implementing Product Agents and Environment

At least the following three entities are required to implement MAPPO: Production-Environment, Machines, Products. The entity "Machines" contains the basic logic of all machines. This class is called to create a machine object. Such a machine object corresponds to the virtual representation of a machine in production. Table 1 shows the parameters which are describing this class. If a machine has a queue of more than one product, the dispatching rule always selects the product with the highest priority for processing.

Table 1. Parameter to describe the machine entity.

Parameter	Explanation
ID	Identification number of the machine object
Processing time	Matrix with all processing times
Queue	Length of the queue in front of the machine object
Status	Boolean: 0 = no disruption and 1 = disruption

The product entity contains the logic with which the products can move through the production. The class is used to initialize the products, each of which is assigned to a product-agent. Each product-agent has a set of values that are used to identify and trace the product through production. Parameter which are describing this class are shown in Table 2.

Table 2. Parameter to describe the product entity.

Parameter	Explanation
ID	Identification number of the product object
Status	Current state the product is in, e.g. processing, moving, waiting
Position	Indicates on which machine the product is currently located
Priority	Priority of the product
Process history	Keeps track of which machines the product has already been on
Complete	Boolean that is set to "True" once the product has completed all processing steps

In the production environment, the machines and the product entity are called and the respective objects are initialized. The production environment sends the observation and the reward to the product-agents, which then send back their respective actions (cf. Fig. 1). The product-agents interact with the production until they are either all processed or the maximum time has been reached. This period of time from the first generation of observations to the last sending of actions is called a training episode. After each training episode, the manufacturing model resets and sends the initial observations, which re-trigger the entire training episode cycle. In the new training episode, the product-agents now have the opportunity to make new decisions and gain new experience. Such training episodes can occur any number of times within a training session.

An observation of a product-agent is a list of values with information about the production and about the product itself. It serves as input for the neural network within the product-agent for selecting an action. All input-values of the neural network are scaled to a value between 0 and 1 before input into the neural network, as this improves the processing quality in the neural network.

4.2   Designing the Reward Function

MAPPO learning is analogous to other reinforcement algorithms. At the start of the learning phase, the actions of the products are purely random. Via the reward function, each product-agent receives a reward according to its action. The goal of the product-agents is to maximize this reward. For this purpose, actions that have led to a high reward are executed more frequently. Other actions, where the reward is very low, are not repeated. After many training episodes, the product-agents have learned a behavior that leads to the highest possible reward and thus to the desired behavior in production.

Decisive for the learned behavior is the reward function. For the MAPPO in the production environment, a negative reward of -1 is given to each product at each time step. With this reward, the product-agents learn a behavior that minimizes the negative reward - the product-agents move along the fastest possible route through production. In addition, the product-agents have different priorities that affect their reward per time step. The higher a product is prioritized, the greater the negative reward the product-agent receives per time step. The negative reward per time step is multiplied by the priority. Thus, products with a higher priority receive a higher negative reward per time step. The reward is mathematically defined as follows:

The episode reward R_a, defined in Formula 1, for a product-agent is the sum of all rewards achieved per time step t of an episode. The reward per time step is calculated as -1 multiplied by the priority of the product-agent P_a.

$$R_a = -1 * \sum_{t=1}^{T} P_a \tag{1}$$

The episode reward of all product-agents R_{tot} is the sum of the episode rewards of all product-agents, see Formula 2.

$$R_{tot} = \sum_{a=1}^{A} R_a \tag{2}$$

5   Validation of the MAPPO

To validate the MAPPO algorithm presented in the previous chapter, it is compared with a heuristic. The heuristic distributes all products evenly to the available machines at the beginning of an episode and routs the products to the nearest machine after the production step is completed. This simple heuristic is intended to replicate the behavior of an employee on the shop floor who always moves products to the next possible machine with the lowest transport time. According to the routings, all products must pass through all machines. The sequence in which the products pass through the machines is not specified. In addition, all products have the same priority. Disruptions are not considered with the test runs. The MAPPO and the heuristics are compared in six different sized environments. On the X-axis Fig. 2 shows the number of machines times the number of products is given. The Y-axis describes the time needed for the products to pass through all machines. The Travel-Time-Matrix is the same for all runs and is extended when another machine is added. The environments differ only in the number of machines and products. In the following, the environments are therefore given as the number of machines times the number of products.

The minimum throughput time for the runs in the 2×3, 3×3, 2×5, and 3×5 environments is determined using a path search algorithm. For the 4×5 and the 4×10 environment, the computational cost of the path search algorithm is too great. The MAPPO leads to the same throughput time as the path search in the first four environments and has thus reached the global optimum. The heuristic is very close to MAPPO for the first three environments. The distance between MAPPO and the heuristic is about 5% in the 3×5 and 4×5 environment. In the 4×10 environment, the difference between MAPPO and heuristic is the largest. The MAPPO is 10% faster in this case. It can be assumed that as the complexity of the environment increases, the difference between MAPPO and heuristic becomes larger. This is particularly interesting for the implementation of the MAPPO in a real production with significantly more machines and products. Advanced heuristics will perform better in these cases than the heuristic used in this example. But the computation of an optimal solution in case of a disruption is time consuming. Due to the way neural networks work, the learned MAPPO can react immediately to disruptions and reroute products even in complex production environments - it thus complements an APS. It can be assumed that the performance of the MAPPO in a static environment can also be transferred to environments with disruptions. For this purpose, disruptions must already be simulated in the environment during the training of the product-agents. The disruptions in the training should be similar to the failure probabilities of the real machines. The training of the product-agents becomes longer due to the larger number of possible states, but can be limited to realistic training scenarios if real failure probabilities are used.

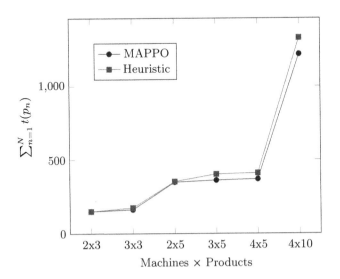

Fig. 2. Throughput time comparison in different static environments

The MAPPO can reach the global maximum if the products are homogeneous. This means that the products have the same routings, processing times and the same priority. In this case, the global optimum also corresponds to the local optimum of all products. If the products have different routings or priorities, the global optimum no longer corresponds to the local optimum. In this case, products with a low priority, for example, would have to let other products pass - thus they would worsen their reward in order to optimize the global reward. However, the experiment shown in Fig. 3 illustrates that MAPPO and other MARL algorithms that rely on a centralized critic are not able to achieve a global optimum with the given reward function.

Figure 3a shows the initial situation. Three product-agents have to decide to which production cell they will go. In this case, each product has to go through only one machine. The processing times of the machines are the same for every product. Product 1 and 2 have a low priority (LP). Product 3 has a high priority and therefore gets a higher penalty for each time step in production, see Sect. 4.2. The experiment is set up so that at least one product has to wait. A global maximum is reached when one LP product waits and the HP product passes through production without waiting. Even in the trained state, the MAPPO keeps product 3 waiting even though it has the highest priority. The product-agents have learned to always bring about their local maximum in different states. Thus, the overall yield improves over all learning episodes until the overall yield converges to a value that represents a local but not a global maximum.

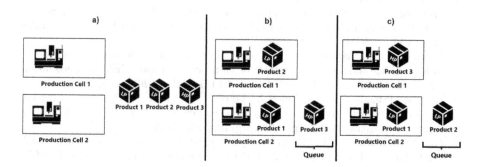

Fig. 3. Product prioritization using the MAPPO. Figure 3a depicts the initial situation. The local optimum of the MAPPO can be seen in Fig. 3b. Figure 3c shows the global optimum for this problem.

6   Conclusion and Outlook

This paper presents an approach for controlling products in a production using multi agent reinforcement learning. The developed MAPPO algorithm is presented in this paper and validated in a production scenario. The MAPPO is compared with a simple heuristic in a static environment. Several test runs are carried out in environments of different sizes and the throughput time of the

MAPPO is compared with that of the heuristic. The MAPPO achieves the minimum throughput time in smaller production environments with homogeneous products. The MAPPO also performs better than the heuristic in larger environments. It can be assumed that the performance of the MAPPO in static environments can also be transferred to environments with disruptions. In this case, the corresponding disruptions must occur in the training runs. However, if the products are no longer homogeneous, the MAPPO cannot generate a global production maximum - in this case, a local optimum is generated, in which each product-agent optimizes its own reward. Future work will investigate whether the MAPPO can also be used to induce a global production maximum for inhomogeneous products. In addition, the MAPPO must also be applied to larger production environments with disruptions. The results of these investigations could then be compared with state-of-the-art heuristics from APS. It can be assumed that the MAPPO holds great optimization potential for production. The MAPPO can react to disruptions without additional computation. Especially for complex cell-based productions with many possibilities for the product to pass through the production online scheduling systems will be necessary. Further studies on the MAPPO will show whether it can meet all production requirements.

References

1. Baer, S., Turner, D., Mohanty, P.K., Samsonov, V., Bakakeu, J.R., Meisen, T.: Multi agent deep q-network approach for online job shop scheduling in flexible manufacturing. In: International Conference on Manufacturing System and Multiple Machines, ICMSMM 2020 (2020)
2. Cadavid, J.P.U., Lamouri, S., Grabot, B., Fortin, A.: Machine learning in production planning and control: a review of empirical literature. IFAC-PapersOnLine 52(13), 385–390 (2019). https://doi.org/10.1016/j.ifacol.2019.11.155
3. Fera, M., Fruggiero, F., Lambiase, A., Martino, G., Elena, M.: Production scheduling approaches for operations management. In: Schiraldi, M. (ed.) Operations Management. InTech (2013). https://doi.org/10.5772/55431
4. Gabel, T., Riedmiller, M.: Scaling adaptive agent-based reactive job-shop scheduling to large-scale problems. In: 2007 IEEE Symposium on Computational (2007). https://doi.org/10.1109/SCIS.2007.367699
5. Gyulai, D., Pfeiffer, A., Nick, G., Gallina, V., Sihn, W., Monostori, L.: Lead time prediction in a flow-shop environment with analytical and machine learning approaches. IFAC-PapersOnLine 51(11), 1029–1034 (2018). https://doi.org/10.1016/j.ifacol.2018.08.472
6. Lowe, R., Wu, Y., Tamar, A., Harb, J., Abbeel, P., Mordatch, I.: Multi-agent actor-critic for mixed cooperative-competitive environments (2017). http://arxiv.org/pdf/1706.02275v4
7. OroojlooyJadid, A., Hajinezhad, D.: A review of cooperative multi-agent deep reinforcement learning (2019). http://arxiv.org/pdf/1908.03963v3
8. Roesch, M., Linder, C., Bruckdorfer, C., Hohmann, A., Reinhart, G.: Industrial load management using multi-agent reinforcement learning for rescheduling. In: 2019 2nd International Conference on Artificial Intelligence for Industries (AI4I), pp. 99–102. IEEE (2019). https://doi.org/10.1109/AI4I46381.2019.00033

9. Schuh, G., Stich, V.: Produktionsplanung und -steuerung 2. Springer, Heidelberg (2012). https://doi.org/10.1007/978-3-642-25427-7
10. Schulman, J., Wolski, F., Dhariwal, P., Radford, A., Klimov, O.: Proximal policy optimization algorithms (2017). http://arxiv.org/pdf/1707.06347v2
11. Silver, D., et al.: Mastering the game of go with deep neural networks and tree search. Nature **529**(7587), 484–489 (2016). https://doi.org/10.1038/nature16961
12. Waschneck, B., et al.: Optimization of global production scheduling with deep reinforcement learning. Procedia CIRP **72**, 1264–1269 (2018). https://doi.org/10.1016/j.procir.2018.03.212
13. Zanakis, S.H., Evans, J.R., Vazacopoulos, A.A.: Heuristic methods and applications: a categorized survey. Eur. J. Oper. Res. **43**(1), 88–110 (1989). https://doi.org/10.1016/0377-2217(89)90412-8

Operation Twins: Synchronized Production-Intralogistics for Industry 4.0 Manufacturing

Mingxing Li[1]([⊠]) [iD], Daqiang Guo[1,2] [iD], and George Q. Huang[1] [iD]

[1] Department of Industrial and Manufacturing Systems Engineering,
HKU-ZIRI Lab for Physical Internet, The University of Hong Kong, Hong Kong,
People's Republic of China
{mingxing, dqguo, gqhuang}@hku.hk
[2] Department of Mechanical and Energy Engineering,
Southern University of Science and Technology, Shenzhen,
People's Republic of China

Abstract. The widespread adoption of Industry 4.0 technologies in factories are transforming manufacturing operations management. Multiple resources are interconnected, massive data are real-timely collected by smart devices to provide visibility and traceability. It is generally acknowledged that real-time data are beneficial for manufacturing operations management. How to utilize these data for facilitating production and intralogistics (PiL) operations management is an emerging challenge. This study proposes a new concept, operation twins, for achieving synchronized PiL operations based on three dimensions of synchronization (cyber-physical synchronization, spatial-temporal synchronization, and data-driven decisions synchronization).

Keywords: Operation twins · Production-intralogistics synchronization · Production and operations management · Real-time visibility and traceability · Industry 4.0 · Smart manufacturing

1 Introduction

Industry 4.0 promises next-generation smart manufacturing. The emerging technologies that enable this revolution and their applications have attracted widespread attention from both scholars and practitioners in the last decade, such as Internet-of-Things (IoT), Digital Twin (DT), Cyber-Physical Systems (CPS), Big Data Analytics (BDA), Additive Manufacturing (AM), Blockchain [1–3]. In contrast, methodological research is rare in the context of industry 4.0 manufacturing, although advanced technologies are revolutionizing production and operations management [4]. For instance, the production and intralogistics (PiL) in a shop floor are inherently coupled by physical flow (e.g., raw materials, WIPs). In conventional management mode, the PiL operations are organized and performed separately by different divisions without considering the overall benefits because it is hard to collect and share the data among the divisions for making coordinated decisions [5, 6].

The advent of various Industry 4.0 technologies provides a promising direction forward and paves the way for the PiL synchronization. Multiple smart devices are

© IFIP International Federation for Information Processing 2021
Published by Springer Nature Switzerland AG 2021
A. Dolgui et al. (Eds.): APMS 2021, IFIP AICT 634, pp. 596–604, 2021.
https://doi.org/10.1007/978-3-030-85914-5_63

deployed in the physical shop floor to capture real-time data, advanced analytics and decision services are integrated into the cyber shop floor [3, 7]. Traditional manufacturing resources are upgraded to smart resources augmented with identification, sensing, and networking capabilities [2]. Hence, how to fully tap the potential of visibility and traceability in Industry 4.0 environments to manage the complexity and uncertainty of PiL operations for better production performance becomes a new challenge [8].

Real-time/online simulation is an effective tool integrated in new production planning and control approaches that can make use of real-time data. Real-time system status is captured as the input, and online simulations are performed to generated new optimal policy or decision [9–11]. These simulation tools connect the information flow and decision flow to implement a closed-loop control for the whole system. The effectiveness of real-time simulation is widely appreciated, while it is too general to abstract the manufacturing systems into two dimensions. For example, the production flow and intralogistics flow in a manufacturing system are highly coupled with complex interactions.

This study proposes a novel concept, operations twins, to achieve PiL synchronization by leveraging advanced Industry 4.0 technologies and methodologies. Section 2 presents the concept of operation twins and how the production flow, intralogistics flow, and information flow are managed via vertical twinning and horizontal twinning. Three dimensions of synchronization (cyber-physical synchronization, spatial-temporal synchronization, and data-driven decisions synchronization) are summarized as the basis for operation twins in Sect. 3. Finally, a simple example is presented to illustrate the application of operation twins in manufacturing.

2 The Concept of Operation Twins

Figure 1 depicts the conceptual framework of the proposed operation twins. Manufacturing operations hold a dominant position in this framework. Production operations (PO) convert materials and components into products by utilizing production resources such as operators, machines, robots, and tools. Intralogistics operations (LO) correspond to the delivery of required resources such as materials, finished products within the plant using forklifts, automated guided vehicles (AGVs), trolleys, etc. With the adoption of frontier Industry 4.0 technologies, the physical operations and resources are mapped to the digital space. The operation twins concept mainly includes two aspects: vertical twinning and horizontal twinning.

2.1 Vertical Twinning

Vertical twinning involves the twinning of production and intralogistics operations and related resources. The PO and LO are inherently complex because they are coupled and entangled by physical flow (materials, WIPs, or finished products). In traditional management mode, PO and LO are managed by different departments to reduce complexity. The information is usually inaccurate, incomplete, and hard to be shared among different departments. The workflow is fluctuated even disrupted due to various disturbances (e.g., material delay, machine failures, stochastic operational time) on the shop floor. Cutting-edge technologies such as IoT and data analytics remove the barriers and promote information sharing within the plant. Hence, it is possible to manage the PO and LO in a coordinated and synchronized manner to improve the overall operational resilience and resource utilization.

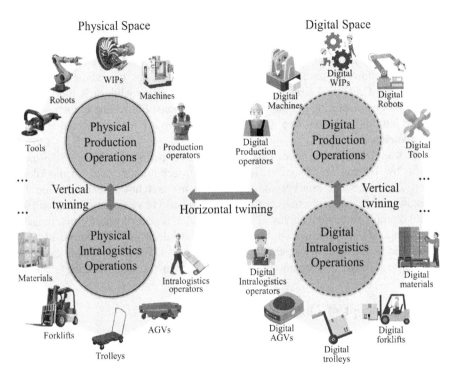

Fig. 1. The conceptual framework of operation twins.

2.2 Horizontal Twinning

Horizontal twinning refers to the twinning of physical and digital operations and related resources. Massive real-time manufacturing data are collected, transmitted, and analyzed thanks to the deployment of Industry 4.0 technologies. All related production and intralogistics resources can be digitized to form corresponding digital representations for real-time simulation and control. PO and LO can also be formulated in digital space with extended visibility and interoperability. Pre-planned operations can be proactively adjusted, ongoing operations can be real-timely monitored, and finished operations can be thoroughly evaluated. Besides, by analyzing the real-time data, the digital space provides real-time feedbacks to support decisions and operations execution in physical space to cope with various uncertainties and enhance efficiency and accuracy.

2.3   The Practical Applicability of Operation Twins

It is noteworthy that the concept of operation twins is closely related to existing concepts such as digital twin [12] and real-time simulation [13]. On the one hand, digital twin is object-oriented; it aims at creating digital representations of manufacturing objects (human, machine, materials, etc.) for real-time monitoring. The concept of operation twins is operations-oriented; manufacturing objects are considered as resources for performing operations, which means operation twins can be more naturally applied in production planning and control processes in practice. On the other hand, real-time simulation focuses on the information flow and decision flow to form closed-loop control of the system. The input system status is usually abstracted so that the interactions and dynamics among the system are often overlooked. For example, in practice, the production and intralogistics for material supply are managed by separate departments that have different KPIs. The concept of operation twins provides a new approach to manage the production flow, intralogistics flow, and information flow in a synchronous and coordinated manner.

3   The Three Dimensions of Synchronization in Industry 4.0 Production-Intralogistics Systems

To establish the operation twin for production-intralogistics synchronization, an overall architecture of synchronized production-intralogistics system is proposed with three dimensions of synchronization, namely, cyber-physical synchronization (CP-Sync), spatial-temporal synchronization (ST-Sync), and data-driven decisions synchronization (DD-Sync), as shown in Fig. 2.

3.1   Cyber-Physical Synchronization (CP-Sync)

The CP-Sync aims at synchronizing the physical shop floor and cyber shop floor to achieve cyber-physical visibility and traceability of the whole plant. As shown in Fig. 2, all physical resources are equipped with smart tags (e.g., RFID, iBeacon, sensors), which can be uniquely sensed, identified and traced by smart gateways, mobiles, industrial wearables, or readers. With the deployment of multiple smart devices, the plant is characterized by hyperconnectivity among physical resources, high-quality real-time data acquisition and transmission. Cyber-physical agents (CP-Agents) are employed to handle various industrial standards/protocols of smart devices and process heterogeneous data from multiple sources to create digital representations with basic facts (e.g., ID, type, quantity), status (e.g., processing, waiting, transferring), spatiotemporal trajectory and so on. Therefore, all manufacturing resources are real-timely monitored and simulated in cyber space to generate insightful feedbacks to physical space, so that cyber space and physical space are seamlessly synchronized. Great interconnectivity of resources, smooth circulation of manufacturing data/information flow, and cyber-physical visibility and traceability serve as solid foundations for further analysis and decision-making.

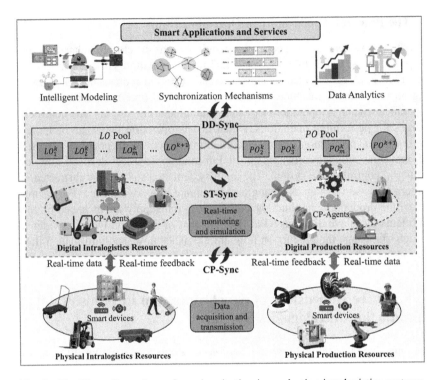

Fig. 2. The Three dimensions of synchronization in production-intralogistics systems.

3.2 Spatial-Temporal Synchronization (ST-Sync)

The ST-Sync aims at ensuring smooth operations execution by synchronizing the required resources within a narrow spatiotemporal window and governing the interactions among smart resources inside. The onsite production execution is subject to the availability of multiple resources (e.g., materials, machines, and humans). Resources-related uncertainty is one of the major challenges in manufacturing execution. Thanks to the cyber-physical visibility and traceability built by CP-Sync. The onsite shop floor situation and detailed information (e.g., the estimated arrival time of materials, machines/operators status) can be easily accessed through smart devices, so that the pending operations in the pools can be organized and executed on a dynamic basis to avoid unreasonable stalls/waits and improve processing efficiency and resource utilization. ST-Sync guarantees the pre-decided production/intralogistics plans/schedules can be completed smoothly under stochastic manufacturing environments (e.g., uncertain operational time, material delays).

3.3 Data-Driven Decisions Synchronization (DD-Sync)

The DD-Sync corresponds to the decision-making process via developing intelligent modeling, synchronization mechanisms, and data analytics. Intelligent modeling establishes the operational logic for critical resources in the PiL process. With embedded algorithms, smart resources can sense and analyze, take actions and interact with each other to enhance overall efficiency. Synchronization mechanisms are designed to coordinate the PO pool and LO pool for supporting decisions based on real-time data (e.g., resource availability, demand change). By incorporating real-time data, the mechanisms will be more resilient and efficient to handle various disturbances and minimize the resulting adverse effects. Besides, data analytics are widely applied, such as data fusion that integrates data from multiple sources to give more accurate results, data mining that uncovers patterns to gain underlying knowledge, etc. For instance, recognizing the frequent spatiotemporal trajectory of materials and humans to facilitate better management and status monitoring. Finally, driven by production data, the combination of these techniques can make the system smarter.

4   An Illustrative Example of Operation Twins

The section presents an illustrative example of the application of operation twins. Considering a simple scenario, there are two orders that request different products, $Order1 = \{B_1, C_1\}$ and $Order2 = \{A_1, A_2, C_2\}$. The original schedule is generated as $\{C_1, C_2, B_1, A_1, A_2\}$ based on the setup requirement and order arrival time.

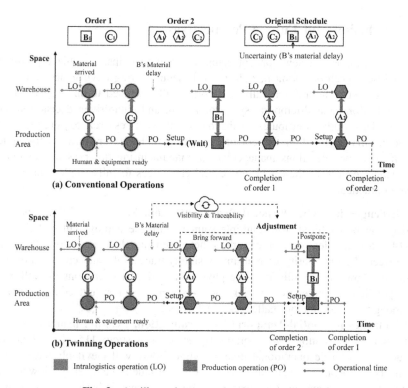

Fig. 3. An illustrative example of operation twins.

When uncertainty (B's material delay) occurs, the following operations have to be postponed and prolong the production process and cause backlog orders. Because in conventional mode (see Fig. 3 (a)), it is hard to identify the uncertainty accurately and quickly, the corresponding information cannot be shared with related departments rapidly so that it is impossible to make decisions to cope with these uncertainties, and the overall production performance deteriorates.

In the twinning operation mode (see Fig. 3 (b)), the uncertainty (B's material delay) can be accurately detected via smart devices, the data and information will be updated in cyber space and shared with intralogistics and production departments (CP-Sync). Based on the information (e.g., estimated delay), corresponding decisions can be made to adjust the operations (DD-Sync). In this example, the operations of A_1, A_2 are brought forward and B_1 is postponed. Finally, onsite operators will perform the adjusted operations accordingly. All required resources will be synchronized into corresponding spatiotemporal windows to ensure smooth execution (ST-Sync). In this way, the adverse effects of uncertainties are minimized.

This simple example is only for illustrating the underlying logic of operation twins in a complete way and how three dimensions of synchronization play a role in the whole process. More comprehensive numerical analyses or case studies will be carried out in the future to verify the superiority of the proposed concept.

5   Conclusion and Future Perspectives

This paper proposed a new concept, namely operation twins, to achieve production-intralogistics synchronization in Industry 4.0 manufacturing environments. The manufacturing operations are vertically and horizontally twinned through cyber-physical synchronization, spatial-temporal synchronization, and data-driven decision synchronization. This study contributes to the methodological research for production and operations management in the era of Industry 4.0. However, how emerging technologies reshape operations management in manufacturing deserves further in-depth discussions. And also, there still are several challenges to fully implement operation twins in practice.

- **Challenges in Cyber-Physical Synchronization.** Massive real-time operational data can be captured from multiple sources with the deployment of IoT devices [14]. How to effectively process these heterogeneous data considering the balance between the granularity of real-time visibility/traceability and computational efficiency, how to faithfully map the physical and digital operations as well as corresponding resources considering their distinct attributes and complex relations among them, are major challenges in CP-Sync.
- **Challenges in Spatial-Temporal Synchronization.** Real-life manufacturing systems are always subject to a certain degree of stochasticity [15]. Uncertain events such as stochastic operational time, machine failure will inevitably have negative effects on operation execution even the overall production efficiency. How to design a mechanism to manage the operation pools on a dynamic basis to achieve spatial-

temporal synchronization for enhancing the overall execution resilience, is a crucial topic in operation twins.

- **Challenges in Data-Driven Decision Synchronization.** Real-time data collection and information sharing make it possible to coordinate and synchronize the decisions of different decision authorities/stakeholders (e.g., production and intralogistics departments in a manufacturing plant) for the global optimum [8]. Therefore, how to formulate novel decision support mechanisms that can fully leverage the potential of abundant IoT data for the coordination of decision-making in manufacturing operations, deserves further explorations.

Acknowledgments. The authors would like to acknowledge partial financial supports from funding sources, including National Key R&D Program of China No. 2019YFB1705401, HKSAR RGC GRF Project (17203518), the 2019 Guangdong Special Support Talent Program – Innovation and Entrepreneurship Leading Team (China) (2019BT02S593), and 2018 Guangzhou Leading Innovation Team Program (201909010006).

References

1. Guo, D., Li, M., Zhong, R., Huang, G.Q.: Graduation Intelligent manufacturing system (GiMS): an industry 4.0 paradigm for production and operations management. Ind. Manage. Data Syst. **121**(1), 86–98 (2021). https://doi.org/10.1108/IMDS-08-2020-0489
2. Zhong, R.Y., Xu, X., Klotz, E., Newman, S.T.: Intelligent manufacturing in the context of industry 4.0: a review. Engineering **3**, 616–630 (2017)
3. Li, M., Zhong, R.Y., Qu, T., Huang, G.Q.: Spatial-temporal out-of-order execution for advanced planning and scheduling in cyber-physical factories. J. Intell. Manuf. (2021). https://doi.org/10.1007/s10845-020-01727-2
4. Olsen, T.L., Tomlin, B.: Industry 4.0: opportunities and challenges for operations management. Manuf. Serv. Oper. Manage. **22**, 113–122 (2020)
5. Luo, H., Wang, K., Kong, X.T., Lu, S., Qu, T.: Synchronized production and logistics via ubiquitous computing technology. Robot. Comput.-Integr. Manufact. **45**, 99–115 (2017)
6. Qu, T., Lei, S.P., Wang, Z.Z., Nie, D.X., Chen, X., Huang, G.Q.: IoT-based real-time production logistics synchronization system under smart cloud manufacturing. Int. J. Adv. Manuf. Technol. **84**(1–4), 147–164 (2015). https://doi.org/10.1007/s00170-015-7220-1
7. Li, M., Jiang, M., Lyu, Z., Chen, Q., Wu, H., Huang, G.Q.: Spatial-temporal finite element analytics for cyber-physical system-enabled smart factory: application in hybrid flow shop. Procedia Manuf. **51**, 1229–1236 (2020)
8. Guo, D., Li, M., Lyu, Z., Kang, K., Wu, W., Zhong, R.Y., Huang, G.Q.: Synchroperation in Industry 4.0 Manufacturing. Int. J. Prod. Econ. **238**, 108171 (2021)
9. Lugaresi, G., Alba, V.V., Matta, A.: Lab-scale models of manufacturing systems for testing real-time simulation and production control technologies. J. Manuf. Syst. **58**, 93–108 (2021)
10. Zhang, L., Zhou, L., Ren, L., Laili, Y.: Modeling and simulation in intelligent manufacturing. Comput. Ind. **112**, 103123 (2019)
11. Faccio, M., Gamberi, M., Persona, A., Regattieri, A., Sgarbossa, F.: Design and simulation of assembly line feeding systems in the automotive sector using supermarket, kanbans and tow trains: a general framework. J. Manag. Control. **24**, 187–208 (2013)
12. Tao, F., Zhang, H., Liu, A., Nee, A.Y.: Digital twin in industry: state-of-the-art. IEEE Trans. Industr. Inf. **15**, 2405–2415 (2018)

13. Ghani, U., Monfared, R., Harrison, R.: Integration approach to virtual-driven discrete event simulation for manufacturing systems. Int. J. Comput. Integr. Manuf. **28**, 844–860 (2015)
14. Kuo, Y.-H., Kusiak, A.: From data to big data in production research: the past and future trends. Int. J. Prod. Res. **57**, 4828–4853 (2019)
15. Hazır, Ö., Dolgui, A.: Assembly line balancing under uncertainty: robust optimization models and exact solution method. Comput. Ind. Eng. **65**, 261–267 (2013)

Risk and Performance Management of Supply Chains

Sustainability Improvement of Coffee Farms in Valle del Cauca (Colombia) Through System Dynamics

Álvaro José Torres Penagos$^{(\boxtimes)}$ ⓘ, Juan Carlos Osorio ⓘ,
and Carlos Julio Vidal-Holguín ⓘ

Escuela de Ingeniería Industrial, Universidad del Valle, Cali, Colombia
{alvaro.penagos, juan.osorio,
carlos.vidal}@correounivalle.edu.co

Abstract. Given the problems generated in the coffee supply chain and iden-tifying the central problem as its low sustainability, especially in Valle del Cauca (Colombia), it is imperative to propose solutions to the current devel-opment of this chain, especially about producers, which are the least benefited. These solutions should allow for balanced growth and be aimed at making it possible to overcome the current socioeconomic system based on predatory and competitive growth at the service of private interests. Thus, sustainability should trigger a profound rethinking about human groups relationships, among them-selves and with the environment, betting on cooperation and defense of the general interest. The purpose should not only be the economic growth of companies, many times increasing the poverty of the inhabitants of the region or the environmental risks, but it should also be the wealth of all the involved parties. In our ongoing research, we plan to use dynamic simulation to evaluate alternatives that consider the sustainability of coffee farms, including elements of profitability, environmental impact, and social development. Preliminary simulation results are shown. This approach should ultimately allow us to find applicable and quantifiable solutions for a sustainable balance in the funda-mental links of the coffee supply chain in the northern region of Valle del Cauca, Colombia.

Keywords: Coffee · Supply chain · Sustainability · System dynamics

1 Introduction

Currently, there is a lot of research on supply chain modeling, most of it with the main purpose of minimizing costs such as inventory, transportation, storage, material han-dling, among others. Less research is devoted to sustainable supply chain modeling that considers the balance between economic, social, and environmental aspects (Drake and Spinler 2013). The integration of these components generates modeling complexity. Brandenburg et al. (2014), Carter and Rogers (2008), and Kannegiesser and Gunter (2013) have conducted literature reviews where the little use of modeling for the analysis of sustainable supply chains that simultaneously include economic, social, and environmental elements is evidenced. In the characterization by Sasikumar and Kannan

© IFIP International Federation for Information Processing 2021
Published by Springer Nature Switzerland AG 2021
A. Dolgui et al. (Eds.): APMS 2021, IFIP AICT 634, pp. 607–617, 2021.
https://doi.org/10.1007/978-3-030-85914-5_64

(2009) and the adjustment made by Brandenburg et al. (2014), supply chain models are classified into mathematical programming methods; simulation methods such as system dynamics, heuristic methods, and hybrid models; and, finally, analytical models such as game theory, multi-criteria methods, and systemic models. Some of the tools that have gained relevance in recent years as methodologies for the analysis of complex problems are the systemic approach and system dynamics.

System dynamics is a methodological paradigm for the investigation of complex systems and is considered a subset of the broader paradigm of simulation models (Meadows and Robinson 1985). In the process of analyzing the sustainability of the coffee supply chain, many elements can be ignored. However, according to Forrester (1987), to understand a system, it is preferable to incorporate variables and interactions even if their representation is difficult and to avoid omitting them, even knowing their importance in the performance of the whole. The idea of this approach is to be able to evaluate in a novel way the impacts of possible management and policy interventions and to observe changes in complex systems Sterman (2001), Thornton and Herrero (2001), and Tedeschi et al. 2011). This paper uses the systemic approach and the system dynamics proposed by Forrester (1987) to analyze some economic, social, and environmental aspects within the coffee supply chain in Colombia that could contribute to its sustainability.

2 Literature Review

Figure 1 shows the connections between articles on 'sustainable supply chains', a first category for reference search. The larger the node size, the more publications are associated with them. The colors represent the year of publication. There is a large volume of publications in sustainability with very similar topics such as carbon footprint, climate change, and life cycle assessment. The graph shows very few social elements; perhaps, more recently, the topics of urban agriculture, food security, and circular economy have been addressed. System dynamics appears as a tool for supply chain sustainability analysis.

In the second category, the keywords 'sustainability and supply chain and coffee' were used, from which 50 documents were obtained. For the bibliometric analysis, only one repetition of keywords was used, since there are very few documents that explore alternatives to improve the sustainability of the coffee supply chain. However, bibliometric analysis showed that coffee certifications, governance, and fair trade are the most researched topics in the search for sustainability in the coffee supply chain. In the last category of 'applications of system dynamics in coffee supply chains', much fewer articles were found. To illustrate, Díaz and Córdoba (2019), carry out a causal analysis in the coffee agricultural system in Cundinamarca, Colombia. With the help of the community, they identified and validated the connection of relevant variables. The authors selected 54 variables in which social, economic, agronomic, and agroclimatic elements were considered, with a focus on the quality of the bean, social capital, the effect of shade on the crop, and the diversification of income from the fruits of the trees used for shade.

A dynamic simulation model was developed by Rachman et al. (2014), who included social, economic, and environmental aspects in the supply chain of Gayo coffee in the province of Aceh, Indonesia. Changes in price, demand, and environmental terms and the effect of certifications were considered. They analyzed the production of an organic fertilizer from the residue of coffee cherry pulp and showed the effect of education and training in social terms. A sustainability indicator of the coffee supply chain is defined, and improvements are evidenced after intervening key factors.

Malik et al. (2019) formulated a model of influences to achieve a sustainable production system in smallholder coffee farmers in Pangalengan, Indonesia. This work seeks to identify the drivers of economics, social quality, technology, and environmental quality that most influence the sustainability of the chain by observing compensating and reinforcing relationships through dynamic interaction. The article concludes that social quality is the most influential driver, and that social quality management and intervention strategies are needed to guarantee sustainability. Hakim et al. (2020) developed a system dynamics model for the supply chain of Gayo Arabica coffee in Indonesia, which seeks to simulate the effects of a hybrid production system, quality engineering, governance, climate change, productivity, and competition on the profitability of the chain. In contrast to Malik et al. (2019), none of the analyzed scenarios generated significant improvements for smallholder farmers.

More recently, Bashiri et al. (2021) investigated the sustainability risks in the Indonesia-UK coffee supply chain by means of systems dynamics combined with multicriteria methods. The authors concluded that improving agricultural productivity is crucial for the coffee supply chain sustainability and that the combination of the applied approaches is better than applying a single tool.

According to the above review, the study of sustainability elements associated with the coffee supply chain using system dynamics is a novel topic and deserves more research.

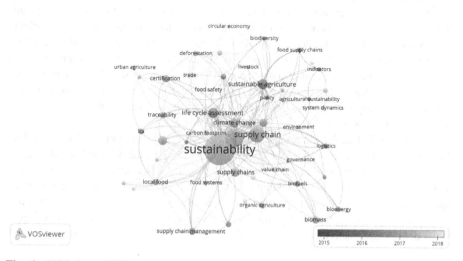

Fig. 1. VOSviewer bibliometric networks of 474 scientific articles on coffee supply chain sustainability from Scopus

3 Problem Statement

The coffee supply chain in Colombia has several drawbacks such as the instability of the international price. According to the National Federation of Coffee Growers (FNC 2018) of Colombia, the grain cost per pound went from \$ 1.60 in November 2016 to \$ 1.00 in May 2019, and although in 2020 and 2021 the price has had rallies above \$ 1.30, there are semesters when the price generates low income in many cases below production costs. Nowadays, coffee multinationals pay 67% less than the price of coffee in 1983 and, although Colombia is the third largest coffee producer in the world and annually the coffee market generates about US\$200,000 million worldwide, producers only have access to less than 10% of that figure (FNC 2018). Although international reference prices can go down, in coffee shops and supermarkets the cost rises progressively. It is calculated that for every pound of coffee sold in the world, producers receive only 7 cents per dollar (FNC 2018). This situation is exacerbated by other problems along the entire supply chain such as logistics costs, especially for producers. According to the national logistics survey (Encuesta Nacional Logística 2018), logistics costs in agricultural companies are around 12.8% of sales in Colombia, concentrated mainly in storage costs with 35.9% and transportation costs with 33.3%.

Another problem is the lack of generational replacement, as confirmed by data from the ceding process registered in the Coffee Information System (Sistema de Información Cafetera-SICA) of the FNC. Between 2005 and 2011, around 3,600 coffee growers in all municipalities were registered, but only 10.2%, a total of 367 growers, were under 35 years old (FNC 2011). At this rate of 10% of new young producers per five-year period, it would take more than ten decades to replace the generations of retiring coffee growers. An additional problematic situation is the replacement of other less sustainable agricultural activities that generate more carbon footprint in the atmosphere, such as cattle raising.

The next problem refers to the lack of additional income on coffee farms to compensate for the seasons of low coffee prices, in addition to the lack of fair trade throughout the entire supply chain that equitably distributes the coffee value chain. According to Potts et al. (2007), although future markets are responsible for establishing the general price context for physical transactions, the ability of producers to impose prices that meet domestic production costs or the costs of maintaining sustainable living standards is also dependent on their capability to negotiate desirable conditions directly with buyers. Producers are often price takers with little capacity to influence the terms of trade in which they participate.

Héctor Fabio Cuéllar, director of the Coffee Growers Committee of Valle in July 2017 stated that, `In the Valle del Cauca (Colombia), 39 of the 42 municipalities grow coffee, especially El Águila, Ansermanuevo, Sevilla, Caicedonia, and Trujillo. The Valle del Cauca has 62,968 ha planted, less than the 70,000 ha registered some years ago; of the total, 37,000 ha are planted with specialty coffee varieties'. This shows that the problems of the coffee supply chain have a very strong influence on the families of Valle del Cauca; concretely, 23,500 families depend on this activity in our department.

To contribute to the sustainability of the coffee supply chain in Valle del Cauca and mitigate or reduce the effects of the problems evidenced here, it is necessary to propose alternative solutions and evaluate the results until a significant improvement in sustainability is achieved. This work proposes an influence diagram and its related Forrester diagram to evaluate such alternatives.

4   Methodology

4.1   Influence Diagram

A diagram of influences was made in which six reinforcement loops were clearly found (Fig. 2). The first one (R1) shows the importance of the permanence of the farmers in the field, the more areas cultivated with the influence of technology, and the improvement of the quality of the coffee bean; so, more income is obtained, improving profitability. The reinforcement loop 2 (R2) shows that the more coffee growers, the less farmer migration to cities, therefore more generational replacement, thus ensuring that employment levels are not reduced in the cities and that consumption is guaranteed, which in turn promotes the purchase of coffee. Because coffee prices are not stable, it is important to compensate the likely reduction in profits with additional income in coffee farms, such as beekeeping, tourism, and pig and chicken raising. Clearly, there are other activities that currently interact with the coffee crops in several coffee farms, although the above three have been selected as the most applicable. In reinforcement loop 3 (R3), investment in tourist attractions on the farms could increase tourist visits, increasing income. Similarly, in loop 4 (R4), the more investment in beekeeping technification and good practices, the greater the production of honey and its derivatives, and therefore the greater the income. The last alternative that was included to increase the income of coffee farmers is the raising of small-scale production animals, such as pigs and chickens. In reinforcement loop 5 (R5), it is observed that if this type of farming is increased, additional income could increase.

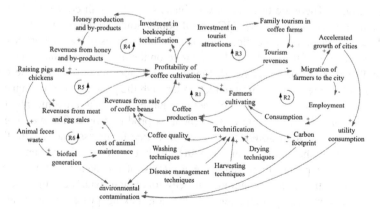

Fig. 2. Influence diagram of the coffee grower link in the coffee supply chain

It is important to note that all the previous loops are constrained by the availability of resources, such as land, water, energy, etc. Animal husbandry has another benefit, in addition to income, which is the generation of biofuel from the waste generated by animals. Many coffee growers cook using firewood, a practice that has several implications. The first is the environmental impact of burning wood. The second is the amount of labor used by farmers to collect firewood, time that can be used in activities related to the crop. Finally, firewood cooking may cause chronic respiratory diseases due to smoke inhalation. Thus, as can be seen in reinforcement loop 6 (R6), the production of more animal waste increases the generation of biofuel that contributes to the reduction of farm costs not only because of the savings in the cooking food method, but also because the biofuel can be used for drying coffee, among other uses.

The diagram of influences shows other important relationships in the sustainability of this chain, such as the utilization and transformation of animal waste into biofuels, avoiding greenhouse gases such as methane, as well as the contamination of aquifers and rivers where these wastes end up. The diagram shows that the technification in all the coffee processes of cultivation, harvesting, and post-harvesting could improve the quality of coffee. Therefore, the coffee could be placed in the market at a better price, in addition to an increase in productivity and yield, generating greater income per hectare planted. Finally, it is observed that the more farmers are cultivating, the greater the reduction of the carbon footprint due to the number of coffee and shade-generating trees planted to improve coffee quality. In the social aspect, we analyze the growing problem in Colombia due to the lack of generational replacement in the countryside. If the coffee farms are profitable, the probability of farmers' migration to cities could be reduced. Migration generates a serious chain effect, producing overpopulation in cities, therefore increasing the environmental damage by the excessive use of resources such as water and energy. In addition to the generation of waste, migration generates less production in the countryside and more dependence on imports affecting food security and the balance of payments.

4.2   Forrester Diagram

The Forrester diagram was made according to the influence diagram and the result is shown in Fig. 3. There are three level variables associated with coffee production, the generation of greenhouse gases (GHG), rural population, and the profitability of coffee farms based on income from coffee sales and the other types of income proposed. The growth or decrease of the rural population based on the increase or reduction of income in the coffee farms is to be analyzed. Finally, we would like to observe the environmental impact of firewood burning reduction through the generation of methane gas by biodigester, as well as the reduction of methane gas emissions to the atmosphere due to animal waste and decomposition of the leachates produced by coffee washing. Information will be collected through field work on coffee farms associated with the variables included in the model. This, together with updated statistical and technical information, are expected to increase the accuracy of the data to obtain simulation results regarding the social, economic, and environmental dynamics suggested in this study. We thus expect to strengthen the decision-making processes associated with increasing the sustainability of the coffee supply chain.

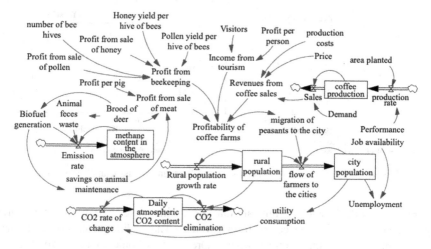

Fig. 3. Forrester diagram of the coffee growers' link in the coffee supply chain

5 Some Selected Simulation Experiments

We have gathered information about some variables from the Forrester diagram; these variables have been simulated to obtain their preliminary behavior at one typical farm. The simulation results indicate that it is important to report on these earliest research advances. Our ongoing research concentrates on the influence of the simulated variables on the non-simulated ones and their correlation. The simulated scenarios considered the following aspects:

- Scenario 1: Only coffee bean production and sales variables for coffee producers.
- Scenario 2: Alternative income sources at coffee farms such as the sales of beekeeping products, farm tourism, and pig raising / meat sales.
- Scenario 3: Some negative environmental impacts at coffee farms and their possible mitigation.

Technical and statistical information was gathered from secondary sources for 60 months (from July 2017 and projected to June 2022), which included data related to the impact of COVID 19 pandemics on coffee and pig meat prices and the reduction of farm tourism.

Figure 4 (a) shows that there are no differences in coffee sales and revenues between scenarios because the other sources of income do not affect coffee harvest. The behavior of coffee sales agrees with the two coffee flowerings that arise in Colombia each year, one from April to June and the most important from October to December. Furthermore, producers' revenues from coffee bean sales depend on coffee international prices and production costs. Accordingly, these revenues might sometimes be very low, and they may be even negative in some periods, generating losses for the producer. (Fig. 4 (b)).

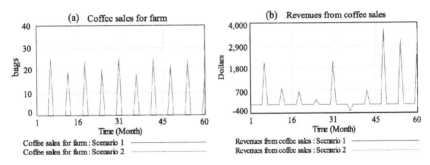

Fig. 4. Simulation of coffee bean sales by farm and its associated profitability

Figures 5 (a), (b) and (c) illustrate that the additional revenue from other sources may be comparable to the coffee bean revenue. The additional income from farm tourism increases in the summer when more tourists come to the farm. Figure 5 (a) reveals a significant reduction of visitors to the farm beginning in month 33 (March 2020) due to the mandatory quarantine caused by the COVID 19 pandemics.

Figure 5 (b) shows some peak production periods of beekeeping products due to the flowering of coffee plants. Each year, a honeycomb generates on average 35 kg of honey and 12 kg of pollen, and the model was run using a typical measure of 1.3 ha per farm, which corresponds to the area of 82 percent of the coffee farms in Colombia (FNC 2018). In addition, the maximum allowed number of honeycombs per hectare is two. As a result, the simulation indicates that the revenue from this activity is not significant.

Figure 5 (d) compares the different revenues. The average monthly revenue from coffee bean sales equals $232 while the average monthly revenue from other income sources equals $153, producing a total monthly average revenue of $385. Although this figure exceeds the minimum monthly wage in Colombia (approximately $252), it can be not enough for the average coffee producer's family group of around 4 people.

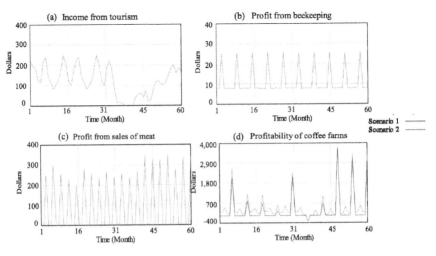

Fig. 5. Behavior of coffee farms with additional sources of income

Finally, Figs. 6 (a) and (b) compare the generation of methane from pig feces in Scenario 2 with and without using a biodigester to produce biogas. It is important to note that the investment on the biodigester was amortized over the analyzed time horizon. A significant reduction in emissions of methane to the atmosphere is shown.

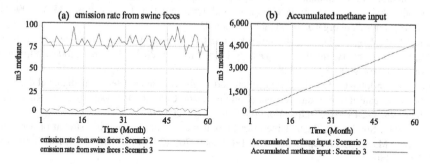

Fig. 6. Methane emissions with and without biofuel generation

6 Conclusions

The study of the sustainable coffee supply chain that considers economic, social, and environmental elements by means of systems dynamics is a topic that deserves more research. As a case in point, several problems have been identified in the coffee supply chain in Colombia, such as the uncertainty in international prices, the small profitability proportion received by coffee growers, and their lack of generational replacement.

To reduce the effects of these factors and improve the coffee supply chain sustainability, we propose system dynamics influence and Forrester diagrams that consider the following improvement alternatives: the permanence of farmers in the field encouraged by better technologies; the production of high-quality beans; and the creation of diverse income sources such as beekeeping, farm tourism, and small-scale animal raising.

According to the influence diagram, these alternatives produce at least six reinforcement loops that could contribute to the economic, social, and environmental sustainability of the coffee supply chain in Colombia. Preliminary runs of the model show that the revenues from other sources different from coffee bean sales may be significant. Besides, the model can be useful to analyze the environmental implications of some production activities such as pig raising and some social impacts of the COVID 19 pandemics, for example, on tourism reduction. Our ongoing research will analyze additional sustainability aspects of selected coffee farms in the region of Valle del Cauca, Colombia.

Acknowledgments. This work was supported by Fondo de Ciencia, Tecnología e Innovación of Sistema General de Regalías (FCTeI-SGR) and Ministerio de Ciencia, Tecnología e Innovación (MinCiencias) of Colombia and by the Universidad del Valle, Cali, Colombia.

References

Bashiri, M., Tjahjono, B., Lazell, J., Ferreira, J., Perdana, T.: The dynamics of sustainability risks in the global coffee supply chain: a case of Indonesia–UK. Sustainability **13**(2), 589 (2021). https://doi.org/10.3390/su13020589

Brandenburg, M., Govindan, K., Sarkis, J., Seuring, S.: Quantitative models for sustainable supply chain management: developments and directions. Eur. J. Oper. Res. **233**(2), 299–312 (2014). https://doi.org/10.1016/j.ejor.2013.09.032

Carter, C.R., Rogers, D.S.: A framework of sustainable supply chain management: moving toward new theory. Int. J. Phys. Distrib. Logist. Manag. **38**(5), 360–387 (2008). https://doi.org/10.1108/09600030810882816

Díaz, M., Córdoba, C.: Estudio de la estructura del agroecosistema cafetero mediante el diagrama de ciclos causales. Estudio de caso (Cundinamarca, Colombia). J. Depopulation Rural Dev. Stud. **28**, 1–24 (2019). https://doi.org/10.4422/ager.2019.08

Drake, D.F., Spinler, S.: Sustainable operations management: an enduring stream or a passing fancy? Manuf. Serv. Oper. Manage. **15**(4), 689–700 (2013). https://doi.org/10.1287/msom.2013.0456

Federación Nacional de Cafeteros de Colombia (FNC). https://federaciondecafeteros.org/wp/publicaciones/. informe de gestión 2011. Accessed 15 May 2019

Federación Nacional de Cafeteros de Colombia (FNC). https://federaciondecafeteros.org/wp/publicaciones/. informe de gestión 2018. Accessed 11 Aug 2019

Forrester, J.W.: Lessons from system dynamics modeling. Syst. Dyn. Rev. **3**(2), 136–149 (1987). https://doi.org/10.1002/sdr.4260030205

Hakim, L., Deli, A., Zulkarnain.: The system dynamics modeling of Gayo Arabica coffee industry supply chain management. IOP Conf. Ser. Earth Environ. Sci. **425**, 012019 (2020). https://doi.org/10.1088/1755-1315/425/1/012019

Kannegiesser, M., Günther, H.-O.: Sustainable development of global supply chains—part 1: sustainability optimization framework. Flex. Serv. Manuf. J. **26**(1–2), 24–47 (2013). https://doi.org/10.1007/s10696-013-9176-5

Malik, A.D., Parikesit, S.W.: Exploring drivers' interaction influencing the adoption of sustainable coffee production system through a qualitative system dynamics modelling, case study : smallholder coffee plantation in Pangalengan, Bandung, Indonesia. IOP Conf. Ser. Earth Environ. Sci. **306**, 012007 (2019). https://doi.org/10.1088/1755-1315/306/1/012007

Meadows, D., Robinson, J.M.: The Electronic Oracle: Computer Models and Social Decisions. Wiley, Hoboken (1985)

Observatorio Nacional de Logística, Colombia. Encuesta Nacional logística 2018. https://plc.mintransporte.gov.co/Portals/0/News/Informe%20de%20resultados%20Encuesta%20Nacional%20Logistica%202018.pdf. Accessed 18 Feb 2021

Potts, J., Fernandez, G., Wunderlich, C.: Trading Practices for a Sustainable Coffee Sector Context, Strategies and Recommendations for Action Prepared as a Background Document for the Sustainable Coffee Partnership. International Institute for Sustainable Development (2007)

Rachman, J., Machfud, S., Raharja, M.: Prediction of sustainable supply chain management for gayo coffee using system dynamics approach. J. Theor. Appl. Inf. Technol. **70**(2), 372–380 (2014)

Sasikumar, P., Kannan, G.: Issues in reverse supply chain, part III: classification and simple analysis. Int. J. Sustain. Eng. **2**(1), 2–27 (2009). https://doi.org/10.1080/19397030802673374

Sterman, J.D.: System dynamics modeling: tools for learning in a complex word. Calif. Manage. Rev. **43**(4), 8–25 (2001). https://doi.org/10.2307/41166098

Tedeschi, L.O., Nicholson, C.F., Rich, E.: Using system dynamics modelling approach to develop management tools for animal production with emphasis on small ruminants. Small Rumin. Res. **98**(1–3), 102–110 (2011). https://doi.org/10.1016/j.smallrumres.2011.03.026

Thornton, P.K., Herrero, M.: Integrated crop–livestock simulation models for scenario analysis and impact assessment. Agric. Syst. **70**(2–3), 581–602 (2001). https://doi.org/10.1016/S0308-521X(01)00060-9

A Study of the Relationships Between Quality of Management, Sustainable Supply Chain Management Practices and Performance Outcomes

Dandutse Tanimu, Yahaya Yusuf[✉], and Dan'Asabe Godwin Geyi

Lancashire School of Business and Enterprise, University of Central Lancashire,
Preston PR1 2HE, UK
{tdandutse,yyusuf,dggeyi}@uclan.ac.uk

Abstract. Extant literature on SSCM practices have paid little attention to quality of management attributes that could influence sustainability implementation in supply chains. The aim of this study is to address this gap by examining the relationship between quality of management, SSCM practices, and business performance. A survey of 192 oil and gas companies was carried out. The data collected was analyses using correlation and multiple regression analysis. The correlation results provide evidence that, quality of management is positively related to the implementation of SSCM practices. The regression results indicate that 18.1% of variance in business performance is explained by quality of management, and 26.4% of the variance is explained by SSCM practices.

Keywords: Quality of management · Sustainable supply chain management · Firm performance

1 Introduction

The notion of sustainable supply chain management (SSCM) has received increasing recognition in both theory and practice, due to several factors supporting its acceptance and adoption such as stakeholder pressures, scarcity of raw materials, competitive pressures, and environmental concerns about the negative impacts of industrial operations [15]. Firms in recent years have focused on employing approaches that simultaneously addresses the economic, social, and environmental issues related to their supply chains [14]. SSCM is deemed as a viable approach that can help firms to effectively integrate economic, social, and environmental considerations, which ultimately leads to competitive advantage [2, 17]. The SSCM approach incorporates the principles of supply chain management (SCM), corporate social responsibility and environmental management with the aim of minimizing environmental destruction while improving the performance of the supply chain [18]. Scholars have utilised the complementary definition of SCM and sustainability literature to introduce a more comprehensive definition of SSCM:

"The strategic integration and achievement of an organisation's social, environmental, and economic goals in the systemic coordination of key organizational business

© IFIP International Federation for Information Processing 2021
Published by Springer Nature Switzerland AG 2021
A. Dolgui et al. (Eds.): APMS 2021, IFIP AICT 634, pp. 618–625, 2021.
https://doi.org/10.1007/978-3-030-85914-5_65

processes for improving the long-term economic performance of the individual company and its supply chain" [1].

In this study, the conceptualisation of SSCM is adopted as it forms the basis for operationalising sustainability concept within the SCM context. In essence, this definition suggests that SSCM is concerned with achieving a balance among the triple bottom line elements. From a holistic perspective, SSCM addresses the economic, social, and environmental goals of the focal firm and its supply chain partners [1]. However, the shift from traditional SCM to a SSCM approach creates substantial pressure on firms to adjust their existing supply chains to meet sustainability needs. While some firms adopt SSCM initiatives due to external pressures, others engage in sustainable practise to improve their reputation and competitiveness [12]. Considering this, it is important for firms to embrace a proactive approach towards achieving a sustainable supply chain, rather than a reactive approach of regulatory compliance [23]. The following section explains the concept of quality of management.

2   Literature Review

2.1   Quality of Management

In defining the concept of quality of management (QOM), it is essential to state the meaning of "quality" and that of "management". Reeves and Bednar [21] define quality as level of excellence, while Smircich and Morgan [22] describes management as the effective and efficient coordination of organisational processes to achieve defined set of goals. The term QOM has been defined differently from different perspectives.

QOM is viewed as the extent to which an organisation is soundly run [19]. In a more elaborate definition, Koch and Cebula [8] states that QOM encompasses management's ability to positively transform their organisation to continuously adapt to the ever-changing business environment. According to Doz and Prahalad [4], QOM is concerned with influencing the individual behaviour of employees to create an effective organisational context. Given the lack of consensus on the definition of QOM among scholars, this study draws from the definitions of "quality" and "management" and propose a more comprehensive definition of QOM concept: QOM is the degree of excellence in the coordination and organisation of business activities to achieve desired outcomes.

The effectiveness of a firm depends on the willingness and ability of managers to facilitate the success of initiatives in the firm [7]. QOM is a necessary antecedent to performance. This assumes that performance is the ultimate management responsibility [7]. In a similar regard, Mcguire et al. [11] asserts that managerial strength or capacity is an important driver of organisational innovations. Thus, the implementation of SSCM initiatives could be influenced by the QOM in an organisation. However, there is a lack of empirical evidence to prove this. Hence, the need to explore the relationship between QOM and SSCM adoption by firms.

Firms with perceived QOM engage in proactive environmental and social practices [19], to lessen the effects of their business operations on the societies and communities in which they operate. More so, QOM is associated with quality of stakeholder relationships [19]. In other words, top management are expected to consider environmental, economic, and social objectives simultaneously to meet the concerns of multiple stakeholders. Therefore, the implementation of SSCM initiatives could be influenced by the QOM in an organisation. However, there is a lack of empirical evidence to prove this. Hence, the need to explore the relationship between QOM and SSCM adoption by firms.

2.2   Sustainable Supply Chain Management (SSCM) Practices

The notion of SSCM has received increasing recognition in both theory and practice, due to several factors promoting its espousal and implementation including stakeholder demands, scarcity of raw materials, competitive pressures, and environmental concerns about the negative impacts of industrial operations [15]. Sustainable supply chain deemed as a viable approach that can help firms to effectively integrate economic, social, and environmental considerations, which ultimately leads to competitive advantage [14]. SSCM offers a wide range of opportunities for an organisation to distinguish itself from its competitors [1]. In their review of the literature Seuring and Müller [17], argued that SSCM is "the management of material, information, and capital flows, as well as cooperation among companies along the supply chain while taking goals from all three dimensions of sustainable development, i.e., economic, environmental, and social, into account which are derived from customer and stakeholder requirements". It was noted in Paulraj et al. [14] that the effective management of an organisation's internal practices (sustainable process and products), as well as external practices (cooperation between suppliers and consumers), help to build a sustainable supply chain.

The philosophy of SSCM encompasses multidimensional activities, comprising of sustainable purchasing [25, 26], which advocates procuring materials with the least environmental impacts; sustainable manufacturing [29], which emphasises internally driven environmental initiatives such as reuse and reproduction; sustainable distribution [23], which facilitates reduction of logistical impacts caused by material flows; and reverse logistics [5, 14], which entails closing the loop through recycling and disposal. In this study, five categories of SSCM practices are considered: sustainable procurement, design, distribution, investment recovery, and social sustainability.

2.3   Organisational Performance

Numerous studies have found that SSCM practices have positive impacts on performance outcomes [5, 14]. SSCM implementation can enhance various processes in supply chains [17]. Major benefits of SSCM include reduction in costs of raw materials and packaging due to the use of recycled materials [25], reduction in environmental risks and improvement in firm's image [12], and improvements in quality of products or processes, flexibility, and delivery speed [15]. Researchers have observed that firms are increasingly adopting SSCM practices to improve relationships, collaboration, competitiveness, and performance of their supply chains [14]. However, many studies on the impact of SSCM practices on organisational performance are either focusing on a particular aspect of performance or structured along a few dimensions only. Thus, this study attempts to shed more light on the impact of SSCM practices on aggregate business performance of supply chains.

3 Methodology

3.1 Data Collation

To answer the research questions, a survey by questionnaire was carried out. After a pre-test, seven hundred and forty (740) questionnaires were emailed to potential respondents taken from the Financial Analysis Made Easy (FAME) database of companies and other databases that host business directories of firms. Both mailed postal and web-based methods was used to send the questionnaire to the operations or supply chain managers of each company, who in some cases delegated certain questions to those in charge of environmental management or quality management. The questionnaire was then preceded by a phone call to identify the appropriate addressee, to announce the sending of the question and to ask for collaboration. A cover letter was attached to each questionnaire. After two weeks a mailing and phone call was made to all the respondent companies that had not replied. This procedure yielded a global response rate of 28.7%. The response rate is considered as representative of earlier studies of organizations by questionnaire. In a previous similar empirical study on sustainability, Luthra et al. [10] achieved a response rate of 24.6%. Of the 213 questionnaires returned, 192 were fully completed and thus deemed valid and usable for the study. Twenty-one incomplete questionnaires were not included in the analysis. Even though poorly completed questionnaires still provides some information, researchers recommend excluding such questionnaires from further analysis to avoid incidence of missing data and to improve the reliability of findings [6].

3.2 The Instrument

The questionnaire is divided into four broad categories of questions. The first category deals with the profile of the respondents. While, the second category contains sustainable supply chain management practices, the basic sustainable initiatives that companies implement. In the third section, the respondents were questioned on the organisational factors such as quality of management. The fourth category questioned respondents on measures of business performance employed in their organisation. Overall, the survey instrument consisted of twenty main questions cover the basic features of a sustainability and quality of management. Some of the questions relate to contextual data sought objective answers, such as market share or profitability. Other includes those which sought to determine the relative importance of the competitive objectives and those indicating the importance of various sustainability practices or performance measures. The managers in the sample were asked to score each of the practices and performance separately on a five-point Likert scare (1 = strongly disagree to 5 = strongly agree; 1 = Very low to 5 = Very high). A scale with balanced keying does avoid the problem of acquiescence bias, but central tendency and social desirability biases are somewhat more challenging to offset [24]. The data analysis of the questionnaire data was carried out using SPSS (statistical Packages for social sciences), one of the most widely used software package for statistical analysis in social sciences.

To make sure that questionnaire data is free of random effects, Kimberlin, C. L., and Winterstein [30] suggest the evaluation of the reliability of the scales used to collect data in a study. Reliability tests assesses the internal consistency of instruments used in measuring research constructs [27]. Measurement items must be highly correlated before they can be considered to meet reliability requirements. The most used technique for testing internal consistency is the Cronbach's coefficient alpha [28]. Accordingly, reliability assessment was conducted for the key research variables, demographics, SSCM practices, QOM, firm performance, and the whole questionnaire.

The result indicates that the Cronbach's alpha of the entire questionnaire is 0.736. In addition, reliability test results for each of the sub-items in the survey instrument indicate that all the sub-items have Cronbach's alphas greater than 0.70. Consequently, this mean that there is a strong internal consistency in the scale of the survey instrument. In the literature, the range for Cronbach's alpha value is 0 to 1, and the closer Cronbach's alpha is to 1, the higher the internal reliability. Reliabilities less than 0.60 are rated to be poor, those in the 0.70 range are acceptable and those from 0.80 and above are considered good [27]. Thus, a Cronbach's alpha value of 0.70 or higher is used to establish reliability of a construct.

3.3 Data Analysis

To enhance our understanding on the influence of organisational factors (such as, QOM) on the implementation of SSCM practices and firm performance, correlation analysis was carried out to assess the relationships among the factors examined. Furthermore, regression analysis was performed to determine causal effects on the links between the independent and dependent variables. Correlation and regression share some similarities however, they serve distinct purposes. While correlation assesses the strength of associations among variables, regression establishes the type of the association which correlation established through estimation and prediction of the value of a dependent variable based upon the values of some independent variables.

4   Results

4.1   Correlations Between the Main Research Constructs

This study followed the guideline provided by [3], which argued that a correlation effect size of less than 0.10 is considered weak, 0.10 to 0.30 is moderate and greater than 0.30 is strong. It is apparent from the correlation coefficients that the relationships between aggregate QOM and SSCM practices ($r = .422, p = .000$) is strong and statistically significant. The relationships of QOM and SSCM practices with organisational performance are ($r = .358, p = .000; r = .472, p = .000$) respectively (see Table 2). These correlation coefficients indicate that QOM and SSCM practices have significant positive impact on the performance of oil and gas companies.

4.2   Regression Analysis

Having identified a positive relationship between quality of management, SSCM practices and the level of business performance, a multiple regression analysis was conducted to evaluate the interactive effects of QOM and SSCM practices on the overall performance of oil and gas companies. The model summary indicates 18.1% of variance in business performance explained by quality of management, and 26.4% of the variance is explained by SSCM practices. From the results, it may be possible to predict the level of performance effect from the level of QOM and SSCM practices in the oil and gas industry. The correlation between QOM and business performance is 0.177. while the correlation between SSCM practices and business performance is 0.344. Approximately 18% ($r^2 = 0.181$) of the variance of the business performance is associated with total quality of management. While 26% ($r^2 = 0.264$) of the variance of the business performance is linked with the overall SSCM practices.

The research has identified a strong relationship between the level of SSCM practices implementation and the level of business performance. While we indicate a weak correlation between the level of QOM and level of business performance. These suggests that QOM may have significant influence on business performance within a short-term, but to maximise the full performance outcomes, organisations need to implement sustainable supply chain practices.

5   Discussion and Implications

This paper, extracted from an ongoing research, contributes to the extant literature on SSCM. Specifically, it explored the relationships between QOM and SSCM practices and their impact on the performance of firms in the oil and gas industry.

The correlation results show that QOM is positively related to SSCM practices. This finding is consistent with previous studies, which noted that top management commitment [20] influence the adoption of SSCM practices by firms. In essence, the implementation of SSCM practices requires top management leadership and commitment [9]. Thus, the higher the QOM, the greater the effectiveness of sustainability implementation and realisation of the full benefits of adopting such practices. Similarly, the results of the regression analysis show that 44.5% of the variance in business performance can be explained by QOM and SSCM practices.

In addition, SSCM practices have been identified to have the highest contributions to business performance in the oil and gas industry. This evidence of a positive link between SSCM practices and performance outcomes is an essential contribution to the ongoing debate on whether it pays to be green/sustainable. While some studies found positive impacts [14], others identified negative impacts [13]. This study confirms that firms could achieve superior performance through the implementation of SSCM practices. Therefore, to attain greater sustainability performance, firms should aim at increasing long-term value through SSCM practices, rather than focusing on short-term economic benefits.

References

1. Carter, C.R., Rogers, D.S.: A framework of sustainable supply chain management: moving toward new theory. Int. J. Phys. Distrib. Logist. Manage. **41**, 46–62 (2008)
2. Carter, C.R., Easton, P.L.: Sustainable supply chain management: evolution and future directions. Int. J. Phys. Distrib. Logist. Manage. (2011). https://doi.org/10.1108/09600031111101420
3. Cohen, J.: 'Statistical power analysis for the behavioral sciences. Technometrics **31**, 499–500 (1988)
4. Doz, Y.L., Prahalad, C.K.: Managing DMNCs: a search for a new paradigm. Strateg. Manag. J. (1991). https://doi.org/10.1002/smj.4250120911
5. Esfahbodi, A., Zhang, Y., Watson, G.: Sustainable supply chain management in emerging economies: trade-offs between environmental and cost performance. Int. J. Prod. Econ. (2016). https://doi.org/10.1016/j.ijpe.2016.02.013
6. Fidell, L.S., Tabachnick, B.G., Fidell, L.S.: Using Multivariate Statistics, 5th edn. Pearson, London (2006)
7. Ghoshal, S., Bartlett, C.A.: Linking organizational context and managerial action: the dimensions of quality of management. Strateg. Manag. J. (1994). https://doi.org/10.1002/smj.4250151007
8. Koch, J.V., Cebula, R.J.: In search of excellent management. J. Manage. Stud. (1994). https://doi.org/10.1111/j.1467-6486.1994.tb00634.x
9. Linnenluecke, M.K., Griffiths, A.: Corporate sustainability and organizational culture. J. World Bus. (2010). https://doi.org/10.1016/j.jwb.2009.08.006
10. Luthra, S., Garg, D., Haleem, A.: The impacts of critical success factors for implementing green supply chain management towards sustainability: an empirical investigation of Indian automobile industry. J. Clean. Prod. (2016). https://doi.org/10.1016/j.jclepro.2016.01.095
11. Mcguire, J.B., Schneeweis, T., Branch, B.: Perceptions of firm quality: a cause or result of firm performance. J. Manage. (1990). https://doi.org/10.1177/014920639001600112
12. Pagell, M., Wu, Z.: Building a more complete theory of sustainable supply chain management using case studies of 10 exemplars. J. Supply Chain Manage **45**, 37–56 (2009)
13. Parast, M.M., Adams, S.G.: Corporate social responsibility, benchmarking, and organizational performance in the petroleum industry: a quality management perspective. Int. J. Prod. Econ. (2012). https://doi.org/10.1016/j.ijpe.2011.11.033
14. Paulraj, A., Chen, I.J., Blome, C.: Motives and performance outcomes of sustainable supply chain management practices: a multi-theoretical perspective. J. Bus. Ethics **145**(2), 239–258 (2015). https://doi.org/10.1007/s10551-015-2857-0
15. Sarkis, J., Gonzalez-Torre, P., Adenso, B.: Stakeholder pressure and the adoption of environmental practices: the mediating effect of training. J. Oper. Manage. (2010). https://doi.org/10.1016/j.jom.2009.10.001
16. Seuring, S.: A review of modeling approaches for sustainable supply chain management. Decis. Support Syst. (2013). https://doi.org/10.1016/j.dss.2012.05.053
17. Seuring, S., Müller, M.: From a literature review to a conceptual framework for sustainable supply chain management. J. Cleaner Prod. **16**, 1699–1710 (2008)
18. Tseng, M., Lim, M., Wong, W.P.: Sustainable supply chain management: a closed-loop network hierarchical approach. Ind. Manage. Data Syst. (2015). https://doi.org/10.1108/IMDS-10-2014-0319
19. Waddock, S.A., Graves, S.B.: Quality of management and quality of stakeholder relations: are they synonymous? Bus. Soc. (1997). https://doi.org/10.1177/000765039703600303

20. Walker, H., Jones, N.: Sustainable supply chain management across the UK private sector. Supply Chain Manage. (2012). https://doi.org/10.1108/13598541211212177
21. Reeves, C.A., Bednar, D.A.: Defining quality: alternatives and implications. Acad. Manag. Rev. **19**(3), 419–445 (1994)
22. Smircich, L., Morgan, G.: Leadership: the management of meaning. J. Appl. Behav. Sci. **18** (3), 257–273 (1982)
23. Vachon, S., Klassen, R.D.: Supply chain management and environmental technologies: the role of integration. Int. J. Prod. Res. (2007). https://doi.org/10.1080/00207540600597781
24. Yusuf, Y.Y., Gunasekaran, A., Musa, A., El-, N.M., Abubakar, T., Ambursa, H.M.: The UK oil and gas supply chains: an empirical analysis of adoption of sustainable measures and performance outcomes. Int. J. Prod. Econ. (2013). https://doi.org/10.1016/j.ijpe.2012.09.021
25. Zhu, Q., Sarkis, J., Lai, K.H., Geng, Y.: The role of organizational size in the adoption of green supply chain management practices in China. Corp. Soc. Responsib. Environ. Manag. (2008). https://doi.org/10.1002/csr.173
26. Zsidisin, G.A., Siferd, S.P.: Environmental purchasing: a framework for theory development. Eur. J. Purch. Supply Manage. (2001). https://doi.org/10.1016/S0969-7012(00)00007-1
27. Sekaran, U., Bougie, R.: Research Methods for Business, 7th edn. Wiley, Hoboken (2016)
28. Cho, E., Kim, S.: Cronbach's coefficient alpha. Organ. Res. Methods **18**, 207–230 (2015)
29. Dües, C.M., Tan, K.H., Lim, M.: Green as the new lean: how to use Lean practices as a catalyst to greening your supply chain. J. Clean Prod. **40**, 93–100 (2013)
30. Kimberlin, C.L., Winterstein, A.G.: Validity and reliability of measurement instruments used in research. Am. J. Health-Syst. Pharm. (2008). https://doi.org/10.2146/ajhp070364

4.0 Transition Methodology for Sustainable Supply Chain Management

Ioana Deniaud[1][✉] [iD], François Marmier[2] [iD],
and Jean-Louis Michalak[1]

[1] Beta, CNRS UMR 7522, University of Strasbourg, Strasbourg, France
deniaud@unistra.fr
[2] ICUBE, CNRS UMR 7357, University of Strasbourg, Strasbourg, France

Abstract. Customers express more and more willingness to consume sustainable products. This is often considered as a requirement by companies and therefore in their whole supply chains. To ensure an overall improvement of the supply chain environmental performance, the transition to 4.0 must encompass all the stakeholders involved. With a view that facilitates the determination of the required transformations of companies on the sustainability criteria, this article sets out to identify a strategy for optimizing the sustainability of the supply chain considering each stakeholder's resources. Based on deductive research, we propose: 1) a methodology for defining a relevant strategy for 4.0 transition of a supply chain, 2) a qualitative model for assessing the maturity of companies and their entire supply chain, with a focus on the fields of the sustainability, characterizing the 4.0 transformation, 3) a decision-making tool, taking into consideration each stakeholder's deviation from clients' requirements, with a view to identifying and prioritizing the development strategy to be followed for a transition to a 4.0 supply chain.

Keywords: 4.0 transformation · Sustainable supply chain · Maturity model

1 Introduction

The great challenge for today's supply chains is to develop strategies to continuously adapt to the new market demand that becomes "smarter", more transparent, more flexible and more agile at all levels [1–3]. Supply chains must therefore combine the advantages of artisanal models, producing customized products, and industrial models based on mass production. In addition to technological and digital parameters, a Sustainable Supply Chain (SSC) should respond to social, societal and environmental dimensions improvement [4, 5].

In conclusion there are multiple and sometimes contradictory objectives: to reduce costs and lead times, to increase the ability to innovate, to offer customized products and services, to meet increased customer demands and sustainability performance criteria. Also, there are many barriers to improving the sustainability of a supply chain. These barriers include a lack of a skilled workforce that understands Industry 4.0, ineffective legislation and controls, ineffective performance evaluation models, and short-term corporate goals [5].

© IFIP International Federation for Information Processing 2021
Published by Springer Nature Switzerland AG 2021
A. Dolgui et al. (Eds.): APMS 2021, IFIP AICT 634, pp. 626–633, 2021.
https://doi.org/10.1007/978-3-030-85914-5_66

In recent years, new organizational concepts have been developed at a steady pace to respond, in part, to these challenges: the ambidextrous enterprise (capable of simultaneously developing innovative and routine projects) [6]; the Lean enterprise (which hunts down waste to reduce costs, increase responsiveness and the level of performance) [7]; the agile enterprise based on decentralized decision-making and organizational learning [8]; the sustainable enterprise that respects the environment [9]. More recently, the concept of enterprise 4.0 [10] builds on the previous concepts by taking advantage of the digital modernization of industrial tools (internet of things, big data, artificial intelligence, cyber-physical systems) [11–13]. Changing market has forced these organizations to revisit their supply chain activities in order to include sustainability effectively [4]. The circular economy associates the supply and demand of supply chain industries to improve resource efficiency [14, 15].

However, most supply chain companies do not know how to make this transition to 4.0. We support the idea that they must be able to carry out a factual diagnosis of the different aspects of the 4.0 transformation of their activities. They also do not know how to set achievable objectives that define a 4.0 transformation strategy. In-deed, it can be difficult for a single company, especially small and medium-sized enterprises (SMEs) whose human and financial resources are limited, to identify the approach to follow and define a new strategy, while being aware of the risks involved [16]. Therefore, it is necessary to support companies, to give them a method and tools to diagnose their level of 4.0 maturity, to define their objectives and priorities in their 4.0 transformation, and more particularly their vision of their sustainable supply chain.

Nowadays, there is no organizational transformation method to help companies to define a strategy for their supply chain transformation towards 4.0. The diagnostics currently used are essentially based on interviews with "auditors", without any structuring methodology or factual results. Based on the state of the art detailed in Sect. 2, we realized that there is no model to guide 4.0 structural transformation of companies and their supply chains. This observation led us to the hypothesis that in order to make a supply chain progress as a whole, it is necessary for each company in this supply chain to be able to project itself through realistic stages by setting achievable objectives with regard to its capacities to evolve towards 4.0.

By conducting hypothetico-deductive research, the objective of this article is to propose a method and tools for the companies to succeed in their transition towards the 4.0 Sustainable Supply Chain. To do so, we need to be able to evaluate the level of performance of a company in relation to an overall objective of the supply chain of which it is a part, and to be able to help it benchmark itself.

The article is structured as follows: (1) we present a state of the art in order to identify the current problematic for the 4.0 transformation to a sustainable supply chain; (2) we list the main fields concerned by this transformation; (3) we propose a tool and an assessment methodology to help the companies in the supply chain to assess themselves and to define priorities in their strategy towards the 4.0 transitions, in line with their supply, while focusing on the sustainability.

2 Literature Review

2.1 Strategic Fields of Transition 4.0

Much research has focused on the technological aspects of Enterprise 4.0 [17] and their implications in the supply chain [3, 12, 18]. The technological aspects mainly concern the concept of the "smart factory", i.e. the creation of an intelligent and learning environment in a company's production system [2, 19]. Driven by the Internet, the real and virtual world of the company is being transformed into the "Internet of Things" to be faster, more efficient and more flexible in terms of production, using "smart big data". Production is connected with the most modern information and communication systems to create a smart, digitally connected supply chain with production largely organized by itself, while building on Lean concepts [20]. This also implies the implementation of cyber-physical systems, having interconnection between products, machines, ecosystem and even consumers, and this at every stage of the product's life from its design to its end of life [11, 21].

The level of maturity refers to the state of an organization in relation to the deployment of its processes and its objectives [22]. We have identified four fields that best represent our global vision of the Supply Chain and the major issues that must be integrated in order to initiate a transformation towards 4.0 industry [23]:

- Product and process design field
- Production, logistics, and maintenance field
- Strategic organization field
- Sustainability field.

2.2 Maturity Evaluation Models

Different maturity models exist in the literature: purely technological oriented [24], quality oriented organizational processes [25], software oriented CMMI (Capability Maturity Model Integration) developed by (Software Engineering Institute, in 2001, and specific for sustainability management based on ISO 14000.

In the last years other specific maturity models were developed for the 4.0 transformation. In the same line as CMMI, [26] proposes a "4.0 Readiness Model" with six levels of maturity named "outsider", "beginner" for newcomers "intermediate", "experienced" for learners, "expert", "top performer" for leaders. This model considers six dimensions: Strategy and organization, smart factory, smart operations, smart products, data-driven services, employees. More recently [21] proposed a model to evaluate a maturity index on 5 levels: Standard, Big Data, Smart Data, Dark Factory, Industrial Ecosystem. They consider five sectors of the company: Business Management, Development, Manufacturing, Supply chain and Service. [27, 28] identified individual logistics subsystems (Purchase logistics, Production logistics, Distribution logistics, After-sales logistics) and three main dimensions (Management, Flow of material, Flow of information) according to which the maturity level of a company should be tested. They considered five maturity levels: Ignoring, Defining, Adopting, Managing, Integrated.

In a recent paper [23] proposed a maturity model allowing the evaluation of supply chain companies. They defined five levels of technological maturity and six levels of organizational maturity of the current situation for the diagnostic model: "1. Basic" and "2. Partial" for newcomers who are starting to question themselves, "3. Managed" and "4. Mastered" for learning companies [2], which have already started a transformation to 4.0, "5. Optimized" and "6. Innovative" for leaders who represent the showcase of the enterprise 4.0. These levels can be likened to "outsider" and "basic", "disciplined" and "adjusted", "optimized expert" and "innovative expert". The latter have already succeeded in achieving the requirements on all aspects of 4.0 transformation, and they are engaged in a continuous innovation process.

On the basis of the four fields identified in Sect. 2.1, we propose a methodology and a detailed diagnostic model, with specific development sustainability field. A concrete application of this methodology which is based on a case study will also be presented.

3 Methodology and Tool

3.1 Methodology for SSC 4.0 Transition

The objective of the methodology (Fig. 1) is to help supply chain managers to succeed in their 4.0 transformation plan. The proposed methodology is based on the PDCA (Plan - Do - Check - Act) methodology. It offers a frame of reference and is applicable to the entire company in order to improve and even innovate by minimizing risks. The idea is that after one or more cycles of the PDCA, the level expected in the 4.0 transformation is reached.

This methodology integrates in the phases "Do" and "Check" a qualitative assessment of the maturity level. The assessment is obtained for each field of the 4.0 transformation. A gap analysis allows to identify the jobs impacted and the skills to be developed. In "Act" phase an action plan is proposed, especially for recruitments and trainings.

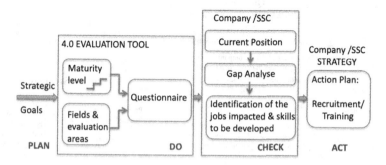

Fig. 1. Methodology to define a 4.0 transformation strategy for SSC.

The purposes of these different steps with regard to the 4.0 transition are detailed in Table 1:

Table 1. Detailed steps of the methodology.

PLAN: Define the supply chain manager's priority objectives in line with the company's strategy. This phase allows to frame the project, to identify all the requirements and expectations for the future development of the company and the supply chain.	DO: Use the 4.0 diagnostic tool : - definition of a maturity scale and its level of control - identifying the fields to be taken into account for the assessment - the realization of a multiple-choice questionnaire for the companies
ACT: Define a prioritized action plan (long, medium and short term) for the entire supply chain as well as for each of its links in relation to the 4.0 strategy: -employees training -new employee recruitment	CHECK: Following the answers to the questionnaire, position the company on each field of the transformation 4.0 : -identification and analysis of gaps between the current situation and the target situation -identification of the job & skills to be developed

The rest of our article focus on the Do and Check steps in order to propose a 4.0 diagnostic tool that will allow us to identify and analyze the gaps in relation to the maturity objectives of the sustainability field linked to 4.0 transformation.

3.2   4.0 Diagnostic Tool for SSC

In [23] we have developed a global model bringing together all the areas of 4.0 transformation previously presented. This model allows us to select the improvement areas and strategies to be adopted so that the supply chain can meet the requirements of the client and the needs of the end customer.

In this paper we focus on "Sustainability field". Figure 2 shows the axis of this field, and the questions concerning it.

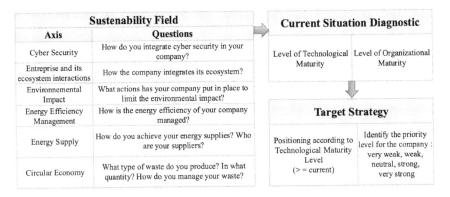

Fig. 2. Diagnostic process for the sustainability field.

Once the responses are done, we should evaluate the current situation concerning each axe. We distinguish two different levels concerning the maturity:

- Level of organizational maturity: one choice between six level proposed by the tool: basic, partial, managed, mastered, optimized, innovative.
- Level of Technological maturity: one choice between the five levels proposed by the tool. For example: for "Energy Supply" axis we propose: 0. Purchase of fossil fuels, 1. Purchase of nuclear energy, 2. Purchase of green energy, 3. Green energy production and 4. Green energy resale.

Concerning the target strategy, we distinguish: the target concerning the technological maturity level, and the priority level according to strategy and available resources.

The gap between current situation and the target strategy is calculated by the tool as shown Fig. 3 presenting the focus on the sustainability field.

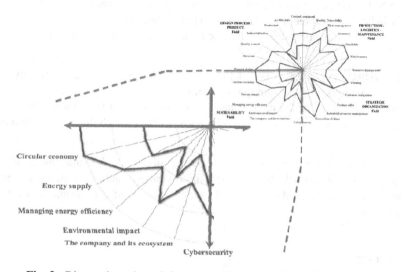

Fig. 3. Diagnostic tool result for sustainability field. (Color figure online)

This representation allows us to quickly see the initial situation (inner curve - blue) and the target situation (outer curve - red).

The gaps between the initial situation and the target situation allow supply chain managers to identify the axis to be improved in each field, and to associate action plans concerning recruiting and training. In this sense, the tool proposes also a list of skills corresponding to each axis.

4 Conclusions and Perspectives

Companies must adapt their organization to meet the new requirements related to Industry 4.0, in a context of sustainable development. Following the literature review we found that there is no organizational transformation method to help companies to define a strategy for their supply chain transformation towards 4.0.

This article aims to propose a methodology and a tool to define the 4.0 transformation strategy for sustainable supply chains. This managerial contribution helps each company, in a personalized way, to design and pilot a strategy of transformation towards 4.0, by prioritizing the axis of development including the essential axis of the sustainable supply chain. Companies will be able to gain in resilience, agility and efficiency, while being sustainable and respectful of people and their environment. They will also be able to integrate more easily into 4.0 supply chains.

These contributions also make it possible to compare companies by sector of activity and typology, to define possible standards and to implicitly develop a "benchlearning" approach.

The tool allows the aggregation of all the evaluations and automatically generates diagrams allowing the company to have a direct visualization of its positioning with respect to the supply chain objectives. It can then build a strategy based on the company's indicators in relation to the supply chain objectives.

During the implementation of the methodology and the tool presented, the main difficulties encountered were the following:

- identifying a contact with sufficient insight and knowledge of the company's processes to complete the entire questionnaire;
- the confidentiality of the data related to the evaluation of the current situation and the levels targeted according to the company's strategy with the prioritization of the axis.

In perspectives, we plan to propose a specific model of risk management, allowing decision-making in the selection of a transition strategy, starting from the characterization of the model of influence of risks on the project of transformation to the 4.0 supply chain.

References

1. Brown, S., Bessant, J.: The manufacturing strategy-capabilities links in mass customisation and agile manufacturing–an exploratory study. Int. J. Oper. Prod. Manag. **23**(7), 707–730 (2003)
2. Prinz, C., Morlock, F., Freith, S., Kreggenfeld, N., Kreimeier, D., Kuhlenkötter, B.: Learning factory modules for smart factories in industrie 4.0. Procedia CiRp. **54**, 113–118 (2016)
3. Barreto, L., Amaral, A., Pereira, T.: Industry 4.0 implications in logistics: an overview. Procedia Manuf. **13**, 1245–1252 (2017)
4. Yadav, G., Luthra, S., Jakhar, S.K., Mangla, S.K., Rai, D.P.: A framework to overcome sustainable supply chain challenges through solution measures of industry 4.0 and circular economy: an automotive case. J. Cleaner Prod. **254**, 112–120 (2020)
5. Kumar, P., Singh, R.K., Kumar, V.: Managing supply chains for sustainable operations in the era of industry 4.0 and circular economy: analysis of barriers. Res. Conserv. Recycl. **164**, 105215 (2021)
6. O'Reilly, C.A., III., Tushman, M.L.: Organizational ambidexterity: past, present, and future. Acad. Manag. Perspect. **27**(4), 324–338 (2013)
7. Womack, J.P., Jones, D.T.: Lean thinking—banish waste and create wealth in your corporation. J. Oper. Res. Soc. **48**(11), 1148 (1997)

8. Alavi, S., Abd Wahab, D., Muhamad, N., Shirani, B.A.: Organic structure and organisational learning as the main antecedents of workforce agility. International J. Prod. Res. **52**(21), 6273–6295 (2014)
9. Elkington, J.: Cannibals with Forks: The Triple Bottom Line of the 21st Century. New Society Publishers, Gabriola Island (1998)
10. Kagermann, H., Wahlster, W., Helbig, J. (eds.): Recommendations for implementing the strategic initiative Industrie 4.0. Final report of the Industrie 4.0 Working Group (2013)
11. Lee, J., Bagheri, B., Kao, H.A.: A cyber-physical systems architecture for industry 4.0-based manufacturing systems. Manuf. Lett. **3**, 18–23 (2015)
12. Hermann, M., Pentek, T., Otto, B.: Design principles for industrie 4.0 scenarios. In: IEEE 49th Hawaii International Conference on System Sciences (HICSS), pp. 3928–3937 (2016)
13. Hofmann, E., Rüsch, M.: Industry 4.0 and the current status as well as future prospects on logistics. Comput. Ind. **89**, 23–34 (2017)
14. Manavalan, E., Jayakrishna, K.: An analysis on sustainable supply chain for circular economy. Procedia Manuf. **33**, 477–484 (2019)
15. Dau, G., Scavarda, A., Scavarda, L.F., Portugal, V.J.T.: The healthcare sustainable supply chain 4.0: the circular economy transition conceptual framework with the corporate social responsibility mirror. Sustainability **11**(12), 3259 (2019)
16. Dossou, P.E.: Impact of Sustainability on the supply chain 4.0 performance. Procedia Manuf. **17**, 452–459. Elsevier (2018)
17. Vaidya, S., Ambad, P., Bhosle, S.: Industry 4.0–a glimpse. Procedia Manuf. **20**(1), 233–238 (2018)
18. Tjahjono B., Esplugues, C., Ares, E., Pelaez G.: What does industry 4.0 mean to supply chain? Procedia Manuf. **13**, 1175–1182 (2017)
19. Faller, C., Feldmüller, D.: Industry 4.0 learning factory for regional SMEs. Procedia Cirp. **32**, 88–91 (2015)
20. Sanders, A., Elangeswaran, C., Wulfsberg, J.P.: Industry 4.0 implies lean manufacturing: research activities in industry 4.0 function as enablers for lean manufacturing. J. Ind. Eng. Manag. **9**(3), 811–833 (2016)
21. Herberer, S., Lau, L.K., Behrendt, F.: Development of an industrie 4.0 maturity index for small and medium-sized enterprises. In: IESM Conference, Saarbrucken (2017)
22. Chrissis, M.B., Konrad, M., Shrum, S.: CMMI 2ᵉEdition - Guide des bonnes pratiques pour l'amélioration des processus - CMMI (r) pour le développement, version 1.2. SEI, Pearson Education France (2008)
23. Deniaud, I., Marmier, F., Michalak, J.-L.: Méthodologie et outil de diagnostic 4.0: Définir sa stratégie de transition 4.0 pour le management de la chaîne logistique. Logistique & Management (28/1), Ed. Taylor & Francis (2020)
24. Nolte, W.L.: Technology Readiness Level Calculator, Air Force Research Laboratory. Presented at the NDIA Systems Engineering Conference (2003)
25. Crosby, P.B.: Quality is Free: The Art of Making Quality Certain. McGraw-Hill, New York (1979)
26. Lichtblau, K., Stich, V.: Industrie 4.0-Readiness, Impuls-Stiftung, Foundation for mechanical engineering, plant engineering and information technology (2015)
27. Batz, A., Oleśków-Szłapka, J., Stachowiak, A., Pawłowski, G., Maruszewska, K.: Identification of logistics 4.0 maturity levels in polish companies—framework of the model and preliminary research. In: Grzybowska, K., Awasthi, A., Sawhney, R. (eds.) Sustainable Logistics and Production in Industry 4.0. E, pp. 161–175. Springer, Cham (2020). https://doi.org/10.1007/978-3-030-33369-0_10
28. Facchini, F., Oleśków-Szłapka, J., Ranieri, L., Urbinati, A.: A maturity model for logistics 4.0: an empirical analysis and a roadmap for future research. Sustainability **12**(1), 86 (2020)

Intuitionistic Fuzzy Cognitive Map Based Analysis of Supply Chain Risks

Gülçin Büyüközkan[1(✉)] ⓘ, Celal Alpay Havle[1,2] ⓘ,
and Orhan Feyzioğlu[1] ⓘ

[1] Department of Industrial Engineering, Galatasaray University,
34349 Istanbul, Turkey
{gbuyukozkan, ofeyzioglu}@gsu.edu.tr
[2] Professional Flight Program, Özyeğin University, 34794 İstanbul, Turkey
celal.havle@ozyegin.edu.tr

Abstract. Supply chains (SCs) are network-like structures and gigantic systems. Such systems are complex and multifaceted. Therefore, they contain many components and risk factors that are directly or indirectly related to each other. The importance of SCs, which has always been important for companies, is increasing day by day. Therefore, it is vital to focus on supply chain management (SCM) and the risk factors encountered in this management process. Plus, the investigation of the cause-effect relationships, evaluation, and analysis of these factors hold a critical role for SCM. Accordingly, this study aims to reveal the risk factors that should be considered in SCM and analyze these factors. Moreover, the causal relationships of these risk factors are aimed to be revealed. For this purpose, Cognitive Map (CM) approach is utilized. The classical CM approach is expanded to the intuitionistic fuzzy (IF) environment and used as the IFCM approach to eliminate the uncertainty and intuition involved in real-life problems and decision-making processes. SC risk factors' importance degrees and causal relations between the factors are displayed and visualized.

Keywords: Supply chain · Supply chain risks · Supply chain risk management · Intuitionistic fuzzy cognitive map

1 Introduction

Nowadays, manufacturing supply chains are disposed to be composed of global, complex relationships and flow between tens and hundreds and thousands of geographically dispersed companies and plants. A supply chain has various members such as facilities, distributors, retailers, suppliers, and their suppliers, installation internal and external logistics providers, and financial institutions [1]. The management of such a structure with many components is crucial. Supply chain management (SCM) is a structure that aims to integrate the management and resource control and flow and oversight of the entire system with multiple suppliers [2]. However, SCM is incorporated with risk management. SCM can be defined as managing risks raised from coordination and collaboration between supply chain members to ensure profitability and sustainability [3]. SC risk management (SRCM), having an influential role in

A. Dolgui et al. (Eds.): APMS 2021, IFIP AICT 634, pp. 634–643, 2021.
https://doi.org/10.1007/978-3-030-85914-5_67

managing business processes and supply chain risks, has many risk sources such as process, control, demand, supply, and environment. Therefore, this study proposes an evaluation framework for supply chain risk analysis and investigates the supply chain risks. The cognitive Map (CM) approach [4] is utilized to analyze these risks with the relationship assumption between criteria. To eliminate the uncertainty, intuition due to human perception, and hesitancy in real-life problems and decision-making processes, the classical CM approach has been expanded to an intuitionistic fuzzy (IF) environment [5]. Hence, the CM is applied as IFCM in this study. A case study is conducted to validate the proposed model in a manufacturing company in Turkey. Importance degree of risks are obtained, and IFCM models of SCRM are visualized.

This study consists of the following sections: Sect. 2 gives a brief literature survey. Section 3 illustrates the IFCM method. The conducted case study is provided in Sect. 4 followingly. Finally, the research is concluded in Sect. 5.

2 Literature Review

SCM is the management of the goods by the flow of finance and information within the network structure of organizations aiming to produce and deliver services or products for customers. Coordination and cooperation of different activities and processes between various functions such as purchasing, logistics marketing, finance and information flow, sales, production, production design are conducted within the network [3].

The SC performance is intrinsically unpredictable. Therefore, managers are often in search of safety measures to be protected from unforeseen situations. In the supply chain process, more efforts are made to check order status frequently. Moreover, distributing necessary inventory and determining the confidence interval of supply times are essential to speed up orders and keep the supply chain performance high. Furthermore, these stocks hide potential hazards until a severe problem arises between the partner due to limited information sharing. This prepares a sub-structure that leads to the formation of risk sources. These risk sources, including delays, disruptions, financial forecasting, intellectual property, purchasing, customers, inventory, and capacity [6], may arise from internal and external supply chains.

This study assumes the existence of relationships between criteria contrary to the principle of criteria independence. This assumption forms the basis for the use of multi-criteria decision-making techniques. The IFCM approach deals with the causal relations between the criteria considering intuition and hesitation. It has a dynamical behavior, and therefore, different scenarios can be conducted for future conditions.

Various studies are dealing with SC risks in the academic literature. A stochastic model was proposed for risk management in global supply chain networks [7]. Supply chain risks are determined in the automotive and electronic industries, and SCRM implementation is emphasized [8]. The performance-based evaluation was performed under the impact of SCRM [9]. Table 1 shows some studies based on SC risks in academic literature.

Table 1. Some SC risks-based studies in the academic literature

Objective of the study	Source
To make performance-based evaluation under the impact of supply chain risk management	[9]
To examine that the research developments in supply chain risk management (SCRM)	[10]
To show the need for supply chain risk management as a management function	[11]
To determine the suited techniques for risk assessment in complex environments in the aspect of the supply chain	[12]
To investigate the assessment of operational risks-based supply chain	[13]
To examine the efficiency to develop a model in the aspect of supply chain risk management	[14]
To emphasize the lack of definition of risk in the perspective of the supply chain in literature	[15]
To research the effect of visibility and risk on cost in the supply chain	[16]
To reduce the risk mitigation in the supply chain with a proposed procedure	[17]

However, there is a limited number of studies using IFCM applications in the literature concerning both SC and SC risks. In these studies, the SC configuration criteria were evaluated using IFCM [18]. A model was developed and analyzed using the IFCM method for sustainable hospital SCM [19]. The IFCM method was used based on a sustainable SCM framework for higher education laboratories [20]. Risks are analyzed concerning the digital supply chain [21]. Hence, this study utilizes the IFCM approach to analyze supply chain risks.

3 Proposed Methodology

This section briefly explains intuitionistic fuzzy sets. Following this, the proposed methodology is to be presented.

3.1 Intuitionistic Fuzzy Sets

IF sets were proposed by Atanassov in 1986 [5], and they can deal with obscurity, intuition, and hesitancy [22]. An IF set can be indicated in a finite set as $A = \{\langle x, \mu_A(x), v_A(x)\rangle | x \in X\}$ where $\mu_A(x), v_A(x) : X \to [0, 1] \mu_A(x)$ and $v_A(x)$ membership and non-membership functions, respectively and here,

$$0 \leq \mu_A(x) + v_A(x) \leq 1. \tag{1}$$

The third component of an IF value which is $\pi_A(x)$ deals with hesitancy.

$$\pi_A(x) = 1 - \mu_A(x) - v_A(x) \text{ where } 0 \leq \pi_A(x) \leq 1, \forall x \in X. \tag{2}$$

3.2   Intuitionistic Fuzzy Cognitive Map Approach

Kosko proposed FCMs, which are network-like structures in 1986 [23], and these structures have causal relationships. Plus, they allow scenario analysis based on their dynamical behavior [24]. FCMs, consisting of nodes, arcs, and their weights, are based on experts' opinions. They are signed weighted graphs [24]. Since real-life problems and decision-making processes include uncertainty, hesitation, and intuition, fuzzy sets [25] may be insufficient to model and solve such issues. Therefore, FCM is extended to IF sets, and it is applied as IFCM [26].

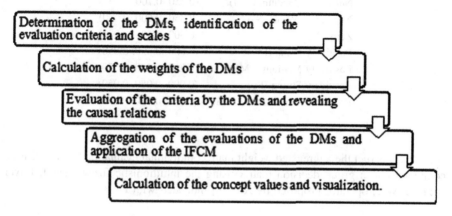

Fig. 1. Computational steps of the IFCM approach

The third component of the IF sets deals with hesitancy in decision-making processes. Computational steps of the IFCM approach presented in Fig. 1 are given as follows [26]:

Step 1: Determine the DMs, identify the evaluation criteria and scales.

Step 2: Obtain the weights of the DMs. The weight of the kth DM (λ_k) is calculated by Eq. (3) adopted from Boran et al. [15] using linguistic terms indicated in Table 2.

Table 2. Linguistic terms to rate the DMs [22, 27].

Linguistic terms	IF values (μ, v, π)
Very unimportant	(0.100, 0.800, 0.100)
Unimportant	(0.250, 0.600, 0.150)
Medium	(0.500, 0.400, 0.100)
Important	(0.750, 0.200, 0.050)
Very important	(0.900, 0.050, 0.050)

$$\lambda_k = \frac{\left(\mu_k + \pi_k\left(\frac{\mu_k}{\mu_k + v_k}\right)\right)}{\sum\limits_{k=1}^{l}\left(\mu_k + \pi_k\left(\frac{\mu_k}{\mu_k + v_k}\right)\right)}, \quad \sum\limits_{k=1}^{l}(\lambda_k) = 1 \tag{3}$$

Step 3: Obtain the judgments of DMs on each concept. Causal relationships and the degree of causalities are determined using the linguistic scale given in Table 3.

Table 3. Linguistic terms for the degree of causality [26].

Linguistic terms	IF values (μ, υ, π)
Negatively Very Strong (NVS)	(0.000, 0.950, 0.050)
Negatively Strong (NS)	(0.050, 0.900, 0.050)
Negatively Medium (NM)	(0.250, 0.700, 0.050)
Negatively Weak (NW)	(0.350, 0.600, 0.050)
Zero (Z)	(0.500, 0.500, 0.000)
Positively Weak (PW)	(0.600, 0.350, 0.050)
Positively Medium (PM)	(0.750, 0.200, 0.050)
Positively Strong (PS)	(0.900, 0.050, 0.050)
Positively Very Strong (PVS)	(0.950, 0.000, 0.050)

Step 4: Construct the aggregated weight matrix. Individual evaluations of the DMs are combined into a group decision matrix using the intuitionistic fuzzy weighted averaging (IFWA) operator proposed by Xu [28] indicated with Eq. (4).

$$w_{ij} = IFWA_\lambda\left(w_{ij}^{(1)}, w_{ij}^{(2)}, \ldots, w_{ij}^{(k)}\right) = \lambda_1 w_{ij}^{(1)} \oplus \lambda_2 w_{ij}^{(2)} \oplus \cdots \oplus \lambda_k w_{ij}^{(k)}$$

$$= \left(1 - \prod_{k=1}^{K}\left(1 - \mu_{ij}^{(k)}\right)^{\lambda_k}, \prod_{k=1}^{K}\left(v_{ij}^{(k)}\right)^{\lambda_k}, \prod_{k=1}^{K}\left(1 - \mu_{ij}^{(k)}\right)^{\lambda_k} - \prod_{k=1}^{K}\left(v_{ij}^{(k)}\right)^{\lambda_k}\right) \tag{4}$$

Step 5: Apply IFCM [26]. IFCM equation is applied to find the value of each criterion. Equation (5) equation is used to calculate concept values at each iteration until convergence.

$$A_i^{(t+1)} = f\left(A_i^{(t)} + \sum_{j \neq i, j=1}^{n} A_j^{(t)}\left(\mu_{ij}(w) - \pi_{ij}(w)\right)\right) \tag{5}$$

where $A_i^{(t+1)}$ indicates the value of the concept C_i at iteration $(t+1)$, $f(x)$ shows the threshold function, which is sigmoid $\left(f(x) = \left(\frac{1}{1+e^{-\alpha x}}\right)\right)$. Here, the growth rate is set to -0.1 $(\alpha = -0.1)$. $A_i^{(t)}$ represents the initial concept value at iteration t. $A_j^{(t)}$ is the concept value at iteration t. $\left(\mu_{ij}(w) - \pi_{ij}(w)\right)$ is applied to reach the weight matrix.

Step 6: Determine concept values.

4   Case Study

A case study is conducted to analyze the SC risks in a manufacturing company. Due to privacy concerns and confidentially issues, the company will be named XYZ. An evaluation model is proposed based on three main dimensions: production and inventory, customer service and delivery, and plant production. Risk factors concerning the main dimensions are determined with the help of decision-makers (DMs). A group of experts, including DMs, is constructed by considering their experience levels, backgrounds, academic careers, positions in the company where they work, and the knowledge levels related to the SC risks. The DMs determined the causality degrees of relationships (edges) between the risk factors using Table 2. Only the evaluations belong to a single DM (DM_1) for the risk factors of Production & Inventory are given in Table 4 due to page limitations.

Table 4. Linguistic terms-based evaluation of PI risk factors

PI risk factors	C_1	C_2	C_3	C_4	C_5	C_6	C_7	C_8
C_1	Z	PS	Z	Z	Z	Z	Z	Z
C_2	Z	Z	Z	Z	PM	Z	Z	Z
C_3	Z	NM	Z	Z	Z	NS	Z	Z
C_4	Z	NW	Z	Z	Z	NW	Z	Z
C_5	Z	Z	PS	Z	Z	Z	Z	Z
C_6	Z	PW	Z	Z	Z	Z	Z	Z
C_7	Z	Z	Z	Z	Z	PM	Z	Z
C_8	Z	Z	Z	Z	Z	PVS	Z	Z

Visualized IFCM model of each main dimension with their sub-criteria are shown in Fig. 2, 3 and 4. Visualization of the IFCM model is performed by Pajek Software. The aggregated weight matrix is used for this. Following that, the concept (risk factor) values are calculated using Eq. (5), and they are given in Table 5 with their ranked orders.

Table 5. Concept values of supply chain risks and their ranked order

Production & inventory		Customer service & delivery				Plant production			
C₂	0.44576	C₄	0.43776	C₇	0.42849	C₁₅	0.41548	C₉	0.40593
C₆	0.44574	C₁₁	0.43364	C₅	0.42696	C₈	0.41406	C₁₄	0.40591
C₁	0.44472	C₃	0.43154	C₂	0.42637	C₂	0.40926	C₅	0.40589
C₄	0.44472	C₆	0.43055			C₆	0.40926	C₁₀	0.40588
C₇	0.44472	C₁₀	0.43004			C₁₁	0.40926	C₁₂	0.40588
C₈	0.44472	C₈	0.43003			C₁₃	0.40926	C₁₆	0.40588
C₅	0.44257	C₁	0.42954			C₄	0.40878	C₁	0.40393
C₃	0.44099	C₉	0.42850			C₃	0.40878	C₇	0.40300

The concept values in Table 5 show that the most critical risk factors for production and inventory are the desired inventory, desired production, and customer demand. Furthermore, when Fig. 2 is examined, it is seen that high customer demand increases the desired production. This triggers production, and consequently, the inventory is influenced. At the same time, desired service level, desired inventory coverage, and plant reliability positively influence desired inventory. If the desired inventory high, then the desired production is increased.

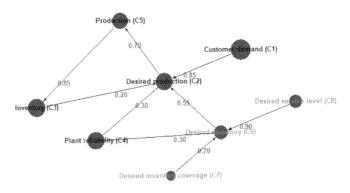

Fig. 2. IFCM model of *production & inventory* risks

As Table 5 states, inventory, demand backlog, and order fulfillment risk factors have greater importance in customer service and delivery risks. When Fig. 3 is examined, it is seen that inventory influences inventory carrying cost and order fulfillment. At the same time, if the order fulfillment level is high, then customer satisfaction is high. Customer satisfaction triggers customer demand, and it causes a demand backlog. Accordingly, the desired shipment will be influenced. On the other hand, high product prices will affect customer satisfaction. However, the product price is determined based on immediate shipment, inventory, inventory carrying cost, and unit shipment cost, which is also influenced by the immediate shipment.

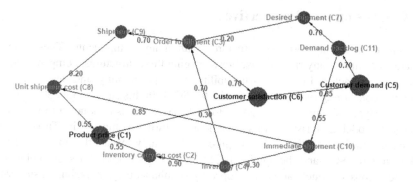

Fig. 3. IFCM model of *customer service & delivery* risks

Finally, the obtained results given in Table 5 shows that customer satisfaction, downtime, and desired production are the most critical factors in plant production risks. Furthermore, Fig. 4 proves that product variety, product price, and product defects significant for customer satisfaction. But the variety of the production increases the setup time, and that increases the manufacturing lead time. The increase in the manufacturing lead time directly increases the unit production cost, and the increased unit production cost increases the price of the product. But the increased product price may influence customer satisfaction negatively.

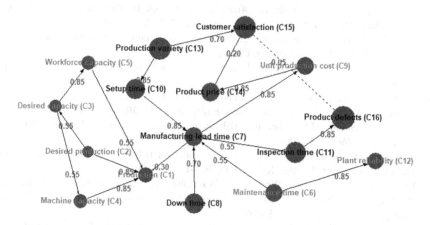

Fig. 4. IFCM model of *plant production* risks.

Manufacturing companies should focus on these risk factors in their SCRM processes. Furthermore, when the IFCM models are examined, it is seen that the submodels have common criteria such as *desired production, plant reliability, production, inventory, and customer satisfaction*. Since these risk factors connected these three subsystems as both influencing and influenced factors, it is possible to propose a general model for supply chain risks.

5 Conclusion and Perspectives

SCs are complex network-like structures with many components. These complex structures contain many risk factors. For managing these structures, companies need to focus on risk factors for their sustainability. Plus, profitability and determination of strategies concerning risks are also crucial for SCM. In this study, a model is proposed for the analysis of supply chain risk factors. A case study is conducted to validate the proposed model and risk factors in a manufacturing company in Turkey. IFCM approach is utilized for the analyzing process. The study reveals the importance of the risk factors for SCs, and the applied IFCM approach is helpful for such problems.

The proposed model can be developed by simultaneously analyzing all sub-criteria of the proposed to see the structure of the whole SC risk system. Interval-valued IF (IVIF) sets can be used to obtain more accurate and sensitive results. Furthermore, sensitivity and scenario analysis can be performed for future studies, and also the results can be compared.

Acknowledgments. The authors would like to give their deep gratitude to industrial experts. This work has been supported by the Scientific Research Projects Commission of Galatasaray University.

References

1. Gaonkar, R.S., Viswanadham, N.: Analytical framework for the management of risk in supply chains. IEEE Trans. Autom. Sci. Eng. **4**(2), 265–273 (2007)
2. Monczka, R., Trent, R., Handfield, R.: Purchasing and Supply Chain Management, chap. 8. South-Western College Publishing, Cincinnati, OH (2015)
3. Tang, C.S.: Perspectives in supply chain risk management. Int. J. Prod. Econ. **103**, 451–488 (2006)
4. Tolman, E.C.: Cognitive maps in rats and men. Psychol. Rev. **55**(4), 189 (1948)
5. Atanassov, K.T.: Intuitionistic fuzzy sets. Fuzzy Sets Syst. **20**(1), 87–96 (1986)
6. Chopra, S., Sodhi, M.S.: Managing risk to avoid supply-chain breakdown. MIT Sloan Manag. Rev. **46**(1), 53 (2004)
7. Goh, M., Lim, J.Y., Meng, F.: A stochastic model for risk management in global supply chain networks. Eur. J. Oper. Res. **182**(1), 164–173 (2007)
8. Blos, M.F., Quaddus, M., Wee, H.M., Watanabe, K.: Supply chain risk management (SCRM): a case study on the automotive and electronic industries in Brazil. Supply Chain Manage. Int. J. **14**(4), 247–252 (2009)
9. Thun, J.H., Hoenig, D.: An empirical analysis of supply chain risk management in the German automative industry. Int. J. Prod. Econ. **131**, 242–249 (2011)
10. Tang, O., Musa, S.N.: Identifying risk issues and research advancements in supply chain risk management. Int. J. Prod. Econ. **133**, 25–34 (2011)
11. Lavastre, O., Gunasekaran, A., Spalanzani, A.: Supply chain risk management in French companies. Decis. Support Syst. **52**, 828–838 (2012)
12. Markmann, C., Darkow, I.-L., Gracht, H.: A Delphi-based risk analysis-identifying and assessing future challenges for supply chain security in a multi-stakeholder environment. Technol. Forecast. Soc. Chang. **80**, 1815–1833 (2013)

13. Tazelaar, F., Snijdersb, C.: Operational risk assessments by supply chain professionals: process and performance. J. Oper. Manag. **31**, 37–51 (2013)
14. Xu, X., Meng, Z., Shen, R.: A tri-level programming model based on conditional value-at-risk for three-stage supply chain management. Comput. Ind. Eng. **66**, 470–475 (2013)
15. Heckmann, I., Comes, T., Nickel, S.: A critical review on supply chain risk – definition, measure, and modeling. Int. J. Manage. Sci. **52**, 119–132 (2014)
16. Nooraie, S.V., Parast, M.M.: A multi-objective approach to supply chain risk management: integrating visibility with supply and demand risk. Int. J. Prod. Econ. **161**, 192–200 (2015)
17. Kırılmaz, O., Erol, S.: A proactive approach to supply chain risk management: shifting orders among suppliers to mitigate the supply side risks. J. Purch. Supply Manag. **23**(1), 54–65 (2017)
18. Dursun, M., Gumus, G.: Intuitionistic fuzzy cognitive map approach for the evaluation of supply chain configuration criteria. Math. Meth. Appl. Sci. **43**(13), 7788–7801 (2020)
19. Mirghafoori, S.H., Sharifabadi, A.M., Takalo, S.K.: Development of causal model of sustainable hospital supply chain management using the intuitionistic fuzzy cognitive map (IFCM) method. J. Ind. Eng. Manage. (JIEM) **11**(3), 588–605 (2018)
20. Purnomo, M.R.A., Anugerah, A.R., Dewipramesti, B.T.: Sustainable supply chain management framework in a higher education laboratory using intuitionistic fuzzy cognitive map. J. Ind. Eng. Manage. **13**(2), 417–429 (2020)
21. Büyüközkan, G., Göçer, F.: Digital supply chain risk analysis with intuitionistic fuzzy cognitive map. In: Data Science and Knowledge Engineering for Sensing Decision Support, pp. 1385–1391 (2018)
22. Boran, F.E., Genç, S., Kurt, M., Akay, D.: A multi-criteria intuitionistic fuzzy group decision making for supplier selection with TOPSIS method. Exp. Syst. Appl. **36**(8), 11363–11368 (2009)
23. Kosko, B.: Fuzzy cognitive maps. Int. J. Man Mach. Stud. **24**(1), 65–75 (1986)
24. Büyüközkan, G., Vardaloğlu, Z.: Analyzing of CPFR success factors using fuzzy cognitive maps in retail industry. Exp. Syst. Appl. **39**(12), 10438–10455 (2012)
25. Zadeh, L.A.: Fuzzy sets. Inf. Control **8**(3), 338–353 (1965)
26. Büyüközkan, G., Havle, C.A., Feyzioğlu, O., Göçer, F.: A combined group decision making based IFCM and SERVQUAL approach for strategic analysis of airline service quality. J. Intell. Fuzzy Syst. **38**(1), 859–872 (2020)
27. Büyüközkan, G., Feyzioğlu, O., Havle, C.A.: Intuitionistic fuzzy AHP based strategic analysis of service quality in digital hospitality industry. IFAC-PapersOnLine **52**(13), 1687–1692 (2019)
28. Xu, Z.: Intuitionistic Preference Modeling and Interactive Decision Making. Springer, Berlin Heidelberg (2014). https://doi.org/10.1007/978-3-642-28403-8

A Classification Tool for Circular Supply Chain Indicators

Asiye Kurt[1,2]([✉]) [iD], Mario Cortes-Cornax[2] [iD], Van-Dat Cung[1] [iD],
Agnès Front[2] [iD], and Fabien Mangione[1] [iD]

[1] Univ. Grenoble Alpes, CNRS, Grenoble INP (Institute of Engineering Univ.
Grenoble Alpes), G-SCOP, 38000 Grenoble, France
{Asiye.Kurt,Van-Dat.Cung,Fabien.Mangione}@grenoble-inp.fr
[2] Univ. Grenoble Alpes, CNRS, Grenoble INP (Institute of Engineering Univ.
Grenoble Alpes), LIG, 38000 Grenoble, France
{Asiye.Kurt,Mario.Cortes-Cornax,Agnes.Front}@univ-grenoble-alpes.fr

Abstract. The Circular Economy approach has gained attention
recently. Supply Chains have an important role in the transition to a
more circular economy. Thus, being able to assess structurally the circularity of multi-activity Supply Chains is essential to help Supply Chain
managers to decide in this transition. An important number of Supply
Chains' indicators are proposed in the literature in the context of sustainability. However, to the best of our knowledge, there is no tool, which
specifically classifies those indicators according to Circular Supply Chain
structures, involving circular activities such as reuse, remanufacturing,
refurbishing and repurposing. The aim of this work is to develop such a
classification tool for indicators in order to assess the circularity of Supply
Chains at the strategic level. This classification tool relies on the three
main principles of circular value creation of Ellen MacArthur Foundation. These principles are converted into different dimensions that could
be applied to the structures of Circular Supply Chains. These dimensions
constitute classification criteria for our tool. In this work, new potential
Circular Supply Chain indicators are also proposed and classified by
the tool. This tool allows and facilitates academics and Supply Chain
managers categorizing and choosing appropriate indicators to assess circularity within Circular Supply Chains.

Keywords: Circular economy · Supply Chain · Classification ·
Circularity indicator

1 Introduction

In order to achieve the goals of sustainability, the world is moving towards a
more circular economy. The Circular Economy (CE) allows an integrated way to

Supported by the French National Research Agency under the "Investissements
d'avenir" program (ANR-15-IDEX-02) through the Cross Disciplinary Program CIR-
CULAR.

handle the Triple Bottom Line of sustainability (economic, environmental and social). Moreover, Supply Chains have an essential role in the transition to a more circular economy [2]. CE involves the transition from the management of linear activities to multiple circular activities running simultaneously [5]. This results in new and complex Circular Supply Chain (CSC) structures, which are much more challenging to manage, evaluate and improve.

Supply Chain Management regarding conceptualization within CE is still at an early stage [12]. Indeed, the need for research on the application of the CE from the Supply Chain perspective has been highlighted [15] along with the need for a measurement methodology to assess circularity performance in Supply Chains [8]. Moreover, CE definitions and what to be measured need to be explored due to the lack of consensus [25]. Furthermore, new CSC structures required by CE bring new factors that could be measured to express circularity.

Therefore, a new framework is needed for academics and Supply Chain managers to understand Supply Chain circularity as well as to support the development and the classification of circularity indicators for new CSC structures. This work aims to fill the aforementioned lack by proposing a classification tool for indicators that are relevant in the assessment of the Supply Chain circularity, based on their structures. This tool is designed relying on the main principles of circular value creation prescribed by the Ellen MacArthur Foundation (EMF) [10,11]. These principles are adapted to the Supply Chain context by proposing different dimensions for each of them regarding the possibilities of CSC structures. Some new potential indicators for each dimension are also proposed in order to illustrate the classification.

The rest of the paper is structured as follows. Section 2 provides a literature background and our positioning. Section 3 introduces our classification tool of CSC indicators illustrated on some CSC structures. Finally, Sect. 4 concludes the paper and gives some insights for future works.

2   Background and Positioning

2.1   EMF Principles and CSC Structures

The CE concept has received increasing attention worldwide in the latter years [15,24]. Ellen MacArthur Foundation (EMF) has emerged as a respected reference in this topic and published different studies about the concept of CE since 2013 [10,11]. The latter proposed four principles of circular value creation: (1) the power circling longer, (2) the power of inner circle, (3) the power of cascaded use, and (4) the power of pure inputs [10,11]. These principles, which have previously been stated in academic publications [28,29], have been gathered by EMF and taken into consideration in recent CE studies [7,30].

On the one hand, the first three principles concern material flows and Supply Chains explicitly. On the other hand, the last principle (the power of pure inputs value creation) is obtained by improving the product's design and the collection activity [10,11]. Therefore, the latter does not directly impact the structure of a Supply Chain, so it is not considered in this work.

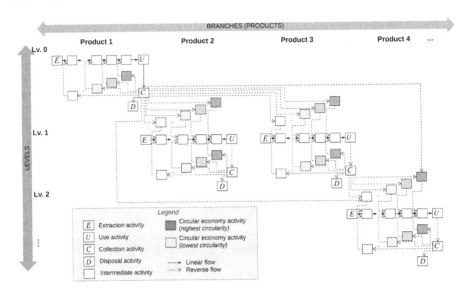

Fig. 1. Circular supply chain structure

Besides, the notion of CSC is relatively recent concerning Supply Chain literature as well. Several studies have been conducted to explore the links between CSC and related concepts such as Eco-Industrial Parks, Environmental, Sustainable and Green Supply Chains, Reverse Logistics and Closed-Loop Supply Chains [4,23,24]. Moreover, some specific works defined the CSC structure as a combination of closed- and open-loops [4,7,12,21]. Closed-loops concern the integration of forward and reverse flows for a specific product. Indeed, used products turn back to the same Supply Chain through CE activities such as direct reuse, reuse with repairing, reuse with refurbishing, reuse with remanufacturing, and recycling [21]. Open-loops allow the integration of different Supply Chains. Used products are introduced in a different Supply Chain through repurposing activities [21]. Repurposing refers to the use of products or materials for a different purpose than the original one.

To clarify CSC structures, we made a further generalization of the Extended Model [21], by adding a flexible number of activities (including the CE ones) and the possibility of integrating multiple Supply Chains to conceptualize CSC structures. Figure 1 presents a CSC structure that contains the integration of several Supply Chains. Each Supply Chain is composed of a material extraction activity (E), a collection activity (C), a use activity (U), a disposal activity (D), as well as a set of manufacturing and distribution activities (blank white squares) and different CE activities (green squares). These activities are connected to each other by direct (solid arrows) and reverse (dashed arrows) flows. The different Supply Chains are connected by open-loops. The integrated Supply Chains have two attributes: branch and level. Branch refers to the type of products produced throughout the Supply Chain (e.g., Product 1, Product 2, etc.). Level refers to the level of requirements of the product produced throughout the related Supply Chain (e.g., Level 0, Level 1, etc.).

Hereafter, we relate the considered EMF principles with the structure of CSCs, in order to highlight value creation potentials through their structures:

The power of circling longer concerns keeping products, components and materials in use as longer as possible. Through a Supply Chain structure, the length of use of products, components or materials could be increased by multiple consecutive closed- or open-loops of circular activities such as reuse, repair, remanufacture, and recycle, etc.

The power of inner circle concerns potential savings on different dimensions: material, energy, labor and pollution. In other words, when the loop is short (with fewer manufacturing activities in the loop), the less a product has to be changed during reprocessing. Having shorter closed- or open-loops means more potential savings in terms of labor, material, energy and pollution and thus, higher circularity. For example, the reuse loop is more circular than the recycling loop as the first one is shorter. Reusing a used product requires few changes. Indeed, the closed-loop related to reuse contains 3 activities: collection, reuse and distribution, while the closed-loop related to recycling contains 4 activities: collection, recycling, manufacturing and distribution. Therefore, choosing the CE activity that creates the shortest loop for a used product allows creating more value by keeping the value already created as long as possible without destroying it. However, we note that returned products and components are not all eligible for all CE activities due to the state of the products or components. Therefore, it is interesting to have multiple CE activities through a CSC, because it may allow choosing among different CE activities to handle used products according to their states in order to provide more savings.

The power of cascaded use concerns material flows across distinct Supply Chains. This could be possible by repurposing the products within different purposes. For example, repurposing electric vehicle batteries in stationary applications. This principle is therefore related to open-loops.

2.2 Indicators and Classifications Considering CE

Indicators that are used in performance measurement influence the decisions to be made at strategic, tactical, and operational levels [16]. These levels concern respectively long-term, mid-term and short term decisions. In Supply Chain Management literature, indicators are classified according to these levels [17]. The strategic level indicators influence the top level management decisions [17], such as Supply Chain design [19] or selection of CE activities [22] that creates closed- and open-loops.

Concerning the classification of CE indicators, significant works have been devoted recently [9, 25, 27]. However, these works do not focus specifically on Supply Chains. Besides the circularity indicators' taxonomies, other classifications of indicators related to CE from different schools of thought are found.

Concerning Green Supply Chain Management Kazancoglu et al. [20] proposed an assessment framework. Concerning Sustainable Supply Chain, the indicators are usually classified according to the Three Bottom Lines (TBL) of sustainability (economic, environmental, and social) [6, 14, 26]. Besides the TBL of sustainability, some frameworks consider other criteria [1] such as Sustainable Supply Chain characteristics (*e.g.*: volunteer focus, resilience focus, long-term focus, flow focus, relationship focus, etc.).

3   A Classification Tool for Circular Supply Chain Indicators

In this section, we introduce a classification tool for CSC indicators relying on the three principles of circular value creation [10, 11] from EMF and the CSC structure. New circularity indicators and some others taken from the literature are classified with our tool in order to illustrate the purpose of our classification tool. We summarized the classification tool with the potential indicators (bold elements) in Fig. 2. As mentioned before, the figure also includes illustrative examples on the right sight of the figure. These examples conform to the CSC structure presented in Fig. 1. Hereafter, we will elaborate each value creation principle and the related dimensions.

The power of circling longer promotes the increase of the time of use of a product within one and/or multiple consecutive loops. This concerns the whole CSC, including closed- and open-loops. The determined dimensions for this principle are described as follows.

Number of consecutive loops is the number of consecutive use through a loop. Having multiple consecutive uses through a loop brings more circularity as the CE promotes keeping resources in the use phase as long as possible [10, 11]. Figure (a) in Fig. 2 illustrates a Supply Chain where three (3) consecutive loops are performed. This could correspond to the consecutive recycling of a product in the same Supply Chain. Another example of an indicator in this dimension is the Circularity [13]. However, the scope of this indicator of Circularity from the literature is tighter than ours, as it covers only one of our dimensions.

Length of use is the length of use of a product obtained as a result of a CE activity. If a CE activity provides an increase in length of use, this results in a more circularity. This aligns with the CE principle to keep resources in use as long as possible [10, 11]. This dimension concerns both closed- and open-loops. The example of figure (b) in Fig. 2 illustrates a scenario where we assume that the closer circular activity to Use adds one (1) unity to the length of use (e.g., years of use) and the other circular activity adds three (3) unities. These values could correspond to a mean of added value for each activity for a product, known by the Supply Chain manager. Another example of an indicator of this dimension, is Longevity [13].

The power of inner circle principle concerns both closed- and open-loops. This principle deals with savings in terms of energy, material, labor, and pollution. These savings are enabled by shortening loops and having multiple loops in the CSC. Note that other related works treat in much more details the savings dimension on looking at different levels of performance resulting in some

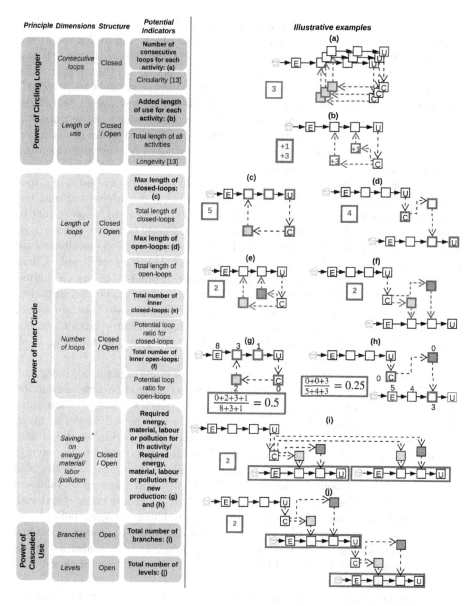

Fig. 2. The classification tool of circularity indicators for supply chains

specific saving indicators [9, 18, 20]. The dimensions related to this principle are described as follows.

Length of loops considers the number of activities of the loop until the Use activity. It is considered that shorter loops result in more circularity [10, 11]. For example, direct reuse (the CE activity that is considered to be "closer" to Use) needs fewer activities to generate new products. This implies that it is more circular than recycling (CE activity "further" from Use) that needs more activities. Recycling has thus a longer length of the loop. Figure 2 illustrates a first Supply Chain where the length of the closed-loop is five (5) (figure (c)) and a second Supply Chain where the length of the loop is four (4) (figure (d)). Note that different potential indicators concerning this dimension could be proposed, such as the maximum length of the loops or the total length of the loops. Length of loops is calculated for one loop; however, the maximum length of the loops and the total length of the loops could be calculated for a Supply Chain (focusing on the output flows of its collection activity) or the whole CSC network (focusing on all the collection activities of the network).

Number of loops considers the number of closed- and open-loops in a specific Supply Chain's product (i.e., not all the network is considered but only the Supply Chain of a specific product). The increased number of loops results in more circularity in CSCs in general. Indeed, the CE should transit to a more complex system, where multiple different CE activities are applied simultaneously through multiple loops [5]. Figure 2 illustrates two examples of Supply Chain where the number of closed-loops and the number of open-loops are calculated (figures (e) and (f)). The number is two (2) in both cases, which correspond to the number of simultaneous CE activities involved in each case. The number of open-loops could be calculated for an individual Supply Chain (focusing on the output flows of its collection activity) or for the whole network (focusing on all the collection activities of the network).

Savings concerns savings obtained in terms of energy, material, labor and pollution as a result of a CE activity or a CSC compared to new production process of a product. This dimension is important since CE seeks to minimize the use of aforementioned resources [10,11] and it is treated in detail in [9, 18,20]. Moreover, our classification tool adds savings on the labor dimension, which is scarcely explored in the literature. A possibility to calculate the savings concerning energy, material, labor, or pollution is illustrated in Fig. 2 as the ratio between the sum of saving values of the linear path and the sum of values of the circular path. The saving values for each activity regarding energy, material, labor, or pollution should be known by the Supply Chain designer beforehand. Therefore, savings' values could be calculated for only one loop, for an individual Supply Chain, or the whole CSC network depending on the quantities of the flows in the considered system. Figure 2 illustrates two examples of closed- and open-loops (figures (g) and (h)).

The power of cascaded use concerns the integration of distinct Supply Chains. This principle concerns the number of levels and the number of branches (explained below) and relates to open-loops as we focus here on repurposing activities. These dimensions are defined as follows.

Number of branches concerns the number of integrated Supply Chains with different product branches. Figure 2 illustrates an example of a Supply Chain with two branches (figure (i)), which means that a repurposed product (or material of a product) could be redirected to two different other Supply Chains.

Number of levels concerns the stages where a product or material could be repurposed with a decreasing requirement level. Figure (j) of Fig. 2 illustrates an example of a Supply Chain with two levels. Note that, different branches could place in the same level, since the related products could have the same requirement level.

The indicators considered in our classification tool allow measuring circularity at the strategic level. In addition, some of the indicators could be applied at all levels (Circularity [13], Longevity [13], Added length of use for each activity and savings dimension's indicators). For instance, indicators in savings dimensions could be calculated at strategic level by using material flow capacity of CSC, and at tactical level by using actual material flow quantity.

Figure 2 only proposes some examples of potential indicators concerning each dimension. Note that some aggregated indicators could consider different dimensions. Our vision is that in order to have a meaningful assessment of CSC, either an appropriate global indicator to measure the circularity of a CSC should cover all the presented dimensions, or a multi-criteria approach is needed. However, the proposed indicators concerning only one dimension are also helpful to give some insights in the comparison and assessment of CSCs. Moreover, these indicators could support selection of CE activities [22] in Supply Chain design. For example, a Supply Chain designer could compare the CE activities by added length of use for each activity (Figure (b) of the Fig. 2).

4 Conclusion

In this work, we proposed a classification tool for CSC indicators based on EMF circular value creation principles. This tool can help academics to analyze existing or new circularity indicators according to CSC structures by using the proposed dimensions as classification criteria. It can also facilitates Supply Chain managers categorizing and choosing appropriate circularity indicators to assess the circularity of CSCs. Moreover, we proposed new potential circularity indicators along with some from the literature (e.g., Longevity) for each dimension in order to illustrate our classification tool. The proposed indicators could support strategic decisions such as selecting CE activities in Supply Chain design.

Nevertheless, this classification tool still needs some improvements. First, while developing this proposal, we did not include the fourth principle of EMF, which is the power of pure inputs. This principle concerns the design process of a product, which we consider out of the scope of the analysis of CSCs. The power of pure inputs also increases collection efficiency [10]. Therefore, a new dimension could be set up to consider the collection and sorting efficiency indicators. Moreover, the design of products is a factor that influences the choice of implementation of CE activities. For example, with the eco-conception approach, the products could be designed for some special CE activities. In this context, Asif et al. [3] proposed product design attributes such as reusability, remanufacturability, and recyclability indexes. These indexes could be helpful to determine a CSC structure as circular as possible according to the design of a product. Second, this classification tool does not include pure economic indicators and social sustainability indicators. Possible integration in the classification tool of these two other dimensions will also be explored. Finally, a future work using the classification tool to categorize more extensively existing indicators in the literature is planned.

References

1. Ahi, P., Jaber, M.Y., Searcy, C.: A comprehensive multidimensional framework for assessing the performance of sustainable supply chains. Appl. Math. Model. **40**(23–24), 10153–10166 (2016)
2. Aminoff, A., Kettunen, O.: Sustainable supply chain management in a circular economy—towards supply circles. In: Setchi, R., Howlett, R.J., Liu, Y., Theobald, P. (eds.) Sustainable Design and Manufacturing 2016. SIST, vol. 52, pp. 61–72. Springer, Cham (2016). https://doi.org/10.1007/978-3-319-32098-4_6
3. Asif, F.M., Lieder, M., Rashid, A.: Multi-method simulation based tool to evaluate economic and environmental performance of circular product systems. J. Clean. Prod. **139**, 1261–1281 (2016)
4. Batista, L., Bourlakis, M., Liu, Y., Smart, P., Sohal, A.: Supply chain operations for a circular economy. Prod. Plann. Control **29**(6), 419–424 (2018)
5. Blomsma, F., Brennan, G.: The emergence of circular economy: a new framing around prolonging resource productivity. J. Ind. Ecol. **21**(3), 603–614 (2017)
6. Corona, B., Shen, L., Reike, D., Carreón, J.R., Worrell, E.: Towards sustainable development through the circular economy–a review and critical assessment on current circularity metrics. Resour. Conserv. Recycl. **151**, 104498 (2019)
7. De Angelis, R., Howard, M., Miemczyk, J.: Supply chain management and the circular economy: towards the circular supply chain. Product. Plann. Control **29**(6), 425–437 (2018)
8. Di Maio, F., Rem, P.C., Baldé, K., Polder, M.: Measuring resource efficiency and circular economy: a market value approach. Resour. Conserv. Recycl. **122**, 163–171 (2017)
9. Elia, V., Gnoni, M.G., Tornese, F.: Measuring circular economy strategies through index methods: a critical analysis. J. Clean. Prod. **142**, 2741–2751 (2017)
10. EMF (Ellen MacArthur Foundation): Towards the circular economy volume 1: An economic and business rationale for an accelerated transition (2013)
11. EMF (Ellen MacArthur Foundation): Towards the circular economy–vol 3: accelerating the scale-up across global supply chains (2014)
12. Farooque, M., Zhang, A., Thurer, M., Qu, T., Huisingh, D.: Circular supply chain management: a definition and structured literature review. J. Clean. Prod. **228**, 882–900 (2019). https://doi.org/10.1016/j.jclepro.2019.04.303
13. Figge, F., Thorpe, A.S., Givry, P., Canning, L., Franklin-Johnson, E.: Longevity and circularity as indicators of eco-efficient resource use in the circular economy. Ecol. Econ. **150**, 297–306 (2018)
14. Gómez-Luciano, C.A., Domínguez, F.R.R., González-Andrés, F., De Meneses, B.U.L.: Sustainable supply chain management: contributions of supplies markets. J. Clean. Prod. **184**, 311–320 (2018)
15. Govindan, K., Hasanagic, M.: A systematic review on drivers, barriers, and practices towards circular economy: a supply chain perspective. Int. J. Prod. Res. **56**(1–2), 278–311 (2018)

16. Gunasekaran, A., Patel, C., Tirtiroglu, E.: Performance measures and metrics in a supply chain environment. Int. J. Oper. Prod. Manage. **21**(1/2), 71–87 (2001)
17. Gunasekaran, A., Patel, C., McGaughey, R.E.: A framework for supply chain performance measurement. Int. J. Prod. Econ. **87**(3), 333–347 (2004)
18. Howard, M., Hopkinson, P., Miemczyk, J.: The regenerative supply chain: a framework for developing circular economy indicators. Int. J. Prod. Res. **57**(23), 7300–7318 (2019)
19. Ivanov, D.: An adaptive framework for aligning (re) planning decisions on supply chain strategy, design, tactics, and operations. Int. J. Prod. Res. **48**(13), 3999–4017 (2010)
20. Kazancoglu, Y., Kazancoglu, I., Sagnak, M.: A new holistic conceptual framework for green supply chain management performance assessment based on circular economy. J. Clean. Prod. **195**, 1282–1299 (2018)
21. Kurt, A., Cung, V.D., Mangione, F., Cortes-Cornax, M., Front, A.: An extended circular supply chain model including repurposing activities. In: 2019 International Conference on Control, Automation and Diagnosis (ICCAD), pp. 1–6. IEEE (2019)
22. Lambert, S., Riopel, D., Abdul-Kader, W.: A reverse logistics decisions conceptual framework. Comput. Ind. Eng. **61**(3), 561–581 (2011)
23. Liu, Z., Adams, M., Cote, R.P., Geng, Y., Li, Y.: Comparative study on the pathways of industrial parks towards sustainable development between China and Canada. Resour. Conserv. Recycl. **128**, 417–425 (2018)
24. Masi, D., Day, S., Godsell, J.: Supply chain configurations in the circular economy: a systematic literature review. Sustainability **9**(9), 1602 (2017)
25. Moraga, G., et al.: Circular economy indicators: what do they measure? Resour. Conserv. Recycl. **146**, 452–461 (2019)
26. Moreno-Camacho, C.A., Montoya-Torres, J.R., Jaegler, A., Gondran, N.: Sustainability metrics for real case applications of the supply chain network design problem: a systematic literature review. J. Clean. Prod. **231**, 600–618 (2019)
27. Saidani, M., Yannou, B., Leroy, Y., Cluzel, F., Kendall, A.: A taxonomy of circular economy indicators. J. Clean. Prod. **207**, 542–559 (2019)
28. Stahel, W.R.: The product life factor. An Inquiry into the Nature of Sustainable Societies: The Role of the Private Sector (Series: 1982 Mitchell Prize Papers), NARC (1982)
29. Stahel, W.R.: The Preformance Economy. Palgrave Macmillan, 2nd edn. London (2010)
30. Vegter, D., van Hillegersberg, J., Olthaar, M.: Supply chains in circular business models: processes and performance objectives. Resour. Conserv. Recycling **162**, 105046 (2020)

Author Index